Our Times/2
Readings from Recent Periodicals

Edited by

ROBERT ATWAN

Bedford Books *of* St. Martin's Press · Boston

For Bedford Books
Publisher: Charles H. Christensen
Associate Publisher: Joan E. Feinberg
Managing Editor: Elizabeth M. Schaaf
Developmental Editor: Jane Betz
Production Editor: Deborah Liehs
Copyeditor: Dan Otis
Text Design: Jean Hammond
Cover Design: Hannus Design Associates
Cover Photograph: Casey McNamara

Library of Congress Catalog Card Number: 89–63882

Manufactured in the United States of America.
5 4 3 2 1
f e d c

For information, write: St. Martin's Press, Inc.
175 Fifth Avenue, New York, NY 10010

Editorial Offices: Bedford Books *of* St. Martin's Press
29 Winchester Street, Boston, MA 02116

ISBN: 0–312–05674–5

Acknowledgments

Kiku Adatto, "The Incredible Shrinking Sound Bite." Copyright © 1990, Kiku Adatto. All
rights reserved.
Carol Ascher, "On Becoming Carol Ascher," excerpted with permission from the women's
studies journal, *Frontiers* (Vol. 10, No. 3), Women's Studies, University of Colorado.
Rita Baron-Faust, "The Anatomy of Addiction." Copyright © 1990 Rita Baron-Faust. Re-
printed by permission of the author.
William J. Bennett, "Why the West?" Copyright © 1988 by *National Review*, Inc., 150 East
35th Street, New York, NY 10016. Reprinted by permission.
Wendell Berry, "An Argument for Diversity," excerpted from *What Are People For?* Copyright
© 1990 by Wendell Berry. Published by North Point Press and reprinted by permission.
Allan Bloom, "Music," from *The Closing of the American Mind.* Copyright © 1987 by Allan
Bloom. Reprinted by permission of Simon & Schuster, Inc.
Victoria A. Brownworth, "Campus Queer Query." Copyright © 1990 by Victoria Brownworth.
Reprinted by permission of the author.
Thomas F. Cash and Louis H. Janda, "The Eye of the Beholder," *Psychology Today*, December
1984. Reprinted with permission from *Psychology Today* Magazine, copyright © 1984
(PT Partners, L. P.).

*Acknowledgments and copyrights are continued at the back of the book on pages 673–75,
which constitute an extension of the copyright page.*

Preface for Instructors

Like its predecessor, *Our Times/2* is a collection of contemporary non-fiction and short fiction intended for use in composition courses. This wealth of very recent writing — most of it published since 1989 and featuring virtually every important American periodical — provides an intriguing and distinctive view of life in America today.

The book has two educational purposes. First, it is especially designed to get students reading, thinking, talking, and writing about the world they live in. Its second aim is to acquaint students with the diverse viewpoints and controversial contents of America's leading periodicals in the hope that they will become regular readers of some of them. To this end, a subscription list describing the periodicals represented in the book appears at the back of *Our Times/2*.

Why a new edition after only two years? The reason is simple: to keep the selections as fresh and topical as possible. Any instructor who wants to use reading material that reflects recent trends and issues knows how quickly anthologies go out of date. To keep *Our Times* current, the book will be revised every two years. But each edition will be available for three years from the publication date. *Our Times/1*, for example, remains available until February 1992.

This second edition has been expanded to seventy selections, fifty-two of which are new. The readings are still grouped, however, into twenty-seven units that treat many of the dominant themes, issues, and ideas of our time. These topics appeal directly to the everyday lives of today's students: the difficulties of parent-teenage conversation, the problems of conflicting identities, the obsession with personal appearance, the value of rock music, the struggle for private space. Represented, too, are a variety of perspectives on some of our country's most compelling social and political issues — AIDS, the homeless, teenage suicide, the drug crisis, and corporate responsibility toward the environment.

Several new and important public issues have been added to this edition: the heated debate over artistic expression, the "outing" of gay men and women, the credibility of television news, the concern with animal rights, the challenges of cultural diversity, and the expectations for America in the rapidly changing world picture. So that the readings hit especially close to home, this edition also features expanded coverage of serious campus issues; besides rape on campus, there are now units on racism, "fighting words," and the canon debate.

A word about the size of these thematic units. In contrast to most thematically arranged readers, which contain a small number of broad categories, *Our Times/2* features a large number of tightly focused units, each with only two or three selections that speak directly to each other. Instead of one large chapter on the media, for example, *Our Times/2* has a smaller unit on television sex role stereotyping and another on television broadcasting of the news. The advantages to using these smaller bite-size units in a composition course should be immediately apparent to instructors: they permit a wider range and variety of topics to be covered in a syllabus; they allow for more focused discussion and writing; and they can be adequately handled in one or two class periods.

The organization of *Our Times/2* and its assignments conveniently conform to the writing agenda of most composition programs. The units themselves are roughly arranged to move from topics close to students' private lives and personal experiences (today's generation, identity conflicts, physical appearance) to topics dealing with more public aspects of American life (drugs, cultural diversity, the environment). The progression of the units is reflected in changes in the types of writing assignments. Generally, the unit assignments in the first third of the book ask students to write personal narrative and reflective essays; in the second third they concentrate on expository and analytical writing; in the final third the assignments ask for argumentative and persuasive papers.

With its emphasis on recent issues and ideas, *Our Times/2* invites class discussion and debate; in fact, the book is carefully designed to facilitate such student responses. Each unit is prefaced by a contextual note that not only helps students find their way into the readings but points the way to future discussion. Key biographical information about the authors is unobtrusively included in footnotes. Each unit ends with a section called "Discussing the Unit," which includes three sets of interlocking study questions and tasks that help students prepare for class discussion and then incorporate that discussion into their own writing. First, a "Suggested Topic for Discussion" lets students know beforehand what main topic their class discussion will cover. This topic gives students a common purpose in reading and helps keep the discussion focused. Second, "Preparing for Class Discussion" gives students questions and ideas to think about so they will come to class with something to say about the topic. Many of these preparatory questions ask the student to do some preliminary writing. Third, "From Discussion to Writing" gives students a writing topic that — without being redundant — draws on and applies the class discussion.

A basic premise of *Our Times/2* is that class discussion — often overlooked as a pedagogical resource — can play an important role in composition by stimulating fresh ideas and creating a social context for writing. Instructors interested in using class discussion as a basis for writing (or in simply eliciting more discussion in general) are encouraged to have their students read "To the Student: A Note on Participating in Class Discussion," which offers some practical advice on how to prepare for and participate in class discussion.

A fuller description of the educational advantages of linking reading, discussion, and writing — along with tips for directing class discussion — can be found in my introduction to the instructor's manual. For teachers interested in using discussion as a basis for composition, the manual for this second edition also includes two new essays on the topic. In "Forming Forums: Encouraging Research, Discussion, and Better Writing," Liz de Beer of Rutgers University offers many practical ideas for using *Our Times/2* in the classroom. In "The Morton Downey Jr. Model: Talk Show Influence on Classroom Discussion," Judith Rae Davis of Bergen Community College in New Jersey provides a provocative view not only of how talk shows influence student attitudes but of classroom discussion in general. Davis's essay, which originally appeared in the October 1989 issue of *Teaching English in the Two-Year College*, won the Best Article of the Year Award presented by that journal.

Prepared by Charles L. O'Neill of St. Thomas Aquinas College, *From Discussion to Writing: Instructional Resources* is bound into the Instructor's Edition of the book. It is an indispensable component of *Our Times/2*. Besides providing a convenient, brief summary of the selections and their relation to the topic, it offers numerous classroom activities for each unit. The manual encourages instructors to use a variety of collaborative tasks, from small-group writing exercises to informal panels and debates. It also contains suggestions for additional reading and research as well as recommendations for supplementing the readings with related and readily available films. Perhaps the most valuable part of the manual, however, is its "Suggestions for Directing Class Discussion." Linked directly to the "Preparing for Class Discussion" questions in the book, these suggestions offer instructors explicit ways to channel their students' reading and preparation into lively and productive discussion — and then into engaging compositions.

Finally, for instructors who don't want to use the class discussion unit, or who don't want to use it all the time, *Our Times/2* contains alternative apparatus. A set of questions, "Points to Consider," follows each selection. These questions can be used by instructors who prefer to concentrate on individual pieces. Instructors who want to give writing tasks based on single selections alone will find in the *Instructional Resources* appropriate assignments that grow directly out of "Points to Consider." The manual also contains a table of contents that groups individual essays into large thematic categories for teachers who would prefer to organize all or some of the selections in different ways.

Acknowledgments

As series editor of the annual *Best American Essays*, I monitor every issue of practically every major national and regional magazine. I would like to thank the many editors and publishers around the country who generously keep me posted on relevant essays and articles. For this edition, I expanded the number of periodicals represented; the selections in *Our Times/2* are drawn from fifty-two different magazines and newspapers. These periodicals represent a full spectrum of regions, interests, and points of view — from *Philadelphia* to *Seattle Weekly*, from *Harvard Business Review* to *The Sciences*, from *Mother Jones* to *The National Review*.

I'd like to thank, too, my students in several writing classes I taught over the past few years at Seton Hall University, where I developed and tried out many of the ideas for this book. I hope some of these students — especially Jane Jubilee, Susan Stoessel, Raymond Piccolini, Nicholas Ghizzone, and Eric Callahan — learned as much from me about writing as I learned from them about teaching. A good part of my thinking about the links between writing and discussion grew out of a 1987 conference at Seton Hall, "Redefining the Essay for the Humanities," in which I participated with (among others) O. B. Hardison of Georgetown University, Donald McQuade of the University of California at Berkeley, William Howarth of Princeton University, Scott Russell Sanders of Indiana University, George Core of the *Sewanee Review*, Kurt Spellmeyer of Rutgers University, Thomas Recchio of the University of Connecticut, Michael Hall of the National Endowment for the Humanities, Jacqueline Berke of Drew University, and Alexander Butrym (the conference director), Barbara Lukacs, and Nancy Enright of Seton Hall.

An early version of this book received some very cogent suggestions from Kathleen Shine Cain of Merrimack College, Michael Meyer of the University of Connecticut, and Thomas Recchio. My publisher, Charles H. Christensen, who brings a Montaignean spirit to these endeavors, helped me fashion and refashion, shape and reshape the project until it reached a "go-ahead" form. Joan E. Feinberg, in the best editorial tradition, not only helped me develop many of my thoughts but contributed many splendid ideas of her own. I also wish to thank several other people at Bedford Books who helped me prepare this new edition. My editor, Jane Betz, participated in so many aspects of *Our Times/2* — the shaping, the selecting, the reviewing, the research, the permissions — that editor seems like the wrong word; collaborator might be better. In addition, I received valuable editorial and research assistance from Beth Castrodale, Ellen Kuhl, and Constance Mayer. Mary Lou Wilshaw, Debbie Liehs, and Laura McCready deserve a great deal of credit for helping to get this second edition through production in a very short time. Once again, I was fortunate to receive Dan Otis's superb copy-editing and perceptive comments. I thank, too, Susan M. S. Brown, who proofread the book.

For their assistance on *Our Times/2*, I'd like to thank a number of friends, colleagues, and reviewers for many helpful suggestions. Charles O'Neill and Matthew Kearney (of Mercer County Community College) provided two enormously useful essay-reviews of the first edition. I also received good ideas from several of the book's users who generously responded to a comprehensive questionnaire: Liz de Beer (Rutgers University), Gunnar Gundersen (Willamette University), Peggy J. Hailey (Rutgers University), Jeanne Pavy (Emory University), Vonnie J. Rosendahl (University of Nevada, Reno), Dian Wyle Seiler (Pace University), and Robert Weinberger (Florida International University).

Working on both editions of *Our Times* would have been far more difficult and certainly far less fun without the help of two good friends, Jack Roberts of Rutgers University and Charles O'Neill of St. Thomas Aquinas College. Both helped in the preparation of apparatus for the book as well as the manual, and much of each edition is informed by their lively and intelligent discussion of topics and selections. They brought to the project a spirit of conversation and inquiry that I am confident will carry over into the classroom. Michael McSpedon generously helped with the proofreading.

Finally, I'd like to thank my family for its patience and contributions. My wife, Hélène, discussed many potential topics with me and helped me choose those that would be most relevant to this collection. My son, Gregory, who just turned seven, liked to interrupt me with such annoying but essential questions as "How do people know what to write about?" or "How do ideas happen?" Two-year-old Emily had few questions but did have some answers. She once jumped on my lap, poked some keys on the keyboard, and dumped a page of text into electronic limbo. I had to rewrite the page. That's one way to make ideas happen.

R. A.

To the Student: A Note on Participating in Class Discussion

Our Times/2 encourages you to view your reading and class discussion as important parts of composition. The book assumes that writing and discussion are closely linked, that each is stimulated and enhanced by the other. By participating in discussion, you approach a writing assignment with an increased awareness of a topic's possibilities; by writing, you open the door to further discussion of the topic. Class discussion allows you to test ideas, explore points of view, share experiences, examine a wide range of opinions. All of these "mind-stretching" activities make a significant difference when you sit down to write.

Like writing, discussion is a learned activity. Learning how to participate in group discussion could be one of the most important skills you can acquire in college. It will be an asset in nearly every course and make you better prepared for a professional career. To be adept at any kind of serious group discussion you must develop a variety of skills — in speaking, listening, thinking, and reading. The following will help you improve your discussion techniques:

1. *Be willing to speak in public.* Good discussion depends on the lively participation of all group members, not (as so often happens) on the participation of a vocal few. Many students, however, do not join discussions because they are afraid to speak extemporaneously in a group. This fear is quite common — so common, in fact, that according to a leading communication consultant, Michael T. Motley, psychological surveys "show that what Americans fear most — more than snakes, heights, disease, financial problems, or even death — is speaking before a group." To take an active role in your education you must learn to overcome "speech anxiety." Professor Motley offers the following advice to those who are terrified of speaking before a group: stop thinking of public speaking as a performance and start thinking of it as communication. He believes that people choke up or feel butterflies in their stomachs when starting to speak because they worry more about how people will respond than about what they themselves have to say. "Most audiences," he reminds us, "are more interested in hearing what we have to say than in evaluating our speech skills."

2. *Be willing to listen.* No one can participate in group discussion who doesn't listen attentively. Attentive listening, however, is not passive hearing, the sort of one-way receptivity we habitually experience when we tune in to our radios, cassette players, and television sets. A good listener knows it is important not only to attend closely to what someone is saying but to understand *why* he or she is saying it. Attentive listening also requires that we understand a statement's connection to previous statements and its relation to the discussion as a whole. Perhaps the most valuable result of attentive listening is that it leads to the one element that open and lively group discussion depends on: good questions. An expert on group dynamics claims that most ineffective discussions "are characterized by a large number of answers looking for questions." When the interesting questions start popping up, group discussion has truly begun.

3. *Be willing to examine all sides of a topic.* Good discussion techniques require that we be patient with complexity. Difficult problems rarely have obvious solutions that can be conveniently summarized in popular slogans. Complex topics are multifaceted; they demand to be turned over in our minds so that we can see them from a variety of angles. Group discussion, because it provokes a number of divergent viewpoints, is an excellent way to broaden our perspectives and deepen our insight into complex ideas and issues.

4. *Be willing to suspend judgment.* Class discussion is best conducted in an open-minded and tolerant spirit. To explore ideas and issues in a free and open manner, you will need to develop a receptivity to the opinions of others even when they contradict your own. Discussion, remember, is not debate. Its primary purpose is communication, not competition. The goal of group discussion should be to open up a topic so that everyone in the group can hear a wide range of attitudes and opinions. This does not mean that you shouldn't form a strong opinion about an issue; rather, it encourages you to be aware of rival opinions. An opinion formed without awareness of other points of view — that has not been tested against contrary opinions — is not a *strong* opinion but merely a stubborn one.

5. *Be willing to prepare.* Effective discussion is not merely impromptu conversation. It demands a certain degree of preparation. To participate in class discussion, you must consider assigned topics beforehand and read whatever material is required. You should develop the habit of reading with pen in hand, underlining, noting key points, asking questions of your material, jotting impressions and ideas down in a notebook. The notes you bring to class will be an invaluable aid in group discussion.

To get the most out of your reading and discussion, take careful notes *during* class. You will want to jot down points that have given you new insights, information that has changed your opinions, positions you take exception to, questions you need to answer, ideas you want to consider more fully. You should think of class discussion as the first step toward your paper, where you can brainstorm ideas, form an approach, discover a purpose. When you sit down to write, you will not be starting from scratch. If you've taken careful notes, you've already begun to write.

Good writing, like nature, abhors a vacuum. That is why most experienced writers work within a climate of ideas generated by reading, discussion, and debate. This climate of ideas permeates their writing. We usually don't have to proceed very far into an essay or article to see how directly the writer is responding to the ideas of others: a literary critic begins an evaluation of a famous novel by citing another critic's opinion; a political commentator starts an argumentative column by summarizing an opponent's position on an issue; a personal essayist launches into an autobiographical episode by quoting a classic writer on a similar theme. As you read the selections in this book you will notice how often the writers are directly engaged in a public exchange of ideas, how often they seem to be participating in discussion *as* they write. This book invites you, too, to write as an active participant and not a passive spectator in the discussion of issues and ideas. It encourages you to write not as an isolated speaker but as part of a community of speakers engaged in the lively pursuit of coming to terms with our times.

Contents

When an African American changed her name she also changed her life.

6   Personal Appearance: How Much Do Looks Count?   112

Looks aren't everything, the saying goes. But are they? One of America's leading pollsters is surprised by our obsession with good looks. . . . A young career woman admits that being beautiful is a definite advantage. . . . Two research psychologists find that good looks are evaluated far differently for men than for women.

7   Public Space: Who Are Its Victims?   130

Public space is space that should be shared equally by all. But often it isn't. A black *New York Times* editor walking alone at night reflects on the fear he automatically produces in others. . . . Constant rudeness makes the life of a young woman in a wheelchair even tougher. . . . An irate citizen raises his voice against the intrusion of music into every corner of American life.

harm of hate speech without introducing censorship. . . . A noted champion of the First Amendment is convinced that such regulation poses a serious threat to individual rights and academic freedom.

11   The Canon Controversy: Whose Classics Are They?   215

When Stanford University recently replaced its traditional Western Civilization course with one that offered a wider, multicultural set of readings, the decision sent shock waves through academia. Was this a signal that the Western intellectual heritage was no longer relevant? Or was it a sign that universities need to broaden their cultural viewpoint? In an address to the students of Stanford, the then secretary of education urges them to study and protect Western values. . . . A Stanford professor disputes the idea of a Eurocentric core curriculum and argues for a multicultural approach to the humanities.

12   Rock: Music or Menace?   239

Is rock music merely the opium of the young masses, or is it a legitimate art form? The controversial author of *The Closing of the American Mind* argues that today's students substitute popular music for serious books. . . . In rebuttal, a Yale professor explores the cultural and aesthetic value of rock.

13   Artistic Expression: What Are Its Limits?   263

The proliferation of obscenity charges in the world of art and entertainment has engendered a new debate about the need for censorship.

An outrageous comedian whose popularity rests on sexist and racist jokes meets with shocking success. . . . A rap group's alleged obscenity must be interpreted within the context of black culture, argues a prominent African-American literary scholar. . . . A federal judge walks us through his decision-making process as he takes the bench in an obscenity case.

14 Outing: Do Gays Have a Right to Privacy?   286

Does the press have the right to make the private lives of gay celebrities public? A recent phenomenon in American journalism is a practice called "outing"—the exposure of public figures as lesbian or homosexuals. The practice of bringing people involuntarily "out of the closet" is defended in the hope that it will lessen the social stigma of homosexuality. A lesbian educator examines the anxieties of gay and straight students toward outing at a prestigious college. . . . A *Village Voice* writer and homosexual takes issue with this controversial practice.

15 Television and Sex Roles: Is TV Defying the Stereotypes?   303

Among the most watched television shows on campus, *Roseanne* and *thirtysomething* are also among the most challenging to America's stereotypical views of male and female behavior. Do these shows represent important changes in public consciousness or is television merely capitalizing on social trends? A prominent feminist writer defends the undainty feminism of Roseanne Barr. . . . Sensitive, quick-witted, introspective, the male characters of *thirtysomething* are just like real guys, right? asks *GQ* magazine in a cover story.

living with the homeless on the streets of New York and gives a vivid account to their day-to-day existence.

21   The AIDS Epidemic: Is Anyone Safe?   452

An estimated 1.5 million people around the nation are infected with the AIDS virus. A young feature writer tells the intimate story of three people who never thought AIDS could happen to them. . . . One of the country's leading experts on AIDS has a ready answer to those who want to know if you can get AIDS from a mosquito. . . . An already famous *New Yorker* short story portrays the impact of the disease on a victim's circle of friends.

22   The Drug Crisis: Is Legalization a Solution?   492

As drug abuse continues to be an insurmountable national problem, more and more experts are wondering if legalization could work. After all, other dangerous addictions are legal—alcohol, cigarettes, gambling—so why not drugs? But the options may not be so simple. A city newspaper editor argues that legalization could be an effective strategy against not only drug abuse but also the crime that prohibition of drugs has created. . . . A well-known expert on crime questions a policy that would socially endorse the use of drugs and argues that the problem can be contained by strict law enforcement.

26   Business and the Public Interest: Can They Work in Harmony?   613

In a chilling speech, a buyout specialist in the movie *Wall Street* claims that corporations are motivated solely and rightly by greed. Is this true? Is it possible to establish better relations between corporate needs and national interests? An advocacy journalist proposes that executives whose corporations have knowingly caused the deaths of innocent citizens be put on death row along with other murderers. . . . American business has begun to show a new respect for our human resources and quality of life, reports the publisher of *Business Ethics* magazine. . . . An investigative journalist discloses how corporations keep an eye on environmental groups that oppose them by donating big wads of money.

27   The Changing World Picture: What Does It Mean for America?   638

The revolutionary changes in the Soviet Union and Eastern Europe have forced Americans to wonder about their own national values and sense of direction. A *Life* magazine essayist and columnist asks what has happened to our great commitment to freedom and equality. . . . Worried about an America nearly gutted by horrendous fiscal policies, a noted economist proposes a plan that would allow us to enter the next century solvent and with our ideals intact. . . . Two Tokyo-based *Newsweek* writers report on why the Japanese think of us as a nation of crybabies.

1

A New Generation:
What Are Its Values?

Do today's young adults constitute a unique generation, a distinct group with its own values, attitudes, and problems? In "A Generation Adrift," Charles Kenney and Robert L. Turner maintain that Americans in their late teens to early thirties—what the authors call the "post-Vietnam generation"—have grown up without the kind of formative conflicts that shaped preceding generations, and consequently possess a much different sense of themselves and their political responsibilities. As Kenney and Turner put it, this is a generation "caught in the middle—not products of Vietnam, but not Nintendo kids, either."

How will this generation respond to the challenge of a new decade? If the 1970s were known as the "me" generation and the 1980s the "mean" generation, what will we label the 1990s? Martha Minow believes that the new decade will test many of our constitutional and communal ideals. In "On Neutrality, Equality, and Tolerance: New Norms for a Decade of Distinction," she proposes several ways to improve human relations in a climate of increasing diversity. "Can we learn," she asks, "to look at perspectives other than our own, and then still others, continually unsettling our assumptions that we know what others think?" As you read Minow's essay, consider how the principles of behavior she recommends for the new decade also bear directly on the principles of effective discussion.

CHARLES KENNEY
AND ROBERT L. TURNER

A Generation Adrift   [BOSTON GLOBE MAGAZINE / September 3, 1989]

The generation of Americans who are now young adults has been, as odd as it sounds, deprived of the adversity that has been so valuable in shaping the American character.

The First and Second World Wars, Korea, Vietnam, the Depression, the civil rights movement, and the assassinations during the 1960s were traumatic experiences that tested the nation's mettle and proved that we as a people, joined together, could meet the stiffest of challenges. Those tests, which ultimately gave us such great confidence, have been crucial to shaping every American generation this century.

Until now. Americans in their late teens to early thirties—a group that accounts for a hefty 25 percent of the American population—are the first of this century to mature in a world where the elusive American ideal of simultaneous peace and prosperity is, for very many of them, at long last a reality. These young men and women were spared the brunt of the Cold War, of Vietnam, and of the domestic chaos and bitter discord of the 1960s. They have grown up in a world without the megachanges of previous decades such as the women's movement, for example, or the sexual revolution that the Pill brought about.

They are the post-Vietnam generation, the 60.3 million Americans born   4 from 1957 to 1971. The oldest of them, now thirty-two, remember Watergate, but they were preteens during the most turbulent parts of the late sixties. The youngest of them, now eighteen, were not even born when Martin Luther King, Jr., and Robert F. Kennedy were killed. The older ones come from the final years of the baby boom, the younger ones from the years when

---

CHARLES KENNEY (b. 1950) is a member of the Boston Globe *staff. He hosts a public affairs show on Channel 7 in Boston. Kenney is currently at work on a book about the rise and fall of Wang Laboratories.*

ROBERT L. TURNER (b. 1943) is a political columnist for the Boston Globe, *where he's worked since 1965. He is the author of* I'll Never Lie to You *(1976) and, most recently,* Dukakis: An American Odyssey *(1988), which he worked on with Charles Kenney.*

American birth rates were declining—now called the baby bust. But what makes this group fascinating is their lack of a common, bonding experience and their failure—so far—to challenge and push the nation as their predecessors did twenty years ago. In a sense they are a generation caught in the middle—not products of Vietnam, but not Nintendo kids, either.

Discussions with pollsters, social scientists, and dozens of Americans of this post-Vietnam generation indicates a tendency toward isolation and individualism, and a lack both of a sense of community with the rest of the country and the community values that bind so many other Americans.

One leading survey analyst, Dottie Lynch of CBS News, says only half-kiddingly that the major experience common to this generation is the shopping mall.

This is a generation of young men and women who are products of the economic Darwinism of the Reagan years that glorified individualism to the point of selfishness. These are the Reagan youth brigades, the young people who helped lock him into the first two-term presidency in thirty years and who voted in large numbers for George Bush.

But now there are signs that the post-Vietnam generation is becoming more active, is seeking a greater humanism and a sense of community than its members find in 1980s America. Increasingly, young people are volunteering for community service. They want stronger environmental protections. And, most significantly, they have been in the thick of the fight the past few months [the summer of 1989] on behalf of abortion rights. Indeed, some political analysts say that this generation—which does not remember an America before *Roe* v. *Wade*,[1] when those rights were not guaranteed—feels so strongly about abortion rights that the Supreme Court's recent decision allowing states to curb those rights may just be the rallying issue their generation has never had.

Perhaps more than anything else, these young Americans share the experience of economic anxiety brought on by the uncertainty about their future standard of living. They toe the conservative line on economic issues as they express a strong desire for economic security. It is ironic that these young people, the first generation to come of age in an America of peace and prosperity, may very well not achieve the level of material success reached by their parents.

Though achieving economic success will present little difficulty for William Landay, he still worries about his financial future as he reflects on other issues that confront his generation. At twenty-six, Landay is smack in the middle of the post-Vietnam generation. In some respects he is atypical: he is from a comfortable background, is a graduate of Yale, and is now a third-

8

---

[1] The controversial 1973 Supreme Court decision which held that state laws restricting abortion were unconstitutional.

year student at Boston College Law School. Landay spent last summer working at one of Boston's more prestigious law firms. He nonetheless has a clear-eyed view of his peers. Landay believes the post-Vietnam generation is "adrift. There doesn't seem to be any commitment. It seems directionless."

Kelly Fallon, twenty-three, is a graduate of the University of Massachusetts at Amherst who now works as a production coordinator at a Boston advertising agency. She is considering getting married within the next year or so and is concerned about the world in which she will raise her children. "In my generation we're a bunch of overachiever, Type-A personalities, or we don't do much of anything," she says. "There's no middle ground. There's no central force to pull us together. There's a lot of apathy. I think my generation is extremely materialistic. Personally, I'm an optimist, but I guess about my generation I don't have a very good view."

One of the more interesting nuggets buried beneath mounds of data   12
about the American people collected last year by the Gallup organization for the Times-Mirror Company was this fact: baby-bust generation members were approximately two-and-a-half times more likely than the average person surveyed to say that they did not know what major events had shaped their views.

Pollsters attribute this ambivalence both to the lack of a single overriding event such as Vietnam or the Depression and to the presence of so many smaller events—from Watergate fallout to the *Challenger* explosion. It is unclear which has left the strongest imprint.

And while there is disagreement over which *event* may have dominated, there is no quarrel about which *person* most influenced this generation. Ronald Reagan was president for as long as many of these young people can remember. He was revered by large numbers of the baby busters, but particularly by the older members of the generation, whose first political recollection was of the waning days of the Carter administration, when American hostages were still held captive in Iran.

Andrew Kohut, president of the Gallup organization, says two events were important to this generation, "One would be Jimmy Carter standing up and saying everything was wrong with America, and the other was Ronald Reagan standing up and saying everything is right with America."

The sharp contrast between Carter's description of America's "malaise"   16
and Reagan's vision of a shining future was very attractive to these young people, says Kohut. Though the historical concept of "American exceptionalism"—the notion that the United States occupies a lofty perch in the world—had been scoffed at by many in the baby-boom generation, Reagan and the post-Vietnam generation embraced it. Under Reagan, these young people grew up in a country at peace and in a time of prosperity for most.

"They like Reagan so much because he instilled pride and confidence in the country and because the country experienced fairly strong economic well-being under his leadership," says Neil Newhouse, senior vice president at the Wirthlin Group, a polling company in the Washington area.

The influence of the Reagan years has made these young people "much more likely to be conservative economically. They want to make money," says Newhouse. "They came of age in the 1980s, when there were no social movements for them to get into. They've focused a great deal of their efforts on getting jobs and making money."

And they admit it. In a Media General–Associated Press national poll last year, eighteen- to twenty-nine-year-olds agreed by large percentages that young people today are "less idealistic" (65 percent) and "more selfish" (71 percent) than young people twenty years ago. But many of today's young people (53 percent) also believe they are "more realistic" than their predecessors.

This realism stems not just from an absence of ideals or social causes 20 but from outright assaults on some of the pillars of modern life: money, technology, and religion.

The Chernobyl nuclear disaster in the Soviet Union opened technology up to question, but the event that raised the most doubts about our reliance on technology was the explosion of the space shuttle *Challenger* in 1986. That disaster, in fact, was listed in a survey of young voters conducted [in 1988] for *Rolling Stone* as the event with the greatest impact on their lives.

Jack Sansolo, a marketing expert who is president of Hill, Holliday, Connors, Cosmopulos, an international advertising agency based in Boston, believes that the 1987 stock market crash was also a crucial event to this generation. "It sent the message that making money is not everything," says Sansolo, "that you can lose it all in minutes."

Newhouse says there were numerous other events that shaped this generation, some large, some small. One reason, he contends, that this generation, for the most part, has an antidrug attitude is because of the 1986 death of basketball player Len Bias from cocaine. As Bias's death curbed their drug use, so, too, has the AIDS epidemic reduced sexual promiscuity. And they were turned off to religion by the scandals involving Jim and Tammy Faye Bakker, Jimmy Swaggart, and Oral Roberts.

Robert Green, a pollster with Penn and Schoen, a New York–based 24 market research firm, says he believes that, more than anything, this generation's attitudes have been shaped by economic frustration.

While America in general was prospering when this group was very young, by the time most were reaching adolescence, the nation was beset with problems that clouded the economic future. It became obvious that many in both the baby-boom and baby-bust generations would never achieve the same level of comfort in their lives as their parents did. The rules of the economic game suddenly changed. There were lines at gas stations. Inflation and interest rates soared. The cost of housing has sent many people in their mid and late twenties back home to their parents, seeking an affordable place to live. In the last dozen years, home ownership among persons under twenty has actually dropped from 32 to 26 percent.

"They have no glue," says social analyst Ralph Whitehead of the University of Massachusetts at Amherst.

In an article about her generation last July, Nancy Smith of the *Washington Post* wrote: "We are a group, of course. But a group of individuals. We have no symbol, no encompassing icon that pulls us together, no public hero who speaks for us. There's no unifying purpose, no common direction."

In a sense, that is the post-Vietnam generation's most striking trait. It 28 has been described as "confused" and "pending," in some ways like the disaffected Lost Generation of the 1920s.

In politics and ideology, these people don't follow the patterns established by the baby boomers. "I consider myself liberal," law student Bill Landay says, "although on certain issues I'm sympathetic to the conversative viewpoint." Though he is "repelled" by the Reagan presidency, Landay worries that government spending is out of control. But he also describes himself as having liberal views on the need for government care for the poor.

Deborah Kosofsky, a thirty-two-year-old producer at a Boston television station, is also split. "I agree with some of the liberal viewpoints, but sometimes I think the conservatives are right," she says. "We have to take care of the poor. I'd like to see everyone get health care. However, sometimes I can be more hard-line, like I think people should be forced to go to work. I'm not in favor of anyone getting a free ride."

As a group, the post-Vietnam generation differs in a number of significant ways from any of its predecessors. More young Americans than ever before have grown up in single-parent households. The number of babies born to single women age twenty to twenty-nine increased from 184,000 in 1975 to 482,000 in 1986, and most of the increase was among white women. More young people are children of divorced parents; the divorce rate has doubled since 1975. Many more are children of working couples.

All of which means the Ozzie-and-Harriet nuclear family has not been 32 a common, shared experience. Glue is lacking for this generation, and so are roots, at least the roots familiar to many waves of young people, either as valued supports or as targets of rebellion. Church attendance is down, for instance. Even as the nation's population increased by 26 million in the past dozen years, church attendance dropped by a million. And while some older people substitute televised religion for churchgoing, the percentage of people eighteen to twenty-nine who say they watch religious TV as often as once a week is barely half that for persons over fifty.

In addition, this generation is far more mobile than any in the past, moving with relative ease from place to place, from job to job, and friendship to friendship. This mobility is driven not by wanderlust but mainly by the search for work.

In many ways they have been pushed to act as adults earlier in life than were the boomers. In 1972 the Twenty-sixth Amendment to the Constitution gave eighteen-year-olds the right to vote. Large numbers of young people are sexually active, but they tend to marry and have families much later. These days, men and women in their late twenties are only half as likely to be married as were men and women of that age in 1975.

It may seem a paradox, but this is a generation of individuals who are self-centered but not necessarily selfish. The economic reality of life has forced them to be financially self-centered, but there are also many who give their time to social and political causes.

There is little tradition of sharing. You can see it in their music. Concerts still attract crowds, but, notwithstanding events such as Live Aid and Farm Aid, there will be no Woodstock for this group. It is a generation without a song—certainly without a single theme song. In the cities, music is absorbed either in isolation, through earphones, or through cranked-up boom boxes.

Not all of this has happened without strain. Indeed, while the national suicide rate has been fairly stable over the last fifteen years, the rate in the fifteen-to-twenty-four age group has jumped by nearly 50 percent. Assigning reasons is not easy, but clearly some in the group have not taken so readily to life alone. Many have been frustrated at the lack of connections, the apparent indifference to others' lives.

Jesse Williamson, nineteen, of Boston, is a junior at Brandeis University who is majoring in sociology and music. Williamson, who plays bass for a local funk-rock band called Between the Wheels, says many people his age feel they are being shortchanged by the generation now in power. On the economy, and especially on environmental damage, Williamson says, "They're upset about what [older] people have done. We've been brought into this, but it's not our fault. To many, it seems overwhelming. There's a feeling that you can't do anything about it."

To many, options for society as a whole seem to be closing in, even as individual possibilities still seem great. The future of education and health care is not as secure as it was a decade ago. Prosperity is something Americans can't control entirely, since it has been threatened by OPEC, the hyperproductivity of Japan, and by mountains of individual, national, and international debt. No one knows just how seriously the world environment is in jeopardy.

If the abortion issue has rallied this generation, it is not only on its own merits, but because constraining reproductive rights is another example of options closing in—of an older generation telling the younger one how to live.

One of the trademarks of the post-Vietnam generation is its racial and economic diversity, and more than any other generation it has a greater tolerance of gays and other groups. Two years ago, demographer Matthew Greenwald pointed out that "the early signs, from two decades of surveying college freshmen by UCLA social scientist Alexander Astin, are that the current group of freshmen are the most tolerant in American society, and the most socially 'liberal.'"

"In the abstract," says Bill Landay, helping others is "very important to me, although I have to admit that in my daily life I'm pretty self-absorbed. Outside my family or close circle of friends I don't do those sorts of community-minded activities."

Landay reflects the conflict between one's own financial success and finding time to help others.

To a twenty-five-year-old Boston tradesman, his own financial success is "the most important thing I could possibly think of." But this man was also one of the few members of this generation interviewed who does volunteer work. He has been a Big Brother for the past two years and spends at least a few hours each week with his little brother.

44

Hal Quinley, senior vice president of Yankelovich Clancy Shulman, a polling firm in Westport, Connecticut, says he believes there is "a reemphasis on identification with community, a longing. These people want a sense of belonging, a sense of community." Volunteerism is increasing, as is union membership, albeit slowly.

Jennifer Gordon, president of Eco-Matrix, a Brookline marketing firm, is one of many who say people start to have much longer-term concerns the minute they become parents. "Younger folks, when they have their first kid, change their view of the world," she says. This helps explain the growing concern for the environment and similar issues in the older members of the post-Vietnam generation.

But the UCLA surveys and other evidence indicate the beginnings of movement at the younger end as well. Jack Sansolo of Hill, Holliday theorizes that this generation is moving toward what he calls a "new humanisim" that will reign in this country in the 1990s. "The nineties began the day the stock market crashed," says Sansolo. It was then that this generation was stunned into looking for values more enduring than a dollar bill or than the materialistic values personified by the likes of Donald Trump.

That is not to say there is any indication of this group shedding its interest in material success. Many of these young people look "to the generation just ahead of them and see people struggling in jobs they are overqualified for, priced out of the housing market, not doing as well as they expected to," states demographer Matthew Greenwald. "And they fear that will be their fate as well unless they make a major effort to change that. Many are doggedly making that major effort."

48

This economic pressure is one fact of life that differentiates the post-Vietnam generation from the baby boomers, says Jim Miller, a *Newsweek* critic and Boston political scientist who has written books about subjects that include rock 'n' roll and the student left of the 1960s. "The baby boomers grew up in a time of the most sustained economic growth in the history of the world and therefore had a sense of utter affluence, which freed up people to experiment with their lives without fear it would wreck what they wanted to do down the road." But only a few years ago, Miller found the college students he was teaching "extremely concerned about making a living and that, given what was happening in terms of rising cost of housing, their concerns about whether they would be able to have the lifestyle their parents had were completely justified."

"It's important to me to be secure," says Landay. "It is not a goal of mine to be fabulously wealthy, although I have to say I run hot and cold on this issue. When I doubt the things I'm doing professionally—doubt whether I like the law, whether I want to be a writer, a politician, an astronaut—the thing I default to is go make lots of money. But then I slap myself around and come out of it."

Says Jesse Williamson: "I want to be a musician, but I don't know what I'm going to do for money," he says. Yet many of his schoolmates at Brandeis are driven by the prospect of financial reward.

But even as they make that effort, there is no overwhelming optimism about the country's future. "I don't feel optimistic at all about America's future, but I'm pretty optimistic about mine. Our generation realizes America isn't superman," says Edward Carbone, a graduate of the University of Massachusetts who works for an engineering firm. Carbone cares deeply about political issues, so much so that he went to work last year in Governor Michael Dukakis's campaign for the presidency. He moved to Pittsburgh, where he took on the distinctly unglamorous task of organizing on Dukakis's behalf.

The post-Vietnam generation will not roll through American life as have the baby boomers, who stretched the educational system, then the job market, and eventually will test the health care and retirement systems. Still, the post-Vietnam generation is now at the age when previous generations have influenced the nation's thinking and values, and this generation is showing signs that it will be no exception.

It is already happening, for instance, on the hottest political issue of the day: abortion.

While the new generation voted for Ronald Reagan and George Bush— both ardent opponents of abortion who favor a constitutional amendment banning it in all or most instances—these same young people are the strongest age group in support of abortion rights for women. Indeed, years from now, social scientists may look back and argue that the Supreme Court's curbing of the *Roe* v. *Wade* decision was the single major event that created this generation's political identity.

"It's the most important political issue to me, and I'm really not a very   56
political person," says Deborah Kosofsky, an ardent supporter of legalized
abortion. "But if I were to give my time to any political issue, it would be
abortion. I feel enormously strong about it."

Kelly Fallon long ago decided to volunteer her time to fight for legalized
abortion. When she was in college, years before the Supreme Court ruling
restricting abortion rights, Fallon joined Mass Choice, an abortion rights
organization. "I thought it was important to stand up for your rights," she
says. "It's a civil right, and I thought it was important to do something about
it."

Edward Carbone believes abortion is "an awful thing, but I'm still very,
very prochoice."

Just how all of this will affect who is elected to the governors' offices
and state legislatures won't be known in most states until November of
[1990]. But already, all across the country, candidates are moving to the left,
and one of the most significant forces doing the pushing is the post-Vietnam
generation.

In a nationwide poll conducted by Media General and the Associated   60
Press last July, after the Supreme Court ruling limiting abortion rights, 54
percent of people forty-five and older said they support *Roe* v. *Wade*, but
support was at 64 percent among eighteen- to twenty-nine-year-olds. Similarly, only 44 percent of the older group thought public funds should be used
even for counseling on the availability of abortions, but funding for counseling was favored by 60 percent of the young people.

One of the throng of political consultants who has looked at the question
is Michael Goldman of Boston, who is advising several prochoice candidates,
including Robert Ambler, a candidate for the state senate who openly flipped
to a prochoice position after the Webster case.

Goldman believes the issue is a driving one for the post-Vietnam generation because they are in their childbearing years. They, or people they
know, "might still have a need, and they don't want some state rep making
that determination," he says.

Their views are especially strong because they came of age after *Roe* v.
Wade was in place, Goldman says. "They don't know any different. They've
always had that protection." Now, he says, many feel: "If the court's not
there for me, I'd better the hell do something about it."

Similarly, this generation has grown up seeing the world environment   64
threatened as never before. DDT killed birds, but Love Canal killed people,
as did Chernobyl. Acid rain threatens whole ecosystems, and vast populations now seem threatened by the greenhouse effect and depletion of the
ozone layer.

There is evidence that the post-Vietnam generation has strong concerns
here. Fully 85 percent of eighteen- to twenty-nine-year-olds in a Media
General–AP poll conducted last May, after the *Exxon Valdez* spill in Alaska,

said they thought the federal government was doing only a poor to fair job of keeping the environment clean. And while this was only slightly higher than the disapproval rating from other age groups, there is some evidence that the younger people are beginning to act on their concerns.

Jennifer Gordon, for instance, is marketing a new brand of disposable, biodegradable diapers. Such a product would have gone nowhere in the seventies, she says, but has a real chance of succeeding with young parents today. "I think they are much more concerned than they were ten years ago," she says.

One area where this generation may have the most impact is volunteerism. Public opinion polls have consistently shown national service to be supported fairly evenly in various age groups, but the post-Vietnam generation has already begun to make a statement with its time, not just its opinions.

In California and Georgia, the cities of New York and Springfield, 68 Massachusetts, and a host of other areas, young people by the hundreds have been volunteering to carry out an enormous variety of services, ranging from conservation to health care to road repair. This will likely be the first generation since the early 1960s to make volunteerism a way of life, and indeed the participation level may well exceed that of the sixties. John F. Kennedy, Jr., who at twenty-nine is squarely in this generation, said last June in Cambridge that, after a long period of dormancy, he has seen growing volunteer and community activity among his peers in the last three years. "A spirit is growing," he said, and one bit of evidence especially pleasing to him is that the Peace Corps, after years of decline, is making a comeback. "It is a tribute to my father, and to all the able leaders of his administration," Kennedy said.

Kelly Fallon may be an example of what Kennedy is talking about. During her years in college she volunteered to work with developmentally disabled adults at the Belchertown State School. She not only helped others but found that the experience "rounded me out, made me feel like more of a person."

No one is suggesting that the spirit of the New Frontier is about to be recaptured. But some college graybeards do say they see in the current undergraduates glimmers of campus activism reminiscent of the sixties.

Overall, the post-Vietnam generation is off to a slow start, absorbed more with individual fulfillment than with common action. The lack of a major, formative crisis as they came of age deprives them not only of a shared experience but also of confidence in themselves as a group—a confidence that was achieved by those who persevered and then prospered after the Depression, by those who won World War II, and by those who helped change the nation in the sixties.

Which leaves the post-Vietnam generation fragmented, isolated, adrift. 72 Its impact is not likely to be felt en masse in major social or political movements—at least not to the extent of its generational predecessors. But like every other generation, it inevitably will make its mark, even if only by nudging the nation along.

Points to Consider

1. The authors argue that today's young adults have been "deprived of the adversity that has been so valuable in shaping the American character." What examples do they offer of this lack of adversity? Why do they see this as a disadvantage and not as an advantage? Do you agree with them on this point?

2. Consider the people the authors interviewed for this article. How many were there? What range of ages and experiences do they represent? Are any major viewpoints missing from the article?

3. Why do the authors regard abortion as such an important issue for this generation? Do you agree with their reasons?

4. What evidence do the authors cite of increasing political activism in this generation? How does the activism differ from that of earlier generations? Do you think activism is less important to this generation than the achievement of personal goals?

MARTHA MINOW

On Neutrality, Equality, and Tolerance:
New Norms for a Decade of Distinction

[CHANGE / January–February 1990]

I have heard the suggestion that if the 1970s were the "me" generation, the 1980s were the "mean" generation. As we ponder a label for the decade just passed, perhaps we can pick a name for the decade upon us, and then make a history to fit. How about this for the 1990s: "the decade of distinction."

Nice sounding, and ambiguous, right? But let me explain. We know the term "distinction" means worthiness, having special honor or recognition. But distinction also means what follows when we distinguish a difference; it means discrimination.

"Discrimination" has acquired the unfortunate implication of illicit or pernicious distinctions, drawn on the basis of race, sex, or other traits of group membership. We know the legacies of that meaning in our legal and social history: disparate and degrading treatment accorded to some people based on the assessment that they were "different." Skin color, sex, religion, physical and mental disabilities, age, sexual orientation—the list of differences that have mattered is the list of historic bases for oppression. Traits of distinction have been used to deny people entrance to colleges and universities and, at times, to deny them any rights.

Lawyers and educators have challenged these historic patterns with noted successes. It was not by accident that the NAACP Legal Defense Fund targeted universities and colleges first, and then public schools, to challenge the practices of racial segregation. Colleges and schools are central to the tasks of democracy and are vehicles for success in America; for these reasons

4

MARTHA MINOW, a 1979 graduate of Yale Law School, is currently a professor at Harvard Law School. She has written a book, titled Making All the Difference: Inclusion, Exclusion, and American Law, *which is scheduled to be published in fall 1990. The article was adapted from a keynote address before the National Association of College and University Attorneys.*

they will continue to be settings for debating the meanings of neutrality, equality, and tolerance, and for struggling to enact those ideals.

If the 1990s are to be years of distinction, then they will be a time to rethink distinctions that have wrongly been made to matter—and to consider distinctions that we should make matter.

But I am getting ahead of myself; let me start at the beginning. Lawyers and educators are inevitable partners as the making and unmaking of distinctions plays out in campus incidents calling for adjudication. Lawyers come to be involved because we are "the experts" in drawing distinctions. The basic problem-solving mode in law, after all, is distinguishing cases. As I tell my first-year law students, *Sesame Street* provides the essential introduction to law in its episode, "Which One of These Things Is Not Like the Other?" The episode engages the viewer in a process of categorization: a chair, a table, a book, and a bed—which one of these is not like the others? Drawing analogies across like cases and distinguishing unlike cases—this is the critical tool for analyzing precedents, interpreting statutes, and persuading decision-makers to accept your view.

I worry, though, that we tend to draw distinctions when we shouldn't— on the basis of race, gender, and other fixed personal traits—and we fail to draw distinctions when we should—distinguishing, say, speech from harassment. Line-drawing itself is not the point. Reaching desired ends is. Drawing lines is a technique to fulfill social purposes rather than a discovery of "real differences" or "real similarities" in the world. We *make* distinctions; we don't just find them.

I ask, then, in the name of the distinctive nineties, how can our line-drawing methods serve rather than obscure the constitutional ideals of equality, neutrality, and tolerance? My take-home message is that serving our ideals will involve learning to understand difference by recognizing diverse points of view. This recognition won't tell us what to do; it may even make things seem more complicated. But until we recognize the contrasting points of view on the meanings of constitutional norms, we won't know what distinctions matter, or to whom they matter.

This all may seem abstract, academic, or mushy. Let me offer into evidence three exhibits to explore our three goals: equality, neutrality, and tolerance.

Well, actually, three cartoons. These are the kind that professors clip out and tape on our office doors, having run out of space on the refrigerator at home.

The first cartoon shows a spotted dog sitting at a typewriter and typing out, "The quick brown dog jumped over the lazy fox."

The second shows a judge with a bulbous nose and bushy mustache, looking down from the bench at a defendant with the same nose and mustache. The judge announces, "Obviously, not guilty!"

In the third cartoon, a first frame shows a minister opening his mail and reading a letter that says, "Dear Minister, I'm sick and tired of your holier-than-thou attitude," signed, "Fed Up." The minister thinks for a minute and writes back, "Dear Fed Up: I forgive you." In the final frame, the minister thinks to himself, "Shame on you!"

What is going on in these cartoons? The best way to kill a joke is to analyze it, I know, but that's what we do in law school, so here goes.

Consider the first cartoon, the one of the dog who types out, "The quick brown dog jumped over the lazy fox." This cartoon highlights problems we have in fulfilling commitments to equality. It shows how prejudices and stereotypes work: they are shorthand to communicate that "we" are better than "they." This is a rather obvious, but not especially funny, point.

What's funny here is that the dog is a member of the group usually   16
identified as the lazy one in the saying, "The quick brown fox jumps over the lazy dog."[1] The cartoon uses the familiar device of surprise or substitution to achieve humor. Working at a level of deeper significance, the cartoon shows the impact of perspective on perceptions of equality and inequality. The cartoon reminds us that even commonplace perceptions of others, captured in sayings that we assume everyone knows and endorses, fall short of universality. They adopt a viewpoint.

We are usually able to remain unaware of our viewpoint *as* a viewpoint because it is reinforced by those we know, those we look to, those who confirm our perceptions—that is, by those who tend to be like ourselves. The cartoon reminds us that when we get a glimpse of the world from the vantage point of someone *we* think different from ourselves, *we* may be the odd or different one. Indeed, we are as different from they as they are from us. Difference is not something intrinsic in the "different" person. It is a comparison.

I have been told that, in Sweden and Norway, people tend to tell a lot of the same jokes—but in Norway they are about Swedes, and in Sweden they are about Norwegians. We may attribute to a group we don't know all the traits we don't like, even as they may do the same to us.

The goal of equality, then, will remain elusive so long as we attribute differences to others and then pretend that differences are discovered, not socially created. Equality will remain elusive so long as we neglect perspectives other than our own that could challenge the labels (like "lazy") we assign.

Consider this in the context of legal equality. Courts have interpreted   20
constitutional and statutory equality provisions to mean that government, employers, and schools must treat all people the same, if they *are* the same. But if they are not the same, if they are "really different," then the demands

---

[1] This now-familiar phrase was originally developed for typing practice; it contains all of the letters of the alphabet.

of equal treatment do not apply. It is unfair to treat people differently if they really are the same; but it is also unfair to treat people the same if they are different.

This points to the complexities of equality. The Supreme Court recognized these complexities in its 1974 opinion in the case of *Lau* v. *Nichols*. The Court ruled that instructing all public school children in English does not accord the *same* treatment to students who primarily speak Chinese as it does to those who speak primarily English. The Chinese-speaking students are denied the same opportunity to learn in the classroom granted to English-speaking students unless the language differences are accommodated in the curriculum.

Accommodation means remaking the ground rules so the difference is not used to exclude. Imagine a student who uses a wheelchair. What is her experience as a college student? If you have worked on issues of accommodation for disabled students, you have thought hard about this. Following a student in a wheelchair around campus is a sobering experience, even when there has been accommodation. Maneuvering a ramp in the snow, managing doorways and tight corners are hard enough. How about the student who joins an organization but who remains foreclosed from ever joining other students at the organization's office because it is inaccessible by wheelchair? A student I know recounted this story, his story, to a judge who is black. Tears sprang to the judge's eyes in recognition of his kindred experiences of segregation.

Does one have to have a kindred experience of discrimination in order to recognize inequality in the treatment of another? It helps, no doubt. But so does talking with others, and asking when differential treatment is injurious, or really necessary, or preferred by those who are treated "differently."

The cartoon of the dog at the typewriter suggests two lessons here. First, 24 you can't know, sitting alone at your typewriter, whether what you or others believe fits the experiences of people unlike yourself. You have to talk with them and learn with them. Second, we can't remedy a past invidious discrimination by drawing simply a new invidious discrimination—by characterizing all dogs as quick and all foxes as lazy.

Equality will remain elusive until everyone pays attention to the perspectives of others. Sometimes this means recognizing—re-cognizing—an issue that seems to be about freedom, from one perspective, but is also about equality, from another point of view.

The incidents at Stanford's Ujamaa House (the African-American theme house) provide an example. A year ago last September, a white student and a black student had an argument over whether Ludwig van Beethoven had any black ancestors; the black student maintained that this was the case; the white student said this was preposterous. The following night a group of white students got drunk and marked up a poster of Beethoven to represent a black stereotype. They then hung the poster outside the dorm room of the black student who had had the argument with the white student. Shortly thereafter a black fraternity poster was defaced with the word "niggers." School officials identified a student responsible for defacing the Beethoven poster, and began disciplinary proceedings. Those proceedings ended last spring with the recommendation of no discipline, citing the student's First Amendment rights.

Professor Patricia Williams, the first black woman to teach at Stanford Law School, has criticized the disciplinary committee for privatizing the matter, for foreseeing no injury to anyone from what it viewed as First Amendment expression. Professor Williams has written about how the incident injured her:

> I am a first black pioneer just for speaking my mind. The only problem is that every generation of my family has been a first black something or other—an experimental black, a "different" black, a hope, a candle and a credit to our race. . . . I wonder when I and the millions of other people of color who have done great and noble things and creative and scientific things—when our achievements will become generalizations about our race and [be] seen as contributions to the larger culture, rather than exceptions to the rule, as privatized and isolated abnormalities. . . . the most deeply offending part of the injury of the Beethoven defacement is its message that if I ever manage to create something as significant, as monumental, and as important as Beethoven's music, or the literature of the mulatto Alexandre Dumas or the mulatto Aleksandr Pushkin's literature—if I am that great in genius, and perfect in ability—then the best reward to which I can aspire, and the most cherishing gesture with which my recognition will be preserved, is that I will be remembered as white . . . maybe even a white man. This should not be understood as a claim that Beethoven's music is exclusively black music, or that white people have no claim to its history or enjoyment; it is about the ability of black and brown and red and yellow people to name their rightful contributions to the universe of music or any other field. It is the right to claim that we are, after all, part of Western civilization. It is the right to claim our existence. . . . The failure of Stanford to acknowledge this level of the harm in the Ujamaa House incident allows students to deface *me*. In the margins of their notebooks, or unconsciously perhaps, they deface me; to them, I "look like a stereotype of a black person," (as [the white student] described it), not an academic; they see my brown face and they draw lines "emphasizing [enlarging] the lips" and coloring in the "black frizzy hair." They add "red eyes, to give . . . a demonic look." In the margins of their notebooks, I am obliterated.

I am moved by Pat Williams's decision to let me and others know a portion of the injury she experienced from this incident. I don't think I'll ever think of it, and others like it, the same way again. We can't really learn about the partiality of our own perspectives without talking with other people about their perspectives, which help us rethink our own.

28

I do not mean here to review the merits of the Stanford decision, nor to tell you how I think other institutions should resolve similar matters in the future, though I am certain you will face them. I do mean to ask, when we do face them, do we have confidence that we know the meanings of these incidents from the perspectives of people we do not know well? Can we imagine, to use the legal tests, what might be the meaning of a "clear and present danger" to a member of a minority group who witnesses an incident like the one at Stanford? Whose are the "average person's sensibilities" to which we lawyers will refer in judging the seriousness of an incident? Or, using the words of the Supreme Court in *Cohen* v. *California,* what kinds of persons do we have in mind in concluding that "no individual actually or likely to be present could reasonably have regarded the words . . . as a direct personal insult"?

In short, can we learn to look at perspectives other than our own, and then still others, continually unsettling our assumptions that we know what others think? This struggle, I think, is critical to the search for equality. It is a process of continual reexaminations of the treatment we allow our institutions to accord people. The lines used to divide people must be scrutinized and rescrutinized to incorporate the perspectives of those who have not in the past been consulted.

Hearing a new perspective does not require deferring to it. The search is not simply for the fox's perspective, or the dog's, but for a perspective that can see them both. That is still a perspective—but it is not one that implies the normal and the deviant, the average and the marginal, but one that looks to the relationships between human beings.

Our second cartoon portrays a judge with a distinctive nose and mustache who declares that a defendant with a similar face is "obviously not guilty." This is a cartoon about the problems of neutrality.

On one level it raises the question, can anyone be unbiased when it comes to judging people one resembles? The cartoon reveals what we who are protectors of the legal system sometimes shield from view: officials are fallible. One predictable form of fallibility is bias toward people like oneself—and perhaps, correlatively, less sympathy toward people unlike oneself. We suffer from partial viewpoints, and risk bias as a result.

We lawyers have developed an oversensitivity to the appearance of bias; with all our talk about professional ethics, attention to the appearance of impropriety almost overshadows concern about wrongdoing itself.

Perhaps it was this concern with appearances that inspired the lawyers defending the law firm of Sullivan and Cromwell in a sex discrimination suit to seek the disqualification of Judge Constance Baker Motley, a black woman, from sitting on the case. They argued that she would identify with those who had experienced race or sex discrimination. Judge Motley explained her decision not to recuse herself this way: "If background or sex or race of each judge were, by definition, sufficient grounds for removal, no judge on this court could hear this case, or many others, by virtue of the fact that all of them were attorneys, of a sex."

Thus several twists present themselves in recognizing the partiality of 36 viewpoints. It is not enough to doubt the objectivity or neutrality of a particular judge who encounters a litigant who resembles herself in some way. It is also important to ask whether the asserted resemblance raises special doubts because the shared trait is itself perceived as different due to assumptions about a more general norm. Did the fact that Judge Motley shared her female gender with the plaintiff who sued the law firm stand out to the defendant because of an assumption that maleness is the norm in the courtroom, in the law firm, and in the application of law?

If these deeper assumptions about difference are at work, the issue of "bias" in judgment actually boomerangs. The question now is whether those who would assume a woman is biased (favorably) about women are themselves biased, though adversely, about women. The recognition of bias and partiality of viewpoint must work both ways. The dangers to neutrality arise as much with those whose viewpoints happen to coincide with the dominant viewpoints as with those whose viewpoint may stand somewhat apart.

For me this raises questions about the law's treatment of another disciplinary action, this one brought by Dartmouth College against members of the *Dartmouth Review,* who had been sanctioned following their treatment of a minority faculty member. The court found a defect in the college's disciplinary process since a committee member had signed a statement prior to participation in the process registering disapproval of the students' conduct. Again, without claiming special knowledge of the case, let me ask, how do you think bias should be treated here? I do not mean to doubt the bias of the member who had publicly announced a view. But why stop the scrutiny for bias there—what about the other members, or any potential members? Why exactly are those members of the Dartmouth community who failed to criticize the students' treatment of a minority faculty member "unbiased"? What does neutral mean here? Shouldn't the search for objectivity start with the recognition that everyone has a bias? And now what are they doing to overcome it?

This reminds me, too, of the search for a jury in the Oliver North case, one that had no exposure to the media coverage of the Iran-Contra hearings. Why does the definition of objectivity mean removal from the public debate over the issues of the day? Are such people neutral when, in some systematic way, they arrange their lives to miss the public debate?

By raising these questions, I do not mean to suggest that bias is never a 40 problem. On the contrary. I think it is a much bigger problem than we usually acknowledge. We either think any knowledge about a subject means bias—as if ignorance about it isn't bias—or we tend to see bias only in people unlike ourselves, and miss what our own actions look like to others.

In this light, I wonder what neutrality means, not just case by case, but in cases taken together. Consider, for example, two decisions made by the same disciplinary committee at Yale in 1986. The committee lifted disciplinary measures that had been imposed against a student who had put up posters satirizing homosexual activities and depicting a particular faculty member and a particular student; the committee said this satire was legitimate speech, protected by the university's commitment to free expression. The very same committee suspended some other students, though, for participating in an antiapartheid sit-in on university premises; the committee concluded that this activity was not protected speech.

Of course, from our legal offices, we can draw sharp distinctions here: speech versus conduct, paper versus bodies, satire versus protest, disrespect for personal reputation and a stigmatized group versus disrespect for property, trespass rules, and school authority. But how do these distinctions appear to gay and lesbian students in the community who wonder if they are now fair game for ridicule, and to students who view apartheid as evil and wonder if the university takes this view seriously?

Deciding what distinctions should matter, too often, happens before we even think about it. We take for granted distinctions we, and others like us, have drawn in the past. We presume and take as starting points for analysis that which we already know well, which inevitably reflects who we are and where we've been—with the likely effect of distinguishing us from others in our own community who have different points of reference and orientation. This isn't neutrality. It's mindless repetition of the nonneutral past.

Even more generally, we stray from neutrality when we take for granted 44 a frame of reference that is familiar to us, without pausing to justify it. We often don't even notice ourselves doing this, because it happens so quickly, especially when we name a problem. I've thought about this in the context of the incidents at Stanford's Ujamaa House. They have often been called by the name "hate speech"; this triggers a free-expression analysis. What we call a problem is halfway toward our treatment of it. Naming categorizes. We use our categories to tell us what to do.

Let's consider how we name the range of recent actions, not just the defaced Beethoven poster and the defaced poster of the black fraternity, but also other incidents that occurred in the past school year: swastikas and Ku Klux Klan graffiti on college walls and sidewalks; the defacement of posters announcing events for women's groups, Third World coalitions, and gay and lesbian groups; notes slipped under dormitory room doors saying "African nigger, go home," and "If you talk once more in favor of abortion, you are going to get fucked"; and a male student wearing to a class on women and the law, a T-shirt saying, "ban women lawyers." We could, and we should, consider the ways in which such actions are similar and different, and when the distinctions should matter in formulating responses. But even before we do this, how do we *name* these incidents? If we call them incidents of "hate speech," haven't we already decided to categorize them as problems of free expression?

"Well," you may be thinking, "that's what they are." And within our current legal culture, that's what most of us would tend to conclude. But this is because we take for granted some lines of thought, and neglect others that may be a bit less familiar. Consider an alternative name—"harassment." As campuses develop codes against sexual and racial harassment, for example, statements and comments that once might have been viewed as simply free expression are now treated as impermissible harassment, depending upon the context.

Consider another alternative name—group defamation. In a classic article on that subject, written in 1942 for the *Columbia Law Review*—years before he wrote *The Lonely Crowd*—David Riesman explained as peculiar an American reluctance to regulate group defamation. This reluctance he attributed both to the heavy legal emphasis on individualism, neglecting the significance of social groups, and to the American focus on capitalism, to the exclusion of concern for reputation based on honor, not merely commercial or financial status. Riesman challenged the conventional American view that, as the number of people within a labeled group expands, "the extravagance of the defendant's statements—or his obvious misanthropy—will discredit him without the need for legal interference." "On the contrary," wrote Riesman, "where the defendant is engaged in exploiting the anxieties or the sadism of his audience, and can count on built-in prejudice, he may increase his credibility as he increases the scope and violence of his lies." Riesman offered Hitler's *Mein Kampf* as his footnote support—a timely reference, not only in 1942.

Especially important for our purposes, Riesman emphasized the significance of social and political context in the development of rules for libel and slander. He noted that "lawyers, trained in the tradition of distinction-drawing and eschewing generalities, may find it difficult to recognize, or to admit, these 'nonlogical' factors in communication, although their training also teaches them the varying meanings which emotion may attach to words." The line that is important, and difficult to draw, is that between social criticism and group defamation; here Riesman recommended the common law technique of "wariness, putting out feelers here and withdrawing them there, as behavior is seen to react to the institutional changes."

Attentive himself to his own social and political context, Riesman wrote that writers hostile to the use of libel law reflected historical fears of the absolutist state or authoritarian church. He wrote: "In the more or less democratic lands, however, the threat of fascism and the chief dangers to freedom of discussion do not spring from the 'state' but from 'private' fascist groups in the community. These groups try to repress criticisms of themselves, sometimes with the help of the government, but more often and more subtly by 'private' pressure and coercion." And this part of Riesman's comment seems particularly timely today: "Or the defamation aims shifted to relatively powerless scapegoats—Negroes, Jews, Mexicans—the attacks which might otherwise be made against the prevailing system. . . . In this

48

state of affairs, it is no longer tenable to continue a negative policy of protection from the state; such a policy, in concrete situations, plays directly into the hands of the groups whom supporters of democracy need most to fear."

Riesman, like others today, suggested that neutrality does not mean an absence of state regulation. The state is not neutral when it permits some private groups to wield power over others. Does this view, however, contravene our liberal, constitutional commitments to freedom and limited state power?

Interestingly, that great prophet of liberalism, John Stuart Mill, in *On Liberty,* wrote about the social tyranny exercised by the majority that is more formidable than many kinds of political oppression, since "it leaves fewer means of escape, penetrating much more deeply into the details of life." He added, "Protection, therefore, against the tyranny of the magistrate is not enough: there needs protection also against the tyranny of the prevailing opinion and feeling; against the tendency of society to impose, by other means than civil penalties, its ideas and practices as rules of conduct." You, therefore, may cite John Stuart Mill in support of contemporary codes against a harassment of minorities that is otherwise silently countenanced by majorities.

Notably, British, Canadian, and Italian laws—and even International 52 Covenants on Civil and Political Rights—give antiracism precedence over freedom of expression. Italy forbids the dissemination of ideas based on racial superiority or race hatred; Britain forbids public speech or publication of threats, insults, and abuse likely to stir up race hatred against any racial group in Britain; Canada's Charter of Rights and Freedoms includes a strong endorsement of free expression but simultaneously limits hate propaganda.

Even in the United States, despite a general disapproval of government restrictions against group defamation, the Supreme Court has unanimously treated as forbidden sex discrimination any sexual harassment that creates a hostile or abusive work environment.

Along with many readers, I do fear threats to freedom of expression, especially in an era when Chinese students are executed for speech and leading government officials seek to amend the constitution to prohibit protests using the American flag. Yet we may act too much out of fear, so much that we neglect to speak out against injuries we should not tolerate. If some acts of hate clearly seem to be harassment or discrimination, shouldn't we treat them as such, and not fear we will lose the ability to draw distinctions in the future? There are ways to name injuries and abuses that we miss if we simply label any or all incidents as forms of "speech."

At the same time, consistent with respecting freedom of expression, can't we develop ways for members of our own communities to express effectively and vividly their own disapproval of acts of hate—ways to shame or shun those who commit them? As members of our communities, committed to free speech, shouldn't you and I speak out against hate speech? Doing nothing, in these circumstances, is hardly neutral.

Thinking back to the judge with the big nose and mustache, I wonder if 56 we can all learn to pause before leaping to the conclusion that we recognize what is before us. Before naming an incident, can we think about the multiple perspectives from which it may be viewed—and named—and analyzed? Given the inevitable impact of our position on our perspectives, and our perspectives on our judgments, can we work for neutrality by searching out perspectives that we do not initially know?

Now for the third cartoon, about the minister, charged with a holier-than-thou attitude, who writes the complainant, "I forgive you." Why is it funny? It notes the self-sealing quality of so many beliefs. The minister recapitulates exactly what he is charged with even in his effort to respond. The cartoon has the quality of a paradox ("I am the most modest person I know"), a paradox created by the boundaries of our own thought. We are un-self-conscious as we repeat the very mistakes we mean to correct.

This problem permeates the search for tolerance in the law. Examples abound in the law's treatment of religious tolerance, women in the workplace, and contrasting sexual orientations, as judges perpetuate traditional distinctions even as they claim to implement commitments to tolerance.

Repeating the intolerance we were trying to avoid sometimes seems more apparent in hindsight. Connecticut was among the first colonies to adopt religious freedom provisions; nonetheless, a Connecticut court found no problem in refusing to accept court testimony from witnesses who declined to swear on the Protestant Bible. The court reasoned that those individuals could make no claim of religious intolerance: they could still practice their own religions. They just could not be called as witnesses in court, and the state's refusal to allow them to testify was ruled not to burden their religious freedom.

But such insensitivities are not from the past only. In 1988, the U.S. 60 Supreme Court rejected an Indian tribe's claim that the government violated the religious freedom of its members by proposing a road that would intrude upon and destroy the tranquility of a sacred site. The Court admitted that the proposed action would burden the religious freedom of the tribe members, and conceded that the government interest was not especially compelling. Nonetheless, the Court rejected the challenge; the majority failed to see this burden as serious and deserving of relief, and found the government action not coercive.

Similarly, in 1984 the Supreme Court rejected a claim that the presentation of a crèche scene on public property unconstitutionally established religion. The Court thereby indicated insensitivity not only to non-Christians, by doubting they would be offended, but also to observant

Christians by suggesting that the crèche presented no religious symbolism but was merely an earmark of the season, like Santa Claus.

These decisions are especially striking compared with moments when the courts seem to understand what they do not understand and implement tolerance by changing the ground rules. For example, in 1987 the Supreme Court considerd whether a state could deny unemployment benefits to a woman who left her job when her employer assigned her to work on her Sabbath. The state law allowed benefits only to those unemployed through no fault of their own. The Court reasoned it would be wrong to treat her religious beliefs as her own "fault" and that the proper question was whether the denial of benefits burdened her religious exercise; the Court answered that the denial posed an unacceptable burden by punishing her religious observance.

I found this recognition of an alternative starting point—the demands of religious observance—specially powerful because it departs from the earlier view that it is no constitutional violation to exclude a person from otherwise available public opportunities when that person chooses to exercise his or her religion. It is wrong to use the norm of the nonreligious person in defining the scope of unemployment benefits. The Court's reasoning was powerful, too, because it showed an understanding of the complexity of choice: one could choose to observe one's religion despite conflict with one's job and still not be properly deemed to be unemployed due to one's own fault.

Tolerance means "inclusion," but actually that is not enough. To many 64 people who have been made marginal in the past, inclusion sounds like, "come on in, but don't change anything." Inclusion sounds like, "you're welcome to join what we do, but we're not going to change what we do." What a different result would emerge if the meaning of tolerance for differences was widely understood to include the varieties of human beings within the norm against which equality is measured!

Notice that this is different from a simple call for inclusion—to include women minorities, for example, within your institution. This is a call for thinking about women, minorities, persons with disabilities, and others in the very definition of the person used to construct the institution. People are made marginal simply because their physical condition, sex, race, or religion wasn't in the minds of those who designed the institution. This is a call for scrutinizing our reluctance to remake our institutions. This is a call to look from the many perspectives of those who still sense rejection or subordination.

If we search out those perspectives, I think we'll come to hear that it is inadequate comfort to those who are injured to call abusive incidents isolated, trivial, or merely symbolic. A black woman I know who works at a predominantly white university recently had the shock of learning of a Ku Klux Klan presence in the university. Her white friends tried to reassure her that there was nothing to fear from such a kooky, marginal group; her response was to ask, "How can I feel safe when my friends don't respect my sense of danger?"

This brings me to the legal treatment of the Gay Rights Coalition at Georgetown University. A group of gay and lesbian students argued that school authorities violated a local ordinance forbidding discrimination on the basis of sexual orientation when they refused to grant official recognition to the gay students' organization. The university had a pretty good argument: it claimed that a governmental requirement to recognize the gay students would violate this Catholic university's right to the free exercise of religion. Given Catholic teaching that homosexuality is sinful, the District of Columbia court found in 1987 that Georgetown could not be compelled to recognize the student organization. The court concluded that mandatory endorsement would indeed amount to "compelled expression in violation of the First Amendment." The court did rule that the student groups were entitled to the tangible facilities afforded to other comparable organizations, but not to university recognition.

In some ways, this may look like a happy compromise; students are 68
assured the use of facilities, and a university can preserve its religiously inspired position. But I wonder where homosexual persons fit in the court's understanding: people to be put up with, or people who are members of the institution and the larger society? By accepting the university's view that recognizing the gay students' group would mean endorsing homosexuality, the court conflated two distinct questions: must the university treat the gay students' group the same way it would any other student group, on the one hand, versus must the university approve homosexuality, on the other. Once again, I am drawing a distinction about the ways we draw distinctions.

The court failed to distinguish university "recognition" from "endorsement." Yet the idea that university "recognition" is the same as "endorsement" is far from obvious. Indeed, the U.S. Supreme Court rejected that view in 1981 in *Widmar* v. *Vincent,* which required a public university to allow an officially recognized student religious group to use school facilities, and noted that university students could not reasonably conclude university endorsement from the "mere fact of a campus meeting place." Moreover, the D.C. court leaves open the possibility that universities may still differentiate on the basis of sexual orientation so long as there are no material disparities. Shades of separate but equal!

To forge a decade of distinction, we need to stop making distinctions out of habit, out of mindless repetition of tradition and familiarity. And we need to learn to make distinctions when our failure to do so wrongly injures or excludes people. All of this means looking at the issues of equality, neutrality, and tolerance from the vantage points of people who were not in mind when our institutions were designed. We can all learn from the occasions when we do glimpse a point of view other than our own. Such occasions can remind us to be more vigilant about presuming that our viewpoint is the only one we need to know.

Looking back at the three cartoons, I think there are lessons to help us hold at bay the legacies of distinctions drawn on the basis of race, sex, sexual orientation, and disability—and lessons to help make even more distinguished our institutions of the future.

The first lesson is for equality. To be meaningful, equality requires looking from multiple perspectives. It means paying attention to contexts and acknowledging the limits of one's own point of view. It doesn't mean caving in to a point of view you don't share; it does mean learning about other points of view rather than pretending yours is the same as everyone's.

The second lesson is for neutrality. Again, to be meaningful, neutrality requires us to look for starting points and expose them to questions; to recognize the partiality of every viewpoint. It also means guarding against disqualifying a viewpoint merely because it is partial. It means learning to consult, collaborate, and participate in overcoming the partiality of everyone's perspective.

The third lesson is for tolerance. To be meaningful, tolerance demands that we expose to view the unstated norms or distinctions we usually rely on and challenge the views embedded in our institutional practices. It means doing more than inviting outsiders to be included—it means listening to their views about what it would take for them to feel included. In colleges and universities, this means dialogue—dialogue about equality, neutrality, and tolerance, about discipline and freedom, about injury and harassment. It means considering the preconditions for participation—the preconditions for assuring that every member of the community feels like a member of the community.

And that means the courage to challenge old distinctions as we make new ones, to be tolerant but also to be intolerant—that is, toward behavior that prevents anyone else from feeling safe in our communities. That would make the nineties truly distinguished.

Points to Consider

1. What various meanings does Minow give to the word "distinction"? Why are these meanings important to her argument?

2. Minow might have used many different kinds of quotations to structure her article. Why do you think she chose the language of three cartoons? Do you think they help her make her points more effectively, or less?

3. Minow presented this essay as a keynote address before the National Association of College and University Attorneys. How has writing for this audience influenced her terminology and the examples she used?

What connections can you find, for example, between her audience and her theme of "distinction"?

4. Minow's goals seem reasonable and humane. But what obstacles might interfere with their implementation? Why might people not be so willing to help promote the ideals of neutrality, equality, and tolerance? How does Minow deal with objections to her proposal?

Discussing the Unit

Suggested Topic for Discussion

Kenney and Turner cite a recent opinion poll claiming that "baby-bust generation members were approximately two-and-a-half times more likely than the average person surveyed to say that they did not know what major events had shaped their views." Consider this comment in relation to your own life. Can you think of any public events that had an important impact on the way you perceive our times?

Preparing for Class Discussion

1. List some of the big national or world events that have occurred in your lifetime. Then go back over your list and jot down next to each event the following information: the main sources of your knowledge of the event (television, newspapers, hearsay, personal experience, etc.) and your emotional response to the event (preferably the way you felt at the time it occurred).

2. Kenney and Turner also cite a survey showing that today's college freshmen "are the most tolerant in American society, and the most socially 'liberal.'" These are characteristics that Martha Minow wants to cultivate as well. Now return to your list. Can you think of any events in your lifetime that played a role in shaping these generational characteristics of tolerance and liberalism? If so, make a note of them; if you think of events that may have had the opposite effect, make a note of them as well.

From Discussion to Writing

According to *Time* magazine, a conference was held recently in which the participants tried (unsuccessfully) to come up with an appropriate name for the age we live in. The authors of the articles in this unit were also concerned about such labels. Kenney and Turner use "post-Vietnam generation" and Martha Minow proposes "the decade of distinction." Based on your reading, reflection, and experience, what name would *you* give to these times or to your generation? Write an essay in which you propose a label for either one; be sure to supply the reasons why you think the label is appropriate.

2

Teenagers and Parents:
Why Can't They Get Along?

Why are relations between parents and teenagers so frequently marked by squabbling, bickering, nagging, arguing, and — at the other extreme — by stubborn silence? Why do these barriers to family communication seem worse today than ever before? What causes this verbal behavior, and which party is at fault: the adolescent or the adult? Or both? Is the constant bickering or monosyllabic sullenness an inevitable part of adolescent development? Or is it culturally conditioned?

These are questions to consider as you read the following essay and short story. In "Bound to Bicker," Laurence Steinberg, a developmental psychologist who has been studying "the day-to-day relationships of parents and young teenagers," reports that "even in the closest of families, parents and teenagers squabble and bicker surprisingly often — so often, in fact, that we hear impassioned recountings of these arguments in virtually every discussion we have with parents or teenagers." In the short story "Shopping," the well-known American novelist Joyce Carol Oates offers a vivid account of one such parent-teenager relationship, a mother and daughter who seem to have exhausted every means of mutual communication except one — shopping.

Bound to Bicker [PSYCHOLOGY TODAY / September 1987]

"It's like being bitten to death by ducks." That's how one mother described her constant squabbles with her eleven-year-old daughter. And she's hardly alone in the experience. The arguments almost always involve mundane matters — taking out the garbage, coming home on time, cleaning up the bedroom. But despite its banality, this relentless bickering takes its toll on the average parent's mental health. Studies indicate that parents of adolescents — particularly mothers — report lower levels of life satisfaction, less marital happiness, and more general distress than parents of younger children. Is this continual arguing necessary?

For the past two years, my students and I have been examining the day-to-day relationships of parents and young teenagers to learn how and why family ties change during the transition from childhood into adolescence. Repeatedly, I am struck by the fact that, despite considerable love between most teens and their parents, they can't help sparring. Even in the closest of families, parents and teenagers squabble and bicker surprisingly often — so often, in fact, that we hear impassioned recountings of these arguments in virtually every discussion we have with parents or teenagers. One of the most frequently heard phrases on our interview tapes is, "We usually get along but . . ."

As psychologist Anne Petersen notes, the subject of parent-adolescent conflict has generated considerable controversy among researchers and clinicians. Until about twenty years ago, our views of such conflict were shaped by psychoanalytic clinicians and theorists, who argued that spite and revenge, passive aggressiveness and rebelliousness toward parents are all normal, even healthy, aspects of adolescence. But studies conducted during the 1970s on samples of average teenagers and their parents (rather than those who spent Wednesday afternoons on analysts' couches) challenged the view that family storm and stress was inevitable or pervasive.

LAURENCE STEINBERG (b. 1952) is a professor of child and family studies at the University of Wisconsin, Madison, and a William T. Grant Foundation Faculty Scholar. His publications include Adolescence *(1985) and, with Ellen Greenberger,* When Teenagers Work: The Psychological and Social Costs of Adolescent Employment *(1986).*

These surveys consistently showed that three-fourths of all teenagers and parents, here and abroad, feel quite close to each other and report getting along very well. Family relations appeared far more pacific than professionals and the public had believed.

Had clinicians overstated the case for widespread storm and stress, or were social scientists simply off the mark? The answer, just now beginning to emerge, seems to be somewhere between the two extremes. 4

The bad news for parents is that conflict, in the form of nagging, squabbling, and bickering, is more common during adolescence than during any other period of development, except, perhaps, the "terrible twos." But the good news is that arguments between parents and teenagers rarely undo close emotional bonds or lead adolescents and their parents to reject one another. And, although most families with adolescents go through a period of heightened tension, the phase is usually temporary, typically ending by age fifteen or sixteen.

My own studies point to early adolescence — the years from ten to thirteen — as a period of special strain between parents and children. But more intriguing, perhaps, is that these studies reveal that puberty plays a central role in triggering parent-adolescent conflict. Specifically, as youngsters develop toward physical maturity, bickering and squabbling with parents increase. If puberty comes early, so does the arguing and bickering; if it is late, the period of heightened tension is delayed. Although many other aspects of adolescent behavior reflect the intertwined influences of biological and social factors, this aspect seems to be directly connected to the biological event of puberty; something about normal physical maturation sets off parent-adolescent fighting. It's no surprise that they argue about overflowing trash cans, trails of dirty laundry, and blaring stereos. But why should teenagers going through puberty fight with their parents more often than youngsters of the same age whose physical development is slower? More to the point: if puberty is inevitable, does this mean that parent-child conflict is, too?

It often helps to look closely at our evolutionary relatives when we are puzzled by aspects of human behavior, especially when the puzzle includes biological pieces. We are only now beginning to understand how family relations among monkeys and apes are transformed in adolescence, but one fact is clear: it is common, at puberty, for primates living in the wild to leave their "natal group," the group into which they were born. Among chimpanzees, who are our close biological relatives, but whose family structure differs greatly from ours, emigration is restricted to adolescent females. Shortly after puberty, the adolescent voluntarily leaves her natal group and travels on her own — often a rather treacherous journey — to find another community in which to mate.

In species whose family organization is more analogous to ours, such as gibbons, who live in small, monogamous family groups, both adolescent 8 males and females emigrate. And if they don't leave voluntarily soon after puberty begins, they are thrown out. In both cases, adolescent emigration helps to increase reproductive fitness, since it minimizes inbreeding and increases genetic diversity.

Studies of monkeys and apes living in captivity show just what happens when such adolescent emigration is impeded. For many nonhuman primates, the consequences can be dire: among many species of monkeys, pubertal development is inhibited so long as youngsters remain in their natal group. Recent studies of monogamous or polyandrous monkeys, such as tamarins and marmosets, have shown that the sexual development of young females is inhibited specifically by their mothers' presence. When the mother is removed, so is her inhibitory effect, and the daughter's maturation can begin in a matter of a few days.

Taken together, these studies suggest that it is evolutionarily adaptive for most offspring to leave their family early in adolescence. The pressure on adolescents to leave their parents is most severe among primates such as gibbons, whose evolution occurred within the context of small family groups, because opportunities for mating within the natal group are limited and such mating may threaten the species' gene pool. It should come as no surprise, therefore, to find social and biological mechanisms that encourage the departure of adolescent primates — including, I think, humans — from the family group around puberty.

One such mechanism is conflict, which, if intense enough, drives the adolescent away. Squabbling between teenagers and their parents today may be a vestige of our evolutionary past, when prolonged proximity between parent and offspring threatened the species' genetic integrity.

According to psychologist Raymond Montemayor of Ohio State University, who studies the relationships of teenagers and their parents, accounts of conflict between adolescents and their elders date back virtually as far as recorded history. But our predecessors enjoyed an important advantage over today's parents: adolescents rarely lived at home much beyond puberty. Prior to industrialization in this country, high-school-aged youngsters often lived in a state of semiautonomy in which they were allowed to work and earn money but lived under the authority of adults other than their parents. Indeed, as historian Michael Katz of the University of Pennsylvania notes, many adolescents actually were "placed out" at puberty — sent to live away from their parents' household — a practice that strikingly resembles the forced emigration seen among our primate relatives living in the wild.

Most historians of adolescence have interpreted the practice of placing out in terms of its implications for youngsters' educational and vocational development. But did adolescents have to leave home to learn their trade? And is it just coincidental that this practice was synchronized with puberty? Historian Alan Macfarlane notes that placing out may have developed to provide a "mechanism for separating the generations at a time when there might otherwise have been considerable difficulty" in the family.

Dozens of nonindustrialized societies continue to send adolescents away at puberty. Separating children from their parents, known as "extrusion," has a great deal in common with the behavior of many nonhuman primates. In societies that practice extrusion, youngsters in late childhood are expected to begin sleeping in households other than their parents'. They may see their parents during the day but are required to spend the night with friends of the family, with relatives, or in a separate residence reserved for preadolescents. Even in traditional societies that do not practice extrusion formally, the rite of passage at puberty nevertheless includes rituals symbolizing the separation of the young person from his or her family. The widespread existence of these rituals suggests that adolescent emigration from the family at puberty may have been common in many human societies at some earlier time.

Conflict between parents and teenagers is not limited to family life in the contemporary United States. Generally, parent-child conflict is thought to exist at about the same rate in virtually all highly developed, industrialized Western societies. The sociological explanation for such intergenerational tension in modern society is that the rapid social change accompanying industrialization creates irreconcilable and conflict-provoking differences in parents' and children's values and attitudes. But modernization may well have increased the degree and pervasiveness of conflict between young people and their parents for other reasons.

Industrialization hastened the onset of puberty, due to improvements in 16 health, sanitation, and nutrition. (Youngsters in the United States go through puberty about four years earlier today than their counterparts did a hundred years ago.) Industrialization also has brought extended schooling, which has prolonged youngsters' economic dependence on their parents and delayed their entrance into full-time work roles. The net result has been a dramatic increase over the past century in the amount of time that physically mature youngsters and their parents must live in close contact.

A century ago, the adolescent's departure from home coincided with physical maturation. Today, sexually mature adolescents may spend seven or eight years in the company of their parents. Put a different way, industrialization has impeded the emigration of physically mature adolescents from their family of origin — the prescription for parent-adolescent conflict.

Puberty, of course, is just one of many factors that can exacerbate the level of tension in an adolescent's household. Inconsistent parenting, blocked communication channels, and extremes of strictness or permissiveness can all make a strained situation worse than it need be. An adolescent's family should seek professional help whenever fighting and arguing become pervasive or violent or when they disrupt family functioning, no matter what the adolescent's stage of physical development.

Given our evolutionary history, however, and the increasingly prolonged dependence of adolescents on their parents, some degree of conflict during early adolescence is probably inevitable, even within families that had been close before puberty began. Telling parents that fighting over taking out the garbage is related to the reproductive fitness of the species provides little solace — and doesn't help get the garbage out of the house, either. But parents need to recognize that quarreling with a teenager over mundane matters may be a normal — if, thankfully, temporary — part of family life during adolescence. Such squabbling is an atavism that ensures that adolescents grow up. If teenagers didn't argue with their parents, they might never leave home at all.

Points to Consider

1. Steinberg distinguishes his own studies of parent-adolescent conflict from those conducted in the past. What sort of studies were done in the past, and how do his studies differ? Why are these differences important to our understanding of parent-adolescent bickering?

2. In his opening paragraph, Steinberg claims that "studies indicate that parents of adolescents — particularly mothers — report lower levels of life satisfaction, less marital happiness, and more general distress than parents of younger children." Consider this statement carefully. Could reasons other than bickering account for this general distress? In what other ways might parents of adolescents differ from parents of younger children? How might these differences account for the problems faced by parents of adolescents?

3. What connection does Steinberg make between bickering and the onset of puberty? How is this connection explained by human evolution? What exactly does Steinberg mean when he says that "fighting over taking out the garbage is related to the reproductive fitness of the species"?

Shopping [MS. / March 1987]

An old ritual, Saturday morning shopping. Mother and daughter. Mrs. Dietrich and Nola. Shops in the village, stores and boutiques at the splendid Livingstone Mall on Route 12. Bloomingdale's, Saks, Lord & Taylor, Bonwit's, Neiman-Marcus: and the rest. Mrs. Dietrich would know her way around the stores blindfolded but there is always the surprise of lavish seasonal displays, extraordinary holiday sales, the openings of new stores at the Mall like Laura Ashley, Paraphernalia. On one of their Mall days Mrs. Dietrich and Nola would try to get there at midmorning, have lunch around 1 P.M. at one or another of their favorite restaurants, shop for perhaps an hour after lunch, then come home. Sometimes the shopping trips were more successful than at other times but you have to have faith, Mrs. Dietrich tells herself. Her interior voice is calm, neutral, free of irony. Ever since her divorce her interior voice has been free of irony. You have to have faith.

Tomorrow morning Nola returns to school in Maine; today will be a day at the Mall. Mrs. Dietrich has planned it for days. At the Mall, in such crowds of shoppers, moments of intimacy are possible as they rarely are at home. (Seventeen-year-old Nola, home on spring break for a brief eight days, seems always to be *busy*, always out with her *friends* — the trip to the Mall has been postponed twice.) But Saturday, 10:30 A.M., they are in the car at last headed south on Route 12, a bleak March morning following a night of freezing rain, there's a metallic cast to the air and no sun anywhere in the sky but the light hurts Mrs. Dietrich's eyes just the same. "Does it seem as if spring will ever come? — it must be twenty degrees colder up in Maine," she says. Driving in heavy traffic always makes Mrs. Dietrich nervous and she is overly sensitive to her daughter's silence, which seems deliberate, perverse, when they have so little time remaining together — not even a full day.

Nola asks politely if Mrs. Dietrich would like her to drive and Mrs.

JOYCE CAROL OATES (b. 1938) is the author of numerous novels and collections of short stories. Among her most important novels are them *(1969),*Wonderland *(1971), and* Do with Me What You Will *(1973). Her recent novels are* You Must Remember This *(1987) and* Because It Is Bitter, and Because It Is My Heart *(1990). She is a professor at Princeton University.*

Dietrich says no, of course not, she's fine, it's only a few more miles and maybe traffic will lighten. Nola seems about to say something more, then thinks better of it. So much between them that is precarious, chancy — but they've been kind to each other these past seven days. Mrs. Dietrich loves Nola with a fierce unreasoned passion stronger than any she felt for the man who had been her husband for thirteen years, certainly far stronger than any she ever felt for her own mother. Sometimes in weak despondent moods, alone, lonely, self-pitying, when she has had too much to drink, Mrs. Dietrich thinks she is in love with her daughter — but this is a thought she can't contemplate for long. And how Nola would snort in amused contempt, incredulous, mocking — "Oh *Mother*!" — if she were told.

Mrs. Dietrich tries to engage her daughter in conversation of a harmless   4
sort but Nola answers in monosyllables, Nola is rather tired from so many nights of partying with her friends, some of whom attend the local high school, some of whom are home for spring break from prep schools — Exeter, Lawrenceville, Concord, Andover, Portland. Late nights, but Mrs. Dietrich doesn't consciously lie awake waiting for Nola to come home: they've been through all that before. Now Nola sits beside her mother looking wan, subdued, rather melancholy. Thinking her private thoughts. She is wearing a bulky quilted jacket Mrs. Dietrich has never liked, the usual blue jeans, black calfskin boots zippered tightly to mid-calf. Mrs. Dietrich must resist the temptation to ask, "Why are you so quiet, Nola? What are you thinking?" They've been through all that before.

Route 12 has become a jumble of small industrial parks, high-rise office and apartment buildings, torn-up landscapes — mountains of raw earth, uprooted trees, ruts and ditches filled with muddy water. There is no natural sequence to what you see — buildings, construction work, leveled woods, the lavish grounds owned by Squibb. Though she has driven this route countless times, Mrs. Dietrich is never quite certain where the Mall is and must be prepared for a sudden exit. She remembers getting lost the first several times, remembers the excitement she and her friends felt about the grand opening of the Mall, stores worthy of serious shopping at last. Today is much the same. No, today is worse. Like Christmas when she was a small child, Mrs. Dietrich thinks. She'd hoped so badly to be happy she'd felt actual pain, a constriction in her throat like crying.

"*Are* you all right, Nola? — you've been so quiet all morning," Mrs. Dietrich asks, half-scolding. Nola stirs from her reverie, says she's fine, a just perceptible edge to her reply, and for the remainder of the drive there's some stiffness between them. Mrs. Dietrich chooses to ignore it. In any case she is fully absorbed in driving — negotiating a tricky exit across two lanes of traffic, then the hairpin curve of the ramp, the numerous looping drives of the Mall. Then the enormous parking lot, daunting to the inexperienced, but Mrs. Dietrich always heads for the area behind Lord & Taylor on the far side of the Mall, Lot D; her luck holds and she finds a space close in.

"Well — we made it," she says, smiling happily at Nola. Nola laughs in reply — what does a seventeen-year-old's laughter *mean*? — but she remembers, getting out, to lock both doors on her side of the car. The smile Nola gives Mrs. Dietrich across the car's roof is careless and beautiful and takes Mrs. Dietrich's breath away.

The March morning tastes of grit with an undercurrent of something acrid, chemical; inside the Mall, beneath the first of the elegant brass-buttressed glass domes, the air is fresh and tonic, circulating from invisible vents. The Mall is crowded, rather noisy — it *is* Saturday morning — but a feast for the eyes after that long trip on Route 12. Tall slender trees grow out of the mosaic-tiled pavement, there are beds of Easter lilies, daffodils, jonquils, tulips of all colors. Mrs. Dietrich smiles with relief. She senses that Nola too is relieved, cheered. It's like coming home.

The shopping excursions began when Nola was a small child but did not acquire their special significance until she was twelve or thirteen years old and capable of serious, sustained shopping with her mother. This was about the time when Mr. Dietrich moved out of the house and back into their old apartment in the city — a separation, he'd called it initially, to give them perspective — though Mrs. Dietrich had no illusions about what "perspective" would turn out to entail — so the shopping trips were all the more significant. Not that Mrs. Dietrich and Nola spent very much money — they really didn't, *really* they didn't, when compared to friends and neighbors.

At seventeen Nola is shrewd and discerning as a shopper, not easy to please, knowledgeable as a mature woman about certain aspects of fashion, quality merchandise, good stores. Her closets, like Mrs. Dietrich's, are crammed, but she rarely buys anything that Mrs. Dietrich thinks shoddy or merely faddish. Up in Portland, at the Academy, she hasn't as much time to shop but when she is home in Livingstone it isn't unusual for her and her girlfriends to shop nearly every day. Like all her friends she has charge accounts at the better stores, her own credit cards, a reasonable allowance. At the time of their settlement Mr. Dietrich said guiltily that it was the least he could do for them — if Mrs. Dietrich wanted to work part-time, she could (she was trained, more or less, in public relations of a small-scale sort); if not, not. Mrs. Dietrich thought, It's the most you can do for us too.

Near Bloomingdale's entrance mother and daughter see a disheveled woman sitting by herself on one of the benches. Without seeming to look at her, shoppers are making a discreet berth around her, a stream following a natural course. Nola, taken by surprise, stares. Mrs. Dietrich has seen the woman from time to time at the Mall, always alone, smirking and talking to herself, frizzed gray hair in a tangle, puckered mouth. Always wearing the same black wool coat, a garment of fairly good quality but shapeless,

8

rumpled, stained, as if she sleeps in it. She might be anywhere from forty to sixty years of age. Once Mrs. Dietrich saw her make menacing gestures at children who were teasing her, another time she'd seen the woman staring belligerently at *her*. A white paste had gathered in the corners of her mouth. . . . "My God, that poor woman," Nola says. "I didn't think there were people like her here — I mean, I didn't think they would allow it."

"She doesn't seem to cause any disturbance," Mrs. Dietrich says. "She just sits — Don't stare, Nola, she'll see you."

"You've seen her here before? Here?"   12

"A few times this winter."

"Is she always like that?"

"I'm sure she's harmless, Nola. She just *sits*."

Nola is incensed, her pale blue eyes like washed glass. "I'm sure *she's* 16 harmless, Mother. It's the harm the poor woman has to endure that is the tragedy."

Mrs. Dietrich is surprised and a little offended by her daughter's passionate tone but she knows enough not to argue. They enter Bloomingdale's, taking their habitual route. So many shoppers! — so much merchandise! Nola speaks of the tragedy of women like that woman — the tragedy of the homeless, the mentally disturbed — bag ladies out on the street — outcasts of an affluent society — but she's soon distracted by the busyness on all sides, the attractive items for sale. They take the escalator up to the third floor, to the Juniors department where Nola often buys things. From there they will move on to Young Collector, then to New Impressions, then to Petites, then one or another boutique and designer — Liz Claiborne, Christian Dior, Calvin Klein, Carlos Falchi, and the rest. And after Bloomingdale's the other stores await, to be visited each in turn. Mrs. Dietrich checks her watch and sees with satisfaction that there's just enough time before lunch but not *too* much time. She gets ravenously hungry, shopping at the Mall.

Nola is efficient and matter-of-fact about shopping, though she acts solely upon instinct. Mrs. Dietrich likes to watch her at a short distance — holding items of clothing up to herself in the three-way mirrors, modeling things she thinks especially promising. A twill blazer with rounded shoulders and blouson jacket, a funky zippered jumpsuit in white sailcloth, a pair of straight-leg Evan-Picone pants, a green leather vest: Mrs. Dietrich watches her covertly. At such times Nola is perfectly content, fully absorbed in the task at hand; Mrs. Dietrich knows she isn't thinking about anything that would distress her. (Like Mr. Dietrich's betrayal. Like Nola's difficulties with her friends. Like her difficulties at school — as much as Mrs. Dietrich knows of them.) Once, at the Mall, perhaps in this very store in this very department, Nola saw Mrs. Dietrich watching her and walked away angrily and when Mrs. Dietrich caught up with her she said, "I can't stand it, Mother." Her voice was choked and harsh, a vein prominent in her forehead. "Let me go.

For Christ's sake will you let me go." Mrs. Dietrich didn't dare touch her though she could see Nola was trembling. For a long terrible moment mother and daughter stood side by side near a display of bright brash Catalina beachwear while Nola whispered, "Let me go. *Let me go.*"

Difficult to believe that girl standing so poised and self-assured in front of the three-way mirror was once a plain, rather chunky, unhappy child. She'd been unpopular at school. Overly serious. Anxious. Quick to tears. Aged eleven she hid herself away in her room for hours at a time, reading, drawing pictures, writing little stories she could sometimes be prevailed upon to read aloud to her mother, sometimes even to her father, though she dreaded his judgment. She went through a "scientific" phase a while later — Mrs. Dietrich remembers an ambitious bas-relief map of North America, meticulous illustrations for "photosynthesis," a pastel drawing of an eerie ball of fire labeled "Red Giant" (a dying star?) which won a prize in a state competition for junior high students. Then for a season it was stray facts Nola confronted them with, often at the dinner table. Interrupting her parents' conversation to say brightly: "Did you know that Nero's favorite color was green? — he carried a giant emerald and held it up to his eye to watch Christians being devoured by lions." And once at a large family gathering: "Did you know that last week downtown a little baby's nose was chewed off by rats in his crib? — a little *black* baby?" Nola meant only to call attention to herself but you couldn't blame her listeners for being offended. They stared at her, not knowing what to say. What a strange child! What queer glassy-pale eyes! Mr. Dietrich told her curtly to leave the table — he'd had enough of the game she was playing and so had everyone else.

Nola stared at him, her eyes filling with tears. Game?   20

When they were alone Mr. Dietrich said angrily to Mrs. Dietrich: "Can't you control her in front of other people, at least?" Mrs. Dietrich was angry too, and frightened. She said "I *try*."

They sent her off aged fourteen to the Portland Academy up in Maine and without their help she matured into a girl of considerable beauty. A heart-shaped face, delicate features, glossy red-brown hair scissor-cut to her shoulders. Five feet seven inches tall, weighing less than one hundred pounds — the result of constant savage dieting. (Mrs. Dietrich, who has weight problems herself, doesn't dare to inquire as to details. They've been through that already.) Thirty days after they'd left her at the Portland Academy Nola telephoned home at 11:00 P.M. one Sunday giggly and high telling Mrs. Dietrich she adored the school she adored her suite mates she adored most of her teachers particularly her riding instructor Terri, Terri the Terrier they called the woman because she was so fierce, such a character, eyes that bore right through your skull, wore belts with the most amazing silver buckles! Nola loved Terri but she wasn't *in* love — there's a difference!

Mrs. Dietrich broke down weeping, *that* time.

Now of course Nola has boyfriends. Mrs. Dietrich has long since given up trying to keep track of their names. There is even one "boy" — or young man — who seems to be married: who seems to be, in fact, one of the junior instructors at the school. (Mrs. Dietrich does not eavesdrop on her daughter's telephone conversations but there are things she cannot help overhearing.) Is your daughter on the Pill? the women in Mrs. Dietrich's circle asked one another for a while, guiltily, surreptitiously. Now they no longer ask. 24

But Nola has announced recently that she loathes boys — she's fed up.

She's never going to get married. She'll study languages in college, French, Italian, something exotic like Arabic, go to work for the American foreign service. Unless she drops out of school altogether to become a model.

"Do you think I'm fat, Mother?" she asks frequently, worriedly, standing in front of the mirror twisted at the waist to reveal her small round belly which, it seems, can't help being round: she bloats herself on diet Cokes all day long. "Do you think it *shows*?"

When Mrs. Dietrich was pregnant with Nola she'd been twenty-nine years old and she and Mr. Dietrich had tried to have a baby for nearly five years. She'd lost hope, begun to despise herself, then suddenly it happened: like grace. Like happiness swelling so powerfully it can barely be contained. I can hear its heartbeat! her husband exclaimed. He'd been her lover then, young, vigorous, dreamy. Caressing the rock-hard belly, splendid white tight-stretched skin. Mr. Dietrich gave Mrs. Dietrich a reproduction on stiff glossy paper of Dante Gabriel Rossetti's *Beata Beatrix*, embarrassed, apologetic, knowing it was sentimental and perhaps a little silly but that was how he thought of her — so beautiful, rapturous, pregnant with their child. She told no one but she knew the baby was to be a girl. It would be herself again, reborn and this time perfect. 28

"Oh, Mother — isn't it *beautiful*?" Nola exclaims.

It is past noon. Past twelve-thirty. Mrs. Dietrich and Nola have made the rounds of a half-dozen stores, traveled countless escalators, one clothing department has blended into the next and the chic smiling saleswomen have become indistinguishable and Mrs. Dietrich is beginning to feel the urgent need for a glass of white wine. Just a glass. "Isn't it beautiful? — it's *perfect*," Nola says. Her eyes glow with pleasure, her smooth skin is radiant. As Nola models in the three-way mirror a queer little yellow-and-black striped sweater with a ribbed waist, punk style, mock-cheap, Mrs. Dietrich feels the motherly obligation to register a mild protest, knowing that Nola will not hear. She must have it and will have it. She'll wear it a few times, then retire it to the bottom of a drawer with so many other novelty sweaters, accumulated since sixth grade. (She's like her mother in that regard — can't bear to throw anything away.)

"*Isn't* it beautiful?" Nola demands, studying her reflection in the mirror. Mrs. Dietrich pays for the sweater on her charge account.

32

Next, they buy Nola a good pair of shoes. And a handbag to go with them. In Paraphernalia, where rock music blasts overhead and Mrs. Dietrich stands to one side, rather miserable, Nola chats companionably with two girls — tall, pretty, cutely made up — she'd gone to public school in Livingstone with, says afterward with an upward rolling of her eyes, "God, I was afraid they'd latch on to us!" Mrs. Dietrich has seen women friends and acquaintances of her own in the Mall this morning but has shrunk from being noticed, not wanting to share her daughter with anyone. She has a sense of time passing ever more swiftly, cruelly.

She watches Nola preening in a mirror, watches other shoppers watching her. My daughter. Mine. But of course there is no connection between them — they don't even resemble each other. A seventeen-year-old, a forty-seven-year-old. When Nola is away she seems to forget her mother entirely — doesn't telephone, certainly doesn't write. It's the way all their daughters are, Mrs. Dietrich's friends tell her. It doesn't *mean* anything. Mrs. Dietrich thinks how when she was carrying Nola, those nine long months, they'd been completely happy — not an instant's doubt or hesitation. The singular weight of the body. A trancelike state you are tempted to mistake for happiness because the body is incapable of thinking, therefore incapable of anticipating change. Hot rhythmic blood, organs, packed tight and moist, the baby upside down in her sac in her mother's belly, always present tense, always *now*. It was a shock when the end came so abruptly but everyone told Mrs. Dietrich she was a natural mother, praised and pampered her. For a while. Then of course she'd had her baby, her Nola. Even now Mrs. Dietrich can't really comprehend the experience. *Giving birth. Had a baby. Was born.* Mere words, absurdly inadequate. She knows no more of how love ends than she knew as a child, she knows only of how love begins — in the belly, in the womb, where it is always present tense.

The morning's shopping has been quite successful but lunch at La Crêperie doesn't go well for some reason. La Crêperie is Nola's favorite Mall restaurant — always amiably crowded, bustling, a simulated sidewalk café with red-striped umbrellas, wrought-iron tables and chairs, menus in French, music piped in overhead. Mrs. Dietrich's nerves are chafed by the pretense of gaiety, the noise, the openness onto one of the Mall's busy promenades where at any minute a familiar face might emerge, but she is grateful for her glass of chilled white wine. She orders a small tossed salad and a creamed-chicken crepe and devours it hungrily — she *is* hungry. While Nola picks at her seafood crepe with a disdainful look. A familiar scene: mother watching while daughter pushes food around on her plate. Suddenly Nola is tense, moody, corners of her mouth downturned. Mrs. Dietrich wants to ask, What's wrong? She wants to ask, Why are you unhappy? She wants to smooth Nola's hair back from her forehead, check to see if her forehead is overly warm, wants to hug her close, hard. Why, why? What did I do wrong? Why do you hate me?

Calling the Portland Academy a few weeks ago Mrs. Dietrich suddenly 36
lost control, began crying. She hadn't been drinking and she hadn't known she was upset. A girl unknown to her, one of Nola's suite mates, was saying, "Please, Mrs. Dietrich, it's all right, I'm sure Nola will call you back later tonight, or tomorrow, Mrs. Dietrich? — I'll tell her you called, all right? — Mrs. Dietrich?" as embarrassed as if Mrs. Dietrich had been her own mother.

How love begins. How love ends.

Mrs. Dietrich orders a third glass of wine. This is a celebration of sorts isn't it? — their last shopping trip for a long time. But Nola resists, Nola isn't sentimental. In casual defiance of Mrs. Dietrich she lights up a cigarette — yes, Mother, Nola has said ironically, since *you* stopped smoking *everybody* is supposed to stop — and sits with her arms crossed, watching streams of shoppers pass. Mrs. Dietrich speaks lightly of practical matters, tomorrow morning's drive to the airport, and will Nola telephone when she gets to Portland to let Mrs. Dietrich know she has arrived safely?

Then with no warning — though of course she'd been planning this all along — Nola brings up the subject of a semester in France, in Paris and Rouen, the fall semester of her senior year it would be; she has put in her application, she says, and is waiting to hear if she's been accepted. She smokes her cigarette calmly, expelling smoke from her nostrils in a way Mrs. Dietrich thinks particularly coarse. Mrs. Dietrich, who believed that particular topic was finished, takes care to speak without emotion. "I just don't think it's a very practical idea right now, Nola," she says. "We've been through it haven't we? I — "

"I'm going," Nola says. 40

"The extra expense, for one thing. Your father — "

"If I get accepted, I'm going."

"Your father — "

"The hell with him too." 44

Mrs. Dietrich would like to slap her daughter's face. Bring tears to those steely eyes. But she sits stiff, turning her wine glass between her fingers, patient, calm, she's heard all this before; she says, "Surely this isn't the best time to discuss it, Nola."

Mrs. Dietrich is afraid her daughter will leave the restaurant, simply walk away, that has happened before and if it happens today she doesn't know what she will do. But Nola sits unmoving; her faced closed, impassive. Mrs. Dietrich feels her quickened heartbeat. Once after one of their quarrels Mrs. Dietrich told a friend of hers, the mother too of a teenage daughter, "I just don't know her any longer, how can you keep living with someone you don't know?" and the woman said, "Eventually you can't."

Nola says, not looking at Mrs. Dietrich: "Why don't we talk about it, Mother?"

"Talk about what?" Mrs. Dietrich asks. 48

"You know."

"The semester in France? Again?"

"No." 52

"What, then?"

"You *know.*"

"I don't know, really. Really!" Mrs. Dietrich smiles, baffled. She feels the corners of her eyes pucker white with strain.

Nola says, sighing, "How exhausting it is."

"How *what?*" 56

"How exhausting it is."

"What is?"

"You and me — "

"What?" 60

"Being together — "

"Being together how — ?"

"The two of us, like this — "

"But we're hardly ever together, Nola," Mrs. Dietrich says. 64

Her expression is calm but her voice is shaking. Nola turns away, covering her face with a hand, for a moment she looks years older than her age — in fact exhausted. Mrs. Dietrich sees with pity that her daughter's skin is fair and thin and dry — unlike her own, which tends to be oily — it will wear out before she's forty. Mrs. Dietrich reaches over to squeeze her hand. The fingers are limp, ungiving. "You're going back to school tomorrow, Nola," she says. "You won't come home again until June 12. And you probably will go to France — if your father consents."

Nola gets to her feet, drops her cigarette to the flagstone terrace and grinds it beneath her boot. A dirty thing to do, Mrs. Dietrich thinks, considering there's an ashtray right on the table, but she says nothing. She dislikes La Crêperie anyway.

Nola laughs, showing her lovely white teeth. "Oh, the hell with him," she says. "Fuck Daddy, right?"

They separate for an hour, Mrs. Dietrich to Neiman-Marcus to buy a 68 birthday gift for her elderly aunt, Nola to the trendy new boutique Pour Vous. By the time Mrs. Dietrich rejoins her daughter she's quite angry, blood beating hot and hard and measured in resentment, she has had time to relive old quarrels between them, old exchanges, stray humiliating memories of her marriage as well, these last-hour disagreements are the cruelest and they are Nola's specialty. She locates Nola in the rear of the boutique amid blaring rock music, flashing neon lights, chrome-edged mirrors, her face still hard, closed, prim, pale. She stands beside another teenage girl looking in a desultory way through a rack of blouses, shoving the hangers roughly along, taking no care when a blouse falls to the floor. As Nola glances up, startled, not prepared to see her mother in front of her, their eyes lock for an instant and Mrs. Dietrich stares at her with hatred. Cold calm clear unmistakable hatred. She is thinking, Who are *you*? What have I to do with *you*? I don't know *you*, I don't love *you*, why should I?

Has Nola seen, heard? — she turns aside as if wincing, gives the blouses a final dismissive shove. Her eyes look tired, the corners of her mouth downturned. Anxious, immediately repentant, Mrs. Dietrich asks if she has found anything worth trying on. Nola says with a shrug, "Not a thing, Mother."

On their way out of the Mall Mrs. Dietrich and Nola see the disheveled woman in the black coat again, this time sitting prominently on a concrete ledge in front of Lord & Taylor's busy main entrance. Shopping bag at her feet, shabby purse on the ledge beside her. She is shaking her head in a series of annoyed twitches as if arguing with someone but her hands are loose, palms up, in her lap. Her posture is unfortunate — she sits with her knees parted, inner thighs revealed, fatty, dead white, the tops of cotton stockings rolled tight cutting into the flesh. Again, streams of shoppers are making a careful berth around her. Alone among them Nola hesitates, seems about to approach the woman — Please don't, Nola! please! Mrs. Dietrich thinks — then changes her mind and keeps on walking. Mrs. Dietrich murmurs isn't it a pity, poor thing, don't you wonder where she lives, who her family is, but Nola doesn't reply. Her pace through the first door of Lord & Taylor is so rapid that Mrs. Dietrich can barely keep up.

But Nola's upset. Strangely upset. As soon as they are in the car, packages and bags in the backseat, she begins crying.

It's childish helpless crying, as though her heart is broken. But Mrs. Dietrich knows it isn't broken, she has heard these very sobs before. Many times before. Still she comforts her daughter, embraces her, hugs her hard, hard. A sudden fierce passion. Vehemence. "Nola honey. Nola dear, what's wrong, dear, everything will be all right, dear," she says, close to weeping herself. She would embrace Nola even more tightly except for the girl's quilted jacket, that bulky L. L. Bean thing she has never liked, and Nola's stubborn lowered head. Nola has always been ashamed, crying, frantic to hide her face. Strangers are passing close by the car, curious, staring. Mrs. Dietrich wishes she had a cloak to draw over her daughter and herself, so that no one else would see.

Points to Consider

1. Why does Mrs. Dietrich feel that at the mall "moments of intimacy are possible as they rarely are at home"? What are these moments like? Is this feeling borne out by her experiences at the mall?

2. Consider the two passages in which mother and daughter see the "disheveled woman." How do their responses to the woman differ? What do their responses tell you about the differences between mother and daughter? Why do you think the author included the "disheveled woman" in the story? What purpose does she serve?

3. Read over the passage dealing with Nola's early adolescence (paragraphs 19 to 21). What information does this passage give us about Nola? What do we learn of her father? Of what relevance is this information to the mother and daughter's present situation?

4. Reread the last two paragraphs. Do you think the final scene represents one of those "moments of intimacy" Mrs. Dietrich longs for? What details in the passage make the answer to that question a complicated one?

Discussing the Unit

Suggested Topic for Discussion

Why do parents and teenagers find it so difficult to talk to each other? Is the problem, as Steinberg claims, a result of evolution or is it, as Oates suggests, related to particular family problems? Or could there be other social and cultural factors at work? In other words, do you think the communication barriers between adults and adolescents are inevitable or resolvable?

Preparing for Class Discussion

1. Steinberg's article and Oates's short story surely provoked memories of your own experiences as an adolescent living at home. How close do you think each writer comes to an accurate portrayal of your own situation? To start your thinking, make a few notes about how your individual experiences either conform or fail to conform to their descriptions.

2. Identify passages in "Shopping" that appear to be examples of what Steinberg would call "bickering." What does bickering mean for Oates? Do you think she sees the problem in the same biological terms as

Steinberg? If Mrs. Dietrich consulted Steinberg about her problems with her daughter, what might he tell her? Do you think she would agree with him?

From Discussion to Writing

To what extent do the difficulties that arise between parents and teenagers revolve around problems of language and communication—things that are said or things that aren't said? Write an essay, based on the readings in this unit, class discussion, and your own experience, in which you identify *one* way that communication between parents and teenagers can seriously break down. Be as specific as possible. Describe how the gap in communication develops and how it can become enlarged over time. Discuss both sides of the problem and how each party contributes to the difficulty.

3

The American Adolescent: What's Happening with Today's Youth?

Today's teenagers are growing up faster, feeling more pressure, and facing greater dangers than ever before,. How are they coping? Although many teenagers are doing just fine, others are struggling. In "A Much Riskier Passage," David Gelman explores what makes the teenagers of the nineties different from the teenagers of earlier generations. According to Gelman, many of the problems of troubled youths have their source in parental neglect. The irony of this situation, however, is that an overwhelming number of teenagers are deciding to become parents themselves. In "The Lives of Teenage Mothers," Elizabeth Marek travels to the Bronx, New York, to talk with a number of unwed young parents.

Each year approximately five thousand American adolescents commit suicide, and another estimated four thousand try. Many suicides take place without warning, leaving family and friends shocked and grieving. Psychologists and social workers have only begun to discover reasons for this second most common cause of death among teenagers, and they are still a long way from providing any solutions. In the meantime, the suicide watch continues, especially at places like Leominster High School in Massachusetts. In "You Wanna Die with Me?" Adrian Nicole LeBlanc examines life in Leominster, where eight high-school students recently killed themselves within less than two years.

A Much Riskier Passage

[NEWSWEEK SPECIAL EDITION / Summer–Fall 1990]

There was a time when teenagers believed themselves to be part of a conquering army. Through much of the 1960s and 1970s, the legions of adolescence appeared to command the center of American culture like a victorious occupying force, imposing their singular tastes in clothing, music, and recreational drugs on a good many of the rest of us. It was a hegemony buttressed by advertisers, fashion setters, record producers suddenly zeroing in on the teen multitudes as if they controlled the best part of the country's wealth, which in some sense they did. But even more than market power, what made the young insurgents invincible was the conviction that they were right: from the crusade of the children, grownups believed, they must learn to trust their feelings, to shun materialism, to make love, not money.

In 1990 the emblems of rebellion that once set teenagers apart have grown frayed. Their music now seems more derivative than subversive. The provocative teenage styles of dress that adults assiduously copied no longer automatically inspire emulation. And underneath the plumage, teens seem to be more interested in getting ahead in the world than in clearing up its injustices. According to a 1989 survey of high-school seniors in forty Wisconsin communities, global concerns, including hunger, poverty, and pollution, emerged last on a list of teenage worries. First were personal goals: getting good grades and good jobs. Anything but radical, the majority of teens say they're happy and eager to get on with their lives.

One reason today's teens aren't shaking the earth is that they can no longer marshal the demographic might they once could. Although their sheer numbers are still growing, they are not the illimitably expanding force that teens appeared to be twenty years ago. In 1990 they constitute a smaller percentage of the total population (7 percent, compared with nearly 10 percent in 1970). For another thing, almost as suddenly as they became a

DAVID GELMAN (b. 1926) is a senior writer at Newsweek, *where he currently writes the magazine's section on the mind. Before coming to work at* Newsweek, Gelman *wrote for* Newsday, *the* New York Post, *and other publications.*

highly visible, if unlikely, power in the world, teenagers have reverted to anonymity and the old search for identity. Author Todd Gitlin, a chronicler of the sixties, believes they have become "Balkanized," united less by a common culture than by the commodities they own. He says "it's impossible to point to an overarching teen sensibility."

But as a generation, today's teenagers face more adult-strength stresses 4 than their predecessors did—at a time when adults are much less available to help them. With the divorce rate hovering near 50 percent, and 40 to 50 percent of teenagers living in single-parent homes headed mainly by working mothers, teens are more on their own that ever. "My parents let me do anything I want as long as I don't get into trouble," writes a fifteen-year-old high-schooler from Ohio in an essay submitted for this special issue of *Newsweek*. Sociologists have begun to realize, in fact, that teens are shaped more by their parents than by their peers, that they adopt their parents' values and opinions to a greater extent than anyone realized. Adolescent specialists now see real hazards in lumping all teens together; thirteen-year-olds, for instance, need much more parental guidance than nineteen-year-olds.

These realizations are emerging just when the world has become a more dangerous place for the young. They have more access than ever to fast cars, fast drugs, easy sex—"a bewildering array of options, many with devastating outcomes," observes Beatrix Hamburg, director of Child and Adolescent Psychiatry at New York's Mount Sinai School of Medicine. Studies indicate that while overall drug abuse is down, the use of lethal drugs like crack is up in low-income neighborhoods, and a dangerous new kick called ice is making inroads in white high schools. Drinking and smoking rates remain ominously high. "The use of alcohol appears to be normative," says Stephen Small, a developmental psychologist at the University of Wisconsin. "By the upper grades, everybody's doing it."

Sexual activity is also on the rise. A poll conducted by Small suggests that most teens are regularly having sexual intercourse by the eleventh grade. Parents are generally surprised by the data, Small says. "A lot of parents are saying, 'Not my kids . . .' They just don't think it's happening." Yet clearly it is: around half a million teenage girls give birth every year, and sexually transmitted diseases continue to be a major problem. Perhaps the only comforting note is that teens who are given AIDS education in schools and clinics are more apt to use condoms—a practice that could scarcely be mentioned a few years ago, let alone surveyed.

One reliable assessment of how stressful life has become for young people in this country is the Index of Social Health for Children and Youth. Authored by social policy analyst Marc Miringoff, of Fordham University at Tarrytown, N.Y., it charts such factors as poverty, drug abuse, and high-school dropout rates. In 1987, the latest year for which statistics are available, the index fell to its lowest point in two decades. Most devastating, according to Miringoff, were the numbers of teenagers living at poverty levels—about 55 percent for single-parent households—and taking their own lives. The record rate of nearly 18 suicides per 100,000 in 1987—a total of 1,901—was double that of 1970. "If you take teens in the fifties—the 'Ozzie and Harriet' generation—those kids lived on a less complex planet," says Miringoff. "They could be kids longer."

The social index is only one of the yardsticks used on kids these days. In fact, this generation of young people is surely one of the most closely watched ever. Social scientists are tracking nearly everything they do or think about, from dating habits (they prefer going out in groups) to extracurricular activities (cheerleading has made a comeback) to general outlook (45 percent think the world is getting worse and 62 percent believe life will be harder for them than it was for their parents). One diligent prober, Reed Larson of the University of Illinois, even equipped his five hundred teen subjects with beepers so he could remind them to fill out questionnaires about how they are feeling, what they are doing, and who they are with at random moments during the day. Larson, a professor of human development, and psychologist Maryse Richards of Loyola University, have followed this group since grade school. Although the results of the high-school study have not been tabulated yet, the assumption is that young people are experiencing more stress by the time they reach adolescence but develop strategies to cope with it. 8

Without a doubt, any overview of teenage problems is skewed by the experience of the inner cities, where most indicators tilt sharply toward the negative. Especially among the minority poor, teen pregnancies continue to rise, while the institution of marriage has virtually disappeared. According to the National Center for Vital Statistics, 90 percent of black teenage mothers are unmarried at the time of their child's birth, although a third eventually marry. Teenage mothers, in turn, add to the annual school dropout rate, which in some cities reaches as high as 60 percent. Nationwide, the unemployment rate for black teenagers is 40 to 50 percent; in some cities, it has risen to 70 percent. Crack has become a medium of commerce and violence. "The impact of crack is worse in the inner city than anywhere else," says psychiatrist Robert King, of the Yale Child Study Center. "If you look at the homicide rate among young, black males, it's frighteningly high. We also see large numbers of young mothers taking crack."

Those are realities unknown to the majority of white middle-class teenagers. Most of them are managing to get through the adolescent years with relatively few major problems. Parents may describe them as sullen and self-absorbed. They can also be secretive and rude. They hang "Do Not Disturb" signs on their doors, make phone calls from closets, and behave churlishly at the dinner table if they can bring themselves to sit there at all. An earlier beeper study by Illinois's Larson found that in the period between ages ten and fifteen, the amount of time young people spend with their families decreases by half. "This is when the bedroom door becomes a significant marker," he says.

Yet their rebelliousness is usually overstated. "Arguments are generally about whether to take out the garbage or whether to wear a certain hairstyle," says Bradford Brown, an associate professor of human development at the University of Wisconsin. "These are not earth-shattering issues, though they are quite irritating to parents." One researcher on a mission to destigmatize teenagers is Northwestern University professor Ken Howard, author of a book, *The Teenage World,* who has just completed a study in Chicago's Cook County on where kids go for help. The perception, says Howard, is that teenagers are far worse off then they really are. He believes their emotional disturbances are no different from those of adults, and that it is only 20 percent who have most of the serious problems, in any case.

The findings of broad-based studies of teenagers often obscure the differences in their experience. They are, after all, the product of varied ethical and cultural influences. Observing adolescents in ten communities over the past ten years, a team of researchers headed by Frances Ianni, of Columbia University's Teachers College, encountered "considerable diversity." A key finding, reported Ianni in a 1989 article in *Phi Delta Kappan* magazine, was that the people in all the localities reflected the ethnic and social-class lifestyles of their parents much more than that of a universal teen culture. The researchers found "far more congruence than conflict" between the views of parents and their teenage children. "We much more frequently hear teenagers preface comments to their peers with 'my mom says' than with any attribution to heroes of the youth culture," wrote Ianni. 12

For years, psychologists also tended to overlook the differences between younger and older adolescents, instead grouping them together as if they all had the same needs and desires. Until a decade ago, ideas of teen behavior were heavily influenced by the work of psychologist Erik Erikson, whose own model was based on older adolescents. Erikson, for example, emphasized their need for autonomy—appropriate, perhaps, for an eighteen-year-old preparing to leave home for college or a job, but hardly for a thirteen-year-old just beginning to experience the confusions of puberty. The Erikson model nevertheless was taken as an across-the-board prescription to give teenagers independence, something that families, torn by the domestic upheavals of the sixties and seventies, granted them almost by forfeit.

In those turbulent years, adolescents turned readily enough to their peers. "When there's turmoil and social change, teenagers have a tendency to break loose and follow each other more," says Dr. John Schowalter, president of the American Academy of Child and Adolescent Psychiatry. "The leadership of adults is somewhat splintered and they're more on their own—sort of like *Lord of the Flies.*"

That period helped plant the belief that adolescents were natural rebels, who sought above all to break free of adult influence. The idea persists to this day. Says Ruby Takanishi, director of the Carnegie Council on Adolescent Development: "The society is still permeated by the notion that adolescents are different, that their hormones are raging around and they don't want to have anything to do with their parents or other adults." Yet research by Ianni and others suggests the contrary. Ianni points also to studies of so-called invulnerable adolescents—those who develop into stable young adults in spite of coming from troubled homes, or other adversity. "A lot of people have attributed this to some inner resilience," he says. "But what we've seen in practically all cases is some caring adult figure who was a constant in that kid's life."

Not that teenagers were always so dependent on adults. Until the nine- 16 teenth century, children labored in the fields alongside their parents. But by the time they were fifteen, they might marry and go out into the world. Industrialization and compulsory education ultimately deprived them of a role in the family work unit, leaving them in a state of suspension between childhood and adulthood.

To teenagers, it has always seemed a useless period of waiting. Approaching physical and sexual maturity, they feel capable of doing many of the things adults do. But they are not treated like adults. Instead they must endure a prolonged childhood that is stretched out even more nowadays by the need to attend college—and then possibly graduate school—in order to make one's way in the world. In the family table of organization, they are mainly in charge of menial chores. Millions of teenagers now have part-time or full-time jobs, but those tend to be in the service industries, where the pay and the work are often equally unrewarding.

If teenagers are to stop feeling irrelevant, they need to feel needed, both by the family and by the larger world. In the sixties they gained some sense of empowerment from their visibility, their music, their sheer collective noise. They also joined and swelled the ranks of Vietnam War protesters, giving them a feeling of importance that evidently they have not had since. In the foreword to *Student Service,* a book based on a 1985 Carnegie Foundation survey of teenagers' attitudes toward work and community service, foundation director Ernest Boyer wrote: "Time and time again, students complained that they felt isolated, unconnected to the larger world. . . . And this detachment occurs at the very time students are deciding who they are and where they fit." Fordham's Miringoff goes so far as to link the rising suicide rate among teens to their feelings of disconnection. He recalls going to the 1963 March on Washington as a teenager, and gaining "a sense of being part of something larger. That idealism, that energy, was a very stabilizing thing."

Surely there is still room for idealism in the nineties, even if the causes are considered less glamorous. But despite growing instances of teenagers involving themselves in good works, such as recycling campaigns, tutorial programs, or serving meals at shelters for the homeless, no study has yet detected anything like a national groundswell of volunteerism. Instead, according to University of Michigan social psychologist Lloyd Johnston, teens seem to be taking their cues from a culture that, up until quite recently at least, has glorified self-interest and opportunism. "It's fair to say that young people are more career-oriented than before, more concerned about making money and prestige," says Johnston. "These changes are consistent with the 'me' generation and looking for the good life they see on television."

Some researchers say that, indeed, the only thing uniting teenagers these   20
days are the things they buy and plug into. Rich or poor, all have their Walkmans, their own VCRs and TVs. Yet in some ways, those marvels of communication isolate them even more. Teenagers, says Beatrix Hamburg, are spending "a lot of time alone in their rooms."

Other forces may be working to isolate them as well. According to Dr. Elena O. Nightingale, author of a Carnegie Council paper on teen roleless-ness, a pattern of "age segregation" is shrinking the amount of time adolescents spend with grownups. In place of family outings and vacations, for example, entertainment is now more geared toward specific age groups. (The teen-terrorizing "Freddy" flicks and their ilk would be one example.) Even in the sorts of jobs typically available to teenagers, such as fast-food chains, they are usually supervised by people close to their age, rather than by adults, notes Nightingale. "There's a real need for places for teenagers to go where there's a modicum of adult involvement," she says.

Despite the riskier world they face, it would be a mistake to suggest that all adolescents of this generation are feeling more angst than their predecessors. Middle-class teenagers, at least, seem content with their lot on the whole. According to recent studies, 80 percent—the same proportion as twenty years ago—profess satisfaction with their own lives, if not with the state of the world. Many teenagers, nevertheless, evince wistfulness for what they think of as the more heroic times of the sixties and seventies—an era, they believe, when teenagers had more say in the world. Playwright Wendy Wasserstein, whose Pulitzer Prize–winning *The Heidi Chronicles* was about coming of age in those years, says she has noticed at least a "stylistic" nostalgia in the appearance of peace-sign earrings and other sixties artifacts. "I guess that comes from the sense of there having been a unity, a together-ness," she says. "Today most teens are wondering about what they're going to do when they grow up. We had more of a sense of liberation, of youth— we weren't thinking about getting that job at Drexel." Pop-culture critic Greil Marcus, however, believes it was merely the "self-importance" of the sixties generation—his own contemporaries—"that has oppressed today's kids into believing they've missed something. There's something sick about my eighteen-year-old wanting to see Paul McCartney or the Who. We would never have emulated our parents' culture."

But perhaps that's the point: the teens of the nineties do emulate the culture of their parents, many of whom are the very teens who once made such an impact on their own parents. These parents no doubt have something very useful to pass on to their children—maybe their lost sense of idealism rather than the preoccupation with going and getting that seems, so far, their main legacy to the young. Mom and Dad have to earn a living and fulfill their own needs—they are not likely to be coming home early. But there must be a time and place for them to give their children the advice, the comfort and, most of all, the feelings of possibility that any new generation needs in order to believe in itself.

Points to Consider

1. According to David Gelman, how have American teenagers changed from the sixties to the nineties? What does Gelman cite as the reason for declining activism among adolescents? To what does he attribute the fact that teenagers have become more career-oriented?

2. As Gelman reports, sociologists now realize that teens are more dependent upon parents than previously believed. How does this information affect your understanding of the way teenagers behave?

3. Why do so many teenagers feel "irrelevant"? What social conditions have contributed to this problem? What do you think our society could realistically offer its youth to foster feelings of self-worth?

4. What does it mean to "destigmatize" teenagers, according to Northwestern professor Ken Howard? What do you think of his position? How does Gelman deal with Howard's assessment of the problem?

ELIZABETH MAREK

The Lives of Teenage Mothers

[HARPER'S MAGAZINE / April 1989]

At two-thirty on a Thursday afternoon in June, when most teenagers, done with school for the day, are hanging out with their friends, the girls I have come to meet are seated in a small office, reaching for cookies with one hand as they settle their babies on their laps with the other. We are at the Kingsbridge Heights Community Center in the Bronx. The center sits at the crossroads of several worlds. The spacious homes of Riverdale dot the rolling green hills to the west; to the south rise the housing projects that cast their shadow on the lower-middle-class single-family homes and the shops which line the blocks closest to the center. The Teen Parenting Program, which provides counseling, education, and health care to teenage parents and soon-to-be parents throughout the Bronx, was started in 1986 with a group of girls from the projects. Once a week the girls in the program, along with their babies and sometimes their boyfriends, crowd into a simply furnished room to drink Coke, munch on snacks, and talk about the difficulties of being a teenage parent.

On this particular Thursday, I have come too. For years I've read about the "problem of teenage parenthood"—children having children. In New York City, teen pregnancies make up 15 percent of all pregnancies and account for more than thirteen thousand births each year. Sociologists and psychologists speculate about social pressures and individual motivation. President George Bush, in his inaugural address, spoke of the need to help young women "who are about to become mothers of children they can't care for and might not love."

But despite the concern voiced by others, we've heard very little from the young women themselves. Are they ignorant about birth control, or are they choosing to get pregnant? What are the conditions of loneliness, poverty, and hopelessness in which having a baby might make sense? What happens

---

ELIZABETH MAREK (b. 1961) graduated from Harvard College in 1984. She works at a school for emotionally disturbed children in New York City. She has written a book, The Children at Santa Clara *(1987), about her experiences at a home for emotionally disturbed adolescents.*

to these girls and their babies? How does having a baby affect their lives? Where do the fathers fit in?

I've come to Kingsbridge because I want to get to know the mothers, most of whom are not much younger than I am. Sophie-Louise, the social worker in charge of the group, introduces me, and the room falls silent. "Well," she laughs, "here we are. Ask away." Looking at the girls, as they tug at a baby's diaper or straighten a barrette, I am not sure where to begin. 4

"Tell me what it's like, having a baby at your age," I ask at last. As if on cue, all heads turn toward Janelle,[1] a heavyset black girl with short, blown-straight hair, who sits in an overstuffed chair with her three-month-old son, Marc, draped across her lap. The baby, dressed in a pale green sleeper embroidered with a blue bunny, is drooling onto her stylish black skirt. She is eating a chocolate cookie and begins to talk about the logistical problems involved in getting to and from high school with an infant. She has just started summer school to make up credits from the classes she missed during her pregnancy. She is seventeen.

"Let's see," she begins. "I get myself up and get the baby up and get myself dressed and get the baby dressed, get my books, get the baby's bag, get the stroller . . ." She laughs. "Do you know how hard it is to get a stroller on the bus? That first day of school, I thought I wasn't going to make it."

Newspaper accounts of teen pregnancy tend to dwell on girls from welfare families. Janelle, however, is the daughter of a retired postal-service clerk and grew up in a small, one-family house in a lower-middle-class neighborhood in the North Bronx. Her childhood was relatively secure: her parents were together and could afford to send her to a Catholic school, where she made friends, got good grades, and dreamed about what she would be when she grew up. "I was gonna finish high school," she says. "Gonna go on to college, like my cousins did. I wanted to get married and have a baby someday, but, really, not now. All through high school I never cut classes, hardly was sick even . . ."

The turning point came when Janelle was fifteen and her parents divorced. "When my parents split, my family just fell apart. My mother only wanted my little sister, so she took her, and then my older sister, she left, too, so it was just me and my father all alone in the house." Feeling unwanted and unloved, Janelle moved into a room in the basement, and her father took over the upstairs. Sometimes they met at breakfast, but other times Janelle went for days without seeing him. "So I started hanging out with a bad bunch of kids," she says, "and cutting classes—I went through an entire year and only got three credits. And then I got pregnant and dropped out." She laughs bitterly. "One thing they don't teach you in high school is how to get a stroller on the bus." 8

---

[1] The names of the young women and their boyfriends and some identifying details have been changed. [Au.]

Lynda, at twenty the mother of a three-year-old girl, nods sympatheti-cally. She is a pretty, young Hispanic woman with long hair pulled away from her face in a ponytail. Three weeks earlier she had graduated from high school, having gone to classes in the evening and worked during the day as a cashier in a small store in Manhattan. Her daughter, Danielle, a small child with blonde hair and a dirty face, walks unsmiling around the edge of the room. There is little interaction between mother and daughter. They neither look at nor speak to each other.

Lynda's family, like Janelle's, could be classified as lower middle class. Unlike Janelle's, Lynda's parents are strict Roman Catholics. On the day Lynda told her father that she was pregnant, he left home. "I guess it was either that or throw me out," she says. A few months later he moved back, but even now, although he allows her to live at home, she feels that he has not forgiven her. Lynda believes that her father, having worked hard to provide the best for her and her siblings, took her pregnancy as a slap in the face.

Leaning back in the circle of her boyfriend's arms, Lynda's large black eyes are ringed with dark circles. "My mother still talked to me, like, at the table, pass the salt and stuff. I think my father blamed her—if you had brought her up right, this wouldn't have happened."

Janelle nods. "My father blamed my mother, too. I don't understand that, though, because he didn't even know that I was pregnant. Now he thinks it's my fault that he didn't know, and I think it's his fault. He was always telling me to stay downstairs, and we never talked. We never did anything. Now all he does is compare me to his sister's children, who are much older. They got jobs, finished college, and he says you make me look so bad, having babies, dropping out of school. But he didn't want to come back to my mother, he didn't want to try to help me. It was all just, 'Don't make me look bad. Don't make me look bad.'"

"So what did he do when he found out you were pregnant?" asks Lynda.

"He never found out! Not until I came home from the hospital. He found out when the baby was a week old."

Lynda's boyfriend, Tony, a construction worker in his early thirties, joins the discussion. "Maybe it's more that he didn't want to know. He wanted to keep it from himself." Tony is not Danielle's father, although he too was a teenage parent and has two boys of his own. He and Lynda have been going out for almost a year. "You know the parents, they blame themselves," he says. "Like maybe they did something wrong with your upbringing."

Janelle lets out her breath in a snort. "Yeah, well now he tells all his friends, 'She's so sneaky.' But I think that if he was really interested, he would have known. I mean, the last day, the day that I gave birth, he went out to the store and said, 'I'll be right back.' And I said, 'Fine, but I won't be here.' But he didn't hear me."

Later, riding home on the subway, I wonder whether, in part, Janelle got pregnant to get her father's attention. Or, perhaps, as one social worker I spoke with earlier suggested, part of the motivation for teenage girls to have babies is a wish to be reborn themselves, to re-create themselves as children, so they can get the love and attention they feel they were denied.

Nine girls, their babies, and a few of their boyfriends are officially enrolled in Sophie-Louise's group, but since the school year ended, only Janelle and Lynda have been coming regularly. The others, Sophie-Louise explains, have drifted away—to the beach, to parties—or are staying home, too overwhelmed by their lives as mothers to make the trip to the center. Janelle and Lynda represent what Sophie-Louise calls the "cream of the crop": the only ones able to structure their lives sufficiently to attend a regular weekly meeting. The others fade in and out.

At the next meeting, I notice that Lynda's boyfriend is missing. Sophie-Louise explains to me privately that Tony and Lynda have been having problems lately. Two new people are present, however: Janelle's boyfriend, Eron, and a new girl, April, a sad-looking black teenager, who brings her five-month-old daughter. April is thin, her ribs jut out below the orange halter top she wears. In contrast to the Calvin Klein jeans Lynda wears, April's jeans are frayed and stained. She sits with her shoulders hunched, as though shielding herself from the vagaries of life. Glancing up, she notices my tape recorder on the table, and she stares at me for a moment before busying herself with the baby on her lap. The baby's dark eyes flicker across her mother's face, but neither of them registers a smile. Sophie-Louise has told me a few facts about April's life: she is the oldest child and lives with her mother, her two siblings, and her baby in a two-room apartment in a housing project in the East Bronx. Seemingly the least equipped to care for an infant, April appears to have been the most determined to have a baby: Kisha was the result of her third pregnancy, the other two having ended in abortions.

As the meeting starts, Janelle reaches across the table with one hand to 20 grab some potato chips, while her other hand effortlessly settles baby Marc in a sitting position on her leg. April, sitting alone at the far end of the couch, shakes off Sophie-Louise's offer of a Coke and, grabbing a handful of Cheez Doodles, drapes a towel over her shoulder so that Kisha can nurse quietly at her breast. April seems to hover on the periphery of the discussion, offering tangential comments or staring fixedly at a spot on the wall. Sophie-Louise finds some rubber cows for Danielle to play with, but the little girl is more interested in building towers of checkers in the corner and knocking them down with excited squeals. Over the din, I ask the girls whether they had planned their pregnancies, and how they felt when they discovered they were pregnant.

As usual, Janelle begins. "At first, you know, I was real scared. I didn't want to have the baby," she says, smoothing her hand over Marc's diaper.

"I was dead set against it. 'Cause you know, I'm just seventeen, and I didn't want to have a baby. I wanted to still go out and have fun with my friends and stuff. But now, you know, it's been three months, and I'm used to it." She pauses. "Of course, I haven't had too much time to myself. Just twice, in three months. I counted it. Twice. The father's family took care of him for a whole day. I couldn't believe it. I was outside and everything was so much fun. But I like being a mom now. I can handle it. All my friends keep telling me, 'Janelle, you're in a closet!' But I'm not in no closet. And if I am, well, they should leave me alone. It's fun in this closet now that I know what I'm doing and everything."

Lynda's mother takes care of Danielle during the day, when she is at work, and again in the evenings, when she attends classes. But Lynda also complains about a lack of freedom. "My mom says, 'Now you are a mother, you have responsibilities.' She will babysit when I go to work or to school, but otherwise, anywhere I go, Danielle goes."

"Did either of you ever think about having an abortion?" I ask.

"Abortion," muses Janelle. "Well, by the time I knew I was pregnant, I was already six months pregnant."

I wonder whether she has misspoken. Surely she can't mean that she had a baby growing inside of her for six months before she was aware of its presence. But, shaking her head, she assures me that it was six months.

"Before that, I had no idea," she says.

Lynda backs her up. "By the time I knew I was pregnant, I was five months."

"Maybe," Sophie-Louise says, "it goes back to what we talked about before. Not knowing because you really didn't want to know."

Lynda is adamant. "No. There was no way I could know. I still had my regular monthly period until I was five months, and that's when I found out. And by then I didn't have much choice because they told me they only did abortions until twelve weeks, and I was way past that. And besides, I don't believe in doing abortions at five months. They say that at three months the baby is still not really formed into a baby, but after that the baby starts forming, and then I feel that it's killing . . ."

April reaches down to straighten Kisha's dress. She speaks for the first time, her voice so soft and low that the rest of us have to strain to hear her. "I didn't know I was pregnant until I was three months. I jumped in a pool and felt something move inside me, and that's when I knew." She pulls her daughter to a sitting position on her lap, pushing a Cheez Doodle into the baby's flaccid mouth.

Janelle pauses and then says quietly, "I don't think I knew, but then I wonder. Maybe somewhere in me I knew, but it was like I was saying, no, I'm not pregnant. I'm not pregnant . . . I was living day-to-day, one day at a time. I would just get up in the morning and do what I needed to do, and not think about it."

As the girls speak, their words reflect their sense of powerlessness. Even 32 their bodies rebel, growing alien creatures without their knowledge, the awareness of their pregnancy dawning only after the possibility for abortion has passed. Does this reflect a yearning for a child? Or is it only a child's way of coping with something too terrifying to acknowledge?

Lynda glances at Danielle, who is still amusing herself with the checkers. She brings the group back to the abortion question. "I think that the girl should just make up her own mind, and then that's it," she says. "Because even if you don't let your boyfriend go, you are still going to get left."

"What do you mean?" Sophie-Louise asks. Like many working mothers, Lynda has an air of perpetual exhaustion. "Sometimes, if you're in love with a guy, and 'I love you' comes up, that's the one thing that always makes you weak. You say, 'Oh, I love you too.' But then it's time for you both to sit down and talk about the situation, you know, after you say, 'Well, I'm pregnant,' and he says, 'Oh, you are?' and he gets happy and everything. This happened to me. And I said, 'I want an abortion.' Then the brainwash would begin, the 'I love you and it's our baby and I'll give you support.' It was like, if I had an abortion, then I didn't love him. I feel that the woman should just make up her own mind, and make her own decision. But he said, 'Oh, I love you, and I'll do this for you, I'll do that for you, and our baby will have this, and our baby will have that.' Now she's two and a half years old, and all he ever got her was a big box of Pampers and socks and T-shirts and twenty dollars and that was it." Suddenly, the resentment in her voice changes to wistfulness. "She's two and a half. And he was going to buy her a baby crib and a bassinet and clothes. Everything . . ."

I have heard stories like this from other girls I talked with and from social workers as well. One fifteen-year-old mother told me that her boyfriend said that if she really loved him, she would have his baby. Despite her mother's urging, she decided against having an abortion. But by the time the baby was born, she and her boyfriend had broken up, and he was expecting another child by another girl in her school. As Sophie-Louise puts it, the guys like to have three or four "pots on different stoves" at the same time—visible proof of their virility.

Sophie-Louise turns to Eron, Janelle's boyfriend. He is seventeen and 36 works two jobs, one in a garage and the other as an attendant at Rye Playland. She asks him how he felt when he found out that Janelle was pregnant. He laughs. "I was scared."

"More scared than me!" Janelle adds. "I mean, you were chicken!" "Well my life was changing, too," says Eron. "I mean, I know guys who just say, oh no, a baby, and then walk off, but I'm not that type of person. My father was never there for me when I was little, so, you know, I don't want that to happen to my son. I don't want him to grow up and hate me and all that. I want to have somebody to love me. Even if me and Janelle don't end up together, I got him to remind me of her."

It interests me that Eron wants the baby as someone to love him. When I ask the girls what they think of this, April rejoins the discussion. Without raising her eyes from her baby, she says, "When my boyfriend found out I was pregnant, he just played it off. He would always play at my stomach, sort of punch me in the stomach.

"Now I don't even let him see her anymore. All he wants to do is play with her, and then give her back when it's time for changing."

"That's tough," Sophie-Louise says. "It takes two to make a baby, but then one of the two doesn't want any of the responsibility. Do you think you can talk to him about it?"

"I don't want to," April says. "I don't even want him to see her. Ever since I was pregnant, he kept saying that he was going to get me some stuff. He lied to his mother, saying that he was going to get me a carriage for the baby, but he didn't get me nothing. I had to do it all. And then I found out that he had some kind of drug addict, some girl in his house, some Puerto Rican girl, and his mother went on vacation and she came back and seen all these suitcases in her room, and she seen this Puerto Rican girl in the house with him. They just did it, right there."

As she clutches Kisha to her breast, I see how absorbed they are in each other. With no job, no boyfriend, nothing to fill her days, the baby is her life. Yet both mother and daughter seem drained.

Janelle looks concerned. "But aren't you worried that she might grow up without having a relationship with her father?"

"Well, I don't even want to see her father anymore," April says. "Her father is crazy! He busted my window one time. I tell you about that? He wanted to see the baby so bad and he was drunk one night, four-thirty in the morning, and he came banging on my door, saying, 'I'm not going nowhere until I see my baby.' So then I brought the baby into my mother's room, because he had cracked the window with a rock and he was making a lot of noise. And then he just left. . . . Besides, I don't want him taking her to his house, 'cause his mother is a crackhead."

April falls silent. Sophie-Louise asks her whether her role in her own family has changed since she got pregnant.

"Oh yeah," April says. "Now, my mother thinks that I have to do everything. You know, when I was pregnant, she tried to make me do more than I was supposed to, more than I did before I was pregnant. Now she says, 'You're no more teenager. You're an adult.' But before that, before I had the baby, I wasn't classified as no adult. So what makes us having a baby be an adult?"

During the next session, the last before the August recess, there is a small "graduation" party for Eron. He feels confident about passing his summer-school course, and when he does, he will officially become a high-school graduate. After the cake is cut and the group settles down, the talk turns to peer pressure. Sophie-Louise has been telling the story of a fourteen-year-old girl she counseled at a local high school. Although the girl had been taught about birth control and abortion and warned about the difficulties facing teen mothers, she became pregnant midway through eighth grade. Speaking with the girl later, Sophie-Louise asked her why, after all they had talked about, had she let this happen. "I don't know," she said. "All my friends have babies. I was beginning to wonder what was wrong with me that I didn't have one too."

The girls in the group laugh at the story. "I don't know about her," Janelle says, "but I knew that seventeen was too young to have a baby. None of my friends have babies. My sister, she just had a baby . . . but it wasn't like I wanted to get pregnant." 48

"Were you using birth control?" I ask.

Janelle's cheeks flush.

"I gotta tell you," she says. "I never used birth control. I mean, now I do, but before, well, I just never thought I would get pregnant. I was like, that can't happen to me. I thought that only happened to the bad girls across town. Who do drugs and stuff. But I didn't do none of that, so I thought I was safe. You know, like when you think it just can't happen to you. To other people *yes,* but not to you."

"I can believe that," Lynda says. "Like, I used to think that if the guy didn't come in you, then you couldn't get pregnant." 52

"Well," says Janelle, "my friend told me once that if you took a bath afterward, then you were safe."

"Or if you do it standing up!"

I could add to the list. A social worker I spoke with said that most of the girls use the chance method. And each month that they don't get pregnant reinforces their belief that they are safe.

The existence of these myths may reflect denial rather than ignorance. As the girls talk, I begin to see why the idea of having a baby might be compelling. There is a sense of loneliness eased, of purpose granted, of a glimmering of hope. 56

Janelle smiles. "But now that I am a mother, I do enjoy it. I mean, he keeps me company all the time, so I never have to be bored or lonely. He's my friend, this little guy. He keeps me so busy that I never have time to get into trouble. And before, I never really had a reason to get up in the morning, to go to school, whatever. But now, because of him, I do."

In Janelle's words, I hear the unspoken wish that, through the baby, the mothers may get a second chance at childhood, that in loving their babies they may almost be loving themselves.

Sophie-Louise asks whether, perhaps, Janelle had some of those thoughts before getting pregnant, whether on some level part of the reason that she did not use birth control was because somewhere inside her she wished for a baby.

Janelle pauses to consider the question. "Well, I don't know. Maybe. You know, I was lonely. My parents had split, and I really didn't have anyone, just me and my father together in the house."

Sophie-Louise turns to April. Despite the fact that Kisha was the result of her third pregnancy, April is unwilling to admit that she had wanted the baby. "It was an accident," she insists. "I mean, I said that this isn't going to happen to me. I was using all kinds of protection. Most times I even had him use protection."

Sophie-Louise seems surprised. "You were using protection?" she asks. "What kind?"

Indignantly, April answers, "Well, I was taking the Pill. I mean, I wasn't taking it all the time, but I was taking it. But I missed a couple of days, I guess. I think I took it on the day before my birthday, but not on my birthday, I don't think . . ."

"So for you it really was an accident," I say. I am surprised when she contradicts me.

"No. I wouldn't really say it was an accident. See, all the other times I got pregnant, my mother made me get rid of it. So I guess part of it was revenge against my mother, like I was gonna get pregnant but not let her know until she couldn't do nothing."

"Not with me," says Lynda. "With me it was just a pure accident. Just a pure accident. I wanted to get an abortion. I said that I was going to have one. But my boyfriend and my parents, my father especially . . . they wanted me to have it. That's when the brainwash began."

It occurs to me that I've been looking for a motivation, a reason why these girls, and others like them, might *choose* to become pregnant. But the more I listen, the more I wonder whether the question of choice is relevant. In all their stories, I hear again and again how little volition these girls feel they have, how little control over the events of their lives. The deadline for school admission passes and April shrugs. Sophie-Louise makes an appointment for Lynda with a job counselor, but Lynda forgets to go. Janelle knows about birth control but doesn't believe "it" will happen to her. Sophie-Louise told me once that these girls exert no more control over their lives than a "leaf falling from a tree." Perhaps having a baby is less a question of ignorance or choice than one of inevitability. Once a girl is sexually active, it is not *having* a baby that requires choice and conscious action, but *not* having one.

Eron shifts in his chair. "You know, all this talk about we didn't want to have the baby, or it was an accident, or whatever . . . I just think it's a waste of time. I mean, now we have the baby. The question is, what are we going to do now?"

Sophie-Louise asks him what he means, and he explains that the cycle of babies having babies, single parents raising single parents, has haunted him as it has haunted most of the teens in the room, and that he feels it can end with them, but only if they are willing to face the realities of their situation. "My father was never there when I was little," he says, "but I don't want him to grow up and hate me and all that . . . That's why I'm going to finish school and do whatever I need to do."

His eyes shine as he speaks of his ambition, but he looks down shyly, as if afraid that someone will mock him. Janelle, however, backs him up with pride and speaks of her own ambition to become a social worker. "It's so easy to go on welfare," she says. "You just sit home and cash a check. But I'm not going to get on welfare, 'cause it makes you lazy. It's addictive."

"I couldn't do that," Eron says. "I'm the kind of person who needs to work." But then the realities of fatherhood seem to descend upon him. "I don't know, though. See, 'cause with a baby, it takes all the money that you don't even have . . ."

At the end of the session, the discussion shifts back to the problems that 72 the girls will encounter when they return to school in the fall. Janelle is telling April that summer school really wasn't so bad. "It was hard leaving him at first," she says, "but I tried not to think about it. And I didn't think about it, because the classes were hard. And I was usually really tired. But I was happy. I just thought about the work, and the time flew by, and I was picking up the baby before I knew it."

Sophie-Louise presses April to consider how she will feel when she is separated from her daughter for the first time. "Have you thought at all about what it's going to be like?" Sophie-Louise asks. "How it's going to feel, emotionally, to be separated?"

April ignores her at first, and then shakes her head no. Sophie-Louise encourages her, suggesting she might feel relief or worry or sadness, but April clearly does not want to pursue the issue. Finally, in frustration, April says, "Look, I haven't thought about it yet. I haven't thought about it because it hasn't happened."

With that, the session ends. Having missed the deadline for entrance to summer school, April stays behind to talk to Sophie-Louise about starting a diploma-geared class in the fall. Danielle tugs at Lynda's arm, asking whether they can finally go to the zoo as she promised. I hear Eron and Janelle bickering about whose turn it is to buy diapers. And I head down the steep hill to the subway that will take me back downtown.

Points to Consider

1. What are some of the predominant stereotypes about teenage mothers? How do the cases of teenagers like Janelle and Lynda challenge these stereotypes?

2. For many teenagers pregnancy is a conscious choice. What reasons does Elizabeth Marek offer for this choice? Can you supply any other reasons for such a decision?

3. What is the predominant attitude to birth control exhibited by these

young women? According to Marek, why do so many teenagers refuse to use birth control? Why does Marek think the failure to use contraceptives is due as much to denial as to ignorance?

4. What does Marek mean by the statement: "Perhaps having a baby is less a question of ignorance or choice than one of inevitability"? Do you accept this appraisal of many teenage parents?

ADRIAN NICOLE LeBLANC

"You Wanna Die with Me?"

[NEW ENGLAND MONTHLY / December 1986]

A lanky girl descends from a yellow school bus. She walks the path leading to her white, clean home surrounded by green fields and mountains. Her older sister washes the car. The girls begin to argue and the younger girl slaps her sister across the face. In her bedroom, the young girl sits and cries. She takes off her baseball hat, pulling her ponytail through the opening above the adjustable band. She picks up a framed picture of her parents. She remembers the time her mother said she didn't love her. She takes her father's rifle out of a closet. As the camera pulls away from the bedroom window, the gun cracks.

The projector clicks off. From the darkened high school auditorium come claps and whistles. Several students mockingly sob and console one another. Others wriggle, their laughter careless, inattentive. Many bite their fingernails and stare indifferently ahead, caught in the numb monotone of a second-period assembly.

"Will those of you who haven't made airplanes out of the HELP cards please put them in your pockets?" asks today's Samaritan, stepping forward. A HELP plane sails past her. Students laugh. The assistant principal beckons

---

ADRIAN NICOLE LeBLANC (b. 1963) is a graduate of Smith College and recently received a Master's of Philosophy degree from Oxford University, where she wrote a thesis on the poetry of Adrienne Rich. She is a 1982 graduate of Leominster High School. She is now the fiction editor for Seventeen magazine.

for help from the teachers lining the perimeter of the gym. They arch their backs, coming off the wall slowly, and ease around the rough room. "Hey, *you!*" a teacher yells, pointing to a boy in the bleachers. "*NOW!*" The boy smirks and bounces down the rows. The teacher pushes him toward the exit.

Imagine you are a student here, at Leominster High. It's the fourth time 4 this year you've had to listen to people talking about depression and death. The white-haired ladies speaking soothingly onstage — representatives of the Samaritans, a suicide-prevention group sent in from Framingham to help you — have already given you their pamphlets. You remain unresponsive to their pleas.

"This is a tough scene, and it's tough to cope," says the Samaritan onstage now, her passé language causing you to roll your eyes. Your neighbor picks lint off his jeans; another stretches and yawns. "Oh, Christ," a student behind you mutters, "here we go again." There's hissing. One girl writes a note to her friend. "You must be mad that you live in Leominster," the Samaritan continues, "because it's only known for one thing these days. Suicide."

Leominster is a largely working-class city of thirty-four thousand, forty miles west of Boston, with a strong French Canadian and Italian heritage. Its usual claim to notoriety is the group of factories that produced the first plastics in the nation. Lately it has had a more somber reputation. Between February 1984 and March 1986, ten Leominster teenagers died sudden, violent deaths, and eight of those committed suicide. This morning's assembly aims to avoid number nine.

"It's always a mistake to kill yourself," says the Samaritan. One boy sleeps through the presentation. A group of "trade rats" from the vocational high school jumps down from the bleachers en masse. The Samaritan tries to continue. "There's *got* to be *someone* you can talk to," she says.

"Listen to her," says the assistant principal, his voice rising. 8

"Listen to each other," says the Samaritan, her face strained and weary. Shoving and hustling one another, students pour down from their seats.

"Pay attention to the signals, keep your eyes open," the Samaritan yells. "Listen!"

"Talk to someone!" screams the assistant principal, lost among a crowd of heads and denim. "And go to your fourth-period class!"

About five weeks before her death, fifteen-year-old Melissa Poirier was 12 beaten up twice in one day. That morning in school she had been jumped in the bathroom. Melissa and the two girls who attacked her were suspended, so Melissa went home. Soon after, one of her assailants went to her house, offering a truce. She asked Melissa to join her and the third girl so they could talk and work out the differences they were having over a boy. Melissa accompanied the girl to Pheasant Run, a derelict ski trail behind the high school where kids often drink and get stoned. The third girl waited beyond the trail. When Melissa arrived, the two girls assaulted her again. One held her down while the other pounded, and then the two traded positions. Half an hour later, Melissa managed to escape to a nearby garage, where she crouched behind a car for over an hour. She then made her way back home, carefully, through the woods.

Melissa was an extremely pretty young girl with thick, long hair, a button nose, shining eyes, and a neat, budding figure. When her classmates finished with her that day, her nose was fractured and both of her eyes were black. The blood vessels on her forehead had broken from repeated blows. Her face was swollen and her ribs were bruised.

"Melissa was tiny, five feet tall, and wicked cute," says one close girl-friend. "The girls never liked her because the guys did. Mel was hassled all the time."

The fight left Melissa despondent. Her mother, who noticed that she was afraid to go outside, encouraged her to see a therapist, but after three sessions, Melissa refused to return.

Andrea Paquette had been Melissa's best friend since fourth grade. The girls had started to grow apart (Andrea became involved with student government, and Melissa with drugs), but the two kept up their morning ritual of a walk before homeroom.

"She cried every day when the bell rang," says Andrea. "She never wanted to go in. Melissa hated school more than anything."

On the average morning at Leominister High, what Melissa Poirier wanted to avoid goes something like this: you might come in on time, drop your books off (if you took any home) but keep your coat on (to look as if you'd just entered the building, without books). You'd head straight for the girls' bathroom. You'd inhale the smoke and shiver; the bathroom is always cold. Graffiti covers the chipped gray paint on the windows and the doorless stalls: "Just because Im no slut doesnt mean I should become a fuckin nun Im no slob like most girls in this fuckin school!" You'd have fifteen minutes to get ready before the heads, the local drug population, took over the washroom. You'd comb your hair and watch your friends comb theirs and lean on a radiator half-covered with hardened wads of gum. You'd try to find your reflection between the black letters of the spray-painted SUCK on a mirror fogged with hair spray. You'd talk and look and tuck in your shirt. You'd put on a little more makeup, comb back your feathered hair one more time, then leave.

In the main corridor, dented light-brown lockers line the cinder-block hallways. Gray paint covers the old graffiti, and new graffiti covers the gray — "Helter Skelter, AC/DC, Led Zeppelin, DIE!" Boys, lined up by now outside the bathroom, shuffle and laugh, arms folded across their chests. Most wear denim jackets and high-tops or leather jackets and work boots. All collars are up.

The boys would tease you those early mornings, especially if they'd been

16

20

smoking or drinking. You would try to get by untouched but very noticed. Some students kept bottles in their lockers and drank in the locker-room shower stalls. Some had gone to McDonald's for breakfast and had dumped out half their Cokes and refilled the cups with booze, usually vodka. Some students didn't drink, of course, but certainly no one thought it strange if someone skipped classes, went to an empty house with a friend, and drank away the afternoon. So you'd lean against the lockers with friends, eyeing everyone but the person you were talking to, trying to see who was out by who was in school that day, and wait for the tardy bell. And then, maybe, you'd go to homeroom. Otherwise, you'd leave.

"And that's if you were one of the good kids," Melissa Poirier's mother says, a year after her daughter's death. "You just try and imagine what it was like to be one of the kids on the other side of the fence, one of the ones inside those detention halls, getting suspended, getting yelled at and punched at and hauled out two times a week. One of the kids called stupid by your teachers and, when you did go to class, one of those who was asked, 'Why did you bother to come?'"

Psychologists say the most dangerous time for a suicidal person is after emerging from depression or crisis. In fact, after planning a suicide, adolescents often look and feel better because a decision has been made, the burden lifted.

"It's like looking through a tunnel," says Susan Warner-Roy, who founded SPACE (Suicide Prevention Awareness Community Education) in 1980. Warner-Roy's own husband, Neil, hanged himself four years ago. "The darkness in the tunnel is the depression, and at the end of the tunnel is the light, the end of pain. To the suicidal kid, the light at the end of the tunnel is death." A couple of days before her death, Melissa's mood began to pick up. For the first time in months, Melissa seemed happy, upbeat.

"I thought to myself, 'Melissa's finally happy,'" says her friend, Andrea.   24
"Her problems are finally over." But despite Melissa's abrupt mood swing, the suicidal symptoms were still apparent: Melissa gave Andrea some brand-new clothes she hadn't worn yet. Melissa wouldn't make plans with Andrea for that afternoon. Melissa had written this poem to Andrea just one week before:

> Andrea Happy Andrea,
>   Joyful Andrea,
>   I Love Andrea,
>   I shall miss her,
> She will hurt but will heal,
>   Andrea is strong
>   Andrea is brave

Andrea has helped a great deal
   She will pull through
She always knew this would
    be the way
   The end of the day!
   My end.

So Melissa Poirier may have been in an especially dangerous frame of mind when she and another friend, Melody Maillet, left Leominster High School early on November 1, 1984. Pushing out the bright yellow doors of a side entrance, Melissa and Melody turned left on Exchange Street and walked the potholed road scattered with Coke cans and trash. The girls probably strolled downtown, past the variety stores and barbershops and tenements, past the pale houses of the plain Leominster streets. They walked past Monument Square, newly renovated and green. They may have walked by the Vietnamese and Cambodian apartments near Red's Variety and the Elbow Lounge. The girls then returned to Melissa's home with a bottle of cheap champagne they'd bought along the way, put on a Pink Floyd album, and began to drink.

The Wall, a series of songs depicting the progressive alienation of a rock star on the downswing, ranked high on the girls' list of revered albums. Each song, metaphorically "another brick in the wall," denotes the social forces propelling the rocker's snowballing anomie — parents, school, his wife — and the failure of the star's struggle to be understood. "Comfortably Numb," Melissa's favorite Pink Floyd song, expresses the rocker's peaking detachment. Melissa doodled the lyrics in her notebooks and in letters to friends:

Hello,/Is there anybody in there . . . I hear you're feeling down . . . Can you show me where it hurts/ . . . I can't explain you would not understand/This is not how I am/I have become comfortably numb . . . /The child is grown/ The dream is gone/And I have become/Comfortably numb.

The final song of the album Melissa quotes verbatim, in one of the five suicide notes the girls left behind:

"Life sucks and then you DIE! *Goodbye cruel world I'm leaving you now and thiers nothin you can Say To make me change my mind!* YES SA! I Love to Die I'd be happier I know it! So Please Let me Go. No hard feelings. Don't Be Sad ReJoyce Its my new beginning! It Didn't hurt I'm free and happy.

Melissa Poirier's mother, Mariette, came home for lunch on that November day and found her daughter and Melody on the floor of the upstairs bedroom, with the Poirier family's 12-gauge shotgun beside them. The medical examiner found high levels of alcohol in the blood of both girls. Exactly how Melissa and Melody committed double suicide remains unconfirmed. Friends believe that Melissa bent forward and leaned on the gun, which was pointed at her stomach, and that Melody climbed on her back. Mariette Poirier says she believes each girl shot herself.

Winnifred Maillet, Melody's mother, suspects foul play. (Susan Warner-Roy's husband, Neil, whose own suicide preceded Melody's by four years, was Winnifred's brother. And Winnifred's son, Bobby, had drowned in 1980.) Since Melody's death more than two years ago, Winnifred has worked to prove that the handwriting in Melody's own suicide note was not her daughter's. The graphology has become an obsessive project. When Winnifred says her daughter was not suicidal, there is an urgent determination in her voice: "We never saw her without the pretty smiling eyes. Always smiling like the dickens. She was always happy." 28

"She went out. She was happy," says Melody's father, Albert, who works in quality control for Digital Equipment Corporation. "She didn't have any problems at all. She had a few problems at school, and was always upset about being put on suspension once in a while, for maybe being tardy or not coming to school, but nothing out of the ordinary."

But Melody's friends feel certain that she was suicidal. One girlfriend says Melody had been asking people to commit suicide with her for a while, sometimes seriously, sometimes as a joke: "You wanna die with me?" Melody would say. "Melissa was the first one to say yes," says the friend. The two girls were known as partying buddies who shared a mutual love for acid rock.

"They dropped acid before an' shit, but they were really getting into it toward the end," says a close girlfriend of Melissa's. "We were losin' them."

Although adamant about Melody's emotional stability, Winnifred Maillet spoke of Melody's devotion to a print still hanging in her daughter's old bedroom among a collection of her things — Van Halen posters, a purple metallic electric guitar, and a black leather jacket she had bought. It shows a young girl who looks startlingly like Melody, a five-foot-eight Canadian beauty with jet black hair, olive skin, and huge, emerald eyes. The girl in the picture is tall and dark, but her eyes are detached, expressionless, complacent, while Melody's were warm. The girl's head is encircled by a lavender halo and she holds lavender feathers and a fan. The girl's skin is death-white. 32

"She loved the purple halo, said it was her purple haze," Melody's mother explains. Winnifred has since surrounded Melody's grave — a small pillar with Melody's picture in a crystal ball on top, leaning on a porcelain unicorn — with purple flowers. Acid rocker Jimi Hendrix popularized Purple Haze in his song about that form of LSD. And Melody referred to the purple haze, and to four of her classmates who died before her, in one of her suicide notes:

Good Bye 'I did cuz I had to' I have to live among the Purple Haze! Tell Cecilia I love her very much! Im took advantage of you without realizing it! But now I will be happy with Jeff Mike David + Scott. 'Mom and Dad I love you' even though I've never tobl you, Im sorry It has to be this way I don't want to hurt anyone I love the Rest of the family very much. . . .

Leominster is not alone. Teenage suicides nationwide have more than doubled since 1960. It's the second most common cause of death among youngsters between the ages of fifteen and twenty-four, and the number two killer among college students. One adolescent commits suicide every two hours. Cluster suicides, as in Leominster, have also continued to climb since the first documented case in Berkeley, California, in 1966. In Plano, Texas, seven occurred in one year. Three teenagers ended their lives in five days in Omaha, Nebraska. In New York's Putnam and Westchester counties, there were five in one month.

But why has Leominster joined this select and tragic group? For one thing, it has a very low residential turnover rate. Many kids in town will go to work in the factories after graduating from high school. It's impossible to know how youngsters interpret these circumstances, of course. But whatever Leominster's particular source of pain, its teenage suicide rate right now is ten times the national average.

Jeffrey Bernier was Leominster's first. On February 22, 1984, Jeff and his friends gathered in the Bernier family's second-story tenement, in the heart of Leominster's French Hill, which was built in the mid-nineteenth century to house Canadian laborers. School had let out early. Jeffrey took a .357 Colt revolver from his father's gun collection and began playing Russian roulette. Ignoring pleas from his friends to stop, Jeffrey placed the muzzle to his throat and pulled the trigger. The bullet passed through his skull and lodged in the ceiling. Jeffrey was fourteen. A teacher described him as a normal boy and an average student who "liked machine shop very much." Jeffrey's father said he had warned his son never to point a gun, at anyone.

Two weeks later, on March 7, 1984, Michael J. Bresnahan, also a freshman at the Trade High School's auto body shop, cut classes with a group of friends. They went to the apartment of Matt Fallon, who wasn't home. There, Alan Arsenault picked up a .30-caliber rifle and shot Michael in the chest. A close friend said they were all very stoned, that it was an accident. Bresnahan's mother described her son as "a good little boy" who was looking forward to his sixteenth birthday and a job that awaited him at a local gas station. "It's a waste of life," she said.

Two months later, on May 11, 1984, the first double suicide struck Leominster. Trade school seniors Scott Nichols and David Dombrowick drove into the concrete loading dock of the RVJ trucking company at what police called "a very high rate of speed." A friend who had been with Scott and David earlier said that they had been driving around, planning their graduation parties (only a few weeks away) and getting high. They had shared seven joints between them in under an hour.

Scott Nichols had been depressed for a long time and had talked about killing himself for over a year. He had recently lost his job, and his girlfriend had split with him. His friends said he also had problems at home.

"After it happened," says Todd Holman, a 1984 graduate who knew both boys from the trade school, "Scott seemed like the person it would have happened to." Both Scott and David had reputations as "serious partiers." Says Holman, "Better life to them just meant better drugs — better mescaline, better pot." But like many of the people who knew him, Holman believes David Dombrowick never intended to kill himself. "People don't like to do things alone in life," Holman says. "Adults don't want to live alone. Kids don't like to be alone, either. Scott just didn't want to die by himself." 40

The Poirier-Maillet suicides followed, bringing the total number of deaths to six. The year after the girls' double suicide was particularly difficult for the high school, says Assistant Principal Peter S. Michaels. Some students made bizarre claims that they were approached by six men in hooded black capes, carrying swords, with the number six scrawled on their foreheads in blood. For weeks after the supposed visit of the hooded men, students unscrewed number nines from the building and turned them upside down. Some students removed numbers from the classroom doors, exempting six. Others drew sixes on their notebooks and papers. They wrote notes to their dead friends on what is sometimes referred to as The Wall, a long cinderblock corridor in the basement of the main school: "Why did you guys leave us?" "We miss you!" "Melissa and Melody live on!"

Nine months passed before Leominster witnessed its seventh teenage death, suicide number five. (Jeffrey Bernier's death in the game of Russian roulette was officially ruled an accident, while Alan Arsenault, who shot Michael Bresnahan, has been convicted of manslaughter.) On August 14, 1985, Randy Cleremont and three friends sat on the railroad tracks behind Nashua Street, drinking. A train approached and they moved. Randy jumped back onto the tracks as the train sped nearer. Thrown twenty-nine feet, he struck a utility pole and slid down a dirt embankment. His friends said he was not drunk. They said he had heard their screams. They said that Randy saw the train, and that he did not want to move.

Two months later, on October 23, 1985, John P. Finn, fifteen, and a friend who remains unidentified walked out of their third-period trade class. Leaving the school by a side entrance, they turned right and traced the battered picket fence circling the wide arch of road leading downtown. They took a left at the first variety store they came upon, passed the recently closed Carter Junior High School, and soon arrived at the home of a friend named Billy Lovetro. John Finn started to tease his friend with a .38-caliber revolver. Feeling uncomfortable, the boy went out on the porch. He heard a shot and told a neighbor to call an ambulance immediately, then ran to school to get help. Finn was Leominster's eighth death in twenty months, suicide number six.

John Finn had been living with the Lovetro family because he had been 44 having problems at home. The local newspaper mentioned John's lingering trademark — "an incredible smile."

On December 31, 1985, Billy Lovetro followed his best friend's lead — he drove into a concrete wall. Earlier, Billy is said to have taken a girlfriend to the spot on Adams Street where the wall stood and had told her, "This is where I'm going to do it." Leominster's superintendent of schools told a reporter, "I just don't know what to do anymore."

The school had handled the first death like any other — a moment of silence in the morning, a planned yearbook dedication, the morning announcement about calling hours. With the second, officials mandated the same procedure and prayed it would be the last. When Melody and Melissa died, the school established a Sudden Death Protocol. The steps, according to guidance counselor Patricia Pothier, were simple: "Don't call school off. Don't lower the flag. Play it low key without being callous. No glamour."

Dr. Pamela Cantor of Newton, Massachusetts, is former president of the American Association of Suicidology. Cantor says there is a contagion effect in these situations. "They must not treat the kid as a hero," she says. "The school must explain the event not as an act of intelligence or coherence but as a tragedy that was the result of stupidity." Calling school off, dedicating the yearbook — such actions, Cantor believes, only heighten the effect of making the dead kid popular. "If you take a kid who is very troubled, with no stature or identity in school," she says, "he sees how the suicides are the center of attention. Other kids might get carried away in the emotion of it all. Their fragility in their depression allows them to see suicide as a model."

In the high school corridors, at hangouts around town, and on the street, 48 the suicides are clearly on the minds of Leominster's teenagers. And they want to talk about it. "Subconsciously, in everyone's mind now, suicide is an option," says Diana DeSantis, a 1986 graduate of Leominster High who was vice-president of her class for four years. "You're upset. You say, 'I'm depressed.' You tell your mother, and it doesn't help. You tell your teacher, maybe, and it doesn't help. So you tell a friend, maybe even a professional — the same. Suicide might be next on the list. It's just higher up on your list of options in Leominster than anywhere else."

"How can you ever get used to it?" asks Matt Mazzaferro, another 1986 graduate, now attending Brandeis. "We were shocked every time. Each one was a whole different person." Mazzaferro modifies the assertion that his peers were looking for glamour. "They were just looking not to be another face in the crowd," he said. "That was their way to make noise." Often, the methods of their deaths are more accurately remembered than any aspect of their lives: people ask, "Was that the one who . . . ?"

"It was my birthday when that last freshman killed himself," says a junior. "At first I was kinda pissed off, you know, 'cause I wanted to have a wicked great day, but afta homeroom it didn't really matter, I didn't give a shit, really. 'Cause it wasn't like it was new or anything, like the first ones. It didn't wreck my day or nothing."

"After the first few the atmosphere was real gloomy around here," says one secretary at the high school. "But by the third or fourth they got numb to it. It isn't such a big deal to them anymore." As one counselor puts it, "The kids are all suicided out." A student says, "I mean, afta *seven*, what difference does one or two make? Christ, you sit in homeroom and they say we haveta have this moment of silence, and you're like, 'Fuck, not again,' but it doesn't *surprise* you. I mean, it's not like some shock or somethin' when you hear it all the time."

Leominster has tried and is still trying. Parents have started support 52 groups; the community has sponsored lectures. The Leominster Youth Committee was formed to look at the problems facing the kids — and then, on March 26, 1986, freshman George Henderson came home from track practice and shot himself in the head, the first suicide in three months.

Henderson's suicide vitiated the by-then usual explanations. The kids who killed themselves had been tough kids — some fought, most drank, most did drugs. They had reputations. Academically, some had special needs. Many of them had problems at home. Diana DeSantis says that, with the exception of George Henderson, all the students who had killed themselves had "the attitude": "They would be the kind of kids who would say, 'Life sucks. Adults suck. The high school sucks. Everything sucks. I just want to party.'"

But George Henderson didn't seem like the other nine at all. He never cut school. He didn't drink or smoke. He was on the honor roll. He was only fourteen and, according to a neighbor, came from a family that "did everything together," from mountain climbing to canoeing. His death seemed to be the one that bothered Leominster's adults most, because George was the first one they really could not understand.

"I don't know why people are so afraid to say it," says one sophomore. "He was the first kid who they didn't think was a real loser."

But the students of Leominster High weren't puzzled by George's suicide. 56 To his peers, he wasn't a model boy — he was a freshman brain who had failed a Spanish quiz, maybe a nice kid, but a nerd, a wimp. His peer category may have been different from that of the students who died before him — he wasn't a burnout, or a head — but in a school that perceives jocks as the in crowd and druggies as cool, George had lost both ways. Being a brain was his marker among the crowd, and faltering grades may have threatened his identity at a time when peer acceptance was acute. "I wouldn't have gotten all upset about getting a warning card or nothing," says a sophomore. "But I can kind of understand how something like that could have really depressed *him*."

"With someone like that you can understand," says a freshman. "School was wicked important and stuff to him."

According to guidance counselors at Leominster High, the deaths have sparked dialogue. They say the students are more willing to talk about their problems, are more alert and more sensitive. "It's brought us closer," says one senior. "All the hugging and crying has made us tighter." But among the students, opinion diverges: "'How are you, are you feeling suicidal today?'" asks a junior sweetly, mocking a counselor. "'I haven't seen you in two years and even though you're flunking all your classes you are doing just fine. Things will be just fine, now, won't they? *Won't* they?'"

Some students harbor anger. They resent the reputation their city has acquired and feel betrayed by the friends who have left them. "Suicide is the ultimate act in selfishness," says a sophomore. "Why bother crying about a selfish brat?" One counselor shares her favorite explanation: "It's the ultimate temper tantrum," she says. "Kids who can't have their lives the way they want them don't want life at all."

Outside the community, too, the response can be just as cold. Leominster and nearby Fitchburg have one of the oldest high school football rivalries in the nation, and school spirit runs deep. Leominster won the game last year, but Fitchburg got its licks in. KILL LEOMINSTER, read the inscription on the Fitchburg rooters' T-shirts, BEFORE THEY KILL THEMSELVES. 60

The dominating ambience of bewilderment and exhaustion makes Leominster's grief difficult to detect. Many adults refuse to discuss the tragedies at all. One student wrote a letter to the editor of the local newspaper after the death of John Finn, asking the community to confront the dangers rather than run away: "I've never felt such a sense of deep loss, pain or fear as during these three years at Leominster High," the letter read. "It's sad to think that some day our children are going to ask us what high school is like. What will we say? I spent most of my high school years mourning the loss of my friends. . . . Somebody must do something. We need help."

Donald Fredd, an English teacher, was so concerned about the section he teaches on existentialism that he has recently modified the course. "Camus and Sartre[1] believe the choice to live is the most profound decision one can make, and you're telling kids that these great thinkers believed the choice must be made every day. That you must get up in the morning and decide

---

[1] Albert Camus (1913–1960), French philosopher, dramatist, and novelist, won the Nobel Prize in 1957; Jean Paul Sartre (1905–1980), the French existentialist philosopher, won the Nobel Prize for literature in 1964.

whether you're going to go through with it or end it right then and there. That it's up to the individual *alone* to decide. In the context of these tragedies I've become slightly paranoid. How will the students take it? How seriously? How literally? What about the real bright ones? What about the ones who are down?"

Teachers, friends, and parents have substantial cause to worry about overlooking the symptoms. The teenagers who took their lives left plenty of clues first, as 80 percent of all suicides do. But "the problem is," says Patricia Pothier, the guidance counselor, "how do you tell the difference between symptoms of suicidal feelings and the normal business of being a teenager in the eighties?" Although preventive and educational measures are being taken, few Leominster residents feel their little city has witnessed its last teenage suicide; those most actively involved in the aftermath still anticipate the next one. "I think it'll slow down," says one graduate who enrolled at the University of Massachusetts this fall. "Maybe at the rate of just one or two a year."

On the morning of a recent Samaritan assembly, a pair of sophomores   64 held a homeroom period of their own in the woods, smoking. But then they reentered the building to hear what the Samaritans had to say. "They just said the usual stuff about suicide like they did last time," says a girl named Celeste in the corridor afterward. "It was dumb," her friend Carol adds.

It is time to go. The two girls start walking down the corridor. Carol turns her head when they are halfway down the hall.

"*You* can leave this school anytime you want," she yells. Then she begins to spin. "An-y-ti-me!" she yells, her voice waving louder and softer with her turns. She spins faster, sending her pocketbook flying, then jerks to a halt. The strap wraps tightly around her thin, young waist.

Points to Consider

1. What are the early warning signs of teenage suicide mentioned in Le-Blanc's article? How accurate do you think these signs are? Could they be interpreted in other ways?

2. Early in the article LeBlanc provides a vivid description of the girls' bathroom at Leominster High. Why do you think she included such a detailed account? Is she making a connection between attitude and environment?

3. Do you agree with Dr. Pamela Cantor that calling off school or dedicating the yearbook as a response to someone's suicide increases the possibility of other suicides? Do you think that students would tend to glamorize their deceased classmate?

4. Why was George Henderson's suicide (see paragraphs 51–56) so disturbing? In what ways did it differ from the town's previous suicides? What does his death tell us about the nature of teenage suicide?

Discussing the Unit

Suggested Topic for Discussion

Two articles in this unit depict the lives of teenagers in very different circumstances. While the teenage mothers portrayed in Elizabeth Marek's article have futures full of uncertainty, for themselves and their children, they are nevertheless trying to survive. Conversely, the students at Leominster High live under much less extreme conditions but apparently have become accustomed to thinking about suicide as a solution to their problems. Consider the difference in mental attitude between these two groups. Do you think that getting pregnant and committing suicide represent different responses to similar adolescent problems or do you think that the different responses develop out of different sets of problems?

Preparing for Class Discussion

1. Suicide prevention groups stress the importance of communication between troubled teenagers and their families and friends. Do you think that talking to someone can help prevent suicide? What other measures might be taken? What would you say or do if you thought one of your close friends was on the verge of suicide? How helpful do you think *you* could be?

2. Committing suicide is one of the most extreme ways that teenagers deal with their problems. Although many adults feel that youth is a problem-free time of life, David Gelman's article shows how adult-size problems have caught up with teenagers. What are these problems? Make a list of the problems that you feel are serious enough to lead to extreme measures like running away or suicide. Do you feel that teenagers tend to exaggerate their problems?

From Discussion to Writing

At some point most teenagers express a desire to "escape" from the pressures of everyday life. Suicide is clearly an extreme form of escape. In an essay (1) explore some specific factors of teenage life that give rise to a desire to escape, and (2) offer some alternative, more healthy, means of escaping. *Be specific* in your examples and your alternative plan.

4

Divided Selves:
How Can We Deal with
Conflicting Identities?

One of the critical problems facing many Americans today is the dilemma of entering mainstream society without denying their own racial and ethnic heritages. This sense of duality can make it extremely difficult for those caught between two worlds to establish a stable and consistent identity. In "Twice an Outsider: On Being Jewish and a Woman," Vivian Gornick discusses her successful struggle to integrate two different but central aspects of her life.

For June Jordan, the struggle to reconcile race and gender with mainstream values has been an especially difficult task: "Waiting for a Taxi" describes the hard choices she must face every day. Yet not everyone who faces a divided identity feels the necessity to make such choices. In "Black *and* Latino," Roberto Santiago describes how he came to understand and accept his dual heritage. While reading these essays, consider how a writer's act of recording such conflicts of identity can play a vital role in helping her or him establish a workable balance between two worlds.

Twice an Outsider:
On Being Jewish and a Woman [TIKKUN / March–April 1989]

When I was growing up, the whole world was Jewish. The heroes were Jewish and the villains were Jewish. The landlord, the doctor, the grocer, your best friend, the village idiot, the neighborhood bully: all Jewish. We were working-class and immigrant as well, but that just came with the territory. Essentially, we were Jews on the streets of New York. We learned to be kind, cruel, smart, and feeling in a mixture of language and gesture that was part street slang, part grade-school English, part kitchen Yiddish. We learned about politics and society in much the same way: down the block were a few Orthodox Jews, up the block a few Zionists, in between a sprinkling of socialists. For the most part, people had no politics at all, only a cautious appetite for the goods of life. It was a small, tight, hyphenated world that we occupied, but I didn't know that; I thought it *was* the world.

One Sunday evening when I was eight years old my parents and I were riding in the back seat of my rich uncle's Buick. We had been out for a drive and now we were back in the Bronx, headed for home. Suddenly, another car sideswiped us. My mother and my aunt shrieked. My uncle swore softly. My father, in whose lap I was sitting, said out the window at the speeding car, "That's all right. Nothing but a bunch of kikes in here." In an instant I knew everything. I knew there was a world beyond our streets, and in that world my father was a humiliated man, without power or standing. By extension, we were all vulnerable out there; but *we* didn't matter so much. It was my father, my handsome, gentle father, who mattered. My heart burned for him. I burrowed closer in his lap, pressed myself against his chest. I wanted to warm the place in him that I was sure had grown cold when he called himself a kike.

That was in the middle of the Second World War—*the* watershed event

VIVIAN GORNICK *(b. 1935) has worked as a journalist for more than twenty years. Her articles and reviews have appeared in the* Village Voice, *the* Nation, *the* New York Times Magazine, *the* Washington Post, *the* Atlantic, *and other publications. Gornick has written five books, among them* Women in Science: Portraits from a World in Transition *(1983) and* Fierce Attachments: A Memoir *(1987).*

for the men and women of my generation. No matter what your social condition, if you were a child growing up in the early 1940s you entered the decade destined for one kind of life and came out of it headed for another. For those of us who had gone into the war the children of intimidated inner-city Jews, 1945 signified an astonishing change in the atmosphere. The end of the war brought frozen food and nuclear fission, laundromats and anti-communists, Levittown and the breakup of the college quota system. The trolley tracks were torn up, and the streets paved over. Buses took you not only to other parts of the Bronx but into Manhattan as well. When my brother graduated from the Bronx High School of Science in 1947 my father said, "Now you can become a salesman." But my cousin Joey had been a bombardier in the Pacific and was now one of the elite: a returned GI at City College. My brother sat down with my father and explained that even though he was not a genius he had to go to college. It was his right and his obligation. My father stared at his son. Now we were in the new world.

When I was sixteen a girl in the next building had her nose straightened;   4 we all trooped in to see Selma Shapiro lying in state, swathed in bandages from which would emerge a person fit for life beyond the block. Three buildings away a boy went downtown for a job, and on his application he wrote "Arnold Brown" instead of "Arnold Braunowitz." The news swept through the neighborhood like wildfire. A nose job? A name change? What was happening here? It was awful; it was wonderful. It was frightening; it was delicious. Whatever it was, it wasn't stasis. Things felt lively and active. Chutzpah was on the rise, passivity on the wane. We were going to run the gauntlet. That's what it meant to be in the new world. For the first time we could *imagine* ourselves out there.

But who exactly do I mean when I say we? I mean Arnie, not Selma. I mean my brother, not me. I mean the boys, not the girls. My mother stood behind me, pushing me forward. "The girl goes to college, too," she said. And I did. But my going to college would not mean the same thing as my brother's going to college, and we all knew it. For my brother, college meant getting from the Bronx to Manhattan. But for me? From the time I was fourteen I yearned to get out of the Bronx, but get out into *what*? I did not actually imagine myself a working person alone in Manhattan and nobody else did either. What I did imagine was that I would marry, and that the man I married would get me downtown. He would brave the perils of class and race, and somehow I'd be there alongside him.

The greater chain of social being obtained. Selma straightened her nose so that she could marry upward into the Jewish middle class. Arnie changed his name so that he could wedge himself into the Christian world. It was the boys who would be out there facing down the terrors of the word "kike," not the girls. The boys would run the gauntlet, for themselves and for us. We would be standing not beside them but behind them, egging them on. And because we knew we'd be behind them, we—the girls—never experienced ourselves directly as Jews. I never shivered inside with the fear of being called a kike. I remember that. Somehow I knew that if I were insulted in that way I might feel stunned, but the fear and shame would be once removed. I knew I'd run home to Arnie, and I'd say, "Arnie, they called me a kike," and he'd look miserable, and I'd say, "Do something!" and the whole matter would be out of my hands the minute I said "Do something." It was Arnie who'd have to stand up to the world, search his soul, test his feelings, discover his capacity for courage or action. Not me. And that is why Arnie grew up to become William Paley, and the other boys on the block—the ones who sneered and raged and trembled, who knew they'd have to run that gauntlet, get into that new world like it or not, and were smart and sensitive, and hated and feared and longed for it all—they grew up to become Philip Roth and Woody Allen. Me and Selma? We grew up to become women.

The confusion is historic; the distinction is crucial.

Woody Allen is exactly my age. I remember as though it were yesterday listening to Allen's first standup comic monologues in the late fifties at the Bitter End Café. We were all in our twenties, my friends and I and Allen. It was as though someone on the block had suddenly found it in himself to say to a world beyond the street, "Listen. You wanna know how it is? This is how it is," and with more courage than anxiety he had shaped our experience. This wasn't Milton Berle or Henny Youngman up there, a Borscht Belt comic speaking half Yiddish, half English, all outsiderness. No, this was one of us, describing how it felt to be our age and in our place: on the street, at a party, in the subway, at home in the Bronx or Brooklyn, and then out there, downtown, in the city. Half in, half out.

Philip Roth, of course, cut closer to the bone. His sentence structure deepened the experience, drove home better than Allen could the pain and the excitement, the intelligence and the anguish, the hilarity and the madness of getting so close you could touch it and *still* you weren't inside.

Behind Allen and Roth stood Saul Bellow, who made the words "manic" and "Jewish" synonymous, whose work glittered with a wild flood of feeling that poured from a river of language, all pent-up brilliance, the intelligence driven to an edge of hysteria that resembled Mel Brooks as much as it did Philip Roth. Although Bellow had been writing since the forties, it was only now in the fifties and sixties that his work and its meaning traveled down from a small community of intellectual readers to the reading populace at large. Here was a street-smart writing Jew who was actually extending the American language, using us—our lives, our idiom—to say something about American life that had not been said before. In the process, he gave us—me and my contemporaries—the equipment to define ourselves, and therefore become ourselves.

These men are on a continuum. From Milton Berle and Mel Brooks to Saul Bellow, Philip Roth, and Woody Allen—the subtle alterations of tone and voice among them constitute a piece of social history, chart a progress of the way Jews felt about themselves in America, embody a fine calibration of rage, resentment, and hunger.

My mother hated Milton Berle, and I understood why—he was hard to 12 take. But I laughed against my will, and I knew he was the real thing. To see the idiom of your life coming back at you, shaped and enlarged by a line of humorous intelligence as compelling as a poem in the sustained nature of its thesis and context, was to experience one of life's deepest satisfactions. When that famous chord of recognition strikes, it is healing—illuminating and healing.

Milton Berle was my first experience of an artist's work applied to the grosser materials of my own environment. Berle, operating at a lower level of genius, was just as sinister as the Marx brothers. It was the wildness of his humor and the no-holds-barred atmosphere that it generated. Berle was coarse and vulgar, fast and furious, frightening in the speed of his cunning and his rage. My mother was repelled. She knew this was Jewish self-hatred at its most vicious.

Mel Brooks was more of the same, only ten years younger, and the ten years made a difference. A few years ago Brooks reminisced about how, when he began writing for Sid Caesar, his mother asked him how much money he was making, and he told her sixty dollars a week. He knew if he told her what he was really making she'd have a heart attack. "The heart," he said. "It would attack her." That story was for us: Woody Allen built on it. Brooks—also marked by a Borscht Belt coarseness that spoke to an uneducated sense of America, a lack of conversance with the larger culture— was still the shrewd, wild Jew talking, but his tone was a bit sadder, a bit quieter than Milton Berle's, less defended against the fears that dominated our lives. The lessened defense was the sign of change.

With Woody Allen, we passed through into a crucial stage of development. Allen built a persona, an identity, a body of work out of the idea of the mousy Jew who makes a fool of the gentile rather than of another Jew. This had not happened before. Its meaning was unmistakable.

The Woody Allen character is obsessed with getting laid. Everyone else 16 does it; he alone can't do it. Everywhere he goes—in the street, on the subway, at a party—he gazes mournfully at the golden shiksas all around him, always beyond reach. It's not a Jewish girl he's trying to get into bed; it's Diane Keaton. The Jewish girl is Brooklyn; Annie Hall is Manhattan.

And what does sexual success mean? It means everything. It means the defeat of all that life bitterly withholds, already characterized by the fact that one has been born a Jew instead of Humphrey Bogart. If Allen can just get that blue-eyed beauty into bed. He wants it so bad he's going to die of it. He's going to expire from this hunger right there before your eyes.

The humor turns on Allen's extraordinary ability to mock himself. He's as brilliant as Charlie Chaplin at making wonderful his own smallness. And he's as successful as Chaplin at making a hero of the little man, and a fool of the withholding world in the person of the pretty girl. When Diane Keaton wrings her hands and moans, "I can't," and Allen blinks like a rabbit and says, "Why? Because I'm Jewish?"—he accomplishes a minor miracle on the screen. The beautiful woman is made ridiculous. The golden shiksa has become absurd, inept, incapable: the insincere and the foolish cut down to size so that Allen can come up to size.

When was the first time I saw it? Which movie was it? I can't remember. I remember only that at one of them, in the early seventies, I suddenly found myself listening to the audience laugh hysterically while Allen made a dreadful fool of the girl on the screen, and I realized that he had to make a fool of her, that he would always have to make a fool of her, because she was the foil: the instrument of his unholy deprivation, the exasperating source of life's mean indifference. I said to myself, "This is dis-*gust*-ting," and as I said it I knew I'd been feeling this way all my life: from Milton Berle to Saul Bellow to Woody Allen. I had always laughed, but deep inside I'd frozen up, and now I saw why. Milton Berle with his mother-in-law jokes, Saul Bellow with the mistresses who hold out and the wives who do him in, Mel Brooks and Woody Allen with the girl always and only the carrot at the end of the stick. Every last one of them was trashing women. Using women to savage the withholding world. Using us. Their mothers, their sisters, their wives. To them, we weren't friends or comrades. We weren't even Jews or gentiles. We were just girls.

At that moment I knew that I would never again feel myself more of a Jew than a woman. I had never suffered as men did for being a Jew in a Christian world because, as a Jew, I had not known that I wanted the world. Now, as a woman, I knew I wanted the world and I suffered.

Hannah Arendt, watching the Nazis rise to power in Germany, had denied the meaning of her own Jewishness for a long time. When she acknowledged it, she did so by saying, "When one is attacked as a Jew, one must defend oneself *as a Jew*. Not as a German, not as a world-citizen, not as an upholder of the Rights of Man [emphasis in original]." I read that and I was ready to change the sentences to read, "When one is attacked as a woman, one must defend oneself *as a woman*. Not as a Jew, not as a member of the working class, not as a child of immigrants."

My father had to be Jewish; he had no choice. When he went downtown he heard "kike." I live downtown, and I do not hear "kike." Maybe it's there to be heard and I'm not tuned in, but it can't be there all that much if I don't hear it. I'm out in the world, and this is what I *do* hear:

I walk down the street. A working-class man puts his lips together and makes a sucking noise at me.

I enter a hardware store to purchase a lock. I choose one, and the man behind the counter shakes his head at me. "Women don't know how to use that lock," he says.

I go to a party in a university town. A man asks me what I do. I tell him I'm a journalist. He asks if I run a cooking page. Two minutes later someone asks me not if I have a husband but what my husband does.

I go to another party, a dinner party on New York's Upper West Side. I'm the only woman at the table who is not there as a wife. I speak a few sentences on the subject under discussion. I am not responded to. A minute later my thought is rephrased by one of the men. Two other men immediately address it.

Outsiderness is the daily infliction of social invisibility. From low-grade humiliation to life-threatening aggression, its power lies in the way one is seen, and how that in turn affects the way one sees oneself. When my father heard the word "kike" the life force within him shriveled. When a man on the street makes animallike noises at me, or when a man at a dinner table does not hear what I say, the same thing happens to me. This is what makes the heart pound and the head fill with blood. This is how the separation between world and self occurs. This is outsiderness alive in the daily way. It is here, on the issue of being a woman, not a Jew, that I must make my stand and hold my ground.

A few years ago I taught at a state university in a small Western town. 28 One night at a faculty party a member of the department I was working in, a man of modest intelligence, said of another teacher who had aroused strong feeling in the department, "He's a smart Jew crashing about in all directions." I stared at this man, thinking, "How interesting. You *look* civilized." Then I said, quite calmly, "What a quaint phrase. In New York we don't hear ourselves described as smart Jews any more. Is that still current out here?" The man turned dull red, and the exchange was at an end.

A few weeks later at another party I saw this same man engaged in conversation with another member of the department, a woman. I knew this woman, and in my view her gifts of mind and spirit were comparable to the man's. She was not a scholar and he was not a scholar. She was not intellectual and neither was he. They were both hard-working university teachers. I watched the two standing together, talking. The woman gestured widely as she spoke, smiled inordinately, fingered her hair. Her eyes were bright; her tone was eager. She exclaimed; she enthused; she performed. The man stood there, pulling at a pipe, silent, motionless, his body slack, his face immobile, his entire being unreadable except for his eyes and his mouth: in them an expression of mockery and patronage as the woman grew ever more frantic in her need to gain a response. It was clear that the harder she tried, the more secure he felt. At a certain point it became obvious that he was deliberately withholding what he knew she needed. I was watching a ritual exchange of petition and denial predicated on a power structure that in this instance turned wholly on his maleness and her femaleness.

I watched these two for a long time, and as I watched I felt my throat tighten, my arms and legs begin to tingle, a kind of sick feeling spread through my chest and belly. I wanted to put her up against the wall, but I wanted to put him through the wall. I realized I'd been absorbing this kind of thing twenty times a day in this department, in this university, in this town; and it was making me ill.

This daily feeling, this awareness of the subtle ways in institutional life that the most ordinary men accord each other the simplest of recognitions and withhold these recognitions from the equally ordinary women with whom they work, is palpable, and it burns inside every woman who experiences it—whether she is aware of what is happening or has numbed herself to what is happening.

When I hear an anti-Semitic remark I am hurt, I am angered, but I am not frightened. I do not fear for my life or my livelihood or my right to pursue the open expression of my convictions. When I hear a sexist remark I feel all of the above. I feel that stomach-churning rage and pain that tells me that I am in trouble, that I am up against threat and wipeout. I am in the presence of something virulent in the social scheme directed against me not because of what I actually am but because of an immutable condition of birth. Something I might once have experienced as a Jew but today can feel only as a woman.

Bellow, Roth, Allen: these are writers who have had only the taste of their own lives as the stimulus for creative work—and a rich, lively taste it has been: tart and smart, full of bite and wisdom. But these writers were allowed to become so fabulously successful precisely because the stigma of Jewishness was fading even as they were recording it. When Bellow wrote *Herzog,* being Jewish was no longer the open wound it had been when he wrote *The Victim*; and by the time Allen and Roth were coming into their own they were far more integrated into the larger world than their work suggested. Therefore, for Allen or Roth to go on making the golden shiksa the foil, or for Bellow to keep portraying the Jewish intellectual who can't arrive as his foil, is tiresome and unpersuasive. It does not speak to the lives that any of us are now living. Such work strikes no chord of recognition; it strikes only chords of memory and sentiment. The thing about outsiderness is that one feels it in the flesh every day; one feels oneself invisible in the ordinary social way. These are requirements of the conditon.

This invisibility once made Jews manic and blacks murderous. It works on women in a variety of ways:

I leaned across the counter in the hardware store and said to the man who had told me women didn't know how to use the lock I'd chosen, "Would you say that to me if I were black?" He stared lightly at me for a long moment. Then he nodded, "Gotcha," he said.

To the man at the university party I explained my work in great and careful detail. The man, a sixty-year-old Ivy Leaguer, was frankly puzzled at why I spoke of something fairly simple at such excessive length. I knew this was the first time he had heard what I was *really* saying, and I didn't expect it to sink in. What I did expect was that the next time he heard a woman speak these words, they would begin to take hold.

At the dinner party in New York I made a scene. I brought harmless sociability to an end. I insisted that everyone see that the little social murders committed between men and women were the real subtext of the evening, and that civilized converse was no longer possible unless this underlying truth was addressed. I did this because these were liberal intellectuals. They had heard it all before, many times, and *still* they did not get it. It was as terrible for me to go home that evening with the taste of ashes in my mouth as it was for everyone else—we had all come expecting the warm pleasures of good food and good conversation—but I couldn't have lived with myself that night if I hadn't spoken up. Just as I would have had to speak up if the conversation had suddenly turned politely anti-Semitic. Which it would not have in this company.

The Jewishness inside me is an education. I see more clearly, can think more inventively, because I can think analogously about "them" and "us." That particular knowledge of being one among the many is mine twice over. I have watched masters respond to "them" and "us," and I have learned. I wouldn't have missed being Jewish for the world. It lives in me as a vital subculture, enriching my life as a writer, as an American, and certainly as a woman.

Points to Consider

1. Vivian Gornick begins her essay with the statement: "When I was growing up, the whole world was Jewish." What does she mean by this statement? When did she realize the whole world wasn't Jewish?

2. Why did Gornick not feel fear when faced with anti-Semitism? Why does she believe that the situation was different for Jewish men? According to Gornick, why didn't Jewish women of her own generation ever experience themselves directly as Jews?

3. Why does Gornick foster a resentment toward famous Jewish men like Woody Allen, Philip Roth, and Saul Bellow? Why did their work play a central part in Gornick's recognition that she felt more of a woman than a Jew?

4. Why does Gornick feel more threatened by a sexist remark than by an anti-Semitic remark? According to the author, what aspects of American life have changed? What has the author learned from her life as a Jew in America that can be applied to her life as a woman? Do you think the situations are analogous?

Waiting for a Taxi [THE PROGRESSIVE / June 1989]

We weren't doing anything. We hadn't hurt anybody, and we didn't want to. We were on holiday. We had studied maps of the city and taken hundreds of photographs. We had walked ourselves dizzy and stared at the other visitors and stammered out our barely Berlitz versions of a beautiful language. We had marveled at the convenient frequency of the Metro and devoured vegetarian crêpes from a sidewalk concession. Among ourselves, we extolled the seductive intelligence and sensual style of this Paris, this magical place to celebrate the two-hundredth anniversary of the French Revolution, this obvious place to sit back with a good glass of wine and think about a world lit by longings for *Liberté, Egalité, Fraternité*.

It was raining. It was dark. It was late. We hurried along, punch-drunk with happiness and fatigue. Behind us, the Cathedral of the Sacred Heart glowed ivory and gorgeous in a flattering wash of artificial, mellow light.

These last hours of our last full day in Paris seemed to roll and slide into pleasure and surprise. I was happy. I was thinking that, as a matter of fact, the more things change, the more things change.

I was thinking that if we, all of us black, all of us women, all of us 4 deriving from connected varieties of peasant/ immigrant/persecuted histories of struggle and significant triumph, if we could find and trust each other enough to travel together into a land where none of us belonged, nothing on Earth was impossible any more.

But then we tried to get a cab to stop for us, and we failed. We tried again, and then again. One driver actually stopped and then, suddenly, he sped away almost taking with him the arm of one of my companions who had been about to open the door to his taxi.

This was a miserable conclusion to a day of so much tourist privilege and delight, a day of feeling powerful because to be a sightseer is to be

JUNE JORDAN (b. 1936) is a leading poet of international acclaim. She has written numerous books, including Kikamo's Story *(1981),* On Call: Political Essays *(1985), and* Naming Our Destiny: New and Selected Poems *(1989). Jordan's numerous poems, articles, essays, and reviews appear frequently in publications nationwide. She is now a professor of Afro-American studies and women's studies at the University of California, Berkeley.*

completely welcome among strangers. And that's the trick of it: No one will say "no" to freely given admiration and respect. But now we had asked for something in return—a taxi. And with that single, ordinary request, the problems of our identity, our problems of power, reappeared and trashed our holiday confidence and joy.

I am looking for a way to catch a taxi. I am looking for an umbrella big enough to overcome the tactical and moral limitations of "identity politics"—politics based on gender, class, or race. I am searching for the language of a new political consciousness of identity.

Many of us function on the basis of habits of thought that automatically concede paramount importance to race or class. These habits may, for example, correlate race with class in monolithic, absolute ways: i.e., white people have, black people have not, or, poor people equals black people. Although understandable, these dominating habits of thought tend to deny the full functions of race and class, both.

If we defer mainly to race, then what about realities of class that point to huge numbers of poor white people or severe differences of many kinds among various, sometimes conflicting classes of black people?

Or, if we attend primarily to factors of class, then we may mislead ourselves significantly by ignoring privileges inherent to white identity, per se, or the socially contemptible status of minority-group members regardless of class.

Both forms of analysis encourage exaggerated—or plainly mistaken—suppositions about racial or class grounds for political solidarity. Equally important, any exclusive mode of analysis will overlook, or obviate, the genuine potential for political unity across class and race boundaries.

Habits of racial and class analyses also deny universal functions of gender which determine at least as much, if not more, about any citizen's psychological, economic, and physical life force and well-being. Focusing on racial *or* class *or* gender attributes will yield only distorted and deeply inadequate images of ourselves.

Traditional calls to "unity" on the basis of only one of these factors— race or class or gender—will fail, finally, and again and again, I believe, because no simple one of these components provides for a valid fathoming of the complete individual.

And yet, many of us persist in our race/class habits of thought. And why is that? We know the negative, the evil origins, the evil circumstances that have demanded our development of race and class analyses. For those of us born into a historically scorned and jeopardized status, our bodily survival testifies to the defensively positive meanings of race and class identity because we have created these positive implications as a source of self-defense.

We have wrested, we have invented positive consequences from facts of unequal conflict, facts of oppression. Facts such as I am black, or I do not have much money, or I am Lithuanian, or I am Senegalese, or I am a girl, or my father mends shoes, become necessary and crucial facts of race and class and gender inside the negative contexts of unequal conflict and the oppression of one group by another, the oppression of somebody weak by somebody more powerful.

Race and class, then, are not the same kinds of words as *grass* and *stars*. *Gender* is not the same kind of noun as *sunlight*. *Grass, stars,* and *sunlight* all enjoy self-evident, positive connotations, everywhere on the planet. They are physical phenomena unencumbered by our knowledge or our experience of slavery, discrimination, rape, and murder. They do not presuppose an evil any one of us must seek to extirpate.

I am wondering if those of us who began our lives in difficult conditions defined by our race or our class or our gender identities, I am wondering if we can become more carefully aware of the limitations of race and class and gender analyses, for these yield only distorted and deeply inadequate images of ourselves.

There is another realm of possibility: political unity and human community based upon concepts that underlie or supersede relatively immutable factors of race, class, and gender: the concept of justice, the concept of equality, the concept of tenderness.

I rejoice to see that last year, more than eight million American voters— black and white and Latino and Asian and Native American and straight and gay and lesbian and working-class and Ivy League—voted for Jesse Jackson.

I rejoice to see that 300,000 people demonstrated for prochoice rights in Washington, D.C., on April 9, 1989. Of that 300,000, an estimated 100,000 who stood up for women's rights were men.

I rejoice at this good news, this happy evidence of moral and tactical outreach and response beyond identity politics. This is getting us where all of us need to go.

On the other hand, the hideous despoiling of Prince William Sound in Alaska, the Exxon spill of ten million gallons of oil contaminating three thousand square miles of those previously clear and lovely waters, makes plain the total irrelevance—the dismal inadequacy—of identity politics, or even national politics. From the torn sky of Antarctica to the Port of Valdez in Alaska, we need vigilant, international agencies empowered to assure the survival of our life-supporting environments.

But we are creatures of habit. I consider myself fortunate, therefore, to keep coming upon immediate, personal events that challenge my inclinations toward a politics as preoccupied with the known old enemies as it is alert to the potential for new allies.

Less than a month ago, I traveled to Liverpool, England, for the first time. I brought with me a selection of my poetry that includes poems written during the 1960s, during the civil rights revolution. I had heard about the poverty characteristic of much of Liverpool, but I was not ready for what I encountered face to face.

One of my hosts was Ruth Grosvenor, a young black woman who described herself, at lunch, as a half-caste Irish-Caribbean. I asked her for more detail about her family background, and she told me about her mother, who had grown up in Ireland so poor she regularly used to dig in the pig bins, searching for scraps of edible garbage. And for additional pennies, her mother was given soiled sanitary napkins to launder by hand.

Ruth's mother, of course, is white. I had lost my appetite, by now, completely, and I could not comprehend the evident cheeriness of Ruth, who had moved on in conversation to describe the building success of the Africa Art Collective in Liverpool that she codirects.

"But," I interrupted, "what about your mother? What has happened to her?"

"Oh," Ruth told me, instantly switching subjects but not altering her 28 bright and proselytizing tone, "my mother is very happy. She remarried, and she has her own little flat, at last. And she has a telephone!"

I felt mortified by the contrast between what would allow me, a black woman from America, to feel happy and the late and minimal amenities that could ease the daily experience of a white woman living in England. To speak with Ruth's mother, to speak for Ruth's mother, I would certainly have to eschew facile notions of race and class correlation. On the basis of class alone, Ruth's mother might very well distrust or resent me. On the basis of race alone, I might very well be inclined to distrust or resent Ruth's mother.

And yet, identity politics aside, we both had infinitely more to gain as possible comrades joined against socioeconomic inequities than we would conceivably benefit from hostilities exchanged in serious ignorance of each other.

After our lunch, we drove to the Liverpool public library, where I was scheduled to read. By then, we were forty-five minutes late, and on arrival we saw five middle-aged white women heading away toward an old car across the street. When they recognized me, the women came over and apologized: They were really sorry, they said, but they had to leave or they'd get in trouble on the job. I looked at them. Every one of them was wearing an inexpensive, faded house dress and, over that, a cheap and shapeless cardigan sweater. I felt honored by their open-mindedness in having wanted to come and listen to my poetry. I thought and I said that it was I who should apologize: I was late. It was I who felt, moreover, unprepared: what in my work, to date, deserves the open-minded attention of blue-collar white women terrified by the prospect of overstaying a union-guaranteed hour for lunch?

Two and a half weeks after Liverpool, I sat sorting through my messages 32 and mail at the university where I teach. One message kept recurring: a young black man—the son, in fact, of a colleague—had been accused of raping a young white woman. The message, as delivered by my secretary, was this: call so and so at once about the young black man who supposedly raped some white woman.

I was appalled by the accusation leveled against the son of my colleague. I was stunned to learn that yet another female student, of whatever color, had been raped. I felt a kind a nausea overtaking me as I reread the phone messages. They seemed to assume I would commit myself to one side or the other, automatically. The sides, apparently, were Young Black Man versus Young White Woman.

I got up from my desk and snatched the nearest newspaper I could find. I needed to know more. As best I could tell, the young black student could not have raped anybody; he has several witnesses who establish him off campus throughout the evening of the alleged assault. As far as I can tell, the young white woman had been raped and she was certain, if mistaken, about the face and the voice of her assailant.

I declined to make any public comment: I do not yet know what the truth of this terrible matter may be. I believe there is a likelihood of mistaken identification on the part of the victim. And I believe that such a mistake, if that is the case, will have created a second victim, the wrongly accused black student. But these are my opinions merely. And I cannot comprehend why or how anyone would expect me to choose between my gender and racial identities.

I do not agree that rape is less serious than any other heinous felony. I do not agree that the skin color of a female victim shall alienate me from a gender sense of unity and peril. I do not agree that the mistaken accusation of a black man is less than a very serious crime. I do not agree that the genuine gender concerns that I embody shall alienate me from a racial sense of unity and peril.

But there is a route out of the paralysis of identity politics, even here, in this ugly, heartbreaking crisis. There is available to me a moral attachment to a concept beyond a gender and race. I am referring to the concept of justice, which I am prepared to embrace and monitor so that justice shall equally serve the young black man and the young white woman. It is that concept and it is on behalf of both the primary and the possible second victim of yet another on-campus rape that I am willing to commit my energies and my trust.

Returning to the recent rainy evening in Paris, I am still looking for an umbrella big enough to overcome the tactical and moral limitations of identity politics.

Yes, I am exhilarated by the holiday I enjoyed with my friends, and I am proud of the intimate camaraderie we shared. But somebody, pretty soon, needs to be talking, sisterly and brotherly, with the taxi drivers of the world, as well.

1. Why does June Jordan use the act of "waiting for a taxi" as a metaphor for her experience as an African-American woman? What does the taxi represent for Jordan? What does she believe will enable her "to catch a ride"?

2. Why does Jordan think it is necessary to move beyond what she labels "identity politics"? What are the tactical and moral limitations of such politics? Does she witness any positive signs that Americans are putting aside the limiting categories of race, class, and gender?

3. How did Jordan's experience in Liverpool, England, change her ideas about race and class? Why do such distinctions tend to divide people who might otherwise have much in common if such distinctions did not exist?

4. What concept does Jordan believe requires a "moral attachment" beyond gender and race? What particular incident provided Jordan with an opportunity to exercise this view? Does such a view endanger Jordan's identity more than if she had made a choice between her gender and her race?

ROBERTO SANTIAGO

Black *and* Latino   [ESSENCE / November 1989]

"There is no way that you can be black and Puerto Rican at the same time." What? Despite the many times I've heard this over the years, that statement still perplexes me. I *am* both and always have been. My color is a blend of my mother's rich, dark skin tone and my father's white complexion. As they were both Puerto Rican, I spoke Spanish before English, but I am

ROBERTO SANTIAGO *(b. 1963) is a staff writer for* Emerge *magazine in New York City. In addition, he free-lances for* Omni *magazine and has published articles in the* Village Voice, Hispanic *magazine, and other publications. He is currently working on a novel.*

totally bilingual. My life has been shaped by my black and Latino heritages, and despite other people's confusion, I don't feel I have to choose one or the other. To do so would be to deny a part of myself.

There has not been a moment in my life when I did not know that I looked black—and I never thought that others did not see it, too. But growing up in East Harlem, I was also aware that I did not "act black," according to the African-American boys on the block.

My lighter-skinned Puerto Rican friends were less of a help in this department. "You're not black," they would whine, shaking their heads. "You're a *boriqua* [slang for Puerto Rican], you ain't no *moreno* [black]." If that was true, why did my mirror defy the rules of logic? And most of all, why did I feel that there was some serious unknown force trying to make me choose sides?

Acting black. Looking black. Being a real black. This debate among us   4
is almost a parody. The fact is that I am black, so why do I need to prove it?

The island of Puerto Rico is only a stone's throw away from Haiti, and, no fooling, if you climb a palm tree, you can see Jamaica bobbing on the Atlantic. The slave trade ran through the Caribbean basin, and virtually all Puerto Rican citizens have some African blood in their veins. My grandparents on my mother's side were the classic *negro como carbón* (black as carbon) people, but despite the fact that they were as dark as can be, they are officially not considered black.

There is an explanation for this, but not one that makes much sense, or difference, to a working-class kid from Harlem. Puerto Ricans identify themselves as Hispanics—part of a worldwide race that originated from eons of white Spanish conquests—a mixture of white, African, and *Indio* blood, which, categorically, is apart from black. In other words, the culture is the predominant and determinant factor. But there are frustrations in being caught in a duo-culture, where your skin color does not necessarily dictate what you are. When I read Piri Thomas's searing autobiography, *Down These Mean Streets*, in my early teens, I saw that he couldn't figure out other people's attitudes toward his blackness, either.

My first encounter with this attitude about the race thing rode on horseback. I had just turned six years old and ran toward the bridle path in Central Park as I saw two horses about to trot past. "Yea! Horsie! Yea!" I yelled. Then I noticed one figure on horseback. She was white, and she shouted, "Shut up, you f——g nigger! Shut up!" She pulled back on the reins and twisted the horse in my direction. I can still feel the spray of gravel that the horse kicked at my chest. And suddenly she was gone. I looked back and, in the distance, saw my parents playing Whiffle Ball with my sister. They seemed miles away.

They still don't know about this incident. But I told my Aunt Aurelia   8
almost immediately. She explained what the words meant and why they

were said. Ever since then I have been able to express my anger appropriately through words or action in similar situations. Self-preservation, ego, and pride forbid men from ever ignoring, much less forgetting, a slur.

Aunt Aurelia became, unintentionally, my source for answers I needed about color and race. I never sought her out. She just seemed to appear at my home during the points in my childhood when I most needed her for solace. "Puerto Ricans are different from American blacks," she told me once. "There is no racism between what you call white and black. Nobody even considers the marriages interracial." She then pointed out the difference in color between my father and mother. "You never noticed that," she said, "because you were not raised with that hang-up."

Aunt Aurelia passed away before I could follow up on her observation. But she had made an important point. It's why I never liked the attitude that says I should be exclusive to one race.

My behavior toward this race thing pegged me as an iconoclast of sorts. Children from mixed marriages, from my experience, also share this attitude. If I have to beat the label of iconoclast because the world wants people to be in set categories and I don't want to, then I will.

A month before Aunt Aurelia died, she saw I was a little down about the whole race thing, and she said, "Roberto, don't worry. Even if—no matter what you do—black people in this country don't, you can always depend on white people to treat you like a black." 12

Points to Consider

1. Roberto Santiago describes himself as *both* black and Puerto Rican. Why do you think other people have difficulty accepting this dual identity?

2. Why do Puerto Ricans who "look" black often reject the title of "black"? What factors other than skin color influence their decisions? Why doesn't Santiago reject this label?

3. According to Santiago's aunt, why doesn't the cultural taboo surrounding interracial marriage that exists in the United States exist in Puerto Rico?

4. What is the irony, pointed out to Santiago by his aunt, about being bicultural in the United States? What does this irony say about American attitudes toward race?

Discussing the Unit

Suggested Topic for Discussion

The three essays in this unit raise similar questions about the minority experience in America. Without losing sight of their differences, consider what these authors have in common. What problem do they share? In your opinion, which of the three offers the best solution to this problem?

Preparing for Class Discussion

1. Vivian Gornick chooses to answer attacks on women as a woman, rather than as a Jew or a member of some other category. June Jordan prefers to appeal to principles beyond gender when making decisions about particularly difficult issues involving her identity as a woman. How do these two authors' approaches differ? Which approach do you prefer and why?

2. In his essay, Roberto Santiago offers another approach to dealing with questions of identity: he refuses to accept the labels others place upon him even though in doing so he risks being labeled an iconoclast. What do you think about Santiago's approach to questions of racial identity? Can you think of other ways to come to terms with biculturalism?

From Discussion to Writing

Everyone has had, at least once in his or her life, the feeling of living in two worlds at the same time. In an essay, describe an experience in which you had to adjust to the ways of another culture or a predominant social group. Record in detail your thoughts and emotions at the time. In what ways was the experience positive? In what ways was it negative? Did you find you were able to maintain your own identity?

5

Names and Identity: Does It Matter What We're Called?

"What's in a name?" asks Shakespeare's Juliet—"that which we call a rose/By any other name would smell as sweet." Yet not everyone has agreed with Juliet's widely quoted remark. For many people, names—whether of persons, places, or things—possess vital social, cultural, and political signif-icance. Our personal names are not merely, as Juliet suggests, arbitrary labels, but can be powerful forms of identification. Our names echo the past; they often carry with them a spectrum of information about our family's origins, social position, race, heritage, and religious affiliation. In "On Becomng Carol Ascher," Ascher describes the ways a woman's identity can be inap-propriately attached to another's name. By legally changing that name, she discovers, she can forge a new and independent identity for herself.

"What's your *real* name?" people continually ask the journalist Itabari Njeri, who then assures them that Itabari Njeri is her "real, legal name." Born Jill Moreland in Brooklyn, New York, she changed her name in the 1970s; the prominent black literary figure Amiri Baraka suggested Itabari (a Swahili corruption of an Arabic name for an esteemed, trustworthy per-

96

son), and her mother contributed Njeri (a Kikuyu word for "worthy of a warrior"). With a sense of humor Njeri describes how her name usually affects both whites and blacks, but more importantly she introduces us to the central theme of this chapter: "the fundamental issue of identity and nomenclature."

CAROL ASCHER

On Becoming Carol Ascher [FRONTIERS / 1989]

My aunt told me an old Jewish story when I changed my last name. "Each person has three names," she said. "The first is given by one's parents, who dream of their child's happy future. The second is the name used when people call one an ugly or embarrassing name. The third is the name one chooses oneself: the important name." For most women, that third name has long been the name of the husband who, like a prince, was supposed to save them. My married name, Lopate, had held that promise once. Yet there came a time, after ten years of no longer being married (coinciding with nearly as many years of being a feminist) when my former husband's name felt like the second kind of name. I was ashamed of it, humiliated by its reminder of a discontinued legal tie and an emotional bond it seemed to perpetuate in sticky ways. We'd had no children to worry about. I needed a name of my own, a third name.

In 1978, after much seemingly pointless talk with close women friends about what to do about my married name, I thought I would write about the problem. Writing can either goad me toward action or soothe my nerves after I have acted or been unable to act. My piece was entitled "What's in a Name," and began: *She is thinking about changing her name.*

CAROL ASCHER (b. 1942) is a free-lance essayist and short story writer. Her stories and essays have appeared in numerous periodicals, including Ms., Arts Revue, *the* New York Times, *the* Nation, *and the* Village Voice. *She is the author of* The Flood *(a novel, 1988) and* Simone de Beauvoir: A Life of Freedom, *and coeditor of* Between Women: Biographers, Novelists, Critics, Teachers, and Artists Write about Women.

Here I am, thirty-six years old, a woman who has worked all her adult life, who has been in the women's movement for nearly a decade. Here I am, assertive and competent, and I can't find a name for myself.

She's looking for a good name

Disgusted, I was obviously trying to shame myself into action—a bad strategy, since it divides me into the aggressor and the one who is bent on self-protection. Besides, I'm so stubborn in the face of my own intimidation that I should have known I wouldn't budge.

My father, a Viennese whose last name is Bergman [I went on to explain] is dead. My mother, who still bears his name, was born in Berlin, an Ascher. My birth certificate reads "Carol Ann Bergmann"—Carol in honor of a wealthy woman who gave my parents visas so that they could leave the refugee camp where they had met to come to this country; Ann for no apparent reason; and Bergmann, with two n's (when was it shortened?) from my father's Austrian Jewish patrilineage. Bergmann means mountain man or *Social group* miner. Lopate, a Russian name, means shovel. I used to think that a Lopate should be useful to a Bergmann, and maybe it has been. However, people often assume the name is Italian or Spanish. Once I was even inadvertently flown across the country for a job interview by a university hoping to fill its Hispanic quota. *How the spelling could change the name of a person and tell where they're from*

The thought of my former husband's remarrying and another woman becoming a Lopate made me queasy, but so far I had been lucky. I thought of returning to my birth name via a hyphenated "Bergman-Lopate," and had some legal documents done up this way, but the image seemed more married than if I retained a single last name. My feminist superego harassed me. "Women who want to break free of the patrilineal naming system," I wrote, "can use their mother's first names with an English suffix." In my case, the name would be Ellenchild. Carol, daughter of Ellen. But the memories of leading my refugee mother through the labyrinths of a new culture *Maze,* were too strong for me to let go so easily of my German-Jewish name.

One spring day I rode my bicycle uptown to the Museum of Natural   4
History to buy a hundred postcards on which I planned to write everyone I knew about my change back to Bergman, the name on all my public school grade cards all the way up to my B.A. I still remember the postcards: a blood red background with an African mask representing a god of judicial decisions in rich brown. I hurriedly filled out my first card and rushed to my friend, Paul, who lives in a fifth-floor walkup two blocks from the museum.

"You can't change your name now, after all these years," he insisted, as he stood at the stove to boil me water for tea. "It's so self-destructive. Carol, you just never take yourself seriously. You belittle your past, your social presence. You're a writer. If you change your name to Bergman now, it'll be like starting from scratch. Nobody will know who you are."

As I sipped my tea, I felt he was onto something. A book and many articles in small magazines already had the name Lopate affixed to them. Yet, as was somehow typical of me, I felt I could start afresh. Did I really believe that my public presence was so small that I would lose nothing by a change of name? I kept looking wistfully at the postcard he had dropped on the kitchen table. What was I going to do if respect for myself meant keeping my married name? When I finally climbed on my bike to ride home, I had ninety-nine unused blood red postcards with African masks on them. The god of judicial decisions seemed to have been wrong—for the time being.

It seemed that I could not push past the slightest obstacle to return to my father's name. A lot of people—famous, infamous, and ordinary—are called Bergman. Yet the actual name (including its rustic meaning) had little to do with it. "I had a problematic relationship with my father," I would apologize to friends, and add somewhat disingenuously that my former husband had looked more kindly on my ambition, which was why I was keeping his name. Then one day I blurted: "I'm tired of being married to my father, as it is." And this perhaps was the deeper truth. If one can't let go of a husband, there may well be a father lurking behind.

My little manuscript, "What's in a Name?" had begun with the wrong tactics and could not push me to a resolution. It ended suddenly in the deepest of feminist depression:

> I see young women, even women my age, taking on new married names. I imagine they think it's forever, but even without divorce, what's the sense of losing a name? What devastation we as women go through in being chosen for "holy wedlock." What a senseless repair in trying to find our own names.

Then in August, while hiking in the woods, I imagined a short story called, "In the Shadow of a Name." I was thinking of a woman painter who still retained the name of her former, now famous, artist husband. But in my mind was also my own last name, and how my former husband's writing career, which had suddenly taken off, would make me feel about being a Lopate in the years ahead. "The story should look back on her life," I wrote in my journal. "It should be like living in the shadow of a gloomy mountain." Having discovered the futility of harassing myself into change, I must have hoped that fiction would serve me in coming to peace with my married name. Yet who would choose to live on the sunless side of a mountain? The story was never written: I couldn't convince myself enough of the resignation I sought even to begin.

And then one frosty night in January 1979 I had a dream, and in the morning I had a new name. In the dream, I was a witch in a wide black hat, flying happily through the air with a flock of large, fluffy, white bird-cats.

"You've changed Bergman to Birdlady," said Bob, who was my lover then, and who to this day sees the puns in my dreams.

"Ascher Birdlady," I said smiling—having lifted off the mountain, without thinking, I had added my mother's family name.

And then over Sunday breakfast, he interviewed me on my new, happily transcended state:

> *Bob*: I guess I really want to know how you were able to leave the ground.
>
> *Ascher Birdlady*: Ah, I think it wasn't so much leaving as no longer being there. So now it takes an effort to lower myself to the ground: a little like what it must be like for you to dive to the bottom of a deep lake. But lifting back off into the sky is a release from effort, a kind of letting go.
>
> *Bob*: You're quite lucky. Most people don't realize this.
>
> *Ascher Birdlady*: It amazes me now the effort people use to hug the ground. Why, if they would just let go, they would be up in the sky like me!
>
> *Bob*: But isn't it scary to be up there all the time? Aren't you ever afraid?
>
> *Ascher Birdlady*: Well, first I'm not always up there. I've come down a bit to talk to you. I come down when I want. The trouble is, I may want to come down less and less. As for fear, it's the other side of joy. There's such joy in being able to move my body freely on all sides.
>
> *Bob*: But don't you get buffeted around by the wind?
>
> *Ascher Birdlady*: Well, you know, one only feels buffeted if one is terribly sure where one ought to be. If one is just flying around, the currents only offer amusement and diversion. Sometimes they even give one the little push in an interesting direction one hadn't thought of.

As happy as I felt that morning, my unsuccessful attempts to change my name were not conducive to a certainty that I could carry through. Nevertheless, this time I seemed to have unfettered energy and daring. At a big party a few days later, I found myself announcing gaily, "I'm changing my name to Ascher, my mother's family name." "Oh," people said, "terrific." My two close women friends, from whom I needed confirmation for every important decision, seemed uncannily relaxed about the change.

So I telephoned my friend Paul by the museum. Over rice and beans in a Chinese-Cuban restaurant, I told him my new plan. And he argued forcefully and sweepingly against it. Although Ascher was a better name for a writer than Bergman—more unusual, he conceded me this—I was merely going further out on a limb, this time cutting myself off from all those who had known me before the age of twenty-two. High school friends, neighbors from childhood—he was eloquent about the scores of people who might have leapt at the sight of a story signed by Carol Bergman—would now be lost for good. This in addition to all those who had finally learned to look for work by Carol Lopate.

"Are you afraid of being friends with a nobody?" I asked, suddenly feeling I was onto his own vain fears. He gave me a quick grin. And, as he continued his attack, I silently wondered if my women friends took my career insufficiently seriously. No matter, I knew I was going to change my name.

She decided to change her name to Ascher mother's family names

The next morning, I called my mother in California and excitedly told her my plans. I didn't expect her to be comfortable with the idea of my becoming an Ascher. She and I tended to misunderstand each other on much simpler things. But I hoped she would find a way to share in my decision.

"It's a Jewish name, you know," she said, her voice coming across the line crisp with worry.

"Yes, I know. It's one of the twelve tribes of Israel." Did she want me to hide from a future holocaust with a disguised name?

"I feel a little bad for your father," she said next.   20

To this, I really had nothing to say, for I was holding back my own peculiar regret.

"Anyway, whatever you do with your life, it's your life," she continued, as if trying to step out of my way.

"It's just a little funny," she added after a moment. "Most people go forwards, but you go backwards." Was she hoping that I would invent an altogether new name, or, more likely, that I would remarry and take yet another man's name?

"Edith and Gerhard will be pleased," she said finally, giving what must   24 have been an ambivalent affirmation; for these were her older brother and his wife—Aschers. A childless couple to whom I had always felt close, and who, as I realized, I was somehow turning into new parents. Yet it was also true that I was taking my mother's name.

Although in Germany my new name would have been spelled A-S-C-H-E-R, my mother and two of her brothers had Americanized it into A-S-H-E-R. Which would I choose? For a week I was announcing my new name and simultaneously asking how I ought to spell it. Not surprisingly, friends and acquaintances alike had immediate and strong opinions based on their own associations. How important the spelling it's to them Hard to pick,

And then one morning I knew I would spell it ASCHER, and I wrote Aunt Edith and Uncle Gerhard to tell them I was changing my name to theirs. I was worried about the letter. I couldn't exactly ask their permission, since I already knew I was going to use their name. Yet I wanted their blessing. When two weeks went by with no mail from them, I told myself that I could not expect belated support from my relatives for my idiosyncratic journey. I would survive, even if they were uneasy, angry, or upset. I had even warned them, "Since I write, you may sometimes be uncomfortable when people you know ask if you are related to Carol Ascher, because you may not always agree with what I write."

One thing I felt sure of: with my own name, I would give more energy and courage to my writing—and to pushing my work. In naming myself, I was untying the ropes that held me back and freeing myself to fly. But, of course, that is what my witch dream had said.

And then I got a thick envelope with separate handwritten letters from   28 my aunt and uncle, each welcoming me to their name. My aunt began with the old Jewish story about the three names. She said she was moved to have a "visible bond" to express the emotional one that existed between us and reassured me that she would not be embarrassed by anything I wrote. My uncle, who was about to celebrate his seventy-fifth birthday, received my new name as a gift. "Love and affection are blessings, often blooming in hidden places," he wrote expansively in his old German script. "They give me happiness and make me feel grateful. They also make me ask, what did I do to deserve it? But the mind does not find the answer. Something in me tells that grace drops from heaven like manna that once fell from the sky on the hungry children of Israel."

Over the next week I wrote, designed, and had printed the most carefully planned announcement of my life. I wanted the paper, the ink, the wording, everything, to be perfect. "This is to tell you," "It is my pleasure," "I am proud to announce," were all tried, until I decided upon:

This is to inform you that I am
changing my name from
Carol Lopate
to
Carol Ascher
my mother's family name

Many woman came up. and proud of her. she was glad,

This was printed in clean bright blue on a cream card. And this time I had five hundred postcards.

Since I had never seen such an announcement, I had no idea what reactions it would elicit. But I went page by page through my current and old address books, writing out a postcard to everyone I knew or had known. (To the extent that I could help it, I would not disappear.) When I went to meetings or parties, I gave out the cards. "How funny," my only critic, a woman at a film premiere, said, as she turned to get another glass of wine. For the rest, people congratulated me and showed pleasure and excitement— even envy at what I had done.

Suddenly I was discovering over and over that women I thought I knew well were ashamedly still carrying former husbands' names. One man confided wistfully that he had long toyed with changing his name; like many last names of European Jews, it had been forced on his forefathers by a town official in the eighteenth century to make them accessible for taxation and conscription. A white Southerner now living in New York confessed with shame that the only other people in the phone book with her last name were black families, descendants of slaves owned by her forefather. Others told me that their names had been altered—by themselves, their parents, immigration officials. On a writing assignment, I met a Greek American with the odd name Perry-Perdikides. Being a new connoisseur, I asked him what his name implied. He had changed his name to Perry when he came to this country, he said, after being warned that no one would be able to say *many people felt the same but never had they do anything about it*

Perdikides. Now he wanted his Greek name back, but since he was known as Mr. Perry, he had settled on the compromise, hyphenated name. A year earlier, when I had tried writing an article on changing my name, I had assumed that the problem of last names was solely a woman's problem. Now I saw that it was also a wider one: part of the suffering of so many in any disenfranchised or minority group.

"Okay," my former husband had said amiably, when I told him of my new name. He seemed so understanding that I was almost hurt. Until one day I met him standing with a woman friend of his on a street corner. "We were just talking about a story of yours," he greeted me.

"Did you say I wrote it under my new name, Ascher?" I asked, beaming at them both.

"Of course not," he said. "I'm not going to brag that you're no longer a Lopate."

Others who have changed their names will not be surprised that people instantly agreed and remembered to call me by my new name. Yet it continually thrilled me to see that I needed only to tell someone that I was now Carol Ascher for that person to turn to the next one and introduce me by my new name. I had hung on for years to an outgrown sense of my powerlessness that seemed retrospectively to be encapsulated in my name. Now every day I watched myself take new charge of my public presence.

The bank, two department stores, the public library, even the motor vehicle bureau, all agreed to change my name. Only Master Charge refused to let me rid myself of Lopate. I called an old friend, Emily, a feminist lawyer. "You have a civil right to use any name you like," she laughed, "just as long as you're not changing your name to evade the law." But her argument about my rights did not impress Master Charge. They were concerned with credit, they told me, and credit does not transfer without a court order.

Which was how I decided to change my name legally. The cost of an attorney for a legal change of name was then about $300, unless one went to a legal clinic, where it could be as low as $125. In addition, there would be filing and publishing fees. Emily told me that I could act without counsel, and she gave me a copy of a legal petition to imitate and listed the steps, from getting a docket number in the Supreme Court of New York, to having the petition signed by a judge and posting a notice in a legal newspaper, to filing the petition in the Court. "It's not hard," Emily assured me in that breezy style she has maintained through years of grinding legal practice. "It's just that you have to wait here and come back there, and they lose everything at least once." Though I was afraid of the time it would take, I didn't want to pay a lawyer. More important, I didn't want to lose my wonderful change-of-name experience into someone else's hands.

It was now early spring, and as the days grew fine, I began to be a regular visitor to the courts. This was all very new and exciting, as well as disturbing at times. My journal recalls the day of March 26, 1979:

Her new name is easy and well accepted by friends and family

Just now as I turned in my documents on the third floor of the Superior Court of New York, having gotten my index number for twenty-five dollars in the cellar below, I was called up to translate for a festively dressed Haitian couple who wanted to get married. When I explained in French that the court clerk was asking for her immigration papers, she fled from the room in terror, her bridegroom running after her. And so my successful intervention in the law on my behalf was saddened by these Haitians running from their marriage because at least the bride is obviously an illegal alien.

Legally giving up my father's name, Bergman, reawakened the deep loss I had suffered at his death. I didn't want to go back on relinquishing his name. But I was struck by how little I had ever known about him, and how confined in years and content my relationship to him had been. Once again, I found myself mourning for him.

Joan Didion once wrote that the answer to "Why I write?" lies in the sound of the words I, I, I. Changing my name was in this like writing. For months, the focus on my name threw my past and present back at me. Going over my birth certificate, my marriage license, and my divorce decree as I prepared my petition had been like looking in different mirrors.

One morning, an envelope lay in my mailbox addressed to Carol Ascher 40 in my mother's fine but sturdy handwriting. How strange—I suddenly understood—for her to be addressing me by her childhood name! As if we were sisters, or I were even her mother. Inside the envelope, the letter mentioned nothing about my changed name; but the message, as best my mother could convey it, was on the envelope. She would call me by her name. That was enough.

Points to Consider

1. How does Carol Ascher's mother react to her daughter's proposed change of name? What are her objections? Are they resolved by the essay?

2. What role do the writer's aunt and uncle play in the change of name? What psychological implications does Ascher suggest this change of name has in her relationship with them? In what ways does their response differ from her mother's?

3. Why does Ascher not want to use her father's last name but accepts her mother's father's last name? Do you think she has merely substituted one patrilineal system for another? How do you think she would argue this point?

4. Why do you think Ascher concludes her essay in the way she does? What does this anecdote suggest about the complexity of her relationship with her mother?

What's in a Name? [THE LOS ANGELES TIMES / January 29, 1989]

The decade was about to end when I started my first newspaper job. The seventies might have been the disco generation for some, but it was a continuation of the Black Power, post–civil rights era for me. Of course in some parts of America it was still the pre–civil rights era. And that was the part of America I wanted to explore. As a good reporter I needed a sense of the whole country, not just the provincial Northeast Corridor in which I was raised.

I headed for Greenville ("Pearl of the Piedmont"), South Carolina.

"*Wheeere*," some people snarled, their nostrils twitching, their mouths twisted so their top lips went slightly to the right, the bottom ones way down and to the left, "did you get *that* name from?"

Itabiddy, Etabeedy. Etabeeree. Eat a berry. Mata Hari. Theda Bara. And   4
one secretary in the office of the Greenville Urban League told her employer: "It's Ms. Idi Amin."

Then, and now, there are a whole bunch of people who greet me with: "Hi, Ita." They think "Bari" is my last name. Even when they don't, they still want to call me "Ita." When I tell them my first name is Itabari, they say, "Well, what do people call you for short?"

"They don't call me anything for short," I say. "The name is Itabari."

Sophisticated white people, upon hearing my name, approach me as would a cultural anthropologist finding a piece of exotica right in his own living room. This happens a lot, still, at cocktail parties.

"Oh, what an unusual and beautiful name. Where are you from?"   8

"Brooklyn," I say. I can see the disappointment in their eyes. Just another home-grown Negro.

Then there are other white people who, having heard my decidedly

ITABARI NJERI is on the staff of the Los Angeles Times. *She is a graduate of Boston University and the Columbia University School of Journalism, and she has written for the* Miami Herald, *the* Greenville News, *and National Public Radio in Boston. Njeri recently published her first colllection, called* Every Good-bye Ain't Gone *(1990). This essay, which originally appeared in the* Los Angeles Times *in a different form, is excerpted from that book.*

northeastern accent, will simply say, "What a lovely name," and smile knowingly, indicating that they saw *Roots* and understand.

Then there are others, black and white, who for different reasons take me through this number:

"What's your *real* name?" 12

"Itabari Njeri is my real, legal name," I explain.

"Okay, what's your original name?" they ask, often with eyes rolling, exasperation in their voices.

After Malcolm X, Muhammad Ali, Kareem Abdul-Jabbar, Ntozake Shange, and Kunta Kinte, who, I ask, should be exasperated by this question-and-answer game?

Nevertheless, I explain, "Because of slavery, black people in the Western 16
world don't usually know their original names. What you really want to know is what my slave name was."

Now this is where things get tense. Four hundred years of bitter history, culture, and politics between blacks and whites in America is evoked by this one term, "slave name."

Some white people wince when they hear the phrase, pained and embarrassed by this reminder of their ancestors' inhumanity. Further, they quickly scrutinize me and conclude that mine was a post–Emancipation Proclamation birth. "You were never a slave."

I used to be reluctant to tell people my slave name unless I surmised that they wouldn't impose their cultural values on me and refuse to use my African name. I don't care anymore. When I changed my name, I changed my life, and I've been Itabari for more years now than I was Jill. Nonetheless, people will say: "Well, that's your *real* name, you were born in America and that's what I am going to call you." My mother tried a variation of this on me when I legalized my traditional African name. I respectfully made it clear to her that I would not tolerate it. Her behavior, and subsequently her attitude, changed.

But many black folks remain just as skeptical of my name as my mother 20
was.

"You're one of those black people who changed their name, huh," they are likely to begin. "Well, I still got the old slave master's Irish name," said one man named O'Hare at a party. This man's defensive tone was a reaction to what I call the "blacker than thou" syndrome perpetrated by many black nationalists in the sixties and seventies. Those who reclaimed their African names made blacks who didn't do the same thing feel like Uncle Toms.

These so-called Uncle Toms couldn't figure out why they should use an African name when they didn't know a thing about Africa. Besides, many of them were proud of their names, no matter how they had come by them. And it should be noted that after the Emancipation Proclamation in 1863, four million black people changed their names, adopting surnames such as Freeman, Freedman, and Liberty. They eagerly gave up names that slave masters had imposed upon them as a way of identifying their human chattel.

Besides names that indicated their newly won freedom, blacks chose common English names such as Jones, Scott, and Johnson. English was their language. America was their home, and they wanted names that would allow them to assimilate as easily as possible.

Of course, many of our European surnames belong to us by birthright. We are the legal as well as "illegitimate" heirs to the names Jefferson, Franklin, Washington, et al., and in my own family, Lord.

Still, I consider most of these names to be by-products of slavery, if not actual slave names. Had we not been enslaved, we would not have been cut off from our culture, lost our indigenous languages, and been compelled to use European names.

The loss of our African culture is a tragic fact of history, and the conflict it poses is a profound one that has divided blacks many times since Emancipation: do we accept the loss and assimilate totally or do we try to reclaim our culture and synthesize it with our present reality?

A new generation of black people in America is reexamining the issues raised by the cultural nationalists and Pan-Africanists of the sixties and seventies: what are the cultural images that appropriately convey the "new" black aesthetic in literature and art?

The young Afro-American novelist Trey Ellis has asserted that the "New Black Aesthetic shamelessly borrows and reassembles across both race and class lines." It is not afraid to embrace the full implications of our hundreds of years in the New World. We are a new people who need not be tied to externally imposed or self-inflicted cultural parochialism. Had I understood that as a teenager, I might still be singing today.

Even the fundamental issue of identity and nomenclature, raised by Baraka and others twenty years ago, is back on the agenda: are we to call ourselves blacks or African-Americans?

In reality, it's an old debate. "Only with the founding of the American Colonization Society in 1816 did blacks recoil from using the term African in referring to themselves and their institutions," the noted historian and author Sterling Stuckey pointed out in an interview with me. They feared that using the term "African" would fuel white efforts to send them back to Africa. But they felt no white person had the right to send them back when they had slaved to build America.

Many black institutions retained their African identification, most notably the African Methodist Episcopal Church. Changes in black self-identification in America have come in cycles, usually reflecting the larger dynamics of domestic and international politics.

The period after World War II, said Stuckey, "culminating in the Cold War years of Roy Wilkins's leadership of the NAACP," was a time of "frenzied integrationism." And there was "no respectable black leader on the scene evincing any sort of interest in Africa—neither the NAACP or the Urban League."

This, he said, "was an example of historical discontinuity, the likes of which we, as a people, had not seen before." Prior to that, for more than a century and a half, black leaders were Pan-Africanists, including Frederick Douglass. "He recognized," said Stuckey, "that Africa was important and that somehow one had to redeem the motherland in order to be genuinely respected in the New World."

The Reverend Jesse Jackson has, of course, placed on the national agenda the importance of blacks in America restoring their cultural, historical, and political links with Africa.

But what does it really mean to be called an African-American?

"Black" can be viewed as a more encompassing term, referring to all 36
people of African descent. "Afro-American" and "African-American" refer to a specific ethnic group. I use the terms interchangeably, depending on the context and the point I want to emphasize.

But I wonder: as the twenty-first century breathes down our necks— prodding us to wake up to the expanding mélange of ethnic groups immigrating in record numbers to the United States, inevitably intermarrying, and to realize the eventual reshaping of the nation's political imperatives in a newly multicultural society—will the term "African-American" be as much of a racial and cultural obfuscation as the term "black"? In other words, will we be the only people, in a society moving toward cultural pluralism, viewed to have no history and no culture? Will we just be a color with a new name: African-American?

Or will the term be—as I think it should—an ethnic label describing people with a shared culture who descended from Africans, were transformed in (as well as transformed) America, and are genetically intertwined with myriad other groups in the United States?

Such a definition reflects the historical reality and distances us from the fallacious, unscientific concept of separate races when there is only one: *Homo sapiens*.

But to comprehend what should be an obvious definition requires knowl- 40
edge and a willingness to accept history.

When James Baldwin wrote *Nobody Knows My Name*, the title was a metaphor—at the deepest level of the collective African-American psyche— for the blighting of black history and culture before the nadir of slavery and since.

The eradication or distortion of our place in world history and culture is most obvious in the popular media. Liz Taylor—and, for an earlier generation, Claudette Colbert—still represent what Cleopatra—a woman of color in a multiethnic society, dominated at various times by blacks—looks like.

And in American homes, thanks to reruns and cable, a new generation of black kids grow up believing that a simpleton shouting "Dy-no-mite!" is a genuine reflection of Afro-American culture, rather than a white Hollywood writer's stereotype.

More recently, *Coming to America*, starring Eddie Murphy as an African 44 prince seeking a bride in the United States, depicted traditional African dancers in what amounted to a Las Vegas stage show, totally distorting the nature and beauty of real African dance. But with every burlesque-style pelvic thrust on the screen, I saw blacks in the audience burst into applause. They think that's African culture, too.

And what do Africans know of us, since blacks don't control the organs of communication that disseminate information about us?

"No!" screamed the mother of a Kenyan man when he announced his engagement to an African-American woman who was a friend of mine. The mother said marry a European, marry a white American. But please, not one of those low-down, ignorant, drug-dealing, murderous black people she had seen in American movies. Ultimately, the mother prevailed.

In Tanzania, the travel agent looked at me indignantly. "Njeri, that's Kikuyu. What are you doing with an African name?" he demanded.

I'd been in Dar es Salaam about a month and had learned that Africans 48 assess in a glance the ethnic origins of the people they meet.

Without a greeting, strangers on the street in Tanzania's capital would comment, "Oh, you're an Afro-American or West Indian."

"Both."

"I knew it," they'd respond, sometimes politely, sometimes not.

Or, people I got to know while in Africa would mention, "I know another 52 half-caste like you." Then they would call in the "mixed-race" person and say, "Please meet Itabari Njeri." The darker-complected African, presumably of unmixed ancestry, would then smile and stare at us like we were animals in the zoo.

Of course, this "half-caste" (which I suppose is a term preferable to "mulatto," which I hate, and which every person who understands its derogatory meaning—"mule"—should never use) was usually the product of a mixed marriage, not generations of ethnic intermingling. And it was clear from most "half-castes" I met that they did not like being compared to so mongrelized and stigmatized a group as Afro-Americans.

I had minored in African studies in college, worked for years with Africans in the United States, and had no romantic illusions as to how I would be received in the motherland. I wasn't going back to find my roots. The only thing that shocked me in Tanzania was being called, with great disdain, a "white woman" by an African waiter. Even if the rest of the world didn't follow the practice, I then assumed everyone understood that any known or perceptible degree of African ancestry made one "black" in America by law and social custom.

But I was pleasantly surprised by the telephone call I received two minutes after I walked into my Dar es Salaam hotel room. It was the hotel operator. "Sister, welcome to Tanzania. . . . Please tell everyone in Harlem hello for us." The year was 1978, and people in Tanzania were wearing half-foot-high platform shoes and dancing to James Brown wherever I went.

Shortly before I left, I stood on a hill surrounded by a field of endless 56 flowers in Arusha, near the border of Tanzania and Kenya. A toothless woman with a wide smile, a staff in her hand, and two young girls at her side, came toward me on a winding path. I spoke to her in fractured Swahili and she to me in broken English.

"I know you," she said smiling. "Wa-Negro." "Wa" is a prefix in Bantu languages meaning people. "You are from the lost tribe," she told me. "Welcome," she said, touching me, then walked down a hill that lay in the shadow of Mount Kilimanjaro.

I never told her my name, but when I told other Africans, they'd say: "*Emmmm,* Itabari. Too long. How about I just call you Ita."

Points to Consider

1. Why does Njeri want to describe how *both* whites and blacks react to her change of name? Are the reactions what you might expect?

2. What do people mean by "real" name and "original" name? Why doesn't Njeri accept these terms?

3. Njeri's essay makes us aware not only of what personal names mean but of the names we use to designate ethnic groups. She uses the terms "black," "Afro-American," "African-American," and "Negro." Why does she vary these terms? Which one does she seem to consider most appropriate?

4. How did Africans respond to Njeri's name? How did her experiences there demonstrate the complexities of identity and nomenclature? Consider her final paragraph. How do you think it should be read?

Discussing the Unit

Suggested Topic for Discussion

Consider Juliet's famous question: "What's in a name?" Is Juliet correct: would a rose by any other name smell as sweet? Or is she wrong: does something's name directly affect our responses to it? (A writer recently wondered how we would regard roses if they were called "scarletina stinkworts.") In short, how much power do names possess?

Preparing for Class Discussion

1. Itabari Njeri says that "When I changed my name, I changed my life." Do you think that by changing your name you can change the person you are? Based on their essays, how different do you think Ascher's and

Njeri's identities were before their name changes and after? Which writer do you think underwent the greater change of identity. Why?

2. Compile a list of all the reasons you can think of for why people change their names (for example, marriage, the restoration of an immigrant's true name, celebrityhood, ethnic heritage, etc.). How do you evaluate these reasons—do you find some more compelling than others? Which reasons do you most approve of? Which least?

From Discussion to Writing

Many people complain about their first or last names. Some dislike the names their parents gave them, some don't like the connotations, and others don't feel their names really fit the image they have of themselves. What name (first, last, or both) would you select if you were to rename yourself? Write an essay in which you propose the name you would take and then provide the reasons for making the change. If you have already changed (or modified) the name you were born with, discuss the reasons you did so in your essay. (If you are happy with your name and would not want to change it, write your essay about why you like your name and what it means to you.) No matter which way you proceed, be sure to confront the issue of names and personal identity.

6

Personal Appearance:
How Much Do Looks Count?

How can we account for the enormous popularity of health clubs, home fitness equipment, and fad diets, and our unprecedented reliance on cosmetic surgery? Do Americans simply care more today about their personal health? Or are they worried to death about how good they look?

In a recent survey, the well-known pollster Louis Harris concluded that "a solid majority of the American people are close to being obsessed with their physical appearance." In "Mirror, Mirror on the Wall: Worry over Personal Appearance," Harris reports on his figures (96 percent of all Americans surveyed said they would like to change something about their looks) and offers a few observations about their significance. He suggests that the fear of not being physically "acceptable" may be one of the dominant worries of young people in our time.

But what of young people who are not just physically acceptable but are actually beautiful? Are their lives happier, more rewarding? In "Born Beautiful: Confessions of a Naturally Gorgeous Girl," Ellen Paige (a pseudonym) describes the everyday advantages of good looks in our society. She doesn't always say what we might expect her to say: "If you were hoping to hear that being beautiful isn't all it's cracked up to be, I'm going to disappoint. It *is* what it's cracked up to be — and more."

Readers, however, should evaluate the Harris poll and Paige's "confessions" in a more thorough intellectual context. According to psychologists Thomas F. Cash and Louis H. Janda in "The Eye of the Beholder," attractive people do possess many social and professional advantages. But there are major differences in how attractive women and attractive men are perceived. These differences, they maintain, can have serious consequences, and thus "thorns appear on the rose of beauty."

LOUIS HARRIS

Mirror, Mirror on the Wall: Worry over Personal Appearance [INSIDE AMERICA / 1987]

How Often Do People Think About How They Look?

Two out of every three adults in the United States say they fidget, fuss, take furtive glances in windows and mirrors, and study other people's reactions to the way they look. It is not overstating it to report that a solid majority of the American people are close to being obsessed with their physical appearance.

The biggest difference, of course, is between men and women. While 54 percent of men say they often think of their physical appearance, a much higher 75 percent of women say the same. And 40 percent say they spend a lot of time on how they look. Many years ago, sociologist David Riesman invented the phrase "other-directed," meaning that most Americans were more concerned with what others thought of them than what they thought of themselves. The segments of the population who spend the most time tinkering with themselves to look better are young people, those in the highest

---

LOUIS HARRIS (b. 1921) is one of America's leading public opinion specialists. He has conducted many landmark studies on topics ranging from racial relations to presidential elections. His polls have been used by corporations, government agencies, foundations, the news media, and both political parties. "Mirror, Mirror on the Wall: Worry over Personal Appearance" originally appeared as a chapter in Harris's Inside America (1987).

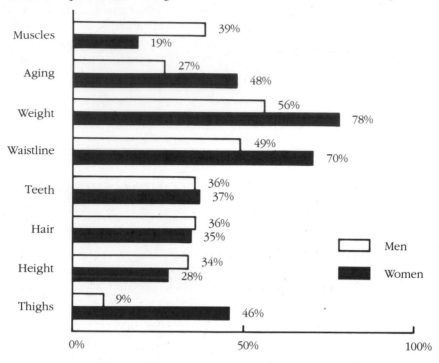

income brackets, big city residents, residents of the Northeast, the best-educated, blacks, singles, and, of course, women.

But perhaps the depth of Americans' obsession with and insecurity over their looks emerged when people were asked if they would like to change something about their personal appearance. A nearly unanimous 96 percent said they would, 94 percent of all men and 99 percent of all women.

Here is what men want changed about their physical appearance [also see the graph]:

- 56 percent volunteer that they would like to change their weight, a sign that a majority of men have the vanity about fitness normally associated with women.
- 49 percent would like to trim their waistline.
- 39 percent would like to develop their muscles, a sign of the macho residue in American life.
- 36 percent want to change their teeth.

- 36 percent would change their hair if they could. Baldness in particular worries men, despite the myth that bald men are more virile.
- 34 percent would like to change their height, most to be taller. To be short is ignominy among American men.
- 27 percent would like to find a way not to show the evidence of aging. This is an area of sly attentiveness for men; many use hair dye, for example, without telling anyone about it.
- 21 percent want to change their overall physique. Men as well as women worry about their shape.
- 20 percent would like to change their complexion.
- 19 percent would change their nose if they could.

Women have a longer and more substantial list of changes they would like to make in their physical appearance:

- 78 percent would change their weight. Fully 35 percent would like to lose twenty-five pounds or more, another 16 percent from sixteen to twenty-five pounds, and 14 percent between eleven and fifteen pounds. Obviously, American women are close to being obsessed with weight and, as a later chapter reveals, are not doing a very effective job of fulfilling their desire.
- 70 percent are worried about their waistline, tied closely to their weight problem, and would like nothing more than to trim it.
- 48 percent would like to make changes to cover up telltale signs of aging.
- 46 percent would like to change their thighs if they could find a way.
- 38 percent would like to do something about their buttocks, again a slimming problem.
- 37 percent want to change their teeth.
- 35 percent would like to change their hair (presumably something they can do).
- 34 percent would like to change their legs, a formidable task.
- 33 percent are really concerned about their wrinkles.
- 32 percent would like to change their bust.
- 29 percent would like to overhaul their entire physique.
- 28 percent wish they could change their height, often to become taller.
- 26 percent would like to have a different complexion.
- 21 percent would like to change their nose.
- 21 percent would like to change their hands.

- 19 percent would like to change their muscles, meaning to have less of them.
- 18 percent would change their feet, mostly to make them smaller.
- 16 percent would change the entire shape of their face.
- 9 percent would change their ears.

Observation

These rampant obsessions of both men and women about their looks have produced an obvious boon for the cosmetics industry, plastic surgery, diet doctors, fitness and shape advisers, fat farms, and a host of other enterprises.

To some extent, these attitudes suggest the positive and healthy attribute of really caring about one's person. But they are also just as indicative of a compulsion to be better looking and hence more acceptable at any cost. The insecurity of being rejected for not looking right physically is partly the artifact of advertising designed to capitalize on these fears and apprehensions.

There was a time a little while ago when people wanted to go back to a natural look, as was evidenced by women forgoing makeup and hair dyeing. Now the dominant desire is to *be acceptable*, whatever that might mean. To have others admire one's looks now ranks high on the lists of both men and women, especially the young, even if those looks are only superficial and wildly deceiving. The race to make one's physical appearance stunning in order to be admired is on in full force in America in the late 1980s.

8

Points to Consider

1. The Harris poll indicates a wide difference between men and women with respect to their worry over personal appearance. What are some of the differences? How would you account for these differences?

2. Go over the individual features that make up the male and female lists. What physical characteristics do you find missing? How important do you think these missing items are?

3. In his attempt to explain the results of his poll, Harris says, "Now the dominant desire is to *be acceptable,* whatever that might mean." What do you think being acceptable means? How does someone know when he or she is acceptable? Where would you find the standards of acceptability?

Born Beautiful: Confessions
of a Naturally Gorgeous Girl [MADEMOISELLE / February 1988]

My blind date is trudging up the four flights to my New York apartment. I'm waiting, in suspense. Will he be a little like William Hurt? Have a touch of Tom Hanks's winsomeness? When there's one flight to go, I can't wait any longer. I poke my head out the door and over the bannister to check him out. Not bad — except that he looks like his best friend just died.

Until he glances up and sees me. In a second his brow relaxes, his eyes brighten, a wave of visible relief sweeps across his face. He grins and bounds up the last few steps. Why is this man suddenly so cheerful? I already know the reason: it's because I'm pretty. And does this little scene make me feel great? Well, yes. But I'm used to it.

I've been pretty most of my life, except for a few awkward phases. I know this because people tell me — both directly and in more subtle ways (like the way my blind date's face did). Sometimes when I look in the mirror, I can see what they mean; other times — as with every woman who has her good and bad days — I can't. But even when I can't, there's no denying the effect of my good looks; it wraps around me like a cocoon, my magic charm. Being beautiful can keep pain at bay.

It's like this: I've made a stupid mistake at work and am feeling embarrassed and worthless — or my ego has been bruised by a particularly bad fight with my boyfriend. So I put on something I think I look great in and head for the door. Outside, what happens usually cheers me up: men turn and react appreciatively as I walk by. I don't mean they catcall or harass me (although no woman on earth can successfully escape that kind of attention). And I'm not talking about the chorus of whistles you get from construction workers or truck drivers. I mean that nice-looking men, well-dressed, carry-

4

ELLEN PAIGE (b. 1958) is a pseudonym for a free-lance writer based in New York City. Born and raised in Los Angeles, she graduated from the University of California at Berkeley with a B.A. in English. Paige has lived in New York City since 1980 and frequently contributes articles to such publications as Self, Savvy Woman, Mademoiselle, *and* Health Magazine.

ing briefcases — men I might want to go out with — check me out in a way I think is flattering. Women also look at me, but in a different, more investigative way. They eye me, taking in everything as if they're gathering details, maybe shopping for a new look for themselves.

Sure, I'd probably feel even better if my boss told me how smart I was or if my boyfriend showed up on my doorstep apologetic and holding roses. But who can count on that happening? What I can count on are the turned heads, the appreciative glances, the "hey, beautiful." And that goes a long way toward making me feel good.

Shallow, you say? Dating success shouldn't depend on how pretty someone is; a setback at work shouldn't be soothed by skin-deep compliments. Maybe not, but it's also undeniable: looks count. If you were hoping to hear that being beautiful isn't all it's cracked up to be, I'm going to disappoint. It *is* what it's cracked up to be — and more.

By now you're probably wondering what I look like. Most of what I know about my looks comes from other people, who tell me I'm the earthy, natural type. But I do know my features are small and even, my brown eyes and hair are a good match, I'm tall and fit, and I can look sexy and sophisticated when I want. I wasn't the type of child adults cooed over; my parents let me know they were proud of my looks, partly because all parents do, but mainly to instill confidence. For the most part; though, beauty was not a big deal in my family. There was some sibling rivalry between my younger sister and me that we now know stemmed from the disparity in our looks — she kept her baby fat well into her teens and I didn't.

I suppose she was right to be jealous of my looks, because in school,   8 beauty was definitely a big deal. Being cute had a lot to do with the number of friends I had. My popularity certainly wasn't due to my outgoing personality (I was and am very shy) or my academic record (unremarkable). Girls, I could tell, admired my looks, but it was the boys who first let me know they thought I was good-looking, usually by threatening to pummel my little brother after school if he didn't dish the latest dirt on me. (Unfortunately he always complied, which accounts for how the entire fifth grade knew when I got my first bra.) As I got older, the boys got braver and started to say things — not compliments exactly, but as close to them as adolescents ever get. Sometimes it was flattering, and I liked it. But other times it was unsettling.

I'm at the beach. I'm thirteen and an "older" man (actually a boy of about eighteen) is talking to me while I wait on line for ice cream. He asks me how old I am. When I tell him, he stops cold, steps back, and stares at my skimpy bikini, and says one word: "Wow." The way he utters that word — slowly, solemnly — is a revelation, both frightening and enlightening. I realize then that beauty bestows power.

I was just starting to get wise to what my looks could mean to me when I headed to high school. That's where I got an advanced degree in "pretty politics." Once, in the restroom, I overheard someone say about me, "She's pretty and she knows it." Translated, that meant I was vain, conceited, stuck-up. Nice girls, you see, weren't supposed to know they were pretty. I got the message. I learned to deny what was as obvious as the nose, and every other feature, on my face. The way to be liked — and being liked is paramount to a teenager — was to be pretty and *not* know it. So I tried hard to get voted Best Personality; I always won Best-Looking instead.

In high school there were no secrets. Our reputations as freshmen followed us to senior year. When I went to college, though, to a university the size of a small city, I faded into the crowd. I no longer stood out because of the way I looked. In fact, there were many girls in my dorm, not to mention on the whole campus, who were more than my equals in the looks department. Instead of feeling inferior, I was less self-conscious about my appearance. The pressure was off, and that let me relax enough to start enjoying my looks. When someone told me I was attractive, I felt as though I'd earned the compliment. "Pretty" was no longer just a label that showed my high-school status.

Once during the summer between my sophomore and junior years, I ran into a guy I knew from high school. He was surprised to hear I was studying biology at a prestigious university. "You never seemed like the type," he said. Maybe I should have been offended, but instead I just laughed; I *was* the type, and always had been. But college had freed me from my looks.

Now that I'm on my own, out of school and working in New York, it's become clearer exactly what being attractive can do for me. It doesn't guarantee glamour, excitement, or adventure, or that I'll marry Mr. Right. But it does make some good things come my way — and make life more comfortable.

For one thing, people notice me: a waiter at a nearby café gives me delicious whole wheat rolls for free; a grocery clerk offers me (but not my date) change for the bus; the guy working out next to me breaks training to flirt. After they've noticed me, people usually want to get to know me, and that's helped to open some doors. My looks hold people's attention long enough for me to strut my stuff — to show them I can produce. If my looks intrigue someone, I don't mind using them. That doesn't mean I'd wear a bustier and miniskirt to a job interview, but I don't try to hide my looks either. It's highly unlikely that someone will hire me on appearance alone, but at least I'll get the interview.

I haven't quite figured out why my looks intrigue. It seems to boil down to simple curiosity; maybe people wonder if I have as much luck in other areas as I've had with my looks. But people do seem attracted to attractiveness, pleased by it, happy to be in the company of it.

I know I am. Sometimes just being with someone I think is good-looking

12

16

makes me feel special by association. I don't choose my friends because they're beautiful, but still, looks *are* alluring. People tend to assign positive traits to those they find attractive. That's why new acquaintances often seem to have decided that they like me almost as soon as we've met. My appearance can speed up the process that makes people choose to be my friends.

It's my first day on the job at a publishing house. I'm making the rounds, introducing myself to co-workers. One woman is so absorbed in her work, and so uninterested in meeting the new kid on the block, that she doesn't even look up when she says hello. A few days later, she suddenly becomes cordial, even palsy. I realize that I've passed her test; she's sized me up and I look right. She's intrigued, I can tell, not by who I am — she's barely spoken to me before this burst of chumminess — but rather by how I look.

The effect of my looks is even more apparent in my romantic involvements. I'm not the first to have noticed that people pair up with their equals — 10s with 10s, 7s with 7s, and so on. Studies have proven it. It's certainly true for my boyfriend, Josh, and me. I think he's at least as good-looking as my friends tell me I am. But there's one big difference: my looks matter more to him than his do to me. I'm not sure why, but it doesn't bother me. In fact, I'm happy Josh is proud of the way I look. If I thought he loved me only for my looks, that would be different.

But then there are those middle-of-the-night doubts. What if he wakes up one day and sees me looking lousy? I don't mean being caught without makeup, since I rarely use cosmetics anyway. What I'm talking about is getting older. I worry about it. So I work out — a lot, sometimes two hours a day. Makeup can disguise the effects of aging, but exercise can actually delay them. I won't hand over my looks to age without a fight. I worry that if time robs me of my beauty, I'll also lose my magic, the power my looks give me. I've felt a twinge of this already. At my ten-year high-school reunion last year I panicked that my former classmates would think I'd gone downhill, and I'm not sure that some of them didn't. But before I started yearning for my old Best-Looking banner, I told myself that nobody looks as good as they did when they were seventeen.

I guess admitting that losing my looks worries me is a giveaway that I care about them a great deal. But while I have them, I might as well capitalize on them. If they can make me feel better when I'm blue, why not?

It's a Sunday, a couple of years ago. I'm out running errands when I bump into Craig — a man I've just started dating. He's friendly, but not exactly passionate in his hello — not like last Friday night, anyway. I ask him if he'd like to catch a movie tonight, but he hedges. He then tells me that he's started seeing his old girlfriend again. The next moment, he hops in a cab and is gone. I feel like I've been socked in the stomach, but I catch

20

a glimpse of myself in a store window and automatically think, "Well, at least I look good." It doesn't bring Craig back, but I do feel better.

When I feel good about my looks, others pick up on it. The day I met my current boyfriend, I was feeling fabulous about my work, my friends, and the way I looked. I was waiting in the tiny backseat of a Triumph for a ride home from a party when there he was — a gorgeous man scrunching his six-foot-one frame in beside me. He was first attracted to me, he says, mostly by my looks, but also my attitude — enough to fold himself in two to sit next to me.

This doesn't happen every day, though. Let me dispel the myth that pretty women have men knocking down doors or squeezing into sports cars just to be near them. I've gone through several long and lonely stretches without a single eligible man in sight, stretches made worse by the loaded question, "How come a pretty girl like you doesn't have a boyfriend?"

True, being pretty may help me catch a man's eye across a room or spark his interest during a brief encounter in an elevator, but more often I end up getting propositioned by overly aggressive guys who aren't my type at all. During my dating dry spells, I used to rationalize that men must have assumed that I had a boyfriend and were afraid to ask me out. Although there's no way to prove it, I don't really think this was often the case. Instead, the reasons I found it hard to meet the right men were the same reasons all women have trouble meeting men — but that's another story.

There can be a kind of beauty backlash in other social situations, too. I've noticed some women giving me nasty looks for no apparent reason; I've also felt them act strangely aloof. Rather than instantly *liking* me because of how I look, they seemed to take an instant *dislike* to me. That they may have been jealous doesn't make me feel any better about their reactions.

My exercise class is small: only two other women and our instructor. It's hard to ignore the fact that my classmates won't talk to me. I am shy, but at least I try to be friendly. I try small talk in the locker room, but I get no response. I ask our instructor, Todd, why he thinks they're so aloof. "Two reasons — you're tall and lean. Period," he says. That's ridiculous. Judy has a great job and Beth's got a husband worth bragging about. Two things I envy them for. How can they be jealous of me? I'm hurt, but I'm also angry. How can they judge me on such trivial grounds? But then I think: How can I be annoyed if they judge me negatively on looks alone, when I love it if people assume I'm great just because I'm attractive?

Still, all things considered, if you ask me how I'd like to be known, I'd say I'd rather be considered intelligent. Why then, I wonder, was I so disappointed after I met my boyfriend's brother for the first time? He told Josh later he thought I was really bright. Didn't he think I was sort of, well . . . beautiful?

Points to Consider

1. Why do you think the writer used a pen name for this essay? What problems does she avoid by doing so?

2. Why do you think she begins her essay with a "blind date"? What does that incident permit her to do? How does it help characterize her right from the start?

3. Note the author's choice of words to describe herself: "pretty," "beautiful," "good-looking," "attractive," "cute." Are these all close synonyms? How would you rank them on an ascending scale of physical appearance? Why does she use "pretty" most of the time? Does the word have any descriptive value?

4. The author worries about being considered "shallow" (paragraph 6). Why is this a problem, given her theme? How does she try to counter that label? Do you think she sounds shallow? Why or why not?

THOMAS F. CASH
AND LOUIS H. JANDA

The Eye of the Beholder   [PSYCHOLOGY TODAY / December 1984]

Ask most people to list what makes them like someone on first meeting and they'll tell you personality, intelligence, sense of humor. But they're probably deceiving themselves. The characteristic that impresses people the most, when meeting anyone from a job applicant to a blind date, is appear-

---

THOMAS F. CASH (b. 1947) and LOUIS H. JANDA (b. 1946) are associate professors of psychology at Old Dominion University in Virginia and are currently writing a book on the psychology of physical appearance and body image. Professor Cash is the author of many journal articles on body image; Professor Janda has written several psychology textbooks and is the author of How to Live with an Imperfect Person *(1985).*

ance. And unfair and unenlightened as it may seem, attractive people are frequently preferred over their less attractive peers.

Research begun in the early 1970s has shown that not only do good looks influence such things as choice of friends, lovers, and mates, but that they can also affect school grades, selection for jobs, and even the outcome of a trial. Psychologist Ellen Berscheid of the University of Minnesota and psychologist Elaine Walster, then at the University of Wisconsin, were among the first researchers to deal with the topic of attractiveness. Their seminal 1974 paper on the subject showed that the more attractive a person, the more desirable characteristics others will attribute to him or her. Attractive people are viewed as being happier, more sensitive, more interesting, warmer, more poised, more sociable, and as having better character than their less attractive counterparts. Psychologist Karen Dion of the University of Toronto has dubbed this stereotypical view as: "What is beautiful is good."

Our current work at Old Dominion University in Norfolk, Virginia, with colleagues and students, focuses on the role that appearance plays in judgments made about people. Our studies have been done in a variety of settings: basic research laboratories, beauty and cosmetics industry labs, plastic and reconstructive surgery practices, psychiatric hospitals, and psychotherapeutic consulting rooms.

One topic that has led to many avenues of research is how attractiveness influences sex-typing — the tendency of people to attribute certain stereotypical qualities to each sex. Besides being perceived as sensitive, kind, interesting, and generally happy, attractive people tend to fit easily into sexual stereotypes, according to a study done by Barry Gillen, a social psychologist in our department.

Gillen speculated that attractive people possess two types of "goodness," one related to and the other unrelated to their sex. To test this hypothesis he showed a group of students photographs of both men and women of high, moderate, and low attractiveness, as determined by the previous rankings of students according to a seven-point scale (contrary to popular belief, researchers usually don't use the Bo Derek scale of 10). The judges were asked to rate the subjects according to the masculinity, femininity, and social desirability scales of the Bem Sex Role Inventory. Gillen's study found that attractive women were perceived as being more feminine, and that attractive men were viewed as being more masculine than their less attractive counterparts. This suggests a second stereotype: "What is beautiful is sex-typed."

One implication of Gillen's work that we wanted to test was whether good looks are a disadvantage for some people, especially women, in work situations that conflict with sexual stereotypes. By the late 1970s, there was already a sizable body of literature documenting the problems women face because of sex-role stereotypes. We speculated that attractive women might be at a real disadvantage when they aspire to occupations in which stereotypically masculine traits — such as being strong, independent, and decisive — are thought to be required for success.

To test that possibility we did a study with Gillen and Steve Burns, a student in our department, in which professional personnel consultants were hired to rate a "job applicant's" suitability for six positions. We matched the positions for the skill required, the prestige offered, and the degree of supervisory independence allowed. Two jobs were stereotypically masculine (automobile salesperson and wholesale hardware shipping and receiving clerk), two feminine (telephone operator and office receptionist), and two were sex-neutral (motel desk clerk and photographic darkroom assistant).

Each of the seventy-two personnel consultants who participated received a résumé package for an individual that contained the typical kinds of information that a job applicant might submit: academic standing, a list of hobbies and interests, specific skills and recommendations from teachers and counselors. All of the résumés were identical with the exception of the name ("John" vs. "Janet" Williams) and the inclusion of a photograph of the applicant. Photographs showed either an extremely attractive applicant or an unattractive one, previously judged on an attractiveness scale.

The results documented the existence of both sexism and "beautyism." On the sexism front, men were given stronger endorsements by the personnel consultants for the traditionally masculine jobs, while women were rated higher for the traditionally feminine jobs. Men were also judged to have just as much chance of success on the neutral jobs as on the masculine ones, while women were perceived to be less likely to succeed on the neutral jobs than on the feminine ones.

"Beautyism" had several facets: attractive men were favored over their less attractive male competitors for all three types of jobs. Similarly, attractiveness gave women a competitive edge against other women, but only for traditionally female or neutral jobs. When it came to jobs inappropriate to society's traditional sex roles, the attractive women were rated lower than their less attractive female competitors.

These findings gain support from a subsequent study by Madeline Heilman and Lois Saruwatari, psychologists at Yale University. They examined the effects of appearance and gender on selection for both managerial and nonmanagerial jobs. Male and female students in a business administration class received résumé packages for equally qualified candidates. Each résumé included a photograph of either an attractive or unattractive man or woman. Being attractive was always an advantage for men. Attractive men received stronger recommendations for hiring, were judged to have better qualifications, and were given higher suggested starting salaries than unattractive men for both the managerial and the nonmanagerial positions.

Among women, however, those who were less attractive actually had a significant edge over their more attractive peers when seeking a place in management, a traditionally masculine occupation. Good looks were an advantage only when women were applying for the nonmanagerial positions. Attractiveness resulted in lower salary recommendations when the women were viewed as stepping into an out-of-sex-role position.

If they want a men's job they have to look less attractive.
because men's job a more masculine,
an attractive women are more feminine.

Heilman says that her findings "imply that women should strive to appear as unattractive and masculine as possible if they are to succeed in advancing their careers by moving into powerful organizational positions."

So, beauty — at least in a woman — doesn't always pay in the work place, nor does it guarantee higher marks in the classroom. Recently, we tested the notion that attractiveness can work against women attempting to cross sex-role boundaries in academic as well as work settings. We constructed a series of essays, purportedly written by college freshmen, that were equivalent in quality, but which varied in the "masculinity" or "femininity" of the topic. The essays were accompanied by photographs of attractive and unattractive "authors."

The masculine topics were "How to Hunt Safely" and "How to Buy a Used Motorcycle," and the feminine topics were "How to Make a Quilt" and "How to Give a Manicure." The essays were read and judged by 216 female college students.

Once again, attractiveness proved to be an advantage for the men, regardless of the sex-typing of the essay topic. For the women, however, beauty was an advantage only when they stuck to a feminine topic. When they were presented as authors of the masculine essays, the attractive women were given a lower score relative to their less attractive peers.

16

It is clear that beauty can be a double-edged sword for women. Attractive women are viewed as having a host of desirable personality characteristics, except the ones needed to step out of prescribed sex roles.

What are the specific cues for gender role stereotyping? Grooming — the way people dress, use cosmetics, and style their hair — appears to be a factor. The differing ideal physiques — thin for women, more muscular for men — also influence gender stereotyping, according to recent experiments by Purdue psychologists Kay Deaux and Laurie Lewis. People who are tall, strong, sturdy, and broad-shouldered — regardless of gender — are viewed as more likely to have masculine personality traits, to fit the assertive, bread-winner role, and to hold a traditionally masculine occupation. Meanwhile, people who are dainty, graceful, and soft in voice and appearance are expected to have typically feminine traits, roles, and occupations.

How does grooming affect sex-typing of attractive women, especially as it relates to their employability? This question was partially answered by a series of studies in which we asked male and female corporate personnel consultants to judge how qualified various attractive women, shown in photographs, were for jobs in corporate management. In the first study, we showed sixteen personnel managers photographs of women wearing various types of clothing, jewelry, hair styles, and cosmetics. The results showed that the more sex-typed, or "feminized," the grooming styles, the less likely were personnel consultants to judge the women to be potential managers.

In a second study, personnel consultants judged businesswomen photographed under two different grooming conditions: one very feminine and made up, the other plainer and less sex-typed. The more feminine style

20

more feminine = less competent

included longer hair or hair styles that concealed the face; soft sweaters, low necklines, or ruffled blouses; dangling jewelry; and heavy makeup. In the other condition "candidates" wore tailored clothes with a jacket, subtle makeup, and either short hair or hair swept away from the face. These criteria were chosen on the basis of descriptions given by judges in the previous study.

more masculine = competent

Once again the corporate personnel consultants made choices suggesting that the less feminine the appearance, the more competent the woman, even though the candidates had been perceived by the consultants as equally attractive under both conditions. Specifically, candidates groomed in a more feminine style were perceived to be less managerial; less intrinsically interested in work; less likely to be taken seriously by others; more illogical and overemotional in critical decision-making; less financially responsible; more helpless and dependent on the influences of others; sexier and more flirtatious in social relations; and less assertive, independent, and self-confident than those groomed in a less sex-typed style.

In the third phase of this project, male and female executives and managers from more than two hundred corporations in major cities nationwide were shown applications containing photographs of attractive businesswomen in various grooming styles and asked how they thought they would fare in the corporate world. Once again, candidates groomed in a less sex-typed style were expected to have a better chance at reaching the management levels of the corporate structure, to be offered higher salaries, and to be afforded greater social acceptance and credibility on the job than when they were groomed in a more traditionally feminine manner. These effects were especially prominent when the judges were men, often the gatekeepers of corporate management.

These studies, taken together, suggest that grooming style has a definite effect on whether women are sex-typed, and thus whether they are viewed as having good management potential. To some extent, our research has confirmed what many people always suspected: if a woman wants to succeed in a man's world, she had better not look too feminine. Several "dress for success" books have made it to the best-seller list by advising women to get ahead in business by wearing their hair short, using cosmetics sparingly, and wearing conservative suits. Our research suggests, sadly, that the advice is sound.

It is interesting how deeply ingrained these attitudes are. Many people, both men and women, who are seriously concerned and offended by the sexism in our society never question this dress-for-success formula, which has different standards for men than it does for women. Men must follow certain clothing norms in the office in regard to neatness and formality, but not masculinity. No one would suggest to a man that he try not to look too masculine when he shows up at the office or expect him to comb his hair one way for the office and another way when he goes out to dinner. It is

24

doubtful that any man has ever been advised not to look too good if he wants to be taken seriously at the next board meeting. But rules of dress for women are far more complex.

Prejudices are slow to fade away. It will be interesting to see if grooming styles for women become more flexible as they move up the corporate ladder in greater numbers and become more powerful.

Attractive women can face problems outside the boardroom as well. Everyone wants to be thought of as desirable and attractive, but a woman's beauty can invite unwanted advances and treatment as a sex object. Perhaps, then, it should come as no surprise that social psychologist Harry Reis of the University of Rochester found attractive women to be more distrustful of men than were their plainer counterparts.

Our research has also confirmed that a third stereotype exists: "What is beautiful is self-centered." We've found that many people assume that attractive people are vain and egotistical. After all, if what is beautiful is good, then the beautiful people must know how wonderful they are. Further, people of low and average attractiveness are often reluctant to choose extremely attractive mates for fear of losing them. In fact, breakups are more common among couples who are mismatched on attractiveness. So once again, thorns appear on the rose of beauty.

We have been discussing how people judge and react to the attractiveness of others. What about people's perceptions of themselves? Currently, in collaboration with Barbara Winstead, a psychologist at Old Dominion, we are examining how body images — the feelings people have about their own appearance — influence their lives. Surprisingly, how people view their own level of attractiveness has almost nothing to do with how others view them. People whom others consider beautiful may not like their looks at all. Conversely, people whom others might judge as downright unattractive or even ugly feel completely comfortable with their appearance.

Using our newly developed Winstead-Cash Body Self-Relations Questionnaire, we are beginning to accumulate evidence that body image may have as much impact on one's life as external evaluations of beauty. In a study with Steve Noles, a graduate student in the Virginia Consortium for Professional Psychology, for example, we have found a greater vulnerability to depression among people who place importance on being good-looking yet see themselves as less attractive than they really are.

Aristotle once maintained that "beauty is a greater recommendation than any letter of introduction." In many respects he was right. But then again, maybe he should have collected more data.

Points to Consider

1. What connection do the authors find between attractiveness and "sex-typing"? What subsequent studies did this connection lead to?

2. Why did the authors coin the word "beautyism"? What does the word mean? How does it differ from sexism? What did they discover about "beautyism" and the job market?

3. In their experiment with freshman essays, why do the authors use only female college students as graders?

4. The authors' experiments are often based on photographs. Though they never question it, do you think judgments made on the basis of photographs are scientifically reliable? Do you think the use of photographs affects the validity of their results?

Discussing the Unit

Suggested Topic for Discussion

All three essays in this unit suggest that a person's physical appearance is coming to be of paramount importance in our society. Do you think this trend will result in serious forms of social and economic discrimination? Will people who are not considered physically "acceptable" face increasing difficulties in school, in society, and on the job? Will attractive people possess unfair advantages? Do you think that anything can — or should — be done about the problem?

Preparing for Class Discussion

1. Consider the matter first from a personal point of view. How would you fit into the Harris poll? Do you worry about how you look, or do you think such worries are trivial? Have you ever thought that you were being seriously evaluated — for a college grade or a job — on the basis of whether your appearance made a favorable or unfavorable impression? If so, what was the occasion?

2. Consider the disadvantages of good looks. Make a note of the disadvantages mentioned in the essays by Paige and by Cash and Janda. How many disadvantages can you come up with? Do they pertain only to women? Can you think of disadvantages to male good looks? How serious do you think these disadvantages are? Are they so serious that most unattractive people would prefer to remain unattractive?

From Discussion to Writing

The philosopher Schopenhauer wrote that we all proceed with people on the basis of an unspoken rule that everyone *is* as he or she *looks.* In other words, we all seem to think — despite evidence to the contrary — that we can judge people mainly by their physical appearance. Consider your own appearance and how you think it affects other people's assessment of you. In an essay try to describe yourself as accurately and as objectively as you can. In the course of your essay, consider the following questions: do you think others see you as you see yourself or do you think there is often a disparity between the way you see yourself and how others see you? What mistakes do you think other people make about the way you look and the way you actually view yourself? Do you think the way other people assess your appearance has made a big difference in your life?

7

Public Space:
Who Are Its Victims?

Public space means something different to everyone. How easily we do such ordinary things as walk about, play, shop, use mass transit, or simply wait for someone often depends on who and where we are. In one part of the country, automobiles stop for pedestrians; in another they seem prepared to run people down as they step from the curb. The crowded sidewalks of a big city mean one thing to a "street-smart" teenager and quite another to an elderly citizen. Our experiences of public space — though often taken for granted — exert a powerful influence not only on the quality of our lives but on our sense of personal identity.

As you read the following three short essays, you will see what being out in public can mean to three different people: Brent Staples, a black journalist walking alone in a city late at night; Cheryl A. Davis, a woman in a wheelchair struggling with mass transit; and Richard Hill, an irate citizen fed up with the intrusion of music ("decibel bullying") into every nook and cranny of America. Though their annoyances are different, these writers share a plight familiar to all of us: the experience of having our peace and privacy rudely disturbed and our patience sorely tested.

BRENT STAPLES

Just Walk on By: A Black Man Ponders His Power to Alter Public Space [MS. / September 1986]

My first victim was a woman — white, well dressed, probably in her early twenties. I came upon her late one evening on a deserted street in Hyde Park, a relatively affluent neighborhood in an otherwise mean, impoverished section of Chicago. As I swung onto the avenue behind her, there seemed to be a discreet, uninflammatory distance between us. Not so. She cast back a worried glance. To her, the youngish black man — a broad six feet two inches with a beard and billowing hair, both hands shoved into the pockets of a bulky military jacket — seemed menacingly close. After a few more quick glimpses, she picked up her pace and was soon running in earnest. Within seconds she disappeared into a cross street.

That was more than a decade ago. I was twenty-two years old, a graduate student newly arrived at the University of Chicago. It was in the echo of that terrified woman's footfalls that I first began to know the unwieldy inheritance I'd come into — the ability to alter public space in ugly ways. It was clear that she thought herself the quarry of a mugger, a rapist, or worse. Suffering a bout of insomnia, however, I was stalking sleep, not defenseless wayfarers. As a softy who is scarcely able to take a knife to a raw chicken — let alone hold it to a person's throat — I was surprised, embarrassed, and dismayed all at once. Her flight made me feel like an accomplice in tyranny. It also made it clear that I was indistinguishable from the muggers who occasionally seeped into the area from the surrounding ghetto. That first encounter, and those that followed, signified that a vast, unnerving gulf lay between night-time pedestrians — particularly women — and me. And I soon gathered that being perceived as dangerous is a hazard in itself. I only needed to turn a corner into a dicey situation, or crowd some frightened, armed person in a

BRENT STAPLES *(b. 1951) is on the editorial board of the* New York Times. *He holds a Ph.D. in psychology from the University of Chicago and has worked at a variety of newspapers, including the* Chicago Sun Times.

foyer somewhere, or make an errant move after being pulled over by a policeman. Where fear and weapons meet — and they often do in urban America — there is always the possibility of death.

In that first year, my first away from my hometown, I was to become thoroughly familiar with the language of fear. At dark, shadowy intersections in Chicago, I could cross in front of a car stopped at a traffic light and elicit the *thunk, thunk, thunk, thunk* of the driver — black, white, male, or female — hammering down the door locks. On less traveled streets after dark, I grew accustomed to but never comfortable with people who crossed to the other side of the street rather than pass me. Then there were the standard unpleasantries with police, doormen, bouncers, cab drivers, and others whose business it is to screen out troublesome individuals *before* there is any nastiness.

I moved to New York nearly two years ago and I have remained an avid   4
night walker. In central Manhattan, the near-constant crowd cover minimizes tense one-on-one street encounters. Elsewhere — visiting friends in SoHo,[1] where sidewalks are narrow and tightly spaced buildings shut out the sky — things can get very taut indeed.

Black men have a firm place in New York mugging literature. Norman Podhoretz[2] in his famed (or infamous) 1963 essay, "My Negro Problem — And Ours," recalls growing up in terror of black males; they "were tougher than we were, more ruthless," he writes — and as an adult on the Upper West Side of Manhattan, he continues, he cannot constrain his nervousness when he meets black men on certain streets. Similarly, a decade later, the essayist and novelist Edward Hoagland extols a New York where once "Negro bitterness bore down mainly on other Negroes." Where some see mere panhandlers, Hoagland sees "a mugger who is clearly screwing up his nerve to do more than just *ask* for money." But Hoagland has "the New Yorker's quick-hunch posture for broken-field maneuvering," and the bad guy swerves away.

I often witness that "hunch posture," from women after dark on the warrenlike streets of Brooklyn where I live. They seem to set their faces on neutral and, with their purse straps strung across their chests bandolier style, they forge ahead as though bracing themselves against being tackled. I understand, of course, that the danger they perceive is not a hallucination. Women are particularly vulnerable to street violence, and young black males are drastically overrepresented among the perpetrators of that violence. Yet these truths are no solace against the kind of alienation that comes of being ever the suspect, against being set apart, a fearsome entity with whom pedestrians avoid making eye contact.

[1] A district of lower Manhattan known for its art galleries.
[2] A well-known literary critic and editor of *Commentary* magazine.

It is not altogether clear to me how I reached the ripe old age of twenty-two without being conscious of the lethality nighttime pedestrians attributed to me. Perhaps it was because in Chester, Pennsylvania, the small, angry industrial town where I came of age in the 1960s, I was scarcely noticeable against a backdrop of gang warfare, street knifings, and murders. I grew up one of the good boys, had perhaps a half-dozen fist fights. In retrospect, my shyness of combat has clear sources.

Many things go into the making of a young thug. One of those things   8
is the consummation of the male romance with the power to intimidate. An infant discovers that random flailings send the baby bottle flying out of the crib and crashing to the floor. Delighted, the joyful babe repeats those motions again and again, seeking to duplicate the feat. Just so, I recall the points at which some of my boyhood friends were finally seduced by the perception of themselves as tough guys. When a mark cowered and surrendered his money without resistance, myth and reality merged — and paid off. It is, after all, only manly to embrace the power to frighten and intimidate. We, as men, are not supposed to give an inch of our lane on the highway; we are to seize the fighter's edge in work and in play and even in love; we are to be valiant in the face of hostile forces.

Unfortunately, poor and powerless young men seem to take all this nonsense literally. As a boy, I saw countless tough guys locked away; I have since buried several, too. They were babies, really — a teenage cousin, a brother of twenty-two, a childhood friend in his mid-twenties — all gone down in episodes of bravado played out in the streets. I came to doubt the virtues of intimidation early on. I chose, perhaps even unconsciously, to remain a shadow — timid, but a survivor.

The fearsomeness mistakenly attributed to me in public places often has a perilous flavor. The most frightening of these confusions occurred in the late 1970s and early 1980s when I worked as a journalist in Chicago. One day, rushing into the office of a magazine I was writing for with a deadline story in hand, I was mistaken for a burglar. The office manager called security and, with an ad hoc posse, pursued me through the labyrinthine halls, nearly to my editor's door. I had no way of proving who I was. I could only move briskly toward the company of someone who knew me.

Another time I was on assignment for a local paper and killing time before an interview. I entered a jewelry store on the city's affluent Near North Side. The proprietor excused herself and returned with an enormous red Doberman pinscher straining at the end of a leash. She stood, the dog extended toward me, silent to my questions, her eyes bulging nearly out of her head. I took a cursory look around, nodded, and bade her good night. Relatively speaking, however, I never fared as badly as another black male journalist. He went to nearby Waukegan, Illinois, a couple of summers ago to work on a story about a murderer who was born there. Mistaking the reporter for the killer, police hauled him from his car at gunpoint and but for his press credentials would probably have tried to book him. Such episodes are not uncommon. Black men trade tales like this all the time.

In "My Negro Problem — And Ours," Podhoretz writes that the hatred 12 he feels for blacks makes itself known to him through a variety of avenues — one being his discomfort with that "special brand of paranoid touchiness" to which he says blacks are prone. No doubt he is speaking here of black men. In time, I learned to smother the rage I felt at so often being taken for a criminal. Not to do so would surely have led to madness — via that special "paranoid touchiness" that so annoyed Podhoretz at the time he wrote the essay.

I began to take precautions to make myself less threatening. I move about with care, particularly late in the evening. I give a wide berth to nervous people on subway platforms during the wee hours, particularly when I have exchanged business clothes for jeans. If I happen to be entering a building behind some people who appear skittish, I may walk by, letting them clear the lobby before I return, so as not to seem to be following them. I have been calm and extremely congenial on those rare occasions when I've been pulled over by the police.

And on late-evening constitutionals along streets less traveled by, I employ what has proved to be an excellent tension-reducing measure: I whistle melodies from Beethoven and Vivaldi and the more popular classical composers. Even steely New Yorkers hunching toward nighttime destinations seem to relax, and occasionally they even join in the tune. Virtually everybody seems to sense that a mugger wouldn't be warbling bright, sunny selections from Vivaldi's *Four Seasons*. It is my equivalent of the cowbell that hikers wear when they know they are in bear country.

Points to Consider

1. Why does Staples begin by talking about his first "victim"? How is he using that word? In what sense was she a "victim"?

2. How does the behavior of his first "victim" affect his own identity? How does it force him to see himself?

3. How does Staples feel about his "victims"? Does he think they are acting foolishly or irrationally? Does he sympathize with them?

4. How has Staples altered his own public behavior as a result of his experiences? Would you do the same?

CHERYL A. DAVIS

A Day on Wheels [THE PROGRESSIVE / November 1987]

"Man, if I was you, I'd shoot myself," said the man on the subway platform. No one else was standing near him. I realized he was talking to me.

"Luckily, you're not," I said, gliding gracefully away.

For me, this was not an unusual encounter; indeed, it was a typical episode in my continuing true-life sitcom, "Day on Wheels."

A train ride can be an occasion for silent meditation in the midst of 4 mechanical commotion. Unfortunately, I rarely get to meditate.

I attract attention. I pretend to ignore them, the eyes that scrutinize me and then quickly glance away. I try to avoid the gratuitous chats with loosely wrapped passengers. Usually, I fail. They may be loosely wrapped, but they're a persistent lot.

I use a wheelchair; I am not "confined" to one. Actually, I get around well. I drive a van equipped with a wheelchair-lift to the train station. I use a powered wheelchair with high-amperage batteries to get to work. A manual chair, light enough to carry, enables me to visit the "walkies" who live upstairs and to ride in their Volkswagens.

My life has been rich and varied, but my fellow passengers assume that, as a disabled person, I must be horribly deprived and so lonely that I will appreciate any unsolicited overture.

"Do you work?" a woman on the train asked me recently. 8

I said I did.

"It's nice that you have something to keep you busy, isn't it?"

Since we are thought of as poor invalids in need of chatting up, people are not apt to think too hard about what they are saying to us. It seems odd, since they also worry about the "right" way to talk to disabled people.

"How do you take a bath?" another woman asked me, apropos of 12 nothing.

One day, an elderly man was staring at me as I read the newspaper.

CHERYL A. DAVIS (b. 1945) is an associate at the Center for Investigative Reporting in San Francisco. An independent journalist, she is currently writing a series of articles and consulting with television stations on disability issues.

"Would you like to read the sports section?" I asked him.

"How many miles can that thing go before you need new batteries?" he responded.

When I was a little girl, I once saw a woman whose teeth looked strange. 16 "Mommy, that lady has funny teeth," I said. My mother explained that it was not *comme il faut* to offer up personal observations about other people's appearances. I thought everyone's mommy taught that, but I was wrong.

For many years, I was in what some of us call "the phyz-diz-biz" — developing housing and educational programs for disabled people. I was active in the disability-rights movement. I went to "special" schools offering the dubious blessing of a segregated education. As a result, I have known several thousand disabled people, at one time or another, across the United States.

For those whose disablement is still recent, the gratuitous remarks and unsolicited contributions can be exceptionally hurtful. It takes time to learn how to protect yourself. To learn how to do it gracefully can take a lifetime.

Many of us take the position that the people who bother us are to be pitied for their ignorance. We take it upon ourselves to "educate" them. We forgive them their trespasses and answer their questions patiently and try to straighten them out.

Others prefer to ignore the rude remarks and questions altogether. I 20 tried that, but it didn't work. There was one woman on the train who tipped the scales for me.

"You're much too pretty to be in a wheelchair," she said.

I stared straight ahead, utterly frozen in unanticipated rage.

Undaunted, she grabbed my left arm below the elbow to get my attention.

"I said, 'You're much too pretty to be in a wheelchair.'" 24

In my fury, I lost control. Between my brain and my mouth, the mediating force of acquired tact had vanished.

"What do you think?" I snapped. "That God holds a beauty contest and if you come in first, you don't have to be in one?"

She turned away and, a moment later, was chatting with an old woman beside her as if nothing had been said at all. But I was mortified, and I moved to the other end of the train car.

For that one lapse, I flagellated myself all afternoon. When I got home, 28 I telephoned one of my more socially adroit disabled friends for advice.

Nick is a therapist, a Ph.D. from Stanford, and paraplegic. "How do you deal with the other bozos on the bus?" I asked him.

"I just say, 'Grow up,'" Nick answered.

That was a bit haughtier than I could pull off, I told him.

"Well, look," he said, "if those words don't do it, find something else. 32 The main thing is to get them to stop bothering you, right?"

"Yes, but — "

"But what?"

"Nick, If I'm *too* rude, they won't learn a thing. They'll just tell themselves I'm maladjusted."

"Then tell them their behavior is inappropriate."   36

"Inappropriate. That's marvelous!" I decided to try it next time.

"Next time" arrived last week. I didn't see the man coming. I was on the train platform, and he approached me from behind and tapped me on the shoulder.

"What's your disability?" he asked, discarding civilities.

I turned and looked at him. "That is not an appropriate question to ask   40
a stranger," I said quietly.

"Well, *I* have schizophrenia," he said proudly.

"I didn't ask you."

"I feel rejected," he said.

"Well, then don't say things like that to people you don't know."   44

The train came and we got on together. I offered him a conciliatory remark, and he quieted down. Clearly he was not the best person for my new approach, but I think I'm headed in the right direction.

Points to Consider

1. What sort of attention does Davis routinely attract? What disturbs her most about this attention?

2. Which of the many comments directed to her bothered her most? Why? In what ways was it different from the others?

3. How does Davis want to respond to people? Why? How have the unwanted attentions of others affected her behavior?

4. What is the significance of the final incident in the essay? Does it resolve her problems? How does it put her experiences into a new perspective?

RICHARD HILL

Could We Please Have Some Quiet, Please?

[THE AMERICAN VOICE / Winter 1989]

> It is the light of course but it is necessary that the place be clean and pleasant.
> You do not want music. Certainly you do not want music.
>
> —*Ernest Hemingway,* "A Clean, Well-lighted Place"

A few years ago, I was lying on a gurney outside an operating room when I realized I was listening to the 1001 Strings' rendition of the Rolling Stones' "(Can't Get No) Satisfaction," brought to me by a car dealer. What if I died on the table, I asked the nurse, and that was my last memory of this life? Wouldn't they please turn it off? "Don't worry," she said, "you'll be asleep soon." Later an emergency room nurse told me that she and others loathed the music, that there had been sabotage, and that the administrator now locked up the controls.

It sounded strangely familiar. But this couldn't have happened before. This could only happen in . . . Brave New World. That was it! I asked my son to bring a copy from home and found it: "The synthetic music plant was working as they entered the hall and left nothing to be desired . . . 'Progress *is* lovely, isn't it?'" The speaker is Lenina Crowne, a model citizen of Aldous Huxley's dystopian[1] hive of general issue happiness. She can't stand silence. "'But it's horrible,' said Lenina, shrinking back from the window. She was appalled by the rushing emptiness of the night . . . 'Let's turn on the radio. Quick!' She reached for the dialing knob on the dashboard and turned it at random." Bernard is a misfit who prefers silence. "'I want to look at the sea in peace,' he said. 'One can't even look with that beastly noise going on.'"

I didn't die, and in my own misfit recovery began to realize that we (or

---

[1] Antiutopian.

RICHARD HILL (b. 1941) is a free-lance writer who regularly contributes to several magazines, including Harper's, Esquire, *the* American Voice, *and* Omni. *He holds a Ph.D. from Florida State University and his recent mystery novel is* Riders on the Storm. *Hill is currently at work on another novel.*

someone) have wired our lives with "beastly noise." Most of the North Carolina ski resorts broadcast music onto the slopes. You have a choice of hard-rock, soft-pop, or "beautiful music" slopes, but not a choice of a quiet slope where you can hear your skis on the snow. I heard about one health club that pipes rock into the swimming pool—and I mean *into* the swimming pool—on underwater speakers. If your hearing is still sound, if you've not already assumed the body-snatcher, glassy rictus of the musical hostage, if, like me, you've had a rude awakening, you'll already know that some kind of music oozes or thumps its way into most of our activities—usually uninvited and too damned loud. Even Musak's turned up the volume.

Musak's original "research" argued its industrial usefulness, advised 　4 low volume, offered only instrumentals, and admitted to situations where even those were inappropriate—such as where workers are expected to think. Now the company offers also "foreground" music—mostly pop vocals at a much louder volume—and new "research" from new hireling scientists showing, no doubt, that the human race has changed drastically just in time to welcome a new marketing gimmick. Musak's imitators, particularly the commercial "beautiful music," "soft pop," Top 40, and other format stations search desperately for listeners—from the kid on the next beach blanket to the corporate giant—who will turn them on and leave them on. And so our stores, offices, public buildings, malls, phone lines, and parking lots resound with music selected for us according to formulas we don't understand for purposes not made clear by people we don't know.

Nor do taste or courtesy play much part in the theater of neighborhoods, apartment buildings, streets, parks, and beaches, where anybody with a few bucks for hardware can implant *his* soundtrack into *your* brain. One Tampa station hired a billboard urging its listeners to "Crank it up!" So abandon conversation, forget bird song, wind, waves, silence. The harbingers of spring are now the thump of pop percussion and the whine of the Top 40 vocalist.

Few of us like this decibel bullying, yet most of us submit. Have we, like Huxley's bottled people, lost our right to choose? Is music now a duty of citizenship rather than an individual option? Why do we put up with it?

Why do they do it to us—besides the obvious motives of the broadcasters themselves? Businesses offer conflicting rationales: one manager said music speeded customers through the store and made room for others; another said it slowed customers so they could buy more. Neither manager seemed ashamed of his attempt to manipulate customers. Both worked for K-Mart. The ski resort manager I interviewed said the music kept his customers from being bored.

A look at the "research" sponsored by the music merchants suggests 　8 little evidence either way. It isn't clear that management at any level understands its use of background music. Nor do they seem to have any notion of what an appropriate volume would be. Once it's turned on, the stuff whines, yelps, moans, shouts, and chatters like some dim relative everyone is politely trying to ignore. It is probably a factor in America's declining productivity; Robert Pirsig suggests this argument in *Zen and the Art of Motorcycle Maintenance*. Worse, this constant exposure to amplified mediocrity seems a threat to our sanity—customers and employees—whether we know it or not.

Unaware? A common response, delivered with a frozen grin, is: "I tune it out." But we're just beginning to understand the physiological and psychological consequences of all the "tuning out" we're forced to do, and to realize that at deeper and significant levels we cannot tune it out, but are absorbing and reacting to every sound, every syllable. Those who appear more relaxed in its presence are usually those who are already addicted to it; purveyors of alcohol, tobacco, chocolate, and coffee can make the same claim (and hire their own researchers). And even if this manipulation does in fact profit merchants, can we afford to let them do it? Has anyone ever asked you if you *wanted* music?

How can any group agree for long about what occasions need what kinds of music, and how loud? What does it say about us and our respect for music that we should even try? If the argument is that it enhances our lives, why not allow people to throw their cologne on us or force-feed us spinach or make us pray for the same reason? Sex enhances our lives, too, but rape's still a crime. How is it that the human race has survived so many centuries without background music if, in fact, it is as indispensable as some would claim?

The sad truth seems to be that many of us have come to need such management, a constant supply of thoughts and moods not our own. The Japanese (who else?) have actually experimented with mood smells to improve worker performance, and one Japanese entrepreneur describes this generation of ska-wired[2] consumerists as Shin Jin Rui, or the New Human Beings.

One day in my old gym, I'd had my lifetime limit of Hall and Oates and 12 yanked the radio plug. What I saw on a young friend's face was very like drug withdrawal. I asked him to describe his feelings. "It [silence] makes me feel [here he shuddered] mellow. My energy's gone. It's like somebody pulled my plug!"

One summer I drove to Cedar Key, Florida, for some quiet, and happened upon a reenactment of a Civil War battle. It was charming for a while. But into that scene drove a kid about eighteen with his Trans-Am vibrating to heavy metal broadcast by that same "crank-it-up" station. He sat in almost total self-absorption, his mating call drowning out the sounds of nineteenth century cannon. He never suspected he wasn't more fascinating than the battle until he was surrounded by members of a Confederate platoon—with

---

[2] Ska: a version of reggae.

fixed bayonets and working weapons but firing blanks. Finally they got attention. "Be quiet!" we were all yelling by then. "Shut up!"

Loud car stereos are a safety hazard as well as noise nuisance. Some are now designed specifically for sheer volume. In one "boom car" contest, the winner generated 154.7 decibels of sheer noise, more than twice as loud as a jet taking off. Emergency sirens measure only 120 decibels, and permanent hearing damage begins at around 115. CBS News reports that California has started issuing tickets.

Can we act only in such extreme cases? Have we forgotten that Americans in particular (Thoreau's different drummers) have a history of resisting any who would dictate our thoughts? Huxley called our century the Age of Noise and saw the "prefabricated din" of radio, in particular, as part of the strategy of merchants to keep us from any kind of spiritual peace that might make their products unnecessary. Milan Kundera and John Updike have examined in their fiction the totalitarian and pornographic abuses of music. One of Kundera's characters describes public music as pursuing her like a pack of hounds. Updike's little aliens regard music as the highest and rarest form of erotic pleasure, which makes their stay on earth much like captivity in a Times Square movie house. This may seem a minority view, but our republic was designed to protect nonconformists—from their government, the "majority," and one another. My freedom to play music stops where your ears begin. John Stuart Mill has already worked it out for us in "On Liberty."

Somebody's bound to ask: "Don't you like music?" I love music. I've played in a symphony orchestra and jazz and blues groups. I've written for *Rolling Stone*. I've been listening to rock 'n' roll since before I stood in line all night for a ticket to see Elvis. Music is important to me. I think we should all be free to listen, or not listen. Music is much too important to turn it into wallpaper or propaganda. Life is too interesting to let it be drowned out by somebody else's soundtrack.

Somebody's bound to say: "There are other issues so much more important—the nuclear threat, world hunger. Isn't this energy wasted on something trivial?" Nobody reading this has ever died from starvation or nuclear disaster; *every*one has been the victim of dozens of daily indignities, muggings, little murders of our own sense of privacy and beauty. Nobody in *Brave New World* was nuked or starved either, but they were spoiled slaves, leading lives of guaranteed managed mediocrity. Pierre DeLattre argues, "The nagging emotion of our times is an almost daily disappointment amounting to grief. Because this emotion does not destroy us quickly and dramatically but erodes us a little at a time, like acid rain eating away at a statue, its cause is not immediately clear to all of us." DeLattre recommends beauty as the focus of a new consciousness.

Maybe I was radicalized that day I had to listen to Olivia Newton-John in the steambath. I'd gone there to relax, not polish my image. The treeneck

towels and guarded the controls told me it was policy,
do, nothing I could do. Phooey. Not long ago, I got a large
op putting everybody in the United States on musical hold.
it's time you did your part. We have nothing to lose but

'er

1. Why does Hill begin with a reference to Aldous Huxley's *Brave New World*? How does that reference enlarge the scope of his complaint? How does it provide a theme for the entire essay?

2. What do you think disturbs Hill most about the presence of uninvited music? Its quality? Its volume? Or are there other issues?

3. "My freedom to play music stops where your ears begin," Hill argues. Do you find this rule reasonable? What are the difficulties of enforcing this rule? Do you think it would convince someone to stop playing loud music?

4. Does Hill view himself as a minority or majority with respect to this issue? What reasons does he give for why we have "wired our lives" with noise? Do you think his reasons are sufficient? For what additional reasons do some people behave like "decibel bullies"?

Discussing the Unit

Suggested Topic for Discussion

The problems of public behavior in this unit cover an area in which manners, customs, and civil rights overlap. Discuss how the difficulties faced by each writer have repercussions that go beyond the issues of rudeness and incivility.

Preparing for Class Discussion

1. As Richard Hill puts it, "*every*one has been the victim of dozens of daily indignities." Do you regard this everyday victimization as trivial or serious? Do you simply put up with these indignities or do you try to do something about them? How do people usually respond to your complaints?

2. Consider the violations of peace and privacy that occur at college. Write down what you believe to be the most serious types of rude or intrusive behavior on campus. Do you think your complaints are shared by many

other students, or would you be considered in the minority? Make
too, about what you think should be done about such violations.

From Discussion to Writing

Think of times when you have been a victim of public space: while
driving, walking, shopping, using mass transit, eating out, or in some
other situation. Choose an experience that you thought involved not
only rudeness or incivility but a violation of your privacy or freedom
of movement. Use this personal experience as the basis of an essay in
which you describe what it was like for you to "alter public space."

8

Sex on Campus: Date or Rape?

Several recent studies reveal that one in every eight female college students is a victim of rape. Of these, more than half were raped by first or casual dates or by romantic acquaintances. Over the past few years, "date rape" has quickly become an issue of major concern on college campuses throughout the United States. In "Dangerous Parties," Paul Keegan returns to his alma mater to find some answers in a highly publicized case in which a college first-year student, after a night of heavy drinking, was allegedly raped by three male students. Keegan examines the reactions of the parties involved in the case, the administration, and other students. He examines, too, the overall atmosphere of campus life — especially the drinking — to see how it contributes to sexually aggressive behavior.

Why do most people, including many university administrators, deny the existence of "date rape"? In "Date Rape: The Story of an Epidemic and Those Who Deny It," Ellen Sweet supplies some answers to this and related questions. She then examines the measures being taken by colleges that do recognize the problem and the ongoing efforts to change attitudes about rape. In doing so, she raises important questions about sex roles and the expectations college students place on each other.

Crime writer Ann Rule provides the bleakest picture yet of the problem. In "Rape on Campus," she reveals that a large number of teenage men and women think it is acceptable behavior for the male to force the female to engage in intercourse if he has paid for the date. She goes on to demonstrate the need for sexual education programs for college students.

As you read the essays, ask yourself how they challenge your own perceptions about what constitutes rape.

PAUL KEEGAN

Dangerous Parties [NEW ENGLAND MONTHLY / February 1988]

I love the University of New Hampshire, its green lawns, its beautiful turn-of-the-century structures, the little paths that snake through the woods to classroom buildings hidden in the trees. I went to college here from 1976 to 1980. It's Everyman's school, ten thousand kids on two hundred acres, cheap and easy to get into for New Hampshire students, expensive and more prestigious for the 39 percent from out of state. Almost everyone can find their niche here, as I eventually did.

But it's the darker side of college life that took me back recently, the side that can emerge at a place like UNH after a night of partying at a bar like the Wildcat. The Wildcat is a pizza-and-beer joint in Durham, a small town that for nine months of the year is overrun by students. Steve Karavasilis, the owner, will pour you a draft beer for a dollar or a pitcher for $3.75. The Wildcat's signature is a wall of windowpanes that creates a huge, moving mosaic of Main Street. That's where guys sit down with a pitcher to watch girls.

Steve has hung a sign clearly stating that you can't be served unless you are at least twenty-one. But somehow, last February 19, on a cold and clear Thursday night, two twenty-year-old sophomores named Chris and Jon, and a nineteen-year-old sophomore named Gordon, sat here and shared several pitchers of beer with a group of friends. The three were buddies who lived on the fourth floor of UNH's Stoke Hall. They were happy-go-lucky guys

---

PAUL KEEGAN (b. 1958) is a contributing editor at New England Monthly. His articles have appeared in many periodicals, including Mother Jones, Down Beat, National Journal, and the Boston Globe.

with a boyish charm and a bag of fraternity pranks. Jon and Gordon had recently become brothers at Sigma Alpha Epsilon. Jon, from Manchester, New Hampshire, was the character of the bunch, a slick talker who always wore his SAE hat, even when he walked to the shower carrying his soap and shaving cream in a six-pack carton. Gordon was tall and good-looking, a little moody, some thought. He was from Rochester, New York. And Chris, of Lexington, Massachusetts, was not a fraternity brother, but he had lots of friends at SAE.

The boys arrived at the Wildcat that Thursday night sometime between nine-thirty and ten o'clock and drank about six beers apiece. At about twelve-fifteen, they went out into the freezing night and headed back to their dorm, where they encountered an eighteen-year-old freshman named Sara who had been drinking heavily at a fraternity party. One by one, each of the three boys had sex with her. As the incident proceeded, witnesses said, Jon bragged in the hallway that he had a "train" going in his room and then gave his friends high fives, as a football player might do after scoring a touchdown.

Sexual assault, if that is what happened here, goes on at every college in America. About one woman student in eight is raped, according to a government survey. Ninety percent of these are victims of "acquaintance rape," defined as "forced, manipulated, or coerced sexual intercourse by a 'friend' or an acquaintance." Its most repugnant extreme is gang rape. Bernice Sandler of the Association of American Colleges says she has documented evidence of more than seventy incidents of this nationwide in the past four or five years. They usually involve fraternities and drugs or alcohol, she says, and the men nearly always contend that it wasn't rape, that they were merely engaged in group sex with a willing partner.

That was precisely the defense used by the UNH boys when they were arrested five days later. Jon and Chris were charged with aggravated felonious sexual assault, punishable by a maximum of seven and a half to fifteen years in prison, and Gordon with misdemeanor sexual assault. All three pleaded innocent, claiming Sara was a willing and active participant in everything that went on. Sara says she had a lot to drink and does not remember what happened.

Like friends of mine who went to other schools, I remember hearing vague tales about such incidents. What makes this case unique is that everyone on campus soon learned the details of what happened that night, and the turmoil that exploded was unlike anything UNH has experienced since the late sixties.

Four days after *Foster's Daily Democrat,* in nearby Dover, mistakenly reported that the boys had confessed to the crime, three life-sized male effigies were hung from a ledge at UNH's Hamilton Smith Hall along with a huge banner that read BEWARE BOYS, RAPE WILL NOT BE TOLERATED. When the accused were allowed to stay on in Stoke Hall, someone sprayed a graffiti message to UNH President Gordon Haaland on the walkway leading to his office: GORDON, WHY DO YOU ALLOW RAPISTS TO STAY ON CAMPUS? And senior Terry Ollila was barred from taking part in the university's judicial proceedings against the three because she was overheard saying, "I want to see these guys strung up by their balls."

Room 127 of Hamilton Smith Hall, where I struggled through Psychology 401, can feel claustrophobic when all of its 170 seats are full. It was here, in late spring, that the controversy, after simmering for months, began to heat up again. Thanks to a shrewd defense lawyer trying to reverse the tide of opinion running against his clients, the normally private student disciplinary hearings were held in public.

Jon, Chris, Gordon, and eleven other witnesses had their backs to the audience as they testified to the five Judicial Board members facing them across a large table. But they could feel the crowd close behind, hear the shuffling of feet, the coughing, the whispering. For four extraordinary evenings, witnesses nervously described what they had seen and heard, and the hearings soon became the hottest show in town. When sophomore John Prescott described how he had interrupted the alleged assault, he could hear women behind him whispering encouragement: "Yeah, good answer." When the testimony became graphic, the crowd gasped. At one point, when the defense began asking about the alleged victim's previous sex life, Sara's father leapt to his feet shouting.

Finally, in the early morning hours of May 7, the board found all three boys not guilty of sexual assault. Gordon, cleared of all charges, wept with relief. Jon and Chris were suspended for the summer and fall terms for violating a university rule entitled "Respect for Others."

It was at this point that the campus, poised at the precipice for months, 12 went over the edge. Four days later, a hundred people, including Sara, turned out for an "educational forum" that turned into a shouting match and led Dan Garvey, the normally easygoing associate dean of students, to storm out of the room. The next day more than two hundred people showed up at a protest demonstration that was crashed by a group of about twenty fraternity members and boys from the fourth floor of Stoke. "Dykes!" they yelled. "Lesbians! Man-haters!" Then it got much uglier. "Look out, we're gonna rape *you* next!" shouted one. "I had Sara last night!" cried another.

Unrattled, the protesters acted out a satire of a rape trial and read a list of demands: the university should nullify the hearings, make a public apology to Sara, and expel all three boys. As the group began marching to the office of Dean of Student Affairs J. Gregg Sanborn, they encountered Sanborn on the sidewalk. More than a dozen of them surrounded him, linked arms, and said they wouldn't let him go until he promised to respond to their demands.

Sanborn agreed, but in his response he defended the university's handling of the affair. Demonstrators marched to his office, announced they were relieving him of his duties, and hung a HELP WANTED sign from the flagpole. After a weekend of altercations between demonstrators, fraternity members, and other students, campus police arrested eleven protesters for criminal trespass. As the semester ended, a shaken President Haaland wrote an open letter advising everyone to return to UNH next fall "ready to examine our moral behavior."

Until then, I had followed the public agonies of my school from a distance. Incidents like the one in Stoke Hall were rare, I knew, and most nights at UNH were probably filled with the warm times among good friends that I remembered so vividly. Still, each new development also triggered less pleasant memories about college life, until finally I decided that I had to go back and find out exactly what was going on at my old school — or, for that matter, at virtually every school. In truth, though, I suspected I already knew.

When I moved into Stoke Hall as a freshman, in the fall of 1976, the place terrified me. It is a hulking, Y-shaped, eight-story monster, made of brick and concrete, crammed with 680 students. We called it the Zoo. It was named after Harold W. Stoke, president of UNH during the baby-boom years that made high-rise dorms necessary on campuses across America. After a tearful good-bye to my parents, I introduced myself to my roommate, who was stoned, and then I ventured into the hallway to meet my new neighbors. They seemed much older than I, standing in front of their open doors bragging to each other about how much beer they'd drunk last night and how many times they'd gotten laid.

I lasted about two weeks in Stoke, then found an opening in another dorm. My new roommate was Ed, a born-again Christian with a terrible sinus condition who would sit on the edge of his bed and play his guitar, accompanying himself by wheezing through his nose. He was engaged in this favorite hobby the cold January afternoon I returned from the holidays with four friends. My buddies pushed me into the room, laughing and screaming and dancing and tackling each other. Devout Ed looked up from his guitar in disgust and amazement, wheezed, and said, "What happened to *you?*"

What was happening to me, dear Ed, wherever you are, is that I was learning to drink, one of the two major components of a college education. The other, of course, is sex, and soon enough I learned about that, too.

When I returned to Durham last fall, I wasn't surprised to discover that some things don't change. Drinking is still the number one social activity, and beer the beverage of choice. As for sex, you want to try it but you're scared of it, so you usually get drunk before deciding anything. Thus, it's common to get drunk without having sex, but rare to have sex without being drunk.

Drinking remains a surefire way of getting to know someone in a hurry. This is necessary partly because of the tendency of college kids to travel in

16

20

packs. Everybody goes to parties, not on dates, to get to know people, and at that age, the last thing you want to be is different. There are also practical considerations: hardly anyone has a car. The students' universe is Durham and the campus, for at least the first two years. And on weekends, there isn't anything to do on campus but party.

What has changed dramatically, however, is where the kids party. Today's students were incredulous at my stories about the huge keg blowouts in our dorms. UNH banned kegs from dorms in 1979, my senior year, when New Hampshire raised the drinking age. Then, in 1986, the university stopped serving alcohol at the student union pub when it found itself in the embarrassing position of selling liquor to minors that it couldn't seem to keep out. This leaves just two options for freshmen and sophomores who aren't lucky enough to know an upperclassman with an apartment: they can drink in their rooms with the door shut, or they can go to fraternity parties.

Frats were decidedly uncool in the sixties but began to come back in the mid-seventies. During my visit I couldn't help but notice all the new frat houses that had popped up. Today, UNH has fourteen frats with twelve hundred members. Their growing influence seems to have worsened the drinking problem. "All the drinking has gone underground," Paul Gowen, chief of the Durham police, told me. "At least bars are controlled environments where they're obligated to cut you off if you have too much to drink. But wearing a headband and marking it every time you chugalug a sixteen-ounce beer is not exactly what I would call a controlled environment."

Madbury Road, also known as Fraternity Row, looks exactly as you might expect: aristocratic old houses line one side of the street, set back from the road on small hills, with wide lawns stretching in front. Several frat members told me that a spate of bad publicity in the last few years over the usual offenses — alcohol poisonings, vandalism — has made this a period of retrenchment for the Greeks. Parties are now smaller and more exclusive. Posted outside the door are signs that say BROTHERS AND INVITED GUESTS ONLY. "Invited guests" means girls, preferably freshmen. The logic is circular: girls go to frat parties because they're the only place to drink and meet boys, who, in turn, joined the frat because that's where the parties are where you drink and meet girls.

Fraternity Row is only half a block up the hill from Stoke Hall. Forty percent of Stoke's residents last spring were freshman girls — 250 of them — which makes the dorm an integral, if unofficial, part of the Greek system. Just out of high school, freshman girls are not yet wise to the ways of fraternity boys. On any Thursday, Friday, or Saturday night on Madbury Road, after about ten o'clock, you'll see clusters of girls marching up from Stoke and the other dorms beyond, toward whichever houses are having parties that night.

There they find the beer, and the boys. Because the fraternity houses stand on private property, police can't go into a frat without probable cause. To protect themselves from the occasional sting operation, most frats now post at the door an enormous boy-man with a thick neck who, with deadly seriousness, asks every girl who enters the same question: "Are you affiliated with or related to anyone affiliated with the liquor commission or any other law enforcement agency?" The girls will either say "No" or "Jeez, you've asked me that *three* times" before he lets them through.

One Friday night last fall I asked a fraternity member to take me to a party, and he agreed on the condition that I not identify him or the fraternity. We met at about eleven o'clock and walked to the frat house for what is known, without a trace of irony, as a Ladies' Tea. We squeezed past about eight guys standing near the door and descended a flight of stairs into the darkness. My first sensation was the overpowering stench of stale beer, and when we reached the bottom, I could see its source. Enormous puddles covered most of the basement floor. Standing in it were a couple of hundred kids jammed into a room the size of a two-car garage, picking up their feet and dropping them into the puddles — dancing — as rock blasted from two enormous speakers. The only illumination came from two flashing lights, one blue, the other yellow.

We pushed our way toward a long wooden bar with a line of frat boys behind it. They stood watching a wave of girls surging toward the corner where the beer was being poured, each girl holding an empty plastic cup in her outstretched hand. Two boys were pouring beers as fast as they could. My guide fetched two beers and told me one hundred tickets to the party were sold to girls, at three dollars apiece. Adding in girlfriends and sorority girls, he said, there were probably between one hundred fifty and two hundred girls in the house. "How many guys?" I shouted. "Oh, probably about seventy."

I asked how many kegs they'd bought tonight, and he led me behind the bar, past the sign that said BROTHERS ONLY BEHIND BAR — NO EXCEPTIONS. In the corner stood a walk-in wooden refrigerator with a "Bud Man" cartoon character painted on the door. Twelve empty kegs were stacked outside it. We opened the refrigerator and found fourteen more fresh kegs of Busch, their blue seals unbroken. Two others were hooked up to hoses that ran out to the bar. My host told me that Anheuser-Busch has student representatives on campus who take the orders, and the local distributor's truck pulls right up to the back door to drop the kegs off. A guy pouring beer said they'd probably go through twenty kegs tonight.

I asked a stocky senior whose shirt was unbuttoned to the middle of a hairless chest whether his frat gets into much trouble. "Oh, once in a while there will be some problems," he said. "You know, if somebody rapes somebody or if there's an alcohol thing." When I asked about the rape controversy he started to get angry.

"Everybody's singling fraternity guys out," he said. "I took a women's studies class last spring because I heard it would be easy. Ha. There were about twenty-five girls and three guys. They started giving me all this shit just because I was in a fraternity. What was I going to say? 'Yes, I think rape is a good thing'? I don't need that shit. So I dropped it and took Introduction to Film," he concluded. "All I had to do for it was sit there and watch movies."

I asked if he thought the rape issue was mostly about girls having sex and then changing their minds the next day. "Absolutely," he said. "I'll bet you guys twenty dollars each I could get laid tonight, no problem. But you know what? If I'm in bed with a girl and she says, 'I'm tired,' and then goes to sleep, you know what I'm thinking? I'm thinking handcuffs."

We walked back into the crowd and I asked where the bathroom was. My guide pointed to a door in a dark corner. When I pushed it open, I was assaulted by the stench of urine, and realized I was standing in a shower. Bits of soap were scattered around. A boy stood peeing on the tile floor. "So this is the urinal," I said, trying not to breathe. "Yep," he said, zipping up his pants, "just aim into the drain."

Later, at around one-thirty, I counted five couples on the dance floor making out. "You've Got to Give It to Me" by J. Geils was playing. Just before I left, I noticed a boy dancing with a very attractive girl. They were bathed in yellow light, circling a beer puddle. Her back was to me, but he saw that I was looking at her. The boy smiled broadly at me, knowingly, then looked at the girl, then back at me. It was all he could do to keep from giving me the thumbs-up sign.

That was a typical weekend night; what happened on the traumatic night of February 19, 1987, I pieced together from police records, the testimony of witnesses, and conversations with most of the participants.

On that night, a freshman named Karen decided she was not in the mood to party with the other girls on the fourth floor of Stoke Hall. She was still upset about her grandfather, who had died in the fall. Also, a boy she liked was not treating her well. Karen told the others she'd rather just stay in her room and study. Her friend Sara, however, would have none of it. "Come on," she told Karen. "You never have any fun. What you need is to go out with your friends and have a good time."

This was typical Sara. She was popular, cute, fun-loving, and smart — she'd had a 3.9 grade point average the previous semester. She planned to be a biology major, and her friends marveled at how easily subjects like botany and chemistry came to her. But Sara was also a real partyer. It was not unusual for her to get everybody else on the floor psyched up to go out. And that night, excitement on the fourth floor was running high. There was a Ladies' Tea at Pi Kappa Alpha, a fraternity behind Stoke. The mood was infectious. Finally, Karen smiled and gave in.

Sara was in her room with her best friend, Michele, drinking rum and Cokes and listening to Steve Winwood. By the time they left for the party forty minutes later, Sara had consumed two rum and Cokes, and had finished up with a straight shot. Finally, a little after ten, Karen and two other girls, Noelle and Tracy, were ready, and all five headed out into the cold night. The temperature was hovering around zero as they walked to the three-story frat house they called Pike.

The basement wasn't yet crowded. Sara and Karen squeezed up to the small curved bar. Each grabbed a plastic cup of beer and challenged the other to a chugging contest. Karen won. They laughed and went back for another. As the night wore on, Sara became preoccupied with a Pike brother named Hal who was pouring beer. Michele noticed that Sara was drinking fast so she'd have an excuse to return and talk with him. But Hal acted cold, which hurt Sara's feelings.

Within an hour, Michele saw Sara dancing wildly. Later, she saw her leaning against a post, looking very spaced out. When Michele asked her something, Sara didn't seem to hear her. Linda, a freshman who also lived at Stoke, was looking for a friend when she noticed Sara leaning against the wall. "Where's Rachel?" Linda shouted. When Sara didn't respond, Linda repeated the question, this time louder. Sara merely stared straight ahead. Finally, Linda shook her and screamed, "*Where is she?*" This elicited only a mumble, so Linda gave up.

At about twelve-thirty, Michele, Noelle, and Tracy decided to leave, but Sara said she wanted to stay longer. Karen and Sara agreed there was no reason to leave, since they were both having a good time. They assumed they'd go back together later. At length, Karen staggered upstairs, threw up, and passed out. When she awakened she was lying on the floor near the bathroom. By then, the party was over and Sara was gone.

At about twelve-thirty that night, Jon, Chris, and Gordon were returning to Stoke after their night at the Wildcat. The three sophomores were probably legally intoxicated but not out of control. Chris decided to go up to the fifth floor, while Jon and Gordon went to the fourth, where all three lived. They headed to one of the girls' wings, and on the way, dropped their pants around their ankles and raced down the hall, a favorite prank. They stopped to visit Laura, a dark-haired freshman who used to date Jon, and her roommate, Linda, who had tried to talk to Sara at the party. No one was in, so they left a note: "We came to see you in our boxer shorts — Jon and Chris."

On the way back to their wing, the two boys saw a girl in the hallway. She was looking for Scott, she said. Noticing her shirt tail sticking out of the zipper of her pants, Gordon tugged on it playfully and said, "What's this?" Both boys laughed.

Before going into his room, Jon asked the girl if he could have a good-night hug, which, he says, she gave him. He then asked for a good-night kiss, and she complied. When the couple backed toward the door, Gordon decided to leave the two of them alone. Without exchanging a word with her, Jon had sex with the girl in his room. After about twenty minutes, he walked down the hall to Gordon's room, where Gordon was already in bed. "I just did it with a girl; she's really horny," Jon told him. Still in his underwear, Gordon decided to check out what was happening. He says he entered Jon's room out of curiosity, without any sexual intentions. But once inside, he changed his mind.

Meanwhile, Jon raced up to the fifth floor to tell his roommate, Chris, 44 what was going on. The two went downstairs to their room. When they reached the door, the boys were surprised to see Linda and Laura, the girls they had left the note for about an hour earlier.

Wordlessly, Chris slipped into the room while Jon, in jeans and T-shirt, stayed outside with the girls, casually discussing the night's partying. The girls saw nothing unusual about Chris going into his own room at one-thirty in the morning, and Jon was being his normal smooth-talking self. But when they drifted near the door, according to the girls' account, Jon said, "Don't go in. Gordy's in there doing really bad things with a drunk girl." (Jon denies using the words *bad things* and *drunk*.)

Oh, *really?* the girls said. "We were kidding around with Jon," recalls Laura. "It wasn't like, 'Oh my God, that's awful.' Usually, if you're in someone's room, it's because you want to be." Even though Chris was in the room, too, it's not terribly unusual to go to bed while two people are having sex in the bunk below you. What the girls didn't know was that it was Chris having sex with the girl while Gordon (whose activities with her had not included actual penetration) waited inside for them to leave so he could sneak back to his own room.

Soon Laura and Linda said good-night to Jon. As they passed John Prescott's room, they saw that the sophomore resident assistant was at his desk studying. Laura was a good friend of his, so they stopped in. After some small talk, the girls half-jokingly asked him how he could let such wild stuff go on in his wing and told him about Gordon and the drunk girl.

"It's not my job to monitor people's sex lives," Prescott told them. "But 48 I'll look into it anyway, out of the goodness of my heart."

Prescott, a hotel administration and economics major from Hudson, New Hampshire, went to the room and knocked. When no one answered, he opened the door and saw two figures silhouetted on a bed. (He would later learn it was Jon, having a second round with the girl.) Prescott also saw Chris, sitting on a couch next to the bed, watching. (Chris maintains he was simply getting dressed.) According to Prescott, Chris looked up laughing and whispered, "Get out," waving him away. After telling Chris several times to come out into the hall and being told to go away, Prescott barked, "Get out here *now*." Chris at last obeyed. "I was tense and nervous," Prescott remembers. "You don't confront your friends like that all the time."

Prescott asked if the girl had passed out, and Chris said no. "I want that girl out of the room," Prescott said.

"Oh, come on," Chris replied.

"Is she really drunk?" Prescott asked.   52

Chris nodded and laughed, Prescott says, although Chris denies this.

"Do you know that what you're doing could be considered rape?" Prescott said.

"No, it's not," Chris answered.

"You guys are going to learn one of these days that someone is going to   56 wake up the next day and think that what happened was wrong, even if she wanted to be in there," Prescott said. "I want that girl out of the room." Chris finally agreed, but said he had to talk to her first.

Despite his role as the enforcer and voice of reason, Prescott nonetheless thought the events on his floor were entertaining — so much so that he went to see two of his friends and told them what had happened. "'Wow! No way! Unbelievable!'" Prescott remembers them saying. "We were all laughing. It was funny, in a sick kind of way."

As Prescott and his friends went out into the hallway, Jon emerged from the room and walked toward them. When he reached the group, two of the boys said, he gave Prescott's friends high fives. Then he continued past them, slapping the air at knee level, giving low fives to other members of the imaginary team.

Prescott says Jon proceeded to tell the three of them in great detail what he had done with the girl and how he had gone to get Gordon and Chris. All three remember that during this conversation Jon told them he had a "train" going in his room. (Jon denies both the high fives and the train reference.) As the boys were talking, Linda and Laura returned, "not because we were worried about what had happened," Laura remembers. "We were still just hanging out." Then Joe, another freshman on the floor, joined the group. A discussion ensued between the five boys and two girls about whether the boys' behavior was wrong. "Someone said, 'Hey, a drunk girl is fair game,'" Laura recalls, "which made Linda and me a little defensive, obviously." One of the boys suggested that maybe Joe could "get lucky, too." Joe walked toward the door — just to see what was happening, he says.

Inside, Chris was now alone with the girl. She got dressed, and for the   60 first time there was verbal communication: Chris told her a lot of people were in the hallway talking about them and watching the door. He carefully explained how she could avoid them. Just as Joe reached the room, the door opened and the crowd saw a girl walk out, her shirt untucked. Without looking up, she disappeared into the stairwell.

To their astonishment, everyone recognized Sara, the girl who lived on the same floor. They had all simply assumed it was someone they didn't know, maybe a high school girl. Suddenly the atmosphere in the hallway changed. Linda and Laura were outraged. "You *assholes!*" one of them screamed. "How could you *do* such a thing?" No one was more shocked than Jon: "You mean you *know* her?" It was at that moment that Jon and Chris heard her name for the first time.

By now there were six witnesses, two of them girls who didn't seem to understand the boys' point of view. This was trouble. Chris and Jon decided to talk to Sara to forestall misunderstanding.

When Giselle, Sara's roommate, heard voices calling "Sara, Sara, Sara," she thought she was dreaming. But when she looked up from her bed, she saw two boys bent over her roommate's bed, shaking Sara's shoulder. "What the hell are you doing in here?" she demanded.

"We have to talk to Sara," they said. "It's very important."   64

Giselle got up. Sara was lying on her side with a nightshirt on. "You okay?" Giselle asked, shaking her gently. Sara nodded. "Do you want to get up?" she asked. Sara shook her head: no. "I don't think she should get up," Giselle said.

But they pleaded with her, so Giselle shrugged and went back to bed. A moment later, she saw Sara standing in the middle of the room, wrapping herself in a blanket. One of the boys held her left arm with his right arm. This must have been, Giselle thought later, to prevent her from falling back into bed.

When the three were out in the hallway, Chris and Jon say, they all agreed on what had happened so there could be no misunderstanding later. Chris then suggested that Jon leave so he could talk to Sara more easily. Alone, they began kissing. They walked a few steps and opened the stairwell door. Then, at some time between three and four in the morning, beneath a window through which a slice of Pi Kappa Alpha was visible, near a heating vent painted the same blue as the walls around them, Chris and Sara got down on the landing and had sex again.

What is most puzzling about the way the kids in Stoke reacted to the   68
incident is that for at least three days, until Sara first spoke with a counselor, no one called it rape. Even Prescott, who had used the term when he talked to Chris outside the room, insists that his main concern was the *perception* that it was rape, not whether it actually was. "These guys were my friends. My concern was *not* for the woman in that room. My concern was for the men. But look where it got me. Now when I see Gordon and say hi, he just gives me a blank look."

Prescott is thin and earnest-looking, with short blond hair and an angular face. Clearly, the incident has taken its toll on him, yet he talks about it willingly. Over the weekend, he told a friend what had happened, setting off the chain reaction of gossip that eventually led to Sara herself; only then did she go to the police. But Prescott's motives, he freely admits, were entirely base. "You know why I told him?" Prescott says today. "I wanted to astonish him."

But why didn't Prescott consider the possibility that the girl in the room was raped? "I just assumed she was willing, since I didn't know any differently," he says. "I saw her walk out of the room. Look, that's how sex happens here. Most scoops happen after parties, and guys go to parties to scoop."

But *three* guys? "It doesn't surprise me that much," he says. "You hear stories about that kind of thing all the time. I don't expect it to happen, but I'm not ignorant that it goes on. I'm not naive. My fault was in not going to see her *right* away, when she walked back to her room. Then there would be no question. I keep asking myself why I didn't. I don't know. I was like a pendulum swinging back and forth, and finally I just had to try to look at this objectively and make a judgment." He stares into space. "You know, I still can't make one."

Linda, who was one of the witnesses who recognized Sara when she 72 emerged from the room, is transferring to another school. Last spring she took one look at the huge crowds at the Judicial Board hearings and walked away. The next day she was convinced that telling her story was the right thing to do; now she's not so sure. Fraternity members are mad at her, and she's disillusioned about the socal life at UNH. "I guess rape happens all the time here," she says, sitting on the bed in her dorm room, wearing shorts and a UNH sweatshirt. "You know, at home, I'd get really drunk and black out and wake up at my boyfriend's house. It wouldn't matter because I was with friends. When I came to school here, people would tell me, 'Linda, don't get so drunk. You're a pretty girl. People may want to take advantage of you.'" She looks down at her hands in her lap and says softly, "I didn't believe that anyone would do something like that. But it's true, they will."

It was a brilliant September day, warm and sunny, when I at last began to feel good about my old school again. President Haaland had called a special convocation to undertake the moral reexamination he had promised in the spring. Sara had transferred to another school; Jon and Chris would soon plead guilty to misdemeanor sexual assault, for which they would each serve two months in prison. The court would also compel them to write a letter of apology to Sara. The misdemeanor charge against Gordon would be dropped altogether.

"Universities have thrived because they are driven by a core set of values," Haaland told the crowd of three thousand. "These shared values are free inquiry, intellectual honesty, personal integrity, and respect for human dignity." Then he announced a series of concrete steps: to make the job of coordinating the sexual-assault program a full-time position; to publicize sexual assault cases; to improve lighting, continue the escort service for women, hire a full-time coordinator for the Greek system, and improve conditions in Stoke Hall. At the end, everybody sang the UNH alma mater: "New Hampshire, alma mater/All hail, all hail to thee!"

At the outdoor reception following the convocation some of the demonstrators who had trapped him on the sidewalk now chatted amiably with Dean Sanborn. "It just floored me that the administration got up there and actually said the word *rape*," said one. "Last year we couldn't even get them to say the word *woman*." The demonstrators, Sanborn told me, "deserve some credit for the change that's occurring."

I wish I could end the story there, when the sky was blue and everything 76 seemed fine again. But then I made one last trip to Durham. Rape crisis programs and well-lit pathways are important, of course, but they don't answer the question that occurred to me when I met some of this year's freshman class.

Ogre, as his friends call him, is a short, compact freshman whose boxers stick out from beneath his gray football shorts. On the door of his room is a sign that says FISH DEFENSE HQ, and if you ask him about it he'll tell you with a deadpan look that mutant radioactive fish with lungs are attacking us all, that they've already got Peter Tosh[1] and John F. Kennedy. If it weren't for Ogre's regiment, consisting of Opus and Garfield, his stuffed dolls, they'd probably have gotten him, too. Ogre is a funny kid.

While I chatted with Ogre in his room, we were joined by a thin fellow with a blond crewcut, wearing a T-shirt with BUTTHOLE SURFERS silk-screened across three identical images of a bloated African belly with a tiny penis below it. His eyelids drooped: our visitor was zonked. I asked him who the Butthole Surfers were, and he explained they were punk musicians, "not hard-core punk, but definitely influenced by hard-core, for sure." The subject soon turned to acquaintance rape, and the Buttonhole Surferite said he'd never heard of it. Ogre had. "You know, those notices we've been getting in our mailbox about rape, with the phony scene where she says no and he says yes," Ogre explained. "Oh, yeah," the kid nodded.

Then Ogre summed up what he'd learned from the incident last spring: "You don't shit where you sleep," he said. "You don't have sex with someone in your dorm. It causes too many problems. You've got to face them the next day."

Ogre had been in college only two weeks when he made those remarks, 80 so there's hope that eventually he'll grow up. Perhaps he will even think of other metaphors for making love. For my old school — and, I'd guess, for far too many others — the question is, What will he do in the meantime?

[1] Jamaican reggae musician and singer who often performed with Bob Marley; Tosh was shot to death in 1987.

Points to Consider

1. As Keegan reports, "Drinking is still the number one social activity" at the University of New Hampshire. To what extent did excessive drinking contribute to the rape?

2. At least one fraternity brother thought "the rape issue was mostly about girls having sex and then changing their minds the next day." What does such a statement reveal about some of the prevailing attitudes toward campus rape?

3. Resident assistant John Prescott insisted that "his main concern was the *perception* that it was rape, not whether it actually was." What does Prescott's comment mean? Do you think he believed a rape was being committed?

4. What is your response to the university's action following the rape? Were the rights of the victim protected? Were the rights of the accused upheld? Were you surprised by the Judicial Board's decision to find all three of the accused not guilty of sexual assault?

ELLEN SWEET

Date Rape: The Story of an Epidemic and Those Who Deny It [MS. / October 1985]

It was the beginning of spring break when I was a junior. I was in good spirits and had been out to dinner with an old friend. We returned to his college [dorm]. There were some seniors on the ground floor, drinking beer, playing bridge. I'm an avid player, so we joined them, joked around a lot. One of them, John, wasn't playing, but he was interested in the game. I found him attractive. We talked, and it turned out we had a mutual friend, shared experiences. It was getting late, and my friend had gone up to bed, so John offered to see me safely home. We took our time, sat outside talking for a while. Then he said we could get inside one of the most beautiful campus buildings, which was usually locked at night. I went with him. Once we were inside, he kissed me. I didn't resist, I was excited. He kissed me again. But

ELLEN SWEET (b. 1942) is currently managing editor of Fifty Plus. *She was formerly a senior editor of* Ms., *where she coordinated the Ms. Magazine Campus Project on Sexual Assault. Sweet was also a consulting editor of a book on the same subject —* I Never Called It Rape *(1988).*

when he tried for more, I said no. He just grew completely silent. I couldn't get him to talk to me any more. He pinned me down and ripped off my pants. *I couldn't believe it was happening to me . . .*

Let's call this Yale graduate Judy. Her experience and her disbelief, as she describes them, are not unique. Gretchen, another student victim of date rape (or acquaintance rape, as it is also called), had known for five years the man who invited her to an isolated vacation cabin and then raped her. "I considered him my best friend," she says on a Stanford University videotape used in discussions of the problem. "I couldn't believe it. *I couldn't believe it was actually happening to me.*"

Such denial, the inability to believe that someone they know could have raped them, is a common reaction of victims of date rape, say psychologists and counselors who have researched the topic and treated these women. In fact, so much silence surrounds this kind of crime that many women are not even aware that they have been raped. In one study, Mary P. Koss, a psychology professor at Kent State University, Ohio, asked female students if they had had sexual intercourse against their will through use of or threat of force (the minimal legal definition of rape). Of those who answered yes, only 57 percent went on to identify their experience as rape. Koss also identified the other group (43 percent) as those who hadn't even acknowledged the rape to themselves.

"I can't believe it's happening on our campus," is usually the initial response to reports such as Koss's. She also found that one in eight women students had been raped, and another one in four were victims of attempted rape. Since only 4 percent of all those reported the attack, Koss concluded that "at least ten times more rapes occur among college students than are reflected in official crime statistics." (Rape is recognized to be the most underreported of all crimes, and date rape is among the least reported, least believed, and most difficult to prosecute, second only to spouse rape.)

Working independently of Koss, researchers at Auburn University, Alabama, and more recently, University of South Dakota and St. Cloud State University, Minnesota, all have found that one in five women students were raped by men they knew.

Koss also found a core group of highly sexually aggressive men (4.3 percent) who use physical force to compel women to have intercourse but who are unlikely to see their act as rape. These "hidden rapists" have "oversubscribed" to traditional male roles, she says. They believe that aggression is normal and that women don't really mean it when they say no to sexual advances. Such men answer "True" to statements like "most women are sly and manipulating when they want to attract a man," "a woman will only respect a man who will lay down the law to her," and "a man's got to show the woman who's boss right from the start or he'll end up henpecked."

In Koss's current study, one respondent who answered yes to a question about obtaining intercourse through physical force, wrote in the comment, "I didn't rape the chick, she was enjoying it and responding," and later, "I feel that sex is a very pleasant way to relieve stress. Especially when there are no strings attached."

"He acted like he had a right, like he *didn't believe me,*" says a coed from Auburn University on a videotaped dramatization of date rape experiences. And several weeks later, when she confronts him, saying he forced her, he says no, she wanted it. "You raped me," she finally tells him. And the picture freezes on his look of incredulity.

Barry Burkhart, a professor of psychology at Auburn, who has also studied sexual aggression among college men, found that 10 percent had used physical force to have intercourse with a woman against her will, and a large majority admitted to various other kinds of aggression. "These are ordinary males operating in an ordinary social context," he says. "So what we conclude is that there's something wrong with that social context."   8

The something wrong is that our culture fosters a "rape supportive belief system," according to social psychologist Martha Burt. She thinks that "there's a large category of 'real' rapes, and a much smaller category of what our culture is willing to call a 'real' rape. The question is, how does the culture manage to write off all those other rapes?" The way it's done, says Burt, currently director of the Social Services Research Center at the Urban Institute in Washington, D.C., is by believing in a series of myths about rape, including:

- It didn't really happen (the woman was lying);
- Women like rape (so there's no such thing as rape);
- Yes, it happened, but no harm was done (she wasn't a virgin; she wasn't white);
- Women provoke it (men can't control themselves);
- Women deserve it anyway.

It's easy to write off date rapes with such myths, coupled with what Burt calls our culture's "adversarial sexual beliefs": the gamesmanship theory that everybody is out for what they can get, and that all sexual relationships are basically exploitive and predatory. In fact, most victims of date rape initially blame themselves for what happened, and almost none report it to campus authorities. And most academic institutions prefer to keep it that way, judging from the lack of surveys on date rape — all of which makes one wonder if they don't actually blame the victim, too.

As long as such attacks continue to be a "hidden" campus phenomenon, unreported and unacknowledged by many college administrators, law enforcement personnel, and students, the problem will persist. Of course, the term has become much better known in the three years since *Ms.* reported on the prevalence of experiences such as Judy's and Gretchen's. (See "Date Rape: A Campus Epidemic?" September 1982.) It has been the subject of talk shows such as *The Donahue Show* and TV dramas (*Cagney and Lacey*). But for most people it remains a contradiction in terms. "Everybody has a stake in denying that it's happening so often," says Martha Burt. "For women, it's self-protective . . . if only bad girls get raped, then I'm personally safe. For men, it's the denial that 'nice' people like them do it."

The fault has not entirely been that of the institutions. "Ten years ago, we were telling women to look over your shoulder when you go out at night and lock your doors," says Py Bateman, director of a nationally known rape education program in Seattle, Alternatives to Fear. The prevailing myth was that most rapes were committed by strangers in dark alleys.

"If you have to think that sixty to eighty percent of rape is by people you know — that's hard to deal with," says Sylvia Callaway, who directed the Austin, Texas, Rape Crisis Center for more than eight years before leaving last July. "No rape center in a university community would be surprised that the university is not willing to deal with the problem."

Statistics alone will not solve the problem of date rape, but they could help bring it out into the open. Which is why *Ms.* undertook the first nationwide survey on college campuses. The *Ms.* Magazine Campus Project on Sexual Assault, directed by Mary P. Koss at Kent State and funded by the National Center for the Prevention and Control of Rape, reached more than seven thousand students at a nationally representative sample of thirty-five schools, to find out how often, under what circumstances, and with what aftereffects a wide range of sexual assaults, including date rape, took place.

Preliminary results are now ready, and the information is no surprise. Participating schools were promised anonymity, but each will receive the results applying to its student body. Our hope is that the reaction of "we can't believe it's happening on our campus" will be followed by "what can we do about it — now."

Just how entrenched is denial of this problem today? One gauge might be the difficulty our own researchers had in persuading schools to let us on campus. For every college that approved our study, two others rejected it. Their reasons (in writing and in telephone conversations) were themselves instructive: "we don't want to get involved," "limited foreseeable benefit," "too volatile a topic," "have not had any problems in this area," "worried about publicity," "can't allow surveys in classroom," "just can't invest the time now," "would be overintrusive," "don't want to be left holding the bag if something goes wrong."

Several schools rejected the study on the basis that filling out the questionnaire might upset some students, and that we were not providing adequate follow-up counseling. (Researchers stayed on campus for at least a day after the distribution of the questionnaire, gave students listings of

12

16

counselors or rape crisis centers to consult if anything upset them, and offered to meet with school personnel to brief them.) But isn't it less upsetting for a student to recognize and admit that she has been the victim of an acquaintance rape than to have buried the trauma of that rape deep inside herself?

"It's a Catch-22 situation. You want a survey to publicize a problem that has tremendous psychological implications. And the school says, 'Don't do it, because it will get people psychologically upset,'" admits John Jung, who heads the human subjects review committee at California State University/Long Beach (a school that declined our study).

One wonders just who are the "people" who will get most psychologically upset: the students, or their parents who pay for their educations, or the administrators who are concerned about the school's image. "There may have been an episode here," said John Hose, executive assistant to the president of Brandeis University, "but there is no cause célèbre surrounding the issue. In such cases, the reaction of Student Affairs is to encourage the student to be in touch with her parents and to take legal action."

"Student Affairs" at Brandeis is headed by Rodger Crafts, who moved   20 to this post about a year ago from the University of Rhode Island. "I don't think we have a significant problem here because we have a sophisticated and intelligent group of students," said Dean Crafts. As for the University of Rhode Island, more students there are "first generation college attenders," as he put it, and therefore have "less respect" for other people. Vandalism and physical harm are more likely to occur with "lower educational levels." Respect for other people goes along with "intelligence level."

Back at the University of Rhode Island, the counseling center is sponsoring a twelve-week support and therapy group this fall for male students who are coercive and abusive in their relationships with women. Even though Nancy Carlson, director of Counseling and Career Services, is enthusiastic about such programs and workshops she notes, "the awareness about date rape has been a long time coming."

Another school where administrators were the last to confront the challenge to their school's self-image is Yale. Last year, two student publications reported instances of date rape on campus that surprised students, faculty, and administration. "There are no full statistics available on rape between students at Yale anywhere. . . . There is no mention of rape in the 1983–1984 Undergraduate Regulations. There is no procedure for a victim to file a formal complaint of rape with the university. But there is rape between students at Yale," wrote Sarah Oates in the *Yale Daily News*. Partly in response to such charges, current Yale undergraduate regulations now list "sexual harassment" under "offenses that are subject to disciplinary action" — but still no mention of rape.

Yale students brave enough to bring a charge of sexual harassment may go before the Yale College Executive Committee, a specially convened group of faculty, administrators, and students that can impose a series of penalties, graduated in severity, culminating in expulsion. All its hearings and decisions are kept secret (but can in theory be subpoenaed in a court of law). But Michael McBride, current chair of the committee, told me that cases of date rape have come up during the past year, leading in one instance to a student being asked to "resign" from the university, and in another, the conclusion that there was not "sufficient evidence." (In Judy's case, described at the beginning of this article, the senior she charged was penalized by being denied the privilege of graduating with his class. But she claims that after he demanded that the case be reconsidered, he was fully exonerated.) Said McBride, "What surprised me the most was how complicated these cases are. It's only one person's word against another's. It's amazing how different their perceptions can be."

Judy chose to take her case before the Executive Committee rather than   24
report it to the local police, because she felt she would have complete confidentiality and quick action. Actually, there were many delays. And then, because the man she accused hired a lawyer, she was forced to hire one too. As a result, the meeting felt very much like a jury trial to her, complete with cross-examinations that challenged her truthfulness and raised excruciatingly embarrassing questions.

Judy's lawyer felt that such painful questions were necessary. But it seems as if the lesson feminists in the sixties and seventies worked so hard and successfully to make understood — not to blame the victim for stranger rape — is one that will have to be learned all over again in the case of acquaintance rape. Only this time, the woman who reports the rape suffers a triple victimization. Not only is she attacked and then not believed, but she carries the added burden of losing faith in her own judgment and trust in other people.

In a recently published study of jurors in rape trials, University of Illinois sociologist Barbara Reskin found that jurors were less likely to convict a man if the victim knew him. "Consent is the preferred rape defense and gets the highest acquittal rates," Reskin observes. "In a date rape situation, I would think the jury would assume that the woman had already accepted his invitation in a romantic sense. It would be a matter of how *much* did she consent to."

Personal characteristics also influence jurors, Reskin says. Those she studied couldn't imagine that certain men would commit a rape: if they were attractive, had access to sexual partners such as a girlfriend or a wife. More often than not, they'd say, "But he doesn't look like a rapist." Reskin imagines that this pattern would be "magnified in date rape, because these are men who could get a date, they're not complete losers."

It may turn out that solutions to the problem will turn up at places with   28
a less genteel image to protect. Jan Strout, director of Montana State, Women's Resource Center, wonders if schools such as hers, which recognize that they are dealing with a more conservative student body and a "macho

cowboy image," aren't more willing to take the first step toward acknowledging the problem. A group called Students Against Sexual Assault was formed there two-and-a-half years ago after several students who were raped or resisted an attempted rape "went public." With men and women sharing leadership, this group is cosponsored by the Women's Resource Center and the student government.

Admitting to the problem isn't easy even when data is available, as doctoral student Genny Sandberg found at University of South Dakota. Last spring, she announced the results of a dating survey she coauthored with psychologists Tom Jackson and Patricia Petretic-Jackson. The most shocking statistic: 20 percent of the students (most from rural backgrounds and living in a rural campus setting) had been raped in a dating situation. The state board of regents couldn't believe it. "I just think that that's absolutely ridiculous," former regent Michael Rost said, according to the Brookings *Daily Register*, "I can't believe we would allow that to occur. If it is true, it's a very serious problem." Regent William Srstka agreed, "If this is true it's absolutely intolerable."

Following testimony by one of the researchers, the board changed its tune. Members are now discussing how to begin a statewide education and prevention program.

An inspiring example of how an administration can be led to new levels of consciousness took place at the University of Michigan earlier this year. Spurred by an article in *Metropolitan Detroit* magazine, a group of students staged a sit-in at the office of a university vice-president who had been quoted as saying that "Rape is a red flag word. . . . [The university] wants to present an image that is receptive and palatable to the potential student cohort," and also that "Rape is an issue like Alzheimer's disease or mental retardation [which] impacts on a small but sizable part of the population. . . . Perhaps it has to become a crisis that is commonly shared in order to get things done."

The students who spent the entire day in Vice-President Henry Johnson's 32 office claimed that rape had already become a crisis on their campus. They presented a list of twelve demands, ranging from a rape crisis center on campus to better lighting and installation of outdoor emergency phones. By the end of the day, Johnson had started to change his mind. Although he insisted that he had been misquoted and quoted out of context in the press, he told me that "I did not realize [before that] acquaintance rape was so much of a problem, that it was the most prevalent type of rape. There is a heightened awareness now on this campus. Whether we as a faculty and administration are as sensitive as we should be is another issue — and that will take some time."

In the meantime, members of the Michigan Student Assembly Women's Issues Committee (one of the groups active in organizing the protest) took their demands before the school's board of regents. The result: a $75,000 program for rape prevention and education on campus, directly reporting to Johnson's office. "We'll now be in a position to document the problem and to be proactive," says Johnson. Jennifer Faigel, an organizer of the protest, acknowledges a change in the administration's awareness but says the students themselves, disappointed in the amount of funding promised for the program, have already formed a group (Students Organized Against Rape) to develop programs in the dorms.

In just the three years since *Ms.* first reported on date rape [in 1982], several new campus organizations have sprung up and other ongoing programs have surfaced.

But the real measure of a school's commitment to dealing with this problem is the range of services it provides, says Mary Harvey, who did a nationwide study of exemplary rape programs for the National Center for the Prevention and Control of Rape. "It should have preventive services, crisis intervention, possibilities for long-term treatment, advocacy, and women's studies programs that educate about violence. The quality of a university's services to rape victims can be measured by the degree to which these other things are in place."

Minimally, rape counselors and educators feel, students need to be   36
exposed to information about date rape as soon as they enter college. Studies show that the group most vulnerable to acquaintance rape are college freshmen, followed by high school seniors. In Koss's original survey, for example, the average age of the victim was eighteen.

"I'd like a program where no first-year students could finish their starting week at college without being informed about the problem of acquaintance rape," says Andrea Parrot, a lecturer in human service studies at Cornell University, who is developing a program to train students and dorm resident advisers as date rape awareness counselors. Parrot and others admit that this would be a bare minimum. Handing out a brochure to read, even conducting a workshop on the subject during the busy orientation week and counting on students voluntarily attending, needs to be followed up with sessions in dormitories or other living units. These are the most common settings for date rapes, according to a study by Parrot and Robin Lynk.

So how do we go about changing attitudes? And how do we do it without "setting student against student?" asks Gretchen Mieszkowski, chair of the Sexual Assault Prevention Committee at the University of Houston/Clear Lake. Chiefly a commuter campus, with a majority of married women students, Clear Lake nevertheless had seventeen acquaintance rapes reported to the local crisis hot line last year. "We had always focused on traditional solutions like lighting and escort services at night," Mieszkowski says. "But changing lighting in the parking lot is easy; it's only money."

Many who have studied the problem of rape education believe it has to begin with college-age women and men talking to each other more frankly about their beliefs and expectations about sex. Py Bateman of Alternatives

to Fear thinks it has to start earlier, among teenagers, by developing rudi-
mentary dating skills at the lower end of the sexual activity scale. "We need
to learn more about holding hands than about sexual intercourse."

Bateman continues: "We've got to work on both sides. Boys don't know   40
what they want any more than girls do. The way our sexual interaction is
set up is that boys are supposed to push. Their peers tell them that scoring
is what counts. They're as divorced from intimacy as girls."

Gail Abarbanel of the Rape Treatment Center at Santa Monica Hospital
agrees. Her center conducts educational programs for schools in Los Angeles
County. In a recent survey of more than five thousand teenagers, she found
a high degree of misconception and lack of information about rape: "Most
boys say yes to the question, 'If a girl goes back to a guy's house when she
knows no one is home, is she consenting to sex?' And most boys believe that
girls don't mean no when they say it."

Women clearly need to get more convincing, and men clearly need to
believe them more. But until that ideal time, Montana State's Jan Strout
warns, "Because men have been socialized to hear yes when women say no,
we have to scream it."

Points to Consider

1. Sweet claims that most rapes go unreported and that date rape is reported
    even less often than other rape. Why do you think this is the case?

2. Social psychologist Martha Burt believes that our culture fosters an
    atmosphere conducive to rape. Examine her reasons for this belief. Do
    you agree with her theory "that all sexual relationships are basically
    exploitive and predatory"?

3. Are most colleges prepared to deal with the problem of "date rape"? Is
    your own? Why do so many schools seem unwilling to acknowledge the
    problem?

4. In a recent survey, most teenage males answered "yes" when asked "if
    a girl goes back to a guy's house when she knows no one is home, is she
    consenting to sex?" What are some of the reasons for this answer?

Rape on Campus [GOOD HOUSEKEEPING / September 1989]

In the fall of 1988, Moira, a slender but athletic redhead, began her freshman year at a prestigious Southern California university. Planning to major in premed and go on to medical school, she was enthusiastically carrying a heavy load of math and science courses and making friends in the coed dorm where she lived.

Then, one Saturday night in December, her whole life changed when she attended a dorm "floor party." Moira had had a little to drink but was not intoxicated when a boy named Dan, whom she knew only slightly, suggested she go to his room, where, he said, "most of our buddies are."

She had no reason to be wary of a "dorm brother," so she went with him—only to find when they got to the room that no one else was there. Dan closed the door and moved toward Moira. She pushed him away, but he was strong enough to throw her down on the bed and rape her.

Moira heard loud pounding on Dan's door—several of his friends, laughing. Startled, he moved off her—just enough to give her a chance to escape. Half-dressed, she rushed screaming down the hall to her own room, where she threw off her clothes, took a shower, then lay shivering and nauseous on her bed. 4

Witnesses who had heard her cries for help could have helped substantiate her story when she went to the university dean the next day—but they didn't. When word got around the dorm, most of Dan's friends were angry that Moira had tried to get Dan "in trouble." After all, she'd gone to his room, hadn't she? Wasn't she inviting something to happen?

She took her semester finals in a daze, and from then on her grades spiraled down. She couldn't sleep or eat. Most of all she couldn't stop replaying the attack in her mind, berating herself for how stupid she'd been. She even began to doubt her own sense of what had happened. By going to

---

ANN RULE (b. 1935) has written numerous books on crime, including The Stranger Beside Me *(1980) about serial killer Ted Bundy,* Lust Killer *(1983),* The Want Ad Killer *(1984),* The I-5 Killer *(1984), and* Small Sacrifices *(1987). She is now at work on a book titled* If You Really Loved Me, *about an Orange County, California, murder case. Rule, who once worked as a police officer, now writes full time. She lives in Seattle.*

the boy's room *had* she signaled that she wanted to have sex? Close to a nervous breakdown, she finally dropped out of college. The happy eighteen-year-old who started her college life so successfully will never go back to the university; she may never return to college at all.

Shocking and poignant as Moira's case is, it is not a rare freak occurrence. Rape has become increasingly common on college campuses across the country. Most often the incidents are "acquaintance" or "date" rapes that do not end in severe injuries—although certainly there is serious psychological damage. Sometimes, though, a sexual attack ends in murder.

In January 1989 a group of some 250 psychologists, law enforcement officers, and students who attended the Third Annual Conference on Campus Violence at Towson State (Maryland) University estimated that 13 to 25 percent of all college women become victims of rape or attempted rape. A 1985 survey of thirty-two campuses conducted by *Ms.* magazine, the National Institute of Mental Health, and Mary P. Koss, a professor of psychiatry at the University of Arizona School of Medicine, puts the ratio at closer to one in six within a one-year period. Dr. Koss further found that most of the rapes occurred on campus and that 84 percent of the women *knew* their assailants. Sexual violence has now surpassed theft as the number-one security concern at U.S. universities.

Most parents of today's students remember a different, gentler campus life in which men and women lived in separate dorms and adhered to curfews. Today male and female students often share the same dorms, and there simply aren't the demarcation—privacy—lines there once were. Someone who only looks familiar may be mistakenly assumed to be trustworthy just because he's a fellow student—as was Moira's rapist. Nor is it unusual to see a stranger walking the corridors and assume he lives on the next floor. How does an intruder get in? Students quickly learn to prop open doors or bypass locks so they can come and go easily. In 1989 few colleges provide a campus police force.

Alcohol and drugs, widely used at campus parties, can be catalysts for an offender while rendering his victim less able to resist attack. Most parents are unaware that rehabilitation programs for criminals—sometimes sex offenders on probation or parole—often take place on college campuses. This puts convicted sex offenders in the classroom right next to students, sometimes even living in the same dorm. Yet privacy laws forbid disclosure of offenders' identities.

But there is a deeper, more complex root cause of campus rapes than mixed-set dorms and drugs and alcohol. The sad fact is that some young men of the current college generation hold dangerously outdated ideas about women and sex. They feel that if a girl allows a boy to visit her room—or if she drinks too much—she is necessarily inviting sexual activity. There is evidence that the misconceptions are learned early. A recent survey of 1,700 students, ages twelve to fifteen, conducted by a Rhode Island Rape Crisis Center revealed a shocking attitude: One-fourth of the boys and one-sixth of the girls thought a man had the right to "force" a woman to have sexual intercourse if he had spent money on her on a date.

What leads "nice, respectable" young men to feel they have a right to   12
force sex? Mark Stevens, a psychologist at the University of Southern California, believes that the confusion of sexuality with violence begins with the old notion of "scoring." "The attitude that women are objects and that treating them in a demeaning way makes a boy 'cool' and in control gets passed along from peers, older brothers, and media images—especially those in the pornographic magazines," says Stevens.

Recent headlines dramatizing the rise in sex offenses by teenagers show just how early these attitudes are formed: the Glen Ridge, New Jersey, scandal, for instance, in which five eighteen-year-old boys have been charged with sexually attacking a mentally impaired seventeen-year-old girl; the brutal rape and beating of a female jogger in New York City's Central Park by a gang of youths, at least one as young as fourteen.

More and more campuses are now conducting rape-prevention courses that spread the message that forced sex is *wrong*. Mark Stevens conducts such a workshop at USC in which he tries to teach young men to be more empathetic to women and to view sexuality in a sensitive, humane way. The University of Florida, Cornell University, and UCLA, among others, also have excellent programs in place.

It's not just young men who need new conditioning. Young women take in the same social messages as men do, and they can be just as confused about sexuality. Freshman girls, eager to appear sophisticated, are particularly vulnerable targets for date rape. When it does happen, it's easy for the victim to feel that it was somehow her fault. Humiliated, ashamed, many young women want only to shove the memory of what happened into the farthest corner of their minds. Like Moira, many tragically drop out of college rather than live so close—sometimes next door—to the man who has attacked them.

Given this tendency to blame themselves, it's not hard to understand   16
why so many college women are reluctant to report a rape. And often it does seem prudent not to, since university officials often are either unable—or unwilling—to deal with the issue. For one thing, rape is difficult to prove in court. For another, they don't want to admit to any laxity in campus security. Security measures cost money and, more expensive to colleges, bad publicity can hurt enrollment.

Gail Abarbanel, founder and director of the Rape Treatment Center at the Santa Monica (California) Hospital Medical Center, has heard a long list of college rape horror stories in which the victims' rights were treated as if secondary to those of their assailants. One young woman suffered through fourteen interviews with college officials, but her attacker was never even called to answer her charges. In another case, a seventeen-year-old freshman girl felt she had no choice but to drop her charges against a star college athlete when she was told by school authorities that he could have a number of his teammates appear as character witnesses, but she could not even bring in her mother or a friend to speak for her.

Abarbanel finds that it is still rare for most colleges to hold disciplinary hearings for students accused of rape. "I can think of only one such hearing in sixty cases," she says.

Traumatic as rape is, there can be even worse dangers on campus. It took a particularly chilling tragedy—and two devastated but determined parents—to finally call attention to the serious problem of lax campus security. Always careful about keeping their own security system on at home, Connie and Howard Clery of Bryn Mawr, Pennsylvania, had been reassured to see that the Lehigh University dorm where their daughter, Jeanne, lived had three locks—on an outside door, an inner door at the stairwell, and a door at each floor. The students' rooms each had locks, too.

Secure in the belief that the locked outer doors kept strangers out, Jeanne and her roommate often left their room door unlocked so the latecomer wouldn't have to fish out her key. On the night of April 5, 1986, Jeanne's roommate had a date; Jeanne left the door unlocked for her, then went to sleep. Someone else entered Jeanne's room—her rapist and murderer.

Perhaps startled when Jeanne awakened and found him rifling through her things, possibly planning to attack her all along, the intruder tried to cut her throat with a bottle, beat and raped her . . . then strangled her to death.

The murderer, Joseph Henry, a fellow student who lived in another dormitory, was arrested two days later. He had been able to enter his victim's dorm because—not a surprise—the latch on the outer door had been left propped open.

The grieving Clerys sued Lehigh University for negligence and were awarded a purported $2 million. They have used the money to form Security On Campus, a clearinghouse for information on college safety, and to lobby for state bills stressing campus safety—so that other parents' children would be protected from violent crime. In 1988 they helped get enacted a bill requiring every college in Pennsylvania to provide prospective students with information relating to the school's crime statistics and security measures upon request. Thanks in part to their efforts, similar legislation has been passed in Florida and Tennessee and is pending in New York, New Jersey, Massachusetts, and California.

If many universities have instituted rape-prevention courses, most still refuse to discuss their responsibility to provide adequate security. In 1983 a

freshman at Cornell University, Erin Nieswand, was
by an irrational young man who had paced the hall
for more than an hour, carrying a loaded rifle. The
suing Cornell. In papers filed in court, however, the u
had any legal duty to provide adequate security fo
Clarkson College (Potsdam, New York) sophomore
viciously attacked and raped on campus. She died a
college officials denied they had any responsibility.

What can parents do to protect the youngster they are sending off to
college? The Clerys have formulated a questionnaire on campus security that
they urge parents to send in with each college application. Another excellent
resource, the Santa Monica Rape Treatment Center, provides helpful bro-
chures. Of course, parents should check out campus living arrangements for
themselves. Then they may want to give their college-bound daughter this
advice:

1. If you intend to drink, drink moderately.
2. Don't give out too much information about yourself to a new acquain-
    tance or a stranger.
3. *Always* lock your dorm-room door.
4. Never walk alone on campus at night. If you must attend an evening
    class, arrange for a good friend to escort you.
5. Walk across campus confidently, head up, shoulders back. If you look
    depressed, ill, or distracted you are a prime target.
6. Don't automatically trust police badges, men with "broken" arms or
    legs, or men with a sad "story."

But more important than offering safety advice to a daughter, says Mark
Stevens, is instilling good sexual values in *both* boys and girls. He especially
urges parents to start early in conveying to boys that sex means infinitely
more than "scoring"—and that "no" to a sexual invitation means *no*. For
if their sons grow up learning to respect women, to have a sense of responsibility toward them, parents won't have to be so concerned about sending
their daughters off to college armed with self-defense strategies.

Points to Consider

1. Why were many of the witnesses to Moira's rape unwilling to testify on
    her behalf? What was the predominant attitude among her attacker's

ny did Moira begin to feel that she was to blame for her own

you feel that the presence of coed dormitories increases the potential for sexual violence among students? What other conditions on college campuses may contribute to the increasing number of rapes? How can colleges provide a safer environment for their female students?

3. According to psychologist Mark Stevens, what leads young men to believe they have the right to force women to have sex? What kinds of media images contribute to this perception? What other reasons can you provide for such attitudes?

4. What does Ann Rule believe is the most effective measure that can be taken against rape? What kinds of sexual values does she encourage parents to instill in their children? Do you feel that most men who commit date rape are aware that what they are doing is wrong?

Discussing the Unit

Suggested Topic for Discussion

Sweet writes that "the prevailing myth [formerly] was that most rapes were committed by strangers in dark alleys." The three essays in this unit challenge this conventional view. Do you think these essays force us to alter our views about how rape should be defined?

Preparing for Class Discussion

1. Some people believe that one of the most common misconceptions about rape is that it is a sexual act rather than a violent crime. Why has this misconception persisted in our culture? Why is it important to view rape as an act of violence?

2. In the articles, women speak of their experiences with rape. Consider their statements as you reread the essays and make notes about what the statements have in common. Then consider statements by men and do the same. Compare the two sets of comments and draw some conclusions about the different ways that men and women view rape.

From Discussion to Writing

As the three selections in this unit reveal, date rape appears to be an especially acute problem on college campuses. Why do you think this is the case? What aspects of college life seem to contribute to the problem? Do you think the college itself bears any responsibility for date rape, or do you think it is a problem the students themselves must deal with? Does your college have a policy concerning the problem? Write an essay in which you consider these questions. Consider, too, the extent of the problem on your own campus and ways you think it should be handled.

9

Racism on Campus:
How Can We Explain It?

At the University of Wisconsin fraternity brothers conduct a mock slave auction and perform skits in blackface. At Arizona State University the campus erupts in an antiblack race riot. At the University of Michigan, the student-run radio station broadcasts racial slurs and white supremacist pamphlets find their way into dormitories. Our colleges and universities, traditionally strongholds in the fight against racism in America, now find themselves the sites of race-related violence. In spite of attempts by administration, faculty, and students at these institutions to put an end to racism on campus, the number of such incidents continues to increase. In "Disillusioned in the Promised Land," Trey Ellis demonstrates how relations between the races seem to have taken a turn for the worse on campuses across the nation.

Some analysts, however, think that while the problem may be similar in form to other kinds of racism in the United States, student racism has at its roots a very different kind of racial conflict. Shelby Steele believes that "racial tension on campus is the result more of racial equality than inequality," and he explains his belief in "The Recoloring of Campus Life." Finally, in "Black and White at Brown," well-known columnist Pete Hamill shares his impressions after his visit to an Ivy League school where a recent series of race-related incidents has shocked university officials and students alike. While reading these essays, consider your experiences with racism on campus and try to decide whether or not the writers have portrayed the problem accurately.

TREY ELLIS

Disillusioned in the Promised Land

[PLAYBOY / June 1989]

Here's some verse from one of many fliers that were slipped under the doors of various University of Michigan black students last year:

Nigger, nigger, go away,
For the white man is here to stay.
Everywhere you look,
Everywhere you'll see
The menacing branches of a tree,
And from that tree,
What do *we* see?
The beautiful sight of my friends and me,
Laughing at your dangling feet.
So be forewarned
And do be scared,
For I, nigger child, *will* see you there.
Take your black asses back to Africa,
Before it's too late.

Last year, Peter O. Steiner, dean of Michigan's College of Literature, Science and the Arts, announced, "Our challenge is not to change this university into another kind of institution where minorities would naturally

---

TREY ELLIS (b. 1962) has published essays in a number of magazines, including Interview *and* Playboy. *His first novel,* Platitudes, *came out in 1988. Ellis, who lives in New York City, is currently at work on another novel.*

flock in much greater numbers. I need not remind you that there are such institutions—including Wayne State and Howard University." Sensing an ally, the student pamphleteers followed up quickly with more fliers:

"Niggers, get off campus!" they wrote. "Dean Steiner was right."

The smart money should start investing in Ann Arbor copy centers.   4

The YPSILANTI CITY LIMITS sign slides past my eyes for the first time in seventeen years; I feel old. Four years out of Stanford, I'm back in Ypsilanti, suburb of Ann Arbor, cradle of the University of Michigan, where my father and mother taught and where I napped on an oval rug and ate Nutter Butters in the campus nursery school.

My nursery class of 1967 was fashionably diverse: blacks, whites, Asians, Jews, Catholics, Protestants. You couldn't have stopped us from hugging and holding hands—just like the kids in the Benetton ads today. Our only fear was not outrunning Ruthie, a frisky-lipped white girl also known as the Kissing Cootie.

This year's freshmen weren't born yet in 1967. By the time Ronald Reagan took office, they were ten. If my childhood saw the explosion of progressivism, theirs witnessed its opposite—the systematic strangulation of liberal values. Having been educated to the old-fashioned intolerance of the Reagan years, this year's incoming frosh has found far more to fear than just a premature kiss on the lips.

At home in New York, I'd read about the University of Michigan's   8 recent racist incidents; but surely, it couldn't have changed that much, I'd thought, heading west. After cruising State Street in person and hitting up both black and white Michigan students for the real deal, however, I hardly recognized my home town. I was going back—I just didn't know how far.

Here's the story of black U of M student Regina Parker (not her real name). Her parents have just hauled her footlockers and posters and radio up to her room and are driving back to Flint, Michigan, proud of their eighteen-year-old, all grown up. Regina thinks, How about a little Gap Band on the stereo to celebrate my new life as a collegian? Then in walks her new white roommate, who plugs in a new forty-watt sound system and cranks up the greatest hits of REO Speedwagon. After months of squabbling, Regina's roommate promises," I'm gonna make life hell for you." Eventually, the white girl gives up and moves out. But it's not over. Some white guys, upset by the loss of a soulmate, start calling Regina the word—nigger—and late at night, while other U of M students are out distributing leaflets, the white guys regularly hurl blocks of ice at the black girl's door. Says Regina, "I thought about jumping out of school, out of the window."

Most of us would have dropped out or maybe dropped somebody with a punch and been kicked out, but Regina took a course in ego aerobics— she checked out the Center for Afro-American and African Studies (C.A.A.S.). The center reminded her that there are black doctors of political science, of sociology and most other disciplines, that blacks, indeed, finish school. In high school, she had been a cheerleader and believes, as ex-cheerleaders will, that "everybody used to be my friend—blacks and whites." In any case, Regina did not imagine when she arrived from Flint that she would ever voluntarily stay away from white folks. Now Regina, like other black students here, believes only separatism will pull her through.

When I was in fourth grade, my father took a job as a campus psychiatrist at Yale. We lived in Hamden, a not-very-ritzy Italian and Irish New Haven suburb, where I met a new kind of off-campus creature. I was doing yardwork one day when a big white seventh-grader walked by.

"Keep raking, Toby," he taunted. At the time, Alex Haley's *Roots,* the   12
miniseries, was breaking TV viewing records nationwide. I had been glued to it. That white boy profoundly rocked my world. Naturally, I wanted to fillet his back with my rake the way the slave master had whipped Kunta Kinte until he had given up his African name for Toby. But the seventh grader was bigger and older, so I stood there alone silently in my own damned front yard.

Later, I transferred to Phillips Academy, Andover, one of the oldest boarding schools in the country and the high school home of Humphrey Bogart (before he was booted), Jack Lemmon, and George Bush. By the time I got there, it was a progressive, coeducational junior think tank, ruled by hippie wanna-bes playing twelve-string guitars and reading *Howl.* But the colonial town of Andover, squatting just north of Boston, offered me no such protection from traditional American values. It was the kind of town where a nine-year-old boy could freely shriek the word—nigger—at me from his school-bus window. If he eventually made it as far as college, he'd likely drive his primer-splotched Camaro an hour or so west to attend the University of Massachusetts at Amherst.

An excellent school with one of the nation's first Afro-American studies departments, where Bill Cosby got his Ed.D. and where James Baldwin lectured, U Mass Amherst also boasts the first notable campus race riot of the modern era. After the last game of the 1986 world series, fifteen hundred disgruntled white Red Sox fans took out their disappointment on twenty or so black students, including then-sophomore Yancey Robinson, who was "stomped on the ground and beaten with bats and clubs," in the words of one witness. The Red Sox fans assumed that all black students came from New York and therefore must be Mets fans.

Last year, two black freshmen were attacked by five white freshmen. The black guys had been seen with a white girl.

At U Mass, only 2.7 percent of the students are black. Most of the   16
students come from eastern Massachusetts, from Andover, the other Boston suburbs, and parts of the city itself. One famous Boston locale, South Boston,

made headlines in 1974, when "Southies" rioted and stoned school buses rather than let black kids be bused there.

I'm getting another note pad from my trunk in the U Mass parking garage near the student union when a Toyota with Massachusetts plates, driven by a white guy in a baseball cap with another beside him in the front and a blonde in the back, drives into the garage. "Yo!" yells the driver in mock black B-boy, to the great amusement of his passengers as they drive past willfully only inches from my foot. Great, I think, running down the ramp after them—my very own racial incident. With luck, they'll be Southies, and I'll interview them. It will be like Oprah's broadcast from Georgia's all-white Forsyth County. But I lose them in the spiral of the garage, give up and go back to the student union to check out the Earth Foods Café, the People's Market and the Central American Solidarity Association, the hotbeds of U Mass progressivism. The Pioneer Valley, home of U Mass, Smith, Mount Holyoke, Amherst, and Hampshire, is, in fact, as liberal an area as our nation knows.

I see two white guys who look like possible Southies sitting in front of the union. Instead, David Martin, an economics major, is from Dorchester, another hard-scrabble urban Boston neighborhood, and Robert Thompson, a communications major, comes from down near the Cape. But they were both at the Red Sox riot and agree that there is a lot of racism on campus.

"U Mass reflects the attitude of Massachusetts in general," Robert says and splits for class.

"They bring the attitude up here," says David. He has a classic Boston-Irish accent—the "here" comes out *he-ah*—and he tells me he is going to try boxing in the Golden Gloves this *summah*. A tough and friendly street kid with feathered hair, he wears acid-washed jeans and jeans jacket buttoned up to the neck, brown loafers with white socks. "Kids in my neighborhood don't wear ripped-up jeans, tie-dyed T-shirts," he tells me, jerking his chin toward a fashionably unkempt barefoot couple. His Dorchesterites are a dwindling working-class people whose urban neigborhood blackens as they, the last European immigrant offspring in America to make it, finally do. 20

David is a latter-day Bowery Boy, as alienated from this pastoral college life as many of the black students. "Suburban kids don't know what goes on in the city," he says. "People look at city kids here like they're some kind of maggot."

Here at U Mass, he has found other divisions besides white and black, Irish and not; you can hear him struggling to modernize his lifelong ethno-centric allegiances. "Of course, you'll have some, uh, city kids up here," he says. "My grandpa came from Ireland. He experienced racism." WASP New Englanders still have contempt for the Boston Irish. David and his friends don't like the children of the D.A.R. much, either. "We used to go up to

Milton [a tiny Boston suburb], beat kids up. That's when we were young, but that's all changed.

"This is much better than the city; it's good to get away. It's so quiet here. . . . But it feels kind of good to stay with kids of your own kind," he confesses, hinting at his own sense of isolation. Maybe that's why the traditions of his roots seem to be undergoing a transformation: "Racism is passed down from generations, but I'm still not prejudiced," he tells me, "and my friends aren't as bad as they used to be. Because there's nothing you can do. I don't want to die because some guy wants to play ball in the park."

I walk through the student-union building looking for black students to interview, but most I pass look away. It is a campus dotted with insular black strays, trying to be invisible. Usually, at a college, when you pass other blacks on the street or in the student union, you acknowledge them. Yo, what's up? Nothing much. All right. At the University of Michigan, a school of comparable size but with twice as not-very-many blacks, folks *waved* at me *from their cars*. But at U Mass, instead of consolidating their tiny community, a dozen black organizations compete for the same members and money.

Black students here complain of severe "creeping," gossipy backbiting. "Smile at your face, talk behind your back," says Scott Thompson, an industrial-engineering major. He and his friends tell me of fist fights between rival black factions at last year's Funkathon concert, just like those between white frat boys. You'd hope blacks would see the bigger picture.

Margaret Jones, a psychology major, Afro-American studies minor, sits by herself in one of the student-union cafeterias, watching a soap. She says white students smile when they tell her she "doesn't sound black," as if it's a compliment. She has heard it a million times. Jones is not yet used to being a living science project, a lab rat.

Even in good situations, minority students remain curiosities—objects of social vivisection. Maybe that's one reason even brilliant black students burn out and don't graduate: "What is that you're putting in your hair?" "What *does* Jesse really want?" "Whitney Houston's really attractive—don't you think?" Just a day of racial Q. & A. tires you out. Try to imagine four years of it. Can't? Neither can a lot of black students. At such humongous labyrinths as U Mass and UC Berkeley, about three black students in four drop out. At the University of Michigan, if you're black, your chances of getting out with a degree are 30 percent. Universities with a primarily black enrollment graduate percentages in the 90s. No wonder Denise Huxtable chose Hillman College.

The problem is that both sides need to be educated about each other. It's not only that the white kids see the blacks as illiterate athletes or affirmative-action-lottery winners. The blacks see the whites as callous and corny, garden-variety rich kids. But those polarities are seldom acknowledged

24

28

publicly. That's why "the occupation" was an event of such magnitude at U Mass.

Jones's eyes widen as she tells me about it. After those two black freshmen were beaten up and after the university nibbled off yet another classroom in the black-studies building, hundreds of black students stormed New Africa House and locked its doors. Jesse Jackson and Mike Dukakis called the school's chancellor in support of the students. "I was almost in tears," says Jones. Not since Isaac Hayes had a hit has the campus black community knitted together so tightly. And yet, now it is over and I discover a campus again dotted with strays, separate and alone.

As a black student entering Phillips Academy at Andover, I had the option of choosing a black roommate to watch my back, but I integrated. I think I felt then as neoconservatives feel now: black separatism is as bad as segregation and talk about racism and bigotry is distasteful.

At Stanford, I snapped out of my naiveté. I chose to have a black roommate in the black dorm. Ujamaa, the black cultural house, half black, half white by population, is a mini black college within a mostly white university. The sense of safety in numbers that Jones felt during the New Africa House occupation existed in "Ooj" year round. Thanks to this dorm and the relatively large number of black students at Stanford (approaching 10 percent), 87 percent of its black students graduate.

My senior year, I worked on a committee that demanded that the works 32 of women and minorities be added to the reading list of the mandatory freshman Western Culture class. Our demands didn't get very far, but last year, after much screaming and lobbying from both the Black Student Union and campus conservatives, the Stanford faculty senate finally agreed to open up the reading list.

Before that fight, Stanford had been racially tranquil. The campus looks like a golf course and most of the students were as political as a seven iron—until then–Secretary of Education William J. Bennett got wind of the reading-list debate and decided to take sides. The proposed changes, the way Bennett apparently saw them, would bring down the cornerstones of the culture. The Black Student Union, the women, and the other protesters were not broadening Western civilization, he said, they were trashing it.

Bennett goosed the proto-yuppies into action—miraculously, they started giving a damn. Where previously the white students had had no visible gripes, Bennett supplied them with a cause. Last year, a group of freshmen printed up T-shirts saying ARYAN BY THE GRACE OF GOD. This year, in Ujamaa, somebody added the word NIGGER to a poster for a black fraternity. But more specifically, the new white consciousness got political. Every Stanford student organization exists on fee assessments voted on by the entire student body. The Black Student Union had always easily won approval; but last year, in a climate that feels increasingly alien to black students, it lost (until, after a fracas, overseas-studies votes were added to the tally and the B.S.U. squeaked by).

Black students are five times more likely than whites to drop out of a mainly white university. And those are middle-class, well-prepared black students. Walter Allen, director of the National Study of Black College Students and professor of sociology and Afro-American and African Studies at Michigan, told me: "Universities don't go to the street corner; they take the cream of the crop now more so than ever. Yet it's not a supportive environment. Fully seventy-five percent of black students report they don't feel a part of campus life."

Be that as it may, affirmative action has become a dirty phrase. Syndi- 36 cated columnists Rowland Evans and Robert Novak concluded last spring that affirmative action itself "is the only plausible explanation" for the rise in campus racism. It's like blaming the miniskirt for the rape.

Vanessa Gibson, a Mount Holyoke student from Detroit, is in a sociology class. The discussion lights on poverty and all eyes respectfully turn to her. Like Cliff Huxtable, Vanessa's dad is an obstetrician-gynecologist. Her mother is a schoolteacher. The talk eventually centers on low test scores among blacks and, again, all eyes face her. She argues that plenty of blacks score well on the college boards. The other women are silent, but after class, one white classmate pulls her aside to compare S.A.T. scores. Gibson wins and the white girl walks away. Gibson isn't trying to separate herself; it just happens.

The most famous case of campus racism created international notoriety for the University of Mississippi. In 1962, a month before I was born, a riot over the admission of its first black student, James Meredith, ended with two people dead and 375 wounded.

At the Memphis airport on my way to Ole Miss in Oxford, I tell the white, born-again shuttle-bus driver that I'm on my way to Ole Miss.

"You know there's a time change in Mississippi," the Tennessean tells 40 me. "You turn the clock back twenty-five years."

Actually, Oxford is a charming college town with a Benetton store across the street from Square Books, where you can buy both Capote and cappuccino. Both face the county courthouse and a white obelisk commemorating the Confederate dead.

I drive past another Civil War monument approaching the Lyceum, Ole Miss's administration building. Giant letters on the neoclassical pediment proclaim RANDOLPH UNIVERSITY and I'm sure I'm lost. In fact, the campus *has* turned its clock back twenty-five years—for the filming of *Heart of Dixie,* a movie about a sixties Southern deb turned civil rights activist starring Ally Sheedy, Virginia Madsen, and Phoebe Cates.

The campus needed little alteration for the film: a gray-bearded "rebel" colonel remains the official school mascot, and Confederate flags, while no longer officially endorsed by the university, pop up frequently at football games. Blacks are even more underrepresented at Ole Miss than at U Mass—7.5 percent in a 40-percent-black state—only at Ole Miss, you don't get called nigger as often.

After a basketball game last year, a car filled with white boys passed Charlsy Wise and her friends, screeching "Niggers!" as they drove by. A white student approached Charlsy and her friends and apologized. "That was real nice," she says. "They've had so many problems here that people bend over backward to be race considerate."

Not everybody. Arson is suspected in last August's burning of Phi Beta Sigma house, which was about to be the first black frat house on fraternity row. Yet, in response, white Mississippians were "race considerate." The interfraternity council swiftly pledged to raise $20,000 to rebuild Phi Beta Sigma house. The university and the alumni association have also donated money.

Segregation on campus remains nearly absolute. Barbara Britten, a black student from Oxford, finds Ole Miss "more divided than high school. There, most of my friends were white," she remembers, "but at Ole Miss, you're frowned on if you run with a group of white people or vice versa."

Derek Nelson, a white student with an earring, who comes from the heart of Klan country, complains that some white students choose Ole Miss "*because* there aren't going to be too many blacks here."

To kill time the night before graduation, I go to the Hoka, a dilapidated, ex-hippie restaurant/movie barn to watch what's playing. It turns out to be John Waters's civil rights dance farce, *Hairspray*. On the screen, a black teenaged boy says, "Our love is taboo." His white girlfriend snuggles up and coaches him, "Go to second, go to second." At Ole Miss, a few of the black track stars now have white girlfriends, so I ask Charlsy if any of the black women go out with white men on campus. She says, "I've never seen that, except on TV."

Unsurprisingly, separateness of the races here is as ingrained as in the North. But here I sense an aggressive dedication to reversing the pattern that is absent at the Northern schools. James Brown, assistant dean of students, a black ex–pro linebacker, has helped institute programs to make sure students stay in school once they're admitted. Now, about 70 percent of the black students graduate. "When I start talking about this, I get happy, because I can make a difference," Brown says. "I see this state as a new frontier." And Toni Avant, Ole Miss class of 1986 and an admissions counselor, recruits the state's best black students. If they don't have transportation to visit the school, says Avant, she drives out and gets them.

At the class of 1988's graduation, Governor Ray Mabus, Ole Miss class of 1969, is the commencement speaker. As the organ pipes "Pomp and Circumstance," the basketball floor fills with black caps and gowns. Parents happily collapse in the stands, finally shaded from the sticky broil of the Mississippi sun. One especially proud black family takes up nearly a whole row and shines smiles from grandpa to toddlers as their graduate files past, breaking rank for a moment to beam back.

Despite "entrenched interests to be discomforted," testifies the liberal governor in dramatic contrast to former governor Ross Barnett, who defended the whiteness of Ole Miss by physically blocking Meredith from registering. No matter the intentions of those who have reshackled minority progress in a decade that "in many ways has sanctified selfishness," the state and the country will not truly live up to their potential for equality and for good, he proclaims, "unless we succeed in educating *all* our children."

Amen. And just singing "Ebony and Ivory" won't make it so.   52

Points to Consider

1. What does Trey Ellis mean by the phrase "the systematic strangulation of liberal values"? Does he view this phenomenon as a major factor in the recent surge of racial incidents on college campuses? Does Ellis note any rise in race-related violence in noncollege environments?

2. Why do some black students advocate separatism as the only way of getting through college? Does Ellis himself agree with such students? Does he offer any alternative ways of coping with the problem of racism as a black student?

3. One professor of Afro-American and African Studies at the University of Michigan told Ellis that "fully 75 percent of black students report they don't feel a part of campus life." Do you think that many nonblack students feel this way as well? What factors other than race might contribute to a student's sense of isolation?

4. Does Ellis seem surprised by what he learns about race relations at the University of Mississippi? Why does he believe that some Southern universities have a greater commitment to reversing the pattern of separatism on campus than many of their Northern counterparts?

SHELBY STEELE

The Recoloring of Campus Life

[HARPER'S MAGAZINE / February 1989]

In the past few years, we have witnessed what the National Institute Against Prejudice and Violence calls a "proliferation" of racial incidents on college campuses around the country. Incidents of on-campus "intergroup conflict" have occurred at more than 160 colleges in the last three years, according to the institute. The nature of these incidents has ranged from open racial violence—most notoriously, the October 1986 beating of a black student at the University of Massachusetts at Amherst after an argument about the World Series turned into a racial bashing, with a crowd of up to three thousand whites chasing twenty blacks—to the harassment of minority students, to acts of racial or ethnic insensitivity, with by far the greatest number falling in the last two categories. At Dartmouth College, three editors of the *Dartmouth Review*, the off-campus right-wing student weekly, were suspended last winter for harassing a black professor in his lecture hall. At Yale University last year a swastika and the words "white power" were painted on the school's Afro-American cultural center. Racist jokes were aired not long ago on a campus radio station at the University of Michigan. And at the University of Wisconsin at Madison, members of the Zeta Beta Tau fraternity held a mock slave auction in which pledges painted their faces black and wore Afro wigs. Two weeks after the president of Stanford University informed the incoming freshman class last fall that "bigotry is out, and I mean it" two freshmen defaced a poster of Beethoven—gave the image thick lips—and hung it on a black student's door.

In response, black students around the country have rediscovered the militant protest strategies of the sixties. At the University of Massachusetts at Amherst, Williams College, Penn State University, UC Berkeley, UCLA,

---

SHELBY STEELE (b. 1946) is a history professor at San Jose State University and a graduate of the University of Utah. He has published numerous articles on civil rights and affirmative action, and he wrote the PBS special Seven Days in Bensonhurst. Steele's first book, The Content of Our Character: A New Vision of Race in America, was published in 1990.

Stanford, and countless other campuses, black students have sat in, marched, and rallied. But much of what they were marching and rallying about seemed less a response to specific racial incidents than a call for broader action on the part of the colleges and universities they were attending. Black students have demanded everything from more black faculty members and new courses on racism to the addition of "ethnic" foods in the cafeteria. There is the sense in these demands that racism runs deep.

Of course, universities are not where racial problems tend to arise. When I went to college in the mid-sixties, colleges were oases of calm and understanding in a racially tense society; campus life—with its traditions of tolerance and fairness, its very distance from the "real" world—imposed a degree of broad-mindedness on even the most provincial students. If I met whites who were not anxious to be friends with blacks, most were at least vaguely friendly to the cause of our freedom. In any case, there was no guerrilla activity against our presence, no "minefield of racism" (as one black student at Berkeley recently put it) to negotiate. I wouldn't say that the phrase "campus racism" is a contradiction in terms, but until recently it certainly seemed an incongruence.

But a greater incongruence is the generational timing of this new problem 4
on the campuses. Today's undergraduates were born after the passage of the 1964 Civil Rights Act. They grew up in an age when racial equality was for the first time enforceable by law. This too was a time when blacks suddenly appeared on television, as mayors of big cities, as icons of popular culture, as teachers, and in some cases even as neighbors. Today's black and white college students, veterans of *Sesame Street* and often of integrated grammar and high schools, have had more opportunities to know each other—whites and blacks—than any previous generation in American history. Not enough opportunities, perhaps, but enough to make the notion of racial tension on campus something of a mystery, at least to me.

To try to unravel this mystery I left my own campus, where there have been few signs of racial tension, and talked with black and white students at California schools where racial incidents had occurred: Stanford, UCLA, Berkeley. I spoke with black and white students—and not with Asians and Hispanics—because, as always, blacks and whites represent the deepest lines of division, and because I hesitate to wander onto the complex territory of other minority groups. A phrase by William H. Gass—"the hidden internality of things"—describes with maybe a little too much grandeur what I hoped to find. But it *is* what I wanted to find, for this is the kind of problem that makes a black person nervous, which is not to say that it doesn't unnerve whites as well. Once every six months or so someone yells "nigger" at me from a passing car. I don't like to think that these solo artists might soon make up a chorus or, worse, that this chorus might one day soon sing to me from the paths of my own campus.

I have long believed that trouble between the races is seldom what it appears to be.[1] It was not hard to see after my first talks with students that racial tension on campus is a problem that misrepresents itself. It has the same look, the archetypal pattern, of America's timeless racial conflict— white racism and black protest. And I think part of our concern over it comes from the fact that it has the feel of a relapse, illness gone and come again. But if we are seeing the same symptoms, I don't believe we are dealing with the same illness. For one thing, I think racial tension on campus is the result more of racial equality than inequality.

How to live with racial difference has been America's profound social problem. For the first hundred years or so following emancipation it was controlled by a legally sanctioned inequality that acted as a buffer between the races. No longer is this the case. On campuses today, as throughout society, blacks enjoy equality under the law—a profound social advancement. No student may be kept out of a class or a dormitory or an extracurricular activity because of his or her race. But there is a paradox here: on a campus where members of all races are gathered, mixed together in the classroom as well as socially, differences are more exposed than ever. And this is where the trouble starts. For members of each race—young adults coming into their own, often away from home for the first time—bring to this site of freedom, exploration, and now, today, equality very deep fears and anxieties, inchoate feelings of racial shame, anger, and guilt. These feelings could lie dormant in the home, in familiar neighborhoods, in simpler days of childhood. But the college campus, with its structures of interaction and adult-level competition—the big exam, the dorm, the "mixer"—is another matter. I think campus racism is born of the rub between racial difference and a setting, the campus itself, devoted to interaction and equality. On our campuses, such concentrated microsocieties, all that remains unresolved between blacks and whites, all the old wounds and shames that have never been addressed, present themselves for attention—and present our youth with pressures they cannot always handle.

I have mentioned one paradox: racial fears and anxieties among blacks and whites bubbling up in an era of racial equality under the law, in settings that are among the freest and fairest in society. And there is another, related paradox, stemming from the notion of—and practice of—affirmative action. Under the provisions of the Equal Employment Opportunity Act of 1972, all state governments and institutions (including universities) were forced to initiate plans to increase the proportion of minority and women employees— in the case of universities, of students too. Affirmative action plans that establish racial quotas were ruled unconstitutional more than ten years ago in *University of California Regents* v. *Bakke*. But quotas are only the most

8

---

[1] See my essay, "I'm Black, You're White, Who's Innocent? Race and Power in an Era of Blame," *Harper's Magazine,* June 1988. [Au.]

controversial aspect of affirmative action; the principle of affirmative action is reflected in various university programs aimed at redressing and overcoming past patterns of discrimination. Of course, to be conscious of patterns of discrimination—the fact, say, that public schools in the black inner cities are more crowded and employ fewer top-notch teachers than white suburban public schools, and that this is a factor in student performance—is only reasonable. However, in doing this we also call attention quite obviously to difference: in the case of blacks and whites, racial difference. What has emerged on campus in recent years—as a result of the new equality and affirmative action, in a sense, as a result of progress—is a *politics of difference,* a troubling, volatile politics in which each group justifies itself, its sense of worth and its pursuit of power, through difference alone.

In this context, racial, ethnic, and gender differences become forms of sovereignty, campuses become Balkanized, and each group fights with whatever means are available. No doubt there are many factors that have contributed to the rise of racial tension on campus: What has been the role of fraternities, which have returned to campus with their inclusions and exclusions? What role has the heightened notion of college as some first step to personal, financial success played in increasing competition, and thus tension? Mostly what I sense, though, is that in interactive settings, while fighting the fights of "difference," old ghosts are stirred, and haunt again. Black and white Americans simply have the power to make each other feel shame and guilt. In the "real" world, we may be able to deny these feelings, keep them at bay. But these feelings are likely to surface on college campuses, where young people are groping for identity and power, and where difference is made to matter so greatly. In a way, racial tension on campus in the eighties might have been inevitable.

I would like, first, to discuss black students, their anxieties and vulnerabilities. The accusation that black Americans have always lived with is that they are inferior—inferior simply because they are black. And this accusation has been too uniform, too ingrained in cultural imagery, too enforced by law, custom, and every form of power not to have left a mark. Black inferiority was a precept accepted by the founders of this nation; it was a principle of social organization that relegated blacks to the sidelines of American life. So when today's young black students find themselves on white campuses, surrounded by those who historically have claimed superiority, they are also surrounded by the myth of their inferiority.

Of course it is true that many young people come to college with some anxiety about not being good enough. But only blacks come wearing a color that is still, in the minds of some, a sign of inferiority. Poles, Jews, Hispanics, and other groups also endure degrading stereotypes. But two things make the myth of black inferiority a far heavier burden—the broadness of its scope and its incarnation in color. There are not only more stereotypes of blacks than of other groups, but these stereotypes are also more dehumanizing, more focused on the most despised of human traits—stupidity, laziness, sexual immorality, dirtiness, and so on. In America's racial and ethnic hierarchy, blacks have clearly been relegated to the lowest level—have been burdened with an ambiguous, animalistic humanity. Moreover, this is made unavoidable for blacks by the sheer visibility of black skin, a skin that evokes the myth of inferiority on sight. And today this myth is sadly reinforced for many black students by affirmative action programs, under which blacks may often enter college with lower test scores and high-school grade point averages than whites. "They see me as an affirmative action case," one black student told me at UCLA.

So when a black student enters college, the myth of inferiority com- 12 pounds the normal anxiousness over whether he or she will be good enough. This anxiety is not only personal but also racial. The families of these students will have pounded into them the fact that blacks are not inferior. And probably more than anything, it is this pounding that finally leaves a mark. If I am not inferior, why the need to say so?

This myth of inferiority constitutes a very sharp and ongoing anxiety for young blacks, the nature of which is very precise: it is the terror that somehow, through one's actions or by virtue of some "proof" (a poor grade, a flubbed response in class), one's fear of inferiority—inculcated in ways large and small by society—will be confirmed as real. On a university campus, where intelligence itself is the ultimate measure, this anxiety is bound to be triggered.

A black student I met at UCLA was disturbed a little when I asked him if he ever felt vulnerable—anxious about "black inferiority"—as a black student. But after a long pause, he finally said, "I think I do." The example he gave was of a large lecture class he'd taken with more than three hundred students. Fifty or so black students sat in the back of the lecture hall and "acted out every stereotype in the book." They were loud, ate food, came in late—and generally got lower grades than the whites in the class. "I knew I would be seen like them, and I didn't like it. I never sat by them." Seen like what? I asked, though we both knew the answer. "As lazy, ignorant, and stupid," he said sadly.

Had the group at the back been white fraternity brothers, they would not have been seen as dumb *whites,* of course. And a frat brother who worried about his grades would not worry that he would be seen "like them." The terror in this situation for the student I spoke with was that his own deeply buried anxiety would be given credence, that the myth would be verified, and that he would feel shame and humiliation not because of who he was but simply because he was black. In this lecture hall his race, quite apart from his performance, might subject him to four unendurable feelings—diminishment, accountability to the preconceptions of whites, a powerlessness to change those preconceptions, and, finally, shame. These are the feelings that make up his racial anxiety, and that of all blacks on any campus. On a white campus a black is never far from these feelings, and even his unconscious knowledge that he is subject to them can undermine his self-esteem. There are blacks on every campus who are not up to doing good college-level work. Certain black students may not be happy or motivated or in the appropriate field of study—*just like whites*. (Let us not forget that many white students get poor grades, fail, drop out.) Moreover, many more blacks than whites are not quite prepared for college, may have to catch up, owing to factors beyond their control: poor previous schooling, for example. But the white who has to catch up will not be anxious that his being behind is a matter of his whiteness, of his being *racially* inferior. The black student may well have such a fear.

This, I believe, is one reason why black colleges in America turn out 34 percent of all black college graduates, though they enroll only 17 percent of black college students. Without whites around on campus the myth of inferiority is in abeyance and, along with it, a great reservoir of culturally imposed self-doubt. On black campuses feelings of inferiority are personal; on campuses with a white majority, a black's problems have a way of becoming a "black" problem.

But this feeling of vulnerability a black may feel in itself is not as serious a problem as what he or she does with it. To admit that one is made anxious in integrated situations about the myth of racial inferiority is difficult for young blacks. It seems like admitting that one *is* racially inferior. And so, most often, the student will deny harboring those feelings. This is where some of the pangs of racial tension begin, because denial always involves distortion.

In order to deny a problem we must tell ourselves that the problem is something different than what it really is. A black student at Berkeley told me that he felt defensive every time he walked into a class and saw mostly white faces. When I asked why, he said, "Because I know they're all racists. They think blacks are stupid." Of course it may be true that some whites feel this way, but the singular focus on white racism allows this student to obscure his own underlying racial anxiety. He can now say that his problem—facing a class full of white faces, *fearing* that they think he is dumb—is entirely the result of certifiable white racism and has nothing to do with his own anxieties, or even that this particular academic subject may not be his best. Now all the terror of his anxiety, its powerful energy, is devoted to simply *seeing* racism. Whatever evidence of racism he finds—and looking this hard, he will no doubt find some—can be brought in to buttress his distorted view of the problem, while his actual deep-seated anxiety goes unseen.

Denial, and the distortion that results, places the problem *outside* the self and in the world. It is not that I have any inferiority anxiety because of my race; it is that I am going to school with people who don't like blacks.

This is the shift in thinking that allows black students to reenact the protest pattern of the sixties. Denied racial anxiety-distortion-reenactment is the process by which feelings of inferiority are transformed into an exaggerated white menace—which is then protested against with the techniques of the past. Under the sway of this process, black students believe that history is repeating itself, that it's just like the sixties, or fifties. In fact, it is the not-yet-healed wounds from the past, rather than the inequality that created the wounds, that is the real problem.

This process generates an unconscious need to exaggerate the level of   20
racism on campus—to make it a matter of the system, not just a handful of students. Racism is the avenue away from the true inner anxiety. How many students demonstrating for a black "theme house"—demonstrating in the style of the sixties, when the battle was to win for blacks a place on campus—might be better off spending their time reading and studying? Black students have the highest dropout rate and lowest grade point average of any group in American universities. This need not be so. And it is not the result of not having black theme houses.

It was my very good fortune to go to college in 1964, when the question of black "inferiority" was openly talked about among blacks. The summer before I left for college I heard Martin Luther King, Jr., speak in Chicago, and he laid it on the line for black students everywhere. "When you are behind in a footrace, the only way to get ahead is to run faster than the man in front of you. So when your white roommate says he's tired and goes to sleep, you stay up and burn the midnight oil." His statement that we were "behind in a footrace" acknowledged that because of history, of few opportunities, of racism, we were, in a sense, "inferior." But this had to do with what had been done to our parents and their parents, not with inherent inferiority. And because it was acknowledged, it was presented to us as a challenge rather than a mark of shame.

Of the eighteen black students (in a student body of one thousand) who were on campus in my freshman year, all graduated, though a number of us were not from the middle class. At the university where I currently teach, the dropout rate for black students is 72 percent, despite the presence of several academic-support programs; a counseling center with black counselors; an Afro-American studies department; black faculty, administrators, and staff; a general education curriculum that emphasizes "cultural pluralism"; an Educational Opportunities Program; a mentor program; a black faculty and staff association; and an administration and faculty that often announce the need to do more for black students.

It may be unfair to compare my generation with the current one. Parents do this compulsively and to little end but self-congratulation. But I don't congratulate my generation. I think we were advantaged. We came along at a time when racial integration was held in high esteem. And integration was a very challenging social concept for both blacks and whites. We were remaking ourselves—that's what one did at college—and making history. We had something to prove. This was a profound advantage; it gave us clarity and a challenge. Achievement in the American mainstream was the goal of integration, and the best thing about this challenge was its secondary message—that we *could* achieve.

There is much irony in the fact that black power would come along in 24 the late sixties and change all this. Black power was a movement of uplift and pride, and yet it also delivered the weight of pride—a weight that would burden black students from then on. Black power "nationalized" the black identity, made blackness itself an object of celebration and allegiance. But if it transformed a mark of shame into a mark of pride, it also, in the name of pride, required the denial of racial anxiety. Without a frank account of one's anxieties, there is no clear direction, no concrete challenge. Black students today do not get as clear a message from their racial identity as my generation got. They are not filled with the same urgency to prove themselves, because black pride has said, You're already proven, already equal, as good as anybody.

The "black identity" shaped by black power most powerfully contributes to racial tensions on campuses by basing entitlement more on race than on constitutional rights and standards of merit. With integration, black entitlement was derived from constitutional principles of fairness. Black power changed this by skewing the formula from rights to color—if you were black, you were entitled. Thus, the United Coalition Against Racism (UCAR) at the University of Michigan could "demand" two years ago that all black professors be given immediate tenure, that there be special pay incentives for black professors, and that money be provided for an all-black student union. In this formula, black becomes the very color of entitlement, an extra right in itself, and a very dangerous grandiosity is promoted in which blackness amounts to specialness.

Race is, by any standard, an unprincipled source of power. And on campuses the use of racial power by one group makes racial or ethnic or gender *difference* a currency of power for all groups. When I make my difference into power, other groups must seize upon their difference to contain my power and maintain their position relative to me. Very quickly a kind of politics of difference emerges in which racial, ethnic, and gender groups are forced to assert their entitlement and vie for power based on the single quality that makes them different from one another.

On many campuses today academic departments and programs are established on the basis of difference—black studies, women's studies, Asian studies, and so on—despite the fact that there is nothing in these "difference" departments that cannot be studied within traditional academic disciplines. If their rationale truly is past exclusion from the mainstream curriculum, shouldn't the goal now be complete inclusion rather than separateness? I think this logic is overlooked because these groups are too interested in the power their difference can bring, and they insist on separate departments and programs as a tribute to that power.

This politics of difference makes everyone on campus a member of a 28 minority group. It also makes racial tensions inevitable. To highlight one's difference as a source of advantage is also, indirectly, to inspire the enemies of that difference. When blackness (and femaleness) becomes power, then white maleness is also sanctioned as power. A white male student at Stanford told me, "One of my friends said the other day that we should get together and start up a white student union and come up with a list of demands."

It is certainly true that white maleness has long been an unfair source of power. But the sin of white male power is precisely its use of race and gender as a source of entitlement. When minorities and women use their race, ethnicity, and gender in the same way, they not only commit the same sin but also, indirectly, sanction the very form of power that oppressed them in the first place. The politics of difference is based on a tit-for-tat sort of logic in which every victory only calls one's enemies to arms.

This elevation of difference undermines the communal impulse by making each group foreign and inaccessible to others. When difference is celebrated rather than remarked, people must think in terms of difference, they must find meaning in difference, and this meaning comes from an endless process of contrasting one's group with other groups. Blacks use whites to define themselves as different, women use men, Hispanics use whites and blacks, and on it goes. And in the process each group mythologizes and mystifies its difference, puts it beyond the full comprehension of outsiders. Difference becomes an inaccessible preciousness toward which outsiders are expected to be simply and uncomprehendingly reverential. But beware: In this world, even the insulated world of the college campus, preciousness is a balloon asking for a needle. At Smith College, graffiti appears: "Niggers, Spics, and Chinks quit complaining or get out."

Most of the white students I talked with spoke as if from under a faint cloud of accusation. There was always a ring of defensiveness in their complaints about blacks. A white student I spoke with at UCLA told me: "Most white students on this campus think the black student leadership here is made up of oversensitive crybabies who spend all their time looking for things to kick up a ruckus about." A white student at Stanford said: "Blacks do nothing but complain and ask for sympathy when everyone really knows they don't do well because they don't try. If they worked harder, they could do as well as everyone else."

That these students felt accused was most obvious in their compulsion 32 to assure me that they were not racists. Oblique versions of some-of-my-best-friends-are stories came ritualistically before or after critiques of black students. Some said flatly, "I am not a racist, but . . ." Of course, we all deny being racists, but we only do this compulsively, I think, when we are working against an accusation of bias. I think it was the color of my skin, itself, that accused them.

This was the meta-message that surrounded these conversations like an aura, and in it, I believe, is the core of white American racial anxiety. My skin not only accused them, it judged them. And this judgment was a sad gift of history that brought them to account whether they deserved such an accounting or not. It said that wherever and whenever blacks were concerned, they had reason to feel guilt. And whether it was earned or unearned, I think it was guilt that set off the compulsion in these students to disclaim. I believe it is true that in America black people make white people feel guilty.

Guilt is the essence of white anxiety, just as inferiority is the essence of black anxiety. And the terror that it carries for whites is the terror of discovering that one has reason to feel guilt where blacks are concerned— not so much because of what blacks might think but because of what guilt can say about oneself. If the darkest fear of blacks is inferiority, the darkest fear of whites is that their better lot in life is at least partially the result of their capacity for evil—their capacity to dehumanize an entire people for ther own benefit, and then to be indifferent to the devastation their dehumanization has wrought on successive generations of their victims. This is the terror that whites are vulnerable to regarding blacks. And the mere fact of being white is sufficient to feel it, since even whites with hearts clean of racism benefit from being white—benefit at the expense of blacks. This is a conditional guilt having nothing to do with individual intentions or actions. And it makes for a very powerful anxiety because it threatens whites with a view of themselves as inhuman, just as inferiority threatens blacks with a similar view of themselves. At the dark core of both anxieties is a suspicion of incomplete humanity.

So the white students I met were not just meeting me; they were also meeting the possibility of their own inhumanity. And this, I think, is what explains how some young white college students in the late eighties can so frankly take part in racially insensitive and outright racist acts. They were expected to be cleaner of racism than any previous generation—they were born into the Great Society. But this expectation overlooks the fact that, for them, color is still an accusation and judgment. In black faces there is a discomforting reflection of white collective shame. Blacks remind them that their racial innocence is questionable, that they are the beneficiaries of past and present racism, and that the sins of the father may well have been visited on the children.

And yet young whites tell themselves that they had nothing to do with 36 the oppression of black people. They have a stronger belief in their racial innocence than any previous generations of whites, and a natural hostility toward anyone who would challenge that innocence. So (with a great deal of individual variation) they can end up in the paradoxical position of being hostile to blacks as a way of defending their own racial innocence.

I think that is what the young white editors of the *Dartmouth Review* were doing when they shamelessly harassed William Cole, a black music professor. Weren't they saying, in effect, I am so free of racial guilt that I can afford to ruthlessly attack blacks and still be racially innocent? The ruthlessness of that attack was a form of denial, a badge of innocence. The more they were charged with racism, the more ugly and confrontational their harassment became. Racism became a means of rejecting racial guilt, a way of showing that they were not ultimately racists.

The politics of difference sets up a struggle for innocence among all groups. When difference is the currency of power, each group must fight for the innocence that entitles it to power. Blacks sting whites with guilt, remind them of their racial past, accuse them of new and more subtle forms of racism. One way whites retrieve their innocence is to discredit blacks and deny their difficulties, for in this denial is the denial of their own guilt. To blacks this denial looks like racism, a racism that feeds black innocence and encourages them to throw more guilt at whites. And so the cycle continues. The politics of difference leads each group to pick at the sore spots of the other.

Men and women who run universities—whites, mostly—also participate in the politics of difference, although they handle their guilt differently than many of their students. They don't deny it, but still they don't want to *feel* it. And to avoid this *feeling* of guilt they have tended to go along with whatever blacks put on the table rather than work with them to assess their real needs. University administrators have too often been afraid of their own guilt and have relied on negotiation and capitulation more to appease that guilt than to help blacks and other minorities. Administrators would never give white students a racial theme house where they could be "more comfortable with people of their own kind," yet more and more universities are doing this for black students, thus fostering a kind of voluntary segregation. To avoid the anxieties of integrated situations, blacks ask for theme houses; to avoid guilt, white administrators give them theme houses.

When everyone is on the run from his anxieties about race, race relations 40 on campus can be reduced to the negotiation of avoidances. A pattern of demand and concession develops in which each side uses the other to escape itself. Black studies departments, black deans of student affairs, black counseling programs. Afro houses, black theme houses, black homecoming dances and graduation ceremonies—black students and white administrators have slowly engineered a machinery of separatism that, in the name of sacred difference, redraws the ugly lines of segregation.

Black students have not sufficiently helped themselves, and universities, despite all their concessions, have not really done much for blacks. If both faced their anxieties, I think they would see the same thing: academic parity with all other groups should be the overriding mission of black students, and it should also be the first goal that universities have for their black students. Blacks can only *know* they are as good as others when they are, in fact, as good—when their grades are higher and their dropout rate lower. Nothing under the sun will substitute for this, and no amount of concessions will bring it about.

Universities and colleges can never be free of guilt until they truly help black students, which means leading and challenging them rather than negotiating and capitulating. It means inspiring them to achieve academic parity, nothing less, and helping them see their own weaknesses as their greatest challenge. It also means dismantling the machinery of separatism, breaking the link between difference and power, and skewing the formula for entitlement away from race and gender and back to constitutional rights.

As for the young white students who have rediscovered swastikas and the word "nigger," I think they suffer from an exaggerated sense of their own innocence, as if they were incapable of evil and beyond the reach of guilt. But it is also true that the politics of difference creates an environment which threatens their innocence and makes them defensive. White students are not invited to the negotiating table from which they see blacks and others walk away with concessions. The presumption is that they do not deserve to be there because they are white. So they can only be defensive, and the less mature among them will be aggressive. Guerrilla activity will ensue. Of course this is wrong, but it is also a reflection of an environment where difference carries power and where whites have the wrong "difference."

I think universities should emphasize commonality as a higher value 44 than "diversity" and "pluralism"—buzzwords for the politics of difference. Difference that does not rest on a clearly delineated foundation of commonality not only is inaccessible to those who are not part of the ethnic or racial group but is antagonistic to them. Difference can enrich only the common ground.

Integration has become an abstract term today, having to do with little more than numbers and racial balances. But it once stood for a high and admirable set of values. It made difference second to commonality, and it asked members of all races to face whatever fears they inspired in each other. I doubt the word will have a new vogue, but the values, under whatever name, are worth working for.

Points to Consider

1. For Shelby Steele, what are the primary causes of racial tension on college campuses? What does he see as the paradoxes of student racism?

2. Why does Steele think that affirmative action programs foster bad feelings between black and white students? Does he believe that such feelings can be averted? Does he believe that such feelings would have existed without affirmative action?

3. What does Steele cite as the major source of anxiety among black students at predominantly white institutions? What does he cite as the major source of anxiety among white students?

4. Steele says that most of the white students he interviewed were defensive with regard to their attitudes toward black students. What reason does Steele give for their defensiveness? Can you think of some other reasons?

PETE HAMILL

Black and White at Brown   [ESQUIRE / April 1990]

Providence, R.I. When I was young and laboring as a sheet-metal worker in the Brooklyn Navy Yard, I sometimes imagined myself as a student on a college campus. This impossible vision of the Great Good Place was constructed from scraps of movies and magazine photographs, and was for me a combination of refuge and treasure-house. The hard world of tenements and street gangs was replaced in my imagination with buildings made of red brick laced with ivy, and a wide, safe quadrangle where ancient oaks rose majestically to the sky. There was an immense library, offering the secrets of the world. The teachers were like Mr. Chips, at once stern, wise, passionate, and kind. And, of course, there were impossibly beautiful women, long of limb and steady of eye, talking about Fitzgerald or Hemingway, walking beside me on winter evenings with snow melting in their hair.

I never made it. I went to other schools of higher learning: the Navy, Mexico, newspapers. I had absolutely no regrets. But when I walked onto the campus at Brown University recently, that old vision came flooding back. There before me were the buildings, the trees, the open quadrangle that I had ached for as a boy. There were the lights, like molten gold, in the library.

PETE HAMILL (b. 1935) writes a monthly column for Esquire, *in which "Black and White at Brown" appeared. He also contributes to other periodicals, including* Cosmopolitan, Life, *the* New York Times Magazine, *and the* Village Voice. *Hamill is the author of several novels and collections of nonfiction, including* Flesh and Blood *(1977) and* Loving Women *(1989).*

There were the fine young women. I wondered how anyone here could be unhappy.

But I knew that at Brown, and on many similar campuses around the nation, the malignant viruses of the outside world had proved impossible to resist. The worst of these was that ancient curse: racism. Last year, the Justice Department reported racial incidents on seventy-seven campuses, from state universities to the most elite academies, ranging from jokes to full-scale brawls. This was an increase of almost 50 percent over the year before, and Brown, the most liberal of the eight Ivy League schools, was not immune. This struck me as a heartbreaking phenomenon. I grew up believing that racism was a consequence of ignorance. But 80 percent of the students at Brown had finished in the top 10 percent of their high schools. If they were racist, the nation was doomed. I went to take a look.

At the Wriston Quad, everyone I saw was white. At the other campus,   4 called Pembroke (it was once a separate school, for young women), blacks chose to "hang" with blacks. On a visit to a cafeteria, I noticed blacks generally sat with blacks, whites with whites. I heard tales (from whites) of pledges from one of the black fraternities marching around campus in paramilitary style ("They look like the Fruit of Islam, for Christ's sake"). I heard blacks complain about white "insensitivity," or outright racism (shouts of "nigger" from white fraternity houses, watermelon jokes). Whites who called themselves liberals complained about black separatism, symbolized by the hermetic clustering of blacks around the college's Third World Center. One white student said, "It's self-segregation, and they've chosen it, not us." One black student said, "When the whites see more than two blacks at a time, they think about calling the cops instead of saying hello."

None of this, of course, was like Mississippi in the fifties, when the White Citizens Councils owned the night. But it wasn't trivial, either. Many of the discussions here referred to two distinct series of events: The Incidents and The Attacks. The Incidents took place last spring. In April racist graffiti appeared in the West Andrews residence hall on the Pembroke campus. The message NIGGERS GO HOME was found in an elevator, MEN and WOMEN were crossed out on lavatory doors and replaced by WHITES and NIGGERS. Racist words were also written on the doors of minority students' rooms and on posters.

Then, on April 28, a flyer appeared on a bathroom mirror, again in West Andrews. It said: "Once upon a time, Brown was a place where a white man could go to class without having to look at little black faces, or little yellow faces or little brown faces, except when he went to take his meals. Things have been going downhill since the kitchen help moved into the classroom. Keep white supremecy [sic] alive! Join the Brown chapter of the KKK today."

Brown president Vartan Gregorian reacted the next day with righteous fury. He addressed a crowd of 1,500 students on the Green, threatened to expel anyone guilty of spreading racism or homophobia, and said, "There are many outlets for racism and bigotry in this country. Brown will not be one of them, I assure you of that." By all accounts, it was a tough, persuasive performance. Students later presented Gregorian with that quintessential element of the sixties, a List of Demands. He answered them the following week, and although his petitioners weren't completely satisfied, the racist graffiti stopped. The identity of the faceless yahoo was never discovered.

In the fall, The Attacks started. Within a period of three months, twenty-seven students were assaulted in the streets immediately adjacent to the Brown campus. All but four of the victims were white. All of the attackers were young blacks. Seven of the assaults were accompanied by robberies, but the others appeared to be simple cases of underclass black kids arbitrarily beating the crap out of rich white kids. On one level, they were a variation on traditional town-gown conflicts. But the racial factor was impossible to ignore. Gregorian was angered again, called for help from the Providence mayor and police chief, beefed up campus security, but was reluctant publicly to characterize The Attacks as racially motivated. "Until we have clear evidence one way or the other," he said in a letter to parents, "we are treating them as what, in all cases, they clearly were—assaults or assault and battery."

But on campus, there was a continuing discussion of the racial context of the violence. Some black students said that the outsiders were aware of The Incidents in the spring and The Attacks were their way of striking back at racism. This interpretation—the Mugger as Freedom Fighter—infuriated other students. Some whites noted that the organized black students were quick to complain about words directed at blacks, but were generally silent when punches were directed at whites.

"The blacks don't want to admit that there's black racism," one white student told me. A black student seemed to confirm this: "There can't be black racism, it objectively can't exist. When a man fights back against his oppressor, that's not racism."

Out there in the real world, of course, there is as much evidence of black racism as there is of white racism. I've met West Indian blacks who look down upon American blacks, light-skinned blacks who can't abide dark-skinned blacks, southern blacks of the old Creole aristocracy who are uneasy with (or terrified by) the homeboys from the housing projects, and blacks of all classes and pigments who hate whites because they are white. Racism is a grand refusal to see individuals as individuals, each responsible for his or her own actions. No race is immune to the virus.

But at Brown, there are some specific institutions that seem to exacerbate the wounds they are intended to heal. All freshman minority students are invited to come to the campus three days early to take part in the Third World Transition Program (TWTP). The intention of the program is honorable: to help minority students feel comfortable in this new environment, where whites are in the majority. Hearing about it from some minority

8

12

students, I realized that if I'd ever made it to a place like Brown, I might have been singled out for the same kind of help, as a Catholic among WASPs, as a semihood from Brooklyn among the gentry. I also knew that I would have resisted with full fury any attempt to register me in the Street Punk Transition Program. I'd have held off anybody who draped a fatherly arm over my shoulder to tell me I had been so severely maimed by poverty that I needed special help.

So I found myself agreeing with much of the criticism of the TWTP at Brown. It is race-driven; it assumes that nonwhites are indeed different from other Americans, mere bundles of pathologies, permanent residents in the society of victims, and therefore require special help. "They're made to feel separate from the first day they arrive," one alumnus said. "And they stay separate for the next four years." During those three intense days of TWTP, critics say, friendships are forged within a group that excludes whites. By the time white students arrive on campus, defensive cliques have already been formed, racist slights or insensitivities are expected (perhaps even welcomed as proof of the victim theory), and the opportunity for blacks to know whites more intimately (and vice versa) is postponed during a long process of testing that is sometimes permanent.

The term *Third World,* as used at Brown, is itself laughable; I can't believe that even a semiconscious professor would allow such slovenly usage in the classroom. The grouping includes, for example, Japanese and Japanese-American students in an era when Japan is virtually the center of the First World. It also includes those minority students from financially privileged backgrounds who came down the track of prep schools and grew up infinitely more comfortable than most whites. Alas, at Brown, *Third World* is not used to describe people from developing nations (or from economically deprived sectors of the United States); it is a racial concept that includes everyone who is not Caucasian.

That some forms of racism exist at Brown and other campuses is undeniable; they are American institutions, after all, and there is racism in American society at all levels. But after I talked with students, faculty, administrators, and a few alumni, the deeper reasons for the emergence of campus racism remained vague and provisional. In one report, Gregorian suggested some possibilities: "The economic dislocations of the 1980s, a shared sense of 'brotherhood and risk,' ignorance of the civil rights struggles of the sixties and seventies, rampant consumerism, cynicism, narcissism." The Reagan years.

There are other possibilities. Many of today's college students were born 16 in the sixties. The more radical students might have a certain nostalgia for that era, when the goal of every young American wasn't limited to the service of greed. There could be other factors: the growing stupidity of all Americans, the decay of high schools, a reaction to twenty years of affirmative-action programs that are perceived by some as giving blacks unearned advantages, a spreading reaction to the disorder of the underclass. I don't have a single explanation for the phenomenon of campus racism, and I don't think anybody else does, either.

But walking around campus, talking to students, I found my own reactions shifting between anger and envy. In their desire to be what Brown students call P.C. (politically correct), some of these privileged young people seemed to be denying themselves the fullest experience of the social and intellectual feast at which they were guests. Too many black students were postponing (perhaps losing) the chance to learn to function in the country Out There, where blacks make up only 13 percent of the population, and where, for good or bad, true power is attained through compromise and connection. Instead of getting to know white people (thus demystifying them, forging alliances with them on the basis of a common experience), the separatists substitute too much sixties-style oratory about empowerment for hard thought. They waste precious hours on such arcane matters as whether the words *black* or *African American* are P.C.

Worse, by insisting upon being special cases, by institutionalizing the claim to victimhood, by using imprecise nomenclature ("white America," whatever that might be), they become perfect foils for true racists. On campus, those whites who might start with a vague prejudice against blacks find easy reasons to give it a harder form. White liberals, committed to integration, throw up their hands (often too easily) and give their energies to other matters. All of this is both infuriating and sad. If anything, black students with true pride in themselves and their race should be demanding the destruction of the patronizing, self-limiting concept of a Third World ghetto on campus. That would take some courage. But in an era when all of Orwell's "smelly little orthodoxies" are being swept away, nobody should waste a single precious hour on being politically correct. There's too much to do Out There.

That was the basis for my feelings of envy. These young people were the most fortunate of all Americans. While some of them continued arguing the gnarled social issues of the postwar period, *their* century was being shaped by the great changes sweeping across the Soviet Union and Central Europe. The wasteful ideological contests that had mauled my generation were swiftly becoming obscure. That meant these young people were free to enter a new century that might be infinitely better than the dreadful one now coming to its exhausted end. And they could only make that exciting passage with the intellectual tools they acquired at places like Brown. With any luck, in *their* time even the ugly idiocies of racism would become a wan memory.

So I envied them that splendid prospect, as I did their certainties, and   20
their passions, and yes, the red-brick buildings and the libraries, and all the fine young women coming across the quad in the wintry light with snow melting in their hair.

Points to Consider

1. Why did the news of a 50 percent increase in racial incidents at Brown University shock Pete Hamill? What was his fundamental assumption about racism?

2. In Hamill's view was there a link between the off-campus attacks directed toward white students and the antiblack incidents on campus? Why did some black students' remarks about these attacks infuriate white students?

3. Why isn't Hamill supportive of the Third World Transition Program? What does he feel are its dangers? What is the assumption underlying such a program?

4. What is the source of the anger that Hamill admits to feeling toward both white and black students during his visit to Brown? Do you think his anger is justified?

Discussing the Unit

Suggested Topic for Discussion

While both Shelby Steele and Pete Hamill take black students' charges of racism quite seriously, Steele feels that many black students could spend their time more wisely if they stopped demonstrating and concentrated on their studies, whereas Hamill suggests that they stop separating themselves from white students. Do these writers feel that such measures might help to eliminate racism on campus? To what extent do the writers in this unit believe that black students should assume responsibility for their victimization?

Preparing for Class Discussion

1. While Trey Ellis seems to support some form of black separatism on campus, Pete Hamill believes that the negative effects of separatism far outweigh its advantages. Consider your own feelings about separatism. Do you think it is merely a form of self-imposed segregation, or is it a necessary strategy for black survival at predominantly white colleges and universities?

2. Shelby Steele feels that one problem facing black students is the shared perception among blacks and whites that the notion of entitlement is based more and more upon race than upon constitutional rights and

standards of merit. According to Steele, what gave rise to this perception? How do you think such a perception might be corrected?

From Discussion to Writing

One of the worst aspects of racism is that it often prevents its victims from formulating a positive sense of identity. At the same time, separatism, or voluntary withdrawal of minority groups from predominantly white campus communities, seems to promote an unrealistic view of social reality, since only about 13 percent of Americans are black. Educators worry that upon graduation, many black students who successfully created a predominantly black environment for themselves as undergraduates may find it difficult to adjust to the integrated world outside. Write an essay in which you explore the possibility of black students forging a positive identity in a multiracial setting. Consider your own college or university. Do you feel that prevailing student attitudes will permit greater cooperation between blacks and whites to end racism on campus? What do you think is the greatest obstacle to such cooperation?

10

Fighting Words:
Is Free Speech
Threatened on Campus?

In response to a disturbing increase in the amount of racist, sexist, and otherwise offensive speech on campus, many college and university administrators have deemed it necessary to place sanctions on speech that creates a "hostile and intimidating environment" and interferes with the education of victims of the verbal abuse. These sanctions have been labeled unconstitutional by many legal scholars, but other experts on the law have argued the opposite view. In "On Racist Speech," Stanford University law professor Charles R. Lawrence III makes a strong case for restrictions on free speech by appealing to the United States Supreme Court's landmark decision in the case of *Brown* v. *Board of Education*.

Although instituting sanctions may significantly reduce the frequency of racist and sexist remarks on campus, how will the educational process be affected? According to Nat Hentoff, a noted champion of First Amendment rights, these measures pose a serious threat to the very idea of the university and the spirit of academic freedom and free inquiry. In "Free Speech on the Campus," Hentoff provides a frightening description of the silence that is currently descending on America's campuses.

CHARLES R. LAWRENCE III

On Racist Speech

[THE CHRONICLE OF HIGHER EDUCATION / October 25, 1989]

I have spent the better part of my life as a dissenter. As a high-school student, I was threatened with suspension for my refusal to participate in a civil-defense drill, and I have been a conspicuous consumer of my First Amendment liberties ever since. There are very strong reasons for protecting even racist speech. Perhaps the most important of these is that such protection reinforces our society's commitment to tolerance as a value, and that by protecting bad speech from government regulation, we will be forced to combat it as a community.

But I also have a deeply felt apprehension about the resurgence of racial violence and the corresponding rise in the incidence of verbal and symbolic assault and harassment to which blacks and other traditionally subjugated and excluded groups are subjected. I am troubled by the way the debate has been framed in response to the recent surge of racist incidents on college and university campuses and in response to some universities' attempts to regulate harassing speech. The problem has been framed as one in which the liberty of free speech is in conflict with the elimination of racism. I believe this has placed the bigot on the moral high ground and fanned the rising flames of racism.

Above all, I am troubled that we have not listened to the real victims, that we have shown so little understanding of their injury, and that we have abandoned those whose race, gender, or sexual preference continues to make them second-class citizens. It seems to me a very sad irony that the first instinct of civil libertarians has been to challenge even the smallest, most

---

CHARLES R. LAWRENCE III (b. 1943) is a professor of law at Stanford University. He has published many articles in law journals, including "The Id, the Ego, and Equal Protection: Reckoning with Unconscious Racism" (Stanford Law Review, 1987). Lawrence has also cowritten a book, The Bakke Case: The Politics of Inequality *(1979). A longer version of this article appears in the February 1990 issue of* Duke Law Journal *under the title "If He Hollers Let Him Go: Regulating Racist Speech on Campus."*

narrowly framed efforts by universities to provide black and other minority students with the protection the Constitution guarantees them.

The landmark case of *Brown* v. *Board of Education* is not a case that 4 we normally think of as a case about speech. But *Brown* can be broadly read as articulating the principle of equal citizenship. *Brown* held that segregated schools were inherently unequal because of the *message* that segregation conveyed—that black children were an untouchable caste, unfit to go to school with white children. If we understand the necessity of eliminating the system of signs and symbols that signal the inferiority of blacks, then we should hesitate before proclaiming that all racist speech that stops short of physical violence must be defended.

University officials who have formulated policies to respond to incidents of racial harassment have been characterized in the press as "thought police," but such policies generally do nothing more than impose sanctions against intentional face-to-face insults. When racist speech takes the form of face-to-face insults, catcalls, or other assaultive speech aimed at an individual or small group of persons, it falls directly within the "fighting words" exception to First Amendment protection. The Supreme Court has held that words which "by their very utterance inflict injury or tend to incite an immediate breach of the peace" are not protected by the First Amendment.

If the purpose of the First Amendment is to foster the greatest amount of speech, racial insults disserve that purpose. Assaultive racist speech functions as a preemptive strike. The invective is experienced as a blow, not as a proffered idea, and once the blow is struck, it is unlikely that a dialogue will follow. Racial insults are particularly undeserving of First Amendment protection because the perpetrator's intention is not to discover truth or initiate dialogue but to injure the victim. In most situations, members of minority groups realize that they are likely to lose if they respond to epithets by fighting and are forced to remain silent and submissive.

Courts have held that offensive speech may not be regulated in public forums such as streets where the listener may avoid the speech by moving on, but the regulation of otherwise protected speech has been permitted when the speech invades the privacy of the unwilling listener's home or when the unwilling listener cannot avoid the speech. Racist posters, fliers, and graffiti in dormitories, bathrooms, and other common living spaces would seem to clearly fall within the reasoning of these cases. Minority students should not be required to remain in their rooms in order to avoid racial assault. Minimally, they should find a safe haven in their dorms and in all other common rooms that are a part of their daily routine.

I would also argue that the university's responsibility for insuring that 8 these students receive an equal educational opportunity provides a compelling justification for regulations that insure them safe passage in all common areas. A minority student should not have to risk becoming the target of racially assaulting speech every time he or she chooses to walk across campus. Regulating vilifying speech that cannot be anticipated or avoided would not preclude announced speeches and rallies—situations that would give minority-group members and their allies the chance to organize counter-demonstrations or avoid the speech altogether.

The most commonly advanced argument against the regulation of racist speech proceeds something like this: we recognize that minority groups suffer pain and injury as the result of racist speech, but we must allow this hate mongering for the benefit of society as a whole. Freedom of speech is the lifeblood of our democratic system. It is especially important for minorities because often it is their only vehicle for rallying support for the redress of their grievances. It will be impossible to formulate a prohibition so precise that it will prevent the racist speech you want to suppress without catching in the same net all kinds of speech that it would be unconscionable for a democratic society to suppress.

Whenever we make such arguments, we are striking a balance on the one hand between our concern for the continued free flow of ideas and the democratic process dependent on that flow, and, on the other, our desire to further the cause of equality. There can be no meaningful discussion of how we should reconcile our commitment to equality and our commitment to free speech until it is acknowledged that there is real harm inflicted by racist speech and that this harm is far from trivial.

To engage in a debate about the First Amendment and racist speech without a full understanding of the nature and extent of that harm is to risk making the First Amendment an instrument of domination rather than a vehicle of liberation. We have not known the experience of victimization by racist, misogynist, and homophobic speech, nor do we equally share the burden of the societal harm it inflicts. We are often quick to say that we have heard the cry of the victims when we have not.

The *Brown* case is again instructive because it speaks directly to the   12
psychic injury inflicted by racist speech by noting that the symbolic message of segregation affected "the hearts and minds" of Negro children "in a way unlikely ever to be undone." Racial epithets and harassment often cause deep emotional scarring and feelings of anxiety and fear that pervade every aspect of a victim's life.

Brown also recognized that black children did not have an equal opportunity to learn and participate in the school community if they bore the additional burden of being subjected to the humiliation and psychic assault contained in the message of segregation. University students bear an analogous burden when they are forced to live and work in an environment where at any moment they may be subjected to denigrating verbal harassment and assault. The same injury was addressed by the Supreme Court when it held that sexual harassment that creates a hostile or abusive work environment violates the ban on sex discrimination in employment of Title VII of the Civil Rights Act of 1964.

Carefully drafted university regulations would bar the use of words as assault weapons and leave unregulated even the most heinous of ideas when those ideas are presented at times and places and in manners that provide an opportunity for reasoned rebuttal or escape from immediate injury. The history of the development of the right to free speech has been one of carefully evaluating the importance of free expression and its effects on other important societal interests. We have drawn the line between protected and unprotected speech before without dire results. (Courts have, for example, exempted from the protection of the First Amendment obscene speech and speech that disseminates official secrets, that defames or libels another person, or that is used to form a conspiracy or monopoly.)

Blacks and other people of color are skeptical about the argument that even the most injurious speech must remain unregulated because, in an unregulated marketplace of ideas, the best ones will rise to the top and gain acceptance. Our experience tells us quite the opposite. We have seen too many good liberal politicians shy away from the issues that might brand them as being too closely allied with us.

Whenever we decide that racist speech must be tolerated because of the   16
importance of maintaining societal tolerance for all unpopular speech, we are asking blacks and other subordinated groups to bear the burden for the good of all. We must be careful that the ease with which we strike the balance against the regulation of racist speech is in no way influenced by the fact that the cost will be borne by others. We must be certain that those who will pay that price are fairly represented in our deliberations and that they are heard.

At the core of the argument that we should resist all government regulation of speech is the ideal that the best cure for bad speech is good, that ideas that affirm equality and the worth of all individuals will ultimately prevail. This is an empty ideal unless those of us who would fight racism are vigilant and unequivocal in that fight. We must look for ways to offer assistance and support to students whose speech and political participation are chilled in a climate of racial harassment.

Civil rights lawyers might consider suing on behalf of blacks whose right to an equal education is denied by a university's failure to insure a non-discriminatory educational climate or conditions of employment. We must embark upon the development of a First Amendment jurisprudence grounded in the reality of our history and our contemporary experience. We must think hard about how best to launch legal attacks against the most indefensible forms of hate speech. Good lawyers can create exceptions and narrow interpretations that limit the harm of hate speech without opening the floodgates of censorship.

Everyone concerned with these issues must find ways to engage actively in actions that resist and counter the racist ideas that we would have the First Amendment protect. If we fail in this, the victims of hate speech must rightly assume that we are on the oppressors' side.

1. On what grounds is it possible to support the protection of racist speech from government intervention? What other alternatives exist for combating racist speech?

2. What does Charles R. Lawrence III cite as the central problem in the debate over racist speech? How has the fight for freedom of expression come into conflict with the fight against racism?

3. What kind of racist speech falls into the category of "fighting words," the sole exception to First Amendment protection? According to Lawrence, why does racist speech work against freedom of expression?

4. How can the Supreme Court's landmark decision in the antisegregation case of *Brown* v. *Board of Education* be extended to cover "the psychic injury inflicted by racist speech"? According to Lawrence, why would the regulation of certain kinds of speech not open "the floodgates of censorship"?

NAT HENTOFF

Free Speech on the Campus   [THE PROGRESSIVE / May 1989]

A flier distributed at the University of Michigan some months ago proclaimed that blacks "don't belong in classrooms, they belong hanging from trees."

At other campuses around the country, manifestations of racism are becoming commonplace. At Yale, a swastika and the words WHITE POWER! were painted on the building housing the University's Afro-American Cultural Center. At Temple University, a White Students Union has been formed with some 130 members.

Swastikas are not directly only at black students. The Nazi symbol has

---

NAT HENTOFF *(b. 1925) is a staff writer for the* Village Voice *and the* New Yorker *and a columnist for the* Washington Post. *He has written widely on the subject of free speech, and recently published the book* The First Freedom: The Tumultuous History of Free Speech in America *(1989).*

been spray-painted on the Jewish Student Union at Memphis State University. And on a number of campuses, women have been singled out as targets of wounding and sometimes frightening speech. At the law school of the State University of New York at Buffalo, several women students have received anonymous letters characterized by one professor as venomously sexist.

These and many more such signs of the resurgence of bigotry and know- 4
nothingism throughout the society—as well as on campus—have to do solely with speech, including symbolic speech. There have also been physical assaults on black students and on black, white, and Asian women students, but the way to deal with physical attacks is clear: call the police and file a criminal complaint. What is to be done, however, about speech alone—however disgusting, inflammatory, and rawly divisive that speech may be?

At more and more colleges, administrators—with the enthusiastic support of black students, women students, and liberal students—have been answering that question by preventing or punishing speech. In public universities, this is a clear violation of the First Amendment. In private colleges and universities, suppression of speech mocks the secular religion of academic freedom and free inquiry.

The Student Press Law Center in Washington, D.C.—a vital source of legal support for student editors around the country—reports, for example, that at the University of Kansas, the student host and producer of a radio news program was forbidden by school officials from interviewing a leader of the Ku Klux Klan. So much for free inquiry on that campus.

In Madison, Wisconsin, the *Capital Times* ran a story in January about Chancellor Sheila Kaplan of the University of Wisconsin branch at Parkside, who ordered her campus to be scoured of "some anonymously placed white supremacist hate literature." Sounding like the legendary Mayor Frank ("I am the law") Hague of Jersey City, who booted "bad speech" out of town, Chancellor Kaplan said, "This institution is not a lamppost standing on the street corner. It doesn't belong to everyone."

Who decides what speech can be heard or read by everyone? Why, the 8
Chancellor, of course. That's what George III used to say, too.

University of Wisconsin political science professor Carol Tebben thinks otherwise. She believes university administrators "are getting confused when they are acting as censors and trying to protect students from bad ideas. I don't think students need to be protected from bad ideas. I think they can determine for themselves what ideas are bad."

After all, if students are to be "protected" from bad ideas, how are they going to learn to identify and cope with them? Sending such ideas underground simply makes them stronger and more dangerous.

Professor Tebben's conviction that free speech means just that has become a decidedly minority view on many campuses. At the University of Buffalo Law School, the faculty unanimously adopted a "Statement Regarding Intellectual Freedom, Tolerance, and Political Harassment." Its title implies support of intellectual freedom, but the statement warned students that once they enter "this legal community," their right to free speech must become tempered "by the responsibility to promote equality and justice."

Accordingly, swift condemnation will befall anyone who enages in "remarks directed at another's race, sex, religion, national origin, age, or sex preference." Also forbidden are "other remarks based on prejudice and group stereotype."

This ukase is so broad that enforcement has to be alarmingly subjective. Yet the University of Buffalo Law School provides no due-process procedures for a student booked for making any of these prohibited remarks. Conceivably, a student caught playing a Lenny Bruce, Richard Pryor, or Sam Kinison album in his room could be tried for aggravated insensitivity by association.

When I looked into this wholesale cleansing of bad speech at Buffalo, I found it had encountered scant opposition. One protester was David Gerald Jay, a graduate of the law school and a cooperating attorney for the New York Civil Liberties Union. Said the appalled graduate: "Content-based prohibitions constitute prior restraint and should not be tolerated."

You would think that the law professors and administration at this public university might have known that. But hardly any professors dissented, and among the students only members of the conservative Federalist Society spoke up for free speech. The fifty-strong chapter of the National Lawyers Guild was on the other side. After all, it was more important to go on record as vigorously opposing racism and sexism than to expose oneself to charges of insensitivity to these malignancies.

The pressures to have the "right" attitude—as proved by having the "right" language in and out of class—can be stifling. A student who opposes affirmative action, for instance, can be branded a racist.

At the University of California at Los Angeles, the student newspaper ran an editorial cartoon satirizing affirmative action. (A student stops a rooster on campus and asks how the rooster got into UCLA. "Affirmative action," is the answer.) After outraged complaints from various minority groups, the editor was suspended for violating a publication policy against running "articles that perpetuate derogatory or cultural stereotypes." The art director was also suspended.

When the opinion editor of the student newspaper at California State University at Northridge wrote an article asserting that the sanctions against the editor and art director at UCLA amounted to censorship, he was suspended too.

At New York University Law School, a student was so disturbed by the pall of orthodoxy at that prestigious institution that he wrote to the school newspaper even though, as he said, he expected his letter to make him a pariah among his fellow students.

Barry Endick described the atmosphere at NYU created by "a host of watchdog committees and a generally hostile classroom reception regarding any student comment right of center." This "can be arguably viewed as symptomatic of a prevailing spirit of academic and social intolerance of . . . any idea which is not 'politically correct.'"

He went on to say something that might well be posted on campus bulletin boards around the country, though it would probably be torn down at many of them: "We ought to examine why students, so anxious to wield the Fourteenth Amendment, give short shrift to the First. Yes, Virginia, there are racist assholes. And you know what, the Constitution protects them, too."

Not when they engage in violence or vandalism. But when they speak or write, racist assholes fall right into this Oliver Wendell Holmes definition—highly unpopular among bigots, liberals, radicals, feminists, sexists, and college administrators: "If there is any principle of the Constitution that more imperatively calls for attachment than any other, it is the principle of free thought—not free only for those who agree with us, but freedom for the thought we hate."

The language sounds like a pietistic Sunday sermon, but if it ever falls wholly into disuse, neither this publication nor any other journal of opinion—right or left—will survive.

Sometimes, college presidents and administrators sound as if they fully understand what Holmes was saying. Last year, for example, when the *Daily Pennsylvanian*—speaking for many at the University of Pennsylvania—urged that a speaking invitation to Louis Farrakhan be withdrawn, University President Sheldon Hackney disagreed.   24

"Open expression," said Hackney, "is the fundamental principle of a university." Yet consider what the same Sheldon Hackney did to the free-speech rights of a teacher at his own university. If any story distills the essence of the current decline of free speech on college campuses, it is the Ballad of Murray Dolfman.

For twenty-two years, Dolfman, a practicing lawyer in Philadelphia, had been a part-time lecturer in the Legal Studies Department of the University of Pennsylvania's Wharton School. For twenty-two years, no complaint had ever been made against him; indeed his student course evaluations had been outstanding. Each year students competed to get into his class.

On a November afternoon in 1984, Dolfman was lecturing about personal-service contracts. His style somewhat resembles that of Professor Charles Kingsfield in *The Paper Chase*.[1] Dolfman insists that students he calls on be prepared—or suffer the consequences. He treats all students this way—regardless of race, creed, or sex.

This day, Dolfman was pointing out that no one can be forced to work   28

[1] A popular 1974 film starring John Houseman as a stern Harvard law professor.

against his or her will—even if a contract has been signed. A court may prevent the resister from working for someone else so long as the contract is in effect but, Dolfman said, there can "be nothing that smacks of involuntary servitude."

Where does this concept come from? Dolfman looked around the room. Finally, a cautious hand was raised: "The Constitution?"

"Where in the Constitution?" No hands. "The Thirteenth Amendment," said the teacher. So, what does *it* say? The students were looking everywhere but at Dolfman.

"We will lose our liberties," Dolfman often told his classes, "if we don't know what they are."

On this occasion, he told them that he and other Jews, as ex-slaves, spoke at Passover of the time when they were slaves under the Pharaohs so that they would remember every year what it was like not to be free.

"We have ex-slaves here," Dolfman continued, "who should know about the Thirteenth Amendment." He asked black students in the class if they could tell him what was in that amendment.

"I wanted them to really think about it," Dolfman told me recently, "and know its history. You're better equipped to fight racism if you know all about those post–Civil War amendments and civil rights laws."

The Thirteenth Amendment provides that "neither slavery nor involuntary servitude . . . shall exist within the United States."

The black students in his class did not know what was in that amendment, and Dolfman had them read it aloud. Later, they complained to university officials that they had been hurt and humiliated by having been referred to as ex-slaves. Moreover, they said, they had no reason to be grateful for a constitutional amendment which gave them rights which should never have been denied them—and gave them precious little else. They had not made these points in class, although Dolfman—unlike Professor Kingsfield—encourages rebuttal.

Informed of the complaint, Dolfman told the black students he had intended no offense, and he apologized if they had been offended.

That would not do—either for the black students or for the administration. Furthermore, there were mounting black-Jewish tensions on campus, and someone had to be sacrificed. Who better than a part-time Jewish teacher with no contract and no union? He was sentenced by—George Orwell would have loved this—the Committee on Academic Freedom and Responsibility.

On his way to the stocks, Dolfman told President Sheldon Hackney that if a part-time instructor "can be punished on this kind of charge, a tenured professor can eventually be booted out, then a dean, and then a president."

Hackney was unmoved. Dolfman was banished from the campus for what came to be a year. But first he was forced to make a public apology to the entire university and then he was compelled to attend a "sensitivity and racial awareness" session. Sort of like a Vietnamese reeducation camp.

A few conservative professors objected to the stigmatization of Murray Dolfman. I know of no student dissent. Indeed, those students most concerned with making the campus more "sensitive" to diversity exulted in Dolfman's humiliation. So did most liberals on the faculty.

If my children were still of college age and wanted to attend the University of Pennsylvania, I would tell them this story. But where else could I encourage them to go?

Points to Consider

1. Does Nat Hentoff notice a trend in the way college and university administrators are handling the recent surge in racist and sexist speech on campus? What approach do most of these administrators take? What particular aspects of administration and faculty attempts to regulate speech worry Hentoff the most?

2. Why does University of Wisconsin professor Carol Tebben feel that students should be allowed to come into contact with "bad ideas"? How would you define these "bad ideas"?

3. Does a commitment to free speech on campus imply support for racist and sexist elements on campus? Does opposition to racist and sexist speech on campus necessarily imply a firm commitment to the elimination of racism and sexism?

4. Why does Hentoff devote much of his essay to relating the case of University of Pennsylvania lecturer Murray Dolfman? Do you feel that Dolfman was "insensitive" in making the comments he made? Does the context of his remarks give support to the black students' charges that they had been humiliated by Dolfman? In your opinion did Dolfman deserve suspension?

Discussing the Unit

Suggested Topic for Discussion

One key word in the debate over free speech on campus is "insensitivity." The term is used most frequently in reference to people whose remarks represent a failure to embrace current "liberal" attitudes about race and gender. Although the charge of "insensitivity" is weaker than the charges of "racism" or "sexism," to be labeled "insensitive" nevertheless amounts to a kind of ostracism. How are we to know what kinds of speech could be called "insensitive"? Is it possible to establish consistent guidelines for evaluating such language? At what point does "insensitivity" become "racism" or "sexism"?

Preparing for Class Discussion

1. Virtually no campus in America has remained untouched by the recent proliferation of racist and sexist speech and other forms of expression. Can you recall any recent incidents at your own college or university that involved racism or sexism? Compare your examples with those depicted in Nat Hentoff's essay. Pay special attention to how these incidents were handled by the administrations at those schools. How did your own administration handle the problem?

2. Charles R. Lawrence III's argument proposes that certain restrictions must be placed on the freedom of speech if the First Amendment is to fulfill its purpose. What do you think of the notion that in order to preserve freedom we must limit freedom? Do you think that racist and sexist speech could be successfully curtailed through regulation? If it could, would you support such measures?

From Discussion to Writing

Suppose the administration of your college or university was considering a proposal asking all students and faculty to pledge to abstain from the use of language that could be construed as offensive in classrooms, dormitories, dining halls, and other common spaces. Anyone who violated the pledge would be penalized with public condemnation and possible suspension. You have been asked whether you agree to the new proposal. Write your response in the form of an essay in which you weigh the relative advantages and disadvantages of the proposed measure. Do you feel that eliminating racist, sexist, and otherwise offensive speech from your campus is worth this self-imposed restriction on your own freedom of expression? Or do you feel that the introduction of such restrictions would have too many negative effects? In your essay be sure to substantiate your position with examples and relevant evidence.

11

The Canon Controversy: Whose Classics Are They?

Achebe instead of Aristotle? Mishima instead of Machiavelli? Shange instead of Shakespeare? Why are many American colleges and universities casting off some of Western civilization's most influential works in favor of lesser-known non-Western texts? In 1988, Stanford University scrapped its popular first-year course, Western Culture, in order to establish a wider, more multicultural context for the intellectual growth of its students. The installation of the new course, Cultures, Ideas, and Values, sparked a lively debate throughout academia that quickly spilled over into the public arena. One of the first statements by a major public figure on this issue occurred when William Bennett, then secretary of education, addressed the students of Stanford urging them to continue their support for Western values. In his speech, "Why the West?" Bennett sets forth the reasons for his belief that our European heritage must remain the primary focus of liberal studies across America.

Bennett's opinions met with much opposition; his detractors claimed that the multicultural approach is necessary to overcoming the dangers of Eurocentrism. In "Humanities for the Future: Reflections on the Western Culture Debate at Stanford," Mary Louise Pratt, a Stanford professor, argues for this approach while revealing the major issues behind the controversy.

As you read these selections, consider the kinds of charges each side makes against the other. What assumptions can you make about the debate, given the accusatory tone used by people on both sides of the issue?

WILLIAM J. BENNETT

Why the West? [NATIONAL REVIEW / May 27, 1988]

One of the most cherished achievements of Western civilization is its tradition of free and open debate. In particular, the university has served, and should of course continue to serve, as a forum for the free exchange of ideas—an exchange in which all opinions, even those that may be unfashionable or unpopular, are welcomed and even encouraged. In this spirit of open inquiry, I appreciate the opportunity to speak here at Stanford on the subject, "Why the West?"

Stanford's decision . . . to alter its Western Culture program was not a product of enlightened debate, but rather an unfortunate capitulation to a campaign of pressure politics and intimidation. For evidence of this, let me briefly turn to the sequence of events as I understand it from press accounts and from individuals at Stanford.

The Western Culture program was established in 1980. By all accounts, the program was immensely popular with both faculty and students—in fact, a good many students considered it their most worthwhile academic experience at Stanford. In the spring of 1986, a small but very vocal group of students called on the university to abolish the program. In its place, they proposed a course that would emphasize the "contributions of cultures disregarded and/or distorted by the present program." This marked the beginning of a steady stream of charges against the existing course, and

---

WILLIAM J. BENNETT (b. 1943) is former director of the Office of National Drug Control Policy. He has had a key role in forming the United States's antidrug policies since he assumed this position in 1989. This article is adapted from a speech Bennett gave at Stanford University in April of 1988, when he served as secretary of education under Ronald Reagan.

against the Western tradition that sustained the existing course—charges of racism, sexism, imperialism, elitism, and ethnocentrism.

The Stanford administration appointed a task force to evaluate the   4 program. The group's preliminary report—which was to become the basic working document for the "Cultures, Ideas, and Values" (CIV) course that replaced Western Culture—prompted a great deal of discussion and debate among faculty and students alike. What is unfortunate is that one side of the debate was, in certain subtle and not so subtle ways, discouraged from making its case. Supporters of the proposal were encouraged to air their views, and they did so frequently and forcefully—in the papers, at rallies, and during demonstrations. Last spring some members of the so-called Rainbow Agenda student group occupied President Donald Kennedy's office for five hours and released a set of ten demands, one of which was the adoption of the task-force proposal. So far as I know, no one was punished or even censured for this occupation. When, however, opponents of the proposal ventured words of criticism, they were publicly taken to task by the administration for reacting too hastily or harshly.

Last fall, a faculty-senate subcommittee met to consider the CIV proposal. Students disrupted this meeting, chanting, "Down with racism, down with Western Culture, up with diversity." One participant in the interruption was quoted as saying, "The [subcommittee] was getting a bit timid and we wanted them to be well aware of the dedication to changing the Western Culture program." The subcommittee got the message and sent the proposal on to the faculty senate for prompt consideration.

The faculty senate deliberated, discussed, and amended the CIV proposal at several meetings. But at the meeting on March 31, there was a heightened sense of urgency. By this point the issue had been publicized extensively, and many simply wanted to get it over with. The proponents of CIV demanded that the matter be brought to a swift and certain conclusion. Amendments proposed by the faculty senate's steering committee that would have shifted CIV to a more Western orientation were unacceptable, they said. President Kennedy urged the senate not to allow the prospect of a "best" proposal to undermine its chances of a "very good" one.

Why was it so necessary for the senate to make its decision on that particular day? More important, why was it so necessary for the senators to accept the proposal without the steering committee's amendments? The answer may be found in the answer to my next question: Why were there two hundred angry CIV supporters apparently ready to disrupt the meeting if a vote on a particular amendment went the "wrong way"? "We would have walked in. We would have interrupted," a student leader was quoted as saying.

Many more instances, much more evidence could be adduced. But this   8 much is clear: CIV was primarily a political, not an educational decision.

The tactics of intimidation that were employed throughout the debate's two-year history not only brought about CIV's success; they were—and they continue to be—central to CIV's meaning. The cultivation and promotion of "diversity" is held up as the primary goal of CIV, but its supporters have done much to discourage free and open debate of the issue.

There have been attempts to portray CIV as a minor pedagogical change—a slight alteration in a single Stanford freshman requirement. Indeed, at first blush, CIV has an air of intellectual respectability to it. The plan for the new course contains the language of something intellectually promising—it talks about "diversity," "self-understanding," and "the common intellectual experience." But the fact is that the old core reading list of fifteen significant works in Western philosophy and literature has been thrown out. Instead, CIV instructors will decide year by year what the content of the course will be. And following the guidelines set down on March 31, the instructors must include works by "women, minorities, and persons of color," and at least one work per quarter that explicitly deals with race, gender, or class. Does anyone doubt that selecting works based on the ethnicity or gender of their authors trivializes the academic enterprise? Does anyone really doubt the political agenda underlying these provisions?

The events of the past two years at Stanford, therefore, serve as a striking example of what Allan Bloom has called "the closing of the American mind." In the name of "opening minds" and "promoting diversity," we have seen in this instance the closing of the Stanford mind. Observing the events from close by, the distinguished American philosopher Sidney Hook has written that he regards "as far more significant than the ultimate constitution and fate of the course in Western culture, the manner in which the discussion at Stanford has so far been conducted." Professor Hook finds that matter of discussion deeply troubling for American higher education. And so do I.

Life, of course, will go on. In fact, now that the debate appears to be over, one can predict what is likely to happen. First, I believe, Stanford will be praised for being "forward-looking," "progressive," and "innovative." Second, other universities will decide that they should change their programs in the same or similar ways. Third, Stanford will continue to prosper. Some alumni will be uneasy about what has happened here, but only a few of them will withhold their support from the university on that account. Fourth, I suspect that this will be only the beginning—the first of many chapters. The methods that succeeded in pushing CIV through the faculty senate have shown that intimidation works—that intimidation *can* take the place of reason. The loudest voices have won, not through force of argument, but through bullying, threatening, and name-calling. That's not the way a university should work.

Fifth and finally, Stanford will be harmed—though perhaps not visibly, 12 perhaps not for a while—by these recent events. I say "not visibly" because many of those who deplore what has transpired here will not say so publicly. They know that speaking out against CIV will invite charges of racism—an utterly false but highly damaging accusation. To his credit, President Kennedy recently spoke out against such name-calling, such McCarthyism of the left. But the name-calling, having been tolerated for so long, is not likely to cease. For now the defenders of Western culture will mostly confine themselves to talking quietly with one another about what has happened. But they know what they know, and others around the country know it too: that for a moment, a great university was brought low by the very forces that modern universities came into being to oppose—ignorance, irrationality, and intimidation.

Our universities should oppose these forces because our universities are the bearers, the transmitters, of Western civilization. And above all else, Western civilization stands for the claim that the life of the mind can and should prevail over ignorance, irrationality, and intimidation. That is why it is ironically appropriate that the issue on which Stanford capitulated was whether a course in Western civilization should be included in the freshman curriculum. The issue of the merits of the course came to stand for the issue of the merits of Western civilization as a whole. The core issue under debate is: Why the West?

Why must we study, nurture, and defend the West? I'll give you four reasons. First, because it is ours. It is the culture in which we live and in which most of us will continue to live, whether our grandparents are African or Asian, Hungarian or Mexican, Muslim or Shinto. Our institutions and ideals—our schools and universities and their great, still honored traditions, our churches and synagogues, our government and laws, even our notions of friendship and family—have all acquired their shape and significance through the course of Western history, largely though not exclusively through the European experience. To be sure, China, India, Africa, and other societies and cultures have made contributions to our institutions and ideals. Where contributions have been made, they must be acknowledged. Where new contributions emerge, they must be included. Historically, this has in fact been the standard Western practice: Western civilization is strong in part because it is open—it studies and learns from others.

The second reason we must study the West is that it is good. It is not all good. There are certainly great blots on its record. Nevertheless, the West has produced the world's most just and effective system of government: the system of representative democracy. It has set the moral, political, economic, and social standards for the rest of the world. To quote Allan Bloom, "Our story is the majestic and triumphant march of two principles: freedom and equality." And those principles now define no less than a universal standard of legitimacy.

This leads me to the third reason—the reason that Western civilization's   16 critics seem to have entirely missed: the West is a source of incomparable intellectual complexity and diversity and depth. Western civilization is emphatically *not* an endorsement of a particular "party line." On the contrary, the West's long history of self-critical dialogue is one of its greatest strengths. Since the time of Socrates, what has distinguished the West is its insistence, in principle, on the questoning of accepted ways and beliefs—its openness to the appeal to nature, to use Socratic terms, as opposed to mere convention. It is true that the West has often failed, beginning with the death of Socrates, fully to live up to this principle—but the principle has always animated the Western experience.

The point of contemporary higher education is this: the classics of Western philosophy and literature amount to a great debate on the perennial questions. To deprive students of this debate is to condemn them to improvise their ways of living in ignorance of their real options and the best arguments for each. In the tradition of Peter Abelard, our civilization offers a great *sic et non* on the human condition. Consider the point/counterpoint of Western thought. On the ends of government, whom do we follow—Madison or Marx? On the merits of the religious life—Aquinas or Voltaire? On the nobility of the warrior—Homer or Erasmus? On the worth of reason—Hegel or Kierkegaard? On the role of women—Wollstonecraft or Schopenhauer? The study of Western civilizations is not, then, a case for ideology; it is a case for philosophy and for thoughtfulness. It considers not only the one hand, but the one hand *and* the other—and, just as often, the third and fourth hands as well. Those who take the study of the West seriously end up living a variety of different lives and arriving at a diversity of opinions and positions. And for this there is unparalleled tolerance and encouragement.

Indeed, some of the West's greatest teachers and statesmen are those who have participated most vigorously in this continual process of dissent, discussion, and redirection. In our time, this tradition is well exemplified by the Reverend Martin Luther King, Jr. Reverend King immersed himself in the writings of the great philosophers: "from Plato to Aristotle," as he wrote, "down to Rousseau, Hobbes, Bentham, Mill, and Locke." These great thinkers—these *Western* thinkers—helped teach and inspire Reverend King to tear down the ugly injustices of Jim Crow.

It is true that Reverend King was also inspired by the example of a non-Western—Gandhi. We should give credit where credit is due, and we should study Gandhi's thought and deeds, as we should study the thought and deeds of others from outside the West. But I would add that in this case, when we study Gandhi, we shall see that Gandhi was himself very much indebted to such Western philosophers as Henry David Thoreau, and to such Anglo-American traditions as the rule of law. So even in studying Gandhi's East, one cannot escape the West. Now, of course, nothing stops Stanford from requiring a course in non-Western traditions of thought; indeed much commends such an idea. But such an idea in no way diminishes the importance, the necessity, of studying the West.

Each year since becoming education secretary, I've been invited to the 20 Martin Luther King Center to deliver an address marking Reverend King's birthday. And each year I speak of how Reverend King drew strength and purpose from his education, an education in the Western intellectual tradition. Last year, at Stanford, Reverend King's birthday was marked by Jesse Jackson leading a group of students in the now famous cry: "Hey, hey, ho, ho, Western Culture's got to go." Just a week earlier, I had been at the King Center talking about Reverend King's self-proclaimed debt to Western thought. Either Reverend King was right, or Reverend Jackson is right. I'll stand with King.

This brings me to my final reason for studying and protecting the West and its unique tradition of open discourse and philosophic inquiry: we must do so because the West is under attack. Oftentimes the assault comes from outside the West, but sometimes, sadly, it comes from within. Those who attack Western values and accomplishments do not see an America that— despite its imperfections, its weaknesses, its sins—has served and continues to serve as a beacon to the world. Instead, theirs is an America hopelessly tainted—tainted by racism, imperialism, sexism, capitalism, ethnocentrism, elitism, and a host of other "isms." Such rhetoric has been used over and over again as a justification for the abolition of the Western Culture program here at Stanford. As one member of the Stanford community has said: "The Western Culture program gives intellectual justification to sexism, racism, and national chauvinism." So, the assertion goes, by diminishing the study of the West in our colleges and universities, we can make an important step toward ridding the world of these unholy "isms."

I would remind those critics that it is Western civilization that has taught much of the world about the evils of "sexism, racism, and national chauvinism." Indeed, it is the West that has given us the very language used to attack the West here at Stanford. After all, where do the concepts of rights, equality, and, yes, diversity come from? It is in the West, it is from the West, that we have learned—over time, through struggle, after bloodshed—to stand squarely behind liberty and equality for all people. An honest study of the West will provide the reasons for its protection. But how are we to protect the West if we set about systematically robbing ourselves of opportunities to know and study it?

Let me therefore say to Stanford students: study the West, study it well and thoughtfully, and build on that study as you continue your education. In saying "study the West," I don't mean study *only* the West. Of course not. But if what I've said here is even partly true, the West is worthy of your study.

Let me close with a quote from William James. Speaking at a Founder's Day celebration on this campus in 1906, James set forth his vision for Stanford's "ideal destiny":

> Can we not, as we sit here today, frame a vision of what [Stanford] may be a century hence, with the honors of the intervening years all rolled up in its traditions? Not vast, but intense; . . . a place for . . . training scholars; devoted to truth; radiating influence; setting standards.

Now, almost "a century hence," we can ask whether Stanford has lived up to James's vision. For the moment, in this instance, I believe it has not. But it is not too late. Stanford can turn the events of the past two years to its advantage by rejecting sloganeering and political pressure. In so doing, Stanford would be true to its purpose as, in James's words, a place devoted to truth and setting standards.

Points to Consider

1. Is William Bennett justified when he calls the decision to adopt CIV a political rather than educational decision? What evidence does he offer for his conclusion?

2. What does Bennett feel is the great irony of CIV supporters' claim that such a course introduces much-needed diversity into the curriculum? How does the study of Western values create a context for the discussion of educational alternatives?

3. Why does Bennett invoke the figures of Dr. Martin Luther King, Jr., and Gandhi to support his views on the West? Is it significant that both of these men advocated passive resistance to oppressive political structures?

4. How does Bennett depict the supporters of curricular reform? Does his scenario of a radical special interest group that was able to pressure a timid Stanford University administration into making the reforms seem feasible? How else might the reforms have come about?

MARY LOUISE PRATT

Humanities for the Future: Reflections on the Western Culture Debate at Stanford

[THE SOUTH ATLANTIC QUARTERLY / Winter 1990]

> SWM, 38, 5'10", N/S, Stanford scientist, average-looking, a bit eccentric, blindingly brilliant, phenomenally funny, amazingly humble, likes jogging, bicycling, all things done with racquet-like instruments, movies, literature and most aspects of western civilization, but most interested in a reasonably attractive and intelligent 25–45 PA female capable of being interested in me. Send photo & brief description of your life, liberty and pursuits of happiness. Box 65C.

This singles ad appeared late last summer in the personals column of a local weekly serving the communities of Palo Alto, California, and neighboring Stanford University. Apart from its intriguing characterization of the "Stanford scientist," I quote it here to suggest the extent to which Stanford's long and intense debate over its Western culture curriculum last year permeated local life. In the semiotics of representation and identity, "Western civilization" remains a constant and intensely meaningful point of reference.

The debate which took place at Stanford during the winter of 1988 and the resulting reform of the Western culture requirement received a great deal of national attention, largely due to the involvement of then Secretary of Education William Bennett, who chose to use the Stanford case as a platform to advocate his views, quite literally making a federal case out of it. Perhaps because of Bennett's own partisanship, the account of the Stanford debate in the national press had a shape somewhat different from the local experience. As other institutions face similar struggles, fuller accounts of the work-

---

MARY LOUISE PRATT (b. 1948) is a professor in the Department of Spanish and Portuguese and the Department of Comparative Literature at Stanford University. She is also the chair of the Program in Modern Thought and the Nina Crocker Faculty Scholar. She has written and cowritten several books, including Women, Politics, and Culture in Latin America *(1990) and* Imperial Eyes *(1991).*

ings of change at Stanford may be helpful. At the same time, there is an urgent need to formulate the concerns that so unexpectedly made freshman book lists an object of wide public concern. What nerves had been touched?

Histories of Western culture curricula in the United States point to the Western civilization course instituted at Columbia University in 1919 as a main antecedent for such courses all over the country. One recent account, however, notes that the Columbia course had a direct antecedent of its own, a War Issues course instituted in 1918 at various universities, including Columbia. Its aim was "to educate recently conscripted American soldiers about to fight in France . . . to introduce [them] to the European heritage in whose defense they were soon to risk their lives."[1] A new tie to Europe was constituted in relation to a national imperative.

Current struggles over Western culture curricula—both challenges to them and reactionary attempts to reassert them—also emerge from urgently felt national imperatives. Among these is an imperative to reimagine cultural and civic identity in the United States in the wake of vast changes produced by the decline of its global hegemony, the rapid internationalization of capital and industry, the immigrant implosion of the "Third World" onto the "First," and the democratization of American institutions and political processes that occurred in the two decades prior to 1980. The question can be posed in Pierre Bourdieu's sometimes helpful language: what is to count as "cultural capital" in a culturally plural nation and a globalized human world? How will that capital be constructed and deployed, how will people be asked to identify with it? How might the United States project itself into the future as a cultural and political entity? In the words (a few of which I've emphasized) of one speaker in the Stanford debate:

> The character of U. S. society is changing. More and more North Americans insist on affirming the specificity of their class, ethnicity, gender, region, race, or sexual orientation, rather than melting into the homogenizing pot. They see such affirmations as *intrinsic to their citizenship*. Culture, literature, and the academy have been important sites for the affirmations: it will be neither productive nor comfortable to commit ourselves only to resisting these developments, rather than engaging with them.

Having acquiesced to change, by what visions will United Statesians be guided into a future where they and their society will be different from what they are now? What is the United States trying to become? What are the options?

---

[1] See Gilbert Allardyce, "The Rise and Fall of the Western Civilization Course," *American Historical Review* 87 (1982): 695–743, cited by Herbert Lindenberger in his admirable essay, "On the Sacrality of Reading Lists: The Western Culture Debate at Stanford University," to appear in the British journal *Comparative Criticism,* Fall 1989. [Au.]

The world is full of multicultural, multiethnic, multilingual nations, so there are plenty of models around. Indeed, Bloom, Bennett, Bellow, and the rest (known by now in some quarters as the Killer B's) are advocating one of them: to create a narrowly specific cultural capital that will be the normative *referent* for everyone, but will remain the *property* of a small and powerful caste that is linguistically and ethnically unified. It is this caste that is referred to by the "we" in Saul Bellow's astoundingly racist remark that "when the Zulus have a Tolstoy, *we* will read him." Few doubt that behind the Bennett-Bloom program is a desire to close not the American mind, but the American university, to all but a narrow and highly uniform elite with no commitment to either multiculturalism or educational democracy. Thus while the Killer B's (plus a C—Lynne Cheney, the Bennett mouthpiece now heading the National Endowment for the Humanities) depict themselves as returning to the orthodoxies of yesteryear, their project must not be reduced to nostalgia or conservatism. Neither of these explain the blanket contempt they express for the country's universities. They are fueled not by reverence for the past, but by an aggressive desire to lay hold of the present and future. The B's act as they do not because they are unaware of the cultural and demographic diversification under way in the country; they are utterly aware. That is what they are trying to shape; that is why they are seeking, and using, national offices and founding national foundations.

Many citizens are attracted to Bloom's and Bennett's pronouncements, on the other hand, out of fairly unreflected attachments to the past (including their own college experience), and simply have trouble seeing how good books could possibly do any harm. Many people are perfectly ready for change but remain deeply anxious about where it is all supposed to be heading. Other visions of the cultural and educational future in the United States, then, are likely to generate as much interest as the Killer B's, if they can be effectively introduced into the national discussion. The attention drawn by Bloom's intellectually deplorable *Closing of the American Mind* and Bennett's intellectually more deplorable "To Reclaim a Legacy" most directly reflects not levels of enthusiasm for their programs (though much enthusiasm does exist), but levels of anxiety that have developed around the issue of national cultural identity. Even among the many people ready for change, one seems to hear voices asking, "If I give up white supremacy, who am I? Am I still American? Am I still white? If I give up homophobia, who am I? Am I the same as gay? If I give up misogyny, am I still a man? a woman? an American? If I learn Spanish, does it make me Mexican? What ties me to these gays, these feminists, these Salvadorans, these Vietnamese, these Navaho, these white people?" And perhaps more acutely, "What ties them to me?" The sooner answers to these questions are attempted, the better. What, indeed, would it mean to adopt the "nonhierarchical, intercultural perspective on the study of culture and the West" called for by one Stanford humanist (a classicist, at that)? What can cultural citizenship and identity be in a radically plural society enmeshed in relentlessly globalizing relations? Can there be transnational national culture? Can it be good?

Alongside the understandable apprehensions such questions generate (especially late in a century), it should be possible to create some excitement and curiosity. After all, this could become, perhaps has become, a fabulously energetic and revealing cultural experiment. It has tremendous imaginative appeal. Does the United States not badly need to revitalize its image and understanding of itself? Is there not much to be learned about the fluid global cultureways that bring the music of Soweto into living rooms across the United States, and make *The Cosby Show* the most popular TV program in South Africa? Is there not much to be learned about the past by rereading it in the light of contemporary intercultural understanding?

Stanford adopted its first Western civilization course in 1935, and, like many other universities, abolished it around 1970. Efforts to restore a requirement began around 1975 on the part of a group of senior faculty in literature, classics, and history. By 1978 a two-year pilot program had been approved and in 1980 a new year-long required course began for all incoming students. It consisted of several tracks corresponding roughly to different departments and schools, and sharing a core reading list that became the focus of the controversy. It is interesting to note that the notorious reading list was not part of the original proposal for the requirement. The list evolved during the pilot program out of desire to guarantee a "common intellectual experience," a phrase that acquired great importance in the subsequent debate without acquiring any greater specificity of meaning. Here is the much-discussed list:

ANCIENT WORLD

Required:
Hebrew Bible, Genesis
Plato, *Republic,* major portions of
    books 1–7
Homer, major selections from *Iliad,*
    Odyssey, or both
At least one Greek tragedy
New Testament, selections
    including a gospel

Strongly recommended:
Thucydides
Aristotle, *Nicomachean Ethics,*
    Politics
Cicero
Virgil, Aeneid
Tacitus

MEDIEVAL AND RENAISSANCE

Required:
Augustine, *Confessions,* 1–9
Dante, *Inferno*

Strongly recommended:
Boethius, *Consolation of*
    Philosophy

More, *Utopia*
Machiavelli, *The Prince*
Luther, *Christian Liberty*
Galileo, *The Starry Messenger, The Assayer*

Aquinas, some selection which illustrates the structure of a Thomistic question
A Shakespearean tragedy
Cervantes, *Don Quixote*
Descartes, *Discourse on Method, Meditations*
Hobbes, *Leviathan*
Locke, *Second Treatise of Civil Government*

MODERN

Required:
Voltaire, *Candide*
Marx and Engels, *Communist Manifesto*
Freud, *Outline of Psychoanalysis, Civilization and Its Discontents*
Darwin, *Selections*

Strongly recommended:
Rousseau, *Social Contract, Confessions, Emile*
Hume, *Enquiries, Dialogues on Natural Religion*
Goethe, *Faust, Sorrows of Young Werther*
Nineteenth-century novel
Mill, *Essay on Liberty, The Subjection of Women*
Nietzsche, *Genealogy of Morals, Beyond Good and Evil*

Participants in developing the course say that in its specifics the list was not intended to be written in stone. It represented a series of compromises rather painfully hammered out by a committee, inevitably through some of the crudest kind of horse-trading—Catholics for Protestants, poets for scientists, Italians for Germans. In the end, ironically, the difficulty of negotiating the list was one source of its permanence: the process had been so painful and so lacking in intellectual integrity that no one expressed the slightest desire to repeat it.

In any case, regardless of its specific content, the list did the job of shaping the requirement in, for many people, unnecessarily narrow ways. Indeed, its extreme narrowness clearly contributed to the breakdown of the program at Stanford. Most conspicuously, the list installed a specific historical paradigm: one quarter for ancient world, one for medieval-renaissance, and one for the past five hundred years. Implicit in the sequence was the canonical narrative of origins deriving the present from classical Greece via the Italian Renaissance and the Franco-German Enlightenment, a narrative that begins and ends with European lettered high culture. (Where is America?) Clearly, teachers of the course could question that implicit narrative, and some did. But to do so in a consistent or structured way involved teaching against the grain of the syllabus, an extremely difficult pedagogical task that often confused students more than it empowered them.

Second, the list not only lays down a Eurocentric paradigm, but also embodies a very restricted sense of Europe. France and even England are barely represented in the required readings; Iberia, Eastern Europe, and Scandinavia not at all. Only "high" culture is represented, an exclusion that has long been under challenge not just by the Black Students' Union, but by whole schools of mainstream literary and historical scholarship. One thinks of the scholars at Princeton's Center for European Studies, or the Berkeley-based new historicism, movements that are in no way radical or critical of the West, but which refuse to give "high" culture or belles lettres a monopoly on cultural understanding. Many Stanford scholars were troubled by the fact that the course organized itself around authors and orthodoxies rather than around problematics or issues, and that it therefore took *as* orthodoxies matters that were actually under serious debate in their fields. Translated into practice, this amounted to a structure of exclusion of faculty who took other perfectly legitimate approaches to culture and to the West, as well as of faculty who worked in non-European literatures and cultures. "For some scholars," said one colleague, "to see a book or an entire cultural tradition as if it were a self-contained whole is like listening to only one side of a phone conversation. For these scholars there is no place in the current program."

Third, the list implicitly suggests a monumentalist attitude to the texts as great works whose interest and value were sui generis. Again, teachers were of course not forbidden to adopt a critical attitude, but to do so required teaching from the negative position of a counter-discourse or a heresy. What you couldn't do was embark positively on a different project or way of thinking, even one that was equally celebratory and equally Eurocentric. An attempt was made to set up a critical track, a course titled "Conflict and Change in Western Culture." In many ways this course was extremely successful, but its founders were constantly hampered by the structure of center and periphery into which they were locked. To bring in other texts was always to bring in "Other" texts. In the end, this structure of otherness comprises, depending on your perspective, the main *obstacle to* or the main *bulwark against* relational approaches to culture. "The *notion* of a core list," argued one teacher in the history track,

> is inherently flawed, regardless of what kind of works it includes or excludes. It is flawed because such a list undermines the critical stance that we wish students to take toward the materials they read. . . . A course with such readings creates two sets of books, those privileged by being on the list and those not worthy of inclusion. Regardless of the good intentions of those who create such lists, the students have not viewed and will not view these separate categories as equal.

The asymmetry can be exemplified by a remark made in support of retaining the core list. Referring to the autobiography of the West African Olaudah Equiano, published in England in the late eighteenth century, one English scholar argued that students "who have studied Genesis, Aquinas, and Rousseau have a good chance of understanding with some precision what the ex-slave Olaudah Equiano meant when he spoke of 'that first natural right of mankind . . . independency.'" The remark, true enough in a way, easily invites some troubling inferences. Would one want to suggest that students who have *not* studied Genesis, Aquinas, and Rousseau have *no* chance of understanding Equiano? That Equiano himself would not have understood liberty without his European education? Neither inference is true in the slightest. There are plenty of readings that can serve to illuminate Equiano to American students, and these certainly include Rousseau, Aquinas, and Genesis. As for Equiano himself, no slave ever needed Rousseau or anybody else to know the difference between freedom and slavery, though a slave might find Rousseau helpful (as Equiano did) in attempting to argue matters with the enslavers. It is not from Europeans that enslaved peoples have learned how to construct cultures that conserve a sense of humanity, meaningful life, and an abiding vision of freedom in the face of the West's relentless imperial expansion. Indeed, it is essential to reverse the direction of inference and note that students who have read Equiano have a good chance of understanding what Rousseau meant in talking about human rights and equality. From there follows the question many find deeply but unnecessarily disturbing: to what extent was Rousseau influenced indirectly by the African slaves, whose fearsome rebellions and unquenchable demands for change echoed constantly back to Europe from the colonial frontier? From an intercultural perspective, the initial statement about Equiano taken by itself reproduces a monumentalist cultural hierarchy that is historically as well as morally distortive.

Many critics felt that the Western culture program set a tone for the humanities as a whole at Stanford, in the words of one Latin Americanist, making "second-class citizens out of faculty whose work focuses on non-European literatures, on noncanonical writers, on European literatures not included in the core, or on the West in dialogue with other parts of the world." In terms of faculty, in the years the Western culture program was in place, classics outgrew all the departments of modern languages and literatures; a Europeanist comparative literature department was founded; the English department continued to boast four medievalists while African, African-American, and Caribbean literatures in English were represented by a single half-time faculty member (whose tenure was hotly contested), and so-called "Commonwealth" literature not at all. The curriculum in French continued to include not a single course in Franco-African or even Quebecois literature. The number of Chicano faculty remained the same in 1988 as it was in 1972. A new humanities center, on the other hand, did assert a

12

broader range, successfully seeking out interdisciplinary scholars and grants to fund minority and Third World fellows.

The opposition to the Western culture curriculum that eventually coalesced at Stanford was there pretty much from the beginning. In the planning stages, it turned out, no fewer than seven other proposals for a culture requirement had been made and set aside. Several of these involved intercultural perspectives and heavily non-European materials. Right from the start many faculty in relevant fields chose not to participate in the course, including what was described as a near boycott by minority, women, and younger faculty. Then a beginning assistant professor, I recall vividly being asked to teach a section in one of the tracks. When I objected to the absence of the Iberian world and the Americas from the core list, I was told I might be invited to give a lecture on things written in Spanish since *Don Quixote*, "if I thought there was anything worth talking about." But really, the senior historian said, the advantage of the assignment was that it would help me avoid getting caught in a "Hispanic rut."

The fact that the course excluded or marginalized the work of many of the university's own humanities faculty made it a good deal more expensive than anticipated. Several hundred thousand dollars a year were needed to pay instructors on short-term contracts, most of them recent Ph.D.'s in the humanities. Many of these teachers did not share the monumentalist project, and they too became an impetus for change, as they introduced other materials and perspectives in their sections. By the time the reform was proposed, the core list was widely tampered with and no longer enforced. Some people were teaching against the grain—but the grain was still very much there. Organized student advocacy of reform was a consistent and essential component throughout the three-year process. Student momentum began to coalesce during Rainbow Coalition activity for the 1984 election, and through the intense antiapartheid activity of 1985–86. A coalition of student groups, including the Black Students' Union, the Movimiento Estudiantil Chicano de Aztlan (MEChA), the Stanford American Indian Organization, the Asian American Student Association, and Students United for Democracy in Education formed to exert continuous pressure on the reform process, from within and without.

The chronology of the reform process ran roughly as follows:

1. In the spring of 1986 the dean of undergraduate studies, a European 16 historian and the first woman to hold the position, appointed a task force to review the Western culture requirement and produce recommendations for the faculty senate's Committee on Undergraduate Studies. The task force consisted of three undergraduate students, two senior historians (one Europeanist and one African-Americanist), a senior philosopher (who had helped draft the original requirement), a senior woman classicist (who had

taught in the "critical" track of the course), a senior Chicano administrator, and one of the lecturers in the program.

2. Throughout the 1986–87 academic year the task force met regularly, speaking with all the relevant parties and anyone else who wished to address them. In the spring of 1987 they released an interim report calling for a reconception and restructuring of the requirement. This trial balloon provoked a great deal of discussion and response that was quite polarized.

3. In the late autumn of 1987, believing it had the support of all relevant parties, the task force released a revised report and recommendations to the Committee on Undergraduate Studies. The report argued (in passages later deleted) that "courses that do not acknowledge in some degree both the cultural diversity of Europe and the even greater diversity of our present American society have increasingly come to seem intellectually inadequate"; such courses, moreover, "have been open to the charge of being socially irresponsible, however unintentionally and inadvertently, for they seem to perpetuate racist and sexist stereotypes and to reinforce notions of cultural superiority that are wounding to some and dangerous to all in a world of such evident diversity." The report recommended a modified requirement called Culture/Ideas/Values (CIV) structured around a series of ground rules rather than a core list. Four instructional objectives were proposed which can be summarized as follows: increasing understanding of cultural diversity and interaction within the United States and elsewhere; engaging students with works that have intellectual importance "by virtue of the ideas they express, their mode of expression, or their influence"; developing critical thinking; and increasing skills in reading, reasoning, arguing, and analyzing texts. Requirements for social, geographical, and historical diversity would mean courses designed to "confront issues relating to class, ethnicity, race, religion, gender, and sexual orientation; to include the study of works by women, minorities, and persons of color"; to study works from at least one European and at least one non-European culture in their own historical and cultural context; and to involve at least six to eight centuries of historical depth.

4. In January of 1988 the new recommendations headed for the floor of the faculty senate with committee approval. At this juncture, opponents of the reform surprised many by introducing counterlegislation which retained the status quo but added one woman and one black writer to the core list for the third quarter of the course. This polarizing move set the stage for the debate that went on through the winter and into the spring. The faculty senate at Stanford is an elected body of fifty-five faculty members which inevitably includes a high proportion of senior scholars and former administrators. Given Stanford's composition, the senate is dominated numerically by faculty from the sciences and professional schools. Advocates of the reform were unprepared for a floor fight in the senate, most of whose members had not been educated as to the stakes and the issues. Senators

were prone to support the familiar status quo. On the other hand, the election of this particular senate had involved, for the first time, a small effort to promote women candidates. Though this was not done with the Western culture debate in mind, the four women elected each made crucial contributions on behalf of the reform.

It would be absurd to summarize the untold hours of meetings, statement writing and reading, corridor talk, cynical maneuvering, and brutal negotiating sessions that followed. Despite the Machiavellian dimensions, two decisions in particular gave the process a democratic character that lends credence to the outcome. First, the weekly faculty/staff newspaper announced that it would print all statements on the matter that it received, from any person. An extraordinary number and range of people responded, making this newspaper the main medium for the community debate. Within the senate, it was likewise decided that anyone who signed up to make a statement would be permitted to do so, whether or not they were a member of the senate, and again many people responded, including student representatives. Thus, within the local taboos on, say, openly racist or openly Marxist language, a fairly full range of views was expressed, with deep conviction and eloquence on all sides. (The scientists, one should note, showed no reservations about expressing themselves on the matter, though it proved extremely difficult to communicate the issues to them.) The five senate meetings on the subject were opened to anyone who requested visitor status, though visitors could not participate. As a result, senate meetings uncannily reproduced the very core-periphery structure that was under debate. In a large round amphitheater, the senators, overwhelmingly senior white men, sat in the middle while up around the outside were gathered the women faculty, the minority faculty, the students, the black and Chicano administrators, all the "other Americans" not authorized to speak, but speaking powerfully through their bodily presence. There we were on the margins, we said, but *we were in the room,* and something had to be constructed that came to grips with that fact.

Perhaps the biggest surprise for naive observers like myself as we listened and read was what some of us came to call the "willful ignorance" factor. It was saddening to hear academics saying please don't make me read anything new. I refuse to agree there are things I am ignorant of that are important and worthwhile. "Does that make me a racist?" one old friend and colleague asked. What would Aretha Franklin reply, I wondered. At the same time, especially given the rantings of the official right, it is important to affirm the thoughtfulness and intellectual quality of the discussion that took place at Stanford, and to give you some examples. It was, for example, George Will and not an academic colleague who, amazingly, called for courses that "affirm this fact: America is predominantly a product of the Western tradition and is predominantly good because that tradition is good." It was William F. Buckley, and not a Stanford professor, who displayed his ignorance by declaring that "from Homer to the nineteenth century no great book has emerged from any non-European source." Below I offer some excerpts from what Stanford faculty and students did say, for and against the reform (the quotations are taken from statements published in the campus newspaper):

Con: Education is an exercise of modesty, a process whereby we give up some of ourselves to gain an understanding of that which is *not* ourselves, an understanding of things still shaping us. It's a kind of surrender; we learn that some things are superior in consequence to us, even to our particular gender, to our particular ethnic heritage, to all the parochialism to which we are subject. Then the apparent foreignness of the past, its record of people seemingly *unlike* ourselves, becomes much less foreign and those people much less strange and irrelevant.

Pro: The famous texts of the past cannot continue to live for us if we simply place them on a pedestal and teach our students to worship them. Only if we see them as engaged with the stuff of history, both of the times in which they were written and of those later times, can we give a continuing life to these texts and to our cultural tradition as a whole. Only if we understand how the idea of a Western culture took shape in differing ways over the centuries and how it defined itself in relation to other forms of culture, can we justify giving it the prime consideration . . . to our students.

Con: As a historian of the United States, I would be the last person to deny the ethnic, racial, and cultural complexity of American society. But, from the same perspective, I find it puzzling, if not troubling, to learn that some of the dominant and influential ideas in modern America are to be seen [in the new legislation] as originating outside the West. Few historians of the United States believe that the culture of this country has been seriously influenced by ideas from Africa, China, Japan, or indigenous North America. . . . There is no direct connection between the dominant ideas and institutions in American culture and the cultures of Africa or Eastern Asia. [The roots of American culture], if one is talking about ideas and institutions, are derived overwhelmingly from Europe. To contend otherwise, I think would cause American historians to scratch their heads in amazement.

Pro: A "liberal education" for our time should expand beyond the culture-bound, basically colonialist, horizon that relies, albeit subtly, on the myth of the cultural superiority of the "West" (an ill-defined entity, in any event, whose borders are ludicrously artificial). . . . Does the new, integrated vision of Area One entail our teaching the Greek Hermes and Prometheus alongside the North American Indian Coyote or the West African Anansi and Legba as paradigms of trickster heroes, or Japanese Noh alongside Greek drama or Indian philosophy alongside Plato? If the answer is yes, so much the better.

Pro: I was never taught in Western Culture the fact that the Khemetic or "Egyptian" Book of the Dead contained many of the dialectic principles

24

attributed to Greece, but was written three thousand years earlier, or the fact that Socrates, Herodotus, Pythagoras, and Solon studied in Egypt and acknowledged that much of their knowledge of astronomy, geometry, medicine, and building came from the African civilizations in and around Egypt. . . . I was never told that algebra came from Moslem Arabs, or numbers from India. I was never informed when it was found that the "very dark and wooly haired" Moors in Spain preserved, expanded, and reintroduced the classical knowledge that the Greeks had collected, which led to the "renaissance." . . . I read the Bible without knowing St. Augustine looked black like me, that the ten commandments were almost direct copies from the 147 negative confessions of Egyptian initiates, or that many of the words of Solomon came from the black pharaoh Amen-En-Eope. I didn't learn that Toussaint L'Ouverture's defeat of Napoleon in Haiti directly influenced the French Revolution or that the Iroquois Indians in America had a representative democracy which served as a model for the American system. . . . I'm damned if my children have to go to a school that preaches diversity, then refuses to practice its own values because it was scared.

In the end, the reform legislation was passed, with some substantial amendments. One, for instance, required courses to "include treatment of ancient and medieval cultures"; another required faculty teaching in the program to agree each spring on a set of "common elements" which all tracks would share the following year. The latter amendment, which finally broke the deadlock, is a very big loophole. It leaves open the unlikely possibility of faculty agreeing to restore the entire core list, or of the whole battle being fought over in miniature every spring. At the moment, it seems more likely that the parties will learn to understand each other better through this compulsory conversation. The actual consequences of the reform remain uncertain, however. With only minor alterations, the standard Great Books course *can* continue to exist at Stanford, and nobody is being required to reeducate him or herself. You can certainly talk about gender without challenging sexism, or race without challenging racism, or class without challenging classism. On the other hand, a space has been made for much greater change by those who desire it. Tracks constructed around other understandings of culture and broader perspectives on the West are now possible. Their existence and survival depends, however, on the presence of sufficient faculty to teach them, and the hiring and tenuring of such faculty is not possible without the acquiescence of those who opposed the reform. It is no accident that the final amendment passed by the senate deleted a phrase calling for the recruitment of minority faculty to teach in the new program. In the larger national picture, it seems fair to say that the new program puts Stanford in the vanguard of the rear guard, for other schools have long since left our modest reform behind. (Write, for example, for the catalog of Oglala College in Pine Ridge, South Dakota.)

Three faculty have jointly prepared a course according to the new guide-   28 lines. It is a course called Europe and the Americas which studies the European, African, and native American strands of American cultures, and the history of their interaction in the Americas. Canonical European texts retain a place in the course, but rather than forming its center of gravity, they simply coexist with American, Caribbean, Spanish-American, native-American, and Anglo-American materials. "The complex interactions of colonialism, slavery, migration and immigration," says the course's preamble, "have produced on this side of the Atlantic societies that are highly diverse in origin, and in many cases multicultural and syncretic. European traditions play a prominent and indeed decisive role in these societies, *though by no means the same roles they play in Europe.*" At times the course adopts a comparative perspective—Haitian Vodun and Greek Dionysus are brought together, for instance, in a section on religious syncretism and ecstatic cults; a section on representations of the self juxtaposes the extroverted, historicized self-representation of a Navaho oral history with the confessional modes of St. Augustine and Freud. Historical dialogues are pursued—the legacy of Shakespeare's *The Tempest* in Aimé Césaire's *A Tempest,* José Enrique Rodó's *Ariel,* and Roberto Fernández Retamar's *Calibán* are examined; the give-and-take between European enlightenment discourse on human rights, American independence movements, abolitionism, and slave rebellions is considered; indigenous traditions are traced, from the ancient Mayan *Popul Vuh,* for instance, to the contemporary *testimonio* by Guatemalan indigenous activist Rigoberta Menchu, or from the pre-Columbian Inca state to the Spanish conquest (through Andean eyes) to the great Andean rebellions of the 1780s to the contemporary Quechua poetry of José María Arguedas. Terms like creolization, transculturation, and syncretism are used to develop an approach to culture that is relational and at the same time recognizes the internal fullness and integrity of particular moments and formations.

Approaches to culture and to United States culture such as those this course adopts are widespread in higher education, but are scarcely to be found in official discourse on education, nor in the national media's depictions of the curricular controversy. Partisans of reform have so far had little success at getting across in the public discourse the modes of understanding against which the monumentalist approach seems narrow and impoverished. Few people reading Bloom or Bennett, even those critical of them, can bring to bear a picture of what nonhierarchical, relational approaches to culture are or what people stand to gain from learning them. Stanford's scientists, in being asked to vote for reform, had little idea of what they were voting *for.* How could they not fall back on the common sense of the man in the personals ad I quoted at the beginning who simply likes most aspects of Western civilization? (As the West Texan is supposed to have said against daylight saving time, "If central time was good enough for Jesus Christ, it's good enough for me!") When then Secretary Bennett and Stanford President Donald Kennedy debated the issue on the *MacNeil/Lehrer Report,* neither party possessed a clear picture of alternative visions of culture, the West, or the United States. Bennett knew only vaguely what he was opposing, and Kennedy what he was defending. Lehrer also seemed to be groping for an unknown. And yet, one goes on to wonder, why should the discussion remain in the hands of those three people, a remarkably uniform group? Where are the voices of those who have the most fundamental, bodily stakes in efforts for change? For the moment, those voices are not authorized to speak for "us" all, the way Bennett, Kennedy, and Lehrer can. When they are, change will have occurred.

The final amendments-to-the-amendments on the Stanford reform were resolved in the last week of May 1988. In the days that followed, a series of local events suggested with unexpected clarity the need for the experiment Stanford had embarked on. A student was expelled from his dormitory after a year of disruptive activity directed especially toward a gay resident assistant, culminating in an assault on the resident and the vandalizing of the dormitory lounge. The following evening, ten fraternity brothers, in defense of the expelled student's freedom of speech, staged a silent vigil at midnight outside the dormitory lounge wearing masks and carrying candles, a gesture that seemed to deliberately invoke the customs of the Ku Klux Klan. The reactions of black students who assembled at the site ranged from terror to outrage, and the action was treated by the university as a serious racial and homophobic incident. The ten demonstrators, however, claimed complete ignorance of the associations their vigil invoked. They did not know, they said, that masks and candles at midnight had any connotations—it is just what they thought a vigil was. The following day a group of sorority women, as part of a rush ritual, performed a mock "Indian dance" around a fountain which happened to stand in the doorway of the native American student center. Asked to stop, they refused, later saying they did not intend to offend, or see the dance as offensive. It was just a tradition.

Many people did not believe these students' pleas of ignorance. But either way, the call for educational change was reinforced. If it is possible for young adults to leave the American educational system ignorant of the history of race relations in the United States (not part of standard Western culture curricula), then something needs to change. And if a person who knows the history of race relations and their symbolizations feels free to reenact racist rituals of mockery or intimidation, something needs to change. At the same time, blame must be placed where it belongs. In pleading ignorance, the students were following the example of many of the country's own leaders, for whom ignorance had become an acceptable standard of public life. Throughout their high school and college years these students had looked to a president who consistently showed himself to be both ignorant and utterly comfortable with his ignorance. (The Stanford incidents coincide with Reagan's extraordinary remarks in Moscow about the "coddling" of native Americans.) For many of us exhausted by conflict that spring, these discouraging incidents reminded us of what we were fighting for.

A week later a less weighty event drew local attention, when two California students turned up as the two finalists in the National Spelling Bee. Their names were Rageshree Ramachandran, an Indian-born American from Fair Oaks (who won), and Victor C. Wang, a Chinese American from Camarillo (who came in second). Nothing could have suggested more clearly the multicultural, multiethnic future taking shape on the West Coast. The final words in the spelling bee, the report noted, were these: buddleia (from an Englishman's surname), araucaria (from South American indigenous language), mhometer (from a German electrician's surname, spelled backwards), ovoviviparous (from Latin), caoutchouc (from another South American indigenous language, via French), stertorous (from Latin), and elegiacal (from Greek). "Who makes up these words?" asked Victor Wang as he went down to defeat on "stertorous." Good question, Victor. And as you head on up the educational ladder, I hope you find a system that will give you an honest and imaginative answer.

Points to Consider

1. What is Mary Louise Pratt's attitude toward William Bennett? Why does she feel that his attention to the Stanford controversy adversely affected media coverage of the debate?

2. According to Pratt, what is the origin of courses like Stanford's Western Culture? Does she think that such courses are still necessary? What changes does she think the world has undergone to justify curricular reform?

3. Pratt charges that the Western Culture course not only neglects non-European texts, but also offers only minimal representation of the literatures of England and France. Why would course planners tend to underrepresent those national literatures given their role in our heritage?

4. Does Pratt's careful chronicle of the events at Stanford influence your ideas about the reforms? How does Pratt's account differ from Bennett's description? How does Pratt represent the faculty members who stand against reform?

Discussing the Unit

Suggested Topic for Discussion

The Western canon, the collection of important works of Western culture held in common, is often spoken of as a list of texts that may not be subtracted from or added to. Do you feel that this perception is accurate? As an experiment, try as a class to derive your own first-year "canon." Construct guidelines for the inclusion or exclusion of works from Western culture as well as influential non-Western works. Compare your "canon" with the traditional and the reformed Stanford canons as described by Mary Louise Pratt. What does this experiment teach you about canon formation?

Preparing for Class Discussion

1. William Bennett cites Allan Bloom's *The Closing of the American Mind*, and Mary Louise Pratt is careful to link Bennett with Bloom. Read Bloom's essay "Music" on page 240. Do you find similarities between the attitudes presented in the Bloom essay and the Bennett speech? What assumptions about culture seem to link these two intellectuals?

2. Obtain descriptions of courses in Western civilization or world literature taught at your own college or university. What are the professed goals of such courses? Examine the lists of works covered in these courses. Do they contain works of the kind taught at Stanford before reform? What kinds of non-Western texts, if any, are included in the course description? Do you think the inclusion of such works is important to your understanding of your culture?

From Discussion to Writing

Imagine that you are a member of an academic committee in charge of recommending texts for a revised first-year curriculum. Carefully choose a work you admire and write a recommendation based on the work's educational value and significance for our culture at large. You may make your selection from non-Western literature or from the literatures of minorities, women, or homosexuals. Be sure to offer careful support for your decision.

12

Rock: Music or Menace?

In recent years rock music has come under fire from religious groups, angry parents, and even the United States government. All these groups charge that America's most popular music contributes to problems ranging from falling SAT scores to drug addiction, from vandalism to teen suicide. One recent critique of rock music was written by the University of Chicago scholar Allan Bloom, whose book *The Closing of the American Mind* was seen by many as the eighties' most influential study of the state of higher education. In "Music," Bloom sets forth what he sees as the dangerous effect of rock music on America's youth. According to Bloom, rock music "encourages passions and provides models that have no relation to any life the young people who go to universities can possibly lead, or to the kinds of admiration encouraged by liberal studies. Without the cooperation of the sentiments, anything other than technical education is a dead letter."

In the wake of the controversy generated by Bloom's book, other scholars, such as Yale University's María Rosa Menocal, responded to Bloom's charges. In her essay, "We Can't Dance Together," Menocal takes the stance that rock music does indeed have cultural value, and explores its affinities with the great traditions of music and literature in Western civilization.

Clearly, even though their viewpoints differ sharply, both Bloom and Menocal see rock music as a serious cultural phenomenon. While reading the two essays, consider your own views on rock: do you think the authors are exaggerating the effects of rock on the American mind and heart?

ALLAN BLOOM

Music [THE CLOSING OF THE AMERICAN MIND / 1987]

Though students do not have books, they most emphatically do have music. Nothing is more singular about this generation than its addiction to music. This is the age of music and the states of soul that accompany it. To find a rival to this enthusiasm, one would have to go back at least a century to Germany and the passion for Wagner's operas. They had the religious sense that Wagner was creating the meaning of life and that they were not merely listening to his works but experiencing that meaning. Today, a very large proportion of young people between the ages of ten and twenty live for music. It is their passion; nothing else excites them as it does; they cannot take seriously anything alien to music. When they are in school and with their families, they are longing to plug themselves back into their music. Nothing surrounding them — school, family, church — has anything to do with their musical world. At best that ordinary life is neutral, but mostly it is an impediment, drained of vital content, even a thing to be rebelled against. Of course, the enthusiasm for Wagner was limited to a small class, could be indulged only rarely and only in a few places, and had to wait on the composer's slow output. The music of the new votaries, on the other hand, knows neither class nor nation. It is available twenty-four hours a day, everywhere. There is the stereo in the home, in the car; there are concerts; there are music videos, with special channels exclusively devoted to them, on the air nonstop; there are the Walkmans so that no place — not public transportation, not the library — prevents students from communing with the Muse, even while studying. And, above all, the musical soil has become tropically rich. No need to wait for unpredictable genius. Now there are

ALLAN BLOOM (b. 1930) is professor in the Committee on Social Thought at the University of Chicago, where he also codirects the John M. Olin Center for Inquiry into the Theory and Practice of Democracy. Bloom has published translations of Plato's Republic *and Rousseau's* Emile, *and has coauthored a book on Shakespeare's political plays. He has taught at many universities, including Yale, Cornell, Toronto, and Tel Aviv. "Music" is a chapter from Bloom's* The Closing of the American Mind *(1987). The ideas for this chapter and others in the book originally appeared in an essay in* National Review, *December 10, 1982.*

many geniuses, producing all the time, two new ones rising to take the place of every fallen hero. There is no dearth of the new and the startling.

The power of music in the soul — described to Jessica marvelously by Lorenzo in the *Merchant of Venice* — has been recovered after a long period of desuetude. And it is rock music alone that has effected this restoration. Classical music is dead among the young. This assertion will, I know, be hotly disputed by many who, unwilling to admit tidal changes, can point to the proliferation on campuses of classes in classical music appreciation and practice, as well as performance groups of all kinds. Their presence is undeniable, but they involve not more than 5 to 10 percent of the students. Classical music is now a special taste, like Greek language or pre-Columbian archeology, not a common culture of reciprocal communication and psychological shorthand. Thirty years ago, most middle-class families made some of the old European music a part of the home, partly because they liked it, partly because they thought it was good for the kids. University students usually had some early emotive association with Beethoven, Chopin, and Brahms, which was a permanent part of their makeup and to which they were likely to respond throughout their lives. This was probably the only regularly recognizable class distinction between educated and uneducated in America. Many, or even most, of the young people of that generation also swung with Benny Goodman, but with an element of self-consciousness — to be hip, to prove they weren't snobs, to show solidarity with the democratic ideal of a pop culture out of which would grow a new high culture. So there remained a class distinction between high and low, although private taste was beginning to create doubts about whether one really liked the high very much. But all that has changed. Rock music is as unquestioned and unproblematic as the air the students breathe, and very few have any acquaintance at all with classical music. This is a constant surprise to me. And one of the strange aspects of my relations with good students I come to know well is that I frequently introduce them to Mozart. This is a pleasure to me, inasmuch as it is always pleasant to give people gifts that please them. It is interesting to see whether and in what ways their studies are complemented by such music. But this is something utterly new to me as a teacher; formerly my students usually knew much more classical music than I did.

Music was not all that important for the generation of students preceding the current one. The romanticism that had dominated serious music since Beethoven appealed to refinements — perhaps overrefinements — of sentiments that are hardly to be found in the contemporary world. The lives people lead or wish to lead and their prevailing passions are of a different sort that those of the highly educated German and French bourgeoisie, who were avidly reading Rousseau and Baudelaire, Goethe and Heine, for their spiritual satisfaction. The music that had been designed to produce, as well as to please, such exquisite sensibilities had a very tenuous relation to American lives of any kind. So romantic musical culture in America had had for a long time the character of a veneer, as easily susceptible to ridicule as were Margaret Dumont's displays of coquettish chasteness, so aptly exploited by Groucho Marx in *A Night at the Opera*. I noticed this when I first started teaching and lived in a house for gifted students. The "good" ones studied their physics and then listened to classical music. The students who did not fit so easily into the groove, some of them just vulgar and restive under the cultural tyranny, but some of them also serious, were looking for things that really responded to their needs. Almost always they responded to the beat of the newly emerging rock music. They were a bit ashamed of their taste, for it was not respectable. But I instinctively sided with this second group, with real, if coarse, feelings as opposed to artificial and dead ones. Then their musical sans-culotteism won the revolution and reigns unabashed today. No classical music has been produced that can speak of this generation.

Symptomatic of this change is how seriously students now take the famous passages on musical education in Plato's *Republic*. In the past, students, good liberals that they always are, were indignant at the censorship of poetry, as a threat to free inquiry. But they were really thinking of science and politics. They hardly paid attention to the discussion of music itself and, to the extent that they even thought about it, were really puzzled by Plato's devoting time to rhythm and melody in a serious treatise on political philosophy. Their experience of music was as an entertainment, a matter of indifference to political and moral life. Students today, on the contrary, know exactly why Plato takes music so seriously. They know it affects life very profoundly and are indignant because Plato seems to want to rob them of their most intimate pleasure. They are drawn into argument with Plato about the experience of music, and the dispute centers on how to evaluate it and deal with it. This encounter not only helps to illuminate the phenomenon of contemporary music, but also provides a model of how contemporary students can profitably engage with a classic text. The very fact of their fury shows how much Plato threatens what is dear and intimate to them. They are little able to defend their experience, which has seemed unquestionable until questioned, and it is most resistant to cool analysis. Yet if a student can — and this is most difficult and unusual — draw back, get a critical distance on what he clings to, come to doubt the ultimate value of what he loves, he has taken the first and most difficult step toward the philosophic conversion. Indignation is the soul's defense against the wound of doubt about its own; it reorders the cosmos to support the justice of its cause. It justifies putting Socrates to death. Recognizing indignation for what it is constitutes knowledge of the soul, and is thus an experience more philosophic than the study of mathematics. It is Plato's teaching that music, by its nature, encompasses all that is today most resistant to philosophy. So it may well be that through the thicket of our greatest corruption runs the path to awareness of the oldest truths.

Plato's teaching about music is, put simply, that rhythm and melody, accompanied by dance, are the barbarous expression of the soul. Barbarous, not animal. Music is the medium of the *human* soul in its most ecstatic condition of wonder and terror. Nietzsche, who in large measure agrees with Plato's analysis, says in *The Birth of Tragedy* (not to be forgotten is the rest of the title, *Out of the Spirit of Music*) that a mixture of cruelty and coarse sensuality characterized this state, which of course was religious, in the service of gods. Music is the soul's primitive and primary speech and it is *alogon,* without articulate speech or reason. It is not only not reasonable, it is hostile to reason. Even when articulate speech is added, it is utterly subordinate to and determined by the music and the passions it expresses.

Civilization or, to say the same thing, education is the taming or domestication of the soul's raw passions — not suppressing or excising them, which would deprive the soul of its energy — but forming and informing them as art. The goal of harmonizing the enthusiastic part of the soul with what develops later, the rational part, is perhaps impossible to attain. But without it, man can never be whole. Music, or poetry, which is what music becomes as reason emerges, always involves a delicate balance between passion and reason, and, even in its highest and most developed forms — religious, warlike, and erotic — that balance is always tipped, if ever so slightly, toward the passionate. Music, as everyone experiences, provides an unquestionable justification and a fulfilling pleasure for the activities it accompanies: the soldier who hears the marching band is enthralled and reassured; the religious man is exalted in his prayer by the sound of the organ in the church; and the lover is carried away and his conscience stilled by the romantic guitar. Armed with music, man can damn rational doubt. Out of the music emerge the gods that suit it, and they educate men by their example and their commandments.

Plato's Socrates disciplines the ecstasies and thereby provides little consolation or hope to men. According to the Socratic formula, the lyrics — speech and, hence, reason — must determine the music — harmony and rhythm. Pure music can never endure this constraint. Students are not in a position to know the pleasures of reason; they can only see it as a disciplinary and repressive parent. But they do see, in the case of Plato, that that parent has figured out what they are up to. Plato teaches that, in order to take the spiritual temperature of an individual or a society, one must "mark the music." To Plato and Nietzsche, the history of music is a series of attempts to give form and beauty to the dark, chaotic, premonitory forces in the soul — to make them serve a higher purpose, an ideal, to give man's duties a fullness. Bach's religious intentions and Beethoven's revolutionary and humane ones are clear enough examples. Such cultivation of the soul uses the passions and satisfies them while sublimating them and giving them an artistic unity. A man whose noblest activities are accompanied by a music that expresses them while providing a pleasure extending from the lowest bodily to the highest spiritual, is whole, and there is no tension in him between the pleasant and the good. By contrast a man whose business life is prosaic and unmusical and whose leisure is made up of coarse, intense entertainments, is divided, and each side of his existence is undermined by the other.

Hence, for those who are interested in psychological health, music is at 8 the center of education, both for giving the passions their due and for preparing the soul for the unhampered use of reason. The centrality of such education was recognized by all the ancient educators. It is hardly noticed today that in Aristotle's *Politics* the most important passages about the best regime concern musical education, or that the *Poetics* is an appendix to the *Politics*. Classical philosophy did not censor the singers. It persuaded them. And it gave them a goal, one that was understood by them, until only yesterday. But those who do not notice the role of music in Aristotle and despise it in Plato went to school with Hobbes, Locke, and Smith, where such considerations have become unnecessary. The triumphant Enlightenment rationalism thought that it had discovered other ways to deal with the irrational part of the soul, and that reason needed less support from it. Only in those great critics of Enlightenment and rationalism, Rousseau and Nietzsche, does music return, and they were the most musical of philosophers. Both thought that the passions — and along with them their ministerial arts — had become thin under the rule of reason and that, therefore, man himself and what he sees in the world have become correspondingly thin. They wanted to cultivate the enthusiastic states of the soul and to re-experience the Corybantic possession deemed a pathology by Plato. Nietzsche, particularly, sought to tap again the irrational sources of vitality, to replenish our dried-up stream from barbaric sources, and thus encouraged the Dionysian and the music derivative from it.

This is the significance of rock music. I do not suggest that it has any high intellectual sources. But it has risen to its current heights in the education of the young on the ashes of classical music, and in an atmosphere in which there is no intellectual resistance to attempts to tap the rawest passions. Modern-day rationalists, such as economists, are indifferent to it and what it represents. The irrationalists are all for it. There is no need to fear that "the blond beasts" are going to come forth from the bland souls of our adolescents. But rock music has one appeal only, a barbaric appeal, to sexual desire — not love, not *eros,* but sexual desire undeveloped and untutored. It acknowledges the first emanations of children's emerging sensuality and addresses them seriously, eliciting them and legitimating them, not as little sprouts that must be carefully tended in order to grow into gorgeous flowers, but as the real thing. Rock gives children, on a silver platter, with all the public authority of the entertainment industry, everything their parents always used to tell them they had to wait for until they grew up and would understand later.

Young people know that rock has the beat of sexual intercourse. That is why Ravel's *Bolero* is the one piece of classical music that is commonly known and liked by them. In alliance with some real art and a lot of pseudo-art, an enormous industry cultivates the taste for the orgiastic state of feeling connected with sex, providing a constant flood of fresh material for voracious appetites. Never was there an art form directed so exclusively to children.

Ministering to and according with the arousing and cathartic music, the lyrics celebrate puppy love as well as polymorphous attractions, and fortify them against traditional ridicule and shame. The words implicitly and explicitly describe bodily acts that satisfy sexual desire and treat them as its only natural and routine culmination for children who do not yet have the slightest imagination of love, marriage, or family. This has a much more powerful effect than does pornography on youngsters, who have no need to watch others do grossly what they can so easily do themselves. Voyeurism is for old perverts; active sexual relations are for the young. All they need is encouragement.

The inevitable corollary of such sexual interest is rebellion against the parental authority that represses it. Selfishness thus becomes indignation and then transforms itself into morality. The sexual revolution must overthrow all the forces of domination, the enemies of nature and happiness. From love comes hate, masquerading as social reform. A world view is balanced on the sexual fulcrum. What were once unconscious or half-conscious childish resentments become the new Scripture. And then comes the longing for the classless, prejudice-free, conflictless, universal society that necessarily results from liberated consciousness — "We Are the World," a pubescent version of *Alle Menschen werden Brüder*,[1] the fulfillment of which has been inhibited by the political equivalents of Mom and Dad. These are the three great lyrical themes: sex, hate, and a smarmy, hypocritical version of brotherly love. Such polluted sources issue in a muddy stream where only monsters can swim. A glance at the videos that project images on the wall of Plato's cave since MTV took it over suffices to prove this. Hitler's image recurs frequently enough in exciting contexts to give one pause. Nothing noble, sublime, profound, delicate, tasteful, or even decent can find a place in such tableaux. There is room only for the intense, changing, crude, and immediate, which Tocqueville warned us would be the character of democratic art, combined with a pervasiveness, importance, and content beyond Tocqueville's wildest imagination.

Picture a thirteen-year-old boy sitting in the living room of his family home doing his math assignment while wearing his Walkman headphones or watching MTV. He enjoys the liberties hard won over centuries by the alliance of philosophic genius and political heroism, consecrated by the blood of martyrs; he is provided with comfort and leisure by the most productive economy ever known to mankind; science has penetrated the secrets of nature

12

---

[1] German song: "All Men Will Be Brothers."

in order to provide him with the marvelous, lifelike electronic sound and image reproduction he is enjoying. And in what does progress culminate? A pubescent child whose body throbs with orgasmic rhythms; whose feelings are made articulate in hymns to the joys of onanism or the killing of parents; whose ambition is to win fame and wealth in imitating the drag-queen who makes the music. In short, life is made into a nonstop, commercially prepackaged masturbational fantasy.

This description may seem exaggerated, but only because some would prefer to regard it as such. The continuing exposure to rock music is a reality, not one confined to a particular class or type of child. One need only ask first-year university students what music they listen to, how much of it, and what it means to them, in order to discover that the phenomenon is universal in America, that it begins in adolescence or a bit before and continues through the college years. It is *the* youth culture and, as I have so often insisted, there is now no other countervailing nourishment for the spirit. Some of this culture's power comes from the fact that it is so loud. It makes conversation impossible, so that much of friendship must be without the shared speech that Aristotle asserts is the essence of friendship and the only true common ground. With rock, illusions of shared feelings, bodily contact, and grunted formulas, which are supposed to contain so much meaning beyond speech, are the basis of association. None of this contradicts going about the business of life, attending classes, and doing the assignments for them. But the meaningful inner life is with the music.

This phenomenon is both astounding and indigestible, and is hardly noticed, routine and habitual. But it is of historic proportions that a society's best young and their best energies should be so occupied. People of future civilizations will wonder at this and find it as incomprehensible as we do the caste system, witch-burning, harems, cannibalism, and gladiatorial combats. It may well be that a society's greatest madness seems normal to itself. The child I described has parents who have sacrificed to provide him with a good life and who have a great stake in his future happiness. They cannot believe that the musical vocation will contribute very much to that happiness. But there is nothing they can do about it. The family spiritual void has left the field open to rock music, and they cannot possibly forbid their children to listen to it. It is everywhere; all children listen to it; forbidding it would simply cause them to lose their children's affection and obedience. When they turn on the television, they will see President Reagan warmly grasping the daintily proffered gloved hand of Michael Jackson and praising him enthusiastically. Better to set the faculty of denial in motion — avoid noticing what the words say, assume the kid will get over it. If he has early sex, that won't get in the way of his having stable relationships later. His drug use will certainly stop at pot. School is providing real values. And popular historicism provides the final salvation: there are new lifestyles for new situations, and the older generation is there not to impose its values but to help the younger one to find its own. TV, which compared to music plays a comparatively small role in the formation of young people's character and taste, is a consensus monster — the Right monitors its content for sex, the Left for violence, and many other interested sects for many other things. But the music had hardly been touched, and what efforts have been made are both ineffectual and misguided about the nature and extent of the problem.

The result is nothing less than parents' loss of control over their children's moral education at a time when no one else is seriously concerned with it. This has been achieved by an alliance between the strange young males who have the gift of divining the mob's emergent wishes — our versions of Thrasymachus, Socrates' rhetorical adversary — and the record-company executives, the new robber barons, who mine gold out of rock. They discovered a few years back that children are one of the few groups in the country with considerable disposable income, in the form of allowances. Their parents spend all they have providing for the kids. Appealing to them over their parents' heads, creating a world of delight for them, constitutes one of the richest markets in the postwar world. The rock business is perfect capitalism, supplying to demand and helping to create it. It has all the moral dignity of drug trafficking, but it was so totally new and unexpected that nobody thought to control it, and now it is too late. Progress may be made against cigarette smoking because our absence of standards or our relativism does not extend to matters of bodily health. In all other things the market determines the value. (Yoko Ono is among America's small group of billionaires, along with oil and computer magnates, her late husband having produced and sold a commodity of worth comparable to theirs). Rock is very big business, bigger than the movies, bigger than professional sports, bigger than television, and this accounts for much of the respectability of the music business. It is difficult to adjust our vision to the changes in the economy and to see what is really important. McDonald's now has more employees than U.S. Steel, and likewise the purveyors of junk food for the soul have supplanted what still seem to be more basic callings.

This change has been happening for some time. In the late fifties, De Gaulle gave Brigitte Bardot one of France's highest honors. I could not understand this, but it turned out that she, along with Peugeot, was France's biggest export item. As Western nations became more prosperous, leisure, which had been put off for several centuries in favor of the pursuit of property, the means to leisure, finally began to be of primary concern. But, in the meantime, any notion of the serious life of leisure, as well as men's taste and capacity to live it, had disappeared. Leisure became entertainment. The end for which they had labored for so long has turned out to be amusement, a justified conclusion if the means justify the ends. The music business is peculiar only in that it caters almost exclusively to children, treating legally and naturally imperfect human beings as though they were ready to enjoy the final or complete satisfaction. It perhaps thus reveals the nature of all our entertainment and our loss of a clear view of what adulthood or maturity is, and our incapacity to conceive ends. The emptiness of *values* results in the acceptance of the natural *facts* as the ends. In this case infantile sexuality is the end, and I suspect that, in the absence of other ends, many adults have come to agree that it is.

It is interesting to note that the Left, which prides itself on its critical approach to "late capitalism" and is unrelenting and unsparing in its analysis of our other cultural phenomena, has in general given rock music a free ride. Abstracting from the capitalist element in which it flourishes, they regard it as a people's art, coming from beneath the bourgeoisie's layers of cultural repression. Its antinomianism and its longing for a world without constraint might seem to be the clarion of the proletarian revolution, and Marxists certainly do see that rock music dissolves the beliefs and morals necessary for liberal society and would approve of it for that alone. But the harmony between the young intellectual Left and rock is probably profounder than that. Herbert Marcuse appealed to university students in the sixties with a combination of Marx and Freud. In *Eros and Civilization* and *One Dimensional Man* he promised that the overcoming of capitalism and its false consciousness will result in a society where the greatest satisfactions are sexual, of a sort that the bourgeois moralist Freud called polymorphous and infantile. Rock music touches the same chord in the young. Free sexual expression, anarchism, mining of the irrational unconscious and giving it free rein are what they have in common. The high intellectual life . . . and the low rock world are partners in the same entertainment enterprise. They must both be interpreted as parts of the cultural fabric of late capitalism. Their success comes from the bourgeois's need to feel that he is not bourgeois, to have undangerous experiments with the unlimited. He is willing to pay dearly for them. The Left is better interpreted by Nietzsche than by Marx. The critical theory of late capitalism is at once late capitalism's subtlest and crudest expression. Antibourgeois ire is the opiate of the Last Man.

This strong stimulant, which Nietzsche called Nihiline, was for a very long time, almost fifteen years, epitomized in a single figure, Mick Jagger. A shrewd, middle-class boy, he played the possessed lower-class demon and teenaged satyr up until he was forty, with one eye on the mobs of children of both sexes whom he stimulated to a sensual frenzy and the other eye winking at the unerotic, commercially motivated adults who handled the money. In his act he was male and female, heterosexual and homosexual; unencumbered by modesty, he could enter everyone's dreams, promising to do everything with everyone; and, above all, he legitimated drugs, which were the real thrill that parents and policemen conspired to deny his youthful audience. He was beyond the law, moral and political, and thumbed his nose at it. Along with all this, there were nasty little appeals to the suppressed inclinations toward sexism, racism, and violence, indulgence in which is not now publicly respectable. Nevertheless, he managed not to appear to contradict the rock ideal of a universal classless society founded on love, with the distinction between brotherly and bodily blurred. He was the hero and the model for countless young persons in universities, as well as elsewhere. I discovered that students who boasted of having no heroes secretly had a passion to be like Mick Jagger, to live his life, have his fame. They were ashamed to admit this in a university, although I am not certain that the reason has anything to do with a higher standard of taste. It is probably that they are not supposed to have heroes. Rock music itself and talking about it with infinite seriousness are perfectly respectable. It has proved to be the ultimate leveler of intellectual snobbism. But it is not respectable to think of it as providing weak and ordinary persons with a fashionable behavior, the imitation of which will make others esteem them and boost their own self-esteem. Unaware and unwillingly, however, Mick Jagger played the role in their lives that Napoleon played in the lives of ordinary young Frenchmen throughout the nineteenth century. Everyone else was so boring and unable to charm youthful passions. Jagger caught on.

In the last couple of years, Jagger has begun to fade. Whether Michael 20 Jackson, Prince, or Boy George can take his place is uncertain. They are even weirder than he is, and one wonders what new strata of taste they have discovered. Although each differs from the others, the essential character of musical entertainment is not changing. There is only a constant search for variations on the theme. And this gutter phenomenon is apparently the fulfillment of the promise made by so much psychology and literature that our weak and exhausted Western civilization would find refreshment in the true source, the unconscious, which appeared to the late romantic imagination to be identical to Africa, the dark and unexplored continent. Now all has been explored; light has been cast everywhere; the unconscious has been made conscious, the repressed expressed. And what have we found? Not creative devils, but show business glitz. Mick Jagger tarting it up on the stage is all that we brought back from the voyage to the underworld.

My concern here is not with the moral effects of this music — whether it leads to sex, violence, or drugs. The issue here is its effect on education, and I believe it ruins the imagination of young people and makes it very difficult for them to have a passionate relationship to the art and thought that are the substance of liberal education. The first sensuous experiences are decisive in determining the taste for the whole of life, and they are the link between the animal and spiritual in us. The period of nascent sensuality has always been used for sublimation, in the sense of making sublime, for attaching youthful inclinations and longings to music, pictures, and stories that provide the transition to the fulfillment of the human duties and the enjoyment of the human pleasures. Lessing, speaking of Greek sculpture, said "beautiful men made beautiful statues, and the city had beautiful statues in part to thank for beautiful citizens." This formula encapsulates the fundamental principle of the esthetic education of man. Young men and women were attracted by the beauty of heroes whose very bodies expressed their nobility. The deeper understanding of the meaning of nobility comes later, but is prepared for by the sensuous experience and is actually contained in it. What the senses long for as well as what reason later sees as good are thereby not at tension with one another. Education is not sermonizing to children against their instincts and pleasures, but providing a natural continuity between what they feel and what they can and should be. But this is a lost art. Now we have come to exactly the opposite point. Rock music encourages passions and provides models that have no relation to any life the young people who go to universities can possibly lead, or to the kinds of admiration encouraged by liberal studies. Without the cooperation of the sentiments, anything other than technical education is a dead letter.

Rock music provides premature ecstasy and, in this respect, is like the drugs with which it is allied. It artificially induces the exaltation naturally attached to the completion of the greatest endeavors — victory in a just war, consummated love, artistic creation, religious devotion, and discovery of the truth. Without effort, without talent, without virtue, without exercise of the faculties, anyone and everyone is accorded the equal right to the enjoyment of their fruits. In my experience, students who have had a serious fling with drugs — and gotten over it — find it difficult to have enthusiasms or great expectations. It is as though the color has been drained out of their lives and they see everything in black and white. The pleasure they experienced in the beginning was so intense that they no longer look for it at the end, or as the end. They may function perfectly well, but dryly, routinely. Their energy has been sapped, and they do not expect their life's activity to produce anything but a living, whereas liberal education is supposed to encourage the belief that the good life is the pleasant life and that the best life is the most pleasant life. I suspect that the rock addiction, particularly in the absence of strong counterattractions, has an effect similar to that of drugs. The students will get over this music, or at least the exclusive passion for it. But they will do so in the same way Freud says that men accept the reality principle — as something harsh, grim, and essentially unattractive, a mere necessity. These students will assiduously study economics or the professions and the Michael Jackson costume will slip off to reveal a Brooks Brothers suit beneath. They will want to get ahead and live comfortably. But this life is as empty and false as the one they left behind. The choice is not between quick fixes and dull calculation. This is what liberal education is meant to show them. But as long as they have the Walkman on, they cannot hear what the great tradition has to say. And, after its prolonged use, when they take it off, they find they are deaf.

Points to Consider

1. What specific dangers does Bloom think rock music presents? In using Plato to criticize rock, what philosophical assumptions does he make? Do you think these assumptions are valid?

2. What do you think of Bloom's charge that rock music "has one appeal only"? What is that appeal? Do you think Bloom is correct?

3. Consider the passage (paragraph 13) in which Bloom describes the scene of a teenager in a living room. How would you describe the quality of Bloom's language here? Is it appropriate to such a scene taken out of real life? Would the scene be characteristic of your own life?

4. How does Bloom's argument differ from other arguments opposing rock music? Does he seem especially concerned with rock's effects on aspects of human life other than serious culture?

"We Can't Dance Together"[1]   [PROFESSION 88 / 1988]

> Maybe this small attachment to my past is only another case of what Frank
> Zappa calls a bunch of old guys sitting around playing rock 'n' roll. But as
> we all know, rock 'n' roll will never die, and education too, as Henry Adams
> always sez, keeps going on forever.
>
> —*Thomas Pynchon, Introduction to* Slow Learner, *xxxiv*

Anyone who teaches Petrarch's lyric magnum opus, vulgarly known as
the *Canzoniere,* is eventually bound to reveal to his or her students the rather
delicious irony that Petrarch actually thought—or at least said, repeatedly—
that writing in the vernacular, the language of the masses and the vulgar,
was not a particularly worthwhile or dignified enterprise. I, at least, get a
somewhat malicious pleasure from pointing out that it is, of course, because
of his magnificently "vulgar" collection of love songs that Petrarch is at all
remembered—and that he is such an integral part of canonical Western
culture. The irony is a double one: first, if his statements can be taken at
face value, Petrarch was terribly wrong in his assessments of the relative
merits of his vernacular versus his "classical" writings; second, we have now,
following his obviously misguided thinking on the matter and in blatant
disregard of the historical lesson, "classicized" the love songs—which were

---

[1] "Hey nineteen / That's Retha Franklin / She don't remember / The Queen of Soul / It's hard
times befallen / The sole survivors / She thinks I'm crazy / But I'm just growing old. . . . Hey
nineteen / No we can't dance together / No we can't talk at all . . ." (Steely Dan, "Hey
Nineteen").

   This paper is written in memory of Clifton Cherpack, who did not quite make it to sixty-
four. [Au.]

---

*MARÍA ROSA MENOCAL (b. 1953) holds a doctorate in Romance phil-
ology and is currently a professor in the Spanish and Portuguese Department
at Yale University. She has written two books:* The Arabic Role in Medieval
Literary History *(1987) and* Writing in Dante's Cult of Truth from Borges
to Boccaccio *(1991). The original version of this essay contained several
direct quotations from popular songs, which had to be deleted because of
copyright regulations.*

so successful precisely because they weren't "classical" in the first place.[2] When one reads Allan Bloom's derisive comments about music in *The Closing of the American Mind,* which are characterized by a remarkably similar disdain for popular love lyrics and the accompanying reverence for the "great tradition," one can't help but wonder, at least for a split second, if Bloom doesn't have a manuscript of rock lyrics stashed away someplace. Well, it was just a split second.

In fact, a first reading of Bloom, of the chapter entitled "Music" in particular, should logically lead one merely to shrug one's shoulders at his stereotypically retrograde views. I spent several months ticking off all the reasons why writing a response to Bloom's book was, is, even on the face of it, a waste of time and a somewhat self-indulgent exercise. It struck me as significant, however, that other reviewers, no matter how negative, rarely mentioned his ravings about music, tending to be concerned with more "serious" issues about education he raises. Even the witty and intelligent review in *Rolling Stone,* which lays many of Bloom's pretenses bare ("he is peddling fundamentalism for highbrows" [Greider 39]) essentially passes over Bloom's substantive comments about music—in great measure, no doubt, because for anyone reading that journal his comments are too ludicrous even to require a response, their silliness exposed just by their being quoted. But because, as the example of Petrarch so clearly indicates, the multiple and complex issues revolving around the question of "vulgar" love lyrics and the canonical literary tradition are much too important to and central in our profession to be left to the occasional college newspaper refutation by a student music reviewer, I decided to respond.

I do so acknowledging the following limitations. First, I do not pretend to be in any way comprehensive or systematic in my treatment of rock, and the examples I have chosen are idiosyncratic, personal, and relatively random, the music that happened to come to mind. I am not a scholar or an expert in this area, nor is this a research paper on rock.[3] I am a middling to

---

[2] See Vickers's extraordinary article for a much fuller discussion of these issues. Her appreciation of the parallels between Petrarch's work and that of one rock group, Survivor, as well as her detailed and sensitive exploration of the complexities of the relationship between popular and "classical" culture is exemplary. I am indebted to her for allowing me to read a prepublication version of the article. [Au.]

[3] Nevertheless, I have been asked to provide scholarly documentation for the songs and lyrics I quote. This is both perfectly reasonable and appropriate, given that I am, in part, claiming that much of rock and its lyrics is a cultural phenomenon to be treated like any other—and thus a song should be quoted as we would quote a poem. It is also true, however, and also part of my argument, that "everyone" knows that, for example, "When I'm Sixty-Four" is on the Beatles's *Sgt. Pepper* that came in 1967 and that the lyrics of a remarkable body of rock are part of the active memory of many people. Thus the citations and quotations that follow are representative of the communal knowledge and memory of rock—a reflection of the living lyrical tradition. The "Works Cited" listings reflect ex post facto documentation, in some cases incomplete. Note that many artists avoid putting dates on their albums. [Au.]

average, at best, connoisseur of the genre. But my examples are not unrepresentative (although they in fact represent a minuscule selection of the full range), and someone else's personal sampling would have comparable validity. Second, I will not address in any great detail the much larger issues Bloom raises, although they are, perforce, the backdrop for the music chapter and, more important, they reflect an ideology within which his rejection of rock must be understood. But those are other reviews.[4] And for the sake of my argument—in sum, that Bloom is, from a scholarly point of view, wrong about what rock and roll is—I will attempt to suspend any sustained rebuttal that involves opinion as to what culture (and thus rock and roll) ought to be.

Bloom's argument about rock has three major elements: (1) that rock music and its lyrics are limited to "sex, hate and a smarmy, hypocritical version of brotherly love" (74), with an emphasis on sex: "rock music has one appeal only, a barbaric appeal, to sexual desire—not love, not *eros,* but sexual desire undeveloped and untutored" (73); (2) that rock's values (or lack thereof) are, at worst, antagonistic to fundamental cultural values and, at best, lie well outside other lasting cultural pursuits: "Rock music encourages passions and provides models that have no relation to any life the young people . . . can possibly lead, or to the kinds of admiration encouraged by liberal studies. . . . [A]s long as they have the Walkman on, they cannot hear what the great tradition has to say" (80–81); (3) that rock is a musical-lyrical genre that concerns youth and children overwhelmingly: "Never was there an art form directed so exclusively to children" (74). Let's take these elements in that order.

Bloom's assertions about the poverty and limitations of rock's themes are perhaps the most excruciating in their simple lack of factualness—and there is such an embarrassment of riches available as counterargument that it is difficult to know where to start. What *is* true, certainly, is that the richest thematic mine is that of love—and more often than not, love that is in some way unsatisfying, unhappy, or unfulfilled. But many, if not most, of rock's classic love songs are about a great deal more—or less—than sex. From the Beatles' basically silly "Michelle, my belle, these are words that go together well" (which reveals the metaliterary preoccupation of rock as well) to Dylan's charming ditty "You're Gonna Make Me Lonesome When You Go," which includes a refusal of other types of love poetry ("Situations have ended sad / Relationships have all been bad / Mine've been like Verlaine's and Rimbaud's / But there's no way I can compare / All them scenes to this affair / You're gonna make me lonesome when you go"), to the troubled and tortured love of Neil Young's "Now that you've made yourself love me / Do you think I can change it in a day?" there are few, if any, of the variations

4

[4] See especially David Rieff's scathing comments about Bloom's cultural-ideological posture. [Au.]

and variegations of "classical" love poetry that have not found lyrics in the rock canon.

Even if we limit ourselves to the writing of the artists mentioned above, Bloom's generalization not only crumbles but has to be replaced by the realization that rock's obsession with love and with its own expressions of the longing for love are next of kin to those same obsessions in all other lyrical schools. Thus, the Beatles's hymn to enduring, perfect, and as yet unfound love in "I Will" . . . is neatly counterbalanced by their wistful and hopeful projection about a perhaps nonexistent future in the classic "When I'm Sixty-Four." . . . Dylan's repertoire of love songs (although it is fair to say that he is far from being known as a love lyricist) is scarcely less representative of these ties to lyric antecedents. From the early, bittersweet "Don't Think Twice It's All Right" about the pain of failed love ("Well it ain't no use to sit and wonder why, babe / If you don't know by now . . . When your rooster crows at the break of dawn / Look out your window and I'll be gone / You're the reason that I'm traveling on / But don't think twice, it's all right . . . But I wish there was something you would do or say / To try and make me change my mind and stay . . .") to the famous "Just like a Woman" (satirized by Woody Allen in *Annie Hall*) to other, much more difficult and hermetic songs such as "Queen Jane Approximately" ("When all the flower girls want back what they have lent you / And the smell of their roses does not remain / And all of your children start to resent you / Won't you come to see me, Queen Jane?"), his long and varied career as a lyricist is reminiscent of a poetic ancestry he is quite conscious of following.[5] And the centrality of the broken heart to the lyric tradition is simply and touchingly reflected in Neil Young's "Only Love Can Break Your Heart." . . .

The interesting question, of course, is why and how the preoccupation with love and its expression in rock is so reminiscent of other lyrical traditions, so like other schools and canons that are now studied, by and large, in a more rarefied atmosphere. From twelfth-century Persian courtly poetry to Petrarchism in Renaissance Europe to opera in the last century, love and its many problems—sometimes sexual, sometimes not—are of overwhelming and enduring fascination and are perhaps the ultimate inspiration for poetry and lyrics—an inspiration that all these lyrical schools are also explicitly conscious of and that is often the focus of metaliterary interest itself. Taken as a whole, rock exhibits, theme for theme, much the same concerns as those of the traditions we have now classicized. In one example, the preoccupation with unsatisfactory love becomes the subject or object of poetry and creates, in turn, the association between the lyricist or singer and the lover. Self-

[5] Dylan, who changed his name from Robert Zimmerman to one that linked him explicitly with the great tradition, has written dozens of songs whose lyrics explicitly harken back to all manner of poetic schools, from the Bible . . . to Petrarch . . . to the great poetic struggle of modernism. . . . [Au.]

reflection and metalyrical concerns include the glory and fame that will be achieved through the singing or poetry: some examples are "So You Want to Be a Rock 'n' Roll Star," "Do You Believe in Magic?" and that early and enduring anthem of rock, "Johnny B. Goode." . . . Thus, what is critical is not merely that Bloom (and others) have got it wrong but that ignorance prevents them from seeing that rock is in so many ways like parts of the "great tradition." And one is then, indeed, led to the question of whether rock resembles these traditions because it is descended from them or because some sort of universal parallelism is at work—a question that, because of our Bloom-like prejudices, has scarcely been asked, let alone answered.[6] As for the sexuality, well, indeed, some rock lyrics are sexual, even, perhaps, exclusively and pointedly and vulgarly sexual. But sexuality, too, is far from uniquely modern, and Mick Jagger's "Satisfaction" and "Let's Spend the Night Together" pale, in both vulgarity and explicitness, beside some of the songs of the venerated William of Aquitaine.

But while rock may thus mimic earlier lyric schools in its fascination with the generative power of unhappy love, it has exploited a much fuller range of themes, including the historicopolitical one that Bloom dismisses as "a smarmy, hypocritical version of brotherly love." Once again the generalization alarmingly misrepresents the remarkable range of topics covered and views expressed. Many of rock's earliest masterpieces, written in the late sixties and early seventies, were, in fact, politically committed, and opposition to the war (and the draft) and sympathy for the civil rights movements were major conditioning and influential currents. But as often as not, the lyrics produced in this climate were most conspicuously informed by and interwoven with the other musical and lyrical traditions that are such important components of rock: black, particularly spiritual, music and the sort of folk tradition that Joan Baez's songs rely on so heavily. Remnants of these strains, pervasive in rock even today, explain the centrality of the Talking Heads's "Take Me to the River" and Eric Clapton's (and others') recordings of "Swing Low, Sweet Chariot." And while there are plenty of examples of virtually unmediated protest (Country Joe and the Fish's "What are we fighting for? / Don't ask me I don't give a damn / Next stop is Viet Nam . . ." is a classic, certainly, as is Dylan's even more famous "The Times They Are A-Changin'"), much of the "political" lyrics of rock are infinitely more complex.

The Band, for example, specialized in songs that reflected back on the Civil War South, and by giving the poet a Confederate voice in "The Night They Drove Old Dixie Down," they brilliantly underscored, without ever being explicit, the universal tragedy of war. The currently popular U2 plumbs the complex problems and no-win situation of Northern Ireland in equally subtle ways. Finally, many rock lyricists have made their points by merely

6 The one exception I know of is Vickers's article. [Au.]

taking over or only slightly rewriting "classics" from other traditions: Prince sings the Lord's Prayer with remarkable effect; the Byrds sang Ecclesiastes in "Turn, Turn, Turn." If these are smarmy versions of brotherly love, so be it. In fact, what is stunning here is that rock's connections with the "great tradition" are often quite explicit, markedly intertextual, and ultimately impossible to ignore. The extent to which Bloom's second major objection to rock—that it has no cultural ties or links or avenues beyond itself—is simply mistaken comes very much to the fore here.[7]

But above and beyond specific songs that are strictly and obviously tied, intertextually, to any number of classic texts outside the rock tradition, rock's place in contemporary society is a major link to a number of cultural phenomena that we now, from a safe distance, view as canonical. In fact, it is telling that Bloom does acknowledge the great impact of rock: at the outset of the chapter he goes on at some length, and with considerable accuracy, about the unique role rock plays in society and about rock's importance, unparalleled in recent history. He begins the chapter, in fact, noting that "[n]othing is more singular about this generation than its addiction to music. This is the age of music and the states of soul that accompany it. To find a rival to this enthusiasm, one would have to go back at least a century to Germany and the passion for Wagner's operas" (68). And, having remarked that one crucial difference between rock and the German passion of the last century is that rock is much less elitist (i.e., it cuts across class boundaries more), he goes on to note the great change that has occurred in the role music and its lyrics play in this century: "The power of music in the soul . . . has been recovered after a long period of desuetude" (69). In acknowledging this rather remarkable turn of events, this existence in the late twentieth century of a status for music and its lyrics that did not always exist and when it did was a major cultural institution and a central part of the culture, Bloom is implicitly recognizing what he will explicitly deny later on: the cultural centrality of the rock phenomenon. In fact, Bloom even goes on to note that this is the first generation he has taught that fully understand Plato's opposition to music, something earlier generations, for whom music was "background," were incapable of understanding. And since Bloom explicitly recognizes the enormous impact per se of the phenomenon, his refusal to see its cultural impact is grounded, explicitly, in what he sees as its failure to address issues other than sex—an opinion that, as I have tried to suggest, cannot be substantiated.

What can be substantiated is the perhaps radical-sounding assertion, already implicit in Bloom's comments, that the rock phenomenon is a twen-

---

[7] The British punk tradition, which I know scarcely at all and thus do not discuss more fully, includes a number of "singings" of important texts. I am grateful to a student, Kirsten Thorne, for bringing to my attention "The Wasteland," by the Mission U.K., and "In Dulce Decorum," by the Damned, where the text is a speech of Winston Churchill's. [Au.]

tieth-century version, in many if not in most of its details, of what at other times and in other places have been major lyrical schools with resounding impact in the cultures that produced them. Poetry, after all, had long ago ceased to be "lyrical" in the etymological sense of the word, an integral part of music. For most people—and many scholars—poetry is what was and is written down to be read and what is published in poetry journals or in the *New Yorker* or in anthologies. Poetry in that form not only is substantively different from lyrics but is rarely (and then only for a minuscule percentage of the population, now or in any other period of history) a living part of one's cultural or spiritual experience. But rock is much like opera and even more like the phenomenon of the troubadours in twelfth- and thirteenth-century Europe, when lyricists started singing in the vernaculars rather than in the long-dead Latin. Rock is poetry that is aggressively and self-consciously a part of the living tradition that, in great measure because it is attached to music, plays a fundamental and vital cultural role for many more people. In this regard, as in various others, Bloom's assertion that rock makes it difficult for young people to have a passionate relationship to the art and thought that are the substance of a liberal education is almost perversely skewed.

The truth is the opposite: the person, young or otherwise, for whom poetry is a living form that resonates daily in the mind and soul is quite capable of appreciating not only the poetry of the troubadours or of Petrarch, so similar in other ways, but, more important, the great lyrical power of poetry in and of itself. Members of this generation, as Bloom likes to put it, are the first in a long time, thanks to rock, to be in a position to understand the impact and repercussions of many earlier lyrical phenomena. They should be able to grasp, for example (particularly if we as mediators can simply point out the parallels), what is moving, rather than dusty and mechanical and arcane, in a previous generation's songs—much more so, I would argue, than people who don't know why tears have been shed at Lennon's "Imagine" or who don't think of love in the haunting structures of "Here, There, and Everywhere," or who might not hear the ecstasy and triumph of the Grateful Dead's "Touch of Grey" . . . , so often sung last summer by Jerry Garcia, who could have been grandfather to many in the audience. For those whose poetic sensibilities have incubated in the heart and soul and tapping feet, Puccini's sentimental arias can be truly moving and Verdi's triumphal choruses can stir, vicariously if nothing else, the same sentiments stirred at Woodstock.[8] The list of ways in which the experience of rock is enlightening vis-à-vis the "great tradition" is seemingly endless: students who know full well that a strong lyric tradition thrives on the seemingly paradoxical combination of parameters and restraints, and the individual creativity that

12

---

[8] Lest the connection appear farfetched I note that in the movie *The Killing Fields* the two most emotionally wrenching scenes are accompanied by Puccini's "Nessun dorma" and Lennon's "Imagine." [Au.]

thrives within the tradition and the repetition of commonplaces, can eventually read the medieval and Renaissance lyric traditions with a fuller appreciation of their astonishing repetitiousness. And those same "students" of rock, because rock has included, and continues to include, a substantial "trobar clus"[9] strain, those students who have learned instinctively to appreciate everything from "Lucy in the Sky with Diamonds" . . . to "Third World Man," by Steely Dan ("When he's crying out / I just sing that Ghana Rondo / E l'era del terzo mondo / He's a third world man"), bring an important background to the study of the myriad canonical schools of hermetic lyrics that have produced poets as varied as Arnaut Daniel, the Spanish mystics, Mallarmé, and that fellow splicer of lines from the Italian, Ezra Pound.

Bloom's third major misapprehension is actually rather touching—or pathetic: that rock's appeal is exclusively to the young, that rock is a phenomenon of a "generation," that it affects his "students," and so on. This notion is belied by the simple facts of chronologies, celebrated every year as one great rock star after another turns forty or fifty and as those who grew up on rock are now bringing up children of their own. Toward the end of this chapter Bloom depicts a pathetic scenario where the poor parents who have struggled to provide a good life and who wish only the best for their child watch on, terrified and helpless, as their thirteen-year-old boy is mesmerized by MTV and its attendant horrors. This is a remarkable fantasy; the parents are, likely as not, especially if they are highbrow and college-educated, the ones who watch MTV and who introduced rock to their child in the first place. And while they may care less for their child's currently preferred groups and lyrics than for their own classics, they are probably not much concerned since it has become clear that their classics are becoming *the* classics and that their child will be listening to the Beatles, as well as to the Beatles's progeny. But more telling than even those fundamentals are columns on contemporary music that now appear regularly in the *New Yorker,* that holy sanctum of haute culture, and articles in academic journals that reflect the extent to which the centrality of rock can no longer be defined in generational terms at all.[10]

In fact, many of Bloom's (and others') misapprehensions about rock and its impact are rooted in remarkably clichéd notions about the general poverty of "youth culture" and a commensurate (and I believe equally illusory) aggrandizement of the degree of "high culture" in earlier societies and generations. Thus, to take but one example, Bloom dismisses the powerful argument that, in fact, there is a significant revival of interest in classical music by saying that even if there is, only 5 to 10 percent of the population

---

[9] A complex writing style adopted by some twelfth-century Provençal poets.

[10] A recent issue of *Stanford French Review* contains an article entitled "The Grateful Dead: Corneille's Tragedy and the Illusion of History." [Au.]

is affected. Does he believe that much more than that has ever had a serious interest in classical music? The serious listener does, indeed, listen seriously to all sorts of music. And not only is "Roll Over, Beethoven" tongue-in-cheek, ultimately, but twenty or so years down the line it may well end up on the same shelf as the Ninth. Likewise, it is obvious that, as with all other schools or cultural phenomena, there is a lot of trash out there and a part of the audience at every concert has never heard of Ecclesiastes. So what else is new? Are we to pretend that everyone who listened avidly to Wagner knew all the allusions? Don't we all know that for every Mozart there were hundreds of Salieris? Rock is no better and probably no worse. There is little doubt that many people who listen to much that is marvelously lyrical in rock, that is poetic and moving, never get past the beat, and, also undoubtedly, much of what has been written and will continue to be written will never amount to anything in posterity.

But it is nonsense—or wishful thinking—to say, as Bloom does, that when we take the Walkmans off after years of listening to rock there will be nothing left. *Au contraire*. It is a pity Bloom has listened so little, for, given the great concern for culture and the educational tradition he claims to be championing, he is thus almost perversely depriving himself of access to a richly variegated and (in the very cultural terms he wishes to see the "liberal tradition") an enormously influential phenomenon. We cannot afford to ignore Bloom's misapprehensions about music, because the nature of his misunderstanding is so intimately tied with the debates now raging, not just at Stanford but nearly everywhere, about what constitutes the canon of "Western civilization." And the educator, particularly in the field of literature and literary culture, who like Bloom walks about deaf to our living lyric tradition is a less able explicator and mediator of the literary traditions and canonized poets that are the fundamental intertexts for the troubadours of our own time. It might alter both the tenor and the substance of these discussions considerably if we were to recognize that a great deal of what is being listened to on the Walkmans is the great tradition very much alive and well—and as Pynchon sez, rock 'n' roll will never die, and education keeps going on forever.

Works Cited

The Band. "The Night They Drove Old Dixie Down." *The Band*. Capitol, CDP 7 46493 2, n.d. on original album.
Beatles. "Here, There and Everywhere." *Revolver*. Capitol, CDP 7 46441 2, 1966.
———. "I Will." No title [*White Album*]. EMI-Capitol, CDP 7 46443 2, 1968.
———. "Michelle." *Rubber Soul*. EMI-Capitol, CDP 7 46440 2, 1965.
———. "When I'm Sixty-Four." "Lucy in the Sky with Diamonds." *Sgt. Pepper's Lonely Hearts Club Band*. EMI, CDP 7 46442 2, 1967.
Berry, Chuck. "Johnny B. Goode."

————. "Roll Over, Beethoven."

Bloom, Allan. *The Closing of the American Mind: How Higher Education Has Failed Democracy and Impoverished the Souls of Today's Students.* New York: Simon, 1987.

Byrds. "So You Want to Be a Rock 'n' Roll Star." *The Byrds.* Columbia, G 30127, n.d.

————. "Turn, Turn, Turn." *Turn, Turn, Turn.* Columbia, CG 33645, n.d.

Clapton, Eric. "Swing Low, Sweet Chariot." *Time Pieces,* RSO, 800 014-2, 1975.

Country Joe McDonald. "I-Feel-like-I'm-Fixin'-to-Die Rag." *Woodstock.* Atlantic-Cotillion, SD 3-500, 1970.

Dylan, Bob. "Don't Think Twice It's All Right." *The Freewheelin' Bob Dylan.* Columbia, CK 8786, n.d.

————. "Queen Jane Approximately." *Highway 61 Revisited.* Columbia, CK 9189, 1965.

————."Just like a Woman." *Blonde on Blonde.* Columbia, CK 841, n.d.

————. "You're Gonna Make Me Lonesome When You Go." *Blood on the Tracks.* Columbia, X 698, 1974.

————."The Times They Are a-Changin'."

Grateful Dead. "Touch of Grey." *In the Dark.* Arista, ARCD 8452, 1987.

Greider, William. "Bloom and Doom." *Rolling Stone* 8 Oct. 1987: 39–40.

Lennon, John. "Imagine."

Lovin' Spoonful. "Do You Believe in Magic?"

Pynchon, Thomas. *Slow Learner.* New York: Bantam, 1984.

Rieff, David. "The Colonel and the Professor." *Times Literary Supplement* 4–11 Sept. 1987: 950, 960.

Rolling Stones. "Let's Spend the Night Together." *Flowers.* Abkco, 75092, 1966.

————. "Satisfaction."

Steely Dan. "Hey Nineteen." "Third World Man." *Gaucho.* MCA Records, MCAD-37220, 1980.

Talking Heads. "Take Me to the River." *Stop Making Sense.* Sire, 25186-1, 1984.

Vickers, Nancy. "Vital Signs: Petrarch and Popular Culture." *Romanic Review,* January 1988.

Young, Neil. "Only Love Can Break Your Heart." "I Believe in You." *After the Gold Rush.* Reprise, 2283-2, 1970.

Points to Consider

1. Why does María Rosa Menocal begin her discussion of the cultural importance of rock music with a brief glance at the poetry of Petrarch, one of the greatest poets of the Italian Renaissance?

2. What is the nature of Menocal's response to Bloom's charge that rock music's themes are limited strictly to "sex, hate, and a smarmy, hypocritical version of brotherly love"? Does Menocal consider rock lyrics' preoccupation with love a negative characteristic?

3. Why does Menocal discuss the roots of lyric poetry? Why does she feel

that understanding lyric poetry's development is crucial to understanding rock music as a cultural phenomenon?

4. What does Menocal think of Bloom's idea that rock music belongs only to youth? Does she feel that the impact of rock can only be understood in generational terms?

Discussing the Unit

Suggested Topic for Discussion

Both Bloom and Menocal seem to think that rock music should be taken seriously, whether or not one finds it valuable. Do you think, like Bloom, that rock music poses a serious danger to education and culture? Or do you believe, like Menocal, that rock music can approach the level of serious art?

Preparing for Class Discussion

1. According to Bloom, rock music occupies the central place in a teenager's life. How central is rock to your own life? Calculate as precisely as you can the number of hours you listen to rock music a day, then determine what that would add up to over a period of weeks or months. Does rock exert a great influence over your own life, or do you view it as merely another form of entertainment?

2. Carefully examine the passage in which Bloom considers rock star Mick Jagger (paragraph 19). How does Bloom's description compare with accounts of Jagger you might find in popular magazines such as *People* or *Rolling Stone*? Rewrite a few lines of the Bloom passage as they might have appeared in one of these periodicals. What does this exercise tell you about Bloom's style and attitude? Do you think Bloom's message could be successfully conveyed by a more casual style?

From Discussion to Writing

Choose a rock singer or group you particularly like or dislike. Considering only words and music, write an essay in which you describe and analyze the singer's or group's appeal or lack of appeal. Discuss whether you think the music has serious social and cultural significance. Do you think the music reaches the level of an art form? How important to your appreciation are these concerns?

13

Artistic Expression: What Are Its Limits?

While women's groups organize boycotts of Andrew "Dice" Clay's new movie, the bad-boy comic continues to work his audiences into a frenzy with his sexist and racist brand of humor. Rap group 2 Live Crew's album *As Nasty as They Wanna Be* is banned for obscenity by a federal court, but not before the album sells 1.3 million copies. Washington, D.C.'s, prestigious Corcoran Gallery removes from an exhibition Andres Serrano's "Piss Christ," a photograph of a crucifix immersed in a bottle of urine, but religious groups wonder why the gallery would display such a work in the first place. Although America has traditionally championed freedom of expression, we may be quickly moving into an era when certain kinds of expression will no longer be permitted. The trend toward greater censorship seems to be the result of a concomitant rise in offensive language and messages in art and popular entertainment. Gerri Hirshey's "The Comedy of Hate" tries to place comics like Andrew "Dice" Clay and Sam Kinison within a larger social context, focusing almost as much on their audiences as on the comics themselves. Does the success of these comics indicate that tolerance in America has ended?

Tolerance is Henry Louis Gates, Jr.'s, plea in "2 Live Crew, Decoded" as he argues for the acceptance of African-American vernacular traditions as legitimate forms of expression. In an attempt to defend the rap group against the charges of obscenity that led to the banning of their hit record, Gates maintains that the survival of these traditions is necessary for the preservation of African-American identity.

Finally, Richard A. Posner, a judge, looks at the legal and ethical aspects of exhibiting works of art that many consider to be offensive. To what extent can the government interfere in the artistic process? Can withholding government subsidies be considered a form of censorship? Posner's analysis takes us to the very heart of the issues surrounding works like "Piss Christ" or the highly controversial photographs by the late Robert Mapplethorpe.

The Comedy of Hate [GQ / August 1989]

Take your date to an Andrew "Dice" Clay show, sit in the front row, and Dice, who talks and dresses like an X-rated Fonz, will want to know if sweet Maria there was good the first time you banged her. Yeah, so how'd she get that way? The Diceman says he can see the stretch marks around her mouth. "Hey," he hollers, "YOU WEARIN' PANTIES, HONEY?" He'll do a pretty minute on yeast infections and oral sex. Then he'll apologize to her, hold up a glass of water in a toast.

"Here's to you, sweetheart . . ."

Maria smiles.

". . . SUCKIN' MY DICK!"   4

An evening of raw Dicetude averages twenty dollars a ticket. Devotees stand in line, bribe the ushers to seat them and their dates up front. After the show, couples come up and thank Dice for the customized abuse.

These days, working "blue" is boffo, disgusting is delightful, even hip in certain tattooed rings of the celeb inferno. Cher graced a Dice show in

GERRI HIRSHEY (b. 1950), a free-lance writer, is a contributing editor at Rolling Stone *and* Vanity Fair *magazines. Her book* Nowhere to Run: The Story of Soul Music *was published in 1984.*

264   **Artistic Expression: What Are Its Limits?**

L.A. recently, alongside Sylvester Stallone, Billy Idol, and heavy metalists Guns N' Roses.

Clubs and cable shows are cashing in on shockucomics, who are telling jokes so dirty, sexist, homophobic, and racist that audiences often gasp before they laugh. They favor chicks-are-all-sluts jokes. Spick jokes. Dick jokes. Gay-bashing jokes. AIDS jokes.

"Rebel comics" they call themselves. Others have called them heavy-metal comics, even neo-Nazi. They've been picketed, banned from certain colleges, reviled in print—and paid handsomely for their outrages. Bad boys are selling out clubs, colleges, rock venues. Headliners such as Sam Kinison and Andrew "Dice" Clay have albums, videos, and HBO specials. Dice has been signed by Twentieth Century Fox to play a rock-and-roll detective in *Ford Fairlane* and by ABC to star in a mid-season–replacement sitcom called *Sal Man. The Diceman Cometh*, as his cable special warned. 8

To better appreciate the gritty gestalt of bad-boy humor—the comics and the crowds—come with me into the belly of the beast:

It's Valentine's Day, at the outset of Sam Kinison's Outlaws of Comedy tour. The Outlaws are barnstorming the country, grossing up to $100,000 a night in medium-sized venues. It's all very rock and roll: they have a bus. Babes in lingerie. Head-banger fans.

Tonight's show is at Manhattan's Felt Forum, and it's sold out—five thousand fans screaming Kinison bits to one another, nodding shaggy heads to the heavy-metal music crashing from huge speakers. They're mostly male, mostly young, and *psyched,* cruising the aisles with a beer in each hand.

There will be three opening acts, then Kinison, all of it billed as a benefit for Lenny Bruce's destitute mother, Sally Marr. Such *nice* boys. 12

First up is Allan Steven, telling penis jokes, urbane anti-immigrant jokes. "Hey, fuck you, I was *bawwwwwn* here."

This gets a big laugh from a fan wearing a sweatshirt that reads "THE WHITE STUFF." Second is Mitchell Walters, a fat guy in tennis shoes, who's grabbing at his crotch within a minute of hitting the stage. More penis jokes. Then: "Women. Bottom line—they're bitches, right?"

Whaaahooo. The crowd is cheering. Barking. *Yeeeeah, brother.*

Now here's Carl LaBove, offering tips for dealing with a troublesome date: "Just snap off her left tit and leave her in a corner somewhere. . . ." 16

Wheeeeeeoooooo. Arf, arf.

LaBove does impressions, too. No candy-ass Brando or Nicholson. He's swinging back and forth, imitating a pair of *testicles.* Finally, LaBove is telling the one about the two dead guys trying to get into Heaven. One got killed by a jealous husband. God likes his attitude, lets him in. Next guy comes up. One of *them.* God asks how he died. LaBove bends over, whines, and points to his backside. *Blam!* God slams the door. Seems God has an attitude about AIDS victims.

Whaaaaahooooooo. The dead-fag bit gets the biggest yowl of the night.

Amazingly, at this moment, Rambo appears through the smoke, backlit 20
by red and blue spotlights.

Yes, it's Stallone, slapping outstretched palms as he struts down the aisle
through the delirious throng. Cameras are following his Deltoid Force en-
tourage, since Kinison hopes to sell the evening's work to cable.

Once Stallone is seated, Kinison follows him down the aisle, a fat, leering
little Jabba the Hutt with a half-dressed babe on each arm. Two and a half
minutes into his act, Kinison, too, has his hand over his genitals. He tells
AIDS jokes, though not the one that got him in so much trouble recently
("Just because a few fags fucked some *monkeys* . . . they want us to wear
rubbers?"). He digresses into drugs, dildos, vaginal sprays, talks about ram-
ming Jack Daniel's bottles into women's vaginas, slapping them, copulating
on altars, having sex while on amyl nitrate.

Minutes later, Lenny Bruce's eighty-two-year-old mother is on the video
screen, thanking these nice boys from her home in California. She's talking
to Kinison: "Don't work to the mothers and fathers. Work to the kids,"
she's saying. "That's what you got here. You got the next generation."

Whaaaahooooo. Fuckin' A. 24

It is some indication of the bad-boys' market penetration that I overheard
San Diego schoolboys reciting the Diceman's dirty rhymes ("Hickory dickory
dock, some chick was suckin' my . . .")

But it's mostly adults who are buying this nasty, masturbatory humor.
Why this sudden appetite for homo and poo-poo jokes? Is it some kind of
fin de siècle decadence? A middle-class nod to skinhead sentiment?

"It is a cyclical thing," says Tony Hendra, former *National Lampooner*
and author of *Going Too Far,* a history of modern comedy. "What's going
on now is an extreme version of what happened with the postwar comics of
the late forties and early fifties. Back then, there was an informal competition
as to who could be more disgusting. Jack Carter was not as disgusting as
Buddy Hackett, who was only outdone by a guy called B. S. Pulley, who, in
the end, threatened to piss on people in the audience."

One exploration for the recent success of shock-value humor has to do 28
with the sudden expansion of the comedy scene itself. There is far more
room for mediocrity, and amid all the tired bad-date jokes, shockucomics
are sure to get noticed. Blue stand-ups who once had to wait until 2 A.M. to
go on in front of six drunks are now headliners in fern bars–cum–comedy
clubs.

According to Barry Weintraub, a stand-up comic and publisher of *Comedy USA,* an industry newsletter, the number of clubs that showcase comedy
has increased over the last decade to three hundred, about sixty times the
number of clubs operating in 1979. Given this boom, plus HBO's commit-

ment to comedy specials and its new comedy channel, it stands to reason that even a mediocre jokemeister can now make a living.

"[Comedy] is the thing now," says one stand-up who's survived ten years in the clubs. "It's been a constant build. A comic today, with one or two little shots on TV, can make anywhere from fifteen hundred to twenty-five hundred dollars a week headlining in little clubs. Middle acts get eight hundred dollars plus airfare."

And cruising down this comedic eight-lane is the bad boy, cutting through the "my wife, she's so fat" shticklock with stuff that makes you hit the brakes and say, *Whaaaaaaaa?* Quality control often goes out the window when an art form goes mainstream with such screaming speed. And in a flooded market, the purveyors find their own level of customer.

"In the sixties," says Weintraub, "comedy clubs were sort of under- 32 ground, hip things, heavy on political humor, some in-crowd drug stuff. Now comedy is reaching everybody. And there really are, of necessity, two camps. You've got the more intellectual guys—the Jerry Seinfelds, Jay Lenos; and you've got the other end—Sam and Dice and the guys who used to clear rooms just a few years ago."

There are also new avenues of promotion. These former room-clearers have learned how to dress better, to walk and talk their attitude with rock-star insouciance. Kinison has the berets, shoulder-length hair, and fat-boy overcoats, even a rock video that features him rolling in a pit with preacher's pet Jessica Hahn. Dice has more than a hundred leather jackets.

Most important, they have airtime. Grist-hungry cable networks can find it in their budgets to champion the outlaw. Given the impossibility of the fabled "shot on Carson" for a filthy mouth, cable has been the key to "breaking" bad boys. More specifically, the comics credit Rodney Danger-field's cable specials. "Without Rodney putting me on the first HBO special I'd still be struggling," Kinison has said. Dice, too, got his shot on a Dangerfield HBO show.

But if Dangerfield gave these comedic Cro-Magnons an open mike and airtime, it was the richest, most bankable bad boy who offered comics a grand vision of what dick jokes and designer leathers can do.

It was Eddie Murphy who was first picketed by angry gays for homo- 36 bashing in his concert film *Delirious*. Murphy, who trumped up the comic-as-outlaw rock-star conceit. His second concert film, *Raw*, is a stultifying exercise in mass-market misogyny, studded with toilet, pussy, and "fat, buck-toothed bitch" jokes. *Raw* was shot in bass-heavy concert verité with excited-fan interviews and limos-and-leather opening scenes.

The material wasn't new, just the pose and the venue. Blue humor has always been with us; Redd Foxx was doing dick and bathroom jokes before Murphy was out of training pants. But never before had a nation's number-one box-office attraction stood up, held his crotch, and talked about taking

Brooke Shields to the Grammys "and fuckin' her afterwards"—for major theatrical release.

As justification, he tossed out the benediction of Richard Pryor, who told him, "Whatever the fuck makes the people laugh, SAY THAT SHIT."

Invoking Pryor to defend suck-my-dick jokes is about as specious as the Outlaws' smarmy "tribute" to Lenny Bruce. Pryor and Bruce talked dirty to make you hear astringent comic truths. Fueling their attacks on almost everything square was a righteous rage—a hipster morality that, for all its darkness, did dare to hope for a better world. And if, as one journalist wrote of Bruce's work, it was "super-ego humor: a brave voice calling from the nursery," the bad boys do little more than reach into their diapers.

Shockucomics are not great thinkers; their success relies on the scuzziest   40
worldview. And putting a pious face on their "art" is dubious indeed. At the end of the Outlaws' Lenny Bruce tribute, Kinison and his boys sobered up for a bit of unctuous bilge on preserving the First Amendment—a law that justly defends their right to be gross. But consider this:

In 1961, Lenny Bruce was arrested and tried for saying the word "cock-sucker" onstage.

In 1989, a comic can stand up in a public club in Atlanta and say, unafraid, that "any disease that kills niggers and fags can't be all bad."

Which is more obscene?

The bad boys' success is, of course, dependent upon finding an audience.   44
That they have is the most grotesque aspect of the phenomenon. But, given the intensely polarized America left in the wake of the Reagan years—deteriorating race relations, the rise of Aryan youth movements, skinheads, and ex-Klansmen who can win state office—it's not surprising.

"There's a lot of rabble to be roused these days," says Tony Hendra. "With some of these shows, I don't see as it's much different than going to a Klan meeting. I have a rule of thumb to size up an audience. Do you find it funnier to see someone stronger and bigger trip and fall? Or someone smaller and weaker?"

So when Dice suggests a policy for the homeless—beat them up and scream, "Geddouda here, ya fuckin' bum"—there is hearty applause. And there is great audience participation when he leads the anti-immigrant chant: "If you don't know the language, *get the fuck outta the country.*"

Who are these people? Kinison's and Dice's shows have a high representation of heavy-metal head-bangers and leather-jacketed Trans Am types, but they are not all drawn from Archie Bunker Land. I saw some young Wall Streeters at the Outlaws show, their yellow power ties limp with mirth and Miller Lite. And Kinison's management says that the Midwest venues sold best of all.

Bad boys insist that their audiences are savvy enough to know they aren't 48 racists. That it's *just a joke.* Kinison often invokes the Archie Bunker defense, as other blue boys do, saying that he merely pushes the envelope further than did sexist, racist pea-brain Archie on prime time. The hole in the simile is that bad boys work without a Meathead—the conscience character who pointed up Archie's sins, just in case anyone missed the point.

There is no denying the sheer ugliness in the room when men and women who truly feel their jobs threatened by foreign Hyundai-mongers, who have felt the reverse sting of affirmative action, are served up a heady mix of vicious racial slurs and vodka on the rocks. Look closely at the laughing faces. Watch men and women pumping their fists for Spick and Jap and "fat, smelly bitch" jokes. It's about as funny as footage of the march on Selma.

No matter, it pays.

Kinison has said he didn't mind the AIDS-information inset that Warner Bros. Records slipped into the sleeve of his album to appease outraged advocacy groups. It was in the stores, he said, "but not at the bank." Responding to frank questioning from Bob Costas on his show *Later,* Kinison reminded him, "I haven't exactly gone unrewarded for my efforts. It's a *lot* of money."

Smilin' Sam declined to be interviewed for this article, declaring through 52 his publicist that, after a burst of unfavorable articles, he has "sealed himself off."

This left the Diceman to clarify the lure of loutism. And, surely, it is the Legend of the Diceman—a tough climb out of comedy hell—that illustrates the sweet six-figure victories of a guy who puts attitude *über alles.* For ten years, ten long fuckin' years, people were putting him down, guys from the old neighborhood saying "Howya doin' wit yer little comedy act?" Gives a guy a certain view of humanity.

"People are *nasty,*" says Dice. "Maybe that's why my humor has got a lot of attitude to it, 'cause nobody likes to see people do good."

Dice talks in heavy Brooklynese but declines to "pinpoint" where he is from, or disseminate any other personal data. (In fact, Andrew "Dice" Clay is Andrew Silverstein, early thirties, a stand-up who has been working for nearly eleven years, and who lived for some time in a boardinghouse for comics in L.A. run by Mitzi Shore of the Comedy Store.)

It had been suggested that Dice is most comfortable talking at his home 56 in Hollywood, so I visited him there. I found him in the company of his girlfriend, Kathleen "Trini" Monica, who appears as his love interest in the HBO special, and his boyhood friend and road manager, "Hot Tub" Johnny West, a skinny guy from Brooklyn with a heavy-metal mallcut.

Hot Tub has gotten Dice's things ready for this chat—water, cigarettes, pad and pen—and configured them precisely on the coffee table. "No!" he'd said as I lowered myself onto the sofa. "*Dice* sits there." Hot Tub likes to stick around because every interview Dice gives is the *best,* you know?

Trini sticks around, too, seated quietly at a table near the pullman kitchen. The Dice den is a modest Hollywood apartment, with a drum set ("I'm playin' since I'm seven") and an exercise machine in the living room. The man who rants about hogs, pigs, and fat, ugly chicks is wearing a tank top over astoundingly hairy shoulders; he is overweight—but training hard, since his movie starts shooting very soon. Here's a guy who says he used to steal steaks with Sam Kinison when they were both gasping for mike time as the Comedy Store. Now Twentieth Century Fox sends him juicy checks; William Morris collects them.

"It's always been a struggle," he says.

Like all show-biz legends, the Diceman's saga has an Inspirational Moment. It happened when Andrew Silverstein went to the movies one day—and it changed his life: "I saw *Rocky.* It gave me the inspiration to make something of myself. Somethin' positive. I came into show business."

So young Andrew started playing discos. He toted a boom box to Xenon and Blossoms doing Travolta bits, a little Rocky, whatever got a reaction. He says he went out West because he "got bored" with the attitude of East Coast clubs and comics who dumped on the guy in the leather jacket doing Travolta impressions, long past the happy daze of the Fonz and Sha Na Na.

When Dice got to Hollywood, there was another Moment: "I got right into the Comedy Store. First audition." The other comics hated him straightaway.

"I did twenty-eight minutes, which you're only supposed to do three. I'll never forget guys yellin' at me. I go, 'Hey, I came three thousand miles, I'll do what I have to do.'"

Dice worked the L.A. scene for seven hard years, stuck in the 2 A.M. spot. "You got to go on late 'cause nobody will follow you, but yet three-quarters of the audience is gone."

Dice shakes his head. "It was like fightin' a two-edged sword or whatever."

All this time, he was also auditioning for acting parts (he has appeared on TV in *Crime Story* and onscreen in *Casual Sex?,* in macho/hood parts). It was humiliating. "For the most part, they're just mean, nasty, cutthroat, backstabbing fucks in this town, and that goes from comics to producers to studio execs."

Just how young Andrew converted to total Dicetude is explained with Moment No. 3. It happened at the Comedy Store: "One night, I just went on and started talking about my own views on stuff. I want to make it in this business, and to make it, you got to be yourself. So I just threw the rest of the act away and started doing my own thing."

Now this is a tad confusing. Over and over, Dice says he is *acting* the 68
bad-boy character—"Definitely." And what does he think other stand-ups
are doing—those with less defined personas? "They're not acting. Just look
at 'em. They're *whining*."

Suggest that Dice's bits are somewhat, ummm, penile, and he gets defensive. "You call it dick humor, I think it's a lot more."

But with the exception of one series of actor impressions, Dice does not
do a single extended bit without direct reference to either the penis, the
vagina, the sex act, the rectum, or excretion. "It's very funny stuff," he says.
"A lot of it people *do*. And I'm up there talking about it, and it's hilarious
to them."

He says they know it's an act. "When I open up my special, going, 'I
got my tongue up this chick's ass in a bank'—that's funny. 'Cause everybody
knows this guy didn't go into a bank and put his tongue up this chick's ass."
Here Dice cracks himself up. Trini is giggling, and, lying beneath the exercise
machine, Hot Tub is hooting.

"I know the fans come to see me because they know this guy isn't for 72
real," says Dice, recovering. "If I really meant all the things onstage, there
wouldn't be a person in the room, because they would just say this is just
nasty, mean, violent humor. Anybody with a brain could see right through
me."

Who does he think his audience is?

"Everybody, once they loosen up. I'm not going for a little cult following."

Who does he see at the front tables?

"You think you're going to get every beer-drinking type of blue-collar 76
worker, and in the meantime, you're getting all these attorneys in there.
Doctors. Yuppies, that's who's comin' to see me. You see these women come
in with their *jooo*-lery and their fancy dresses."

One thing that angers Dice is that while interviewers ask about his gay-
bashing stuff, the racial stuff, they never ask about his antidrinking-and-
drug campaign. I confess I missed it and later go back to the HBO tape. It's
two lines, stating that if the Diceman wants to get high, he bangs his head
against a wall.

Chastened, I ask Dice about the racial riffs, in particular a bit about
Third World persons that goes like this: "You got these people, I don't know
what they are—not white, not black, like *urine-colored*, you know, walk
around with their fuckin' laundry on their head . . . with that *smell*, they
never heard of soap, these fuckin' people."

"*Urine*-colored?" I squeak. Dice cracks up again.

"I mean, that's very funny just hearing you say it," he says. "*Yoo-rine*- 80
colored people. Ahhhh."

Hot Tub is clutching himself on the rug.

But seriously, Dice is getting tired of defending his stuff, when others are getting away with it. He cites Jay Leno's *Tonight Show* Jap-bashing: "He'll talk about the foreigners who own 7-Eleven, and it's okay."

Here's Dice on the Japanese: "Look at these Japs—you could blindfold these people with dental floss. . . . They're taking over. Didn't we drop two bombs on 'em a few years ago?"

True, no *Tonight Show* writer could come up with such zingy material. 84

"What about the blacks?" he says. "I rip them apart."

This is true—I had forgotten. In his act, he imitates a shuffling, whining black named Moby, and suggests that he snake out toilets with his huge penis.

"It's all *jokes*. It used to be Polish or Italian or Jew jokes. So it's just who I'm pickin' on at the time."

Dice also picks on his peers. 88

On "generic comics" like Jerry Seinfeld: "Nobody gives a shit about losing socks in a laundry machine—that's not funny."

On Kinison: "I don't even listen to him anymore."

On Letterman: "A jerk-off. I look at this guy and I see no confidence. He's weak. I don't like weak people." Dice is particularly venomous about Letterman, who, he insists, is too personally threatened to have him booked on his show, though "everybody from his producer to his talent coordinator has come to me a hundred times going, 'We want you on the show.'"

(Says Bob Morton, Letterman's talent coordinator, "I can virtually guar- 92 antee you that no one here ever told Dice we wanted him to appear. We can't use his kind of stuff—which I told him in person when I went to check out his act three years ago.")

Hot Tub is getting antsy now, suggesting we end things, since he and the Diceman have a standing appointment with Stallone's *personal trainer,* George Pipsick. Stallone—"a personal friend"—set it up.

Hot Tub is hectoring his friend nervously. "Getcha sneakers on—if we're not there he'll *cancel us*. Jeezus, move."

Hot Tub brings the Diceman's sneakers.

"Schmuck, geddoudaheah. . . ." But Dice is putting on the sneakers. 96

Hot Tub is punching at the phone frantically, mumbling into the receiver. "We're on our way, honest, we're *there*, Gawge. Come on, cut us a break."

"Aaassshole. I'm doin' an interview." Dice is talking about his forth-coming ABC series. "It'll be number one, 'cause I'm funnier than anybody that's on TV. It'll be beeootiful, prime time. . . ."

He'll be doing stand-up too, but in rock arenas. "A couple of ten-thousand- to fifteen-thousand-seaters, just to say I did it."

Will Dice crap out when his character gets old? 100

"It's not gonna be a flash in the pan. I'm going to go on to movie stardom and TV stardom—I'm gonna cover all of it. When I get bored, I'll quit."

He doesn't pay much mind to the critics, the jealous comics. Yank his chain, honey, and he just gets BIGGER.

"Like they say, every knock's a boost."

He taps a cigarette on his ear, puts it down to tie the sneakers.

104

"If I wasn't big enough to talk about, you wouldn't mention my name. That's the beoooooty of it."

Points to Consider

1. To what does Gerri Hirshey attribute the recent proliferation of "bad-boy" comics? How does she link this phenomenon to the resurgence of comedy in general?

2. Why does Hirshey feel that comics specializing in blue humor are wrong to invoke the comedy of the late Lenny Bruce and Richard Pryor as forerunners for their own comedy? Why does she feel that profanity was acceptable in Bruce and Pryor?

3. What sorts of people make up the audiences at an Andrew "Dice" Clay or Sam Kinison performance? Why does Hirshey include the fact that Kinison has an easier time selling out in the Midwest than anywhere else?

4. How do comics like Clay and Kinison defend themselves against charges of racism? Why does Hirshey feel that the example of Archie Bunker cannot be used by these comics? Does she think the audiences that go to see these comics are themselves racist?

HENRY LOUIS GATES, JR.

2 Live Crew, Decoded   [THE NEW YORK TIMES/June 19, 1990]

The rap group 2 Live Crew and their controversial hit recording "As Nasty as They Wanna Be" may well earn a signal place in the history of First Amendment rights. But just as important is how these lyrics will be interpreted and by whom.

For centuries, African-Americans have been forced to develop coded ways of communicating to protect them from danger. Allegories and double meanings, words redefined to mean their opposites ("bad" meaning "good," for instance), even neologisms ("bodacious") have enabled blacks to share messages only the initiated understood.

Many blacks were amused by the transcripts of Marion Barry's sting operation, which reveals that he used the traditional black expression about one's "nose being opened." This referred to a love affair and not, as Mr. Barry's prosecutors have suggested, to the inhalation of drugs. Understanding this phrase could very well spell the difference (for the mayor) between prison and freedom.

2 Live Crew is engaged in heavy-handed parody, turning the stereotypes   4
of black and white American culture on their heads. These young artists are acting out, to lively dance music, a parodic exaggeration of the age-old stereotypes of the oversexed black female and male. Their exuberant use of hyperbole (phantasmagoric sexual organs, for example) undermines—for anyone fluent in black cultural codes—a too literal-minded hearing of the lyrics.

This is the street tradition called "signifying" or "playing the dozens," which has generally been risqué, and where the best signifier or "rapper" is the one who invents the most extravagant images, the biggest "lies," as the

---

Henry Louis Gates, Jr. (b. 1950) is the John Spencer Bassett Professor of English and Literature at Duke University. He frequently contributes articles and reviews to periodicals and journals, including Critical Inquiry, Black American Literature Forum, Antioch Review, *and* New York Times Book Review. *He is the author of several books, including* Black Literature and Literary Theory *(1984) and* The Signifying Monkey, *which won a 1989 National Book Award.*

culture says. (H. "Rap" Brown earned his nickname in just this way.) In the face of racist stereotypes about black sexuality, you can do one of two things: you can disavow them or explode them with exaggeration.

2 Live Crew, like many "hip-hop" groups, is engaged in sexual carnivalesque. Parody reigns supreme, from a take-off of standard blues to a spoof of the black power movement; their off-color nursery rhymes are part of a venerable Western tradition. The group even satirizes the culture of commerce when it appropriates popular advertising slogans ("Tastes great!" "Less filling!") and puts them in a bawdy context.

2 Live Crew must be interpreted within the context of black culture generally and of signifying specifically. Their novelty, and that of other adventuresome rap groups, is that their defiant rejection of euphemism now voices for the mainstream what before existed largely in the "race record" market—where the records of Redd Foxx and Rudy Ray Moore once were forced to reside.

Rock songs have always been about sex but have used elaborate subterfuges to convey that fact. 2 Live Crew uses Anglo-Saxon words and is self-conscious about it: a parody of a white voice in one song refers to "private personal parts," as a coy counterpart to the group's bluntness. 8

Much more troubling than its so-called obscenity is the group's overt sexism. Their sexism is so flagrant, however, that it almost cancels itself out in a hyperbolic war between the sexes. In this, it recalls the inter-sexual jousting in Zora Neale Hurston's novels. Still, many of us look toward the emergence of more female rappers to redress sexual stereotypes. And we must not allow ourselves to sentimentalize street culture: the appreciation of verbal virtuosity does not lessen one's obligation to critique bigotry in all of its pernicious forms.

Is 2 Live Crew more "obscene" than, say, the comic Andrew "Dice" Clay? Clearly, this rap group is seen as more threatening than others that are just as sexually explicit. Can this be completely unrelated to the specter of the young black male as a figure of sexual and social disruption, the very stereotypes 2 Live Crew seems determined to undermine?

This question—and the very large question of obscenity and the First Amendment—cannot even be addressed until those who would answer them become literate in the vernacular traditions of African-Americans. To do less is to censor through the equivalent of intellectual prior restraint—and censorship is to art what lynching is to justice.

Points to Consider

1. Why, according to Henry Louis Gates, Jr., have African-Americans been forced to develop a special way of expressing themselves? Is there reason to believe that the members of 2 Live Crew need to use such coded language?

2. To what does Gates see 2 Live Crew's controversial lyrics as a response? Why does Gates feel that parody is a useful tool in the fight against racist stereotypes of black sexuality?

3. Do you agree with Gates's formula that the group's "sexism is so flagrant ... that it almost cancels itself out"? Would Gates apply similar reasoning to flagrant racist comments? What qualification does Gates add to guard against misinterpretation of his statement?

4. Why does Gates believe that 2 Live Crew is perceived as more threatening than Andrew "Dice" Clay? Why does Gates think that the rap group is being singled out for obscenity? According to Gates, what does the group represent to many Americans?

RICHARD A. POSNER

Art for Law's Sake [THE AMERICAN SCHOLAR / Autumn 1989]

There is persistent, perhaps intensifying, controversy over offensive art. It is well illustrated by the recent brouhaha over "Piss Christ." A photograph (which I have not seen) by Andres Serrano of a plastic crucifix immersed in a bottle of the artist's urine, "Piss Christ" won a prize funded by a federal grant, sparking proposals to attach conditions to public support of the arts that would prevent future public subsidies of blasphemous, obscene, or otherwise offensive works. The questions raised by the Serrano work were shortly afterward exacerbated by the removal from the Corcoran Gallery of an exhibition, also supported by public funds, of photographs by the late Robert Mapplethorpe on subjects homoerotic and, some have argued, sadomasochistic into the bargain. Among the photographs (which, again, I have not seen) is one that is reported to show a black man urinating into the mouth of a white man. But I shall concentrate on "Piss Christ," which poses the issue of public regulation of offensive art in a particularly useful way.

RICHARD A. POSNER (b. 1939) is a judge on the United States Court of Appeals for the Seventh Circuit and a senior lecturer at the University of Chicago Law School. He is the author of The Federal Courts: Crisis and Reform *(1985) and* Law and Literature: A Misunderstood Relation *(1988).*

Despite or perhaps because of my being a member of the judiciary, I do not want to discuss the legality of proposals to restrict public funding of offensive art. I want instead to discuss the larger philosophical and jurisprudential issues raised by such art. Concretely, I want to argue that nowadays there is no objective method of determining what is art or what is offensive, and to consider whether, if this is right, it implies that offensive art should get a lot, or a little—or even no—protection from governmental interference, however that interference should be defined in this setting. For example, is it interference when the government grants, or when it withdraws, a subsidy to the arts?

When we say that lead is heavier than aluminum or that an automobile is faster than a rickshaw, we make a statement that can be verified by methods independent of the tastes or personal values of the people doing the verifying. A Communist, a nudist, a Jehovah's Witness, and a follower of Ayn Rand will all agree on how to test such propositions and on how to interpret the test results. Such "observer independence" gives the propositions about lead and automobiles truth value, makes them objective. It is quite otherwise if we say that "Piss Christ" has, or does not have, artistic value. The problem is not that artistic value is not a thing which a work either has or has not, for in this respect artistic value is no different from weight or speed, being like them an attribute or property rather than a thing. You don't take apart a Maserati and announce, "This is the carburetor and that is the speed." Similarly, "Piss Christ" is not a composite of urine, a bottle, a crucifix, a photograph, and artistic value.

But while it is possible to make objective measurements of physical properties such as weight and speed, it is not possible to make such measurements of artistic value, because people having different values and preferences do not agree and cannot be brought to agree on how to determine the presence of that attribute or even how to define it. A moralistic critic such as Tolstoy might think that the most important question about "Piss Christ" from an artistic standpoint is its likely effect on belief in Christianity. A Marxist critic might agree, and might further agree with Tolstoy that "Piss Christ" would undermine that belief, yet they would disagree about whether this made the work valuable or pernicious. Even if everyone to whom judges are willing to listen agrees that a work has no artistic value, we know from historical experience that it may; later generations may find such value in the work even though the artist's contemporaries did not. Conversely, a work highly valued in its time, or for that matter in later times, may eventually come to seem thoroughly meretricious. Artistic value is something an audience invests a work with, and as the tastes of audiences change, so do judgments of artistic value. About all that can be said in a positive vein is that the longer a work is held in high repute the likelier it is to continue to be held in high repute. This is the "test of time" that Samuel Johnson, David Hume, and George Orwell thought the only objective test of artistic merit.

If, to take a concrete example, the Homeric epics are still being read more than twenty-five hundred years after they were composed, then chances are they will continue to be highly regarded for some time; their appeal is robust and resists cultural change.

So far, though, all we have established is an inductive generalization, not an explanation. We could try to figure out what such durable works as the *Iliad* and *Hamlet* and Raphael's madonnas and *The Marriage of Figaro* and the "Ode on a Grecian Urn" and the Louvre's "Winged Victory of Samothrace" have in common and call that the key to artistic value. But this sort of thing has been attempted for millennia without success, and it now seems clear that the quest is a snipe hunt, so diverse are the durable works of the Western tradition. Conceivably we might identify a *necessary* condition of artistic survival—that a work have a certain "omnisignificance" or, less portentously, a certain ambiguity or generality that enables it to be taken in different ways in different times and places. But the distinction between a necessary and a sufficient condition is critical here, for we would not concede artistic value to every work that crossed some threshold of ambiguity or generality. "Piss Chirst" deals with a fundamental concern of humankind, religion, and does so in a distinctly ambiguous way. Serrano denies harboring any blasphemous intent and indeed claims—for all I know, with complete sincerity—that "Piss Christ" is a Christian commentary on the debasement of religion in modern America. The work may have artistic or even moral value, and then again it may not; it may soon come to be thought a worthless bit of trash. If it seems altogether too slight and ephemeral a work to have *any* chance of winning a secure niche in art history, let us remind ourselves that Marcel Duchamp's toilet seat, one of the objets trouvés of the Dadaist movement, has won such a niche along with Goya's disgusting painting "Saturn Eating His Children."

The conclusion to which I am driven is that ascriptions of artistic value or valuelessness to "works of art"—especially to contemporary works of art—are arbitrary. And so with offensiveness, another property of, not a thing found in, a work. "Piss Christ" is no more a compound of urine, a bottle, a crucifix, and offensiveness than it is a compound of urine, a bottle, a crucifix, a photograph, and artistic value. Again this property, offensiveness, is largely, perhaps entirely, a matter of public opinion rather than of correspondence to or causation by something that is observer-independent, something akin to the forces that determine weight and speed in accordance with the laws of physics.

This is not a problem when public opinion is united, as perhaps it is over the offensiveness of certain particularly graphic or degrading types of visual obscenity. With specific reference to "Piss Christ" one might be tempted to argue that, while there may be no consensus on what is art, there is a consensus, in Western societies anyway, that the public display of excreta is offensive. Consensus is a highly fallible warrant of truth, yet we might grant it provisionally objective status, even when it is local and temporary—a consensus in our society today, although not in all others and perhaps not in ours tomorrow. But it is a mistake to suppose that there is a consensus concerning the offensiveness of public displays of excreta. If samples of diabetics' or addicts' urine, or the feces of sufferers from Crohn's disease or cancer of the colon were displayed at a medical convention, we would not think the display offensive. It is all a matter of context and purpose. The question of the offensiveness of "Piss Christ" is therefore connected to the question of its artistic value. Those who find the work artistically valuable will not be offended by the (photographic) presence of urine, which they will consider integral to the work's value. Those who find the work blasphemous and barren of artistic value will consider the display of urine gratuitous and hence, given our culture's feelings about excreta, offensive. A few people may find the work both offensive and aesthetic, as many find Ezra Pound's *Cantos* or Vachel Lindsay's *Congo*. Their judgment on whether "Piss Christ" should be suppressed will depend on how offensive, and on how aesthetic, they find it, and on their personal sense of the proper balance between art and insult.

All this (to turn now from philosophy to jurisprudence) would have little or nothing to do with law if law had its own values, if it were morally autonomous. But for the most part it does not and is not. The law that entitles the victim of negligence to collect damages from the injurer is parasitic on—has no life apart from—social norms concerning what is careful and what is careless behavior. The prohibition in the First Amendment against government's abridging freedom of speech or freedom of the press, broadly conceived to include artistic as well as political and scientific expression, is parasitic in the same sense of social norms concerning artistic as well as other "speech" values and offensiveness and other speech harms such as violence. If a speaker urges a mob to lynch a prisoner because his guilt is so plain that a trial would be a waste of time and money, the speaker will be punishable for incitement to violence, because the danger of the speech will be felt to outweigh its value in drawing attention to the problematic character of due process. But if instead he writes a book urging the masses to rise up and liquidate the bosses, he will not be punishable, because such books are thought to have some value and not to be very dangerous, although citizens of Communist states may want to dispute both points. If our society thought such books were dangerous, they would be suppressed. Practical considerations, rather than the text or the eighteenth-century background of the First Amendment, guide the application of the amendment to today's problems.

Certain forms of obscenity are considered by virtually everyone in our society (including many of the consumers of obscene works) to be completely worthless and highly offensive, and they are suppressed without much ado, although, it must be added, also without much success. But the consensus

8

that condemns the extremely obscene does not extend to the class of works illustrated by "Piss Christ," which are thought valuable and nonoffensive by some, worthless and offensive by others, worthwhile but offensive by a handful. If there is no objective way to arbitrate such a disagreement, what should the courts do? More broadly, what are the implications for law of the kind of cultural relativism that I am describing?

There are three possibilities here, of which the first two reflect a desire to secure definiteness in law at any price. The first is to forbid *any* governmental interference with "art," no matter how offensive the "art." This approach does not escape subjectivity entirely; rather, it pushes inquiry back a stage, to the question of whether the work in question *is* art (and also to what counts as governmental "interference"). If a work is sufficiently offensive, it is classified as obscene, and therefore as non-art.

At the other extreme is the judicial-hands-off approach: courts are the forum of principle, there are no principles to apply to questions of aesthetic merit and offensiveness, so let the political branches do what they want with these questions. Such an approach is likely to appeal to those who are especially protective of courts—who want the judges to shine and believe that the judicial escutcheon is tarnished when the judges mess in indeterminate questions such as artistic value and offensiveness.

The third possible approach, the intermediate or pragmatic, is to acknowledge that the problem of relativism, moral as well as aesthetic, so strikingly presented by a work such as "Piss Christ," is a general feature of American, and perhaps of any, legal controversy. Judges need not feel they must shy off merely because the issues raised by offensive art are spongy. That's just the way things are in law; the nature of the legal enterprise ensures that judges will frequently find themselves wrestling with indeterminate questions, because those are the questions least likely to be settled without recourse to lawsuits that have to be pressed all the way to the Supreme Court or to another high appellate court before the question can be answered. Judges struggle with such questions all the time yet somehow manage to retain that minimum of public respect which is indispensable to the effectiveness of a court system. They are unlikely to forfeit it if they venture—with appropriate caution—into the controversy that eddies around issues of value and taste in purported works of art. The significance of the qualification will, I hope, become clearer as I proceed.

The first thing to note about this venture is that although artistic value 12 is largely, perhaps entirely, unknowable, there is little doubt that art is valuable. If this seems a paradox, consider: the lesson of history is that many of the scientific theories in which we firmly believe today are almost certainly false, just as Euclidean geometry as a theory of spatial relations, the geocentric theory of the solar system, the luminiferous ether, the spontaneous generation of bacteria, and Newton's laws of motion are now known to be false after having been believed by the scientific community for centuries.

Yet the fallibility of scientific theory does not lead a sensible person to doubt the existence, growth, or value of scientific knowledge. Even if every current scientific theory is someday falsified, we will still be able to make atomic bombs, fly airplanes, and immunize people against polio. Likewise it is a fact that art museums are thronged, that works of art command huge prices, that some people devote a lifetime to the study of art, and, more to the point, that many people would feel a profound sense of deprivation if the French Academy had succeeded in suppressing Impressionist art just as they feel that the world is a poorer place because so little classical Greek sculpture has survived.

If we grant that art has value and add that the censorship of art has a dreadful historical record, we can derive, in order to guide judicial review of controversies over offensive art, a presumption in favor of letting the stuff be produced and exhibited to whoever is willing to pay the price of admission. The Supreme Court's recent decision in the flag-burning case illustrates the presumption. Flag burning is an offensive, inarticulate, and immature mode of political communication (at least when the flag is our own), but as long as one is burning a flag one bought and paid for, before a willing audience, the flag burning contributes, however feebly, to the marketplace of ideas without impairing anybody's property rights.

We can bolster the presumption in favor of a permissive judicial attitude toward offensive art by noting that the "test of time" that is the closest we seem able to get to an objective measure of artistic value presupposes, like natural selection in the theory of biological evolution (which the test of time resembles), the existence of variety, from which history makes its selections. The whole thrust of censorship is to reduce variety, to suppress outliers, and by doing this it interferes with the test of time and impoverishes art's legacy to the future.

I don't mean "presumption" in any fancy lawyer's sense. I just mean that judges should be highly suspicious of anything that smacks of censorship. But since it is only a presumption that I am defending, judges should also be sensitive to arguments for rebutting it in particular cases, even at the risk of occasionally being found guilty by history of the sort of folly illustrated by the audience that was scandalized when *The Playboy of the Western World* was first performed in 1907 because Synge used the word "shift" for a woman's slip. There is such a thing as worrying too much about history's verdict on one's actions.

Consider a case in which the presumption in favor of freedom of artistic 16 expression was successfully rebutted. The case was decided by my court years ago, and since it is quite over and done with, I can discuss it without violating professional proprieties.

The case, *Piarowski* v. *Illinois Community College*, involved a small junior college near Chicago that, being public, was subject to the constitutional limitations on restricting free expression. The artist in the case, who was the chairman of the college's art department, made an improbable effort to fuse his two loves—the making of stained-glass windows and the art of Aubrey Beardsley—by making stained-glass versions of some of Beardsley's illustrations from Aristophanes' comedy *Lysistrata*. The illustrations, like the comedy, are bawdy even by today's standards (how fitting that they should be on public display in the Victoria and Albert Museum in London). They are, of course, line drawings of white men and women—Greeks. To transpose the drawings to the stained-glass medium, the artist in my case used pieces of colored glass for each of the figures, and the colors had to contrast. He made the innocent but, as it turned out, unfortunate choice of amber glass for the women and white glass for the men. As a result, one of the stained-glass windows depicts a brown woman, naked except for stockings, on her knees, embracing in an attitude of veneration the huge white phallus of a robed man. The other two windows depict brown women passing wind and masturbating, respectively.

The artist hung the windows in the art department's annual exhibition of faculty work, held in an alcove (the "gallery") off the main corridor of the college (the "mall," as it is called), on the ground floor. As the college has only one building, the exhibition was visible to all students, faculty, and visitors, whether or not they wanted to see it—more especially as there is no wall between the gallery and the mall. The first group to complain was the cleaning staff, which was black. Most of the students in the college are black, and they, too, were offended by the stained-glass windows and complained to the president of the college, who ordered the artist to shift the display from the first-floor corridor to a smaller exhibition room on the fourth floor, a room normally used for exhibiting photographs but suitable for exhibiting other works of art as well. When the artist refused, the president took down the stained-glass windows and placed them in his office. The artist sued the college, alleging a violation of the First Amendment.

Having studied photographs of Aubrey Beardsley's illustrations for *Lysistrata,* I find the stained-glass pastiches to be essentially free of both artistic value and offensiveness. Beardsley's charm is in the line, and it is lost when lines give way to chunks of colored glass. On the other hand, there was no contention that the chairman of the art department was attempting a commentary on race or sex; he was merely trying to use different colors, vaguely human, to distinguish the figures in the windows from one another. And the very crudeness of the windows neutralizes any obscene impact. For the reasons stated earlier, however, I have no basis for confidence in my or any other judge's ability either to evaluate the artistry of the stained-glass windows or to gauge their offensiveness to a community in which Aubrey Beardsley is not a household word.

A "hands-off-relativist" might take the position that since issues of artistic and moral taste are not objective, the artist should have lost his suit even if the college had refused to allow him to exhibit his stained-glass

20

windows anywhere on (or for that matter off) the campus. This was not the court's view, but neither did we think the Constitution *entitled* him to exhibit his windows in the most public place in the college. The college's president had offered an alternative place of exhibition that, while indeed less conspicuous, was by the same token less offensive. Racial sensitivities are a fact in our society, and if, as I have argued, offensiveness ultimately is no more objective than artistic value, neither is it less so. The college president's action seemed a reasonable compromise, and the court gave judgment for the college. In so doing, we affirmed that "academic freedom" is a two-way street. It is the freedom of a college to manage its affairs without due judicial interference no less than it is the freedom of the teacher or scholar to teach or write or, in this case, create works of art without undue interference by the state (for remember that this was a public college, and hence an arm of the state). A further point worth making is that the power of a single junior college to affect the art scene by shunting offensive works to less conspicuous places of exhibition is distinctly limited. But of course the example might prove catching.

So particularistic and fact-specific—so pragmatic—a mode of adjudication that led to the judgment for the college, and that implies that the scope of First Amendment protection may be different for works of art than for political or scientific works, is not to everyone's taste. Lawyers have a predilection for rules, and there indeed are many occasions when hard-edged rules are preferable to fuzzy standards, but controversies over offensive art may not be one of them. It is not even clear that art would be helped rather than hindered by a rule that forbade any and all public regulation of offensive art. Such a rule—a rule that gave privileged status to the *flaunting* of offensive art—might engender public hostility to art that would be out of all proportion to the benefits in artistic freedom gained. On the other hand, a rule that gave government carte blanche to suppress art deemed offensive by any vocal, assertive, politically influential group in our diverse, teeming, and (let us face it) rather philistine society could impair the future of art, a costly consequence. So perhaps the watchword in First Amendment cases having to do with art should indeed be *caution*.

Points to Consider

1. Why does Richard A. Posner believe that objective judgment of artistic value is impossible? Why doesn't he think that artistic value is a component of the work of art?

2. What role does consensus play in measuring artistic value or, conversely, offensiveness? Why, according to Posner, does consensus make the court's job easier? Is there any consensus about a work like "Piss Christ"?

3. On what grounds does Posner make his argument that a work of art can

be offensive while possessing artistic value? Do you tend to see these two terms as mutually exclusive? What does your answer to this question tell you about your own views on art and on freedom of expression in general?

4. What are Posner's three alternatives for dealing with art widely considered offensive? Which one of the three does he endorse? Does his decision in the case of *Piarowski* v. *Illinois Community College* reflect his stated preference for the "pragmatic" approach to such cases?

Discussing the Unit

Suggested Topic for Discussion

Andrew "Dice" Clay defends his comedy by saying that his audience knows that what he does on stage is an act. "Anybody with a brain," he says, "could see right through me." Gates pursues a similar line of defense for 2 Live Crew, insisting that their songs are merely parodies of black sexual stereotypes and in no way meant to be taken literally. Why do you think that Clay and Gates take this particular approach? Why do Clay and Gates feel that these explanations diminish the offensive quality of the comedy and music, respectively?

Preparing for Class Discussion

1. Using Posner's discussion of the role of consensus in relation to the arts, can you think of a work of art or some aspect of popular culture that is deemed offensive by almost everybody? Why do you think your choice was considered offensive by most people? Try to devise a set of guidelines for determining offensiveness. Compare your guidelines with those of other students in your class.

2. Because of America's commitment to freedom of expression, comics and musicians feel at liberty to say or play anything they want. As things stand, artists and performers have a right to offend, and you have a right to be offended. At what point do you think that the protection of one person's freedom of expression interferes with another person's right not to be subjected to obscenity? How can such a conflict be resolved?

From Discussion to Writing

Although many people who protest the offensiveness of works like "Piss Christ" or of comics like Andrew "Dice" Clay claim that society is harmed by constant exposure to such obscenity, few have demonstrated an actual negative effect on society as a whole. Why is it difficult to measure such long-term effects? If such things cannot be measured, must we believe there is no effect? Write an essay in which you take a position on artistic expression. Would you propose limits? If so, of what sort? Who would establish them?

14

Outing: Do Gays Have a Right to Privacy?

Three weeks after the death of Malcolm Forbes, the editors of *OutWeek,* a popular gay and lesbian weekly, ran a cover story alleging that the famous multimillionaire was homosexual. The publication of the controversial report ignited a raging debate in our nation's media about the ethics of "outing," the practice of exposing public figures who have chosen to remain silent about their homosexuality. Not surprisingly, "outing" continues to gain attention in the press, since the practice raises profound questions about the nature of public life and privacy in America, issues that reach far beyond the confines of the gay community.

Although the arguments for "outing" take many forms, most of its supporters seem to agree that awareness of the large number of gay people in public life would not only encourage other homosexuals to stop hiding the truth about their sexuality, but also foster more widespread public acceptance of gay life among heterosexuals. In "Campus Queer Query," Victoria A. Brownworth, a lesbian activist, describes the reactions of American college students to "outing" and offers her own defense of this new form of gay activism. Not all gay people support the practice, however, and in "The Art of Outing," Richard Goldstein examines the possible disadvantages and questions the ethics of this radical trend in American journalism.

VICTORIA A. BROWNWORTH

Campus Queer Query [OUTWEEK / May 16, 1990]

This year outing has become as popular as voguing. Everyone has a point of view on how or whether to do it, to whom, and the level of outrageousness involved. In the still-as-apathetic-as-the-eighties nineties it's one of the few issues to goad liberal and conservative alike. Even college campuses are aware of outing and students have big questions.

Last month I was a featured speaker at the Pride Week festivities of Haverford and Bryn Mawr colleges. My topic was the subversion of gay culture by heterosexual society and the talk was attended by a refreshingly large number of students—male and female, white and nonwhite in nearly equal numbers. Because much of the talk focused on denial of homosexuality—either by the heterosexual culture or by gay artists and writers themselves—many of the early questions in the period following the lecture focused on closeting and, by extension, outing.

So what do the students of two of America's most prestigious colleges think about outing? They love it and it scares them to death. After nearly an hour and a half of questions, the consensus was that outing is a good thing to do to people who are dead (Forbes), evil (Ritter and Roy Cohn), or working against us (oops, we haven't outed him yet), but not something to do to anyone gay who might ever do anything nice or helpful for other gays. Including themselves. For as one young black woman said, "How can we be sure that as we're outing these people we can stay safe?"

In short, how do young gays and lesbians out the people they don't like—the gays they believe should be "exposed" for their internalized homophobia—while remaining safely cocooned in the closet themselves? 4

These students had serious questions about the long-range effects of outing and the ethics of it. They also wanted to talk about the techniques: how to out homophobic college administrators, for example. But the more

---

VICTORIA A. BROWNWORTH (b. 1954) teaches English and writing at the Community College of Philadelphia and writes regularly for the Village Voice, the Nation, OutWeek, and the Advocate. She has written five books, most recently a book on women film directors called Camera Obscura: Interviews with Women Film Directors in America and Europe (1991).

questions they asked, the more apparent was their underlying fear: to participate in outing must you be out yourself?

I have been on both sides of the outing issue since before it was called outing. In the fifteen years I've been writing for the gay and mainstream press I've had occasion to "out"—sometimes intentionally and sometimes by accident. When I was in my early twenties I had a lot of sympathy for closeted queers. When I hit thirty it stopped completely.

In telling these students the story of my own activism—being expelled from my high school for being a lesbian (in the enlightened seventies, no less), being arrested in "zaps" of antigay organizations, media, and the like, being a token lipstick lesbian on television talk shows, and basically taking on the day-to-day homophobia from a very public place—I also told them that I have no patience any longer for anyone in the closet. I told them that every gay man and lesbian woman who "passes" (and tries to) oppresses me further and reaps the benefits of my activism while hiding the strength of our numbers from the people to whom those numbers would make a difference.

When we talk about outing, what are we really talking about? We're 8 talking about exposing the collaborationists, we're talking about exposing those who think they'll never get marched to the gas chambers because "nobody knows."

We know outing has arrived because it is suddenly a mainstream media topic. Outing has become a matter of "ethics" for the liberal left who liken it to McCarthy tactics and red-baiting; the neo-cons are gloating because they see it as the final feeding frenzy before we kill ourselves off. But outing is, in reality, a civil rights tactic. Radical yes, but then so was refusing to move to the back of the bus.

Talking with these students and listening to their fears of coming out, the threat they believe is posed to them specifically, individually, by the outing issue made me believe even more strongly in the need for just such tactics. Here are eighteen-, nineteen-, and twenty-year-olds poised on the brink of the rest of their lives and they have the chance of being openly gay and facing the possibility of discrimination that is very real or hiding it and facing the reality of a double life for all eternity. Yet because they cannot look to the huge and compelling variety of gay and lesbian models—from the Hermann Goerings and Roy Cohns to the boys and girls next door—because they continue to be closeted from them, they think there is only one choice that makes sense. That choice is the one they see practiced most often: climbing into the closet, changing pronouns, faking heterosexuality, and praying every day of their life that no one finds out. This is the choice we offer our gay and lesbian youth.

Outing has become an essential in the quest for gay and lesbian rights, gay and lesbian equality. The big question is: is outing ethical? Is outing politically correct?

These questions come from the same source as the oppression that fuels 12 them. Let's reverse those questions and, instead of blaming the activists striving for equal rights, let's shift the blame to the self-proclaimed victims. Is it ethical to stay in the closet, pass for straight, assume the mantel of heterosexual privilege and enjoy its benefits while those who are openly gay suffer the oppression of their minority status? Is it ethical to turn a deaf ear to AIDS? Is is politically correct to ignore the fact that gays and lesbians have absolutely no rights under the law?

This is why outing cannot be equated with red-baiting and this is why outing should be welcomed rather than feared by the gay and lesbian youth of America. Outing represents a step toward freedom, a step toward acknowledgement of our diversity and our vast numbers. Gays and lesbians are the largest single minority in the United States, yet because of the huge number who remain silent and closeted, we appear to the heterosexual society to be far smaller and, as a consequence, less strong, less politically powerful, less financially powerful, less self-determinant.

One student asked me if outing didn't represent a threat to the privacy of the individual. In one sense it does, most certainly, yet if we look at the history of oppression, the most virulent backlash has been directed toward those groups who were able to "pass" as members of the majority group— like the majority of Jews in Germany in the final days of the Weimar Republic.

Blacks, Asians, Hispanics, and women cannot "pass." Gays and lesbians can. And as long as we perpetuate the theory that in passing we can augur change from within, we perpetuate the whole cycle of oppression. When we try to pass there is always the possibility we will be uncovered. Outing represents the refutation of that level of oppression, the oppression of passing. Passing only gives the illusion of allowing us access to power; yet by forcing us to pass, to be other than who we really are, the culture maintains its dominance over us. It has disallowed us ourselves.

In urging these students to come out now, to acknowledge themselves 16 and to declare themselves, I also asked that they refute the role of collaborationist—not simply in their own oppression, but in the oppression of others as well.

One student asked what if we outed someone who really wasn't gay, wouldn't we destroy that person's life?

The answer to that is self-evident. As long as fear surrounds gayness, rather than affirmation, there will be denial. And until the gays and lesbians of the world begin to assume with the same level of arrogance that heterosexuals have assumed—until we operate on the assumption that everyone is gay until proven otherwise—we are not going to shift the balance of power.

There is a radicalism attached to outing that is different from any other gay rights activism. Because at the heart of outing is a refutation of internalized homophobia; participating in outing makes the statement that anyone can be gay and that as a group we can accept that. That's a major leap toward self-love and independence. And quite simply, until we believe and *act* like we are *worthy* of the same legal protections, rights, and privileges awarded the heterosexual society, we won't achieve them.

This is the lesson I wanted to teach those students last month: that they are in charge of their own freedom. That outing should become a tool for them toward that freedom. That until heterosexuals can be presumed gay until proven otherwise, until being called gay isn't the worst thing that can happen to you, there is going to be a struggle. And the best way to participate in that struggle is to come out, acknowledge yourself, and refuse to be placed in the closet.

We will not have equality and we will not have legal rights until the closet doors in this country—on every level—are ripped off their hinges and their occupants declared.

20

Points to Consider

1. According to Brownworth, what are the greatest fears among young gays and lesbians in relation to "outing"? Would the continued exposure of gay public figures help to magnify or eliminate such fears?

2. The author reserves her most severe criticism for gay men and women who attempt to "pass" as heterosexual. Do such individuals pose a real threat to the cause of gay rights in this country?

3. Throughout the piece, Brownworth draws analogies between the treatment of Jews in Nazi Germany and the treatment of gays and lesbians in America. Do you think the situation of homosexuals in this country merits such a comparison? Why do you think the author offers such parallels?

4. How does Brownworth answer the student who asks if "outing" is a threat to privacy? What does her answer imply about an individual's right to privacy?

RICHARD GOLDSTEIN

The Art of Outing   [THE VILLAGE VOICE / May 1, 1990]

By now, it seems everyone knows that Malcolm Forbes had a "secret gay life." The revelation—though news to few who traveled in this motor-cycling media-mogul's circles—sent shock waves across the gossip desks of the dailies. *Newsday*'s James Revson, speaking for this city's decent dish-mongers (the ones who follow Marla Maples around), vented no small rage at Michelangelo Signorile, who first blew Malcolm's cover in *OutWeek*. Signorile is Revson's nightmare—a fiercely open gay man whose idea of gossip is to fire salvos at closeted gossip columnists. And his home base is that rarity among gay publications—a hot read—because of how it defines the radical act. *OutWeek*'s auto da fé is the increasingly vitriolic practice of bringing out the rich and famous who happen to be gay.

This impulse has been labeled "outing," and it springs from several sources. One is the memory of growing up gay with the painful illusion that everyone else is straight. If all gay heroes were out, the theory goes, young people wouldn't have to wait until they were grown to discover that ho-mosexuals can make a life—indeed, a very useful one. Then there's the AIDS crisis, which has intensified the relationship between survival and solidarity. For many activists, that's meant impelling the (often closeted) gay elite to use their clout to save lives. Finally, as gay visibility grows, so does rage at the closet as an agent of the cherished fiction that homosexuals can't be teachers, soldiers, baseball players, priests, and even parents. Gay people who do play these roles often must hide the truth about their sexuality, nurturing the very system that bars homosexuals from "sensitive" positions. The paradox of being blocked from realizing your full potential, while others who cling to the closet prosper, is enough to make an avenging angel out of any activist.

This is a bind few heterosexuals can grasp, and it's led to a fairly facile condemnation of outing by straight progs who are usually allies of gay liberation—joined, naturally enough, by closet cases who've made their

---

RICHARD GOLDSTEIN (b. 1944) is the arts editor for the Village Voice. He is the author of One in Seven: Drugs on Campus (1966), The Poetry of Rock (1969), and an anthology of his journalism from the 1960s called Reporting the Counterculture (1989).

peace with this arrangement. But even "new gays" of the nineties—those queers without fears—disagree about the ethics of naming gay names. Should Barney Frank, the openly gay congressman from Massachusetts, have threatened to bring out right-wing closet cases if the G.O.P. persisted in smearing House speaker Tom Foley with homosexual innuendo? Most gay activists say yes, since rank hypocrisy was involved. But should the same standard be applied to Malcolm Forbes, who never harmed a hair on any homo's head (even while mussing it)? The battle rages, between those who insist that liberation hinges on visibility by any means necessary, and those who are convinced that coming out can only have meaning as a voluntary act.

OutWeek fuels the fires in a column called "Peek-a-boo," the kind of 4
list red-blooded guys could pass around a locker room, if they didn't know that just being seen with this magazine identifies you as a major 'Mo. So far, *OutWeek*'s targets have been people whose dirty secrets most of us would like to see exposed: dilettantes and ditsy celebrities. As for gossipmongers, they profit from the secrets of others, so why should their private lives be off limits?

But the problem with outing folks we love to hate is that it can be an exercise in puritanism with a liberated face. In a Stalinist state, Malcolm Forbes would be labeled a "social parasite," and any inference of homosexuality would be welcome as proof of his decadence. Though *OutWeek* tried to claim Forbes for the "gay nation," the honorific rang false. When we bring out a voluptuary or a vulgarian, aren't we trading off our own resentment, and using politics as a cover for contempt?

The horrific history of homophobia is a major reason why even many gay people have profound doubts about outing. Until very recently, homosexuals who rose above their station (as body-servants and buffoons) to shape society lived in constant fear of being brought out as a pretext for being purged—or worse. In 1327, King Edward II, the first Prince of Wales, was punished for his homosexuality with death by a red-hot poker up the ass; a paramour's genitals were cut off and burned before his eyes. As a young man, Frederick the Great of Prussia was forced by his father to watch his male lover hanged for the crime of their bond.

In a kinder, gentler vein, who can forget the uses of gay-baiting in the McCarthy era—or its invocation by Southern conservatives to discredit the civil rights march on Washington in 1963. At the time, several congressmen released a police report on Bayard Rustin, an organizer of the event, who had been arrested for soliciting men. Marx's minions have hardly been more reticent. In 1967, when the students of Prague elected visiting poet Allen Ginsberg king of the May Day parade—in a witty gesture of rebellion—the authorities deported him. To justify that act, they published passages from Ginsberg's diary celebrating the sexual proclivities of Czech youths. In both cases, the revelation of homosexual activity was resisted: the civil rights leadership stood behind Rustin, and the students of Prague gave public readings of "Howl."

The point is that exposure has long been used by the enemies of gay 8 people as an instrument of control. But suddenly, the terms have changed. Conservatives, for the most part, cling to the closet as the only permissible way for a homosexual to live. It's a testament to the gay movement's success that demagogues and divines who single out sodomites can't get beyond their fundamentalist base. These days, the live-and-let-sin ethic prevails in most polite circles, and homosexuals—even when they're the stuff of gossip—are often tolerated as long as they don't break the code. Of course, that means fleeing from contact with young people, escorting members of the opposite sex, and never, never announcing, "I'm gay and happy that way."

There's a direct relationship between this relative relaxation and the fact that openly gay people are bringing closeted homosexuals out, in violation of a longstanding tradition that required sodomites to keep each other's secrets. But is the danger really past? The question is further complicated by the fact that outing is taking place in the full glare of mass media. After all, the word *outing* was coined by *Time* magazine. The subject clearly moves product, and not just gay papers. So far, the major beneficiaries have been supermarket tabs, where the sexuality of studs and starlets has replaced the five-hundred-pound man who gave birth to a dog as front page news. The politics of outing definitely makes strange bedfellows. Take the report that Richard Chamberlain is gay, which recently jumped from the gay press to check-out counters at Food World. Chamberlain denies it, and where does that leave the future of liberation? Do we stake out his home to ascertain if Dr. Kildare is one of us? And what gives gay muckrakers a monopoly on this sleuthing? Imagine a TV show called *Outside Edition,* in which reporters surprise a celebrity with evidence that he or she is gay. (Are you listening, Mr. Murdoch?)

The very prospect that outing might become a mass-phenom—the next logical step after Andrew "Dice" Clay—shows what's ominous about it. Also what's irresistible. For what would happen if Americans were bombarded with infotainment about the sex lives of our heroes and villains? Would the result be a purge of the prominent or a giant sigh of relief; an explosion of fear and loathing or a true picture of sexuality that could shatter stereotypes? The question can't be asked in the abstract. Perhaps a better way to frame it might be: is the pain outing would doubtless cause some individuals worth the gain?

Whatever scenario one imagines, the fact is that outing is here to stay. The new vanguard of gay liberation has begun to question the rules of the game, including the age-old assumption that a closeted gay celebrity is a source of pride. That doesn't apply in an age when openly gay people are struggling for their place in the sun. Why should a candid performer confined to gay cabaret look kindly on a closet case who gets to chat with Arsenio Hall? The entire thrust of gay liberation has been toward removing sex from the arena of privacy and making the personal political in the bluntest terms.

Indeed, the trend throughout American society is toward shattering the 12 boundaries of privacy—and not just in the name of liberation. As it becomes possible to live outside the marriage vows, the talk shows have moved in, unleashing a torrent of titillating detail about sexual practices once regarded as shameful but secret, or at least outside the parameters of prime time. And what began as entertainment has entered the arena of public policy. In Newark, the city council recently voted to publish a broadside with the names of everyone arrested on a drug or sex charge, *prior to conviction*. In many localities, ambitious prosecutors arrange arrests with the media in mind, requiring suspects to walk a gauntlet of cameras and mikes. That's how Rudy Giuliani made a name for himself.

In the years since Nelson Rockefeller died with his pants down, the sex lives of politicians have become prime bait for scholars and sleazebags alike. What FDR could keep to himself JFK could not, and Gary Hart ushered in an age of scrutiny that now subjects anyone who runs for office to the kind of inquiry once reserved for therapy. Even the confidence of the confessional is being challenged in court, and when you add to this expectation of candor the remarkable amount of personal information Americans must provide to squads of information gatherers—from social workers to credit card companies—it's clear that less and less in the realm of human behavior is beyond disclosure.

The potential for repression here is at least as great as the likelihood of liberation, which is why outing distresses those who worry about the regimentation of behavior. But activists who endorse this practice are reacting to an environment in which it seems that *only* homosexuality is beyond the pale. It's one thing, after all, to say that FDR had a mistress or two, quite another to suggest that Eleanor had a lesbian relationship. The result is an elaborate ritual of prevarication that rightly infuriates gays who are out. The same gossip columnists who skewered *OutWeek* for debearding Malcolm Forbes were eager to report his impending marriage to Liz Taylor, even though they must have doubted its credibility—and even though some of these same people are gay.

This rush to preserve the closet is a commonplace of "respectable" journalism. In fact, many publications indulge in a practice that could be called "inning"—ignoring the truth, even when an individual has confirmed that he or she is gay. This has been a regular feature of obituaries, unless a survivor specifically requests otherwise—even when homosexuality had a direct bearing on the cause of death. When Allard Lowenstein was murdered by a young man with whom he'd had a sexual relationship, the *Post*'s James Wechsler attacked *Voice* writer Teresa Carpenter for reporting the fact. When a murdered lesbian was found recently with a picture of her lover and a letter of devotion in her pocket, the *Times* reported that the person in the picture was her boyfriend. Only after a protracted campaign by the Gay and Lesbian Alliance Against Defamation, did the paper of record print a correction.

This discretion does not extend to most other aspects of human identity. Back in the sixties, the *Times* revealed that the head of the New York Ku Klux Klan, a member of the Nazi party, was Jewish. (He killed himself after the story appeared.) But the same sort of contradiction did not move the *Times* to print that Terry Dolan or Roy Cohn was gay, though both men actively pursued antigay politics. Such hypocrisy is what led Larry Kramer to approach Dolan at a gay party, throw a drink in his face, and shout: "You fuck us by night and fuck with us by day." That story—a legend in activist circles—has not been fit to print.

The *Times* has been unable to resist covering the outing of Malcolm Forbes, but it has yet to mention him by name. Instead, the paper has used phrases like "a famous, deceased millionaire." Even in an Op Ed article by Randy Shilts, America's best known openly gay investigative reporter, Shilts was limited to advocating outing by inning. This should come as no surprise in a publication whose famous, deceased den mother, Iphigene Sulzberger, once told a group of activists who demanded coverage of gay life: "Not in my newspaper."

Such forced attempts at delicacy make the absurdity of the closet painfully clear. And the closet is an appropriate context for a discussion of outing. This is a unique institution in contemporary American life, comparable, perhaps, to the quasi secret identity Jews of prior generations were forced to construct. The closet informs homosexuals that, though they may be able to avoid criminal prosecution, they are still members of a class whose legitimacy is subject to attack. What was once considered a humane alternative to oppression—a sphere of privacy within which queers were free to be—has come to be perceived as the foundation of homophobia. In the years since Stonewall, tens of thousands of homosexuals have come out, replacing their shadowy subculture with an array of affinity groups, from Hikin' Dykes to Dentists United for Human Rights. And once the terms of the closet were challenged, it became clear that those who were most attached to this institution did not have the well-being of gay people in mind; their only concern was to spare themselves having to deal with queers in their midst.

This reflex is hardly limited to right-wingers. In fact, affection for the closet ties together social conservatives of the left and right. Murray Kempton has written: "The closet happens to be the single human invention whose consequences have been universally benevolent." In Kempton's addled view, "public discussions of sexuality are always in bad taste," and mayoral proclamations of Gay Pride are "pathetic hypocrisy . . . when gay shame remains an open wound all year round." Jeff Greenfield, a correspondent for ABC News, once wrote in the *Voice* that "gays, like everyone else, have a right to be free of laws making their bedroom habits public offenses." But, to translate this "right of privacy" into a demand for affirmative public action "violates the essential distinction between what is and is not public concern."

From this premise, Greenfield builds a case for distinguishing between the gay movement and other crusades for civil rights. "There is no such thing as the right to be black or female *in private*," he notes. When gays make their sexuality known, they incur a judgment the law should not redress. "It is the public nature of their impulses that 'entitles' me to exercise my prejudice. . . . This is true, not just of homosexuality but of *any* private conduct." For example: "I have a visceral dislike for the foliage of the arriviste. Vuitton bags, digital watches, Bergdorf shopping bags, trigger in me a strong sense of revulsion. . . . If a member of this 'group' came to me for a job garbed in the uniform of the acquisitive, I would refuse out of hand, and I would have a right to refuse." 20

Both Kempton and Greenfield expressed these sentiments in the 1970s, when it was still respectable for straight liberals to be frank about their distaste for gay rights. (Note, in Greenfield's case, the implication that he has a right to regulate the way women in his employ dress. Such a boss might well feel entitled to fire office boys he finds too *obvious*.) They would probably be more subtle about it now, but in neoconservative circles, the closet is still a homosexual's castle. When he was secretary of education, William Bennett once remarked that gays ought to be permitted to teach in schools as long as they didn't "flaunt" their sexuality, a standard John Cardinal O'Connor says he applies in hiring homosexuals at Catholic agencies.

Never mind that flaunting is in the eye of the beholder; that many homosexuals don't choose to be overt but can't help displaying the mannerisms Greenfield finds offensive. What such "decent" men demand as the price for their "tolerance" is an elaborate system of duplicity—ranging from tight control of body language to silence when the subjects of love and lust come up—that they would never accept themselves. Indeed, the restraints of the closet are so close to the demands sexism places on the bodies of women that the result is often read by men like Greenfield as "effeminacy" (or in the case of lesbians, a Garboesque aloofness). What's actually on display is the evidence of human beings in stylized expressions of pain.

This is the daily anguish of the closet—so pervasive and socially sanctioned that it's rarely obvious, even to homosexuals themselves, until they come out. The habit of repressing one's libido in public leads to a variety of vehement compensations in private, from promiscuity to utter prissiness about sex. The ability to form enduring relationships is obstructed by the burden of shame that comes of living in a culture where any expression of same-sex love is greeted with contempt, at best. And even when such bonds are forged, they are never amalgamated into ordinary life. Closeted gay people are deprived of all the rituals that hold people together, from having the boss over for dinner to celebrating an anniversary with friends.

Gay people compensate for this loss of public acknowledgement with a rich subculture of solidarity and special codes—that is, camp—but the inability to integrate sexuality into the world takes an enormous toll. Ask Barney Frank, whose liaison with a hustler may end his political career. As a closeted gay man, Frank lacked the skills to navigate the shoals of sexuality: those are social skills, and the silence, secrecy, and shame that constitute the closet make them difficult for many homosexuals to acquire. In retrospect, Frank has come to understand that the "right to privacy" social conservatives extol is the very device that led him to the brink of self-destruction. 24

So the closet is a pathology, and coming out is part of a larger struggle to integrate desire with one's place in the world. This is what gay liberation is all about, and why, for homosexuals too, the personal is political. But for all the exhilaration and self-acceptance, coming out also brings another kind of clarity. Suddenly, the true dimensions of homophobia are clear: one's relationships with heterosexuals—especially men—grow strained as the alienation becomes more overt; one's response to words like *faggot,* so ubiquitous on the street (and lately in the media) is more aggressive as the violence behind these exercises in free speech becomes clear; and one's vulnerability to discrimination, not to mention banishment from the cocoon of family, increases markedly. Then there is gaybashing, the ultimate enforcer of the closet. Nearly a quarter of all gay men and lesbians say they have experienced violence as a result of their sexuality. In the face of endemic brutality, many who can hide do.

To be truly out is a constant battle between self-assertion and self-preservation. And the fight is never more painful than when other gay people are attacked. To stand against homophobia is to become a target for the bigot inside the gentleman and the packs of roving youths who are the storm troopers of those "reasonable men" in robes of church and state. I speak from the most direct experience, not just as a journalist but as a walker in the city. To hold my lover's hand in public is to risk my life—which is why, in gay circles, such acts of defiance are known as PDAs, for "public displays of affection." Kissing good-by as I leave our car means glancing over my lover's shoulder, for safety's sake. In a hospital, where one fears the biases of medical personnel, I may choose not to hold my lover as we wait in the emergency room, though he is in pain. On the street at night, we walk a pace apart, keeping the distance from each other that straight men expect. The constant threat of violence, as a reminder that the world we shape in our relationship is not the only place we inhabit, is something all minorities face—in fact, it's one reason gay people have a right to claim minority status.

Confronting that threat, by "flaunting" the most ordinary expressions of intimacy, is not a casual act.

Consider this incident, which happened a few weeks ago. My lover and I were strolling through the East Village on a warm evening, when we happened to pass between two women holding hands and a young man shrieking obscenities at them. No one else on the crowded sidewalk seemed to notice that one of the women had turned to fight. We were suddenly faced with a choice: to walk on—since *we* weren't offending this dude by holding hands—or to "come out" by joining the fray. In an instant, I did.

"Go back to Jersey," I shouted in my best Bronx voice. The punk replied,   28 "Hey—I'm from Brooklyn."

"Well, you're in the wrong borough," I insisted. (As a bridge-and-tunnel type, I know how that hurts.)

He wheeled at me, his chest heaving, and I could see he was out of control. "I'll stab you right now," he yelled. Pedestrians were ambling by, oblivious to his twisted face; the two women were nowhere in sight. Now I was his target, and my own adrenaline blinded me to the possibility that he might actually have a knife. But my lover's eyes were the size of silver dollars; he looked like a deer trapped in the headlights of an oncoming semi.

"C'mon faggot," our assailant purred.

"See you in Rikers," I spat back. Fortunately, we were in shouting   32 distance of a police station, and I pointed that out.

"Ah, you're fags, they'll never believe you," he barked. But the green globes of the precinct house gave him pause, and he lumbered away, leaving us to ponder the prospect of sudden death. Under the trembling that coursed through my body was rage that I hadn't obliterated this brute.

Anger and terror: I'm suspended between those two states whenever my sexuality becomes an issue. And, as an out gay man, I insist that it become an issue, because the price of pretending otherwise is my integrity. This sense of living on the brink is a consequence of coming out: along with glory comes the threat. And the result is fury at those who tuck themselves into the closet when it suits them, while drawing sustenance from men and women willing to take the consequences of their candor. This is where my own impulse to bring out the rich and famous arises. And when a closeted homosexual profits from attacking other gay people, the rage becomes explosive.

Unfortunately, the reflex to strike out at assertive gay people may be especially strong among the closeted, who struggle to maintain an illusion of heterosexuality. Father Bruce Ritter, for example, aggressively pursued the antigay agenda of the Meese Commission on Pornography, though he allegedly had homosexual relationships. Roy Cohn had no problem gay-baiting his enemies, which is why activists published broadsides while Cohn was alive with evidence of his homosexuality. And why the panel someone wove for the AIDS quilt in Cohn's honor refers to him as both a bully and a victim of homophobia.

The danger of coming out clarifies the problem with outing, especially when it's aimed at closeted homosexuals who do nothing to harm other gays. Why subject them to homophobia against their will? The question may have special resonance for lesbians, because they face greater economic discrimination than gay men. Add to this disparity in income a pattern of violence that singles out "butch" women, who represent resistance to male authority in a way that "femme" men do not. The punishment may include that signature of male rage, rape. An attitude toward coming out that does not take the complex realities of oppression into account is not a liberated one.

And even if the consequences of coming out are minimal, who can measure personal terror for anyone else? A homosexual who is closeted for the sake of his family may need to understand the futility of that charade, but publishing the news is no way to help someone grow. Nor is bringing out a married homosexual a way to resolve that ambiguity. For some gay people, the closet is the very basis of eroticism. Those fantasies that one is merely "fooling around" may be a delusion, and a self-hating one at that, but policing the libido in the name of liberation is a tyrannical act.

This is not to deny that I detest queers who claim their sexuality is a private matter, and when they benefit from duplicity and denial, I'm sorely tempted to bring them out. But it's not as if my own sexual history is a noble trek; there were endless years of pretense and panic (not to mention indifference to homophobia). I came out with patience and support from gay friends, which helped me cope with the hatred coming at me and the horror within. At the time, I felt flayed, and it would have taken much longer to heal if I'd been outed.

Of course, the folks at *OutWeek* aren't after the obscure; they want celebrity meat. The impulse is understandable, but what would gay life be like if coercion prevailed? The question is tactical as well as moral. For all their sound and fury, gay men and lesbians who come out are a minority within a minority; and when it comes to power and financial clout, we control a meager piece of the pie. If gay activists turned on closeted homosexuals, the result would be a major breach in the community, as rich and famous queers surmised that any contact with or contributions to the cause could become an occasion for outing.

And would the closet really be destroyed? Consider Liberace, whose on- and offstage persona was a gay fantasia, billboard sized. Yet, his legions of fans overlooked their idol's sexual identity, even as they reveled in its acoutrements. The closet does not require evidence of the senses to maintain itself, only the willingness of those who reside within: as long as queers *say* they're straight, the closet will stand, because it's a mechanism of subordination and control. The only way to break this code is to say it isn't so, and no one can do that for anyone else. If outing results in a spate of "role models" who react with denial and shame, what kind of paradigm would that create for young queers? How would that force the straight world to acknowledge that gay is good?

This is not to say that outing is never justified. As the law of libel recognizes, death is an appropriate occasion for candor, even where sexuality is concerned. "Claiming" the deceased is an important aspect of gay scholarship, not to mention journalism. When a public figure dies, his or her sexuality ought to be part of an obituary, whatever distress that may cause the survivors, because without such documentation, the true history of gay life can never be recorded, and without a past, the present can never be put into perspective. If the *Times* won't print the truth, that's what *OutWeek* (and the *Voice*) is for.

As for outing the living, I'm not sure yet when it's right or wrong. But I *am* afraid that reflexive outing would produce a vengeful, riven gay community, in which the confused fear the committed. I don't think there's any honor in the closet, and I'm fully aware that a world where every homosexual announced that fact would be a safer, healthier place. But no one can force a coward to be a hero. And what's lost in the process of coercion may be more significant than what's gained.

As for those who take advantage of the world homophobia creates, by traipsing through the gay community and retreating when it suits them, there is a way to deal with them without blowing their cover—and our consciousness. Shun them, or prod them into change. But let them choose. Something unintended happens when we lose sight of the individual as the agent of sexual politics; some barrier to tyranny is torn away. And gay liberation—like all progressive movements—begins with love of ourselves and each other. As we are.

Points to Consider

1. Richard Goldstein points out that "exposure has been long used by the enemies of gay people as an instrument of control." To what does he attribute gay activists' recent efforts in the name of outing, given "the horrific history of homophobia"?

2. Do you feel that Goldstein is correct when he places outing within the context of the American trend toward destruction of the boundaries of privacy? Do you think that such a trend can be understood as a sign of increasing tolerance in America for alternative lifestyles?

3. Even if the public consequences of "coming out" were minimal, would Goldstein still balk at the idea of exposing someone else's homosexuality? Does he extend these attitudes to the deceased as well?

4. At one point in his essay, the author quotes political analyst Jeff Greenfield: "It is the public nature of [gay people's] impulses that 'entitles' me to exercise my prejudice." Greenfield seems to be saying that ho-

mosexuality is acceptable to him as long as he does not have to acknowledge its presence in public realms. What kinds of attitudes might underlie statements like this one?

Discussing the Unit

Suggested Topic for Discussion

Probably the most important "gay" issue in the American media is the response of the gay community to the AIDS crisis. For this reason it is surprising that neither Brownworth nor Goldstein devotes much time to the question of AIDS in relation to outing. Are there any important connections to be made between the two phenomena? In what ways, if any, has the AIDS crisis prompted gay activists to employ more radical measures like outing in their pursuit of greater civil rights for homosexuals? Can you imagine other factors facing homosexuals that have led many to advocate the exposure of other people's sexuality?

Preparing for Class Discussion

1. It is often reported that at least 10 percent of the people who make up our society are gay, and that most of these individuals choose to conceal their sexuality. Consider how people's attitudes about gay people might change if it turned out that some of your heroes from sports, entertainment, or government were revealed to be gay. In light of your response to this hypothetical situation, do you feel that outing is a good way to overcome homophobic attitudes in America?

2. Throughout the eighties, gays protested in the courtrooms and to the press that their constitutional right to privacy was constantly being violated, and that what they did in their own bedrooms was nobody's business. The recent trend of outing seems to ignore such opinions completely. Consider whether two such divergent attitudes can be reconciled. Is it consistent to tell heterosexuals to respect the privacy of gay people when they see gays exposing one another in the nation's press?

From Discussion to Writing

As both selections in this unit make clear, one of the assumptions behind the practice of outing is that if enough homosexuals in positions of power or public trust were exposed as such, then America would have to acknowledge the valuable contributions gays have made to our nation, and, in turn, homophobic attitudes would decline. Write an essay in which you support or attack this premise. Does it follow from the arguments you have read for and against outing that gay power and the greater acceptance of homosexuals would result from a corresponding increase in awareness about the gays who live among us?

15

Television and Sex Roles:
Is TV Defying the Stereotypes?

America's colleges and universities have traditionally served as testing grounds for new ideas about society, including ideas about gender, so it should not be surprising that two television series that consistently challenge sexual stereotypes are among the most watched on campus. *Roseanne* and *thirtysomething* may not ultimately change the way the roles of men and women are constructed in American society, but they have certainly altered the portrayal of men and women on television. In "The Wretched of the Hearth," Barbara Ehrenreich examines what the sitcom *Roseanne* has to say about working women with families, and more generally how the series represents a new wave of feminism being ushered in by the women of the blue-collar suburbs.

A new kind of male has also made his television debut. According to Stephen Fried in "*thirtysomething:* A Fun House Mirror on American Men," the dramatic series *thirtysomething* provides a glimpse at men engaged in an activity seldom viewed on the small screen: speaking about their feelings in an open, even witty manner. With its honest approach to the problems men face as a result of changing sex roles, *thirtysomething* offers powerful insights into the ways American men think about themselves.

The Wretched of the Hearth   [THE NEW REPUBLIC / April 2, 1990]

In the second half of the eighties, when American conservatism had reached its masochistic zenith with the reelection of Ronald Reagan, when women's liberation had been replaced by the more delicate sensibility known as post-feminism, when everyone was a yuppie and the heartiest word of endorsement in our vocabulary was "appropriate," there was yet this one paradox: our favorite TV personages were a liberal black man and a left-wing white feminist. Cosby could be explained as a representative of America's officially profamily mood, but Roseanne is a trickier case. Her idea of humor is to look down on her sleeping family in the eponymous sitcom and muse, "Mmmm, I wonder where we could find an all-night taxidermist."

If zeitgeist were destiny, Roseanne would never have happened. Only a few years ago, we learn from her autobiography, Roseanne Barr was just your run-of-the-mill radical feminist mother-of-three, writing poems involving the Great Goddess, denouncing all known feminist leaders as sellout trash, and praying for the sixties to be born again in a female body. Since the entertainment media do not normally cast about for fat, loudmouthed feminists to promote to superstardom, we must assume that Roseanne has something to say that many millions of people have been waiting to hear. Like this, upon being told of a woman who stabbed her husband thirty-seven times: "I admire her restraint."

Roseanne is the neglected underside of the eighties, bringing together its great themes of poverty, obesity, and defiance. The overside is handled well enough by Candice Bergen (*Murphy Brown*) and Madonna, who exist to remind us that talented women who work out are bound to become fabulously successful. Roseanne works a whole different beat, both in her sitcom and in the move *She-Devil*, portraying the hopeless underclass of the female

BARBARA EHRENREICH (b. 1941) is a regular columnist for Mother Jones and Ms. magazine. She holds a Ph.D. from Rockefeller University and since 1982 has been a fellow of the Institute of Policy Studies in Washington, D.C. Her personal essays appear in many magazines, and she is the author of several books, most recently Fear of Falling: The Inner Life of the Middle Class (1989) and The Worst Years of Our Lifes: Irreverent Notes from a Decade of Greed (1990).

sex: polyester-clad, overweight occupants of the slow track; fast-food wait-resses, factory workers, housewives, members of the invisible pink-collar army; the despised, the jilted, the underpaid.

But Barr—and this may be her most appealing feature—is never a victim. 4 In the sitcom, she is an overworked mother who is tormented by her bosses at such locales as Wellman Plastics (where she works the assembly line) and Chicken Divine (a fast-food spot). But Roseanne Connor, her sitcom char-acter, has, as we say in the blue-collar suburbs, a mouth on her. When the cute but obnoxious boss at Wellman calls the workers together and an-nounces, "I have something to tell you," Roseanne yells out, "What? That you feel you're a woman trapped in a man's body?" In *She-Devil*, where Barr is unfortunately shorn of her trademark deadpan snarl, revenge must take more concrete forms: she organizes an army of the wretched of the earth—nursing home patients and clerical workers—to destroy her errant husband and drive the slender, beautiful, rich-and-famous Other Woman dotty.

At some point the women's studies profession is bound to look up from its deconstructions and "rethinkings" and notice Roseanne. They will then observe, in article and lecture form, that Barr's radicalism is distributed over the two axes of gender and class. This is probably as good an approach as any. Barr's identity is first of all female—her autobiography is titled *My Life As a Woman*—but her female struggles are located in the least telegenic and most frequently overlooked of social strata—the white, blue-collar working class. In anticipation of Roseannology, let us begin with Barr's contribution to the sociology of social class, and then take up her impressive achievements in the area of what could be called feminist theory.

Roseanne the sitcom, which was inspired by Barr the stand-up comic, is a radical departure simply for featuring blue-collar Americans—and for depicting them as something other than half-witted greasers and low-life louts. The working class does not usually get much of a role in the American entertainment spectacle. In the seventies mumbling, muscular blue-collar males (*Rocky, The Deer Hunter, Saturday Night Fever*) enjoyed a brief modishness on the screen, while Archie Bunker, the consummate blue-collar bigot, raved away on the tube. But even these grossly stereotyped images vanished in the eighties, as the spectacle narrowed in on the brie-and-chardonnay class. Other than "Roseanne," I can find only one sitcom that deals consistently with the sub-yuppie condition: *Married . . . with Chil-dren*, a relentlessly nasty portrayal of a shoe salesman and his cognitively disabled family members. There may even be others, but sociological zeal has not sufficed to get me past the opening sequences of *Major Dad, Full House*, or *Doogie Howser*.

Not that *Roseanne* is free of class stereotyping. The Connors must bear part of the psychic burden imposed on all working-class people by their economic and occupational betters: they inhabit a zone of glad-handed gemeinschaft,[1] evocative, now and then, of the stock wedding scene (*The Godfather, The Deer Hunter, Working Girl*) that routinely signifies lost old-world values. They indulge in a manic physicality that would be unthinkable among the more controlled and genteel Huxtables. They maintain a traditional, low-fiber diet of white bread and macaroni. They are not above a fart joke.

Still, in *Roseanne* I am willing to forgive the stereotypes as markers 8 designed to remind us of where we are: in the home of a construction worker and his minimum-wage wife. Without the reminders, we might not be aware of how thoroughly the deeper prejudices of the professional class are being challenged. Roseanne's fictional husband, Dan (played by the irresistibly cuddly John Goodman), drinks domestic beer and dedicates Sundays to football; but far from being a Bunkeresque boor, he looks to this feminist like the fabled "sensitive man" we have all been pining for. He treats his rotund wife like a sex goddess. He picks up on small cues signaling emotional distress. He helps with homework. And when Roseanne works overtime, he cooks, cleans, and rides herd on the kids without any of the piteous whining we have come to expect from upscale males in their rare, and lavishly documented, encounters with soiled Pampers.

Roseanne Connor has her own way of defying the stereotypes. Variously employed as a fast-food operative, a factory worker, a bartender, and a telephone salesperson, her real dream is to be a writer. When her twelve-year-old daughter Darlene (brilliantly played by Sara Gilbert) balks at a poetry-writing assignment, Roseanne gives her a little talking-to involving Sylvia Plath: "She inspired quite a few women, including *moi*." In another episode, a middle-aged friend thanks Roseanne for inspiring her to dump her chauvinist husband and go to college. We have come a long way from the dithering, cowering Edith Bunker.

Most of the time the Connors do the usual sitcom things. They have the little domestic misunderstandings that can be patched up in twenty-four minutes with wisecracks and a round of hugs. But *Roseanne* carries working-class verisimilitude into a new and previously taboo dimension—the work place. In the world of employment, Roseanne knows exactly where she stands: "All the good power jobs are taken. Vanna turns the letters. Leona's got hotels. Margaret's running England . . . 'Course she's not doing a very good job. . . ."

And in the work place as well as the kitchen, Roseanne knows how to dish it out. A friend of mine, herself a denizen of the low-wage end of the work force, claims to have seen an episode in which Roseanne led an occupational health and safety battle at Wellman Plastics. I missed that one, but I have seen her, on more than one occasion, reduce the boss's ego to rubble. At Chicken Divine, for example, she is ordered to work weekends—an

[1] Community.

impossibility for a working mother—by an officious teenage boss who confides that he doesn't like working weekends either. In a sequence that could have been crafted by Michael Moore, Roseanne responds: "Well, that's real good 'cause you never do. You sit in your office like a little Napoleon, making up schedules and screwing up people's lives." To which he says, "That's what they pay me for. And you are paid to follow my orders." Blah blah blah. To which she says, staring at him for a long time and then observing with an evil smile: "You know, you got a little prize hanging out of your nose there."

The class conflict continues on other fronts. In one episode, Roseanne 12 arrives late for an appointment with Darlene's history teacher, because she has been forced to work overtime at Wellman. The teacher, who is leaning against her desk stretching her quadriceps when Roseanne arrives, wants to postpone the appointment because she has a date to play squash. When Roseanne insists, the teacher tells her that Darlene has been barking in class, "like a dog." This she follows with some psychobabble—on emotional problems and dysfunctional families—that would leave most mothers, whatever their social class, clutched with guilt. Not Roseanne, who calmly informs the yuppie snit that, in the Connor household, everybody barks like dogs.

Now this is the kind of class-militant populism that the Democrats, most of them anyway, never seem to get right: up with the little gal; down with the snotty, the pretentious, and the overly paid. At least part of the appeal of *Roseanne* is that it ratifies the resentments of the underdog majority. But this being a sitcom, and Barr being a pacifist, the class-anger never gets too nasty. Even the most loathsome bosses turn out to be human, and in some cases pathetically needy. Rather than hating the bad guys, we end up feeling better about ourselves, which is the function of all good and humanistic humor anyway.

According to high conservative theory, the leftist cast to a show like *Roseanne* must reflect the media manipulations of the alleged "liberal elite." But the politics of *Roseanne* including its feminist side, which we will get to in a minute—reflects nothing so much as the decidedly unelite politics of Barr herself. On the Larry King show a few weeks ago, Barr said that she prefers the term "working class" to "blue collar" because (and I paraphrase) it reminds us of the existence of class, a reality that Americans are all too disposed to forget. In her autobiography, right up front in the preface, she tells us that it is a "book about the women's movement . . . a book about the left."

Roseanne: My Life As a Woman traces her journey from alienation to political commitment. It must stand as another one of Barr's commanding oddities. Where you would expect a standard rags-to-riches story, you find a sort of rags-to-revolution tale: more an intellectual and spiritual memoir than the usual chronicle of fearsome obstacles and lucky breaks. She was born the paradigmatic outsider, a Jew in Mormon Utah, and a low-income

Jew at that. Within the Mormon culture, she was the "Other" (her own term), the "designated Heathen" in school Christmas pageants, always being reminded that "had we been in a Communist country, I would never have been allowed to express my religion, because 'dissent' is not tolerated there." At home she was loved and encouraged, but the emotional density of the Holocaust-haunted Barr family eventually proved too much for her. After a breakdown and several months of hospitalization, she ran away, at nineteen, to find the sixties, or what was left of them in 1971.

Her hippie phase left Barr with some proto-politics of the peace-and-love variety, three children, and an erratic wage-earner for a husband. It was in this condition that she wandered into the Woman to Woman bookstore on Colfax Avenue in Denver, where she discovered the Movement. Barr seems to have required very little in the way of consciousness-raising. With one gigantic "click," she jumped right in, joined the collective, and was soon occupied giving "seminars on racism, classism, anti-Semitism, pornography, and taking power." If this seems like a rather sudden leap to political leadership, I can attest from my own experience with venues like Woman to Woman that it happens every day.

But even within the ecumenical embrace of feminism, Barr remained the Outsider. "We did not agree anymore," she tells us of her collective, "with Betty Friedan, Gloria Steinem, or party politics within the women's movement," which she believes has turned into "a professional, careerist women's thing." When she found her "voice," it spoke in a new tone of working-class existentialism: "I began to speak as a working-class woman who is a mother, a woman who no longer believed in change, progress, growth, or hope." It was this special brand of proletarian feminism that inspired her stand-up comic routine. "I am talking about organizing working-class women and mothers," she tells us, and her comic persona was her way of going about it.

Middle-class feminism has long admitted the possibility of a working-class variant, but the general expectation has been that it would be a diluted version of the "real," or middle-class, thing. According to the conventional wisdom, working-class women would have no truck with the more antimale aspects of feminism, and would be repelled by the least insult to the nuclear family. They would be comfortable only with the bread-and-butter issues of pay equity, child care, and parental leave. They would be culturally conservative, sensible, dull.

But we had not met Barr. Her stand-up routine was at first almost too vulgar and castrating for Denver's Comedy Works. In her autobiography, Barr offers an example. Heckled by a drunk for not being "feminine," she turned around, stared at her assailant, and said, "Suck my dick." I wish *Roseanne: My Life As a Woman* gave more examples of her early, Denver-era, stand-up style, but the recently released videotape *Roseanne* (made later in a Los Angeles club) may be a fair representation. On it she promotes a product called "Fem-Rage," designed to overcome female conditioning during that "one day of the month when you're free to be yourself," and leaves her female fans with the memorable question: "Ever put those maxi-pads on adhesive side up?"

In *Roseanne,* the sitcom, however, Barr has been considerably tamed. 20 No longer standing bravely, and one must admit massively, alone with the microphone, she comes to us now embedded in the family: overwhelmed by domestic detail, surrounded by children too young for R-rated language, padding back and forth between stove, refrigerator, and kitchen table. Some of the edge is off here. There are no four-letter words, no menstruation jokes; and Roseanne's male-baiting barbs just bounce off her lovable Dan. Still, what better place for the feminist comic than in a family sitcom? Feminist theory, after all, cut its teeth on the critique of the family. Barr continues the process—leaving huge gaping holes where there was sweetness and piety.

All family sitcoms, of course, teach us that wisecracks and swift put-downs are the preferred modes of affectionate discourse. But Roseanne takes the genre a step further—over the edge, some may say. In the era of big weddings and sudden man shortages, she describes marriage as "a life sentence, without parole." And in the era of the biological time clock and the petted yuppie midlife baby, she can tell Darlene to get a fork out of the drawer and "stick it through your tongue." Or she can say, when Dan asks, "Are we missing an offspring?" at breakfast, "Yeah. Where do you think I got the bacon?"

It is Barr's narrow-eyed cynicism about the family, even more than her class consciousness, that gives *Roseanne* its special frisson. Archie Bunker got our attention by telling us that we (blacks, Jews, "ethnics," WASPs, etc.) don't really like each other. Barr's message is that even within the family we don't much like each other. We love each other (who else do we have?); but The Family, with its impacted emotions, its lopsided division of labor, and its ancient system of age-graded humiliations, just doesn't work. Or rather, it doesn't work unless the contradictions are smoothed out with irony and the hostilities are periodically blown off as humor. Coming from Mom, rather than from a jaded teenager or a bystander dad, this is scary news indeed.

So Barr's theoretical outlook is, in the best left-feminist tradition, dialectical. On the one hand, she presents the family as a zone of intimacy and support, well worth defending against the forces of capitalism, which drive both mothers and fathers out of the home, scratching around for paychecks. On the other hand, the family is hardly a haven, especially for its grown-up females. It is marred from within by—among other things—the patriarchal division of leisure, which makes Dad and the kids the "consumers" of Mom's cooking, cleaning, nurturing, and (increasingly) her earnings. Mom's job is to keep the whole thing together—to see that the mortgage payments are made, to fend off the viperish teenagers, to find the missing green sock—but Mom is no longer interested in being a human sacrifice on the altar of "profamily values." She's been down to the feminist bookstore; she's been reading Sylvia Plath.

This is a bleak and radical vision. Not given to didacticism, Barr offers 24 no programmatic ways out. Surely, we are led to conclude, pay equity would help, along with child care, and so on. But Barr leaves us hankering for a quality of change that goes beyond mere reform: for a world in which even the lowliest among us—the hash-slinger, the sock-finder, the factory hand—will be recognized as the poet she truly is.

Maybe this is just too radical. The tabloids have taken to stalking Barr as if she were an unsightly blot on the electronic landscape of our collective dreams. The *New York Times* just devoted a quarter of a page to some upscale writer's prissy musings on Roseanne. "Was I just being squeamish" for disliking Barr, she asks herself: "a goody-two-shoes suburban feminist who was used to her icons being chic and sugar-coated instead of this gum-chewing, male-bashing . . . working-class mama with a big mouth?" No, apparently she is not squeamish. Barr is just too, well, unfeminine.

We know what Barr would say to that, and exactly how she would say it. Yeah, she's crude, but so are the realities of pain and exploitation she seeks to remind us of. If middle-class feminism can't claim Roseanne, maybe it's gotten a little too dainty for its own good. We have a long tradition of tough-talking females behind us, after all, including that other great working-class spokesperson, Mary "Mother" Jones, who once advised the troops, "Whatever you do, *don't* be ladylike."

Points to Consider

1. What segment of American society does *Roseanne* represent? Does Barbara Ehrenreich believe this group is well represented on television? Why do you think it is difficult to portray accurately the daily lives of this group in a way that would be attractive to most television viewers?

2. Does Ehrenreich think that there are major differences between Roseanne Barr and her character Roseanne Connor? Does the real-life Roseanne moderate her attitudes for television? How might the fact that *Roseanne* is a sitcom affect the show's political content?

3. Why does the series *Roseanne* pose a challenge to middle-class feminism? How would you describe the differences between middle-class and working-class feminism?

4. Do you think Roseanne Connor should be considered a role model for working-class women? Think of some other television characterizations of working-class women. Does Barr's character compare favorably or unfavorably with these?

STEPHEN FRIED

thirtysomething: A Fun House Mirror
on American Men [GQ / April 1989]

It was right there in the script for MGM/UA Production No. 8209; no editor on drugs or prankish college intern had slipped the sequence in by mistake. In Scene 28 of *thirtysomething* Episode 29, Elliot Weston was to be shown commencing to masturbate on network television. In prime time. Wearing boxer shorts. Holding one of *those* magazines.

Don't worry, you didn't miss an episode. And if you're one of those people who hate *thirtysomething* and pride themselves on missing it every week, you can't add this to the list of things that annoy you about the program. The scene was ultimately cut on the recommendation of ABC Broadcast Standards and Practices. But you have to admit that there's something powerful about the thought of twenty-one million Americans sitting in front of their televisions on a Tuesday evening and being confronted with one of those truths even your "sensitive, open" guys still prefer to fib about. Once and for all, *we don't read the articles, okay?*

But for every earthshaking nuance that doesn't end up onscreen in *thirtysomething,* plenty do. Although I'll leave it to future generations to ponder what the impact of the masturbation scene might have been, it couldn't have been any more devastating than seeing Elliot and Michael weep together recently over the failure of their business. Sure, guys have lost money before on TV: *Dallas*'s J.R. had some oil wells go bust. *Hill Street*'s J.D. lost his investment in the career of narcoleptic comic Vic Hitler. But never before have two characters had their ambitions dashed so glaringly, their ability to bring home the bacon challenged so brutally—and without any of the self-mocking humor that usually softens the Emmy-winning situation drama's edgiest scenes. This, friends and neighbors, is investigative journalism of the soul, more ground-breaking than "Transsexuals Who

---

STEPHEN FRIED *(b. 1958) is senior editor at* Philadelphia *magazine and a contributing writer at* GQ. *He also contributes articles to* Rolling Stone, *the* Philadelphia Enquirer, *and* Fame. *Fried is currently working on a book about the fashion industry and the late model Gia Carangi, which is scheduled for publication in 1992.*

Shoplift" on *Geraldo,* "Peter Pan Syndrome, the Wendy Dilemma, and Captain Hookworm," on *Oprah,* and "Skinheads with AIDS" on *Morton Downey Jr.* Like most things you've never seen on TV before, it makes you wonder whether there wasn't some *real good reason* you never saw it on TV before. But even the show's detractors can't deny the impact of such scenes on the body politic and especially the male body politic. Jesus. Makes you shudder just to think about it. Five minutes after the show, I was upstairs checking how much was in my IRA.

thirtysomething is certainly not a guy-dominated show. It is, in fact, the 4 first of the intelligent ensemble programs to actually feature gender parity among its principal characters. Of the original seven, only three were men: Michael (played by Ken Olin), his business partner, Elliot (Timothy Busfield), and his best friend, Gary, an English professor (Peter Horton). The one character added last season (Steve Woodman, the boss/boyfriend of terminally single Ellyn, played by Polly Draper) and the two new ones this season (a gay male painter named Russell and Susannah, Gary's new love interest, whose pregnancy will complicate his "no commitments" stand on life) will not change that balance of power. And the major innovation of *thirtysomething* remains its (depending on your perspective) tireless or tiresome exploration of the personal lives of *all* baby boomers and baby owners.

Still, the show was created by two men in their thirties, Marshall Herskovitz and Ed Zwick. And *thirtysomething* certainly tends to revolve around its main male character, the ambivalent adman Michael; producer Richard Kramer refers to the program as "The Sentimental Education of Michael Steadman." Given all this, and the fact that TV men are usually one- or two-dimensional characters at best (not so unlike real men), I don't think it's chauvinistic to suggest that the show's most revolutionary aspect, week in and week out, is the provocative portrait it paints of an emotionally punch-drunk generation of American males.

"When I first saw the script for the pilot," says Melanie Mayron, who plays Michael's cousin, Melissa, an unhappily unmarried free-lance photographer, "what I thought was so unique about it was that the men were portrayed so differently. They were sensitive. They talked about their feelings. They were more like the men I *know,* the kind you never see onscreen or on television."

But the *thirtysomething* men do more than just talk. The show's inherent drama lies in watching the characters constantly being cornered by contemporary quandaries: responsibility versus freedom, sexual variety versus family stability, comfort versus social consciousness, compassion versus competitiveness, sensitivity versus lunkheadedness.

"Our generation is attempting to sort out a thousand mutually exclusive 8 truths," says Olin. "We have had an enormous amount of information, all of it conflicting. So we're very self-involved, and for good reason: we're very hard on ourselves, and it's good we're very demanding. But on the other hand, we're not demanding enough. And it's easy to get paralyzed by all the dichotomies."

And the show's creators seem willing to go to any length to explore the issues that interest them. While last season it was Michael's wife, Hope (played by Mel Harris), who was frazzled by motherhood and Elliot's wife, Nancy (played by Olin's real-life wife, Patricia Wettig), who plunged to the depths when faced with the dissolution of her marriage, this year, it's the men who are in trouble. Gary is denied tenure because he refused to play the game during his six years of teaching; the foundations of his Peter Pan existence are crumbling beneath him. So, too, of course, are Michael's and Elliot's careers—just when Hope becomes pregnant and won't be returning to work full time, and Elliot's separation requires him to support two households. This year, nobody will be able to accuse *thirtysomething*'s characters of being whining yuppies with no responsibilities and no *real* problems to complain about.

"This is what scares me about Herskovitz and Zwick," says Tim Busfield, whose character has gone from being an immature, fun-loving jerk to one of the most compelling, angst-ridden jerks in the history of television. "They'll do *anything* to these characters. I can just hear them: 'Let's have Elliot and Michael get in a car crash and die' . . . just because nobody else would ever do it to two regulars on TV."

There is a scene in the pilot of *thirtysomething* that is probably the most efficient evocation of what the show has to say about men. This particular "walk and talk" (Hollywood lingo for a scene in which characters, um, walk and talk) begins innocently enough with the two guys checking out every pretty girl who parades by.

"What is going *on* here?" Michael wants to know. Here he is, a happily married man with a gorgeous wife and a cute kid—and a sex life even after his gorgeous wife bore his cute kid—and he's still hearing a voice in his head singing, "Gotta flirt."   12

Elliot offers an elaborate theory about australopithecines out on the savanna. "And the ones who win out," he winds up, "are the ones who can spot a great-looking australopithecine rear end at four hundred yards. And the australopithecine girls think, if this guy can spot me from two miles off and beat up all these other apes, he must be one hell of a hunter-gatherer. So I'm just gonna wiggle my rear end a little bit. Two million years [later] . . . you got a bunch of guys in jackets and ties that are supposed to be working, and what are they doing?"

"Looking at women on the street."

"Exactly. *That's* called evolution."

This point, if I may interrupt for a moment, should be marked Exhibit   16
A: the typical *thirtysomething* speech about how contemporary, "sensitive" man is at war with his primal urges to be a cave-mannish boy. "I think this

is a terrible time to be a man, maybe the worst time in history," says Marshall Herskovitz. "Men come into the world with certain biological imperatives. And part of growing up and being a man was always knowing how to channel those imperatives—like, say, aggressiveness—into societally useful ends.

"One way to look at the social changes of the last thirty years is to see that many of the ways in which men channeled their aggressive desires were at the expense of women, children, and men who were lower in the hierarchy. We've rightly done away with a lot of those channels. But we're still left with these biological imperatives and no acceptable channels for them—the most extreme consequence of which, I think, is the increase in violence that we see today.

"Another result is that manhood has simply been devalued in recent years and doesn't carry much weight anymore. And one of the virtues of manhood that was lost was control, discipline. Today, controlling yourself seems like castration. I don't think anybody understood the real precariousness of men's feeling of masculinity. Now we're just drowning in our options."

Back at the walk and talk, Michael is not mollified. "What I don't understand is, what are we supposed to *do* about it?" he, like every other married man, wants to know. "I mean, it's just *there,* right? Are we supposed to suffer, ignore it, have an operation?"

"I don't know," Elliot says.

"Do you think some people actually *do* anything about it?" Michael, married only a couple of years, asks Elliot, a twelve-year vet with two children. "Would *you* ever do it? The real question is: would you ever tell me?"

"Would you?"

"Yes, I would tell you. I would have to tell somebody."

"*That's* the truth."

Let's mark the beginning of this last interchange Exhibit B: the typical *thirtysomething* "raising of the unanswerable question." If Mike Steadman could get a job doing what he does best—stepping outside of life's little daily dramas to address the Big Issues—he'd be a millionaire and wouldn't have to sit around dreaming up bad ad copy. Then let's mark the second part Exhibit C: the proverbial *thirtysomething* "talking about it" sequence, augmented by a bonus "talking about talking about it" and a "making fun of talking about talking about it" clincher.

It's for all this talk that *thirtysomething* takes most of its critical lumps. To some people, it sounds less like conversation than incessant complaining. Perhaps it's because most Americans are unaccustomed to hearing men really discuss their feelings, and anything but stoicism sounds like weenieness. Perhaps it's because most Americans were content *not* hearing men discuss their feelings. Either way, says Olin, the intent of the dialogue device—

nobody on the show pretends that people really talk this way—is misunderstood.

"We've developed a sort of ironic language of complaint," he explains, proving that his English degree from Penn wasn't a waste of time. "It's not to be taken for sincerity or deep reflection of the character's sensibility but rather a way of speaking which is very much something that is true of our peers, I think. It's just a way of keeping your values in check. I don't think it's sincerely saying 'Everything is so bad.' It's just our way of interacting, our way of being hip and deflecting the real, true stuff of your feelings momentarily. Or maybe it's the way our generation has adopted this collective guilt at being so fortunate but, in a lot of ways, abandoning the ideals which brought us to the place we're at.

"But it's meant to be ironic, and if people mistake irony for sincerity,   28
there's nothing we can do about that. It's also a particular sense of humor, and if you don't think it's funny, there's nothing we can do about that either."

One possible implication of the "irony of complaint" theory is that these men—or men in general—don't really discuss how they feel but rather ironically survey all the things they've been told they're *supposed to feel.* Perhaps they are not so much open as they are informed. Perhaps they don't seek to change behaviors currently deemed "socially unacceptable"—you know, sexism, insensitivity, rivalry, lust, sloth—but are searching for a politically correct way to justify themselves.

"I think the general tendency for men is to try and apologize," says Peter Horton. "In the last decades, women have been asserting their rights, and a lot of men feel this strange sense of apology we owe women. I'm not sure it's the right response at all. The notion of blame and fault has been boiling through this entire awakening of gender: it's either women blaming men for dominating or men blaming women for confusing them or in some way trying to emasculate them. I think both feelings are wrong."

As we rejoin our walking-and-talking heroes, we see their conversation take an unexpected turn: Like life or Dan Marino, *thirtysomething* is always a threat to suddenly go deep. Michael notices Elliot is becoming slightly uncomfortable with the banter. It dawns on him that the man he has worked with every day for six years—and has been in business with for two—has a secret.

"You had an *affair.* I don't *believe* it. . . . Does Nancy know?"   32

"*I* don't even know," says Elliot, which is one of the truest things anyone is ever going to say on network television. Then he tries to relate what the affair has done to his life. "Before I did this, I couldn't buy a present for her without blabbing about what it is. I mean, I couldn't keep a secret from her. And then all of a sudden, I'm lying. I'm making things up. And the worst part of it is that it's *totally easy.* It's like there's some psychopath lying around inside me just waiting for a chance to jump out."

"So you'd recommend this to your friends as a worthwhile experience?" Mike asks.

If it please the court, let's mark this passage Exhibits D, E, and F. Exhibit D is Michael Steadman's uniquely premodern shock at the idea of someone's cheating on his wife. Imagine building a television show around a character who loves his wife, loves being married, and self-righteously scorns anyone or anything that challenges the notion that being happily married is the only appropriate way to face the misery of human existence. Gee, there's a radical concept . . . creating a fictional world where the things that are really important are the things that are really important.

This seems especially brave when so much of our popular culture is 36 based on exalting the joys of singleness, and it's especially unusual to see a man lecturing other men (and himself) about their immaturities and responsibilities. Women are usually the ones who tell men how badly they're failing at manliness. Having a man do it would be considered heresy in some cultures—it may very well still be heresy in ours. Maybe I'm underestimating the sensitivity and self-awareness of the average man on the street. But considering all the men I hear who hate the show specifically because "the husband with the suspenders is a wimp," making Michael Steadman the hero of a network TV program in 1989 seems like an incredible act of faith. (And speaking of faith, portraying a character so concerned about religion— being a Jew married to a Christian, and a conflicted Jew at that—is a pretty progressive statement to make in this day and age. "Progressive," that is, because of its nod to concerns currently thought of as regressive.)

Exhibit E is the show's tendency to hammer away at the Power of the Lie. On a program that almost always prefers a therapist's view of a perfect universe over, say, Dick Van Dyke's, not only is honesty the best policy, dishonesty is portrayed as a bigger threat than thermonuclear war. The show is obsessed with the consequences of not just keeping secrets from others but lying to yourself, and this is where it especially touches a nerve for men. Because the message comes through loud and clear that women know themselves better than women know men better than men know women—but men hardly know themselves at all. And the TV world may never get a better example of the consequences of that lack of self-knowledge than the life and times of Elliot Weston.

"Elliot is such a litmus test for so many people," says Herskovitz. "I hear the most wildly disparate opinions about him. I happen to love Elliot. I find him in many ways sad, and I feel for him. He has been very poor in dealing with his feelings.

"In a show we just did, Elliot goes through a real crisis. The episode deals with the important issue of what is passed down through generations of men. We learn that Elliot's father left home when Elliot was a kid. And we come to see that just as Elliot suffers from never having a father who was a father to him, he's now engaged in not being a father to his own son."

And with our last exhibit, we see the ingredient that helps make this high-stakes angst palatable: heaping tablespoonsful of self-effacing humor.

"I don't think we're trying to be Bergman here," says Busfield. "There's not one character on the show that doesn't go, 'Hey, I'm an asshole, y'know, I'm an idiot, okay, so I make mistakes.' Each one of these characters can admit to being insecure, and I think if there's any message you want to give it's this: people who are cold, the hard people, they're the ones who make life difficult, the ones who aren't open enough to say they have a problem. If there's any hope, it's in saying, 'So I'm a weak person, so I can't make up my mind. Kill me.' "

But *thirtysomething* portrays male openness as a double-edged sword. Maybe even a triple-edged one. "There are still real dangers in expressing feelings," says Herskovitz. "The world is still an emotionally dangerous place, especially for men.

"This society objectifies women in terms of beauty and men in terms of wealth and power. I think there is still a real danger if a man is considered weak in this society, and there are still lots of people who will take honest expression of feeling as expression of weakness. A man in that position stands to lose, in his work, at home. What if, by being honest, he makes his wife frightened that he can't support the family? That's going to put up barriers in the relationship."

One recent scene that tackled this issue was in the episode "Politics," in which Michael and Elliot take on a reprehensible political candidate as a client because they need the money. The subtext of the show is that Michael is confronting the fact that fatherhood and business ownership have shifted his political views; everybody on the show, in fact, takes a look at what's left of his or her youthful idealism. Toward the end of the show, Hope and Gary gang up on Michael, who explodes: "I see that spreadsheet in my mind every hour of the day. I never thought it would be like this and I don't particularly like it, but a lot of people depend on me now. . . . I don't talk to either of you about this stuff. So maybe sometimes I think too much about the bottom line. And I know I sound like my father, and, God, I always resented how cautious he was, the nickels and dimes, I was so ashamed of him. I thought he never saw the big picture. . . ."

"Why don't you tell me about this stuff?" Hope wants to know.

"Because it's boring," Michael says.

Which is really only half the answer. The other half is that it's scary, as they find out two episodes later when the spreadsheets show the agency bankrupt. On top of that, funds had been surreptitiously siphoned from the company by the recently single Elliot, who needed money because dates were now "like a hundred bucks a pop even if you hate her guts and'll never see her again." All this, and Hope is pregnant.

"The baby is coming," Michael tells Elliot. "There's no stopping it. At night, I lie awake and I swear I hear it in there, next to me . . . ticking like a bomb."

The real bomb, which has exploded memorably several times during the past two seasons, is Elliot and Michael's risk-filled relationship, which *thirtysomething* constantly uses to explore the bonds—and rivalry—between men. One of last season's most memorable shows was "Competition," in which an agency client makes it clear that he personally prefers Elliot to Michael. This sets off a series of small depth charges, as Michael admits that even though they are partners, he—like most men—always saw himself as the more *crucial* partner. He then begins to painstakingly examine the power implications of everything that happens between the two of them. He's finally pushed over the edge when Elliot beats him in a game of puff basketball— for the first time ever. Then Elliot is literally pushed over the edge and onto the floor by a violent Michael, who has been momentarily transported back to the savanna.

(Another example of Michael's violent side will never be seen by *thirtysomething* viewers. On this season's first episode, Michael tells Hope during foreplay that he wants to do it without birth control that night. She says no, and wriggles free to head into the bathroom for her diaphragm. In the original script, however, Michael was to make an overpowering gesture before letting her up. As he apologizes—according to the script—"she is still looking at him, not letting him off the hook for the force he just tried to use on her." Says Herskovitz, "Kenny Olin had a problem with that gesture, politically. We had many talks about it. I told him it didn't make Michael a rapist, but he felt it would be an example of violence against women. Ultimately, neither I nor the director could convince him to do it.")

"I am deeply competitive," says Ed Zwick of how all this aggressiveness and competitiveness imitates his own life. "I still play in a baseball league, and I've just had to move from shortstop to second base because I lost a step, and I was not happy about it. I can't get into a goofy game of office Nerf ball without it becoming fierce. It's something I'm still learning about myself, how it empowers me and fuels how I approach my life. I've got a two-and-a-half-year-old son, and I can't help but watch when he picks up a stick and his first instinct is to hit something with it."

The competitiveness between the show's characters genuinely mirrors 52 the lives of real men. But Zwick is willing to concede that the closeness of all the characters—especially the relationships between the single and married people—may be more fantasy than documentary.

"It's a very accurate reflection of my life and Marshall's life," he says. "I have friends about whom I'm very vigilant and whose friendships with me have a certain tenure. I prize them, and that's what the show reflects. But it is amazing what happens when you have a kid, the choices you make about time.

"So there is a certain degree of wish fulfillment about this show. The characters have kids and move away from their college town or home, but the show does provide an illusion of continuing sustained involvement with a group of people. To some degree that's probably wish fulfillment for those who write it. And that may be part of the show's appeal—the assumption that it's possible to maintain these relationships. We have a commitment to truth-telling, but within that context you can't deny the quotient of idealizing that takes place. I mean, what is art for if not the fulfillment of deep wishes?"

If it seems as if I'm going out of my way to avoid Peter Horton's character—the eternally uncommitted Gary, who was described in a recent episode as a "peculiar combination of hair and whimsy"—it's only because so far he's been largely overlooked by *thirtysomething*. For all I know, this may reflect contractual arrangements or network biases against characters resembling Bjorn Börg, but it's more likely the result of yet another reality about men that the show portrays: married people, especially married people with babies, find themselves increasingly unable to relate to single people. This phenomenon, based on my empirical research, occurs far more regularly among men, perhaps because most single women—such as Melissa and Ellyn—will, however grudgingly, admit that they really want to be married, while a single man is more likely to fiercely defend his freedom and describe his married friends with some variant of the charming phrase "pussy-whipped."

"Yeah, I think there's a tendency to not look quite as deeply into the single world on *thirtysomething*," says Horton, who has also directed several episodes of the show. "They make some noble attempts at it, but it's hard to just make attempts. There's a certain bias inherent in the fact that Ed and Marshall chose the route they chose. They're both married with small children; that's where their interest lies.

"But let's be realistic. I don't know many married people who are friends with single people. I'm going through a divorce myself [from actress Michelle Pfeiffer], so I've been on both sides. There's probably more closeness between the single and married characters on the show than in real life. The people I spend the most time with are single. It doesn't have much to do with love but just with the mechanics of being.

"That is, unless you work with your friend. Ed and Marshall are very close friends, but that's partially because they have a partnership. One thing that's interesting this season is the whole thing Michael and Elliot go through when their business goes under: when the partnership fails, where's the friendship? That plot line might allow a greater appreciation for the innocence of friendships from college, which began because someone liked you for *you* and not because of any business reasons."

Given the show's bent toward marriage, it should come as no surprise that as Gary has gotten involved with Susannah—she becomes pregnant, they'll move in together, and although they won't marry, they'll raise the

56

child together—he has become more interesting to the show's writers and is featured more prominently in forthcoming episodes. There is, of course, one roadblock to Gary's being accepted as a fellow grown-up. Michael—actually, most everyone—hates Gary's girlfriend.

"Isn't that just great?" Horton laughs. "Finally, here's Gary's ticket into Michael's world, a woman who kindles in him a desire to grow up, a sense of joining the human race, getting some stability and a sense of depth. And Michael doesn't like the ticket." 60

The question that remains, of course, is whether all these unusually realistic TV portrayals of men really mean anything in the larger scheme of things. Sure, some California therapists are prescribing episodes of *thirtysomething* to patients suffering from similar problems. And, yes, the show has created a sort of benchmark vision of a certain generation, so when people are abhorring baby boomers and everything they stand for, at least they're all abhorring the *same* baby boomers. (The abhorrers, of course, are usually boomers themselves; I never cease to be amazed at the *thirtysomething* generation's capacity for self-loathing.) But will mass exposure to a handful of honest male characters really make any impact on American men?

In the mid-seventies, when Ken Olin went to Penn, a communications professor there, Dr. George Gerbner, developed an index for measuring TV violence and began producing yearly data that assured him perpetual media coverage, congressional appearances, and funding. A lesser-known—but more serious—part of his research is something called the Cultural Indicators Project, which posits that most people get most of their information about the way people really are from television. For example, if the only blacks on TV were Jimmie Walker and Redd Foxx, then "people who didn't know better" would believe that all black people said "dy-no-mite" and called everyone "dummy."

The ongoing research project suggests only that TV portrayals can change people's perceptions of others; it doesn't presume to suggest that people are going to pattern their lives after TV characters. But stranger things have happened. Even at its worst, television is an influential medium. And except for occasional glitches—"We still miss in big ways on this show," Olin concedes—*thirtysomething* is television at its best. The writing and acting are consistently excellent—four Emmys in its rookie year—and the film-quality production values (especially the lighting and special effects) are arguably the best in tube history. This, together with the highly personal story lines, makes *thirtysomething* seem more real than almost anything else on television: it's like a soap opera without all the multimillionaires, biker-rapists and cross-dressing priests who serve to reinforce the fictionality. And since the *thirtysomething* generation is a little short on heroes these days, these characters could easily become pretty persuasive role models. (As could the younger blue-collar characters on the new NBC series *Dream Street*, produced by Herskovitz and Zwick and created by their old film-school pal Mark Rosner.)

And given the recent dearth of honorable male heroes in any mass medium—seems like every guy you see on the large or small screen has a Ramboner to blow up or buy out someone—I suppose we could do a lot worse than the men on *thirtysomething*. At their best, these characters actually think about things and try to act responsibly. At their worst, at least when they're being jerks, they *know* they're being jerks. Which I guess is some sort of progress. 64

Points to Consider

1. According to Stephen Fried, how closely do the men on *thirtysomething* approximate their real-life counterparts? Does he think that the show aims at realism? What does his title, "A Fun House Mirror on American Men," imply about his attitude toward the series?

2. According to Marshall Herskovitz, one of *thirtysomething*'s creators, what are the major problems facing today's American male? Does the series offer solutions to these problems or does it merely attempt to depict them?

3. Much of the negative criticism directed at *thirtysomething* charges that its characters complain too much. Do you accept Ken Olin's explanation that the show's "language of complaint" is for the most part ironic?

4. Do you agree with what Fried calls one of the show's major messages, that "men hardly know themselves at all"? From the standpoint of the series, what part does honesty play in a male character's quest for self-knowledge?

Discussing the Unit

Suggested Topic for Discussion

Think about the ways that television's treatment of gender can affect—positively or negatively—our sense of stereotypes. Do you think television accurately reflects changes in our society? Or does television distort social change for its own purposes? To what extent does television replace old stereotypes with new stereotypes?

Preparing for Class Discussion

1. Watch an episode or two of *Roseanne* or *thirtysomething*. Do you feel that the characterization of men and women on these programs is ac-

curate with respect to men and women you know? Pay particular attention to the specific problem addressed by each episode you watch. Does the problem's solution in any way hinge upon a redefinition of traditional sex roles? Do you feel that the problem could have been solved in some other manner?

2. As you watch the show, do you find that there are characters who continue to fulfill traditional sex roles? Do characters sometimes revert to these roles? Under what kinds of circumstances does such behavior occur? Is such behavior approved by the other characters?

From Discussion to Writing

Both Ehrenreich and Fried comment on the possible effects of television on American attitudes. Do you think that series like *Roseanne* and *thirtysomething* make a positive contribution to changing perceptions about men and women? Write an essay in which you consider other television programs that show a concern with gender roles. Discuss the extent to which television can alter or reinforce male and female roles in our society. Be sure to illustrate your points with specific references to the programs.

16

Television Broadcasting:
Does It Distort the News?

Is television news coverage as complete, balanced, and objective as possible? Or has it become another form of television entertainment that merely offers viewers half-hour "docudramas" on a narrow range of issues while reinforcing conventional attitudes and stereotypes? Though newscasters and networks usually claim that they're providing responsible, up-to-the-minute coverage, many critics believe that the quality of television news reporting has seriously deteriorated over the years. In "Antihero," Ishmael Reed wonders what one of America's finest newscasters, the late Edward R. Murrow, would think of today's "performance-oriented" news shows. Reed, who has been monitoring news programs, is especially angered and astonished by television's persistent portrayal of racist stereotypes: "Why," he asks, "are black faces and bodies used to illustrate most social pathologies?"

Kiku Adatto also contrasts today's news coverage with that of the past. By focusing on how the television coverage of the recent 1988 presidential campaign differed from the 1968 campaign, Adatto documents a serious decline in political reporting as newscasters shifted from substantive issues to superficial images. In "The Incredible Shrinking Sound Bite," Adatto argues that in 1988 television news became so attentive "to the way the campaigns constructed images for television that political reporters began to sound like theater critics, reporting more on the stagecraft than the substance of politics." Concerned about serious gaps in television's coverage of major issues, two *TV Guide* writers recently conducted a survey of a dozen prominent social critics and media analysts. The consensus of opinion is reflected in the title of Joanmarie Kalter's and Jane Marion's article: "The Big Stories TV News Is Missing—and Why."

ISHMAEL REED

Antihero [SPIN / May 1990]

Edward R. Murrow's broadcasts from Europe provided me with one of my earliest introductions to the modern writing style. His crisp, dramatic narratives brought the war home to thousands of American radio listeners. After witnessing how the Nazi propaganda machine fictionalized reality and used psychological warfare against unpopular groups, Murrow returned to America vowing to prevent such abuses of media power here. Since his death, Murrow has come to epitomize the great journalist. His documentary, *Harvest of Shame,* about the oppression of migrant workers, became a model for the muckraking journalism of the 1960s. Today's muckraker, perhaps working for a think tank financed by the growers, would probably blame the migrant workers' plight on their personal behavior.

I often wonder what Murrow would think of today's media, with its performance-oriented newsmen, docudramas, instant analyses, and its manipulation by political candidates who are packaged and promoted through media sound bites and guided by media consultants. I wonder what his response would be to a government that manipulates the media so that we may never get all of the facts regarding the Iran-Contra affair, or the invasion

---

ISHMAEL REED (b. 1938) is a prolific writer of fiction, poetry, essays, and plays. He has published his work in numerous journals and magazines, including Fiction, Iowa Review, Rolling Stone, Yale Review, *the* Washington Post, *and* Life. *His* New and Collected Poetry *was published in 1988, and he recently edited a book called* Writin' Is Fightin': Thirty-seven Years of Boxing on Paper *(1988).*

of Panama. I wonder what he would think of technology that Joseph Goebbels would find awe-inspiring and that's often used as a weapon against unpopular groups. It's my impression that the media often behave as though blacks are members of an enemy nation and that they, the media, are a propaganda bureau for a nation at war.

For *Time* magazine, Gorbachev was the man of the decade. For me it was Willie Horton, the prisoner who committed a rape while he was on furlough from a Massachusetts prison. Mr. Horton seemed to epitomize the image of the black male projected by the media in the 1980s—that of a roving, irresponsible predator. It is clear to me that Bush's Willie Horton ad campaign was successful because it was created after a decade of black male bashing by the mass media. "The enemy wants to do something awful to 'our' women," is a classic image used in war propaganda. An ancestor of this campaign was a famous World War II poster depicting a grinning, sinister, buck-toothed Japanese soldier with a nude European woman slung over his shoulder.

As an African-American, I regularly become angry as I watch the racist 4
stereotypes portrayed on television news. Unlike the print media, where one at least has an opportunity to reply with a letter, it's difficult to document the lies and half-truths that are perpetuated about minorities on the Big Tube—they fly by so fast, and it's far more difficult to challenge them. I find myself diving for sheets of paper, the backs of envelopes, napkins, or matchbook covers in order to document these abuses.

Why are black faces and bodies used to illustrate most social pathologies—illegitimacy, crime, illiteracy, alcoholism, drug addiction, spousal abuse, prostitution, AIDS, family abandonment, and abuse of the elderly—when there are millions more whites involved in these activities than blacks?

The media often portray the single black female parent as the source of all the country's poverty problems. Terry K. Adams and Greg J. Duncan challenge that myth in a paper they wrote for the University of Michigan's Survey Research Center in 1988. They write: "Media images of urban poverty often present households headed by young, never-married black women. . . . Data show that this image does not fit most, or even a substantial minority, of the persistently poor living in urban areas."

NBC News even illustrated a story about a white-collar crime with footage depicting blacks, when blacks usually don't commit white-collar crime of the sort that figured in the savings and loan scandals, scandals that may cost the American taxpayers $500 billion, many times the $40 billion spent on welfare and farm subsidies each year.

But of all social "pathologies," none has been attached to blacks in 8
recent years as much as crack—the distribution, possession, and addiction to the substance. When several networks did their video montages summa-

rizing the 1980s, whites were shown doing positive things—blacks were shown smoking crack pipes.

Both the government and the media have made crack a black issue, even though its consumption is more prevalent among whites than among blacks. Jack Anderson and others have been reporting on how crack has reached the suburbs and small towns for at least three years now. He says that in many of these white peach-cobbler communities, parents don't know where their children are, but I doubt these parents will be threatened with jail as was a Los Angeles black mother whose sons were engaged in illegal drug activities, nor will middle- and upper-class pregnant white women who use cocaine be threatened.

George Bush, so as not to embarrass what he views as a white middle-class constituency, and his drug czar William Bennett continue to portray crack addiction as a black problem, making appearances in black neighborhoods and at institutions that are predominantly black. These appearances are obediently covered by the media. Mr. Bush even went along with the staging of a drug buy from a black dealer so that he could say on television that the crack was bought across the street from the White House.

Hodding Carter, appearing on the David Brinkley show the weekend this strange prank was discovered, said you didn't have to go that far from the White House to buy coke. I wonder if the authorities who go around entrapping black politicians interviewed Hodding Carter for an elaboration of his remark, or if two-way mirrors and hidden cameras are set up in those parties in Georgetown frequented by the political elite, where Fawn Hall said she snorted coke on weekends.

The day after his cynical stunt, Mr. Bush posed with a black crack baby 12 and later he was shown on the site of a public housing project in Alexandria, Virginia.

Will Mr. Bush ever pose with a white cocaine baby? Why doesn't he pose in front of the Los Angeles bank that was found to have raised its profits over 2000 percent in ten years to total assets of ten billion dollars through money laundering, or how about before a gun store that sells sophisticated weapons to black youths, no questions asked. Or on Wall Street, where cocaine sales and distribution were the subjects of a long piece published in the *New York Times*. Or better still, will he ever reveal whether he looked the other way as tons of cocaine were dumped into this country by his anticommunist allies? Or, will anybody in the administration ever explain its ties to Craig Spence, a right-wing socialite who was under investigation by the secret service and FBI at the time of his death a few months ago? Mr. Spence had been arrested for cocaine possession and weapons charges in New York on August 15, indicating that the refreshments served to the Washington, D.C., establishment at his million-dollar apartment, where he entertained "key officials of the Reagan and Bush administrations, military officers, congressional aides and US and foreign business people with close ties to Washington's political elite," included more than herbal tea.

And so the administration and the media have successfully used blacks as scapegoats for the crack problem.

The media continued to perpetuate the story that crack is black, even after evidence of widespread cocaine use among whites was supported by a study late last year by the Parents Resource Institute for Drug Education, Inc., which revealed that white teenagers are more prone to drug addiction than are blacks. On the Sunday, January 13, edition of *This Week with David Brinkley*, Mr. Brinkley asked General Clayton Powell about the drug problem as though it were an exclusively inner-city problem.

I decided that something had to be done when I saw one of those 16 pompous, campy, incoherent Roger Rosenblatt essays, carried on the *MacNeil/Lehrer NewsHour*, which associated black youth, as a class, with "evil." This convinced me that television had gone too far. Granted, the alleged attack and rape of a Central Park jogger was cruel, but was this an act on the same level as the Holocaust, the genocide committed by the Khmer Rouge, or the My Lai massacre as Mr. Rosenblatt suggested? And why accompany an essay about the alleged misdeeds of a few black youth with a graphic depicting a nonspecific, dark youthful figure and a commentary about Satanism? And why emphasize the Central Park incident as though it were even worse than those other colossal tragedies? There was a reference to the rape of a disabled child by some middle-class white youth—an event that has since disappeared from public consciousness—that had occurred in New Jersey the week before the commentary, but this was referred to only in passing during Jim Lehrer's introduction to Rosenblatt's essay. And unlike the case of the black youth, no photo of the white youth was shown, another practice of the television networks—concealing the faces of whites who are associated with pathologies.

Unlike the other hit-and-run TV spots that harass black people, I was able to record this commentary on videotape. I showed it to eleven young black professional people a few weeks later, during a meeting about television stereotypes in San Francisco. They were the sort of people who call my generation bitter, but even they agreed with me that something had to be done, and plans for a boycott of television and opinion programs were under way.

You would think commentators and reporters for government-supported television and radio would be less likely to rely on racist stereotypes, but in my monitoring of the media I've found that some of the most careless notions about black life are perpetuated by reporters and commentators on National Public Radio and the Public Broadcasting System.

Typical was the coverage of blacks by NPR's *Weekend Edition* on

Saturday, January 12, and Sunday, January 13, during which there were at least four stories connecting blacks to crack, one about blacks and illiteracy, one about black teenage fathers who abandon their children, and one about homeless blacks, even though most homeless people are white. Sixty percent of the homeless found dead during San Francisco's most recent winter were white males in their forties.

On August 30, 1989, the day the *Times* revealed the extent of cocaine 20 pregnancies among middle-class white women, this shocking story received one line on television news, while the drug addiction of Lawrence Taylor, a black football player, was featured.

Lack of motivation on the part of journalists to dig for the facts accounts in part for the unbalanced view that American audiences receive of black life. One gets the impression that they spend most of their time under the drier, or getting made up, or engaging in such lofty decisions as whether to stand or sit down while delivering the news. I told Mary Beth Grover, who called me to write an article for the Op-Ed page of the *New York Times* about whether there was a conspiracy to dump drugs in the black neighborhood—a notion that was treated with sarcasm and incredulity by Lianne Hansen on NPR's *Weekend Edition*—that it was up to the press to discover whether one exists, rather than dismiss the opinion held by large numbers of blacks as being based upon paranoia. Certainly there's far more evidence— some of which has appeared in her newspaper—than the quoted lines from *The Godfather:* "Let's give it to the [blacks]; they're animals anyway, they're going to lose their souls." And just because those lines were said in a movie doesn't mean that they were untrue. She said that she wanted a ghetto black to say conclusively that there was a white conspiracy. I wasn't her kind of ghetto black, I guess. Howard Kurtz, the journalist who began this debate in the *Washington Post,* erred when he wrote that crack was largely a problem in black communities. He must be getting all his news from television.

Another reason for the stereotypes of blacks in the white media may be that white journalists find it difficult to divorce themselves from cherished myths about black life even though the facts are right in front of their eyes. I'm constantly amazed that my primitive data base—strewn about the room as though some hurricane just blew through, and bookshelves still in disrepair from a recent earthquake—constantly proves to be superior to those of the most sophisticated news-gathering organizations in the world, with millions of dollars' worth of technology at their disposal.

Tom Brokaw seemed jubilant as he celebrated what he called the wresting away of the media by the people from the Communist state in Czechoslovakia. We're not even calling for the wresting away of the media from anybody, and as writers we would be the last to interfere with the First Amendment rights of anybody. We're calling for balance, which is what the minority critics have always called for. Balance. The best and the worst, the brightest and the stupidest, and all gradations in between, of black, Hispanic, and Asian-American life.

When the electronic media, which have the power to topple presidents, 24 arbitrarily, as it turns out, become smug and arrogant and unresponsive to the people, this presents a danger in a democracy. A Reagan appointee even did away with the Fairness Doctrine, which at least pretended to give those with opposing points of view some time to respond to class slander.

If these electronic Leviathans, which have more power than most political institutions, were governments, they would have been toppled long ago.

Points to Consider

1. Reed asks why blacks are "used to illustrate social pathologies." What answer does he give to his own question? Do you find his answer satisfactory? Can you think of other answers to the question?

2. Why does Reed believe that the media have made drug use, especially crack, a black issue? What arguments and evidence does he offer that it isn't a black issue?

3. How does Reed use the example of the Central Park jogger to make his point? Note his comparisons and terminology in discussing that case. How does he play down the episode and why does he do so?

4. Reed claims that the central problem with the media coverage of minorities is "balance." What do you think he means by balance? How can the lack of balance be corrected?

The Incredible Shrinking Sound Bite

[THE NEW REPUBLIC / May 28, 1990]

Standing before a campaign rally in Pennsylvania, the 1968 Democratic vice presidential candidate, Edmund Muskie, tried to speak, but a group of antiwar protesters drowned him out. Muskie offered the hecklers a deal. He would give the platform to one of their representatives if he could then speak without interruption. Rick Brody, the students' choice, rose to the microphone where, to cheers from the crowd, he denounced the candidates that the 1968 presidential campaign had to offer. "Wallace is no answer. Nixon's no answer. And Humphrey's no answer. Sit out this election!" When Brody finished, Muskie made his case for the Democratic ticket. That night Muskie's confrontation with the demonstrators played prominently on the network news. NBC showed fifty-seven seconds of Brody's speech, and more than a minute of Muskie's.

Twenty years later, things had changed. Throughout the entire 1988 campaign, no network allowed either presidential candidate to speak uninterrupted on the evening news for as long as Rick Brody spoke. By 1988 television's tolerance for the languid pace of political discourse, never great, had all but vanished. An analysis of all weekday evening network newscasts (over 280) from Labor Day to Election Day in 1968 and 1988 reveals that the average "sound bite" fell from 42.3 seconds in 1968 to only 9.8 seconds in 1988. Meanwhile the time the networks devoted to visuals of the candidates, unaccompanied by their words, increased by more than 300 percent.

Since the Kennedy-Nixon debates of 1960, television has played a pivotal role in presidential politics. The Nixon campaign of 1968 was the first to be managed and orchestrated to play on the evening news. With the decline of political parties and the direct appeal to voters in the primaries, presidential campaigns became more adept at conveying their messages through visual images, not only in political commercials but also in elaborately staged media

---

Kiku Adatto (b. 1947) has taught at Harvard University and writes about American culture and politics. She is currently working on a book comparing television coverage of the 1968 and 1988 presidential campaigns.

events. By the time of Ronald Reagan, the actor turned president, Michael Deaver had perfected the techniques of the video presidency.

For television news, the politicians' mastery of television imagery posed 4 a temptation and a challenge. The temptation was to show the pictures. What network producer could resist the footage of Reagan at Normandy Beach, or of Bush in Boston Harbor? The challenge was to avoid being entangled in the artifice and imagery that the campaigns dispensed. In 1988 the networks tried to have it both ways—to meet the challenge even as they succumbed to the temptation. They showed the images that the campaigns produced—their commercials as well as their media events. But they also sought to retain their objectivity by exposing the artifice of the images, by calling constant attention to their self-conscious design.

The language of political reporting was filled with accounts of staging and backdrops, camera angles and scripts, sound bites and spin control, photo opportunities and media gurus. So attentive was television news to the way the campaigns constructed images for television that political reporters began to sound like theater critics, reporting more on the stagecraft than the substance of politics.

When Bush kicked off his campaign with a Labor Day appearance at Disneyland, the networks covered the event as a performance for television. "In the war of the Labor Day visuals," CBS's Bob Schieffer reported, "George Bush pulled out the heavy artillery. A Disneyland backdrop and lots of pictures with the Disney gang." When Bruce Morton covered Dukakis riding in a tank, the story was the image. "In the trade of politics, it's called a visual," said Morton. "The idea is pictures are symbols that tell the voter important things about the candidate. If your candidate is seen in the polls as weak on defense, put him in a tank."

And when Bush showed up at a military base to observe the destruction of a missile under an arms control treaty, ABC's Brit Hume began his report by telling his viewers that they were watching a media event. "Now, here was a photo opportunity, the vice president watching a Pershing missile burn off its fuel." He went on to describe how the event was staged for television. Standing in front of an open field, Hume reported, "The Army had even gone so far as to bulldoze acres of trees to make sure the vice president and the news media had a clear view."

So familiar is the turn to theater criticism that it is difficult to recall the 8 transformation it represents. Even as they conveyed the first presidential campaign "made for television," TV reporters in 1968 continued to reflect the print journalist tradition from which they had descended. In the marriage of theater and politics, politics remained the focus of reporting. The media events of the day—mostly rallies and press conferences—were covered as political events, not as exercises in impression management.

By 1988 television displaced politics as the focus of coverage. Like a gestalt shift, the images that once formed the background to political events—the setting and the stagecraft—now occupied the foreground. (Only 6 percent of reports in 1968 were devoted to theater criticism, compared with 52 percent in 1988.) And yet, for all their image-conscious coverage in 1988, reporters did not escape their entanglement. They showed the potent visuals even as they attempted to avoid the manipulation by "deconstructing" the imagery and revealing its artifice.

To be sure, theater criticism was not the only kind of political reporting on network newscasts in 1988. Some notable "fact correction" pieces offered admirable exceptions. For example, after each presidential debate, ABC's Jim Wooten compared the candidates' claims with the facts. Not content with the canned images of the politicians, Wooten used television images to document discrepancies between the candidates' rhetoric and their records.

Most coverage simply exposed the contrivances of image-making. But alerting the viewer to the construction of television images proved no substitute for fact correction. A superficial "balance" replaced objectivity as the measure of fairness, a balance consisting of equal time for media events, equal time for commercials. But this created a false symmetry, leaving both the press and the public hostage to the play of perceptions the campaigns dispensed.

Even the most critical versions of image-conscious coverage could fail to puncture the pictures they showed. When Bush visited a flag factory in hopes of making patriotism a campaign issue, ABC's Hume reported that Bush was wrapping himself in the flag. "This campaign strives to match its pictures with its points. Today and for much of the past week, the pictures have been of George Bush with the American flag. If the point wasn't to make an issue of patriotism, then the question arises, what was it?" Yet only three days later, in an ABC report on independent voters in New Jersey, the media event that Hume reported with derision was transformed into an innocent visual of Bush. The criticism forgotten, the image played on.

12

Another striking contrast between the coverage of the 1968 and 1988 campaigns is the increased coverage of political commercials. Although political ads played a prominent role in the 1968 campaign, the networks rarely showed excerpts on the news. During the entire 1968 general election campaign, the evening news programs broadcast only two excerpts from candidates' commercials. By 1988 the number had jumped to 125. In 1968 the only time a negative ad was mentioned on the evening news was when CBS's Walter Cronkite and NBC's Chet Huntley reported that a Nixon campaign ad—showing a smiling Hubert Humphrey superimposed on scenes of war and riot—was withdrawn after the Democrats cried foul. Neither network showed the ad itself.

The networks might argue that in 1988 political ads loomed larger in the campaign, and so required more coverage. But as with their focus on media events, reporters ran the risk of becoming conduits of the television images the campaigns dispensed. Even with a critical narrative, showing commercials on the news gives free time to paid media. And most of the time the narrative was not critical. The networks rarely bothered to correct the distortions or misstatements that the ads contained. Of the 125 excerpts shown on the evening news in 1988, the reporter addressed the veracity of the commercials' claims less than 8 percent of the time. The networks became, in effect, electronic billboards for the candidates, showing political commercials not only as breaking news but as stand-ins for the candidates, and file footage aired interchangeably with news footage of the candidates.

The few cases where reporters corrected the facts illustrate how the networks might have covered political commercials. ABC's Richard Threlkeld ran excerpts from a Bush ad attacking Dukakis's defense stand by freezing the frame and correcting each mistaken or distorted claim. He also pointed out the exaggeration in a Dukakis ad attacking Bush's record on Social Security. CBS's Leslie Stahl corrected a deceptive statistic in Bush's revolving-door furlough ad, noting: "Part of the ad is false. . . . Two hundred sixty-eight murderers did not escape. . . . [T]he truth is only four first-degree murderers escaped while on parole."

Stahl concluded her report by observing, "Dukakis left the Bush attack   16 ads unanswered for six weeks. Today campaign aides are engaged in a round of finger-pointing at who is to blame." But the networks also let the Bush furlough commercial run without challenge or correction. Before and even after her report, CBS ran excerpts of the ad without correction. In all, network newscasts ran excerpts from the revolving-door furlough ad ten times throughout the campaign, only once correcting the deceptive statistic.

It might be argued that it is up to the candidate to reply to his opponent's charges, not the press. But the networks' frequent use of political ads on the evening news created a strong disincentive for a candidate to challenge his opponent's ads. As Dukakis found, to attack a television ad as unfair or untrue is to invite the networks to run it again. In the final weeks before the election, the Dukakis campaign accused the Republicans of lying about his record on defense, and of using racist tactics in ads featuring Willie Horton, a black convict who raped and killed while on furlough from a Massachusetts prison. . . . In reporting Dukakis's complaint, all three networks ran excerpts of the ads in question, including the highly charged pictures of Horton and the revolving door of convicts. Dukakis's response thus gave Bush's potent visuals another free run on the evening news.

The networks might reply that the ads are news and thus need to be shown, as long as they generate controversy in the campaign. But this rationale leaves them open to manipulation. Oddly enough, the networks were alive to this danger when confronted with the question of whether to air the videos the campaigns produced for the conventions. "I am not into tone poems," Lane Venardos, the executive producer in charge of convention coverage at CBS, told the *New York Times*. "We are not in the business of being propaganda arms of the political parties." But they seemed blind to the same danger during the campaign itself.

So successful was the Bush campaign at getting free time for its ads on the evening news that, after the campaign, commercial advertisers adopted a similar strategy. In 1989 a pharmaceutical company used unauthorized footage of Presidents Bush and Gorbachev to advertise a cold medication. "In the new year," the slogan ran, "may the only cold war in the world be the one being fought by us." Although two of the three networks refused to carry the commercial, dozens of network and local television news programs showed excerpts of the ad, generating millions of dollars of free airtime.

"I realized I started a trend," said Bush media consultant Roger Ailes in the *New York Times*. "Now guys are out there trying to produce commercials for the evening news." When Humphrey and Nixon hired Madison Avenue experts to help in their campaigns, some worried that, in the television age, presidents would be sold like products. Little did they imagine that, twenty years later, products would be sold like presidents.   20

Along with the attention to commercials and stagecraft in 1988 came an unprecedented focus on the stage managers themselves, the "media gurus," "handlers," and "spin-control artists." Only three reports featured media advisers in 1968, compared with twenty-six in 1988. And the numbers tell only part of the story.

The stance reporters have taken toward media advisers has changed dramatically over the past twenty years. In *The Selling of the President* (1969), Joe McGinniss exposed the growing role of media advisers with a sense of disillusion and outrage. By 1988 television reporters covered image-makers with deference, even admiration. In place of independent fact correction, reporters sought out media advisers as authorities in their own right to analyze the effectiveness and even defend the truthfulness of campaign commercials. They became "media gurus" not only for the candidates but for the networks as well.

For example, in an exchange with CBS anchor Dan Rather on Bush's debate performance, Stahl lavished admiration on the techniques of Bush's media advisers:

Stahl: "They told him not to look into the camera. [She gestures toward the camera as she speaks.] You know when you look directly into a camera you are cold, apparently they have determined."

Rather [laughing]: "Bad news for anchormen I'd say."

Stahl: "We have a lot to learn from this. Michael Dukakis kept talking right into the camera. [Stahl talks directly into her own camera to demonstrate.] And according to the Bush people that makes you look programmed, Dan [Stahl laughs]. And they're very adept at these television symbols and television imagery. And according to our poll it worked."

Rather: "Do you believe it?"

Stahl: "Yes, I think I do, actually."

So hypersensitive were the networks to television image-making in 1988   24
that minor mishaps—gaffes, slips of the tongue, even faulty microphones—
became big news. Politicians were hardly without mishap in 1968, but these
did not count as news. Only once in 1968 did a network even take note of
a minor incident unrelated to the content of the campaign. In 1988 some
twenty-nine reports highlighted trivial slips.

The emphasis on "failed images" reflected a kind of guerrilla warfare
between the networks and the campaigns. The more the campaigns sought
to control the images that appeared on the nightly news, the more the
reporters tried to beat them at their own game, magnifying a minor mishap
into a central feature of the media event.

Early in the 1988 campaign, for example, George Bush delivered a speech
to a sympathetic audience of the American Legion, attacking his opponent's
defense policies. In a slip, he declared that September 7, rather than December
7, was the anniversary of Pearl Harbor. Murmurs and chuckles from the
audience alerted him to his error, and he quickly corrected himself.

The audience was forgiving, but the networks were not. All three network anchors highlighted the slip on the evening news. Dan Rather introduced CBS's report on Bush by declaring solemnly, "Bush's talk to audiences
in Louisville was overshadowed by a strange happening." On NBC Tom
Brokaw reported, "He departed from his prepared script and left his listeners
mystified." Peter Jennings introduced ABC's report by mentioning Bush's
attack on Dukakis, adding, "What's more likely to be remembered about
today's speech is a slip of the tongue."

Some of the slips the networks highlighted in 1988 were not even verbal   28
gaffes or misstatements, but simply failures on the part of candidates to cater
to the cameras. In a report on the travails of the Dukakis campaign, Sam
Donaldson seized on Dukakis's failure to play to ABC's television camera
as evidence of his campaign's ineffectiveness. Showing Dukakis playing a
trumpet with a local marching band, Donaldson chided, "He played the
trumpet with his back to the camera." As Dukakis played "Happy Days Are
Here Again," Donaldson's voice was heard from off-camera calling, "We're
over here, governor."

One way of understanding the turn to image-conscious coverage in 1988
is to see how television news came to partake of the postwar modernist
sensibility, particularly the pop art movement of the 1960s. Characteristic
of this outlook is a self-conscious attention to art as performance, a focus
on the process of image-making rather than on the ideas the images represent.

During the 1960s, when photography and television became potent
forces for documentation and entertainment, they also became powerful
influences on the work of artists. Photographers began to photograph the

television set as part of the social landscape. Newspapers, photographs, and commercial products became part of the collage work of painters such as Robert Rauschenberg. Artists began to explore self-consciously their role in the image-making process.

For example, Lee Friedlander published a book of photography, *Self Portrait,* in which the artist's shadow or reflection was included in every frame. As critic Rod Slemmons notes, "By indicating the photographer is also a performer whose hand is impossible to hide, Friedlander set a precedent for disrupting the normal rules of photography." These "postmodernist" movements in art and photography foreshadowed the form television news would take by the late 1980s.

Andy Warhol once remarked, "The artificial fascinates me." In 1988 32 network reporters and producers, beguiled by the artifice of the modern presidential campaign, might well have said the same. Reporters alternated between reporting campaign images as if they were facts and exposing their contrived nature. Like Warhol, whose personality was always a presence in his work, reporters became part of the campaign theater they covered—as producers, as performers, and as critics. Like Warhol's reproductions of Campbell's soup cans, the networks' use of candidates' commercials directed our attention away from the content and toward the packaging.

The assumption that the creation of appearances is the essence of political reality pervaded not only the reporting but the candidates' self-understanding and conduct with the press. When Dan Quayle sought to escape his image as a highly managed candidate, he resolved publicly to become his own handler, his own "spin doctor." "The so-called handlers story, part of it's true," he confessed to network reporters. "But there will be no more handlers stories, because I'm the handler and I'll do the spinning." Surrounded by a group of reporters on his campaign plane, Quayle announced, "I'm Doctor Spin, and I want you all to report that."

It may seem a strange way for a politician to talk, but not so strange in a media-conscious environment in which authenticity means being master of your own artificiality. Dukakis too sought to reverse his political fortunes by seeking to be master of his own image. This attempt was best captured in a commercial shown on network news in which Dukakis stood beside a television set and snapped off a Bush commercial attacking his stand on defense. "I'm fed up with it," Dukakis declared. "Never seen anything like it in twenty-five years of public life. George Bush's negative television ads, distorting my record, full of lies, and he knows it." The commercial itself shows an image of an image—a Bush television commercial showing (and ridiculing) the media event where Dukakis rode in a tank. In his commercial, Dukakis complains that Bush's commercial showing the tank ride misstates Dukakis's position on defense.

As it appeared in excerpts on the evening news, Dukakis's commercial displayed a quintessentially modernist image of artifice upon artifice upon artifice: television news covering a Dukakis commercial containing a Bush commercial containing a Dukakis media event. In a political world governed by images of images, it seemed almost natural that the authority of the candidate be depicted by his ability to turn off the television set.

In the 1950s Edward R. Murrow noted that broadcast news was "an 36 incompatible combination of show business, advertising, and news." Still, in its first decades television news continued to reflect a sharp distinction between the news and entertainment divisions of the networks. But by the 1980s network news operations came to be seen as profit centers for the large corporations that owned them, run by people drawn less from journalism than from advertising and entertainment backgrounds. Commercialization led to further emphasis on entertainment values, which heightened the need for dramatic visuals, fast pacing, quick cutting, and short sound bites. Given new technological means to achieve these effects—portable video cameras, satellite hookups, and sophisticated video-editing equipment—the networks were not only disposed but equipped to capture the staged media events of the campaigns.

The search for dramatic visuals and the premium placed on showmanship in the 1980s led to a new complicity between the White House imagemakers and the networks. As Susan Zirinsky, a top CBS producer, acknowledged in Martin Schram's *The Great American Video Game*, "In a funny way, the [Reagan White House] advance men and I have the same thing at heart—we want the piece to look as good as [it] possibly can." In 1968 such complicity in stagecraft was scorned. Sanford Socolow, senior producer of the *CBS Evening News with Walter Cronkite*, recently observed, "If someone caught you doing that in 1968 you would have been fired."

In a moment of reflection in 1988, CBS's political correspondents expressed their frustration with image-driven campaigns. "It may seem frivolous, even silly at times," said Schieffer. "But setting up pictures that drive home a message has become the number one priority of the modern-day campaign. The problem, of course, is while it is often entertaining, it is seldom enlightening."

Rather shared his colleague's discomfort. But what troubled him about modern campaigns is equally troubling about television's campaign coverage. "With all this emphasis on the image," he asked, "what happens to the issues? What happens to the substance?"

Points to Consider

1. Why does Adatto believe the media now cover political events in a theatrical fashion? What evidence does she offer to support her views? How did this situation come about?

2. What does Adatto argue is the problem with political commercials? What mistakes did the media make in covering the 1988 presidential ads?

3. What tensions existed between the 1988 campaigns and the networks? What did the networks hope to do in their coverage? How were the networks manipulated? Who did the manipulating?

4. Why does Adatto compare the 1988 campaign coverage with the pop art movement of the 1960s? What do they have in common? How does her example of Dukakis's political commercial support her claim?

JOANMARIE KALTER AND JANE MARION

The Big Stories TV News Is Missing—and Why [TV GUIDE / July 22, 1989]

The news . . . it pours out, day by day, hour by hour. By satellite, fax machine, and portable computer it comes, an explosion of information on the morning and evening news shows, on TV's newsmagazines, on network specials and twenty-four-hour cable. Yet could it possibly be that major news stories affecting millions of people are not being adequately reported at all? The sad fact, according to more than a dozen social critics and media analysts polled by *TV Guide,* is an unequivocal yes.

Their consensus was that TV is good at covering news events—indeed, better than ever. But what it fails to do well, according to the critics, is put those events in context. "We get on-the-ground coverage during a disaster

JOANMARIE KALTER (b. 1951) is a free-lance writer based in New York. Her articles have appeared in the New York Times, *the* Christian Science Monitor, Mother Jones, Psychology Today, *and many other publications. Kalter is a graduate of the Columbia Graduate School of Journalism.*

JANE MARION (b. 1963) has been an editor with TV Guide *for three years. She free-lances for a number of other publications, among them* Reader's Digest, the *Philadelphia Daily News, and the* Asbury Park Press *in New Jersey. Marion currently lives in Philadelphia.*

but not the process that shaped it," says Carl Jensen, professor of communication studies at Sonoma State University. The analysts say, for instance, that before shots rang out in Beijing's Tiananmen Square, they heard almost nothing of the breakdown of Chinese Communist Party control; and they learned more about the personal peccadilloes of Defense Secretary–nominee John Tower than of the larger issue—the economic bonds between the Pentagon and its military suppliers.

Here are some of the major issues that critics say are not being covered adequately on television:

Race. "We have in this country a giant racial problem," says Roger   4
Wilkins, senior fellow at the Institute for Policy Studies, "that by and large is being ignored and only being covered in pieces. It's covered as drugs in the street, or murder in Washington, D.C., or too many teenagers having babies. I am talking about taking all these pieces and putting them together, pulling the camera back and looking at the whole picture.

"There's a big group of blacks," says Wilkins, "who have never escaped the long tentacles of slavery. . . . Some are hopelessly dependent, and some are viciously destructive, and our inattention to this problem is costing us enormously."

Class. There's an absence, "an unbecoming discretion," as Todd Gitlin, a professor of sociology at the University of California at Berkeley, puts it, of talk about class. "It's the great taboo of American life." Peggy Charren, president of Action for Children's Television, points out that in this, the world's wealthiest country, one in five children lives at or below the poverty line (and one in two black children). "People don't focus on that. It's a selfish attitude, and it's reinforced when the press ignores it," she says.

But is it fair to say TV has ignored the plight of America's least fortunate? What about those pervasive images of the homeless living in shelters or out of cardboard boxes? "There's been massive coverage of homelessness," says Everette E. Dennis, director of the Gannett Center for Media Studies. But the coverage, he argues, doesn't have much continuity. "It is more human interest, which is a fragment of the real story. We get it city by city; there's not much on the national sweep [of homelessness]. Nor do we get much analysis of the conditions that caused it." Nor, he adds, is much attention given to its solution.

Foreign news. "One of the things that was most striking to me while I   8 was in London," says Deborah Leff, who recently returned from a year's stint there as a senior producer of ABC's *Nightline*, "is how much more time the British press spends reporting foreign news than the American [media do]. For example, the flooding in Bangladesh was the lead story day after day after day, and so was the famine in the Sudan." In contrast, U.S. journalists would cover Third World countries "every now and then."

Economics reporting. "I'm old enough to remember when we hardly had any at all," says Paul Friedman, a former NBC News producer and now executive producer of ABC's *World News Tonight,* "because it was hard to visualize. Then we made enormous progress with graphics, and we all hired economics reporters to be experts, but I still think it's a very difficult subject to make clear . . . unless you have the opportunity to read about it."

Labor news. "Labor coverage has diminished enormously in recent years," says Everette Dennis. "It's now a subset of business coverage—partly because the labor movement doesn't have the political muscle it once did." Plus, he says, "labor as an institution doesn't do a very good job connecting with the media and trying to make its case. Most of the reports about labor tend to be somewhat negative" and reflect more of the point of view of management.

While news-division spokesmen at CBS, NBC, and PBS all declined to comment for this article, at least one network executive, Richard Wald, senior vice president of ABC News, disagrees strongly with critics who perceive shortcomings in TV's coverage of race, class, and other areas. "These are broad generalizations that don't apply to us," says Wald, "and frankly, it's insulting. There are a lot of things to criticize TV for. Those things are not among them."

In reply to the criticism that TV news tends to be event-oriented, Wald says: "I wouldn't say it's more true of TV news than of news in general. News does tend to be spasmodic or episodic, but I think the major news organizations do try to put things into perspective and to examine not only the event but [its] meaning." 12

Wald concedes, however, there are some areas that the networks need to cover more thoroughly. "We should, in general, do a better job on the Pacific nations," he says, singling out Indonesia, as well as "the emerging nations of Southeast Asia. I think we could cover black Africa a bit better. We are professionally guilty because we have a time limitation. We can't add pages."

Some of the other reasons for these oversights are as old as TV news itself. "Anyone who has worked in TV news will tell you the executive producer always asks, 'What are the pictures?' " says Edwin Diamond, director of the News Study Group at New York University. TV, a visual medium, is assumed to demand action and color. And because it's a small-screen picture, the visual image is more powerful when trained on a single person. So, says Diamond, there's an imbalance in Washington, with more coverage of the president and less of Congress.

"It's much easier," says Todd Gitlin, "to cover the microcosmic event and to take for granted the way Washington makes decisions. Things that don't change dramatically are not considered newsworthy in the conventional sense, yet those are much more significant and affect more of human life."

Jude Wanniski, editor of *MediaGuide,* an annual journalism critique, 16 offers another explanation for why these important stories often go unreported: "TV journalists were educated and groomed to be interesting personalities rather than news gatherers and reporters." So, in his judgment, TV covered John Tower when Tower was charged with being a drinker and a womanizer because that "doesn't involve knowledge of [military] procurement requirements or counterforce theory at the Pentagon."

To some degree, say the analysts, such flaws have been exacerbated by the budget cuts in the network news divisions. Says Carl Jensen of Sonoma State, "The bean counters are taking over!" They are less willing to detach reporters to work on long-range pieces, he says, "because investigative reporting is more expensive than public stenography."

This bottom-line mentality, notes Ed Diamond, is responsible for "the biggest scandal in local TV news—the failure to cover state government. That's the biggest uncovered story across the country. They may cover politics well, but government. . . . People barely know what their governor does or the size of the state budget. All they know is the color of the license plates."

As for lingering problems of race and class, "I think a lot of people don't see it and don't want to see it," Roger Wilkins says simply. TV news executives and correspondents, he says, tend to be white and wealthy, living lives that keep them cloistered from the inner-city or rural poor.

"That doesn't mean," says Todd Gitlin, "they are unsympathetic to the poor, but they see them as the well-meaning rich have always seen them, as people who are suffering and deserving of charity." That's why, he says, we see poignant profiles of the homeless more often than stories about housing policy or the growing gap in per capita income. 20

Richard John Neuhaus, director of the Institute on Religion and Public Life, goes further. He finds TV news overlooking "the drama of the quotidian, the everyday economic life of most Americans, paying their bills, sending their kids to college, making very hard decisions between right and wrong." When TV news does turn to "the heartland," he says, "it's a sideshow . . . it's to lift up what's not working and to land on some left-of-center cliché."

The reason? "Most of us in the media," says Neuhaus, "come from somewhere that we quite deliberately left. We decided we could be more free and truly ourselves in the great city. And there's a conscious or unconscious contempt for the people we came from and the places we fled."

According to some of these critics, the outlook is not entirely grim. Overlooked issues do sometimes surface—eventually. Problems of the environment are one. Carl Jensen, for instance, compiles an annual list of ten "censored" stories and notes that pesticides in food, on his list in 1980, has become a hot topic now. Others question whether the TV news audience is even being shortchanged. "Demand produces the supply," says Jude

Wanniski, and if TV news is fast food, that's because it caters to people on the run, who do not need or care for more.

But some critics do see ominous implications in TV's piecemeal approach 24 to the news. Jay Rosen, assistant professor of journalism at New York University, cites coverage of the federal budget deficit. It is well known that the Reagan administration kept a close eye on the TV cameras, providing news of the day in thirty-second sound bites. According to Rosen, "They knew they could cut taxes and increase defense spending and that the long-term consequences of that would be difficult to render on television." Reality, he says, "is starting to accommodate TV in a much larger way than just designing campaign stops so they look good on television." And this, he says, is the ultimate uncovered story of TV news: that its limitations now shape the very strategies of government.

What, then, are the solutions? Says Diamond, "Because I can analyze this doesn't mean it's easy to solve! It only means it's easy to analyze."

Points to Consider

1. According to Kalter and Marion, the consensus of opinion from their survey of news coverage was that television fails to put news events in context. What does this mean? Give an example of how context could be provided. Why do you think context is often lacking?

2. In what sense does the orientation of TV news to events result in limited coverage? What does this orientation fail to take into account?

3. Why are problems of race and poverty so inadequately treated by the news media? What is it about these problems that results in the media's relative inattention to them?

4. Why do the news media concentrate more on the president than on Congress? What picture does this present of our government? How does this imbalance lead to certain news stories' getting more attention than others?

Discussing the Unit

Suggested Topic for Discussion

The selections in this unit cover various inadequacies of television news reporting. Having examined all three articles, consider the problem of responsibility: who seems most to blame for the quality of the news we receive? Is it the news reporters themselves? Is it the networks they work for? Is it the viewing audience whose ratings the networks depend upon? Or is some other factor to blame?

Preparing for Class Discussion

1. Select your favorite half-hour evening national news program. Watch the show with a stopwatch, counting the number of stories and timing each one (this procedure will be easier if you can tape the show as well). How much time was devoted to the kind of issues mentioned in Kalter and Marion's survey? How was political coverage handled? How does it compare with Adatto's analysis? How were minorities portrayed on the show? What was the proportion of time devoted to sports and weather as contrasted to foreign and political news? How much of the half-hour was taken up with commercials and with conversations between members of the news team? Compare the quality of coverage on your show with that of rival shows examined by others in your class.

2. Having examined one show in detail, now consider why that show covered events the way it did. How did the newscasters handle the stories? How were the segments arranged? What type of story took priority? What attitudes in the audience were the newscasters appealing to? What age group and social class do you think the stories were designed to appeal to? Consider, too, if the show satisfied your personal requirements.

From Discussion to Writing

Based on your reading and on your detailed observations of one news program, write an essay in which you propose a way to improve news coverage. What features would you add? What features would you get rid of? How would you select stories and design segments? Be as specific as you can but make sure the improvements you suggest can be incorporated into a half-hour format.

17

Celebrities:
How Do They Affect Us?

figure of speech { similie metaphor hyperbole - exaggeration ux ymoron - put two words with contradict meaning etc.

What does the average American think about fame and famous people? Perhaps we cannot arrive at any sure answers, but if the number of talk shows, newspaper and magazine articles, and radio interviews about or involving celebrities are any indication of our fascination with public figures, then we can surmise that most ordinary people view celebrities as an integral part of the American experience. In "Nymphs and Satyrs," essayist Lewis H. Lapham attempts to account for our national obsession, going so far as to compare our modern-day heroes with the gods and goddesses of the ancient world. According to Lapham, what these media stars represent to most of us is the hope of immortality.

But celebrities are mortal, as was made painfully clear in July 1989 when actress Rebecca Schaeffer was shot and killed at her apartment by a deranged fan. The death of the young star prompted reporter Rod Lurie to write "Guns n' Roses," a detailed look at the growing number of fans who cannot make a distinction between their fantasies and real life.

Finally, in "Senseless," Rick Telander examines another form of fan violence, this time directed against the fans themselves. Each year, a large number of inner-city youths are killed and robbed of their celebrity-endorsed athletic shoes and sportswear. Popular figures like Michael Jordan and Spike

Lee find themselves in the middle of the controversy over whether a pair of sneakers is worth dying for. As you read these pieces think about the ways celebrities wield their influence over the lives of all Americans.

<hr>

LEWIS H. LAPHAM

Nymphs and Satyrs   [HARPER'S MAGAZINE / August 1989]

The religions we call false were once true.

—*Emerson*

At a newsstand in Grand Central Station the other day I was surprised to notice that the celebrities posed on the covers of the magazines imparted a sense of stability and calm to a world otherwise dissolved in chaos. The newspaper headlines brought word of violent change—riots in Beijing, political revisionism in Moscow, near anarchy in Argentina, and moral collapse in Washington—but on the smooth surfaces of the magazines the familiar faces looked as vacant and imperturbable as they had looked for twenty years, as steady in their courses as the fixed stars, as serene as the bronze Buddha in the courtyard at Kamakura. There they all were—Liz and Elvis and Zsa Zsa and Cher; Sammy Davis, Jr., and Joan Collins and Andy Warhol—indifferent to the turmoil of the news, bestowing on the confusion of events the smiles of infinite bliss.

I hadn't expected a row of clichéd photographs to produce so philosophical an effect, and later in the afternoon it occurred to me that I never had properly understood the place and function of celebrity in the American scheme of things. I had thought of celebrities as frivolous and ornamental figures, as toys or pets or metaphors. Clearly this was a mistake. If they

<hr>

LEWIS H. LAPHAM (b. 1935) is the editor of Harper's Magazine, *where he writes a monthly essay. A 1956 graduate of Yale University and a former newspaper reporter and magazine journalist, Lapham is the author of several books, including* Money and Class in America *(1988) and* Imperial Masquerade *(1990).*

could ease the pain of doubt and hold at bay the fear of change, then even the shabbiest of celebrities, like a little crowd of unpainted idols at a roadside shrine, deserved to be appreciated as minor deities. I thought of the lares and penates who protected the citizens of ancient Rome, and, more fancifully, of the nymphs and satyrs and fauns so lovingly construed by the poets of ancient Greece. The pagan imagination endows all the phenomena of the natural world with the traits of human personality. The postmodern imagination, which is also anthropomorphic but more accurately described as post-Christian, reverts to the same device. The old paganism assigns true elements of the divine to rivers and trees and winds and storms. The contemporary paganism assigns similar powers to individuals brushed, no matter how lightly, with the gilding of fame. Which is why famous actors show up on television commercials muttering ritual incantations over the lifeless forms of cameras and automobile tires, why well-known athletes can be seen breathing the gift of life into cans of deodorant and shaving cream, why even dowager movie queens remain capable of awakening with their "personal touch" the spirit dormant in the color of a lipstick or a bottle of perfume. The popular worship of images (whether graven on T-shirts, designer labels, or magazine covers) has become so habitual that we find it easy to imagine celebrities enthroned in a broadcasting studio on Mount Olympus, idly conversing with one another on an eternal talk show. It doesn't matter that they say nothing of interest or importance. Neither did Aphrodite or Zeus. What matters is the hope of immortality. Elvis lives, and so does anybody else who can transform the corruption of the private flesh into the incorruptibility of a public image.

The belief in the transfiguring power of personality derives its modern and egalitarian bona fides from Jean-Jacques Rousseau's romantic pastoral of man as a noble savage at play in the fields of the id, of man set free from laws and schools and institutions, free to declare himself his own government, free to declare himself a god. In a spirit that would be well understood by the editors of *People* magazine, Rousseau's writings reflect his desire to walk into a room and seize the instant and universal approbation of everyone present to focus upon himself all eyes, all praise, all sexual feeling. Precisely the same desire animates the life and work of individuals as sympathetic to the spirit of our age as Lee Iacocca and Shirley MacLaine.

A concise form of the pagan aesthetic was elegantly stated several years   4
ago by a Yale University student named Vincent Renzi, who exhibited himself as a work of art. He did so to satisfy a requirement for a theater project. The other students in the class, crippled by their attachment to the traditional forms of expression, wrote scripts or directed plays.

Renzi entitled his exhibition "My Youth in Literature" and circulated a handbill stating that "from 11:49 P.M. 12 October 1984, until 10:49 P.M. 16 November 1984, the life of Vincent Renzi will be a work of art." The handbill went on to say that prospective critics or patrons could arrange for their "access to the art" through Renzi's curator, a fellow student named

David Hyder. During the course of the exhibition, about forty people attended private "viewings" of Renzi as he made the admittedly banal rounds of his admittedly banal existence. The happy few got to see Renzi do his laundry, walk to class, shave, go the movies, order breakfast in a coffee shop, look into a book or newspaper, sharpen one or two pencils, form an occasional opinion.

Celebrities employ press agents instead of curators, but the rules of the exhibitions, variously entitled "My Youth in Satin" or "My Old Age in a Cask of Brandy," remain the same. The publicists provide "access to the art" and arrange private showings as well as magazine interviews and photo opportunities. Flesh becomes property, which, in a commercial society, is akin to salvation.

A few months after reading about Renzi's exhibition in New Haven, I had further occasion to consider the question of celebrity at the American Museum of Natural History in New York City. To a gathering of celebrities as impressive in its bulk as the stuffed elephants and the polyurethane whale, the president of Columbia Records introduced Michael Jackson as "the greatest artist of all time"—not the greatest recording artist of all time, not the greatest pop singer or dancer of all time, but simply and unequivocally the greatest artist of all time. The hyperbole seemed to me excessive, and at first I thought that the gentleman from Columbia Records merely wished to say that Jackson was extremely rich. This form of politeness is so prevalent in New York and Los Angeles that if a performer in any venue earns an income that can be counted in megabucks, he or she becomes, as if by royal proclamation, an artist. The title is another of the honors that come with the Mercedes, the house in Beverly Hills, the appearances on the Carson show. American celebrity can be defined as wealth incarnate, and its manufacture in the alembics of network television proves the media's power as an alchemist capable of changing crime into philanthropy and lead into gold. Like individuals said to be worth more than thirty million dollars, celebrities become their own masterpieces, rare jewels for whom the world offers more or less satisfactory settings inexpressibly more beautiful than anything else in their art collections.

But even the magnificence of Michael Jackson's fortune didn't adequately explain the phrase "the greatest artist of all time." Why not merely "a sublime artist" or "one of the greatest artists of all time"?

Once again, I missed the allusion to the pagan system of belief and failed to understand that the record promoter might as well have been talking about Dionysus. Only later did I remember what Paul Johnson, the British historian, had said about Adolf Hitler. In his book *Modern Times,* Johnson portrayed Hitler as the first modern rock star, the first totalitarian statesman to conceive of himself as an artist. Long before the advent of Ronald Reagan, Hitler understood that the staging of a leader is more important than what the leader has to say. He set the scenes of his speeches as artfully as the producers of rock videos arrange the visual accompaniments for songs. Recognizing that in Germany politics was music, especially music drama, Hitler derived his effects from the study of Wagnerian opera. At Nuremberg, he experimented with the modern forms of *son et lumière*.[1] Hitler's talent for political costume resulted in the Nazi uniform, which has remained, in Johnson's phrase, "the standard of excellence in totalitarian sumptuary."

It is the standard to which rock musicians, particularly those attempting a synthesis of elegance and sadism, still aspire. The lines of connection between totalitarian art and pagan superstition suggested what the president of Columbia Records might have had in mind when billing Michael Jackson as "the greatest artist of all time." Like so many of his peers in the entertainment and weapons industries, he identified art not with thought or wisdom, not even with skill and ingenuity, but with power.

In *Mein Kampf* Hitler observed that the object of all propaganda was the "encroachment upon man's freedom of will," and toward this end he recommended techniques likely to "whip up and excite . . . the instinctive." The impresarios look for the same effect, and by art they mean, more often than not, the Dionysian burst of feeling that draws a crowd, burns the Reichstag, elects a president, or sells forty million copies of *Thriller*.

If civilization can be defined as an advance toward impersonality— toward a system of justice that doesn't depend on the whim of a judge or a conception of art that relies on something other than applause for celebrity— then the pagan worship of network anchorpersons or cypress trees implies the joyous return to barbarism. 12

Given another few years of deterioration of the nation's schools, I can imagine an American pantheon of celebrities not only imprinted on film but also carved in stone or wood. As matters now stand, too many celebrities come and go too quickly through a market glutted with a publicist's cheap imitations. Nobody knows whether a newly minted celebrity will last as long as a week, whether he or she hasn't been too hastily assembled in Taiwan. The company of immortals could be fixed at a precise number (no more than two thousand but no fewer than one thousand), all of whom grant all interviews, pose for all photographs, answer all questions, and publish their bank accounts and medical histories. The number of places allotted to the professions should reflect the order of precedence operative elsewhere in the society—400 film and television personalities, 250 athletes, 100 rock singers, 100 notorious criminals, 75 faith healers, 50 new millionaires, 25 business magnates, 14 politicians, 9 real estate developers, 6 authors, 4 generals, 3 presidential candidates, 2 foreigners, 1 mathematician, 1 engineer, and 1 saint. The company reserves four places for nonentities—the Cinderella appointments awarded to previously anonymous people who hijack air-

---

[1] French for "sound and light": a dramatic event held at night that presents special light and sound effects and music.

planes, win lotteries or Nobel Prizes, assassinate heads of state, or give birth to quintuplets.

Whenever they go among the common people, the immortals dress in the costumes from which they derive their principal source of reputation. Joe Namath always appears in football uniform, Joan Collins in a peignoir. The immortals ride the subways, stand in line at supermarkets, and travel coach class on commercial aircraft. Their presence comforts the populace with the proof of immortality, prompting people to say to one another that if Kenny Rogers were on this subway, then no thug would dare pull a knife, that if Madonna were on this plane, not even God would dare strike it from the sky.

Every city with any pretension to civic pride probably would maintain a temple dedicated to the worship of celebrity. Wandering divinities on their way to speak in Detroit or play a football game in New Orleans would sit behind a screen in the sanctuary, listening to the dreams of success. The faithful who come to make confession would never know whether they were speaking to Henry Kissinger or Joe Montana. This, of course, would make no difference.

Points to Consider

1. How would you describe Lewis H. Lapham's attitude toward celebrity? According to Lapham, what special function do celebrities perform in American society? Does Lapham view this role as fundamentally positive?

2. Why does Lapham employ the analogy of pagan gods and goddesses to write about celebrity? Do you think that the analogy is a good one? Hollywood publicists of the thirties and forties often described major movie stars as "gods" or "goddesses." Does Lapham use these terms in a similar way?

3. What was Lapham's reaction to the introduction of Michael Jackson at a New York reception as "the greatest artist of all time"? Why is Lapham surprised by the fact that Jackson is referred to as an artist? What ideas must replace more traditional notions about art if Jackson is to be seen as an artist?

4. Why does Lapham offer a futuristic view of celebrity at the end of his essay? Do you think he wants the reader to take this scenario seriously? Why does he attribute this deification of celebrities to the decline of the educational system?

Guns n' Roses [LOS ANGELES / February 1990]

He sits virtually alone in the theater, one of the few art-film showcases in Tucson, as Paul Bartel's *Scenes from the Class Struggle in Beverly Hills* flickers before his eyes. He's not there because of the reviews. The critics have really done their dance of death on this black comedy. Nor have the film's stars drawn him there. He couldn't care less about Jacqueline Bisset and Wallace Shawn. What brings nineteen-year-old Robert John Bardo to this theater is the young actress Rebecca Schaeffer. Like the rest of the nation, his first glimpse of her was on the CBS sitcom *My Sister Sam,* on which she played Pam Dawber's younger sibling—adorable, smart-mouthed, impulsive, flirtatious, and, most important to Bardo, a virgin.

Schaeffer is hardly a major star in the film. She has about eight scenes. It is the shortest one that disturbs Bardo. In it his sweetheart, his *virgin,* lies in bed with Ray Sharkey. Worse, in her next scene she uses the word *hump.* And later talks of using birth-control pills. *Birth-control pills!* Bardo's mind reels. Some sins can be forgiven. Infidelity is not among them. It will be his mission to right the wrong.

This might explain what is on his mind when he returns to his one-story home and says good night to his father, a retired Air Force NCO, and his Japanese-born mother. The reason, perhaps, why he writes to his sister and explains his intentions, his anger and the bitterness overwhelming him. "I have an obsession with the unattainable," he writes. "I have to eliminate [something] I cannot attain."

In his room, cluttered with Beatles posters from the "white album" (whose "Helter-Skelter" set off Charles Manson), are videotapes of most of the episodes of *My Sister Sam.* Now that the show is canceled, Bardo depends on this collection for his entertainment. He doesn't do much else in the evenings (though neighbors now relate how Bardo and his brother made nocturnal runs up and down the street, racing across lawns, cursing and

4

ROD LURIE (b. 1962) is a regular contributor to Premiere, *the* New York Daily News, Los Angeles Magazine, *and other periodicals. Lurie graduated from the U.S. Military Academy at West Point and recently finished serving in the U.S. Army. He is currently working on a book about the celebrity-stalking phenomenon.*

making obscene gestures at passersby). After his freshman year at Pueblo High School, Bardo had dropped out, despite the fact that his grades were all As and Bs and that he had achieved this level of excellence in a school with an attrition rate greater than the national average. After Bardo quit school, he went through a series of odd jobs. Eventually, he found work as a janitor in a Jack-in-the-Box close to home.

A few days after seeing *Class Struggle,* Bardo asks his older brother to purchase a gun for him, a .357 Magnum. Arizona has perhaps the most liberal gun laws in the nation. You can, for example, walk through Tucson with an unconcealed revolver in your belt. There are a few restrictions. One is you have to be at least twenty-one. Bardo needs his brother's help.

It's not long before Bardo has his weapon. The ease with which he obtains the gun is smugly satisfying (Arthur Jackson, the man who stabbed actress Theresa Saldana in 1982, traveled through fourteen states unable to find even one shop that would sell him a gun.)

Star stalkers, for the most part, have long been seen as a kind of occupational hazard—the price of stardom. They were simply the inevitable fruits and nuts—the letter writers, the obscene phone callers—that fame was bound to attract. There have always been star stalkers. In *The Natural,* Robert Redford's baseball phenom is blasted in the stomach by a deranged devotee, played by Barbara Hershey, who believes she can possess him only in death; the story was based on the 1940 shooting of baseball great Eddie Waitkus by Ruth Steinhagen. In the seventies there was Manson. Curiously, the eighties began with several sensational, highly publicized star stalkers. Just before Christmas in 1980 John Lennon was shot to death outside his New York City apartment building by Mark David Chapman, a fan who believed he had to kill the ex-Beatle to protect him from selling out the ideals he had once espoused. Five months later, President Reagan was shot by John Hinckley, Jr., who, it turned out, was trying to kill the president to impress actress Jodie Foster.

Rebecca Schaeffer's murder at the hands of Robert John Bardo last July, however tragic, was perceived by most people as another psychopathic mishap, another deranged sociopathic anomaly that no one can predict or defend against. But what has become clear, in fact, is that Schaeffer's death was not an isolated incident. It is simply the latest occurrence in what has become a new and bizarre wrinkle in the world of criminology, and one that is shockingly commonplace in Los Angeles. Whether because of some fallout from a Me Decade that worshiped money and fame or an electronic media bent on hyping the latest superstar, so-called star stalkers and obsessed fans have increased dramatically—some would say, epidemically—in the eighties. It is a phenomenon that has created a nightmare for local police agencies, which don't have the training or the manpower to deal with it.

Neither the police nor the FBI can provide accurate data on how many stalkers have been monitored, arrested, and prosecuted in the past ten years. Several who were arrested were found unfit to stand trial; in some cases the stars refused to press charges. Many of the incidents are kept quiet for publicity reasons. To be associated with a psychopath is to become indelibly linked with him. (Who can read about Hinckley and not think of Foster?) In the six months after Schaeffer was killed, Michael J. Fox, Michael Landon, David Letterman, Olivia Newton-John, Cher, Sheena Easton, Justine Bateman, Tiffany, Johnny Carson, and newscaster Kelly Lange were all targets of stalkers. And they are but the tip of the iceberg.

According to Gavin de Becker, an L.A.-based private-security analyst who has become the nation's undisputed expert on star stalking and assessing threats to public figures, in 1985 there were some fifteen hundred people his firm considered obsessives who under the right circumstances were capable of a violent act. That number now hovers around six thousand. Last year alone, de Becker's clients—among them Cher, Newton-John, Fox, Saldana, Redford, Tina Turner, and Jessica Lange—received fifty thousand "inappropriate" letters from fans.

And now, at the beginning of the nineties, this deluge of delusion shows no sign of letting up. L.A. has become a star-studded mecca for obsessive fans.

A week after seeing *Class Struggle,* Bardo tells his boss at Jack-in-the-Box that he is quitting. He travels across town to the Anthony Private Detective Agency, located in a small red-brick building close to the University of Arizona. When he enters the office, his clothes are dirty, his hair is unkempt, and he needs a shave. Still, he speaks to one of the detectives with the fluidity you would expect from an honors student. He has a long-lost close friend, he explains. Her name is Rebecca Schaeffer, she's an actress, and he thinks she's living in California. The last time he saw her was at Universal Studios. He has a birthday present for her. He pulls out an eight-by-ten glossy of the actress; on it, she had written a little note and signed it "Love, Rebecca." He also has a batch of letters he claims she wrote.

The detective asks Bardo for all the details he can give on Schaeffer. Since Bardo has read most of the articles written about the actress, he has a good grasp of her history. He tells the detective everything he knows. The detective tells Bardo "no problem." He'll track her down. His fee is thirty-five dollars an hour (whether or not he finds her) or a two hundred fifty-dollar flat rate (paid only if her locates her). Bardo opts for the flat fee.

In the four weeks it takes the agency to find Schaeffer, Bardo mills around the house. Like his father, he spends the majority of the day indoors. The Bardos are one of the few non-Hispanic families in the enclosed community of Midvale Park. The neighbors know little about them.

On July 17, Bardo tells his parents he is going to Los Angeles. This will not be the first time he has boarded a Greyhound for Southern California.

Two years earlier he had shown up on the Warner Bros. lot, where *My Sister Sam* was taped, carrying flowers and an enormous teddy bear. He told the guards at the gate that the gifts were for Schaeffer. They were apprehensive about people trying to get on the set. Only a few weeks before, the FBI had been called in to examine death threats against Pam Dawber.

Bardo was so intent on seeing Schaeffer that the guards called their boss, [16] Jack Egger. Bardo told Egger, a retired Beverly Hills cop, about his adulation for Schaeffer. Egger explained to Bardo there was no way he could get on the set. They were just too busy. He then personally drove Bardo back to his motel. Maybe it was Egger's intention to coax Bardo back into reality. When he dropped Bardo off he gave him the facts of life: "Get Rebecca Schaeffer out of your mind, son. You'll never get to her—not on the set, anyway."

When Egger returned to his office, he called Mimi Webber, Schaeffer's publicist. They agreed Bardo's visit was nothing to worry about. Two days later, Bardo, on his way out of town, called Egger from the bus terminal. He just wanted to thank him for being so kind. "You were like a father to me," Bardo told Egger.

Rebecca Schaeffer and Theresa Saldana are just two of the high-profile cases of movie fans gone amok. Lesser known is the obsession of Ralph Nau, a twenty-seven-year-old Wisconsin farmhand who in 1980 became convinced that Olivia Newton-John wanted him, that she performed for him, and that her films and records were tributes to him. In 1984, after four years of writing bizarre and often frightening letters to the singer-actress, Nau pursued her to Australia. (Earlier, he had traveled to Scotland because he knew Sheena Easton "wanted" him to come live with her.) Newton-John was well aware of Nau. Earlier that year he had shown up at her concert at the Universal Amphitheater and tried to get onstage.

Gavin de Becker was also aware of Nau. Since 1981 de Becker had kept track of hundreds of Nau's letters to Newton-John in order to keep abreast of his plans. Considering Nau a threat to Newton-John (Nau had once killed a dog he thought was trying to prevent him from seeing the singer), de Becker had his staff continue to monitor him.

In the summer of 1984, Nau was arrested in Illinois for killing his autistic [20] baby brother. Psychiatric experts speculated he had bludgeoned his brother because Nau thought the boy, too, was denying him the opportunity to fulfill his romantic destiny. Nau, however, was acquitted when Illinois's Kane County Court found him mentally incompetent, and he was committed to the state mental hospital in Elgin. Nau, however, was never found guilty in a court of law, and he retained the privilege of petitioning for release in sixty days.

In December 1989, Nau was found to be a danger to himself and society and indefinitely committed to the institution. The decision was rendered after the judge had read several of the letters Nau had written to game-show hostess Vanna White as well as to TV anchor Joan Lunden, who, he said, wants him to have sex with her "very, very, very young" children. De Becker, who has been largely responsible for gathering evidence to prosecute Nau, anticipates he will be out in a year.

But Nau wasn't Newton-John's only trouble. In 1980, a drifter and self-taught survivalist from Louisiana named Michael Perry wrote the singer two letters after seeing her in the film *Xanadu*. Both were sent registered. In one, Perry wrote, "Either the dead bodies are rising or else there is a listening device under my mother and father's house. The voices I hear tell me that you are locked up beneath this town of Lake Arthur and were really a muse who was granted everlasting life."

When Perry, who had moved to Los Angeles and begun living in the hills behind the singer's Malibu estate, made his second attempt to get on Newton-John's property, he was spotted by one of de Becker's security guards and identified through a computer in de Becker's headquarters as one of the people on a list of potential threats to Newton-John. He was apprehended by de Becker's men and "escorted" out of the state.

When Perry returned to Louisiana, he slaughtered his parents, his cous- 24
ins, and his baby nephew. The police discovered near the bodies a hit list of ten people. Included were the names of four of the deceased, as well as those of Newton-John, her then-fiancé Matt Lattanzi, and Supreme Court Justice Sandra Day O'Connor. (Perry later said her eyes reminded him of Newton-John's.)

Perry was eventually arrested on a petty-theft charge in a motel two miles from the U.S. Supreme Court. When the police searched his motel room, they found six television sets with OLIVIA scrawled in red on the screens. Though he had been diagnosed as a paranoid schizophrenic by the Feliciana Forensic Facility in 1982, he was found fit to stand trial. He was eventually convicted and sentenced to death row in 1985. Since his incarceration, OLIVIA has been scrawled on the wall of his cell.

Michael J. Fox exudes the same innocence as Newton-John, an approachability that draws a lot of fan mail—much of it from women with frightening delusions.

Tina Marie Ledbetter, a twenty-six-year-old packaging clerk from Camarillo, called herself Fox's "number one fan." She began writing him in 1987. At first her unsigned letters were innocuous enough, though her "crush" drove her family crazy. Posters and photos were plastered to the walls of her room with a religious zeal, the VCR incessantly played *Family Ties* episodes, and there was nonstop clacking on the typewriter as she dispatched some six thousand letters in two years. But for the most part, there was nothing that indicated she was potentially violent.

It was when Fox started dating former costar Tracy Pollan that some- 28
thing broke loose in Ledbetter's mind. Her letters, still unsigned and now

crammed with exclamation points and expletives, demanded Fox give up Pollan and resume his relationship with *Facts of Life* star Nancy McKeon.

When Fox married Pollan in 1988 and it was later announced the couple was expecting, Ledbetter's letters became littered with anti-Semitic remarks and death threats. "Fox felt very threatened," says Los Angeles assistant D.A. Susan Gruber, "but he was more concerned for the safety of his wife and child." Gruber and the police, however, were powerless. Ledbetter's letters were untraceable. But in early 1989 she made the mistake of sending Fox boxes of rabbit droppings via UPS. The shipping labels were easily traced to Ledbetter, and she was soon arrested.

But Ledbetter did not meet the court's definition of insanity—that is, she knew the difference between right and wrong and was aware of the pain her letters caused. And there was no precedent in the courts dealing with a legally sane individual who had harassed a celebrity with letters.

Gruber, with de Becker's help, came across an obscure law: penal code 422, which makes it a crime to make "terrorist" threats against anyone if they cause the victim to have a real fear for his safety or life. Ledbetter pleaded guilty to the charges in May and received three years' supervised probation, plus the ten months' time she'd already served, and a restraining order to stay away from Fox.

PC 422 was also used this past fall against Warren Sevy Hudson. A telemarketer who had been living in a series of motels in Los Angeles, Hudson began sending love letters to KNBC anchor Kelly Lange in 1985. When his mother died, he even sent Lange her fur coats and jewelry. His infatuation gradually turned to frustration when he realized she was never going to return his affections.

He began telling people at his office that he was engaged to Lange. Occasionally he would phone the station and let his delusions bleed into the ear of a receptionist. When Lange traveled to Korea to cover the Olympics, Hudson tried to get his own credentials, claiming he was a KNBC employee.

Eventually, he sent Lange a postcard telling her that he was going to shoot his way into the studio. Last year he showed up at his office with .38-caliber bullets, telling his co-workers he was going to get to Lange. Police were called, and Hudson was taken into custody. In a search of his home the police found a .38 pistol, which had belonged to his father, a retired policeman. Hudson was tried and found guilty under PC 422 in December, and at press time he was awaiting sentencing.

Kenneth Orville Gause was arrested in December at KNBC studios outside *The Tonight Show* for making "terrorist threats" and writing threatening letters to Johnny Carson. In his possession was a sock filled with gravel. "We can't call it a weapon," says Burbank prosecutor Robert Cohen, "but it sure would hurt if you were hit with it."

Gause, a thirty-six-year-old Wisconsin native, calling himself a radio talk-show host, had communicated regularly with Carson and claimed that almost six million dollars of his own funds had been diverted by Carson for personal use. Gause wanted the money back. He declared himself the "King of Goodness" and signed his letters.

As it turned out, according to Cohen, Fred DeCordova, the show's producer, had received warnings from de Becker, who had learned about Gause's fixation with Carson while monitoring Gause on behalf of another of his clients. As of press time, Gause has not gone to trial.

Finding a consensus for the increase in the peculiar crime of star stalking is no easy task. The common denominator, according to experts, is that the rise of stalking can be tied to two themes of the eighties: the inability of government to deal with the mentally ill and, more important, the growing access to celebrity lives through television, video, cable, and tell-all talk shows such as *Donahue* and show-all talk shows such as *Lifestyles of the Rich and Famous*.

Take Bardo, Gause, Jackson, Perry, Ledbetter, Nau, and Hudson. Look at their demographics. Examine their hometowns, their ages, their families' wealth, their jobs. You will not find a common denominator. According to Park Dietz, a local psychologist and expert on obsessed fans who testified at Hinckley's trial, there's no way to draw a composite of the star stalker. "Anyone who tells you he can do that is not being truthful," Dietz says.

What is possible, however, is finding a common thread of behavioral 40 patterns. As a rule, stalkers communicate with their idols in a steady stream of letters that are normally filled with any of several delusions: the author (Bardo, Hudson, Jackson) will have a life of love with the celebrity (Schaeffer, Lange, Saldana); the author is in a business relationship with his obsession (Gause); the author wants to save the celebrity from harm or some miserable fate (Ledbetter); or the author is convinced the celebrity is someone they are not (Nau).

Stalkers also tend to build shrines to their idols. Nau's one-room apartment in Los Angeles was plastered with posters of both Newton-John and Easton. The six television sets in Perry's motel room had been scrawled with OLIVIA. Ledbetter, like Bardo, had videotaped almost one hundred episodes of her icon's TV show, and posters and photos covered the walls of her room.

Stalkers also make frequent attempts to contact the celebrity by letter, phone, or in person. According to de Becker, an attempt at an actual encounter—as in the case with Bardo when he arrived at Burbank Studios—is the clearest sign of a dangerously obsessed fan.

In many cases there is an overwhelming desire to display love for the celebrity. There have been few instances of stalking preceded by hate mail or threats. Love can be a much more powerful and motivating force than hate. Thus, most of the celebrities who become the object of obsessive fixation are generally unthreatening, open types.

"Most celebrity stalkers are not likely to attempt an encounter with an actor who portrays a cold, ruthless, unattached person, such as Larry Hagman or Joan Collins," says Dietz. "They're more likely to go after the approachable, sweet girl-next-door types . . . like Newton-John."

By its very nature, star stalking is particularly frustrating to law-enforcement agencies. The police and FBI are unequipped, and in most instances are not legally able, to act on letters of love and delusion, which are usually the only tangible indicators of a possible threat. After all, there's nothing illegal about writing love letters—no matter how delusional. The only correspondence likely to swing police into action are threatening letters (and then, only when the threats seem rooted in reality). An Iowa farmer threatening to blow up the Universal Amphitheater frightens nobody.

The problems here are threefold: first, people who communicate a threat to, say, Joan Rivers will probably never act on it. In most instances they have vented their rancor through their pen. Second, most correspondence comes from out of state, which usually takes it out of LAPD jurisdiction. When Gause began writing threatening letters to Carson from Wisconsin, even as far back as 1986, what were the chances of the LAPD extraditing him to a California court? Finally, even if an arrest can be made, prosecuting an obsessed fan, who is usually mentally ill, is almost impossible.

Captain Robert Martin, a twenty-three-year veteran of the LAPD and commander of the police's mental-evaluation unit, noted at a meeting of celebrity managers and agents at the Artist's Protection Seminar in the fall of last year, "I hate to tell you, but if we get a letter of threat we're just mildly interested. No crime has been committed, no reports are generated. We don't do anything with it. You call up and say, 'Some screwball's in my neighborhood.' We say, 'Call us when he does something.' I know that's not what you want to hear. But that's the way it is."

"I cannot guarantee you immediate action," says Kenneth Jacobsen, an FBI agent who specializes in interstate threats. "If you call in a panic and say someone is outside your client's house right now, you've called the wrong agency. . . . If we conduct an investigation, are fortunate enough to identify the individual who's doing the threats, and are able to amass a case that is prosecutable under the statutes, I still can't guarantee it will be prosecuted.

"In Los Angeles," he continues, "you are dealing with limited resources and a grossly understaffed U.S. Attorney's office. We have probably the biggest drug problem in the United States right now. We have one of the biggest bank-failure problems. We have rampant white-collar crime. The threat may be important to you, but it's not going to be one of the priorities of the U.S. Attorney's office."

As a result, most often the problem falls into the hands of security personnel, producers, and managers—people with absolutely no training in dealing with mentally ill, obsessed fans. In fact, many times untrained security personnel and publicists actually exacerbate the situation. Some managers and security guards have made it a point to contact obsessed fans with the hope of talking "sense" to them. Phil Little, CEO of West Coast Detectives, uses the tactic, as do Sylvester Stallone's bodyguards.

And then there is the case of Mary Frann, costar of *Newhart,* who became anxious when she kept receiving letters from an admirer in Portland, Maine. The fan had read an article in a tabloid that quoted Frann as saying she wanted a baby but not, at that time, a husband. The fan offered his services. Frann gave the letters to the head of CBS/MTM Studios security, Ed Lujan, who, in turn, handed them over to a representative of a private-security company.

The firm contacted the fan and told him that Frann had moved from the   52
address to which he was writing and that the current owners, who had read the letters, were terrified the fan was a "Manson-style stalker." The security expert was assuming the fan would believe the post office would not forward his letter. The fan later wrote to several other stars, ridiculing MTM for its ineptitude. Obviously, he bragged, since he was called by Frann's representatives, his mail was read by Frann and it affected her—and he was coming closer to an encounter.

De Becker feels contacting the fan is hazardous. "Most people who write inappropriate letters won't attempt an encounter," he says. "It's not on their agenda. If you call them up they may stop writing. But you may be worse off. . . . For a mentally ill person to receive a phone call or visit from a star's representative, it means the person is that much closer to his obsession. Delusions won't shut off. On the contrary, any sort of contact validates the delusion. Letters can't hurt people, but encounters can."

FBI agent Jacobsen concurs. "I know enough about these cases to know there are individuals who when approached [by law enforcement or security personnel] may go into a violent mode. They may decide that everything they've believed about the relationship with the [celebrity] is true and that they have to kill him or her."

While the bottom line is that there is simply no way to defend oneself successfully against the celebrity stalker, the best defenses, for now, are the fan letters. They are, in almost all cases, the first contact with the star and the significant indicator of the author's mental stability and of the chances that he or she will attempt an encounter. De Becker, an innovator in the field, recently appointed by Governor Deukmejian to his advisory board at the Department of Mental Health, has created the first system to detect and track potential stalkers. In his offices are seven computer terminals used to investigate suspect letters. To date, almost 150,000 pieces of correspondence have gone through the system, a program called MOSAIC, which de Becker and his colleague Walter Risler invented.

The program examines several elements: what the menacing aspect to   56
the letter is; how the author perceives himself (is he God or the smartest

man in the world or Farrah Fawcett's lover?); how the object of a letter is perceived (does a letter to Johnny Carson begin "Dear Dad"?); the intensity of the letter; and how many have been sent.

Based on the above data fed into the computer, MOSAIC spits out a rating. A letter writer is assigned a code, ranging from R1 to R3. So-called R3s signify obsessives, whom de Becker will monitor closely. He says Bardo was probably an R3H, the *H* standing for "high."

De Becker's list of R3s contains nearly six thousand cases (people he thinks pose a threat to his clients). Of these, 216 live in Texas, 481 in New York, and 1,372 in California. Of those who live in California, 373 have tried to make contact with celebrities.

But not everyone—including Schaeffer—can afford a private security force like de Becker's, whose services run upwards of a quarter of a million dollars a year. Though the Industry—including the Screen Actors Guild, management firms, and talent agencies—is beginning to recognize and address the problem, most of L.A.'s colony of rich and famous, even semifamous, currently have to rely on the resources of the overworked LAPD. And the system is still ill-equipped to deal with the stalker.

Several bills have been introduced in California in the past year to curb star obsessives. Just after Schaeffer's murder, Assemblyman Michael Roos authored a bill to limit access by outside agencies and individuals to DMV records, where private-detective agencies hired by Bardo and Jackson found the addresses for Schaeffer and Saldana. In August, state senator Dan McCorquodale introduced SB 1065, which amends civil commitment laws to cover stalker situations such as when a mentally ill person continues to pose a hazard to others. Meanwhile, Assemblyman Richard Katz has introduced several bills and amendments that, among other things, allow the state to take away "good time" and "work time" credits from some prisoners, including those who threaten their victims from jail—such as Arthur Jackson, who vows to kill Saldana when he is released from prison next month. Because of Jackson's threats, officials in the D.A.'s and de Becker's offices are making attempts to ensure that Jackson remains incarcerated.

Even so, for now the best defense against a shadowy world of unknown and unbalanced assailants is to be rich enough to afford a private security army—or just lucky enough to avoid contact with an obsessive. Rebecca Schaeffer was neither.

Bardo is riding a westbound bus headed for Los Angeles. In his bag he carries a change of clothes, some toiletries, a copy of J. D. Salinger's *Catcher in the Rye,* a photo of Schaeffer, the address the detective gave him, a list of things to do—and the Magnum. The list is a step-by-step method by which Bardo will kill Rebecca Schaeffer. It's an idea he may have gotten from watching *Billionaire Boys Club,* the television movie about the methodic murder executed by Joe Hunt. Bardo's list calls for an escape. Specifically,

60

he has instructed himself to scratch the serial number off the .357 Magnum and to discard his clothing.

He arrives in Los Angeles early the next morning. He hurries to Sweetzer Avenue and tries to locate the building where the detective indicated Schaeffer lives. He's wearing a yellow T-shirt, jeans, and flip-flops. When he finds it, he's troubled. It just doesn't look like an apartment building. He goes into a minor panic and wanders up and down the street. He stops people on the street and shows them Schaeffer's photo. Nobody helps him. Eventually, Bardo consults his list again and rings the buzzer that was supposed to be hers.

The building's intercom fails to work. It's been that way for months.   64
When Schaeffer hears the buzzing, she must go down to the door to see for herself who the caller is. As she walks down the hallway in her robe, a bullet tears through two panes of glass in the door and enters her chest. As she collapses, Bardo runs.

Later, police will find a yellow shirt in the alley. Close to it is a copy of *The Catcher in the Rye*. On the building's roof they will find a holster. And no other sign of Schaeffer's murderer.

When Bardo gets off the bus in Tucson, he's dazed. He's several miles from his home, near the Congress Street exit of I-10, and he wanders back and forth along the highway. Some witnesses later say they thought he was trying to get himself hit by oncoming traffic. A policeman arrives and comments that Bardo looks upset. Bardo nods, and the two sit on the curb. I killed her, Bardo tells him quietly. The policeman nods understandingly and then reads him his rights. Now, he says, who was it you said you killed? Bardo stares ahead and tells the officer he wants a lawyer. He is arrested on a misdemeanor charge of obstructing traffic and is brought downtown.

A few hours later, police contact Bardo's father, who tells them his son may have killed Rebecca Schaeffer. Tucson homicide detective Phil Mondrian charges Bardo with Schaeffer's murder, and Bardo is assigned a Pima County public defender, Lorrie Lefferts. Until she meets Bardo, her chief notoriety in town has come from being the sister of San Francisco Giants relief pitcher Craig Lefferts.

Lefferts' plan in the extradition hearing is to prove that Bardo is not   68
mentally competent to understand the extradition process. It's a tactic Lefferts does not recall ever being used in Arizona. She figures she has a strong case. The judge before whom Bardo is brought also serves in the capacity of justice of the peace.

Lefferts is stunned that Bardo's hair has been shorn. It gives him a sinister aura. The procedure is simple. Judge Walter Webber gives Bardo a ten-day stay so Lefferts may organize an appropriate defense against the extradition. Because Lefferts wants Bardo examined by a psychiatrist, a process that may take weeks, she returns to the courtroom the next day to ask for a prolonged stay of the extradition. The D.A. questions whether the judge has jurisdiction in the matter. Webber himself is unsure and agrees that Lefferts should seek the stay elsewhere. The D.A. jumps on this development. Maybe Webber didn't have the authority to grant the extradition at all. Wasn't he serving as justice of the peace at the time he granted the stay of extradition? That duty, in fact, rests with superior-court judges. The D.A. races to the phone and tells the LAPD that he thinks they can come and get their man.

Lefferts arrives at her office at eight the next morning. On her desk is a police report explaining that Bardo had been taken from his cell five hours earlier by LAPD officers and put on a plane bound for California.

At present, Bardo is being held in Los Angeles County Jail awaiting trial sometime this summer. City prosecutor Marcia Clark has charged him with murder in the first degree with special circumstances, making him a death-row candidate. Bardo's plea: not guilty.

Points to Consider

1. What reasons does Rod Lurie supply for the current rise in the number of "star stalkers"? According to Lurie, why is it so difficult to determine what kind of person becomes a "stalker"? Do these people have anything in common?

2. What emotion initially seems to fuel the obsessions of most of these dangerous fans? What kinds of celebrities are most likely to become objects of obsessive fixation? In light of your answer, do you think that women or men are more likely to attract such fans? Does Lurie provide evidence for your conclusion?

3. Why does "star stalking" cause so many problems for law-enforcement agencies? What legal measures can be invoked in such cases? Do you think such measures could be considered preventative or are they merely punitive in nature?

4. Lurie believes that greater access to the lives of stars has been afforded by celebrity magazines, talk shows, and interviews. Do you think that these forums provide a realistic picture of celebrity lives? How might this kind of publicity result in greater potential for obsessiveness in their fans?

Senseless [SPORTS ILLUSTRATED / May 14, 1990]

Is it the Shoes? . . .
Money, it's gotta
be the shoes!

—*Mars Blackmon, to Michael Jordan, in a Nike commercial*

For fifteen-year-old Michael Eugene Thomas, it definitely was the shoes. A ninth-grader at Meade Senior High School in Anne Arundel County, Maryland, Thomas was found strangled on May 2, 1989. Charged with first-degree murder was James David Martin, seventeen, a basketball buddy who allegedly took Thomas's two-week-old Air Jordan basketball shoes and left Thomas's barefoot body in the woods near school.

Thomas loved Michael Jordan, as well as the shoes Jordan endorses, and he cleaned his own pair each evening. He kept the cardboard shoe box with Jordan's silhouette on it in a place of honor in his room. Inside the box was the sales ticket for the shoes. It showed he paid $115.50, the price of a product touched by deity.

"We told him not to wear the shoes to school," said Michael's grandmother, Birdie Thomas. "We said somebody might like them, and he said, 'Granny, before I let anyone take those shoes, they'll have to kill me.' "

Michael Jordan sits in the locked press room before a workout at the   4
Chicago Bulls' practice facility in suburban Deerfield, Illinois. He is wearing his practice uniform and a pair of black Air Jordans similar to the ones young Thomas wore, except that these have Jordan's number, twenty-three, stitched on the sides. On the shoelaces Jordan wears plastic toggles to prevent the shoes from loosening if the laces should come untied. Two toggles come in each box of Air Jordans, and if kids knew that Jordan actually wears

---

RICK TELANDER (b. 1948) is a free-lance writer based in Chicago. He contributes articles to Sports Illustrated, Sport, *and other magazines. He has written several books, including* Heaven Is a Playground *(1976),* Joe Namath and the Other Guys *(1976), and* The Hundred Yard Lie: The Corruption of College Football and What We Can Do to Stop It *(1989).*

them, they would never step out the door without their own toggles securely in place. The door is locked to keep out the horde of fans, journalists, and favor seekers who dog Jordan wherever he goes. Jordan needs a quiet moment. He is reading an account of Thomas's death that a reporter has shown him.

For just an instant it looks as though Jordan might cry. He has so carefully nurtured his image as the all-American role model that he refuses to go anywhere, get into any situation, that might detract from that image. He moves swiftly and smoothly from the court to home to charity events to the golf course, all in an aura of untarnished integrity. "I can't believe it," Jordan says in a low voice. "Choked to death. By his friend." He sighs deeply. Sweat trickles down one temple.

He asks if there have been other such crimes. Yes, he is told. Plenty, unfortunately. Not only for Air Jordans, but also for other brands of athletic shoes, as well as for jackets and caps bearing sports insignia—apparel that Jordan and other athlete endorsers have encouraged American youth to buy.

The killings aren't new. In 1983, fourteen-year-old Dewitt Duckett was shot to death in the hallway of Harlem Park Junior High in Baltimore by someone who apparently wanted Duckett's silky blue Georgetown jacket. In 1985, thirteen-year-old Shawn Jones was shot in Detroit after five youths took his Fila sneakers. But lately the pace of the carnage has quickened. In January 1988, an unidentified fourteen-year-old Houston boy, a star athlete in various sports, allegedly stabbed and killed twenty-two-year-old Eric Allen with a butcher knife after the two argued over a pair of tennis shoes in the home the youths shared with their mothers. Seven months later a gunman in Atlanta allegedly robbed an unnamed seventeen-year-old of his Mercedes-Benz hat and Avia hightops after shooting to death the boy's twenty-five-year-old friend, Carl Middlebrooks, as Middlebrooks pedaled away on his bike. Last November, Raheem Wells, the quarterback for Detroit Kettering High, was murdered, allegedly by six teenagers who swiped his Nike sneakers. A month later, seventeen-year-old Tyrone Brown of Hapeville, Georgia, was fatally shot in the head, allegedly by two acquaintances who robbed him of money, cocaine, and his sneakers. In Baltimore last summer eighteen-year-old Ronnell Ridgeway was robbed of his forty-dollar sweatpants and then shot and killed. In March, Chris Demby, a tenth-grader at Franklin Learning Center in West Philadelphia, was shot and killed for his new Nikes.

In April 1989, sixteen-year-old Johnny Bates was shot to death in Houston by seventeen-year-old Demetrick Walker after Johnny refused to turn over his Air Jordan hightops. In March, Demetrick was sentenced to life in prison. Said prosecutor Mark Vinson, "It's bad when we create an image of luxury about athletic gear that it forces people to kill over it."

Jordan shakes his head.

"I thought I'd be helping out others and everything would be positive," he says. "I thought people would try to emulate the good things I do, they'd try to achieve, to be better. Nothing bad. I never thought because of my endorsement of a shoe, or any product, that people would harm each other. Everyone likes to be admired, but when it comes to kids actually killing each other"—he pauses—"then you have to reevaluate things."

We certainly do. In a country that has long been hung up on style over substance, flash over depth, the athletic shoe and sportswear industries (a projected 5.5 billion dollars in domestic sales of name-brand shoes in 1990; more than $2 billion in sweatpants, sweatshirts, and warmup suits) suddenly have come to represent the pinnacle of consumer exploitation. In recent months the industries, which include heavyweights Nike and Reebok as well as smaller players Adidas, Asics, British Knights, Brooks, Converse, Ellesse, Etonic, Fila, L.A. Gear, New Balance, Pony, Puma, Starter, and numerous other makers of sports shoes, caps, and jackets, have been accused of creating a fantasy-fueled market for luxury items in the economically blasted inner cities and willingly tapping into the flow of drug and gang money. This has led to a frightening outbreak of crimes among poor black kids trying to make their mark by "busting fresh," or dressing at the height of fashion.

In some cities muggings for sportswear are commonplace—Atlanta police, for instance, estimate they have handled more than fifty such robberies in the last four months. Yet it is not only the number of violent acts but also the seeming triviality of the booty that has stunned the public. In February, nineteen-year-old Calvin Wash was about to cross Central Park Avenue on Chicago's West Side when, according to police, two youths drove up in a van and demanded that he give them the Cincinnati Bengal jacket he was wearing. When Wash resisted, one of the youths is alleged to have fatally shot him in the back—through the A in BENGALS.

Chicago police sergeant Michael Chasen, who works in the violent crimes division in Area Four, which covers four of Chicago's twenty-five police districts, says his districts have about fifty reported incidents involving jackets and about a dozen involving gym shoes each month. "When you really think about the crime itself—taking someone's clothes off their body—you can't get much more basic," he says.

But of course, these assailants aren't simply taking clothes from their victims. They're taking status. Something is very wrong with a society that has created an underclass that is slipping into economic and moral oblivion, an underclass in which pieces of rubber and plastic held together by shoelaces are sometimes worth more than a human life. The shoe companies have played a direct role in this. With their million-dollar advertising campaigns, superstar spokesmen, and overdesigned, high-priced products aimed at impressionable young people, they are creating status from thin air to feed those who are starving for self-esteem. "No one person is responsible for this type of violence," says Patricia Graham, principal of Chicago's Simeon High, one of the city's perennial basketball powers. "It's a combination of circumstances. It's about values and training. Society's values are out of sync, which is why these things have become important."

12

"The classic explanation in sociology is that these people are driven by peer pressure," says Mervin Daniel, a sociology professor at Morgan State. "What is advertised on TV and whatever your peers are doing, you do it too." Most assuredly, the shoe industry relies heavily on advertising; it spends more than two hundred million dollars annually to promote and advertise its products, churning out a blizzard of images and words that make its shoes seem preternaturally hip, cool, and necessary. Nike alone will spend sixty million dollars in 1990 on TV and print ads that have built such slogans as "Bo knows," and "Just do it," and "Do you know? Do you know? Do you know?" into mantras of consumerism.

What is baffling, however, is the strength of certain sporting products   16
as icons for drug dealers and gangs. In Boston the Greenwood Street gang wears Green Bay Packer garb, the Vamp Hill Kings wear Los Angeles Kings and Raider gear, and the Castlegate gang wears Cincinnati Reds clothes. "The Intervale gang uses all Adidas stuff exclusively—hats, jackets, sweatpants, shoes," says Bill Stewart III, the probation officer at the Dorchester District Court in Boston, one of the busiest criminal courts in the nation. "They even have an Adidas handshake, copying the three stripes on the product. They extend three fingers when they shake hands."

Stewart knows how certain young drug dealers feverishly load up on the latest models of sneakers, tossing out any old ones that are scuffed or even slightly worn and replacing them with new pairs. "I was in a kid's apartment recently and there were about fifty pairs of brand-new sneakers, all top-of-the-line stuff—Adidas, Reebok, and so forth," he says. "I asked the kid's mother how he came into all this stuff. She said she didn't know."

The use of Major League Baseball hats by gangs has prompted some high schools around the nation to ban them from school grounds, and expensive gold chains, major league or major college team jackets, and other ostentatious, potentially troublesome items have also been prohibited. "When I look around sometimes, I think I'm in spring training in Florida," says Stewart.

When informed that baseball caps are being used by gangs as part of their uniforms, Major League Baseball public relations director Richard Levin seemed shocked. "I'm not aware of it at all, nor would I understand why," he said. "Obviously, we don't support it in any way."

Could any respectable U.S. corporation support the use of its products   20
in this way? Absolutely not, said most shoe company executives contacted for this article. You better believe it, said a number of sports apparel retailers, as well as some of the more candid shoe execs.

Among the retailers is Wally Grigo, the owner of three sportswear shops in and near New Haven, Connecticut. Last August, Grigo put a sign in the front window of his inner-city store that reads, IF YOU DEAL DRUGS, WE DON'T WANT YOUR BUSINESS. SPEND YOUR MONEY SOMEWHERE ELSE. "Unfortunately, it'll probably have to stay up forever," says Grigo. "I was doing, I'd say, two thousand dollars a week in drug money sales that disappeared after the sign went up. Our industry is sick, addicted to drug money. We're going through the first phase of addiction, which is total denial."

Before he put up the sign, Grigo had been told by sales reps from two sportswear companies that he should "hook up" the local drug dealers to expose the companies' new products to the neighborhood clientele. After the sign went up, Grigo says, the rep from the smaller company returned and said, "Wally, we're thinking about giving you the line. But, you know, I can't do anything until you cut out the crap and take that sign out of your window. The bulk of our business is done with drug dealers. Wake up!"

Grigo was so stunned that he thought of wearing a wire to record the rep making similar statements. He didn't do so, though, figuring the company's officials would dismiss any evidence by saying the rep was a loose cannon. But Grigo says the companies know what's going on, because the reps are "in the trenches, and they go back and report."

Grigo doesn't want to publicly state the names of the suppliers, for economic reasons. "I'm not afraid of the drug dealers," he says. "But the shoe companies could put me out of business anytime, just by canceling my credit." 24

One obvious question: how does Grigo, or anyone, know when a drug dealer and not a law-abiding citizen is making a buy? "Hey, spend ten minutes in any city store," says Grigo. "When an eighteen-year-old kid pulls up in a BMW, walks down the aisle saying, 'I want this, this, this, and this,' then peels off fifties from a stack of bills three inches thick, maybe doesn't even wait for change, then comes back a couple weeks later and does the same thing, hey . . . you know what I'm saying?"

And what about all those good guys advertising the shoes? What about Nike's Jordan and Spike Lee, the gifted filmmaker and actor who portrays Mars Blackmon, the hero-worshipping nerd in the company's Air Jordan ads? Are they and other pitchmen at fault, too?

"Maybe the problem is those guys don't know what's going on," says Grigo. "There are stores doing five thousand to ten thousand dollars a week in drug money, all over. Drug money is part of the economic landscape these days. Even if the companies don't consciously go after the money, they're still getting it. Hey, all inner-city kids aren't drug dealers. Most of them are good, honest kids. Drug dealers are a very small percent. But the drug dealers, man, they set the fashion trends."

Liz Dolan, director of public relations for Nike, hits the ceiling when she hears such talk. "Our commercials are about sport, they're not about fashion," she says. 28

But the industry's own figures make that assertion extremely questionable. At least 80 percent of the athletic shoes sold in the United States are not used for their avowed purpose—that is, playing sports.

Dolan sighs. She says that all of Nike's athlete-endorsers are quality citizens as well as superjocks. "We're not putting Leon Spinks in the commercials," she says. Then she says that the people who raise the alarm that

Nike, as well as other sports apparel companies, is exploiting the poor and creating crime just to make money are bizarre and openly racist. "What's baffling to us is how easily people accept the assumption that black youth is an unruly mob that will do anything to get its hands on what it wants," she says, excitedly. "They'll say, 'Show a black kid something he wants, and he'll kill for it.' I think it's racist hysteria, just like the Charles Stuart case in Boston or the way the Bush campaign used Willie Horton."

Lee also says he has heard such panic before. "Everybody said last summer that my movie *Do the Right Thing* was going to cause thirty million black people to riot," he says angrily. "But I haven't heard of one garbage can being thrown through a pizzeria window, have you? I want to work with Nike to address the special problems of inner-city black youths, but the problem is not shoes."

Lee is particularly irate because he has been singled out by *New York Post* sports columnist Phil Mushnick as being untrue to the very people Lee champions in his films. In Mushnick's April 6 column headlined, SHADDUP, I'M SELLIN' OUT . . . SHADDUP, he sharply criticized Lee for leading the hype. The caption under four photos—one of Lee; the others of soaring pairs of Air Jordans—said, "While Spike Lee watches Michael Jordan (or at least his shoes) dunk all over the world, parents around the country are watching their kids get mugged, or even killed, over the same sneakers Lee and Jordan are promoting." In his column Mushnick said, "It's murder, gentlemen. No rhyme, no reason, just murder. For sneakers. For jackets. Get it, Spike? Murder." 32

Lee wrote a response in *The National,* the daily sports newspaper, in which he angrily accused Mushnick of "thinly veiled racism" for going after him and other high-profile black endorsers and not white endorsers like Larry Bird or Joe Montana. Lee also questioned Mushnick's sudden "great outpouring of concern for Afro-American youths." Lee wrote, "The Nike commercials Michael Jordan and I do have never gotten anyone killed. . . . The deal is this: let's try to effectively deal with the conditions that make a kid put so much importance on a pair of sneakers, a jacket, and gold. These kids feel they have no options, no opportunities."

Certainly Lee is right about that. Elijah Anderson, a University of Pennsylvania sociologist who specializes in ethnography, the study of individual cultures, links the scourge of apparel-related crimes among young black males to "inequality in race and class. The uneducated, inner-city kids don't have a sense of opportunity. They feel the system is closed off to them. And yet they're bombarded with the same cultural apparatus that the white middle class is. They don't have the means to attain the things offered, and yet they have the same desire. So they value these 'emblems,' these symbols of supposed success. The gold, the shoes, the drug dealer's outfit—those things all belie the real situation, but it's a symbolic display that seems to say that things are all right.

"Advertising fans this whole process by presenting the images that appeal to the kids, and the shoe companies capitalize on the situation, because it exists. Are the companies abdicating responsibility by doing this? That's a hard one to speak to. This is, after all, a free market."

But what about social responsibility? One particularly important issue 36 is the high price of shoes—many companies have models retailing for considerably more than one hundred dollars, with the Reebok Pump leading the parade at $170. There is also the specific targeting of young black males as buyers, through the use of seductive, macho-loaded sales pitches presented by black stars.

"You can quibble about our tactics, but we don't stand for the drug trade," says Dolan. She points out that Nike's fall promotion campaign will include five million dollars worth of "strictly pro-education, stay-in-school" public service commercials that will "not run late at night, but on the same major sporting events as the prime-time ads." Nike is not alone in playing the good corporate citizen. Reebok recently gave $750,000 to fund Project Teamwork, a program designed to combat racism that is administered by the Center for the Study of Sport in Society at Northeastern University.

Nevertheless, certain products wind up having dubious associations—some products more than others. John Hazard, the head buyer for the chain of City Sports stores in Boston, says, "We used to have brawls in here, robberies, a tremendous amount of stealing. But we cut back on 90 percent of it by getting rid of certain products. We don't carry Adidas, Fila, British Knights. Those things bring in the gangs.

"There's a store not far away that carries all that stuff. They have after-hours sales to show the new lines to big drug dealers. They even have guys on beepers, to let them know when the latest shoes have come in. It would be nothing for those guys to buy twenty, thirty pair of shoes to give to all their twelve-year-old runners."

He thinks for a moment. "I don't know if you can really blame the shoe 40 companies for what happens. Not long ago there was a murder, a gang deal, here in Boston. The cops had the murderer, and they were walking him somewhere. It was on TV. The murderer was bent over at first, and then the cops stood him up, and—I couldn't believe it—all of a sudden you could see he was wearing a City Sports T-shirt. There's no way you can control what people wear."

John Donahoe, manager of a Foot Locker store in Chicago's Loop, agrees. "Right now, this is the hottest thing we've got," he says, holding up a simple, ugly, blue nylon running shoe. Behind him are shelves filled with more than one hundred different model or color variations. "Nike Cortez: thirty-nine dollars," he says. "Been around for twenty years. Why is it hot now?" He shrugs. "I don't know."

Assistant manager James Crowder chimes in helpfully, "It's not the price, or who's endorsing it. It's just . . . what's happening."

Keeping up with what's happening has shoe manufacturers scrambling these days. "It used to be you could have a product out and fiddle with it for years, to get it just right," says Roger Morningstar, the assistant vice president of promotions at Converse. "Now, if you don't come out with two or three new models every month, you're dead."

At home I go to my closet and pull out my own meager assortment of sports shoes—nine pairs, all told. A pair of ancient turf football shoes; some nubbed softball shoes; a pair of old running shoes; a pair of original, hideous red-and-black Air Jordans, kept for historical reasons; a pair of Avia volleyball shoes, worn out, though they were never used for their intended purpose; two pairs of low-cut tennis shoes (or are they walking shoes?); a pair of Nike cross-training shoes (though I don't cross-train or even know what it means) in bad shape; a pair of sweat-stained, yet still awe-inspiring hightop basketball Reebok Pumps, a Christmas gift from my sister and brother-in-law. I pick these up. They are happening. 44

There are three colors on them, and the words REEBOK BASKETBALL are stitched in the tongue, right below the wondrous pump itself, colored orange and pebbled to resemble a basketball. On the bottom of the shoes are three colors of textured rubber. And there is an indented section in the heel with clear plastic laid over four orange tubes, and embossed with the words REEBOK ENERGY RETURN SYSTEM. On the back of the hightops there is the orange release valve that, when touched, decompresses the whole shebang.

The shoes haven't changed my hoops game at all, though they are comfortable, unless I pump them up too much and my toes slowly go numb. While I could never bring myself to pay for a pair out of my own pocket, I will admit that when I opened the shoe box on Christmas Day, I was thrilled by the sheer techno-glitz of the things. It was identical to the way I felt when, at the age of eight, I received a Robert-the-Robot.

But can promoting athletic shoes possibly be wrong in a capitalist society? Reebok chairman Paul Fireman was recently quoted as describing the Pump as "a product that's aspirational to a young person"—that is, something to be desired. He added, if prospective buyers couldn't afford the shoes, "that's the place for a kid to get a job after school." What, indeed, is the point of ads if not to inform the public of products that it may or may not need, but that it may wish to buy? Should we demand that the sports shoe industry be held to a higher standard than, say, the junk food industry? The advertising community itself thought so highly of Nike's "Bo knows" spot with Bo Jackson and Bo Diddley that *Advertising Age* named Jackson its Star Presenter of 1989.

What are we looking for here, anyway? 48

"Responsibility," says Grigo, the New Haven store owner. "Have Spike Lee and Michael Jordan look at the camera and say, 'Drug dealers, don't you dare wear my shoes!' Put antidrug labels on the box. I already do at my stores."

"Everybody wants us to do everything," says Nike's Dolan. "It's naive to think an antidrug message on the shoe box is going to change anyone's behavior. Our theme is 'Just do it!' because we want people playing sports, because they'll need more shoes. The healthier people are, the more shoes we'll sell."

Trouble is, young black males—a significant portion of the market—are not healthy right now. In fact, 23 percent of black males between the ages of twenty and twenty-nine are under the supervision of the criminal justice system—incarcerated, paroled, or on probation. According to a 1989 study in the *Journal of the American Medical Association,* a black male is six times more likely to be a homicide victim than a white male. Writes *Washington Post* columnist William Raspberry: "The inability of so many young black men to see themselves as providers, or even as necessary to their families, may be one explanation for their irresponsible behavior." Marc Mauer, of the Sentencing Project, a nonprofit group concerned with disparities in the administration of criminal justice, says, "We now risk the possibility of writing off an entire generation of black men."

Obviously we are talking about something bigger than shoes here. Jordan sits up straight in his chair. It's time for practice to start. "I'd rather eliminate the product [the shoes] than know drug dealers are providing the funds that pay me," he says.   52

Of course drug money is, to a troubling extent, supporting the product, as well as other brands of sneakers and sports apparel. And kids are being killed for them. So what should the shoe companies, the schools, the advertising industry, the endorsers, the media, parents—all of us—do about it?

Do you know? Do you know? Do you know?

Points to Consider

1. If, as Rick Telander argues, the rise in violent crimes related to athletic shoes and other sportswear is due to the promotion of such articles by their manufacturers, what particular aspects of the advertising campaigns might be the source of the problem?

2. What do products like Air Jordan basketball shoes represent to young people? To what extent does celebrity involvement in endorsements create such an impression? Why have these products been adopted by drug dealers and gangs?

3. Spike Lee maintains that society must attempt to "deal with the conditions that make a kid put so much importance on a pair of sneakers, a jacket, and gold." In your opinion, does advertising help to create such conditions? Specifically, what is the message being sent to youths by Air Jordan ads?

4. Sportswear store owner Wally Grigo suggests, "Have Spike Lee and

Michael Jordan look at the camera and say, 'Drug dealers, don't you dare wear my shoes!' " Do you think that Grigo's solution would help to eliminate apparel-related crime? Can you think of other ways that celebrities can be employed to exert a positive influence upon youth?

Discussing the Unit

Suggested Topic for Discussion

Two of the pieces in this unit explore the dangers of fame for both the celebrities themselves and their fans. In "Guns n' Roses," Rod Lurie stresses the role of mental illness in dangerous fan behavior, whereas Rick Telander in "Senseless" tends to cite sociological conditions as the reason for apparel-related crime. America's obsession with celebrity, then, would seem to be the common source for both phenomena. Although Lewis H. Lapham's essay offers some philosophical reasons for our national obsession, how would you explain a celebrity's power to hold our attention and influence our lives? What does fame symbolize in American culture and what needs do celebrities fill in the lives of many fans?

Preparing for Class Discussion

1. Make a list of the people you admire most. How many of the names are those of celebrities? How many are those of people you actually know and with whom you have frequent contact? If you placed a number of celebrities on your list, in what ways do you think they have influenced the way you think and act?

2. In recent years, many celebrities in entertainment have attempted to project a more positive image by promoting social, political, medical, environmental, and other types of causes. Do you think that such involvement improves the images of celebrities? How has such involvement affected your own view of a celebrity's importance in society? How many celebrities can you name who are currently linked with a cause? What kinds of causes are most popular among celebrities?

From Discussion to Writing

Publicity about celebrities often creates unrealistic perceptions of them. To what extent do you think that publicity or advertising campaigns foster obsessive behavior in fans, in relation not only to the celebrities but to the products they endorse? Choose a celebrity and think about the image he or she has created. Write an essay in which you evaluate how the celebrity's image has been responsible for his or her success. What aspects of the image do you find most attractive? Are there any aspects of the image that you find unattractive? Be sure to use examples and evidence to support your conclusions.

18

God or Goddess:
Does It Make Any Difference?

One of the heated religious controversies of our time has focused on the issue of divine gender: why is God perceived as male and how did that perception come about? The issue is a complex one, involving feminist studies, new Biblical scholarship, and recent discoveries in anthropology and archeology. Many studies have concentrated on the role of women and male bias in the Bible, some studies have pursued abstract theological questions pertaining to the nature of divinity, and other examinations — such as the two in this unit — have turned to history, myth, and magic for insights into the cultural processes that led to a male divinity.

Some religious scholars point to the "Big Discovery" as the force behind the evolution of religion in Western civilization. Briefly, the theory of the Big Discovery attempts to explain the historical origins of male dominance in the biological discovery that sperm contribute to conception. Before this discovery, this theory suggests, procreation was apparently seen as uniquely female, and women were therefore accorded a more prestigious role in their cultures.

The importance of the Big Discovery is challenged in Riane Eisler's "Our Lost Heritage: New Facts on How God Became a Man." Using archeological evidence, Eisler constructs a different series of events, one that finds the origins of a male-oriented religion not in the biological discovery of paternity but in prehistoric military invasions that destroyed the world's first true civilizations.

The scholarly side of goddess worship is only one side of the issue. In "Oh, Goddess!" Rusty Unger investigates several groups who participate in goddess ceremonies and profiles some of today's women who have created a new religion from ancient myths and magical practices. Goddess worship, she shows, is not only a subject for historical research but a contemporary reality.

RIANE EISLER

Our Lost Heritage: New Facts on How God Became a Man [THE HUMANIST / May–June 1985]

In the nineteenth century, archeological excavations began to confirm what scholars of myth had long maintained — that goddess worship preceded the worship of God. After reluctantly accepting what no longer could be ignored, religious historians proposed a number of explanations for why there had been this strange switch in divine gender. A long-standing favorite has been the so-called Big Discovery theory. This is the idea that, when men finally became aware that women did not bring forth children by themselves — in other words, when they discovered that it involved their sperm, their paternity — this inflamed them with such a new-found sense of importance that they not only enslaved women but also toppled the goddess.

Today, new archeological findings — particularly post–World War II excavations — are providing far more believable answers to this long-debated puzzle. For largely due to more scientific archeological methods,

---

RIANE EISLER (b. 1931) is codirector for the Center for Partnership Studies and a national and international lecturer. She is the author of Dissolutions: No Fault Divorce, Marriage, and the Future of Women *(1977),* The Equal Rights Handbook: What ERA Means to Your Life, Your Rights, and the Future *(1978), and* The Chalice and the Blade: Our History, Our Future *(1987).*

including infinitely more accurate [archeological, dating methods] such as radiocarbon and dendrochronology,[1] there has been a veritable archeological revolution.

As James Mellaart of the London University Institute of Archeology writes, we now know that there were in fact many cradles of civilization, all of them thousands of years older than Sumer, where civilization was long said to have begun about five thousand years ago.[2] But the most fascinating discovery about these original cultural sites is that they were structured along very different lines from what we have been taught is the divinely, or naturally, ordained human order.

One of these ancient cradles of civilization is Catal Huyuk, the largest 4
Neolithic site yet found. Located in the Anatolian plain of what is now Turkey, Catal Huyuk goes back approximately eight thousand years to about 6500 B.C.E. — three thousand years before Sumer. As Mellaart reports, this ancient civilization "is remarkable for its wall-paintings and plaster reliefs, its sculpture in stone and clay . . . , its advanced technology in the crafts of weaving, woodwork, metallurgy . . . , its advanced religion . . . , its advanced practices in agriculture and stockbreeding, and . . . a flourishing trade. . . ."[3]

But undoubtedly the most remarkable thing about Catal Huyuk and other original sites for civilization is that they were *not* warlike, hierarchic, and male-dominated societies like ours. As Mellaart writes, over the many centuries of its existence, there were in Catal Huyuk no signs of violence or deliberate destruction, "no evidence for any sack or massacre." Moreover, while there was evidence of some social inequality, "this is never a glaring one." And most significantly — in the sharpest possible contrast to our type of social organization — "the position of women was obviously an important one . . . with a fertility cult in which a goddess was the principal deity."[4]

Now it is hardly possible to believe that in this kind of society, where, besides all their other advances, people clearly understood the principles of stockbreeding, they would not have also had to understand that procreation involves the male. So the Big Discovery theory is not only founded on the fallacious assumption that men are naturally brutes, who were only deterred from forcefully enslaving women by fear of the female's "magical" powers of procreation; the Big Discovery theory is also founded on assumptions about what happened in prehistory that are no longer tenable in light of the *really* big discoveries we are now making about our lost human heritage — about societies that, while not ideal, were clearly more harmonious than ours.

---

[1] Radiocarbon dating is a method of establishing the age of prehistoric artifacts by measuring the radioactivity of carbon; dendrochronology is a dating procedure based on counting the growth rings of trees.

[2] J. Mellaart, *The Neolithic of the Near East* (New York: Charles Scribner's Sons, 1975). [Au.]

[3] J. Mellaart, *Catal Huyuk* (New York: McGraw-Hill, 1967), p. 11. [Au.]

[4] Ibid., pp. 69, 225, 553. [Au.]

But if the replacement of a <u>Divine Mother with a Divine Father</u> was not <u>due to men's discovery of paternity</u>, how did it come to pass that all our present world religions either have no female deity or generally present them as "consorts" or subservient wives of male gods?

To try to answer that question, let us look more carefully at the new archeological findings.

8

Logic would lead one to expect what ancient myths have long indicated and archeology has since confirmed: that since life issues from woman, not man, the first anthropomorphic deity was female rather than male. But logical or not, this position was hardly that of the first excavators of Paleolithic caves, some of whom were monks, such as the well-known Abbé Henri Breuil. They consistently refused to see in the many finds of twenty-five-thousand-year-old stylized female sculptures what they clearly were: representations of a female divinity, a Great Mother. Instead, the large-breasted, wide-hipped, bountiful, and often obviously pregnant women these men christened "Venus figurines" were described either as sex objects (products of men's erotic fantasies) or deformed, ugly women.[5] Moreover, in order to conform to their model of history as the story of "man the hunter" and "man the warrior," they refused to see what was actually in the famous cave paintings. As Alexander Marshack has now established, not only did they insist that stylized painting of tree branches and plants were weapons, they sometimes described these pictures as backward arrows or harpoons, chronically missing their mark![6] They also, as Andre Leroi-Gourhan noted in his major study of the Paleolithic, insisted on interpreting the already quite advanced art of the period as an expression of hunting magic, a view borrowed from extremely primitive contemporary societies like the Australian aborigines.[7]

Although Leroi-Gourhan's interpretation of the objects and paintings found in Paleolithic caves is in sexually stereotyped terms, he stresses that the art of the Paleolithic was first and foremost religious art, concerned with the mysteries of life, death, and regeneration.[8] And it is again this concern that is expressed in the rich art of the Neolithic, which, as Mellaart points out, not only shows a remarkable continuity with the Paleolithic,[9] but clearly foreshadows the great goddess of later Bronze Age civilizations in her various forms of Isis, Nut, and Maat in Egypt, Ishtar, Lillith, or Astarte in the Middle

---

[5] See, for example, E. O. James, *The Cult of the Mother Goddess* (London: Thames and Hudson, 1959), and M. Gimbutas, "The Image of Woman in Prehistoric Art," *Quarterly Review of Archeology*, December 1981. [Au.]

[6] A. Marshack, *The Roots of Civilization* (New York: McGraw-Hill, 1972). [Au.]

[7] A. Leroi-Gourhan, *Prehistoire de l'Art Occidental* (Paris: Edition D'Art Lucien Mazenod, 1971). [Au.]

[8] Ibid. [Au.]

[9] J. Mellaart, *Catal Huyuk*, p. 11. [Au.]

East, the sun-goddess Arinna of Anatolia, as well as such later goddesses as Demeter, Artemis, and Kore in Greece, Atargatis, Ceres, and Cybele in Rome, and even Sophia or Wisdom of the Christian Middle Ages, the Shekinah of Hebrew Kabalistic tradition, and, of course, the Virgin Mary or Holy Mother of the Catholic Church about whom we read in the Bible.[10]

This same prehistoric and historic continuity is stressed by UCLA archeologist Marija Gimbutas, whose monumental work, *The Goddesses and Gods of Old Europe,* brings to life yet another Neolithic civilization: the indigenous civilization that sprang up in the Balkans and Greece long, long before the rise of Indo-European Greece.[11] Once again, the archeological findings in what Gimbutas termed the civilizations of Old Europe not only demolish the old "truism" of the "warlike Neolithic" but also illuminate our true past, again showing that here, too, the original direction of human civilization was in some ways far more civilized than ours, with pre-Indo-Europeans living in far greater harmony with one another and the natural environment.

Moreover, excavations in Old Europe, like those unearthed in other parts of the ancient world, show that what brought about the onset of male dominance both in heaven and on earth was not some sudden male discovery. What ushered it in was the onslaught of barbarian hordes from the arid steppes and deserts on the fringe areas of our globe. It was wave after wave of these pastoral invaders who destroyed the civilizations of the first settled agrarian societies. And it was they who brought with them the gods — and men — of war that made so much of later or recorded history the bloodbath we are now taught was the *totality* of human history.

12

In Old Europe, as Gimbutas painstakingly documents, there were three major invasionary waves as the Indo-European peoples she calls the Kurgans wiped out or "Kurganized" the European populations. "The Old European and Kurgan cultures were the antithesis of one another," writes Gimbutas. She continues:

> The Old Europeans were sedentary horticulturalists prone to live in large well-planned townships. The absence of fortifications and weapons attests the peaceful coexistence of this egalitarian civilization that was probably matrilinear and matrilocal. . . . The Old European belief system focused on the agricultural cycle of birth, death, and regeneration, embodied in the feminine principle, a Mother Creatrix. The Kurgan ideology, as known from comparative Indo-European mythology, exalted virile, heroic warrior gods of the shining and thunderous sky. Weapons are nonexistent in Old European

[10] See, for example, R. Eisler, *The Chalice and the Blade: Our History, Our Future* (New York: Harper and Row, 1987); M. Stone, *When God Was a Woman* (New York: Harvest, 1976); E. Neumann, *The Great Mother* (Princeton, NJ: Princeton University Press, 1955). [Au.]

[11] M. Gimbutas, *The Goddesses and Gods of Old Europe* (Berkeley, CA: University of California Press, 1982). [Au.]

imagery; whereas the dagger and battle-axe are dominant symbols of the Kurgans, who, like all historically known Indo-Europeans, glorified the lethal power of the sharp blade.[12]

So while we are still commonly taught that it was to Indo-European invaders — such as the Aechaean warriors, celebrated by Homer, who eventually sacked Troy — that we owe our Western heritage, we now know that they in fact did not bring us civilization. Rather, they destroyed, degraded, and brutalized a civilization already highly advanced along wholly different lines. And, just as the factuality of how these truly savage peoples demoted both women and goddesses to the subservient status of consort or wife has now been established, the fact [that] they brought in warfare with them is also confirmed.

Once again, as when Heinrich Schliemann defied the archeological establishment and proved that the city of Troy was not Homeric fantasy but prehistoric fact, new archeological findings verify ancient legends and myths. For instance, the Greek poet Hesiod, who wrote about the same time as Homer, tells us of a "golden race," who lived in "peaceful ease" in a time when "the fruitful earth poured forth her fruits." And he laments how they were eventually replaced by "a race of bronze" who "ate not grain" (in other words, were not farmers) and instead specialized in warfare ("the all-lamented sinful works of Ares were their chief care").[13]

Perhaps one of the most fascinating legends of ancient times is, of course, that of the lost civilization of Atlantis. And here again, as with the once only legendary city of Troy, archeological findings illuminate our true past. For what new findings suggest is what the eminent Greek scholar Spyridon Martinatos already suspected in 1939: that the legend of a great civilization which sank into the Atlantic is actually the garbled folk memory of the Minoan civilization of Crete and surrounding Mediterranean islands, portions of which did indeed disappear into the sea after unprecedented volcanic eruptions sometime after 1500 B.C.E.[14]

First discovered at the turn of this century, the once unknown Bronze Age civilization of ancient Crete has now been far more extensively excavated. As Nicolas Platon, former superintendent of antiquities in Crete and director of the Acropolis Museum, who excavated the island for over thirty years, writes, Minoan civilization was "an astonishing achievement." It reflected "a highly sophisticated art and way of life," indeed producing some of the most beautiful art the world has ever seen. Also in this remarkable society — the only place where the worship of the goddess and the influence

---

[12] M. Gimbutas, "The First Wave of Eurasian Steppe Pastoralists in Copper Age Europe," *Journal of Indo-European Studies,* 1977, p. 281. [Au.]

[13] Hesiod, quoted in J. M. Robinson, *An Introduction to Early Greek Philosophy* (Boston: Houghton Mifflin, 1968), pp. 12–14. [Au.]

[14] S. Martinatos, "The Volcanic Destruction of Minoan Crete," *Antiquity,* 1939, 13:425–439. [Au.]

of women in the public sphere survived into historic times, where "the whole of life was pervaded by an ardent faith in the goddess Nature, the source of all creation and harmony" — there was still "a love of peace, a horror of tyranny, and a respect for the law."[15]

And once again, it was not men's discovery of their biological role in paternity that led to the toppling of the goddess. It was another, final Indo-European invasion: the onslaught of the Dorians, who, with their weapons of iron, as Hesiod writes, brought death and destruction in their wake.[16]

So the revolution in norms that literally stood reality on its head — that established this seemingly fundamental and sacrosanct idea that we are the creations of a Divine Father, who all by Himself brought forth all forms of life — was in fact a relatively late event in the history of human culture. Moreover, this drastic change in direction of cultural evolution, which set us on the social course that in our nuclear age threatens to destroy all life, was certainly not predetermined or, by any stretch of the imagination, inevitable. Rather than being some mystical mystery, it was the substitution of a force-based model of social organization for one in which both the female and male halves of humanity viewed the supreme power in the universe not as the "masculine" power to destroy but rather as the "feminine" power to give and nurture life.

Another popular old idea about this change was that it was the replacement of matriarchy with patriarchy. But my research of many years shows that matriarchy is simply the flip side of the coin to the *dominator* model of society, based upon the dominance of men over women that we call patriarchy. The real alternative to patriarchy, already foreshadowed by the original direction of human civilization, is what I have called the *partnership* model of social relations.[17] Based upon the full and equal partnership between the female and male halves of our species, this model was already well-established a long time ago, before, as the Bible has it, a male god decreed that woman be subservient to man.

The new knowledge about our true human heritage is still meeting enormous resistance, with traditional "experts" from both the religious and academic establishments crying heresy. But it is a knowledge that, in the long run, cannot be suppressed.

It is a knowledge that demolishes many old misconceptions about our past. It also raises many fascinating new questions. Is the real meaning of

[15] N. Platon, *Crete* (Geneva: Nagel, 1966), pp. 48, 148. [Au.]

[16] Hesiod, see note 13. [Au.]

[17] See, for example, R. Eisler, *The Chalice and the Blade;* R. Eisler "Violence and Male-Dominance: The Ticking Time Bomb," *Humanities in Society,* Winter–Spring 1984, 7:1/2:3–18; R. Eisler and D. Loye, "The 'Failure' of Liberalism: A Reassessment of Ideology from a New Feminine-Masculine Perspective," *Political Psychology,* 1983, 4:2:375–391; R. Eisler, "Beyond Feminism: The Gylan Future," *Alternative Futures,* Spring–Summer 1981, 4:2/3: 122–134. [Au.]

the legend of our fall from paradise that, rather than having transgressed in some horrible way, Eve should have obeyed the advice of the serpent (long associated with the oracular or prophetic powers of the goddess) and *continued* to eat from the tree of knowledge? Did the custom of sacrificing the first-born child develop after the destruction of this earlier world — as the Bible has it, after our expulsion from the Garden of Eden — when women had been turned into mere male-controlled technologies of reproduction, as insurance of a sort that conception had not occurred before the bride was handed over to her husband?

We may never have complete answers to such questions, since archeology only provides some of the data and ancient writings, such as the Old Testament, were rewritten so many times, each time to more firmly establish, and sanctify, male control.[18] But what we do have is far more critical in this time when the old patriarchal system is leading us ever closer to global holocaust. This is the knowledge that it was not always this way: there are viable alternatives that may not only offer us survival but also a far, far better world.

[18] Ibid. [Au.]

Points to Consider

1. What does Eisler's evidence primarily consist of? How does it help give scientific validity to her claims?

2. What does Eisler find wrong with the Big Discovery theory? Why does she find it hard to believe that early civilizations were unaware of biological paternity?

3. What did early archeologists miss in their investigations of prehistoric cultures? Why did they not see these things? What new evidence is available?

4. Why does Eisler reject the "old idea" that the major change in religion and culture was from matriarchy to patriarchy? Why does she find that view of the transformation erroneous?

Oh, Goddess! [NEW YORK / June 4, 1990]

In the Morristown, New Jersey, Unitarian Fellowship Center, in an attic room lit by candlelight, thirteen women have assembled in a circle to celebrate the full moon. That moon is particularly luminous tonight against the rich, deep winter sky, its platinum glow visible from the dormer windows. Among those gathered are a sculptor, a biologist, a professor, and a computer-systems analyst, ranging in age from seventeen to sixty-eight. On the large round mirror on the floor in the center of the circle are a mass of flickering candles and pieces of jade, coral, pumice, and lava. There is a huge conch shell filled with water, a small bronze statue of a fertility goddess, and a long plastic tropical flower. The shell is passed around, each woman anointing the forehead of the person to her left: "I, Donna, bless thee, Tiffany. Thou art Goddess."

The women begin to chant and tap tambourines and shake feathered rattles, their voices occasionally breaking off from the song to trill and hum their own private arias to the glory of the Goddess, the divine female principle that represents for them the mysterious and sacred procreative powers of women inherent in the Earth and its cycles of birth and rebirth. You can almost hear Helen Reddy: "I am woman—hear me roar."

Next, the plastic flower, a ceremonial "talking stick," circulates. Whoever holds it is free to speak. But at least one stunned woman—a visitor and a first-timer—is at a loss for words.

The ceremony is being led by the computer analyst, a well-preserved   4
grandmother with a striking resemblance to Shirley Temple Black. She is wearing a grass skirt and a cowrie necklace with the shells "turned out, like vulvas." In keeping with the Hawaiian motif she has chosen, her self-styled ritual involves a series of hula dances and a taped selection of Hawaiian

RUSTY UNGER (b. 1945) has written articles for the Newsday Magazine, *the* New York Times, Mirabella, Look, Harper's Bazaar, *and other publications. A graduate of the University of Pennsylvania, Unger has worked in book publishing, magazine publishing, and motion pictures. She is the co-editor and writer of* Not the New York Times *(1978) and the humor book* The 90's: A Look Back *(1990).*

songs. After the recitation of an ode to the Hawaiian goddess of the volcano, the women are urged to rise and dance the hula on their own.

Donna Wilshire, a lithe, middle-aged writer and professional performer of Goddess myths ("collages of song, dance, and dramatized verse and history"), watches the performance with her mouth half open. Since the mid-seventies, Wilshire has been a devotee of feminist spirituality and an avid proselytizer for the movement. She fears that tonight's pagan pastiche could be enough to convince a guest that Goddess worship is, well, a little off the wall.

By some estimates, more than a hundred thousand people across the United States worship the Goddess. Notices of their moon circles are pinned to bulletin boards in suburban supermarkets and near the checkout counters of health-food stores. Recently, fliers announcing Goddess meetings have been taped to the mirrors of the women's rest rooms at Merrill Lynch and at a nurse's station in New York Hospital.

While adopting a religion based on the pagan worship of nature may seem extreme, some of the practices have caught on. "You wouldn't believe the number of cars and drivers sitting out on East Ninth Street while some lady in a Chanel suit was inside buying tarot cards or a copy of Robert Graves's *The White Goddess*," says Dee Kissinger, a fortuneteller who used to work at Enchantments, a Goddess store in the East Village.

8

Many of those who dabble become disciples. Since the rebirth of feminism in the seventies and amid growing disenchantment with organized religion, thousands of Americans have moved—to borrow the title of a book by philosopher Mary Daly—beyond God the father.

For some, like Donna Wilshire, goddess worship is the spiritual aspect of feminism. Viewing themselves as an oppressed class, these women have rejected the patriarchal, hierarchical tenets of the Judeo-Christian ethic. (Buddhism is also on their hit list.) Their spiritual quest reaches all the way back to the Stone Age worship of fertility goddesses, to shamanism and witchcraft, where they find strong, holy images of women to revere. This "feminist theology" or "feminist spirituality" celebrates a composite archetype: part Neolithic fertility symbol, part Hera, part woman warrior.

Along the same lines, many worshipers see the Goddess as Mother Nature, and they follow a pantheistic principle that calls for living in harmony with the Earth and its seasons. Many men as well as women who are involved in the antinuclear movement, ecological concerns, or animal rights regard their activities as an outgrowth of this reverence for the Earth Goddess.

But there is another branch of Goddess worship, which has evolved from an older, occult tradition independent of the women's movement. The men and women in this group are followers of "the Craft," or Wicca—which is the Old English word for "witch." The good witches and wizards of Wicca—who are in no way related to satanism, Christianity's dark opposite—believe that theirs is "the old religion" of goddesses like the Roman deity Diana, practiced throughout Europe before the arrival of Christianity.

Despite these nuances, the two groups who worship the Goddess share a basic world view. As expressed in the movement's extensive literature, prehistory is "her-story," a matriarchal golden age dreamily similar to Woodstock—full of peace, love, organic meals, be-ins, and the kind of communal ecstasy one might have experienced at the feet of Janis Joplin (though the physical ideal here is more like Mama Cass). 12

Some give the Goddess political and social veils, but underneath them, she is the Great Mother. Worshiping her—through dance and study, art and herbal medicine, meditation and witchcraft—has resulted in a balanced, natural way of life for many women and quite a few men as well.

In a videotape made at a summer-solstice camp in the Sierra Nevadas, Charlotte Kelly, once married to a minister and now the director of the Women's Alliance in Oakland, California, tells how embracing a feminine deity validated her sense of self. "I took assertiveness training," she says, "but there was no way in which I was really embodying the power of my own womanhood." Church rituals had no meaning for her: "I didn't have any place for the beauty of my own soul."

In a documentary about the movement, dashiki-clad author and teacher Luisah Teish recalls that as a child, "the more I listened to what they had to say about the great bearded white man in the sky, the more I realized he was nobody I could talk to. You couldn't say nothing to the dude. He didn't answer prayers."

Jean Shinoda Bolen, a psychiatrist and the author of *Goddesses in Everywoman,* says she sees the Goddess not as a figurehead but as a "life force, as affiliation, as that which links us all at a deep level to be one with each other and one with nature, and in that, we are all connected with Gaia, or Mother Earth." 16

This grassroots religious movement is a subculture with its own politics, morality, aesthetics, and language. Its inhabitants have redesigned the tarot deck, the calendar, astrology, medicine, ancient history, and the dictionary. ("It's feminist theology, not theo-," says Carol Bulzone, the owner of Enchantments, correcting a customer.) Words like "wimmin," "womon," and "womyn" are ubiquitous. Such elements have trickled into the mainstream, enough to provoke riotous laughter from audiences when satirized in Off Broadway's *Kathy and Mo Show.* And to be sure, some of the activity associated with Goddess worship is as wacky as anything patriarchal societies ever invented.

There is, for example, a book that invites its readers to find their "goddess type." Are you Athena, Aphrodite, Hera, or Demeter? (This is even more fun than being a Leo.)

In the summer-solstice-camp video, a woman intones, "We are the teachers of the New Dawn. We are the Ones." Other participants, wearing horned headdresses, feathered masks, and wispy gowns, dance through the forest, grunting and gesticulating, keening and moaning.

If that doesn't seem extreme, then how about one of the most influential 20 books on Goddess spirituality, Starhawk's *The Spiral Dance,* which has instructions for casting a "Spell to Be Friends With Your Womb": "Light a RED CANDLE. Face South. With the third finger of your left hand, rub a few drops of your menstrual blood on the candle. . . ."

But the Morristown Full-moon Circle is considerably more moderate. This lunar luau is a warm support group, effusive in its praise for the swivel-hipped computer analyst. Still, a nervous Donna Wilshire whispers loudly to her guest, "This isn't typical!"

Actually, there doesn't seem to be a typical feminist spiritual group in the New York area. Moonfire, perhaps the most famous Manhattan group, is not meeting now because its leader, Amethyst, is "feeling burned-out." Goddess worship in the city is a diverse, do-it-yourself proposition that borrows freely from a variety of pagan traditions.

Margot Adler, a Central Park West witch who is a correspondent for National Public Radio and author of *Drawing Down the Moon,* the definitive work on paganism in the United States, identifies two streams of the Goddess movement: "There's the feminist stream and a slightly different one, the neo-pagan Wiccan movement. They have different histories, really, which doesn't mean some people don't move back and forth between them."

Adler, forty-four, the granddaughter of the psychiatrist Alfred Adler, 24 lives with her nonpagan husband in a comfortable, rambling apartment filled with books and plants. With her dark good looks, earthy warmth, and sophisticated intelligence, she makes being a witch seem as reasonable as joining Channel 13.

Adler says she knows of about twenty good-witch covens in Manhattan (with more than 200 members altogether). "As far as Goddess-spirituality groups, there are fewer in New York than in a lot of other places."

Within the two streams of Goddess worship—the feminist and the Wiccan—are further distinctions. Some Wiccan covens are open to visitors, some closed. Some are heterosexual, some are feminist, others are lesbian-separatist. Some followers worship in the nude.

Feminist Goddess groups, or circles, vary, too—with those in the Dianic tradition emphasizing the Greek-goddess archetypes in their rituals and others focusing on herbal healing. The latter call themselves Green Witches or Wise Women. Still others concentrate on Native American teachings and deities.

Naturally, there is some friction among the groups. Certain feminist 28 witches claim that the Craft is "wimmin's religion" and should exclude men, a prospect that upsets traditional witches, who cherish the Wiccan ideal of a male-female balance.

"I do get upset and unhappy when people say Wicca should be exclusively female," says a male witch known in the Manhattan Wiccan community as Black Lotus. "There was a three-day Goddess festival at the New York Open Center [in SoHo] last year that allowed men in only at night. Assuming the Goddess is for women only is silly."

Christopher Hatton, another male witch, says, "My attitude toward the very small group that wants to exclude men is the same as it would be toward men who want to exclude women from religion. I have a very low opinion of them."

Beyond the sexist strife, some East Coast worshipers have problems with the magical Native American branch of the movement. "The shamanistic tradition isn't the Goddess movement," says one New Jersey woman. "Some women are very adamant about not participating in Native American rituals, and now the Native American followers are pissed off. But the medicine wheel is not our symbol. Herbal healing is our tradition as North American witches." (She admits, however, that she and her friends "*have* done sweat lodges.")

Part of the feminist stream, the New Jersey group was formed around   32
Barbara G. Walker, author of *The Woman's Encyclopedia of Myths and Secrets* and seven other scholarly works on the Goddess published by Harper & Row. Women who first met at one of Walker's booksignings at a local store six years ago make up the core of the half-moon circle and another "intellectual support group," explains Donna Wilshire, one of the most enthusiastic members.

Wilshire is an intense, talkative mother of two grown children, with a dancer's body and a mass of curly brown hair framing her heart-shaped face. Her husband of thirty years, Bruce Wilshire, is a professor of philosophy at Rutgers who, she says, "is into shaman journeys." He says that in his marriage to Donna he has had three wives. "The first cooked for me. The second cried a lot. The third is a goddess."

Donna Wilshire grew up in a Catholic boarding home, struggled to become an actress, then spent a decade being "the perfect wife, garnishing every dish with a palette of colors." When she realized in the late sixties that her husband "didn't care about any of that," Wilshire became depressed. Eventually, "he knew something was wrong and brought home books by Betty Friedan and Merlin Stone." Stone's *When God Was a Woman* is a seminal volume for many. Published in 1976, it attempts to document the Goddess cults of Stone Age matriarchal societies in the Near and Middle East and their destruction by patriarchal, Indo-European bad guys.

"This is the best time of my life," Wilshire says. "I'm confident. I'm performing sacred work that combines all the things the world keeps separate. I can use my whole self because that's what the Goddess is: whole."

The lives of Donna Wilshire's friends Nancy Blair and Lynn Peters—   36 slender, attractive sculptors in their thirties—also revolve around the Goddess. The two run Star River Productions, a New Brunswick, New Jersey, company that makes "museum-quality" Goddess statues and jewelry.

Blair, a petite brunette, is passionate about her beliefs. "We used to do full-moon rituals with women we knew from the local co-op and through our business, gathering together to raise energy," she says. "But we've taken it more private. Groups can drain you. In the morning, we arrive at our studio, light candles, maybe write affirmations about our growth, and pray to the Great Goddess to allow divine energy."

As an art student in 1984, Blair saw the Venus of Willendorf, a famous archeological relic and one of the oldest sculptures of a human form yet uncovered, for the first time. "All art-history courses begin with her, but they describe her as just another fertility goddess," Blair says. "Connecting with the Goddess, I got the most incredible feeling right up my spine. It really felt like coming home."

Peters, who is fair-skinned, with dark hair piled atop her head, says, "I feel like Ceres [the Roman goddess of agriculture] some days, or else more like Lilith [a Talmudic demon], or this day I can feel like the Willendorf, an Earth Mother. They're all aspects of the One, so I can really flow with who I am that day."

Four years ago, with two hundred dollars seed money, the artists decided 40 to start a business that would "make images of the divine female available to other women," says Blair. "Last year, we grossed more than one hundred thousand dollars. Now we even have an 800 number." (Feminist spiritual hunger is apparently almost insatiable: a Saugerties, New York, company ships bite-size chocolate Willendorf goddesses around the world for nine dollars a dozen, plus postage.)

Blair and Peters consider themselves part of the Wise Woman, herbal-healing tradition in which female intuition is the guiding force. Manhattan's leading Green Witch is Robin Bennett. Pale, wiry, and articulate, Bennett, thirty-two, teaches an herbal-healing course and holds monthly open gatherings of women in her home to celebrate the new moon. The tiny kitchen in her small high-rise apartment near Union Square is stocked with jars of every imaginable herb. Bennett began studying them at nineteen to find relief from periodontal disease. ("I have perfect trust that my mouth needed to do this for me," she says.)

"I was working with healing already, on an intangible level," Bennett says, "emotional, spiritual, psychological kinds of healing with one of the human potential groups: Let Go & Live. My picture of what spirituality was was totally tied up with what organized religion was, and it didn't speak to me.

"When I met Susun Weed in 1985, the person most behind the reclaiming of the Wise Woman tradition around the world, it changed my whole relationship with spirituality and healing, bringing it more onto the earth.

Susun helped me to put a name to all the things I was doing and to learn there was this whole history of traditional women working this way. To me, the wise woman behind it all is the Earth Goddess."

Susun Weed, the author of *Healing Wise*, runs the Wise Woman Center— a "safe space for deep female healing . . . nourished by woman-only space/ time," according to its pamphlet—in Woodstock, New York. In her forties, Weed looks like a rock superstar—tall and willowy with long, flowing auburn hair, fair, unlined skin, and a dazzling smile. At a workshop called "The Spirit and Practice of the Wise Woman Tradition," held at the New York Open Center last October, she wore an elegant turquoise silk outfit with matching bandanna and exotic jewelry. Twenty women of all ages sat in the familiar circle around candles, baskets overflowing with leafy branches, a black caldron, and a rubber snake in the spiral shape that symbolizes the Goddess.

The day began with "nourishing" chants to the Sacred Corn Mother. Weed's morning lecture on the failings of both scientific and alternative medicine displayed her encyclopedic knowledge of herbs. Participants then used Weed's beaded witch-hazel-wood talking stick to explain why they were there.

Several in the "healing professions" felt disaffected with the medical establishment. A few had cured themselves of painful physical "female" problems. One had come because she was interested in "owning myself since my marriage ended." A fortyish woman—in tears "because [here] I'm allowed to speak"—was attending because "I really love trees." A video producer said, "If we respect ourselves, then we can respect the environment, the rain forest. I know plants have tremendous power." Two young nannies on their day off seemed to be there by accident.

"A lot of women who come into the women's spirituality movement," says Margot Adler, "come into it for reasons that are very personal. They feel like s---, they hate their bodies, they hate themselves. They come into these groups which basically say to you, 'You're the Goddess, you're wonderful.' And that's really a personally important experience for a certain period of time. But then comes the question of where do you go from there? Because then they become very political."

Attunement to nature and one's own inner wisdom, the idea that "every woman is an extension of the Earth Mother," as Weed proclaims, is an attractive idea to harried, fragmented urbanites, especially at a time when the death of nature is being prophesied.

Some of the events at Weed's Woodstock center are earthy, indeed. At last year's "Blood of the Ancients" retreat, held over Labor Day weekend, "we recreated the sacred moon lodge, or menstrual hut," recalls Weed, "and reawakened the old blood mysteries of woman's creativity—pregnancy, birth, lactation, menstruation, and menopause. We reclaimed the blood of peace, thereby bringing an end to war." Living conditions at the center are said to be less than idyllic. It "is really just a shack on a former stone quarry," says one participant, "but there's a beautiful stream and waterfall—you should have seen us, about twenty women all nude at the waterfall."

The plumbing is problematical. "You can't flush the indoor toilet often because it will overflow and there's just one portable toilet outside, so women have to squat on the ground," she says. "After a few days, they stop wearing underpants. There are lots of goats, so you're walking in human and goat s--- all the time. For dinner, it's great—Susun just goes out and picks all sorts of greens and flowers for a big salad."

Such mellow weekend flashbacks to Woodstock '69 are hardly typical of the classic Wiccan covens. "We're more oriented to the balance than to just the Goddess," explains Judy Harrow. A plump brunette who is a health worker and sometime radio producer, Harrow is the high priestess of a Gardnerian coven based in her narrow, homey apartment in Washington Heights. (The Gardnerians are descended from a coven founded in Britain by Gerald Gardner in the early fifties.)

Harrow has lived with the large, bearded man in the photographs on 52 her living-room wall for seventeen years. He and the others in the photographs are all middle-aged, jolly—and nude. Gardnerians almost always worship "sky clad."

In her soft voice, Harrow says she "resents the term 'feminist theology' because 'feminist' is often equated with the term 'separatist.' There are plenty of us feminists who aren't separatists. You don't have to disrespect men in order to respect women. Separatists are part of the picture, though. Certainly, a lot of the art and writing comes out of those groups."

Harrow traces her involvement with witchcraft to being "a forest-oriented, nature-oriented sort of person, more than you'd expect from someone who grew up in the city. And when our consciousness began to raise about ecology, that also became important to me. I heard from friends that there were people who made a religion out of this."

Wicca has given Harrow "a framework. It's become the focus of my life, which was pretty scattered and unfocused." As a high priestess, Harrow says, "I got much more confident and assertive from the experience of being a model for other people, teaching and mentoring." She notes that a support group of coven leaders meets once a month. "It's a very little pond, okay?" she says. "But I'm a decent-sized fish."

There are seven men and women in Harrow's coven: an X-ray techni- 56 cian, a housewife, a student, a secretary, a copy editor, a computer technician, and a computer consultant. During a typical meeting, Harrow says, they will "cast the circle—creating a focus and sense of differentness—and then work on a particular theme. The second half of the meeting will be whatever anybody wants to work on—magic or personal issues."

To work magic, Harrow explains, "we focus our will, our attitude, our personal energy, on our goals—through visualization, through chanting, affirmations, lots of different techniques. If someone is ill and wants to get better or wants to make some other change in their life, wants to change jobs or have a new relationship, whatever. It's a way of making a transference of consciousness. I've seen results again and again: people getting jobs, getting better from illnesses, against the odds. For me, a lot of the magic is completely explainable in terms of psychology, okay? That's big heresy, but it's the truth."

As for *black* magic, "I'm sure it goes on," Harrow concedes, "but it's a whole other world."

Harrow's group belongs to the Covenant of the Goddess, a federation of covens incorporated as a legally recognized church. "In every way, [Wicca] is deepening and growing as a religion and as a culture," she says. "There's more interaction because of the development of weekend gatherings that allow groups to share techniques more than before."

Harrow would like to see "more communication between the academic-feminist-theology community and us. Some of the academic stuff is pretty disconnected with what's going on, and some of what's really going on is pretty shortsighted because there's a philosophical and historical perspective lacking." 60

Margot Adler agrees that the split between Wicca and the Goddess-spirituality movement is a problem. "Most of the Goddess-oriented groups, particularly the lesbian-feminist ones, [are] much more open [than covens] on one level, but they also don't care about the society at large, or certainly the male society." Yet Adler believes that "the whole separatist movement is lessening. Even lesbians are working with men more."

Men are drawn to Goddess worship for many of the same reasons women are. Black Lotus says that as a child, he was "interested in the idea of polytheism, relating to Godhead as not just exclusively male or one particular image. In Wicca, we're used to relating to God the Father and also God the Mother, God the Child and God the Lover, God the Servant and God the Master. This very much enriches one's view, to see divinity in all things." Christopher Hatton's "pagan awareness" began, he says, "when I was reading the old myths and I encountered the concept of Mother Earth. By that, I mean the biosphere—it felt right that this should be treated as a goddess."

Since becoming involved with Wicca in 1971, Margot Adler has seen "the odd acceptance of it. It's permeated mass culture to a certain extent." She points to a new forty-five-dollar coffee-table tome on witchcraft and five different related volumes she's been sent in just the past month. "Hundreds of pagan magazines are flourishing," she notes. "Some of these newsletters that have been going for years have five hundred [subscribers]. Some of them also have ten thousand."

Adler sees further evidence of her religion's growth: "There are all these 64 straight museums having Goddess exhibitions. There was a Goddess festival at the New York Open Center in March of 1989 with two hundred people. That was where Olympia Dukakis 'came out.' " (When she announced her affiliation, Dukakis says, "I felt very vulnerable and tentative sharing with people my own yearnings." Dukakis became involved with Goddess worship when she acted in *The Trojan Women* in 1982. Her character, she says, "rejects the god of Troy and goes back to a more ancient time." Now Dukakis develops improvisational theater pieces based on Goddess myths. Her most recent is called *Voices of Earth*.)

Despite its growth, the future of Goddess spirituality is uncertain. "Is it going to take directions that are really going to be exciting and interesting?" asks Adler. "I think that's still really up for grabs." At a festival held in the Berkshires last fall, she says, "they wanted to create a new women's synthesis, [and] very few people showed up. Clearly, they did not know how to create some kind of new alliance calling on the pagans, the Goddess people, the environmental people. I don't know if that meant it wasn't time yet or whether they just f---ed up."

Serinity Young, an adjunct professor of religion at Hunter College, says that there is a great deal of "cross-fertilization going on between orthodox religions and the Goddess movement. Reformists within the church and the synagogue visit Goddess groups and take the rituals back with them." Young believes that "if the movement can keep its political focus, it will last. If it just becomes about sitting around in the woods and feeling good, it won't."

In New York today, the Goddess movement lacks cohesion—and that may be its most appealing attribute. There is room for the most individualized styles of worship, whether enacting or sculpting powerful feminine images, communing with herbs, or casting spells for success. What can be bad about a belief system that includes women and joy? Celebrating nature's mysteries and women's connection to them clearly feels right to many.

Perhaps only those who are particularly wounded or angry will respond 68 to the more strident and excessive elements of the movement. And sophisticates would probably wince when Robin Bennett tells her New Moon circle to "go with the flow." But the low, modern coffee table in the young Green Witch's simple downtown apartment makes a fairly decent altar. And to the assembled faithful, the guided meditation she leads is as much of a religious rite as Sunday mornings at St. Pat's are to others.

The ages of the ten women—early twenties to early forties—are as diverse as their vocations, which include nurse, photographer, young mother, and writer. They are asked to picture a spiral staircase with a cave at the bottom. The cave is inhabited by their Wise Woman, who has a message for them. The women focus on what they want to get rid of as the moon's cycle ends and what new seeds they want to plant in the coming one.

With a feather, each woman wafts the smoke from the smudge pot—a rich blend of cedar, sage, and mugwort—over the body of the person next to her, sending "supportive wishes." Then everyone drinks herbal tea and, holding the talking stick, says what's on her mind.

Rituals like these—part seder and part consciousness-raising group—may strike some outsiders as silly or strange. But the fact is that these disparate women—who want to connect with something more eternal than *L.A. Law*—are all immensely likable and intelligent. And it's just possible that with the tea, the chants, the good wishes, and the Goddess statue, they'll have a pretty good month.

Points to Consider

1. What is Unger's tone throughout the essay? What attitude seems to dominate the article? What does Unger find silly about goddess worship? What does she consider serious?

2. What do the women Unger interviews seem to have in common? What does this commonality suggest about the types of women most likely to participate in the worship of goddesses?

3. How is the goddess movement split? What are the two leading groups? Which group does Unger seem most sympathetic to? Why?

4. In what ways does the worship of a goddess resemble more traditional forms of ritual and religion? In what ways does it differ? Is there one goddess the women worship, or are there several?

Discussing the Unit

Suggested Topic for Discussion

Consider the different images one has of God and the ways these different images can affect our religion and culture. Do you think the gender of God makes a significant difference? In what ways does it matter whether we think of God as male or female or both or neither?

Preparing for Class Discussion

1. Consider how our traditional male image of God the Father has affected the position of women in organized religions. Do you think it has led to various forms of paternalism and justified a male hierarchy? To what extent is the idea of God as male simply based on symbol or analogy and to what extent does this concept represent a dominant masculine theology?

2. A prominent theologian, Hans Küng, has argued that "Father" is only a symbol for "a transhuman, transsexual, absolutely last/absolutely first reality." In other words, we need not view God as possessing any human sexual characteristics. Does this point of view solve the problem of gender and religion raised by the articles in this unit?

From Discussion to Writing

Which image of God do you personally believe is the best? The traditional male image? A female image? An androgynous image? A genderless image? Or none of the preceding? Write an essay in which you describe your image of God and defend it against rival or alternate images.

19

The Ethics of Dependency:
Addiction or Alibi?

When San Francisco's Mayor George Moscone was killed in 1978, his murderer tried to excuse the crime by claiming that his addiction to junk food (mainly Twinkies) resulted in serious emotional distress. Joel Steinberg, a New York lawyer who beat his young daughter to death, was acquitted in 1988 of a second-degree murder charge by a jury who thought that his cocaine use had severely affected his mental capacities; the jury found him guilty of first-degree manslaughter instead. As more cases like these come to the public's attention, we are confronted with an important question: are people who claim addictive or dependent behavior responsible for their actions?

The issue does not only involve criminal conduct. As Art Levine shows in "America's Addiction to Addictions," there are now programs and treatment centers for people "addicted" to shopping, eating, sex, and gambling. Among some of the many groups treating addictive personalities are Batterers Anonymous, Debtors Anonymous, Emotions Anonymous, and Women Who Love Too Much. In "The Anatomy of Addiction," Rita Baron-Faust examines the self-destructive behavior of women, many of whom "slide into multiple addiction." She accepts the medical diagnoses of addictive behavior. Stanton Peele in "Ain't Misbehavin' " does not. He sees little scientific evidence for most medical claims of dependency and thinks that treating addictions as though they were diseases has "serious ramifications for American society."

ART LEVINE

America's Addiction to Addictions

[U.S. NEWS AND WORLD REPORT / February 5, 1990]

When District of Columbia Mayor Marion Barry tearfully announced that he had "weaknesses" and entered a Florida treatment program last week, he and his aides were also launching a political and legal strategy to portray his addiction problems as a disease—something beyond his control and thus politically less damaging. By going into treatment for chemical dependency, he stood to gain public sympathy and, he and his advisers hoped, prosecutorial leniency. But Barry's downfall and speedy resort to treatment also raise basic questions about the nature and causes of addictions and the role of individual willpower in curbing excessive behavior.

Most medical experts today view alcoholism and drug addiction as chronic diseases with biological, and perhaps genetic, underpinnings. But it was not that long ago that even these excesses were seen as evidence of moral turpitude rather than medical conditions. What worries some addiction experts is society's willingness to expand the definition of addictive disease beyond substance abuse to include a host of excessive behaviors—ranging from shopping to promiscuity—and clinicians' readiness to treat what may be social and will-power problems as medical disorders instead.

Addiction was once seen primarily as a physical dependence on a drug that created severe physical symptoms when the drug was withdrawn. But

---

ART LEVINE (b. 1950) is an associate editor of U.S. News and World Report *and a contributing editor at* Washington Monthly *magazine. He has also written for* Harper's Magazine, *the* Washington Post, *the* New Republic, *and* Spy. *Levine is currently working on an anthology of his humorous pieces.*

that view is changing. "The drug is necessary but not sufficient to cause addiction," notes Jack Henningfield, chief of the clinical pharmacology branch of the National Institute of Drug Abuse. He and others point to the clear effects of social conditions on drug use: for example, the ability of 90 percent of addicted Vietnam veterans to kick their heroin habits once free of the stress of battle. By contrast, three-quarters of other heroin addicts who try to quit fail.

It is this sort of wide variation in addictive patterns that, in part, prompts   4 some critics to question whether substance abuse is truly a disease with an inevitable course if untreated. Furthermore, they argue, the disease model sends a harmful message to abusers. It not only excuses irresponsibility but "indoctrinates them with the idea they're helpless and sick," says Herbert Fingarette, an addiction expert at the University of California at Santa Barbara.

Medical authorities generally dismiss these criticisms, noting that other well-accepted diseases, such as diabetes, lack a simple pattern while still having a physical component. They also argue that disease-oriented treatment programs don't absolve patients of responsibility for their habits, even though they have biological roots. "Once a behavior becomes an addiction, it involves a biological component," points out Dr. Frederick K. Goodwin, a psychiatrist and administrator of the Alcohol, Drug Abuse and Mental Health Administration. But "it starts as a voluntary act, then becomes reflexive and automatic."

Can any behavior become reflexive and automatic—in effect, an addiction? Some experts are inclined to see addiction in any pleasurable behavior that turns compulsive, despite the problems that that can cause. In part because of this looser definition, addiction chic is everywhere: there are now over two thousand meetings each week of groups catering to self-styled sex and love addicts, up at least 20 percent in the past year; there are more than two hundred national Alcoholics Anonymous–style groups in the country, including Messies Anonymous, and there are inpatient therapy programs and self-help groups for those people—called "codependents"—whose main problem is they remain with, and worry too much about, destructive mates. Whether it is excesses in drug taking or even TV watching, Harvey Milkman, a professor of psychology at Metropolitan State College in Denver and coauthor of *Craving for Ecstasy,* argues, "The disease concept may be applied to the entire spectrum of compulsive problem behaviors."

But the prospect of less personal responsibility concerns critics of the would-be addictions. "Creating a world of addictive diseases may mean creating a world in which anything is excusable," says psychologist Stanton Peele, author of the new book *Diseasing of America.* Even some addiction researchers are questioning whether the boom in addiction treatments has gone too far. "It is in vogue now to call any excessive behavior an addiction, and, frankly, the professions are too quick to turn a dollar on this," says

Howard J. Shaffer, director of the Center for Addiction Studies at Harvard Medical School and Cambridge Hospital. And none of the often expensive treatments offered for the alleged behavioral addictions has proved effective, experts say.

Yet researchers exploring the disease models of addiction are often genuinely seeking to understand the underpinnings of some self-destructive, repetitive behaviors that trouble individuals—and baffle scientists. How do we explain someone who buys more pairs of shoes than could ever possibly be worn or gambles away the family home and life savings? 8

The idea of an addictive-personality type has been proposed, but the science is inconclusive. "There is no single characteristic or constellation of traits that is inevitably associated with addiction," notes psychologist Alan Lang of Florida State University, who contributed a chapter on personality to a National Research Council report on habitual behavior. At the same time, his research review points to such predisposing traits as a sense of alienation, impulsivity, and a need for instant gratification.

Despite the controversies over addictions, they have made their way into the legal system as defenses. Defendants claiming "diminished capacity" because of their addictions sometimes succeed: one Vietnam vet accused of drug running was acquitted after a defense expert argued that he was a victim of the "action-addict syndrome." "Is every problem a disease?" asks sociologist Martin Levine of Bloomfield College in New Jersey.

It sometimes seems that way. A leading "sex addiction" theorist, Minnesota psychologist Patrick Carnes, has designed the country's first Sexual Dependency Unit at Golden Valley Health Center in Minnesota. It has offered both inpatient and outpatient treatment to more than one thousand people since 1984. The roughly four-week, sixteen-thousand-dollar treatment includes an AA-style twelve-step program, group therapy, and celibacy pledges. The critics of the sex-addiction movement view it more as a moralistic crusade than as a genuine medical effort.

But for many who consider themselves sex addicts, the damage in their lives can be quite real, even if there is no agreement on what causes their problems. Jamie, a Minneapolis member of Sex Addicts Anonymous, says he lost a few jobs because of his constant search for new sex partners. "Everything else got in the way," he says. And there are some hints of a biological basis for such behavior. New York City psychologist William Wedin recalls one patient, a well-paid executive who began spending thousands of dollars a week on prostitutes and joined a twelve-step sex-addict program. It wasn't until he collapsed on the street one day that doctors diagnosed him as a victim of a stroke, suggesting that an organic brain disorder had probably spurred his flings. Other experts are using antidepressants to successfully treat sexual compulsives. 12

Compulsive gambling may pose the greatest theoretical challenge for addiction researchers. Unlike alcoholism and drug addiction, it involves no toxic substance that might directly affect brain chemistry and lead to physical craving. Yet it is well accepted by such groups as the American Psychiatric Association as an addictive syndrome. The Department of Veterans Affairs offers inpatient and outpatient treatment for gambling at four medical centers. And there may even be a biological factor: in 1988, researchers at the National Institute on Alcohol Abuse and Alcoholism found higher levels of the brain chemical norepinephrine in gamblers, which could signal a mood-regulation disturbance that spurs them to seek greater thrills. It is theoretically possible that others seek the same kinds of rewards through compulsive shopping and sex.

For those who work with such troubled people, the causes are still ultimately mysterious, but Dr. Sheila Blume, who heads the alcohol, chemical-dependency, and compulsive-gambling programs at South Oaks Hospital in Amityville, New York, says, "I'm hopeful a final pathway in the brain will be found." Until the biology of excessiveness is better understood, America's addiction to addiction will no doubt continue.

Points to Consider

1. What is meant by the "disease model" of addiction? How have addictions come to be considered diseases? How does calling an addiction a disease affect the way we treat it?

2. What is the relevance of the statistic (paragraph 3) concerning Vietnam veterans and heroin addiction? How is it used in the argument about the medical nature of addiction?

3. How is the disease model of addiction creating opportunities for exploitation? Who benefits from this concept? Why?

4. Why is the discovery of a biochemical factor in addictive gambling important? Do you think this chemical will explain the causes of heavy gambling? What additional information would you need to know about this chemical before coming to any conclusion?

The Anatomy of Addiction [COSMOPOLITAN / June 1990]

At thirty, Gail was riding high—in more ways than one. She had a glamorous job in television, a condo with a pool and a view in Los Angeles, a late-model Porsche, and a terrific man who wanted to make a commitment. Then she acquired a five-hundred-dollar-a-day cocaine habit—and quickly lost it all.

"When I first got out to L.A. five years ago, everyone was doing coke—at business lunches, at parties. It seemed like part of the whole lifestyle. I never really thought twice about the dangers of trying it. I was insecure, and it made me feel like an insider," Gail recalls. "Cocaine energized me, it made me feel like I could do anything. Then I found I couldn't do without it.

"Before long, it stopped being fun and got really scary. I was freebasing, blowing a hundred and twenty dollars per gram on coke like I used to pop for a pair of shoes or earrings. I made a lot of money, and I was broke all the time," she says.

Gail was an associate producer on a network sitcom. But the frantic up- 4 and-down moods of her growing addiction led to trouble on the set, and she was fired. The word spread that she had "personality" problems, and free-lance work was hard to get. Soon Gail had trouble paying her mortgage. She sold the Porsche to raise cash. But when that money was gone, the bank foreclosed.

"I moved in with my boyfriend. He knew I had a cocaine problem, but after I stole some money from his wallet, he told me either I get help or I get out. But I was still into heavy denial, so he handed me my suitcase."

Gail found shelter with a girlfriend for a few weeks, but then they quarreled and she was left with nowhere to go. She spent a chilly night on the beach, then tried a women's shelter. "It was like the last stop before hell . . . the stench, the noise. I used to spend seventy-five dollars just on nail tips, and now I only had five dollars in my pocket. I was terrified and

RITA BARON-FAUST is a free-lance writer and television producer. She writes articles for Cosmopolitan, Redbook, McCall's, *and* Harper's Bazaar *and has produced television segments for* Physician's Journal Update *and* Health Link Television. *She also reports on medicine for WCBS radio in New York City.*

humiliated," Gail says. "The next day, I got on the phone to a producer friend of mine, and he pulled some strings to get me into a good treatment program."

Although it's disturbing, Gail's story is not unusual. She is only one of the millions of women in this country who are addicted to drugs, alcohol, food, gambling, or sex.

Is There an Addictive Personality?

"The difference between an alcoholic and a person who simply likes to drink is the loss of control," says Sheila Blume, M.D., medical director of alcoholism, chemical-dependency, and compulsive-gambling programs at South Oaks Hospital in Amityville, New York. "A healthy person knows when to stop and sets limits. The addict does not. Her behavior becomes obsessive, destructive. Addicts lose the ability and the desire to take care of themselves."

So what pushes women over the edge? A wide variety of factors make up the anatomy of addiction, although one characteristic common among addicts is low self-esteem. But experts say there's no real evidence of a so-called addictive personality that makes certain people prone to chemical dependency. Research has shown, however, that there are numerous potential "triggers" for addictive behavior. "As many as forty percent of addicts may have underlying psychiatric disorders that drive them to use drugs or alcohol to obliterate bad feelings," says Robert Millman, M.D., director of the Alcohol and Drug Abuse Services at New York Hospital–Cornell Medical Center. Those "bad feelings" include clinical depression, anxiety, and panic disorders. Experts say these conditions may contribute to drug abuse (or result from it) in as many as 70 percent of cases. People who suffer from manic depression and attention-deficit disorder (adult hyperactivity) are also more likely to abuse cocaine. And in cases like these, addicts may be seeking relief from mental or personality problems, not just looking for a high.

"Alcohol is disinhibiting; it loosens up a shy person and calms down a chronically anxious or angry person," says Edward Khantzian, M.D., principal psychiatrist for substance-abuse disorders at Cambridge Hospital in Massachusetts. "Stimulants such as amphetamines and cocaine may be used for a lift by people with depressive tendencies or as an extra accelerant for overactive people. Aggressive and violent people gravitate to opiates, such as heroin." New studies also suggest that some people may have inherited a genetic tendency toward alcoholism.

Pain and Self-Loathing

Ruth, thirty-four, says she believes genetics played a part in her own addiction. Her mother is an alcoholic, and other family members also have drinking problems. "I've been addicted to one thing or another my entire life, and I have never liked myself," says Ruth. "My first drug of choice was books, and I became a compulsive student. When that didn't work, I turned to food and became a compulsive eater. I was fat in high school, and that just reinforced my low self-esteem."

The oldest of seven children, Ruth grew up in the affluent Boston suburb of Brookline. Because of her mother's heavy drinking, Ruth's brothers and sisters grew up out of control. "No one talked about problems in my house. I had these terrible feelings about myself, terrible anger toward my parents. And I had to bottle them up inside," she remembers. "I went to all-girl Catholic schools. But when I started college at sixteen, I had to start interacting with boys. It was then that I discovered beer made me more outgoing when I was with men—and I progressed from beer to wine to vodka." 12

Ruth went on to law school, where she abused diet pills to keep her awake for the long hours of study. She passed the bar exam in 1979, but "I never filled out the papers I needed to be admitted to the Bar Association. I was too out of it," she says. Instead, she worked in low-level jobs—and stayed drunk. "I got up in the morning and my whole goal was oblivion, to get back to sleep. The more I screwed up, the more I hated myself."

Then one night, coming home in a stupor, Ruth was almost raped in the lobby of her building. "For me, that was the bottom. I never went back to work, I rarely got out of bed. I had one dress, nowhere to go, no job, no friends—nothing to do but get high. And when the money ran out, I couldn't even do that. I was one step away from the street, from being a dead person," she recalls. Not long after, Ruth hospitalized herself and began the long climb back to sobriety.

Many addicts have histories that include unhappy childhoods, sexual abuse, violent spouses, failed marriages, and unsuccessful careers, says Dr. Khantzian. "Some of us feel more injured, neglected, or abused because we were either shamed as children or were not sufficiently validated and praised. Drugs are a way to alter those feelings."

The Work-Drug Connection

For women in the work place, alcohol and drug abuse is a multifaceted problem. "Many working women feel underpaid, undervalued, overworked, and overstressed; they're trying to juggle too many roles with too little reward. Some become frustrated and turn to alcohol or tranquilizers," says Reed Moskowitz, M.D., director of the Stress-Disorders Medical Services at New York University Medical Center. "Some women may also feel they lack the aggressiveness to compete in a male-dominated work place, and mistakenly think that drugs such as cocaine will give them that aggressive edge. Other women use drugs or alcohol to be one of the boys at business functions or while entertaining clients. The insecurities that make women feel they won't be accepted on their own terms also contribute to their addiction." And in such professions as entertainment and finance, where the energy level is frenetic and the stakes are high, the use of stimulants is even more common. 16

"Cocaine was everywhere when I started out on Wall Street," admits Carol, twenty-nine. "Here I was, black, a brand new M.B.A., and the youngest woman at my level. Everyone had high expectations for me. My family had struggled to send me to college, then I got this fellowship to a top grad school. I was carrying some heavy baggage."

Then an acquaintance turned Carol on to cocaine.

"This business can be a pressure cooker," says Carol. "Cocaine seemed to keep me on track, help my concentration. But after a while, I would get wired—really tense—and to come down, I needed to take a drink or a Valium. Finally, I was taking so many drugs, I couldn't handle the job."

For Carol, the turning point came when she was swept up in one of the 20
mass arrests of drug buyers and sellers that shook the glass canyons of the financial district in 1985. "I went out to make a buy during lunch, and next thing I knew, I was in handcuffs," she recalls. "I had a good lawyer, so I was never charged. But what did I do when I got home? I popped a Valium. A good friend finally convinced me I'd be throwing away my entire future if I didn't get straight."

The Female Factor

Carol's slide into multiple addiction is not unusual. Experts say that women have different patterns of addiction than men do, and suffer more cross-dependencies—many involving prescription drugs. The latest figures from the National Institute on Drug Abuse show that a shocking 45 percent of the nation's drug abusers between the ages of twelve and thirty-five are women, five million of them between the ages of fifteen and forty-four. According to the National Institute of Alcohol Abuse and Alcoholism, 5.7 million women in this country are problem drinkers, and a survey by the Association of Junior Leagues reports that more than half the women now in treatment are between the ages of eighteen and thirty-four.

Statistics also show that nearly twice as many women as men regularly use tranquilizers. Antidepressants and sedatives are taken by three times more women than men. One reason, says Dr. Blume, is that doctors tend to overprescribe these drugs for women. But women also tend to mix these drugs with alcohol. A survey by Alcoholics Anonymous found that 45 percent of its female members had an addiction to another drug. The number jumps to 64 percent for women under thirty, according to the Association of Junior Leagues survey. "A male alcoholic may take his first drink in the morning, but women may think it isn't proper to drink until evening," says Dr. Blume. "So they take another drug during the day."

Women are also much more sensitive to alcohol than men. Researchers at Mount Sinai School of Medicine and the Alcohol Research and Treatment Center at the Bronx Veterans Affairs Medical Center in New York City found that women get drunk more quickly than men on the same amount of alcohol because their stomachs are less able to break down alcohol.

"A normal woman produces half as much of a stomach enzyme called 24
alcohol dehydrogenase, which breaks down alcohol before it enters the
bloodstream and can damage other organs such as the brain and the liver,"
says Charles Lieber, M.D., professor of medicine and pathology at Mount
Sinai and director of the Alcohol Research and Treatment Center. "We also
found that alcoholism, both in men and women, also decreases this gastric
protective mechanism. But alcoholic women end up with no protection to
speak of, because they start out with lower levels of the protective enzyme
to begin with."

Dr. Lieber says this may explain why women become alcoholics faster
than men, and why such long-term complications as cirrhosis of the liver hit
women earlier and harder. One study found the death rate for women
alcoholics was 50 to 100 percent higher than for alcoholic men.

Women in nontraditional roles (single, divorced, or never married; no
children; and a job in a male-dominated occupation) may be at a greater
risk for addictions of all kinds, says Sharon Wilsnack, professor of neuro-
science at the University of North Dakota School of Medicine. Wilsnack,
who conducted a landmark study of women and alcohol, also found that
many women who abuse alcohol and drugs do so to reduce their sexual
inhibitions. They believe alcohol heightens sexual arousal, when the reverse
is actually true.

Sex itself can also become part of the deadly spiral downward for some
female addicts. "It's not uncommon for women to become so-called cocaine
whores," says Leslie Brewer, director of the Center for Problem Resolution
at the Sun Coast Hospital in Largo, Florida. "These women would literally
do anything for cocaine, and frequently do. They become exploited by the
men supplying their drugs, and get into a self-destructive pattern. They stop
caring about what happens to themselves as long as they have the drugs."

Hooked on Sex

"I must have had sex with more than a thousand guys over the years," 28
says Linda, thirty-nine. "Hey, in the late seventies, people were still sleeping
around and no one was afraid of AIDS or VD. I liked sex. I never thought
it was a problem."

Linda feels her behavior started to become a compulsion after she was
hired as an art director at a Minneapolis ad agency. "I was competing in a
mostly male environment, and I felt I had to hide my sexuality. I wore severe
suits, no short skirts or anything like that," she says. "But I would think
about sex all the time, fantasizing about the guys in the office. After work,
I cruised the bars and picked up men everywhere. I thought it validated me
as a desirable woman."

But then Linda was badly beaten by a lover last summer. "I looked in
the mirror and saw a face that wasn't mine. It was a mass of cuts and bruises.
I was too ashamed to go to my doctor or to the police. I spent the next few
days drunk at home," Linda recalls.

The beating and the possibility that she might have contracted AIDS from so much sexual activity terrified her, and she entered one of the few sex-addiction treatment programs in the country. So far, she's tested negative for AIDS antibodies. But the fear hasn't left her. "I came close to totally self-destructing," she says. "I never considered myself an addict until I entered treatment, but sex is really another kind of drug."

Compulsive Gambling

Another "escape" for troubled women is compulsive gambling, a prob- 32
lem usually associated with men. "One in three compulsive gamblers is a woman," says Henry Lesieur, a professor of sociology at Saint John's University in New York City who studied female gamblers. "But less than five percent of the patients in treatment are women. That's partly because they often get less family support for this problem."

According to Lesieur, "There are two kinds of women gamblers. First, there are the 'adventure seekers,' who are looking for a thrill in what they perceive as a man's world. They're into making money and the excitement. Then there are the 'escape artists,' women who may have alcoholic or abusive husbands, or who had addicted or sexually abusive parents. They are extremely lonely and troubled, and the 'action-adventure' of gambling helps them forget and feel like a different person."

Casey, twenty-six, a data processor, agrees. "I was hooked on the risk, the thrill, the rush I got at the track and in Vegas. My work was dull. My marriage was disintegrating. Gambling really was my escape hatch." Then Casey began losing, and soon her debts threatened to drown her. "I borrowed to the limit on all my credit cards. I got loans from friends. I was always going to win big and pay it all back, but it never happened," she says. "When my husband left, everything collapsed. I couldn't pay the rent, I had no money for food. I was so desperate. I was on the verge of suicide. My sister rescued me and forced me to go to Gamblers Anonymous."

When Food Becomes a Bad Habit

The other cross-addiction likely to turn up in the file of a female addict is food. A 1987 survey by the Renfrew Center, a Philadelphia treatment center for eating disorders, found that more than 40 percent of the women being treated for anorexia or bulimia also had a problem with alcohol and/or drugs. "Compulsive overeating is part of a constellation of addictions that can include alcohol, drugs, shoplifting, and excessive sexual activity," says Leonard Levitz, clinical director of the Renfrew Center. "Many of the same factors that make people susceptible to other addictions also produce eating disorders. A compulsive overeater centers her life around food, the same way an alcoholic does with drinking. Food also acts as a tranquilizer. These people will eat a box of cookies or an entire cake to make themselves feel good or as a way to relieve stress."

Cravings for sweets may also be linked to the same physiological mech- 36 anism that sets off an addiction to drugs. Research at the University of Michigan demonstrated that consuming sweets makes the pleasure enhancers in the brain (called opioid peptides) go into action. Fortunately, it was also found that blocking those peptides can turn off the craving for sweets.

Getting Straight

Treatment programs are finally being designed to tackle the unique problems of female addicts. "With women, you have to be sensitive to the presence of other drugs, particularly prescription drugs. And you have to intervene more quickly if alcohol is involved, because alcoholism hits faster in women and with more deadly force," says Dr. Blume.

At Atlanta's Charter Peachford Hospital, men and women are put into single-sex therapy groups after a standard twenty-eight days of detoxification. "Separate therapy groups allow us to focus on sex-specific issues, such as those of relationships and identity," explains Thomas Hester, director of Medical Services for Addictive Diseases at Charter Peachford Hospital. "Men are more focused on occupations than relationships, while many women have a history of sexual or physical abuse. It's hard to discuss that in a mixed group."

Most treatment programs also require addicts to join a twelve-step self-help program patterned after Alcoholics Anonymous. "The first step is to admit you are powerless over the alcohol or drugs and your life has become unmanageable," explains Dr. Hester. "Step two is acknowledging there is a higher power greater than yourself that can help you fight the addiction. That spirituality is a key to the program."

But even after—or during—treatment, many recovering female addicts   40
switch from one addiction to another, going from drugs to food or sex, for example. So the key to staying straight, say the experts, is *staying* in treatment. "Once people cross the line into compulsive behavior or chemical dependency, that compulsion is always lurking in the shadows, waiting to come out," says Brewer. "People have to continue with self-help groups to maintain the right attitude, the way they view themselves and the world. If they don't, the old thinking and old behavior will come back."

Points to Consider

1. Baron-Faust begins her article with an individual instance of an addictive personality. Why did Gail begin using cocaine? What do you think of her reasons? What do you think of her values? Do you consider her responsible for her behavior? Or do you consider her a victim?

2. Baron-Faust concentrates on women and addiction. Why does she feel that women are prone to different types of addiction than men? What evidence does she offer to support the existence of these differences?

Why does she believe that women are more likely to have multiple addictions than men?

3. Baron-Faust uses several women to illustrate various forms of addiction. Besides their addictive personalities, do they have anything else in common? In your opinion, do their backgrounds and lifestyles contradict or reinforce Baron-Faust's argument?

4. What does Baron-Faust suggest about the causes of addiction? Do you think she leans toward a medical or psychological explanation?

STANTON PEELE

Ain't Misbehavin' [THE SCIENCES / July–August 1989]

Swept up in the hurly-burly of an American presidential campaign, Kitty Dukakis looked to be in her element. Throughout the gaudy carnival of speechmaking and handshaking, she exuded warmth and a kind of kinetic energy that, to many observers, offered a refreshing contrast to the rather stolid manner of her husband, Massachusetts Governor Michael S. Dukakis, the Democratic aspirant. And, though candidate Dukakis was repudiated at the polls, his wife seemed to have emerged a winner—popular and admired, with a lucrative career as an author and lecturer looming before her. But scarcely three months after the election, it was a weary, wistful Kitty Dukakis who appeared on the cover of *Newsweek,* with the headlines ADDICTIVE PERSONALITIES: WHO GETS HOOKED ON DRUGS AND ALCOHOL—AND WHY and KITTY DUKAKIS: HER PRIVATE STRUGGLE.

Inside the magazine were more photographs showing her face haggard and tormented, accompanied by an account of why she had checked herself into Edgehill-Newport, a Rhode Island treatment center for alcohol and drug

---

STANTON PEELE *(b. 1946) is a senior survey researcher at Mathematica Policy Research, Inc., in Princeton, New Jersey. He regularly contributes articles to* Psychology Today, American Political Science Review, *and other journals. Peele is the author of several books on addiction, including* Love and Addiction *with Archie Brodsky (1975) and* Diseasing of America: Addiction Treatment out of Control *(1989).*

dependency. Mrs. Dukakis (who, in the past, had frankly discussed her apparently successful recovery from a twenty-six-year bout with amphetamines) had suddenly begun drinking to excess. As Governor Dukakis said at the time, "She clearly recognizes she has a sickness—and it is a sickness—and she had to deal with it."

Two weeks later, *New York Newsday* ran a front-page photograph of Grace Ann Machate, taken as she followed a flag-draped casket bearing the body of her husband, police officer Robert Machate, down the steps of a Brooklyn church. In the early-morning stillness several days before, Machate, twenty-five years old, had been slain with his own revolver on a deserted city street while attempting to arrest a suspected drug dealer. He was the seventh New York–area law officer killed in the line of duty within a year whose death was tied to drug trafficking. That day's newspaper also carried an Associated Press Wirephoto of Kitty and Michael Dukakis, smiling and waving buoyantly upon arriving home after Mrs. Dukakis's completion of treatment at Edgehill-Newport.

These stories exemplify the range of news about alcohol and drug problems that, through various media, bombards the American public. At one end of the spectrum are tales of high-powered celebrities—entertainers, athletes, political figures—some of whom, like Kitty Dukakis, enter expensive rehabilitation clinics. In stark contrast are grim reports from city streets, where random violence associated with heroin, cocaine, and, recently, crack (a potent, inexpensive cocaine derivative) has infected many neighborhoods, threatening grandmothers, toddlers, and police officers alike. Between these extremes are constant reminders of how substance abuse threatens children of the middle class: one is hard put to find a town in New Jersey, for instance, without a street sign bearing the caution DRUG-FREE SCHOOL ZONE. Similarly, organizations such as Mothers Against Drunk Driving have arisen from suburban, middle-class roots.

In the minds of most Americans, narcotics and alcohol are linked inextricably with addiction, an idea that conjures up images of the crazed user, oblivious to anything but obtaining more of his or her particular poison, who will stop at nothing to get it. To be sure, drugs and alcohol have chemical effects, and withdrawal from habitual use of those substances can elicit a raft of irritating physical sensations. But beyond that, science, and now the public, has embraced the notion that addicts suffer from a physiologically well-defined phenomenon—as Governor Dukakis put it, "a sickness"—even though repeated attempts to prove that addiction is a clear-cut medical condition have been, at best, inconclusive. The addiction-as-disease idea has spread wildly, to encompass not only chemical dependency but also a host of other compulsive behaviors, including gambling, overeating, undereating, shopping, and fornication. The "addiction" issue of *Newsweek,* for example, carried an unrelated story about the travails of Boston Red Sox third baseman Wade Boggs, who was being sued for twelve million dollars by a woman

4

who had long provided him with companionship on road trips. In explaining the liaison, the married Boggs confessed that he was "addicted to sex"—to which his former mistress responded, "I guess what I thought was love was just a disease."

The pervasive and growing influence of the disease model of addiction has serious ramifications for American society. The more psychologists and attorneys dismiss forms of misbehavior as uncontrollable compulsions, the less people are held accountable for their actions—even when they have harmed others. Often, the only penalty for gross, even criminal misconduct is undergoing counseling in a treatment center. Creating a world of addictive diseases may mean creating a world in which anything is excusable, one that must inevitably slide into chaos.

While the word is attached to a growing crowd of compulsive behaviors, addiction still is most commonly associated with narcotics use—so much so that *drug* and *addiction* seem almost synonymous. The drugs most often thought of as addictive are the opiates (derivatives of opium, the dried milky discharge of the poppy plant), which are unsurpassed as pain-killers and sleep inducers and include heroin, morphine, and the milder formula, codeine.

Though opiates have been used commonly for most of recorded history, 8 only since the eighteenth century have their addictive effects been explored in any detail. In one of the earliest descriptions of withdrawal symptoms, written in 1701, the English physician John Jones cited perspiration, frequent urination, loose bowels, depression, and chronic itching as likely results of sudden curtailment of habitual opium ingestion. Similar notes were sounded in scattered English medical journals over the next one hundred and fifty years, and in 1850, Jonathan Pereira, in *Elements of Materia Medica and Therapeutics,* one of the most respected medical manuals of the time, warned that excessive opium intake brings on moral, as well as physical, deterioration and that children of drug addicts were apt to be "weak, stunted, and decrepit."

Despite these caveats, the use of opiates in Europe and the United States spiraled upward. Physicians dispensed narcotics indiscriminately, and for the most part, neither the general public nor the medical profession had any notion that opiates were especially dangerous. While their consumption often was described as addictive, the opiates themselves were not considered any more habit-forming than other pharmacological agents. Indeed, prominent turn-of-the-century pharmacologists, such as Clifford Allbutt and Walter E. Dixon, of England, were just as concerned about withdrawal from caffeine, often resulting from curtailment of habitual coffee drinking:

> The sufferer is tremulous and loses his self-command; he is subject to fits of agitation and depression. He has a haggard appearance. . . . As with other

such agents, a renewed dose of the poison gives temporary relief, but at the cost of future misery.

At that time, according to the English research team of historian Virginia Berridge and psychiatrist Griffith Edwards (writing in 1981, in *Opium and the People,* an extensive review of English opiate use during the nineteeenth century), addiction was viewed as any indulgence in an act that was mildly damaging to health and perhaps a little bit of a nuisance.

In the final quarter of the nineteenth century, a small number of German scientists began to conduct research into drug addiction. In 1878, one of them, the physician Eduard Levinstein, published *The Morbid Craving for Morphia,* in which he described morphia addiction as "the uncontrollable desire . . . to use morphine as a stimulant and a tonic, and the diseased state of the system caused by the injudicious use of the said remedy." And, presaging modern notions, he argued, albeit without experimental evidence, that the compulsion to take narcotics results "from the natural constitution"—that, in effect, drug addicts are victims of physiology. Still, Levinstein remained true to the established view of his time (and, increasingly, our own), making no distinction between addiction to drugs and other "passions," including smoking, gambling, greed, and sexual excess.

The reclassification of drug addiction as a medical condition rather than a passion, vice, or other behavioral phenomenon did not occur as a result of startling new studies of narcotics users or even of animal experiments. Instead, the idea slipped unseen into the realm of conventional wisdom on the coattails of other scientific developments. In finding bacterial and viral causes for infectious diseases, Louis Pasteur, Robert Koch, and other researchers of a century ago helped create a climate in which a medical cure for almost any ill seemed possible. And since drug addiction has physical manifestations, it seemed safe to assume that it, too, was a disease that could be cured, even in the absence of evidence that addiction displays specific symptoms, follows a particular course, or responds to treatment as infectious diseases do.

Coincidental with the medicalizing of addiction was a dramatic rise in   12 the number of drug addicts. The reasons are unclear, but when alcoholism and compulsive drug use gained acceptance as forms of illness, during the 1890s, narcotics addiction had ebbed in England and America. Then, during the next ten years the trend reversed, and by 1910 the level of English opium consumption had returned to its nineteenth-century peaks.

The situation in the United States was in some ways more extreme. Like the English, Americans consumed massive quantities of opium at the turn of the century, especially in the form of patent medicines available at local dime stores and peddled by itinerant salesmen. Another important catalyst for American addiction had come in 1898, with the invention by the Bayer company of the morphine derivative heroin. Legal at the time, heroin was easily administered by syringe and was ten times more potent than its parent drug.

America went on to become the world leader in narcotics addiction. In many nations the opium poppy is cultivated openly, yet addiction is virtually nonexistent: native peoples consider the drug harmless and use it only for ceremonial purposes. European nations—including France, where much of America's heroin supply is processed—also have had negligible addiction problems. Even England has had dramatically lower levels of heroin addiction than the United States. Indeed, drug use in America has come to be surrounded by a kind of mystique, which intensified when control of narcotics began to shift from physicians to government and law-enforcement officials. (In 1914, the Harrison Act, passed by the U.S. Congress, regulated the use of opiates and other drugs.) And as drugs became an object of social disapproval, there was a change in the groups that used them.

During the 1800s, much attention was focused on Chinese opium smoking, but the leading consumers of opium were, in fact, white, middle-class women, who apparently preferred the drug to their husbands' alternative, alcohol. By 1920, however, drugs had moved underground, to urban ghettos, where they were used predominantly by poor immigrant and minority males. Narcotics, especially heroin, had become an exotic source of horror and fascination for Americans. What once had been available at any local apothecary now was seen as the agent of an insidious compulsion that was an inevitable consequence of its use. Still, despite all the research into the pathology of cholera, malaria, influenza, and other diseases, the first quarter of this century passed before any attempt was made to find physiological evidence that narcotics use meant inescapable physical bondage.

The pioneering effort to demonstrate a biomedical basis for addiction   16
in human drug users was begun in 1925, at Philadelphia General Hospital. A team of researchers—an internist, a pathologist, a psychiatrist, and a chemist—administered a series of heavy doses of morphine to a group of drug addicts. To check for signs of physiological addiction, they measured the subjects' body functions and observed their performance on several tasks during withdrawal. But they found little evidence that addiction was much more than a result of the subjects' imaginations. In one of a series of articles based on this research, published in 1929 in the *Archives of Internal Medicine,* two of the Philadelphia physicians, Arthur B. Light and Edward G. Torrance, described the amazing behavior of their most recalcitrant subject, a man who was the quickest to express his displeasure when there was even the slightest delay in the administration of a drug. He refused to continue the experiment thirty-six hours after withdrawal, demanding instead that he be given more morphine. Light and Torrance administered a placebo and were bemused when the man "promptly went to sleep for a period of eight hours," never aware that he had been given "nothing but sterile water."

The researchers noted that, in general, though "the incessant begging and annoying behavior of the addict" during withdrawal "becomes at times almost unbearable," there were no marked changes in their patients' metabolism, circulation, respiration, or blood composition. Light and Torrance did observe such withdrawal symptoms as vomiting, diarrhea, perspiration, and nervousness, but because these occurred inconsistently, they did not appear to indicate a medical syndrome. In fact, the researchers reported that similar symptoms can be found among members of a university football team just before the proverbial big game—symptoms that disappear "when the whistle starting the game is blown."

Over the years, this work has been all but dismissed by the scientific community. Light and Torrance have been accused of ignoring the biological realities of addiction by mistaking physiological withdrawal for malingering. But this criticism fails to account for some of the most striking aspects of their findings. The addicts in their studies had been given extremely high levels of morphine—certainly in comparison with standard doses of narcotics available to American street addicts today—yet, when eventually denied their fixes, they overcame the ensuing withdrawal symptoms and lost their cravings. Some did so under forced regimens of physical exertion (when withdrawal set in, they were made to climb steps, for instance); others, after placebo injections.

In contrast, today's heroin addicts typically manifest severe, unremitting withdrawal symptoms when deprived of the drug at treatment centers—even though, as opposed to the addicts in the 1925 study, they often enter rehabilitation with no detectable concentrations of narcotics in their systems. (Drugs sold on the street typically are mixed with liberal amounts of benign substances, so the user is not exposed to large doses of narcotics.) Nevertheless, physicians continue to maintain that withdrawal and readdiction are inevitable consequences of habitual narcotics use, inherent in the chemical properties of the drugs—and that people who take these drugs are bound to consume them more frequently, compulsively, and invariantly than do users of other, so-called nonaddictive pharmacological products.

One of the most damning refutations of this belief is research into   20
narcotics use by American soldiers who served in Vietnam. A vast proportion of the men used opiates at one time or another during the war. This panicked American officials, who anticipated a wholesale influx of addicts stateside when the veterans returned home. The U.S. Department of Defense commissioned a research team, led by the epidemiologist Lee N. Robins, to study the military drug problem. Robins and her colleagues interviewed more than five hundred men who had used narcotics in Vietnam (identified by urine screening upon their departure) one year and then three years after their return home. Most had received a concentrated form of the drugs while in Southeast Asia, and of those who took narcotics five or more times, nearly three-quarters reported becoming addicted: they suffered significant with-

drawal symptoms when they were forced to stop using heroin for various reasons (they could not get any while out on patrol, for example).

According to all widely accepted ideas about heroin abuse, recovery depends on total abstinence. So, most of the returning soldiers who had been addicts, had they sought the drug back in the United States, should have become readdicted in short order. But Robins discovered that, while fully half of those who had been addicted in Vietnam used narcotics again upon their return home, only one-eighth became readdicted after three years back in the United States. And only half of those who used heroin frequently—more than once a week for what Robins described as "a considerable period of time"—became readdicted.

Robins's research yielded other surprising results. The returning veterans in her sample commonly consumed a variety of drugs besides heroin, including marijuana and amphetamines, though heroin addicts supposedly are possessed by a monomaniacal obsession for heroin. Moreover, their indulgence in heroin was no more compulsive or uncontrollable than their consumption of the other substances. All this evidence calls into question the long-held claim that opiates are special agents of addiction. Remarkably, however, such findings have had virtually no impact on addiction research and theory.

More influential has been a large body of experiments in which rats or monkeys continually self-administer drugs in the laboratory—studies often cited in support of the argument that narcotics are uniquely addictive. Yet, what many of these experiments have demonstrated is that it can be extremely difficult to addict animals. John L. Falk, a behavioral pharmacologist at Rutgers University, in New Jersey, found it necessary to alter the accustomed feeding regimen of rats to get them to drink significant amounts of alcohol. When a normal feeding regimen was resumed, the rats lost nearly all interest in alcohol. As Falk pointed out in a 1983 article entitled "Drug Dependence: Myth or Motive?" these results are consistent with other investigations showing that the motivational power of drugs over animals is "altered radically by seemingly small changes in the behavioral context." For example, many studies in which animals are required to press a bar to earn a narcotic injection have shown that increasing only slightly the number of requisite bar presses can halt the animal's drug consumption.

In one series of experiments, Bruce K. Alexander, a psychologist at Simon   24
Fraser University, in British Columbia, found that rats housed together in a large cage would not choose an opiate solution over water but that rats isolated in small cages drank significantly more of the opiate. Moreover, even after a period of being allowed to drink only the drugged liquid, the animals that had been isolated also chose water over the opiate when they were placed in the roomier cage and could once again enjoy the companionship of other rats. These experiments strongly suggest that drug dependence is a consequence of behavior *and* environment, and that, although animals

and some people will, under certain circumstances, consume drugs excessively and compulsively, it does not follow that narcotics are inherently addictive.

Certainly, the Vietnam experience also served as a kind of laboratory demonstration of how environmental factors can create a climate hospitable to addiction. In Southeast Asia, most American soldiers encountered a range of emotions and sensations unlike anything they had experienced at home: incessant fear, constant physical discomfort, intense loneliness for family and friends, the necessity for killing, a sense of complete helplessness—the inability to control their own destinies or even to know whether they would live to see the next dawn. In this alien world, the numbing, analgesic effects of narcotics were welcomed. But when returned to the secure familiarity of home, most of the men who were hooked in Vietnam—even if they felt moved to take a drug now and again—did not find narcotics addictively alluring.

As Harold Kalant, a pharmacologist at the Addiction Research Foundation, in Toronto, observed after decades of work, given that the drug user or alcoholic often continues to seek the intoxicated state even after completing the period of withdrawal, there can be no pharmacological or biological explanations for this behavior. Clearly, any habit has an impact on a person's body and mind, but interpreting how a pharmacological experience feels, deciding that this feeling is desirable, concluding that it is impossible to live without it, and seeking more of it all are matters of individual perception and choice.

Given that there is no evidence for a purely physiological explanation of addiction, the whole process of labeling a drug addictive is arbitrary at best. One of the more telling examples of this is the evolution of American public policy concerning cocaine. As difficult as it may be to fathom today, cocaine once was an active ingredient in soda pop: Coca-Cola contained a dose of the drug until 1903. Though narcotics researchers have explored the addictive potential of cocaine for the past fifty years in the laboratory, only upon a sudden rise in recreational cocaine consumption, as well as a proportional rise in compulsive use, during the early eighties, did government agencies ordain that the drug be regarded as addictive. In fact, that judgment directly contradicted the most comprehensive experimental findings available.

In a recent survey, investigators at the Toronto addiction-research center 28 found that 20 percent of the recreational cocaine users they studied had frequently been seized by an urge to continue taking the drug, but, even among this minority, most did not become fully addicted. A review of the literature on cocaine use, by the Yale University psychiatrist David Musto, pointed out that less than 10 percent of regular cocaine users descend into a pattern of compulsive, uncontrollable consumption. Nonetheless, we are warned repeatedly that to "say yes" to cocaine is to slide inexorably into chemical bondage and, ultimately, death.

As Berridge and Edwards point out, this publicity campaign echoes an earlier time: "The nineteenth-century discovery that the addict is a suitable case for treatment is today an entrenched and unquestionable premise, with society unaware of the arbitrariness of this come-lately assumption." The researchers add that any suggestion that addicts be "left to their own devices would be dismissed only as outrageous and bizarre." In the light of the failure of researchers to link narcotics addiction or, for that matter, alcoholism with physiology, it seems all the more absurd that so many sexually driven people, compulsive shoppers, and other obsessive types have joined substance abusers in the special programs and treatment centers that have proliferated across the country.

What, exactly, goes on inside these rehabilitation facilities? Certainly, Edwards's disillusionment with them is based, in part, on his own research experience in England (where he is considered the leading psychiatric authority on addiction). In a controlled study of hospital treatment for alcoholism, he and his colleagues found that problem drinkers given a single session of counseling improved just as much as a comparable group receiving the full complement of inpatient and outpatient hospital services, including detoxification programs and follow-up counseling. Similarly, a study by the psychiatrist George Vaillant, of Dartmouth College, checked the progress of hospital-treated alcoholics two and then eight years after their release. Though some had cut down on drinking or ceased altogether, they had done so only in roughly the same proportions as untreated alcoholics.

Still, many graduates of treatment centers passionately proclaim that their lives have been saved by the help they sought. In part, this may be because alcoholics and addicts who enter such treatment programs often are effectively brainwashed into believing they have an incurable disease. The sociologist David R. Rudy, of Morehead State University, in Kentucky, who observed several chapters of Alcoholics Anonymous, reported, in *Becoming Alcoholic*, that a number of those who entered these groups did so believing that they had some kind of drinking problem but not that they had succumbed to uncontrollable alcoholism. Once inside the group, however, they quickly were shown the error of their thinking; new members were pressured into acknowledging that, because of their disease, their drinking was out of control.

This brainwashing exerts a powerful influence on the addict's perception   32
of his or her addiction. An experiment conducted by the psychologist G. Alan Marlatt, of the University of Washington, in Seattle, demonstrated the effects on active alcoholics of believing that one slip off the wagon leads to a binge. Alcoholics in the study were given highly flavored drinks either with

or without alcohol. Some were told that they were drinking liquor, others that they were consuming a nonalcoholic beverage. Marlatt found that alcoholics who believed they were drinking alcohol—whether or not they were—drank significantly more than those who were actually given alcohol without their knowledge. Having learned that even a casual brush with liquor means an inevitable relapse, the alcoholics given the placebo lived out their expectations. But it had nothing to do with physiology.

The fundamental tenet of Alcoholics Anonymous—that alcoholism is never cured—has been imposed upon almost every bad habit imaginable, and as a result, a thriving addiction-treatment industry has developed in the United States. Comparing statistics from 1942 with those from 1976, Robin Room, of the Alcohol Research Group, in Berkeley, California, found that the number of people being treated for alcoholism in America, per capita, had increased twentyfold. And in the ten years since Room's survey, treatment has continued to grow at an alarming rate. Yet Americans over twenty-one drink less today than a decade ago. One explanation for this paradox is that the threshold for labeling a person chemically dependent has been lowered—as with Kitty Dukakis, who referred herself to Edgehill-Newport because she had gotten drunk a few times after years of moderate drinking. By attracting such alcoholics as Mrs. Dukakis, private hospital chains that specialize in treating substance abuse continue to expand.

Meanwhile, new addiction-treatment groups modeled on Alcoholics Anonymous have proliferated, as well. The National Council on Compulsive Gambling, which coalesced from numerous Gamblers Anonymous groups, has grown even more rapidly during the eighties than the AA-inspired National Council on Alcoholism. Sometimes, compulsive gamblers are treated in hospitals, frequently on the same inpatient wards as alcoholics. And there is a National Association on Sexual Addiction Problems, as well as a nationwide network of Sex Addicts Anonymous branches, both of which support hospital treatment for "victims" of compulsive copulation.

Perhaps the most dire consequence of the disease model of addiction is that it has encouraged the abdication of individual responsibility for outrageous conduct. The addict is a victim and, thus, unaccountable for his actions. The misadventures of Wade Boggs, confessed "sex addict," may have provided the public with a measure of titillation. But another recent news event—the object of even more intense public and media preoccupation—had a more chilling aspect: jurors declined to deliver a murder conviction against Joel Steinberg (the disturbed Manhattan lawyer convicted of manslaughter in the fatal beating of his illegally adopted six-year-old daughter, Lisa), partly because they felt Steinberg, a habitual drug user, was under the influence of cocaine at the time of his daughter's death and, so, was not fully responsible.

Certainly, Joel Steinberg may have been impaired by the effects of a drug   36 when he murdered Lisa. But was he suffering from a disease? Is there something in cocaine that interacted with the cells in Joel Steinberg's body to enslave him to the drug? And if so, must we forgive him for killing a child? There is no justification within the realm of science for making that conceptual leap.

Points to Consider

1. Why is the history of drug addiction important to Peele's argument? According to Peele, how did addiction become a "disease"?

2. Of what importance are the experiments conducted in the 1920s by Light and Torrance? Why are their findings dismissed by the scientific community?

3. Why does Peele regard the recent profileration of treatment centers for compulsive shoppers, sex addicts, and other obsessive types as "absurd"?

4. What role has Alcoholics Anonymous played in the recent vogue of addiction? According to Peele, what role does "brainwashing" play in the cure of addiction?

Discussing the Unit

Suggested Topic for Discussion

The three selections in this unit present a wide spectrum of views on the topic of addiction and each cites numerous experts who also offer widely divergent opinions. Which point of view—or which expert opinion—do you agree with most? Do you think the concept of addiction is being unreasonably stretched to excuse irresponsible behavior? Or do you think that recent medical and psychological research is providing a new view of pathological behavior that cannot be socially or legally ignored?

Preparing for Class Discussion

1. Consider how much of your opinion about addiction is shaped by a traditional sense of free will and moral responsibility. What is your instinctive reaction to someone who cites dependency as an explanation for criminal or antisocial behavior? Go through the individual cases referred to in the selections. Which addictions do you personally find silly? Which do you feel deserve sympathy? List the cases in order from the most serious to the most absurd.

2. Though Stanton Peele argues that there is no scientific basis for our belief in an addictive personality, a large number of scientists, doctors, and professionals clearly accept addiction as a serious illness. How do you explain these disagreements among experts? To what extent do these opinions depend upon how we define "addiction"? What definitions of the term can you find in the articles? How do dictionaries and encyclopedias define the word? How would *you* define the term? What does your definition imply about the basis of addiction?

From Discussion to Writing

Derive from your reading a definition of "addiction" that you think accurately conveys the true meaning of the word. Use that definition to shape an essay in which you argue why a specific problem is or is not an addiction. You may choose any type of behavior classified as addictive in the preceding articles—shopping, sex, drugs, alcohol, eating, etc. Be sure to show how your example either fits or doesn't fit your definition of addiction. Support your views with appropriate evidence drawn from the articles and additional sources.

20

America's Homeless:
What Should Be Done?

No one seems sure how many of them there are or who they are, but homeless people have become an increasingly disturbing presence in America's towns and cities. Their plight has caught the attention of politicians, journalists, social reformers, professional groups, and television networks nationwide; homelessness has even surfaced as a theme of several recent Hollywood films. Yet despite all the discussion and debate surrounding the topic, most Americans still know little about the nature of homelessness and the daily conditions of homeless people.

Much of the discussion about homelessness has focused on the causes and the extent of the problem. On one side of the issue are those who, like Jonathan Kozol in "Distancing the Homeless," believe not only that the size of the homeless population is huge and rapidly increasing but that the problem is primarily one of housing and economics. On the other side are those who, like Thomas J. Main in "What We Know About the Homeless," believe that the extent of homelessness has been exaggerated and that the problem has a great deal to do with the mental and physical disabilities of the homeless themselves.

Both the Kozol and Main essays are concerned with explanations of homelessness in America. In "Homeless Bound," Roy Rowan reports on the several weeks in the winter of 1990 that he lived as a homeless person in New York City. By introducing us to some of the people he met on the streets and in shelters, Rowan brings us close to the everyday conditions of homelessness. His essay offers no explanations or interpretations but it convincingly shows us that economic statistics and abstractions always come down to real people and actual places.

JONATHAN KOZOL

Distancing the Homeless   [THE YALE REVIEW / Winter 1988]

It is commonly believed by many journalists and politicians that the homeless of America are, in large part, former patients of large mental hospitals who were deinstitutionalized in the 1970s — the consequence, it is sometimes said, of misguided liberal opinion, which favored the treatment of such persons in community-based centers. It is argued that this policy, and the subsequent failure of society to build such centers or to provide them in sufficient number, is the primary cause of homelessness in the United States.

Those who work among the homeless do not find that explanation satisfactory. While conceding that a certain number of the homeless are, or have been, mentally unwell, they believe that, in the case of most unsheltered people, the primary reason is economic rather than clinical. The cause of homelessness, they say with disarming logic, is the lack of homes and of income with which to rent or acquire them.

They point to the loss of traditional jobs in industry (two million every year since 1980) and to the fact that half of those who are laid off end up in work that pays a poverty-level wage. They point to the parallel growth of poverty in families with children, noting that children, who represent one

---

JONATHAN KOZOL (b. 1936), a writer and teacher, has written several books on educational and social problems, including Death at an Early Age *(1968), which won a National Book Award,* Illiterate America *(1985), and* Rachel and Her Children *(1988), from which "Distancing the Homeless" was adapted for the* Yale Review *(Winter 1988).*

quarter of our population, make up 40 percent of the poor: since 1968, the number of children in poverty has grown by three million, while welfare benefits to families with children have declined by 35 percent.

And they note, too, that these developments have coincided with a time   4
in which the shortage of low-income housing has intensified as the gentrification of our major cities has accelerated. Half a million units of low-income housing have been lost each year to condominium conversion as well as to arson, demolition, or abandonment. Between 1978 and 1980, median rents climbed 30 percent for people in the lowest income sector, driving many of these families into the streets. After 1980, rents rose at even faster rates. In Boston, between 1982 and 1984, over 80 percent of the housing units renting below three hundred dollars disappeared, while the number of units renting above six hundred dollars nearly tripled.

Hard numbers, in this instance, would appear to be of greater help than psychiatric labels in telling us why so many people become homeless. Eight million American families now pay half or more of their income for rent or a mortgage. Six million more, unable to pay rent at all, live doubled up with others. At the same time, federal support for low-income housing dropped from $30 billion (1980) to $9 billion (1986). Under Presidents Ford and Carter, five hundred thousand subsidized private housing units were constructed. By President Reagan's second term, the number had dropped to twenty-five thousand. "We're getting out of the housing business, period," said a deputy assistant secretary of the Department of Housing and Urban Development in 1985.

One year later, the *Washington Post* reported that the number of homeless families in Washington, D.C., had grown by 500 percent over the previous twelve months. In New York City, the waiting list for public housing now contains two hundred thousand names. The waiting is eighteen years.

Why, in the face of these statistics, are we impelled to find a psychiatric explanation for the growth of homelessness in the United States?

A misconception, once it is implanted in the popular imagination, is not   8
easy to uproot, particularly when it serves a useful social role. The notion that the homeless are largely psychotics who belong in institutions, rather than victims of displacement at the hands of enterprising realtors, spares us from the need to offer realistic solutions to the fact of deep and widening extremes of wealth and poverty in the United States. It also enables us to tell ourselves that the despair of homeless people bears no intimate connection to the privileged existence we enjoy — when, for example, we rent or purchase one of those restored townhouses that once provided shelter for people now huddled in the street.

But there may be another reason to assign labels to the destitute. Terming economic victims "psychotic" or "disordered" helps to place them at a distance. It says that they aren't quite like us — and, more important, that we could not be like them. The plight of homeless families is a nightmare. It may not seem natural to try to banish human beings from our midst, but it *is* natural to try to banish nightmares from our minds.

So the rituals of clinical contamination proceed uninterrupted by the economic facts described above. Research that addresses homelessness as an *injustice* rather than as a medical *misfortune* does not win the funding of foundations. And the research which *is* funded, defining the narrowed borders of permissible debate, diverts our attention from the antecedent to the secondary cause of homelessness. Thus it is that perfectly ordinary women whom I know in New York City — people whose depression or anxiety is a realistic consequence of months and even years in crowded shelters or the streets — are interrogated by invasive research scholars in an effort to decode their poverty, to find clinical categories for their despair and terror, to identify the secret failing that lies hidden in their psyche.

Many pregnant women without homes are denied prenatal care because they constantly travel from one shelter to another. Many are anemic. Many are denied essential dietary supplements by recent federal cuts. As a consequence, some of their children do not live to see their second year of life. Do these mothers sometimes show signs of stress? Do they appear disorganized, depressed, disordered? Frequently. They are immobilized by pain, traumatized by fear. So it is no surprise that when researchers enter the scene to ask them how they "feel," the resulting reports tell us that the homeless are emotionally unwell. The reports do not tell us we have *made* these people ill. They do not tell us that illness is a natural response to intolerable conditions. Nor do they tell us of the strength and the resilience that so many of these people still retain despite the miseries they must endure. They set these men and women apart in capsules labeled "personality disorder" or "psychotic," where they no longer threaten our complacence.

I visited Haiti not many years ago, when the Duvalier family was still in power. If an American scholar were to have made a psychological study of the homeless families living in the streets of Port-au-Prince — sleeping amidst rotten garbage, bathing in open sewers — and if he were to return to the United States to tell us that the reasons for their destitution were "behavioral problems" or "a lack of mental health," we would be properly suspicious. Knowledgeable Haitians would not merely be suspicious. They would be enraged. Even to initiate such research when economic and political explanations present themselves so starkly would appear grotesque. It is no less so in the United States.

One of the more influential studies of this nature was carried out in 1985 by Ellen Bassuk, a psychiatrist at Harvard University. Drawing upon interviews with eight homeless parents, Dr. Bassuk contends, according to the *Boston Globe,* that "90 percent [of these people] have problems other than housing and poverty that are so acute they would be unable to live successfully on their own." She also precludes the possibility that illness, where it does exist, may be provoked by destitution. "Our data," she writes, "suggest that mental illness tends to precede homelessness." She concedes that living in the streets can make a homeless person's mental illness worse; but she insists upon the fact of prior illness.

The Executive Director of the Massachusetts Commission on Children and Youth believes that Dr. Bassuk's estimate is far too high. The staff of Massachusetts Human Services Secretary Phillip Johnston believes the appropriate number is closer to 10 percent.

In defending her research, Bassuk challenges such critics by claiming that they do not have data to refute her. This may be true. Advocates for the homeless do not receive funds to defend the sanity of the people they represent. In placing the burden of proof upon them, Dr. Bassuk has created an extraordinary dialectic: how does one prove that people aren't unwell? What homeless mother would consent to enter a procedure that might "prove" her mental health? What overburdened shelter operator would divert scarce funds to such an exercise? It is an unnatural, offensive, and dehumanizing challenge.

Dr. Bassuk's work, however, isn't the issue I want to raise here; the issue   16
is the use or misuse of that work by critics of the poor. For example, in a widely syndicated essay published in 1986, the newspaper columnist Charles Krauthammer argued that the homeless are essentially a deranged segment of the population and that we must find the "political will" to isolate them from society. We must do this, he said, "whether they like it or not." Arguing even against the marginal benefits of homeless shelters, Krauthammer wrote: "There is a better alternative, however, though no one dares speak its name." Krauthammer dares: that better alternative, he said, is "asylum."

One of Mr. Krauthammer's colleagues at the *Washington Post*, the columnist George Will, perceives the homeless as a threat to public cleanliness and argues that they ought to be consigned to places where we need not see them. "It is," he says, "simply a matter of public hygiene" to put them out of sight. Another journalist, Charles Murray, writing from the vantage point of a social Darwinist, recommends the restoration of the almshouses of the 1800s. "Granted Dickensian horror stories about almshouses," he begins, there were nonetheless "good almshouses"; he proposes "a good correctional 'halfway house'" as a proper shelter for a mother and child with no means of self-support.

In the face of such declarations, the voices of those who work with and know the poor are harder to hear.

Manhattan Borough President David Dinkins made the following observation on the basis of a study commissioned in 1986: "No facts support the belief that addiction or behavioral problems occur with more frequency in the homeless family population than in a similar socioeconomic population. Homeless families are not demographically different from other public assistance families when they enter the shelter system. . . . Family homelessness is typically a housing and income problem: the unavailability of affordable housing and the inadequacy of public assistance income."

In a "hypothetical world," write James Wright and Julie Lam of the University of Massachusetts, "where there were no alcoholics, no drug addicts, no mentally ill, no deinstitutionalization, . . . indeed, no personal social pathologies at all, there would still be a formidable homelessness problem, simply because at this stage in American history, there is not enough low-income housing" to accommodate the poor. [20]

New York State's respected Commissioner of Social Services, Cesar Perales, makes the point in fewer words: "Homelessness is less and less a result of personal failure, and more and more is caused by larger forces. There is no longer affordable housing in New York City for people of poor and modest means."

Even the words of medical practitioners who care for homeless people have been curiously ignored. A study published by the Massachusetts Medical Society, for instance, has noted that the most frequent illnesses among a sample of the homeless population, after alcohol and drug use, are trauma (31 percent), upper respiratory disorders (28 percent), limb disorders (19 percent), mental illness (16 percent), skin diseases (15 percent), hypertension (14 percent), and neurological illnesses (12 percent). (Excluded from this tabulation are lead poisoning, malnutrition, acute diarrhea, and other illnesses especially common among homeless infants and small children.) Why, we may ask, of all these calamities, does mental illness command so much political and press attention? The answer may be that the label of mental illness places the destitute outside the sphere of ordinary life. It personalizes an anguish that is public in its genesis; it individualizes a misery that is both general in cause and general in application.

The rate of tuberculosis among the homeless is believed to be ten times that of the general population. Asthma, I have learned in countless interviews, is one of the most common causes of discomfort in the shelters. Compulsive smoking, exacerbated by the crowding and the tension, is more common in the shelters than in any place that I have visited except prison. Infected and untreated sores, scabies, diarrhea, poorly set limbs, protruding elbows, awkwardly distorted wrists, bleeding gums, impacted teeth, and other untreated dental problems are so common among children in the shelters that one rapidly forgets their presence. Hunger and emaciation are everywhere. Children as well as adults can bring to mind the photographs of people found in camps for refugees of war in 1945. But these miseries bear no stigma, and mental illness does. It conveys a stigma in the Soviet Union. It conveys a stigma in the United States. In both nations the label is used, whether as a matter of deliberate policy or not, to isolate and treat as special cases those who, by deed or word or by sheer presence, represent a threat to national complacence. The two situations are obviously not identical, but they are enough alike to give Americans reason for concern.

Last summer, some twenty-eight thousand homeless people were afforded shelter by the city of New York. Of this number, twelve thousand were children and six thousand were parents living together in families. The average child was six years old, the average parent twenty-seven. A typical homeless family included a mother with two or three children, but in about one-fifth of these families two parents were present. Roughly ten thousand single persons, then, made up the remainder of the population of the city's shelters.

These proportions vary somewhat from one area of the nation to another. In all areas, however, families are the fastest-growing sector of the homeless population, and in the Northeast they are by far the largest sector already. In Massachusetts, three-fourths of the homeless now are families with children; in certain parts of Massachusetts — Attleboro and Northhampton, for example — the proportion reaches 90 percent. Two-thirds of the homeless children studied recently in Boston were less than five years old.

Of an estimated two to three million homeless people nationwide, about 500,000 are dependent children, according to Robert Hayes, counsel to the National Coalition for the Homeless. Including their parents, at least 750,000 homeless people in America are family members.

What is to be made, then, of the supposition that the homeless are primarily the former residents of mental hospitals, persons who were carelessly released during the 1970s? Many of them are, to be sure. Among the older men and women in the streets and shelters, as many as one-third (some believe as many as one-half) may be chronically disturbed, and a number of these people were deinstitutionalized during the 1970s. But in a city like New York, where nearly half the homeless are small children with an average age of six, to operate on the basis of such a supposition makes no sense. Their parents, with an average age of twenty-seven, are not likely to have been hospitalized in the 1970s, either.

Nor is it easy to assume, as was once the case, that single men — those who come closer to fitting the stereotype of the homeless vagrant, the drifting alcoholic of an earlier age — are the former residents of mental hospitals. The age of homeless men has dropped in recent years; many of them are only twenty-one to twenty-eight years old. Fifty percent of homeless men in New York City shelters in 1984 were there for the first time. Most had previously had homes and jobs. Many had never before needed public aid.

A frequently cited set of figures tells us that in 1955, the average daily census of nonfederal psychiatric institutions was 677,000, and that by 1984, the number had dropped to 151,000. Subtract the second number from the first, conventional logic tells us, and we have an explanation for the homelessness of half a million people. A closer look at the same number offers us a different lesson.

The sharpest decline in the average daily census of these institutions occurred prior to 1978, and the largest part of that decline, in fact, appeared at least a decade earlier. From 677,000 in 1955, the census dropped to 378,000 in 1972. The 1974 census was 307,000. In 1976 it was 230,000; in 1977 it was 211,000; and in 1978 it was 190,000. In no year since 1978 has the average daily census dropped by more than 9,000 persons, and in the six-year period from 1978 to 1984, the total decline was 39,000 persons. Compared with a decline of 300,000 from 1955 to 1972, and of nearly 200,000 more from 1972 to 1978, the number is small. But the years since 1980 are the period in which the present homeless crisis surfaced. Only since 1983 have homeless individuals overflowed the shelters.

If the large numbers of the homeless lived in hospitals before they reappeared in subway stations and in public shelters, we need to ask where they were and what they had been doing from 1972 to 1980. Were they living under bridges? Were they waiting out the decade in the basements of deserted buildings?

No. The bulk of those who had been psychiatric patients and were 32 released from hospitals during the 1960s and early 1970s had been living in the meantime in low-income housing, many in skid-row hotels or boarding houses. Such housing — commonly known as SRO (single-room occupancy) units — was drastically diminished by the gentrification of our cities that began in 1970. Almost 50 percent of SRO housing was replaced by luxury apartments or by office buildings between 1970 and 1980, and the remaining units have been disappearing at even faster rates. As recently as 1986, after New York City had issued a prohibition against conversion of such housing, a well-known developer hired a demolition team to destroy a building in Times Square that had previously been home to indigent people. The demolition took place in the middle of the night. In order to avoid imprisonment, the developer was allowed to make a philanthropic gift to homeless people as a token of atonement. This incident, bizarre as it appears, reminds us that the profit motive for displacement of the poor is very great in every major city. It also indicates a more realistic explanation for the growth of homelessness during the 1980s.

Even for those persons who are ill and were deinstitutionalized during the decades before 1980, the precipitating cause of homelessness in 1987 is not illness but loss of housing. SRO housing, unattractive as it may have been, offered low-cost sanctuaries for the homeless, providing a degree of safety and mutual support for those who lived within them. They were a demeaning version of the community health centers that society had promised; they were the de facto "halfway houses" of the 1970s. For these people too, then — at most half of the homeless single persons in America — the cause of homelessness is lack of housing.

A writer in the *New York Times* describes a homeless woman standing on a traffic island in Manhattan. "She was evicted from her small room in the hotel just across the street," and she is determined to get revenge. Until she does, "nothing will move her from that spot. . . . Her argumentativeness and her angry fixation on revenge, along with the apparent absence of hallucinations, mark her as a paranoid." Most physicians, I imagine, would be more reserved in passing judgment with so little evidence, but this author makes his diagnosis without hesitation. "The paranoids of the street," he says, "are among the most difficult to help."

Perhaps so. But does it depend on who is offering the help? Is anyone offering to help this woman get back her home? Is it crazy to seek vengeance for being thrown into the street? The absence of anger, some psychiatrists believe, might indicate much greater illness.

The same observer sees additional symptoms of pathology ("negative 36 symptoms," he calls them) in the fact that many homeless persons demonstrate a "gross deterioration in their personal hygiene" and grooming, leading to "indifference" and "apathy." Having just identified one woman as unhealthy because she is so far from being "indifferent" as to seek revenge, he now sees apathy as evidence of illness; so consistency is not what we are looking for in this account. But how much less indifferent might the homeless be if those who decide their fate were less indifferent themselves? How might their grooming and hygiene be improved if they were permitted access to a public toilet?

In New York City, as in many cities, homeless people are denied the right to wash in public bathrooms, to store their few belongings in a public locker, or, in certain cases, to make use of public toilets altogether. Shaving, cleaning of clothes, and other forms of hygiene are prohibited in the men's room of Grand Central Station. The terminal's three hundred lockers, used in former times by homeless people to secure their goods, were removed in 1986 as "a threat to public safety," according to a study made by the New York City Council.

At one-thirty every morning, homeless people are ejected from the station. Many once attempted to take refuge on the ramp that leads to Forty-second Street because it was protected from the street by wooden doors and thus provided some degree of warmth. But the station management responded to this challenge in two ways. The ramp was mopped with a strong mixture of ammonia to produce a noxious smell, and when the people sleeping there brought cardboard boxes and newspapers to protect them from the fumes, the entrance doors were chained wide open. Temperatures dropped some nights to ten degrees. Having driven these people to the streets, city officials subsequently determined that their willingness to risk exposure to cold weather could be taken as further evidence of mental illness.

At Pennsylvania Station in New York, homeless women are denied the use of toilets. Amtrak police come by and herd them off each hour on the hour. In June 1985, Amtrak officials issued this directive to police: "It is the policy of Amtrak to not allow the homeless and undesirables to remain. . . . Officers are encouraged to eject all undesirables. . . . Now is the time to train and educate them that their presence will not be tolerated as cold weather sets in." In an internal memo, according to CBS, an Amtrak official asked flatly: "Can't we get rid of this trash?"

I have spent many nights in conversation with the women who are 40 huddled in the corridors and near the doorway of the public toilets in Penn Station. Many are young. Most are cogent. Few are dressed in the familiar rags suggested by the term *bag ladies*. Unable to bathe or use the toilets in the station, almost all are in conditions of intolerable physical distress. The sight of clusters of police officers, mostly male, guarding a toilet from use by homeless women speaks volumes about the public conscience of New York.

Where do these women defecate? How do they bathe? What will we do when, in her physical distress, a woman finally disrobes in public and begins to urinate right on the floor? "Gross deterioration," someone will call it, evidence of mental illness. In the course of an impromptu survey in the streets last September, Mayor Koch observed a homeless woman who had soiled her own clothes. Not only was the woman crazy, said the mayor, but those who differed with him on his diagnosis must be crazy, too. "I am the Number One social worker in this town — with sanity," said he.

It may be that this woman was psychotic, but the mayor's comment says a great deal more about his sense of revulsion and the moral climate of a decade in which words like these may be applauded than about her mental state.

A young man who had lost his job, then his family, then his home, all in the summer of 1986, spoke with me for several hours in Grand Central Station on the weekend following Thanksgiving. "A year ago," he said, "I never thought that somebody like me would end up in a shelter. Nothing you've ever undergone prepares you. You walk into the place [a shelter on the Bowery] — the smell of sweat and urine hits you like a wall. Unwashed bodies and the look of absolute despair on many, many faces there would make you think you were in Dante's Hell. . . . What you fear is that you will be here forever. You do not know if it is ever going to end. You think to yourself: it is a dream and I will awake. Sometimes I think: it's an experiment. They are watching you to find out how much you can take. . . . I was a pretty stable man. Now I tremble when I meet somebody in the ordinary world. I'm trembling right now. . . . For me, the loss of work and loss of wife had left me rocking. Then the welfare regulations hit me. I began to feel that I would be reduced to trash. . . . Half the people that I know are suffering from chest infections and sleep deprivation. The lack of sleep leaves you debilitated, shaky. You exaggerate your fears. If a psychiatrist came along he'd say that I was crazy. But I was an ordinary man. There was nothing wrong with me. I lost my kids. I lost my home. Now would you say that I was crazy if I told you I was feeling sad?"

"If the plight of homeless adults is the shame of America," writes Fred   44
Hechinger in the New York Times, "the lives of homeless children are the nation's crime."

In November 1984, a fact already known to advocates for the homeless was given brief attention by the press. Homeless families, the New York Times reported, "mostly mothers and young children, have been sleeping on chairs, counters, and floors of the city's emergency welfare offices." Reacting to such reports, the mayor declared: "The woman is sitting on a chair or on a floor. It is not because we didn't offer her a bed. We provide a shelter for every single person who knocks on our door." On the same day, however, the city reported that in the previous eleven weeks it had been unable to give shelter to 153 families, and in the subsequent year, 1985, the city later reported that about two thousand children slept in welfare offices because of lack of shelter space.

Some eight hundred homeless infants in New York City, reported the National Coalition for the Homeless, "routinely go without sufficient food, cribs, health care, and diapers." The lives of these children "are put at risk," while "high-risk pregnant women" are repeatedly forced to sleep in unsafe "barracks shelters" or welfare offices called Emergency Assistance Units (EAUs). "Coalition monitors, making sporadic random checks, found eight women in their *ninth* month of pregnancy sleeping in EAUs. . . . Two women denied shelter began having labor contractions at the EAU." In one instance, the Legal Aid Society was forced to go to court after a woman lost her child by miscarriage while lying on the floor of a communal bathroom in a shelter which the courts had already declared unfit to house pregnant women.

The coalition also reported numerous cases in which homeless mothers were obliged to choose between purchasing food or diapers for their infants. Federal guidelines issued in 1986 deepened the nutrition crisis faced by mothers in the welfare shelters by counting the high rent paid to the owners of the buildings as a part of family income, rendering their residents ineligible for food stamps. Families I interviewed who had received as much as $150 in food stamps monthly in June 1986 were cut back to $33 before Christmas.

"Now you're hearing all kinds of horror stories," said President Reagan,   48
"about the people that are going to be thrown out in the snow to hunger and [to] die of cold and so forth. . . . We haven't cut a single budget." But

in the four years leading up to 1985, according to the *New Republic,* Aid to
Families with Dependent Children had been cut by $4.8 billion, child nutri-
tion programs by $5.2 billion, food stamps by $6.8 billion. The federal
government's authority to help low-income families with housing assistance
was cut from $30 billion to $11 billion in Reagan's first term. In his fiscal
1986 budget, the president proposed to cut that by an additional 95 percent.

"If even one American child is forced to go to bed hungry at night," the
president said on another occasion, "that is a national tragedy. We are too
generous a people to allow this." But in the years since the president spoke
these words, thousands of poor children in New York alone have gone to
bed too sick to sleep and far too weak to rise the next morning to attend a
public school. Thousands more have been unable to attend school at all
because their homeless status compels them to move repeatedly from one
temporary shelter to another. Even in the affluent suburbs outside New York
City, hundreds of homeless children are obliged to ride as far as sixty miles
twice a day in order to obtain an education in the public schools to which
they were originally assigned before their families were displaced. Many of
these children get to school too late to eat their breakfast; others are denied
lunch at school because of federal cuts in feeding programs.

Many homeless children die — and others suffer brain damage — as a
direct consequence of federal cutbacks in prenatal programs, maternal nutrition, and other feeding programs. The parents of one such child shared
with me the story of the year in which their child was delivered, lived, and
died. The child, weighing just over four pounds at birth, grew deaf and blind
soon after, and for these reasons had to stay in the hospital for several
months. When he was released on Christmas Eve of 1984, his mother and
father had no home. He lived with his parents in the shelters, subways,
streets, and welfare offices of New York City for four winter months, and
was readmitted to the hospital in time to die in May 1985.

When we met and spoke the following year, the father told me that his
wife had contemplated and even attempted suicide after the child's death,
while he had entertained the thought of blowing up the welfare offices of
New York City. I would tell him that to do so would be illegal and unwise.
I would never tell him it was crazy.

"No one will be turned away," says the mayor of New York City, as 52
hundreds of young mothers with their infants are turned from the doors of
shelters season after season. That may sound to some like denial of reality.
"Now you're hearing all these stories," says the president of the United
States as he denies that anyone is cold or hungry or unhoused. On another
occasion he says that the unsheltered "are homeless, you might say, by
choice." That sounds every bit as self-deceiving.

The woman standing on the traffic island screaming for revenge until
her room has been restored to her sounds relatively healthy by comparison.
If three million homeless people did the same, and all at the same time, we
might finally be forced to listen.

Points to Consider

1. Why does Kozol think that mental-health explanations of homelessness are unsatisfactory? Why does he believe these explanations are advanced? Who advances them?

2. How does Kozol respond to studies such as Dr. Ellen Bassuk's which show that mental illness precedes homelessness? What does he feel these studies omit?

3. What factors does Kozol believe were responsible for the increases in the number of homeless people since 1970?

4. What does Kozol find offensive about the *New York Times* report of the homeless woman in Manhattan (paragraph 34)? Why does he think the reporter is both wrong in his interpretation and inconsistent in his argument?

5. At the beginning of his essay, Kozol refers to "those who work among the homeless." Who are they and why does he think they understand the homeless better than others do? How does he establish himself as one of these people? What are his contacts with the homeless like? Do you think they help make his essay convincing?

THOMAS J. MAIN

What We Know About the Homeless

[COMMENTARY / May 1988]

In April 1986, Joyce Brown, a former New Jersey secretary (who also calls herself Billie Boggs), had a fight with her sisters with whom she was then living — and hopped on a bus to New York City. Something happened, and she ended up living near the hot-air vent of Swensen's restaurant at Second Avenue and Sixty-fifth Street. She stayed there for a year, during which time her hair became tangled and matted; she insulted passers-by (especially black men, at whom she hurled racial epithets, although she herself is black), she burned the money she was given by sympathetic observers, and she relieved herself on the streets.

Eventually she came to the attention of Project Help, a mobile psychiatric unit that monitors mentally ill homeless people in lower Manhattan. Until recently, Project Help would not involuntarily transport a "street person" to a hospital unless he was an immediate danger to himself or others, and it interpreted that criterion strictly. When the Koch administration decided to apply a less strict interpretation — on the ground that living on the street is dangerous for the mentally ill even if not immediately so — Joyce Brown became the first person removed from the streets to Bellevue Hospital for psychiatric evaluation. She was diagnosed as a chronic schizophrenic, and the city held her in the hospital for twelve weeks, during which time her doctors attempted to obtain permission to have her medicated. But with the aid of Robert Levey, a lawyer from the New York Civil Liberties Union (NYCLU), Miss Brown not only avoided medication but successfully litigated for her release.

At this point, under the guidance of Levey and NYCLU president Norman Siegel, Miss Brown declared that she had been "appointed the homeless spokesperson." After shopping trips to Saks Fifth Avenue, Lord & Taylor,

THOMAS J. MAIN (b. 1955), an alumnus of the University of Chicago and the John F. Kennedy School of Government at Harvard University, is currently working on a Ph.D. in politics at Princeton University. His writings on the homeless have appeared in Public Interest, *the* New York Times, *the* Wall Street Journal, *and* Commentary.

and Bloomingdale's, and dinner at Windows on the World, Miss Brown and her lawyers hit the lecture circuit. She spoke at New York University Law School and at the Cardozo Law School, she was interviewed on *60 Minutes* and *Donahue,* and she received half-a-dozen book and film proposals. Then, on February 18, 1988, Miss Brown, Levey, and Siegel all participated in the Harvard Law School Forum on "The Homeless Crisis: A Street View."

Levey (describing himself as a kind of "warm-up act . . . at a rock   4 concert") spoke first. He wanted, he said, only to raise some questions, of which the key one was why our society had decided to make Joyce Brown into a celebrity. Was it because we wanted to sweep the problem under the rug by focusing on the fate of a single individual who had successfully challenged the city and gotten off the streets? This seemed an odd question and a still odder answer since it was precisely Levey and his colleagues at the NYCLU who had made Joyce Brown a celebrity; and the last thing in the world they had in mind was to sweep the problem of homelessness under the rug.

At length, Miss Brown herself spoke. Her speech was slurred, and she dropped a few lines from her prepared statement, but she certainly gave a creditable performance. The first part of her talk sounded very much as if it had been stitched together out of slogans made familiar by advocates for the homeless: homelessness is caused by policies that help the rich and not the poor; it will be solved only by building low-income public housing; etc. Of her stay in the hospital she said, "I was a political prisoner."

Much more interesting was what Miss Brown called "my street view" of homeless life. She said nothing about her history either of heroin and cocaine abuse or of mental illness. According to her, she had had only two problems in being homeless. The first was police harassment. She claimed that at some point she had been beaten with night sticks and kicked by several police officers. Project Help also had degraded and humiliated her and had denied her what she called "my right to live on the street." Never, she said, had Project Help been of any use, except to offer her a sandwich.

Her second problem was that, obviously, she had been unable to find an apartment, which was why she had ended up on the streets. With no place of her own and since there are no public toilets, she had to use the streets as a bathroom. She did not explain why she did not return to live with her sisters in New Jersey, who had been looking for her during the year she was living on the streets. Moreover, if she had been eager all along to come indoors, what was the point of fighting tooth and nail for the right to live on the streets?

Joyce Brown's claim that she had been beaten by the police also presented   8 difficulties. She provided no details of the event. When she was asked during the question period if she intended to press charges against the police for their abuse, her response was, "Everyone knows New York City cops are killers."

Another difficulty was her complaint of being degraded by Project Help. It is true that for most of the time she was on the streets, outreach workers only offered her sandwiches. The reason for this was that Miss Brown spurned all other help. Project Help workers kept regular tabs on her, they coaxed her to accept further services, such as transportation to washroom facilities and a women's shelter. Miss Brown refused every time.

In other words, until the city decided to bring her inside against her will, Project Help was following exactly the policy that her lawyers told the Harvard audience ought to be followed in these cases: the city kept an eye on her, offered whatever services she would accept, and tried to win her confidence. It was only after months of such attempts that this approach was abandoned.

Joyce Brown ended her talk, received applause, and sat down. Norman Siegel then rose to speak. He too claimed that homelessness was essentially a housing problem, or rather that it was an issue of economic justice and equality and in no sense a mental-health issue, still less a matter of public order or law enforcement. The main cause of homelessness was the construction of high-rise developments for the rich and the destruction of the single-room-occupancy hotels (SROs) that many poor people once lived in. Allowing landlords to warehouse apartments, failing to require developers to build low-income housing, and the unwillingness of the city to redevelop the abandoned apartments it had seized — these were the real problems.

As Siegel saw it, the only way to deal with these problems was by radical political action. Just as law students from Harvard had gone to the South during the 1960s to organize and register blacks as part of a progressive political movement, so in the late 1980s lawyers should go to the bus terminals and park benches of America's cities and organize for economic justice. Homeless people needed "guerrilla legal tactics" in order to win, though "non-legal solutions" pressed forward "in a harassing way," were also important.

Whatever else one may say of the approach that Siegel and Levey put forward at the Harvard Law School Forum, it is very close to the position taken by most advocates and researchers on the homeless. Writers like Jonathan Kozol in his new book, *Rachel and Her Children: Homeless Families in America;* activists like Mitch Snyder of Communities for Creative Non-Violence (CCNV) and Robert Hayes of Coalition for the Homeless; and research centers like New York's Community Service Society all agree with Joyce Brown's lawyers in their general analysis of the problem.

The thrust of this analysis is as follows:

1. Homelessness is a huge problem and it is getting worse. The size of the homeless population is at least two to three million (a figure originally

advanced by CCNV in 1982), perhaps as large as four million, and growing.

2. Homelessness is simply or primarily a housing issue. As Kozol puts it, "The cause of homelessness is lack of housing" due to federal cutbacks and urban redevelopment.

3. Mental illness and other disabilities, such as alcoholism, while frequent among the homeless, have been greatly exaggerated. About one-third of the homeless are members of homeless families, who are neither mentally ill nor otherwise disabled.

4. Radical tactics and objectives are necessary if the problem is ever to be solved. Homelessness is a systemic problem, caused by the structure of the economy and society in general. As such it cannot be effectively addressed either by the charity of the welfare state or by benefits conferred at the whim of legislatures. What is needed is the enactment of a constitutional "right to shelter" that would be enforceable through the courts.

Let us take up these claims one by one, especially as they relate to the Joyce Brown case.

First, as to the size of the homeless population. The CCNV estimate of two to three million as of 1982 was based on an unsystematic telephone survey of shelter providers and advocates. It was never clear just how CCNV went from these local to its national estimates, or even exactly how CCNV defined homelessness.

To try to get things straight, the Department of Housing and Urban Development (HUD) conducted its own survey, released in 1984, which concluded that, as of 1983, there were about 250,000 to 350,000 homeless people in America.

The HUD report was widely attacked. Mitch Snyder of CCNV declared that the officials who had inspired it reminded him "of nothing so much as a school of piranha, circling, waiting to tear the last ounce of flesh." Various methodological critiques were also brought against the report, but their validity remained uncertain in the absence of an independent cross-check of its methods.

Such an independent cross-check was finally completed in 1986 by Richard B. Freeman and Brian Hall of Harvard University in their Report of the National Bureau of Economic Research, "Permanent Homelessness in America?" The bottom line of the Freeman-Hall study was that "the much-maligned" HUD figure of 250,000–350,000 was "roughly correct." Freeman and Hall's exact estimate for 1983 was 279,000 (and Freeman estimates that as of 1988 the number has jumped to about 400,000). Further, the key data on which they based their numbers were confirmed by surveys of homeless people done by other researchers using several different methods in Boston, Chicago, Nashville, Washington, D.C., Phoenix, Pittsburgh, and Los Angeles. I myself have also confirmed these findings in a survey of homeless people in San Diego.

To cite only the example of Chicago: CCNV had reported one estimate of 250,000; later, Coalition for the Homeless cut this by a factor of ten, to 25,000. Neither of these estimates was based on systematic scientific research, nor was either organization willing to say exactly how they were arrived at. Then after two surveys of his own, Peter Rossi of the University of Massachusetts released his conclusions: in the winter of 1986 there were about 2,020 homeless people in Chicago (give or take about 275).

These studies, all independent of one another, using various methodologies, and all arriving at approximately the same conclusions, reinforce one basic point: the estimate circulated by advocacy groups of between two and three (and even up to four) million homeless people is about ten times too high.

When confronted with this evidence, Jonathan Kozol and the others frequently argue (although without ever withdrawing their own claims) that, in Kozol's words, "Whether the number is one million or four million or the administration's estimate of less than a million, there are too many homeless people in America." Or as Chester Hartman, a housing analyst at the Institute for Policy Studies, testified before Congress during its hearings on the HUD report, "the real issue is that in a society with the wealth of the United States, there should not be a single involuntary homeless person."

Now, it is undoubtedly true that homelessness is a tragedy no matter how few or how many people it touches, and it is also true that 400,000 is a large number. But such statements as Kozol's and Hartman's will not do. It is as though someone were to claim that the unemployment rate is 60 percent and then, upon being informed that the real rate is closer to 6 percent, were to respond: "No matter whether the rate is 60 percent or 6 percent, too many people are unemployed. The real issue is that in a society this wealthy not a single person should be involuntarily unemployed."

One final point on the size of the homeless population. Surveys done in Nashville and Boston, and shelter counts in New York, suggest that the growth of the homeless population has leveled off. One should therefore be very skeptical about recent claims by the National Coalition for the Homeless and the U.S. Conference of Mayors that the number of people on the streets has grown by 25 percent over the last year. Homelessness undoubtedly did increase throughout the early 1980s, but it may by now have reached its peak.

What about the cause of homelessness? Is it, as Kozol says, lack of housing? Before we can evaluate this claim, we have to reacquaint ourselves with a few basic facts.

First, it is indeed true that New York (to take a city with an especially large homeless population, and which is the subject of Kozol's recent book) faces serious housing problems. Between 1981 and 1984 the number of apartments renting for under two hundred dollars a month dropped from 437,000 to 256,000. As single-room-occupancy hotels have been torn down for development, thousands of dwelling units for the poor have vanished.

Yet the fact is that, as in most other cities, the housing stock in New York is so large (about 1.8 million rental units), and the number of homeless families is so "small" (about five thousand at any given point and about twelve thousand in the course of a year) relative to that stock, that a simple "lack" of housing cannot be the trouble. The real trouble is that the current housing market is prevented from making a rational allocation of such housing as exists. For the housing market could easily meet the demand that a few thousand homeless families impose on it if it were allowed to, and it could do so in a manner consistent with current standards of decency and fairness.

Again, the Freeman and Hall study throws light on the subject. They   28
report that for the United States as a whole there was no dramatic decline in the number of "affordable" units (i.e., those renting for under $200 in real terms) during the recent increase in homelessness between 1979 and 1983. In central cities, as the case of New York shows, the number of such units did decline during this period (by about 5.4 percent according to Freeman and Hall), but this decline is in itself too small to have caused homelessness. Nor is it correct that the number of public-housing units declined during this same period. In fact, public housing units actually increased from 1,178,000 in 1979 to 1,250,000 in 1983.

What did happen, however, was a sharp rise in the number of people looking for such units. Between 1979 and 1983 the number of poor unattached individuals increased by about 21 percent and the number of poor families by 45 percent.

Yet this increase need not, in itself, have led to homelessness. In an open market, landlords and perhaps some developers would have responded to the new demand by providing more cheap housing. Through some combination of dividing up old units, renovating abandoned buildings, renting out space formerly used as garages and basements and the like, these newly-poor renters could have had their demand met. Admittedly such accommodations would have been of inferior quality, but they would have prevented homelessness.

This demand was never met because housing regulations in New York (and some other cities) made it difficult for the market to adjust. For example, New York offered a bonus of $6,000 to landlords who would put up homeless families. There were few takers, even when the bonus was raised to $9,700. One reason seems to be that participating landlords would have had to spend more than the bonus to bring their buildings up to the required standard.

That homelessness is not due to a lack of housing is also shown by the   32 fact that most homeless families in New York *do* manage to find a place to stay fairly soon after they enter the shelter system. Half leave the system within two to five months, and two-thirds leave within a year. Writers like Kozol who think that most families in welfare hotels are in effect permanently homeless are focusing on the long-term stayers and missing the majority who do leave after several months. In other words, homeless families simply need more assistance in finding housing more quickly in the stock that already exists.

③ Since advocates for the homeless claim that homelessness is entirely or primarily caused by a housing shortage, they typically deemphasize the role that disabilities like mental illness, alcoholism, and drug abuse play in the plight of the homeless. This is the theme sounded by Peter Marcuse, a professor of urban affairs at Columbia University. Marcuse cautions against "blaming the victim," a tendency which (according to him) holds that "The homeless are not like you and me. There is something wrong with them or they wouldn't be homeless." We should, as Louisa Stark, president of Coalition for the Homeless puts it, "Blame the System, Not Its Victims."

To get a sense of how valid such claims are, we have to distinguish for the moment between homeless individuals and homeless families. This approach is controversial. Indeed, one reason that disability among the homeless is sometimes thought to be less of a factor than is popularly supposed is that many of the homeless are members of homeless families. Since these families — especially the children — have much lower rates of mental illness and other disabilities than homeless individuals do, amalgamating the two groups brings the disability rate down. At the same time, however, it conceals the true dimension of disability among homeless individuals. The best way to proceed, therefore, is first to consider individuals and families separately and then to reaggregate them for the total picture.

In some journalistic accounts of homelessness during the mid to late 1970s, all homeless individuals were assumed to be mentally ill. It was thought that most such mentally ill homeless individuals had once been patients in mental hospitals before they were "deinstitutionalized."

It is clear, however, that deinstitutionalization — if by this is meant the policy of reducing the number of patients in mental hospitals with an eye to having them cared for by community mental-health centers — cannot explain the plight of *today's* homeless, because this policy was implemented mostly during the 1960s. Very few homeless people today came to the streets or shelters *directly* from mental hospitals. (In the Freeman and Hall study the number of such people was only 1 percent of the sample.)

On the other hand, while few of the homeless are direct victims of deinstitutionalization, we learn from Freeman and Hall that more than ninety thousand of the people on the streets today would have been in mental hospitals in the days before the policy of deinstitutionalization came into being. Almost all surveys indicate that between a quarter and a third of the homeless are indeed mentally ill. For example, the Freeman and Hall study found 33 percent of its sample to be mentally ill. Rossi, in a survey of eighteen studies of homeless individuals, found that the average rate of chronic mental illness was 36.5 percent.

According to some writers, these findings demonstrate that the perception of the homeless as being mentally ill is merely a stereotype. Thus Louisa Stark tells us that "Although only one-third of homeless people nationwide are mentally disabled, since the early 1980s homelessness has become synonymous in the public mind with mental illness. What we have done, then, is taken one stigmatized illness, alcoholism, and replaced it with another, mental illness, as a stereotype for the homeless." Peter Marcuse presents the other side of this observation when he remarks that "most of the mentally ill are not homeless. More mentally ill are housed than homeless."

But neither of these superficially correct observations can break the link between mental illness and homelessness. For a rate of mental illness of 33 percent is very high. In the general population, according to Freeman and Hall, the rate is less than 2 percent, and it is not much more than that even among the dependent poor: Rossi has found that among individuals receiving General Relief in Chicago the rate of previous hospitalization for mental illness is between 3 and 4 percent.

Further, to say that the majority of the mentally ill are housed and that   40
therefore mental illness is not a key factor in the current homeless problem is like saying that during the 1930s the majority of Americans were employed and that therefore the Depression had nothing to do with unemployment.

Yet those researchers who stress that the majority of the homeless are not mentally ill are making an important point. Just as it is misleading to assume that homelessness is *simply* a housing problem (although it is partly that), so too is it misleading to assume that homelessness is *entirely* a problem of mental illness (although it is partly that, too). There are several other groups among homeless individuals with different problems of their own.

The most obvious are alcoholics and hard-drug abusers. Freeman and Hall report that 29 percent of their sample suffered from alcohol abuse (the rate for the general population is 13 percent), and they found a rate of hard-drug abuse of 14 percent (the rate for the general population is less than 1 percent). My own guess is that something like a fifth to a third of homeless individuals suffer from some combination of these disabilities.

Mental illness, alcoholism, and drug abuse are all regarded as quasi-medical problems. But of course straightforward medical or physical problems can be disabling, too. Indeed, such disabilities turn out to be characteristic of significant percentages of homeless individuals. For example, 36 percent of Rossi's Chicago sample reported "fair" or "poor" health (a level of self-reported ill health roughly twice that of the general population); 28 percent reported a hospital stay of more than twenty-four hours in the last year; and 28 percent were unable to work for health reasons. Also, a survey of over eight thousand clients in New York's shelters for individuals (conducted in 1984 by Stephen Crystal and Mervyn Goldstein, then of New York City's Human Resources Administration) found almost two-fifths had a current medical problem.

It is difficult to extrapolate from these numbers to a hard estimate of physical disability among the homeless. But a safe guess is that about 25 to 30 percent of homeless individuals suffer from such problems.

In addition to such strictly or quasi-medical difficulties, there are problems of a qualitatively different type that can be contributing factors to a spell of homelessness. Thus 41 percent of Rossi's sample had been in jail for periods of longer than forty-eight hours, 28 percent had at some point been convicted by a court and given probation, and 17 percent had felony convictions behind them. And Freeman and Hall found 39 percent of their sample had at some point been in jail.

One objection to regarding a criminal record as a disability characteristic of a subpopulation of the homeless is that such a history might be considered a result rather than a precipitating or contributing cause of homelessness. My experience in San Diego suggests that many homeless people are frequently convicted of misdemeanors like jay-walking or littering as a form of harassment by police. Yet Freeman and Hall found that 61 percent of the time spent in jail by their sample was before the subjects became homeless. This indicates that being convicted of a crime can indeed be a contributing cause of homelessness. Moreover, it is unlikely that minor police harassment can account for a felony conviction rate of 17 percent.

What, then, is the overall picture of disability among homeless individuals? First, these data — dramatic as they are — do not support the idea that homelessness is some "special" problem quite unlike any other social problem. The disabilities involved are not unique to the homeless; they are found among the extremely poor and the underclass in general. In this sense, those who caution against "stereotyping" the homeless have a point.

However, a point which these data highlight with at least equal force is that homeless individuals are much more disabled than the general population or even than the poor in general. Somewhere between 70 and 80 percent of homeless individuals suffer from one or more major disability. Thus Rossi found that 82 percent of his survey had *at least one* of the following disabilities: poor or fair health; previous mental hospitalization; previous stay in a detoxification unit; clinically high scores on psychological tests for depression or psychotic thinking; sentence(s) by a court.

Similarly, the Crystal and Goldstein study of New York's shelters for singles found that 74.9 percent of the men and 70.4 percent of the women suffered from *at least one* of the following disabilities: hard-drug abuse; alcoholism; jail record; less than an eighth-grade education; never employed; physical/medical problems; psychiatric problems; over sixty-five years old.

The homeless, then, are *not* "just like you and me" and most of them *do* have "something wrong with them" which contributes to their being homeless. (We should also keep in mind, however, the approximately 20 to 30 percent of the homeless who are relatively able and who have been described in other studies by Crystal as "economic-only" clients.)

When advocates for the homeless are confronted with figures like the above, they often choose to shift attention away from homeless individuals to homeless families. For example, a recent publication of the National Coalition for the Homeless argues:

> not only is homelessness increasing in numbers, it is also broadening in reach. The old stereotype of the single, male alcoholic — the so called "skid-row derelict" — no longer applies. Increasingly, the ranks of the homeless poor are comprised of families, children, ethnic and racial minorities, the elderly, and the disabled. The face of America's homeless now mirrors the face of America's poor: skid row has become more democratic. Perhaps the starkest indication of this diversity is the fact that, today, the fastest growing segment of the homeless population consists of families with children. In some areas, families with children comprise the majority of the homeless . . . families with children now account for about 30 percent of the homeless population.

Kozol and other advocates also claim that the rate of disabilities like drug abuse and mental illness among such families is very low. Although "Many homeless *individuals* may have been residents of such [mental] institutions," writes Kozol, "in cities like New York, . . . where nearly half the homeless are small children, with an average age of six, such suppositions [of former mental hospitalization] obviously make little sense."   52

There are two questions here: (1) Just how many homeless family members are there and what percentage of the total homeless population do they represent? (2) What are the rates of disability among homeless family members?

As to the question of numbers, the Freeman and Hall study again provides the best source. They estimate that in 1983 there were 32,000 homeless family members, and that in 1985 there were 46,000 such people.

Right away, we can see from the Freeman-Hall data that Kozol is exaggerating wildly when he tells us that 500,000 children are currently homeless. Since only 46,000 members of families were homeless in 1985 (this includes *both* adults and children), homeless families would have had to grow by more than ten times in three years for Kozol's figure even to approach reality — not to mention that there are in fact no more than a *total* of 400,000 homeless people in 1988. The truth is that the widely circulated estimate that families with children represent 30 percent of the total homeless population is more than twice too high.

So far as the question of disability goes, we know roughly what the rates   56 are among homeless individuals, but at this point we do not know enough to conclude either that homeless families suffer from no more disabilities than do other poor families, or that in fact they do have special problems which contribute to their being homeless. Such studies as we do have suggest that the rate of disabilities among such families may be significant. But until better information is available on this subject, we have to regard the confident pronouncements of advocates that homeless families are simply victims of a tight housing market as being largely conjectural.

(4)

What are we to make of the advocates' interpretation of the politics of homelessness? It is important to understand that they see homelessness not as an aberration or a failing but as a natural outcome of the ordinary workings of social policy and the economy in general. As Mitch Snyder of CCNV writes (in collaboration with Mary Ellen Hombs):

> We live in a disposable society, a throwaway culture. The homeless are our human refuse, remnants of a culture that assigns a pathologically high value to independence and productivity. America is a land where you *are* what you consume and produce. The homeless are simply surplus souls in a system firmly rooted in competition and self-interest, in which only the "strongest" (i.e., those who fit most snugly within the confines of a purely arbitrary norm) will survive.

Similar sentiments are expressed by Robert Hayes of Coalition for the Homeless ("the homeless are indeed the most egregious symbol of a cruel economy, an unresponsive government, a festering value system") and by Peter Marcuse of Columbia ("homelessness in the midst of plenty may shock people into the realization that homelessness exists not because the system is failing to work as it should, but because the system *is* working as it must").

Yet it ought to be obvious that homelessness cannot be the result of "a festering value system," or "free-market capitalism," or "a system firmly rooted in competition and self-interest," or any other long-term systemic feature of American society, for the simple reason that all these have remained more or less what they always have been, and so cannot explain the rise of homelessness *now.*

Advocates seem to recognize this at some level, since, after having made sweeping pronouncements against American society in general, they usually concentrate their fire on the Reagan administration's social and economic policies. But while poverty did increase during the Reagan years, the Reagan administration can hardly be blamed either for deinstitutionalization or for the housing policies — such as rent control and byzantine regulations — which in cities like New York have undoubtedly exacerbated the situation.

To sum up: homelessness is a much *smaller* problem, in terms of the number of people affected by it, than is commonly thought, but it is also

60

much more *intractable* than advocates understand. This intractability stems from the fact that the great majority of homeless individuals, and possibly some significant proportion of homeless families, are afflicted with behavioral or medical disabilities or both. Dealing with such problems requires a willingness to assert *authority* — for example, in refusing to allow people like Joyce Brown to live on the streets — as much as it requires an expenditure of resources. Nonetheless, an important part of the problem is economic, and can best be addressed not by building more public housing but by raising the income of the extremely poor and removing regulations which block the allocation of housing to them.

In short, a reformist agenda — one aimed at enabling our mental-health system to treat people who need treatment, at reducing extreme poverty through income supports, and at allowing housing markets to function — can go a long way toward the elimination of homelessness.

This agenda is a far cry from the radical systemic measures such as a constitutional "right to shelter," or the "guerrilla legal tactics" and the "harassing" techniques recommended by Joyce Brown's lawyers and other activists in the field. But it has the virtue of being based on a truthful diagnosis rather than on wild and tendentious analyses which, by simultaneously exaggerating the dimensions of the problem and underplaying its difficulties, make it harder rather than easier to help the homeless at all. In taking up the case of Joyce Brown, and in securing her release, the NYCLU lawyers may have furthered the "delegitimation" (as Peter Marcuse calls it) of a social system they consider evil. But as for Joyce Brown herself, only a short time after her appearance at Harvard, she was found begging on the streets and hurling abuse at passers-by who refused to give her money.

Points to Consider

1. Why does Main open his essay with a discussion of the Joyce Brown case? What does he want to establish about the homeless and their advocates? Why does he end his essay with another reference to Joyce Brown?

2. How does Main go about disputing the claim that homelessness is mainly a housing problem? What concessions does he make to this explanation? Why does he think an open market in real estate will help alleviate the problem? Do you agree?

3. What does Main think about the claim that homelessness is a mental-illness problem? What other disabilities does Main deal with? What does the range of these disabilities indicate to Main about the causes of homelessness?

4. Why does Main believe that homelessness is not a serious economic problem ultimately caused by the "structure of the economy and society in general"?

Homeless Bound [PEOPLE / February 1990]

A large crowd stands waiting for the Staten Island ferry. Hidden behind them, monopolizing the terminal's long wooden benches, are some sixty or seventy homeless men and women in various states—sitting and sleeping, drunk and sober, bearded and shaved, calm and agitated. A few days earlier a social worker had described this transportation hub in Manhattan as a "menagerie." Today it is missing only the Greek mythological ferryman, Charon, to pole the damned across New York Harbor. Most of the people are not just homeless but are also drunks and druggies. An argument is raging between a black man and a drunk blond woman with a hip-high cast covering her left leg. She slashes at the man with one of her crutches until two policemen chase him away. Across the terminal, a loony, shoeless lad is menacing an Asian passenger. "Gonna knock your teeth out," he shouts. "You Jap guys stole my job." The same two cops lead him away, but blaring loudspeakers are now calling for police assistance elsewhere. "NYPD to the change booth!" echoes a plea to help a homeless man who had been knocked down by youths hurdling the turnstiles.

I hadn't come simply as a reporter to cover this stygian scene. Wearing faded jeans, a frayed corduroy jacket, vintage combat boots used in Korea, and with a beat-up pack strapped to my back, I was hoping to blend in with all the vagrants who had converted this old pier into a makeshift hotel. This was my first stop on a scary two-week journey into their murky, purgatorial world. I wanted to report on what I had seen as one of *them*.

I had put off a haircut for several weeks and hadn't shaved for days. Still, I worried. Would this disguise really work? Could I make myself feel truly destitute, or would the safety of my just-temporary plight betray me? I fixed my gaze on a smartly dressed businessman tapping his shoes, impatient for the next boat to depart. He glanced everywhere except at me. That was a good sign. I had joined the estimated three million homeless who, it is said, have become "invisible" to most Americans.

Roy Rowan (b. 1920) belongs to the board of editors at Fortune *magazine. A former correspondent and managing editor for* Life *magazine, Rowan served as bureau chief for Time Inc. in Rome, Tokyo, Bonn, Chicago, and Hong Kong. Rowan is a graduate of Dartmouth University and the author of the critically acclaimed book* The Intuitive Manager *(1986).*

I must admit that they had been largely invisible to me. On my way to   4
work from suburban Greenwich, Connecticut, I would see the sleeping
bodies sprawled over the cold marble or tucked into the recesses of Grand
Central Terminal. In the evening as I headed home, these figures would come
alive, rising like specters out of a Hieronymus Bosch painting, dunning us
commuters with outstretched palms or empty coffee cups. But my personal
involvement was very slight.

My knowledge of their problems was also slight. I knew that a prepon-
derant number were black and that a large percentage were drug addicts,
alcoholics, AIDS victims, or crazies turned loose from overcrowded psycho
wards. And yet there were other homeless people, both black and white,
who almost could have passed for fellow commuters. They were the ones
who intrigued me most. Who were these seemingly sane, reasonably well-
dressed drifters who languish in rail and subway stations, bus depots, bank
vestibules, and stand like frozen statues on the street? How did they fall
between the cracks of our affluent society? Could they ever climb back up?

I had decided to try to learn more about these victims of homelessness
by stepping into their lives, and yet as that day approached, I felt myself
becoming more and more apprehensive. I had heard horror stories about the
knifing and shooting of homeless men, mostly senseless attacks by marauding
youth packs. One old man had been doused with gasoline and set afire. I
had also heard about wild free-for-alls started by "crackheads" in the big
armory shelters of Manhattan and Brooklyn. "Better sleep with your shoes
on or they'll be stolen," I was warned. "Your glasses too."

The day was clear and crisp when I arrived at the Staten Island ferry
terminal. I had fifty dollars stashed in various pockets in small bills, but no
house keys, checks, credit cards, driver's license, or any identification other
than my Medicare card. To my wife's consternation I had removed my gold
wedding band for the first time in thirty-seven years. Shorn of all these
accoutrements, I felt peculiarly weightless. Worse, the desolation made me
feel that perhaps I had made a horrible mistake. Sharing a soldier's danger
as a war correspondent, as I had done, was strangely exhilarating, yet the
prospect of hunkering down with these derelicts seemed only demeaning.

I parked my pack next to an old geezer and asked him if it was possible   8
to spend the night in the terminal. "Yes," he said. "The cops usually don't
bother you." He said his name was Philip Nachamie, and he had lived there
for three weeks. "Once I worked as a clerk for E. F. Hutton," he explained,
pointing in the direction of Wall Street. "Just a few blocks from here."

I decided to board the next boat. Standing on the open bow with the
cold wind whipping my face, I felt suddenly uplifted by the beauty of New
York. The profusion of steel and glass soaring skyward from Manhattan's
southern tip, Miss Liberty standing proudly with sun glinting on her gilded
torch, the spidery span of the Verrazano Bridge stretching across the harbor's

mouth—all striking human accomplishments in a city where thousands lived on the street.

I hadn't been to Staten Island for years, but a social worker had mentioned a place called Project Hospitality, a few blocks from the ferry. A sign on the door warned DON'T EVEN THINK OF DOING DRUGS HERE. A friendly woman at the front desk told me to sign in. "We'll be serving dinner in an hour," she said. "But you can have coffee now."

I still felt queasy in my new role, but I poured myself a cup and sat down. About forty men and women filled the chairs that lined the room. Dinner consisted of mushy Swedish meatballs on a heaping mound of brown rice. Two peanut butter sandwiches were also doled out to each "client," as the homeless are referred to in drop-in centers like this. I pocketed mine for breakfast. "Sorry, but there are no beds available tonight on Staten Island," the woman at the front desk informed me.

I decided to spend the night crossing back and forth on the ferry. Its throbbing engines lulled me right to sleep, but as the ferry docked, a cop rapped his club against the back of my seat. The police, I came to learn, are viewed by the homeless as both enemy and protector. I slipped into the terminal through an exit, then reboarded the boat without paying. By 5 A.M. I had made half-a-dozen round trips, snatching twenty-minute naps en route. Finally I joined the snorers slumped on the benches in the Manhattan terminal.

When the new day dawned, I was camped between a pair of talkative New Englanders. Anthony Joseph Robert Quinn proclaimed himself a lace-curtain Irishman from Boston. His downfall apparently came from growing up with too much money and an unquenchable thirst for whiskey. Having quit Boston College to join the Army in World War II, he married a "very artistic lady" who eventually departed for Palm Beach with his and her money. But I couldn't pry loose the secret of what sent him into oblivion. "You don't have an extra shirt in that pack, lad?" he inquired. "There's nothing under this coat." I had two extra and gave him one. "Bless you. Care for an eye-opener?" he asked, pulling out a pint.

Cecile Sanscartier, an aging but still twinkly-eyed blond woman, was originally from New Bedford, Massachussetts. She moved to New York City, where her husband drove a taxi. One night, she says, he was parked in front of Metropolitan Hospital, and he was shot and killed by holdup men. For several years after his death, Cecile worked in a stationery store but kept falling behind in her rent. Reluctantly last summer she entered a city shelter, where she says, "I was scared of being robbed or raped, and felt like a prisoner. Here I can walk out through the turnstile any time I want." She had been living at the ferry terminal for two months.

After only one night there, I was eager to find a bed. My back ached, and I felt groggy from lack of sleep. I consulted the *Street Sheet*—a nonprofit annual publication, distributed free to New York's homeless, which lists the places they can go for food, shelter, clothing, medical assistance, and legal aid. It included the McAuley Water Street Mission. Within walking distance, it seemed like a good place to begin looking. At McAuley's, you must attend a midday, two-hour Bible class to get a ticket for dinner, a bed, and breakfast. "Food for the soul before food for the body," its homeless lodgers are told, although none seem eager for the religious nourishment. After the Bible class, I spent the rest of the afternoon at a nearby public library writing notes for this article. Warm, with clean bathrooms as well as books and newspapers, branch libraries are homeless havens.

Returning to McAuley's at 5:30 P.M., I joined about ninety men in the chapel. Most were young blacks. First we stored our belongings for the night in a padlocked closet. Then we were interviewed. I was "Roy Brown from Chicago," the cover I had decided to use. "No, I don't have any identification. My wallet was snatched at the bus terminal when I arrived." Many of the homeless, I knew, carried no identification.

Finally we filed downstairs for a thick meat soup that looked more like slabs of beef in gravy. Then everybody marched up to the dormitory, found their assigned bunks, and stripped for the communal showers. Hospital gowns were given out to sleep in because our clothes were hauled away on wheeled racks so they wouldn't be stolen. By seven-thirty everybody was in bed, the aged, handicapped, and grossly overweight having been awarded lower bunks.

Many men at McAuley's were regulars: some with jobs but no place to live, others out looking for work. But none had surrendered to homelessness. There was a laid-off garbage collector from the Bronx, an unemployed bartender from Ireland, a sugar worker from St. Croix whose home had been devastated by Hurricane Hugo, a political refugee from South Africa. "Why," he asked, "does a country like yours, that gives so much food to Africa, have so many hungry people?"

I returned to McAuley's three consecutive nights, making a couple of friends there whom I would be happy to meet again. One was Jimmy Pate, a highly intelligent black man with a close-cropped salt-and-pepper beard. He had managed a Salvation Army shop on Long Island and worked as a messenger in Manhattan. But as a periodic boozer, he would begin swigging gin and get fired. "I haven't had a drink for two weeks," he boasted. "Time to look for a job."

Another was Mark Fitzgerald, a gargantuan Canadian with a black beard so thick all you could see was a pair of blue eyes peeking out above it. He came from Churchill, on Hudson Bay below the Arctic Circle, where "polar bears," he said, "roam the streets like stray dogs." New York he called the "Trapezoid City. No matter what you do, you end up in a trap."

A linebacker in high school in Beaver, Pennsylvania, Fitzgerald once dreamed of a pro-football career. Instead he found work in a Canadian oil field. A series of job changes back in the United States followed, and with each he seemed to pick up more weight, until he tipped the scales at more than four hundred pounds. Finally last December, at twenty-nine, he was hit with a massive heart attack in New York. "They jump-started me twice and kept me in intensive care for ten days," he reported. "That cleaned out my bank account."

Despite his own problems, Mark took pity on me. "I'll buy you a bus ticket to St. Christopher's Inn when I get my next welfare check," he promised. St. Christopher's, he explained, is a retreat in Garrison, New York, for homeless men. It bothered me not being able to level with Mark. But if word got out about what I was doing, it could have been dangerous. "How come you ask so many questions, man?" a McAuley regular had already wondered. My last night there, the director asked if I would like a permanent job manning the front desk. Clearly it was time to move on.

I had been spending my days trudging the streets, investigating different drop-in centers and soup kitchens listed in the *Street Sheet*. Some, I discovered, like the Holy Apostles church in mid-Manhattan, serve hot, sit-down meals for one thousand men and women. *Voices to and from the Streets,* a free homeless newsletter published by the South Presbyterian Church in suburban Dobbs Ferry, even runs a column called Dining Out with Rick C. that rates the soup kitchens for "atmosphere, service and cuisine." Sunday breakfast at St. Bartholomew's Church on Park Avenue received a four-star rating in all three categories. " 'Bum's Rush' is really unnecessary here," it reported, since "everyone has a ticket." But I found Saturday breakfasts at St. Agnes even better. "The coffee cake here is top shelf," commented a toothless table mate, who also advised me, "Stay out of Grand Central. Too many guys over there eager to cut up a white face."

After dinner I checked into the Moravian Coffee Pot, considered a safe 24 haven for older homeless men and women. At first, the reverend in charge was pessimistic about my chances of being assigned to a shelter. But after spying my week-old whiskers and hearing my sad story about being robbed, I was put on a school bus bound for St. Clement Pope Roman Catholic Church in Queens.

During the next few days, I found many surprises among the hundred Coffee Pot clients. There were teachers with master's degrees, shopkeepers, file clerks, secretaries, chambermaids, day laborers, a lawyer, even a TV actor who played in *The Defenders,* and a former opera singer who now sang on Sundays in the First Moravian Church next door. Most were nicely spruced up, since two showers and long racks of donated clothing were available upstairs. Yet they sat around in segregated black or white cliques, complaining about everything from their free meals to the high rent and taxes that had driven them into the street. Consumed by their own misfortune, they showed little concern for each other. When it was announced that a woman there had died during the night, the news hardly caused a murmur.

"I like rich people," a black woman confided. "Poor people are too cruel to each other."

Many Coffee Pot regulars, I was told, draw SSI (Supplemental Security Income) from the federal government for ailments that supposedly prevent them from working. But nobody appeared sick, except for the chronic, croupy cough that plagues practically all the homeless, and which I, too, had picked up. Several times I was tempted to stand up and shout, "Why don't you all go out and get jobs?" Instead, I'd go out myself, prowling the city till dark, seeking homeless people with more poignant stories. I must have looked pretty grubby. Women, I now noticed, leaned away from me on buses and subways.

It was beginning to sink in that sitting around crowded, fetid drop-in centers, standing pressed together in long soup-kitchen lines, and sleeping side by side in shelters, the homeless had precious few moments alone. No wonder so many preferred the parks or streets, where even a cold packing crate to sleep in provided some privacy.

In four nights the Coffee Pot dispatched me to three shelters, each more comfortable than the last. Manhattan's famed Riverside Church, my final resting place so to speak, was called the "Helmsley Palace shelter." Pasta or some other tasty hot dish was served. The beds were well spaced in the men's choir room. There was a shower and a TV. 28

Already into my second week, the time had come to tough it out with the hard-core homeless in places like Tompkins Square Park on the Lower East Side, where police and squatters have been waging continuous warfare; Penn Station, dubbed the "Panama combat zone" because of a proliferation of drugs and guns; the Bowery; Brooklyn; and the big Bellevue shelter, converted from a hospital.

In Tompkins Square Park, with the temperature hovering around 20° F, I warmed myself over a trash-can fire with a group of shivering men, amusing themselves by reeling off their old penitentiary numbers. They eyed me suspiciously when I didn't chime in with mine.

That night I decided to stay on the street as long as my feet could take the cold. Dinner came from a Salvation Army mobile kitchen parked near City Hall. Too cold to sit around, I walked slowly up through Chinatown and SoHo back to the East Village. Along the way many men were leaning against buildings or slumped in doorways, waiting for the "Midnight Run," a church caravan from suburbia that distributes sandwiches and blankets.

"Be careful crossing the street," I kept reminding myself. The sleep deprivation that dims the consciousness of every homeless person was beginning to slow my own reactions. Quite a few street dwellers, I'd heard, get hit by cars. 32

Then I walked three miles back to the Battery. About 2 A.M. I decided to head for John Heuss House, a drop-in center for the chronically homeless and mentally ill, partly supported by Wall Street's Trinity Church. "You don't have a single scrap of paper with your name on it?" the night duty officer asked caustically. Eventually he told me to shove some chairs together and stretch out, as others had done. Every time I reached for a chair, a mentally disturbed man grabbed it away. Only after the duty officer threatened to toss him into the street did I lie down.

Some of the mentally unstable homeless people, I found, sound deceptively sane. Bill Roth, thirty-three, a Long Island letter carrier for eight years, was holding forth brilliantly in Grand Central about the collapse of Communism in Eastern Europe, when he casually mentioned that boxing promoters were sure he could whip Mike Tyson, despite their eighty-pound difference. Later he admitted having been hospitalized for alcoholism and mental problems.

Deinstitutionalizing these troubled people, I realized, not only forces them to flounder helplessly, it also allows them to inflict their insanity on everyone around them—sometimes violently. Right after my homeless stint ended, a deranged man in a midtown subway station was pummeled to death by a passenger he had accosted and spat on.

The next night I was determined to find a real bed. I went back to Staten 36 Island, but with no success. I tried the nearly all-black drop-in center on Bond Street in Brooklyn. James Conway, a homeless chef, who had just been released from the hospital, warned me that a bloody battle royal had erupted there the previous day. I wasn't feeling too comfortable anyway. A black woman had pointed at me and yelled, "Hey, look at the macadamia nut," when I walked in.

Then I remembered that Mark Fitzgerald, my McAuley friend, had high praise for the Fulton Hotel in the Bowery. But a room there, he said, costs $6.50. (Bus, subway, and ferry fares, cough medicine, and repairs to my backpack had already used up thirty-five of my fifty dollars.) Finally I decided to try some panhandling—not an appealing idea, although a man at the Coffee Pot had boasted of picking up $240 in one day.

It was already dark when I arrived in Little Italy, a district of posh restaurants bordering on the Bowery. The streets were filled with fur-coated women from uptown. "Could you help a fella out?" I kept asking. In forty minutes I collected four quarters, a dollar, and a fiver, although my heart wasn't in it. I felt dishonest playing on the sympathy of strangers, knowing that I didn't really need their help.

The Fulton Hotel turned out to be a Chinese flophouse named Fu Shin, where a four-by-six-foot, windowless, tableless, chairless cubicle now costs $8.50. There was barely room to squeeze in between the wall and the bed, covered with a grimy green blanket showing worrisome brown burn holes. A light bulb hung from a false ceiling constructed of wrapping paper and chicken wire.

Here, at least, was a warm place of my own to shed my smelly clothes 40 and sleep. But the cubicle, I discovered about 1 A.M., wasn't really all mine. That's when the cockroaches began running across my face. I sat up in bed the rest of the night reading a *New York Times* salvaged from a sidewalk trash can. By then I was almost looking forward to the Bellevue shelter with its thousand beds.

I wasn't sure they would let me into this city-run, older men's refuge. I lacked the required Human Resources Administration case number. But it was Martin Luther King, Jr.'s, birthday, and the place was down to a skeleton staff. I gave my real name and handed the man at the admitting office my Medicare card for identification. It was 5 P.M. "You'll have to wait till midnight for an emergency bed," he advised. He issued me a dinner slip and pointed down a long, dimly lit corridor to a waiting room where some fifty other emergency-bed candidates were congregated.

This was an angry bunch of men—mad at the armed guards there to keep order, mad at each other, and at the world for the way it had treated them. "Sit up!" snapped a guard, prodding a skinny black fellow sprawled on the floor. "Go 'way, asshole," responded the man. "Is my lying down a security problem?" The guard prodded him again. "You don't even know why I'm lying here, asshole. I got two bullet holes in me." The guard finally gave up, and the bullet holes were never explained.

A trembly, eighty-year-old, bewhiskered white man kept trying to stand up and walk to the bathroom, only to fall back in his chair. The guards ignored him. So did the others in the room. I desperately wanted to offer a steadying hand. Yet, as a reporter, I also wanted to see what would happen. Finally I watched a dark wet spot spread across the old man's lap. Humiliated, he never looked down.

From time to time a woman came and called a few names—the lucky recipients of emergency beds. But at 1 A.M. about twenty of us were still waiting. "Okay, you guys are going to Post Five," barked one of the guards. He led us down two flights to an abandoned lobby and pointed at the marble floor. "Sleep here. You can go outside to pee." The price of homelessness, I had come to understand, is not the hard surfaces you sometimes have to sleep on or the soup kitchen meals that usually leave a strong aftertaste in your mouth. It is the dehumanizing loss of dignity.

After two weeks I felt saturated with these depressing sensations and ready to write. My grubbiness was also becoming unbearable. Sitting in the rear car of the train going home (where my neighbors never ride), I wondered if I would ever run into any of my homeless friends again. Would the deep chasm separating us make such an encounter embarrassing, even though I now know there are talented, intelligent individuals out there among all the derelicts? Never again would I look away when a homeless person approaches. It might be somebody I know.

There are a few I would very much like to see. I would like to find out if Phillip Nordé, a handsome thirty-eight-year-old Trinidadian who says he was the first black man to model clothes on the fashion runways of Europe for Gucci, Valentino, Giorgio Armani, and Missoni, managed to stay off drugs. Having recently returned from a crack rehab center in Vermont, he lives at the Wards Island shelter under the Triborough Bridge. He fears that his problem is genetic. His father and grandfather were both alcoholics. "But crack," he says, "takes over your body, your mind, and your soul."

One man at the Coffee Pot, I believe, will surely break free. He's a Fordham University graduate and a teacher whose periodic mental breakdowns have left him homeless. Nevertheless, he calls his situation "a temporary walk on the downside" and feels his positive attitude won't permit him to stay stuck in that miasma. "You can live without money," he says, "but you can't live without plans." That, I realized, is what had made two weeks of homelessness endurable for me. I always knew I would be going home.

Points to Consider

1. Rowan introduces us to several homeless people, among them Anthony Joseph Robert Quinn, Cecile Sanscartier, and Mark Fitzgerald. How do these individuals and others mentioned in the essay provide us with a sense of the different types of homeless people?

2. Rowan says that he made friends among the homeless and that some of these people he'd like to meet again. Consider the people he liked. What do they have in common? How do they differ from other homeless people?

3. What is the effect of the mythological and literary references in the first two paragraphs? Why does Rowan introduce these terms? What atmosphere do they establish?

4. What part of his experience among the homeless do you feel was most difficult for Rowan? What do you think is the most important thing he learned from his experiences?

Discussing the Unit

Suggested Topic for Discussion

Though Kozol and Main take entirely different positions, both consider it important to explain the causes of homelessness. Why do you think they care so much about explanations? Consider the problem of homelessness in these terms: why is it important for one writer to view homelessness as a serious housing and economic problem and equally important for another that the problem *not* be viewed as such? Discuss the social and political implications behind each view.

Preparing for Class Discussion

1. Read carefully Kozol's conversation with the homeless young man at Grand Central Station (paragraph 43). What do the man's comments suggest about homeless people? Do the manner and substance of his remarks weaken or reinforce Kozol's position? If you could question the man, what would you ask him? Do you find any significant details missing from his talk? Are there facts you'd like to know? Make a short list of some of the personal questions you would ask. Alternatively, think of questions you would ask Mark Fitzgerald in Rowan's essay.

2. In discussion of social and economic problems, statistics play a large part. Consider how statistics are interpreted and employed to support Kozol's and Main's arguments. For example, note in Main's essay (paragraph 38) that one writer thinks that the homeless should not be stereotyped as mentally ill because "only one-third of homeless people nationwide are mentally disabled." Then note that Main's argument is based on the same figure: "For a rate of mental illness of 33 percent is very high." What do these interpretations suggest about arguments from statistics? Make a list of other examples of statistical reasoning in each essay.

From Discussion to Writing

Imagine that you are serving on a commission to examine possible solutions to the plight of the homeless in America. It is your responsibility to draft a specific plan that would help eliminate homelessness. After carefully considering the facts, figures, and interpretations that you read and discussed, prepare a proposal in which you (1) state your explanation of homelessness, (2) rebut opposing explanations, and (3) offer your plan to deal with the problem.

21

The AIDS Epidemic:
Is Anyone Safe?

The first documented case of AIDS (acquired immune deficiency syndrome) within the United States occurred in 1977. At first, the disease was largely confined to a high-risk group, which included homosexuals, intravenous drug users, and some recipients of blood transfusions. Since its appearance, however, the disease has spread at an alarming rate and no segment of the population can be said to be beyond the risk of contracting it in one of its several forms. Lisa DePaulo's "Love and AIDS" presents the stories of three people infected with the virus and provides a powerful account of how their lives and the lives of those around them have been changed by their affliction. We are shown a side of the disease not often seen in medical journals or television news reports.

Although the AIDS crisis continues to gain the attention of the nation's press, the number of newspaper and magazine articles on the subject has fallen significantly over the last several years. The ways in which we as a society respond to the disease will determine the future of millions of Americans. Accordingly, accurate reporting of the progress being made in AIDS research is of the utmost importance to our nation's health. In "Talking AIDS to Death," Randy Shilts, author of the internationally acclaimed *And the Band Played On* expresses his frustration about the state of media coverage of AIDS.

Finally, how would you react if a friend contracted AIDS? How would his or her illness affect your friendship and your perception of the disease? These questions and others are presented in "The Way We Live Now," a short story by Susan Sontag. While reading the story, consider the innovative use of dialogue and the ways the characters think and talk about the disease. Consider, too, how Sontag in her story dramatizes a concrete instance of AIDS and the social contract.

LISA DePAULO

Love and AIDS [PHILADELPHIA / May 1987]

In tears, Lynne Gold[1] ran to a phone booth, fumbled in the pockets of her coat for two dimes and a nickel, and dialed her boyfriend's number.

"Steven," she said, "I'm dying."

She was thirty-four years old. She owned a condo in Bala Cynwyd,[2] was up for a promotion at work, and kept enough in the bank to travel to Europe every year. Her newest possession was in her hands — a letter from the American Red Cross. It read: " . . . The results of this test indicate that it is likely that you have the HTLV-3 antibody in your blood, and have been exposed to the virus sometime in your past. We do not know what the significance of these tests will be for you, but . . ."

"Steven," she repeated. "Did you hear me? *AIDS.*"

4

That day, about a year ago, Lynne had gone home for lunch not knowing what was in store for her. She opened a pint of yogurt and started flipping

---

[1] The names of AIDS patients and some details of their lives have been changed to protect their privacy.

[2] An affluent suburb of Philadelphia.

LISA DePAULO (b. 1961) is a staff writer with Philadelphia *magazine. A graduate of the University of Pennsylvania, she contributes regularly to the magazine and has been an associate editor there since 1987.*

through the mail. A bill from Bloomingdale's, a notice to renew her sub-scription to *Vogue,* and a slip instructing her to pick up a certified letter at the post office.

She'd never gotten one of those before, but she'd heard that they were sometimes sent for traffic violations. "Damn," she thought, "I should have paid that ticket."

On the drive back to work she stopped at the post office and was almost relieved when she saw the envelope and the words "Red Cross." Still, it seemed strange. Over the past four years Lynne Gold had donated blood half a dozen times, ever since her office blood drive, when she learned that her type — AB positive — was rare and in great demand. She figured it was the least she could do. But they never sent her a thank-you letter before.

Then, as she was signing for the letter, she remembered. Her hands   8
started trembling. This time, she recalled, as she had waited in line to give blood, she was asked a few questions: Had she ever had sex with someone who was in a high-risk group for AIDS? Was she an intravenous drug user? She answered no to all of the questions and was told she could donate blood. But that donation would, in fact, be routinely tested for the presence of the AIDS antibody. "That's fine," said Lynne, but as she began to roll up her sleeve she looked at the woman behind the desk.

"If you *do* have it," she asked, "how long before you're notified?"

"Six to eight weeks," the woman said.

Lynne looked at the date on the wall calendar. It was almost seven weeks to the day.

Lynne Gold wasn't naïve about AIDS. She was a health care worker in   12
a social service agency where AIDS was everyday business. It just wasn't *her* everyday business.

As she leaned against the wall of the phone booth, the tears kept rolling down her cheeks. She could think only of three things.

The first: "I'm going to die."

The second: "Why me?"

And the third: *"Who gave this to me?"*   16

Lynne Gold grew up the daughter of a prominent Main Line[3] physician, in a household where the kids were sent to music lessons before they started kindergarten. She recalls that she was well into grade school before she learned that not every kid belonged to the country club or spent part of each winter at the family condo in Florida.

While her brother would go on to become a successful Center City attorney, Lynne never made the grades at Lower Merion High to pursue what her friends called the status jobs. Not that it mattered. At Lower Merion High, you stuck with your own kind, and for Lynne, that meant the rich kids. They all had their sweet sixteen celebrations at the same banquet room.

---

[3] Affluent area that includes a number of Philadelphia suburbs.

Lynne had always been a pretty girl, thin with jet black hair, but she lasted through four years of high school without experiencing so much as her first kiss. Still, she went to all the proms — with guys her parents thought were perfect for her, though she remembers thinking they were creepy.

It was in the heat of the sixties when she arrived at Penn State. She managed to get through her college years without getting involved in the drugs that were widely available on campus. She remembers taking one toke of a joint at a party but she didn't like it and never touched the stuff again. What she *did* get involved in was sex.

She met Chuck in her freshman year at a frat party. He took her to the football games and home to Long Island to meet his parents. When they had sex for the first time, she thought that one day she'd marry him. It was supposed to be that way. He wasn't supposed to just stop calling.

In the days and weeks after Lynne Gold got her letter, she thought a lot about Chuck. Not that it mattered — Chuck was long before 1977, the year that the AIDS virus was first present in this country. But still, the first time with Chuck, in the back seat of his Mustang parked behind the frat house, was, in her mind, the beginning of the end. To think that all those men she had tried to love, as she had tried to love Chuck, could someday come back to haunt her.

Since 1977. She kept repeating it in her mind. That was the year she turned twenty-five and had just broken up with a Penn State professor who had had a thing for her since she took his course. It couldn't have been him, she thought. He's healthy, he's married, he has *kids.*

Since 1977. Most of her social life that year was spent in the clubs along City Line, with girlfriends who'd married well and didn't have to work or worry anymore about finding true love. She wished that she had their lives, and they wished they had hers: back then her boyfriends came and went like the flavor of the month.

Now Lynne Gold had to remember all of them. *Who gave this to her?*

She narrowed it down to three men.

In 1980 she dated a drummer she'd met in a bar. Her girlfriends thought it was the ultimate fantasy — *a rock musician.* They'd never have had the guts. But what bugged Lynne about the drummer — it bugged her then and it bugged her now — was that he was high all the time on marijuana. Still, she never saw a needle — but who *knew*? She never saw the girl he started cheating on her with either.

Or was it Richard? He was in '83. For three months, he took her to all the nicest places. He never thought twice about dropping a couple hundred every time he picked her up in his snazzy little sports car. Then Lynne found out what Richard did for a living. You don't make that kind of money selling used cars — which was what Richard did only when he wasn't selling cocaine. But does being a coke dealer necessarily make you an intravenous drug abuser? Lynne didn't know for sure. All she knew was that Richard had plenty of secrets.

Secrets. Could any of those men she'd known have been gay? She remembers how shocked she was when, at a college reunion, she ran into an old boyfriend — and *his* boyfriend. And all the while she had thought that when they'd gone away for a weekend and done nothing but cuddle in bed, it was because he respected her too much. She continued to search her past, thinking, considering each of the men she'd been sexually intimate with. Not that there were that many. It was hardly a high number for a young woman in the sexually liberated seventies, she thought. Certainly other young women she knew had had more encounters. But now, with the advent of AIDS, the rules had been changed retroactively.

The third name on Lynne's list was there only for longevity. He was the only man she had ever lived with, and it lasted for nearly two years. Alan was the kind of guy she was *supposed* to date — he was Jewish, his parents were rich, and when she visited their house, there was silver on the table and a butler at her service. For two years she had played the role of wife, throwing dinner parties for Alan's business friends and always coming up with the right thing to say. But his parents didn't think Lynne was good enough, and after a couple of dish-throwing episodes, Alan moved out. She was having a tiny flash of poetic justice in thinking that *he* might be the one — Alan, with his perfect house, his perfect lawn, and his perfectly boring sex.

Narrowing it down to three men who *might* have infected her was tough enough. But going back and judging her old lovers was only part of the task. "I know who *I've* slept with," she thought, "but how do I know who *they've* slept with? My God. It could have been anyone."

But the worst part was that all of this seemed like ancient history. By the time she'd hit her mid-thirties the crazy days were over. What she wanted now was children and a normal life. Not only had she become quite particular about her men, but for all those years she was even using condoms most of the time — though mainly because the pill made her feel fat. And besides, she'd been just about monogamous with Steven for the past three years. She'd dated enough losers to know that what she had with Steven, the handsome man she'd met one day on the tennis courts, was good. And maybe forever.

Suddenly, "forever" was taking on a new meaning. Two days after Lynne got her letter, Steven went to a Center City hospital and was tested for the AIDS antibody. For the ten days it took to get the results of the preliminary tests, Lynne agonized. "If I gave this thing to Steven, I'll never forgive myself," she thought. Steven, who'd been sick with all sorts of things as it was.

Steven. She had never even thought of including him on her list. For ten years or more he had been in and out of hospitals for a chronic respiratory ailment, one day out on the tennis courts, the next day barely able to catch his breath — surely it couldn't have been AIDS.

Ten days later, Steven learned he had tested positive. Less than three months later, he died from AIDS.

Lots of people wondered why Lynne didn't show up for the viewing. 36
His friends didn't know why he died; he was forty-four and had had so
many health problems for so long that the question didn't really come up.
The day of the funeral, Lynne slipped into the back of the church and listened
as the Protestant minister eulogized her boyfriend. But she just couldn't bring
herself to follow the trail of cars that led up a hill to the grave site.

She had been with him the night he died, though. He'd started vomiting
and the nurses had asked Lynne to leave the room. As she walked down the
hall, past the window that looked in on the intensive care unit, she waved
and blew him a kiss. She didn't know it would be the last time she'd see him.

What she *did* know at that point was plenty. That Steven never lied to
her, sure, but also that he had been sick long before the complications brought
on by AIDS killed him. In 1982, before there was a test for the AIDS antibody,
he'd had an operation on his lung that required a blood transfusion.

The blood supply was contaminated.

His doctors now believe that it was that transfusion that infected Steven 40
with AIDS.

And so Lynne Gold's "mistake" wasn't the musician, or the coke dealer,
or even Alan with his polished silver. Lynne Gold's mistake was falling in
love with a man who'd had an operation. . . .

Nineteen seventy-seven: Jimmy Carter was in the White House, Elvis
was dead, and Frank Rizzo was mayor.

Meanwhile, twenty-five-year-old Lynne Gold was out hitting the clubs
on City Line. Another young Philadelphia-area woman, Georgianna Cox, a
thirty-eight-year-old from South Jersey, had just signed her final divorce
papers after a seventeen-year marriage to a politician. On Samsom Street, a
college senior named Sean Taylor was nervously shopping the jewelry stores
for an engagement ring.

Ten years later, all three of these people would learn that they have the 44
AIDS virus. One would go on to develop full-blown AIDS. Another would
develop ARC, the "mild" form of AIDS, from which 30 percent eventually
develop AIDS, and from which no one has ever recovered. The third would
remain an asymptomatic carrier of the disease, suspended amid the statistics
that say the longer one carries the virus, the greater one's chances of developing ARC or AIDS.

But back in 1977, there was nothing any of them could have done to
prepare them for what was to come.

When Georgianna Cox became a free woman she still had a couple of
kids to raise and a full-time job. Playing the singles scene as a divorced
woman somehow just "wasn't" an option. But then, as she likes to put it,
she'd never been "a loose woman" anyway.

"I was a product of the fifties," says Georgianna. "We didn't have sex until we got married. And I didn't. I worked very *hard* at that. I was a virgin when I got married."

When she was growing up, she recalls, "all we ever worried about was the clap." 48

Georgianna Cox got the bad news on the phone at work, where she manages a communications company. She only learned about it because she was such a cautious woman: a week earlier, she was told she needed surgery for cervical cancer. She knew that with all she'd been reading about AIDS, there was no way she would get on an operating table without first storing her own blood. It was in that donation that the virus was found.

"*My* blood is infected?" she asked the caller. She felt herself ready to faint. "There must be some mistake."

When she learned at the age of forty-seven that she had gotten the AIDS virus, she was especially appalled. And humiliated. She was a grown woman, her kids were through college. And she had just remarried — to the man of her dreams.

Just two years earlier, at a point in her life when she started to believe she'd be spending the rest of it alone, she'd met Joe. Their eyes locked at a party, and for the first time in Georgianna's life her heart instantly melted. "I'd waited forty-five years for this man," she remembers. 52

Five months later they were married. Joe had the whole reception crowd in tears when he sang a love song he'd written to his new bride. Her children, who were then in their twenties, said they'd never seen their mother happier.

When Georgianna told her children about having AIDS, they refused to eat in her house. But Joe was as loving as he'd ever been. "We'll get through this," he told her, and every night when they went to sleep he whispered over and over how much he loved her. At the same time, they decided that Joe should be tested.

During the week that they waited for Joe's test results, all Georgianna felt was shame. She was a woman who'd never even date a man until she'd seen him several times socially, with friends. In the ten years between her marriages, there'd only been four relationships — long relationships. Why, she still met a former boyfriend's mother now and then for lunch.

Joe already knew about all her lovers, mainly because there wasn't much to tell. But now, Georgianna would have to dredge up everything. For months, the question of how she had been infected baffled her. Even after Joe's test came back negative, she and her best friend of twenty-five years would sit at the kitchen table and go over it again and again. 56

There was only one clue they could come up with, but even the thought of it made Georgianna feel guilty. In 1981, her boyfriend was a journalist who'd moved east from San Francisco for a job at a New Jersey paper. She remembered how exciting it was after seventeen years of marriage to a small-town official to meet a man who filled her head with exotic stories almost beyond her imagining. One night they sat in bed going through a pile of snapshots from Lewis's life. She particularly loved the pictures from San Francisco — the Golden Gate Bridge, the steep streets and cable cars. *And the gay parade.* She remembered stopping at that snapshot, but Lewis just teased her. "It's a big event in San Francisco," he said. She felt embarrassed for even asking. My God, she thought, I'm really showing my age, and the one thing she did *not* want to be viewed as was old-fashioned.

But night after night, as she sat up with her best friend, she kept remembering that funny feeling. That single snapshot kept popping up in her mind, as clear as on the night she first saw it. Could there really have been *that* many secrets? And the more she thought about it, the guiltier she felt for assuming . . . well, just because Lewis had gone to the gay parade. . . .

She continued to wonder until the following June, six months after she'd tested positive, when she picked up the morning newspaper, turned to the obituary page, and learned how she'd been exposed to AIDS. "My God," she thought, reading Lewis's death notice, "I never knew he was that young."

To Sean Taylor, who'd just turned twenty-nine, the news came as less   60 of a shock. Even though for six years he'd been married to Susan, the girl he met in his college dorm at West Chester. All the guys wanted Susan, with her deep green eyes, long blond hair, and dancer's trim body. And Susan wanted Sean.

When she asked him out, the guys all wanted to know what Sean's secret was. How did he ever get Susan? Sean was just as shocked. His experience as a womanizer at that point was limited to two dates in high school — one with the minister's daughter, whom he took to see *Romeo and Juliet* against his parents' wishes (there was a shot of their naked backs in the film), and whom he kissed just once at her front door. The other was with another girl he met in church — he took her to a tamer movie and barely got a peck.

For three years, Sean and Susan were West Chester's golden couple. They went to all the games and dances and slipped poetry underneath each other's doors. When he finally gave her the ring, their families responded with a huge wedding and a honeymoon trip to the Bahamas.

Six years later, when Sean came home to tell Susan the news, she was sitting in the kitchen of their suburban Philadelphia home with their one-year-old baby. He had two things to tell his wife: that he had AIDS, and that all those years, when she suspected another woman, she had been wrong. What there had been was other men.

At the time Sean Taylor was diagnosed, back in 1983, doctors didn't   64 know exactly how the AIDS virus was transmitted. Nor was there a test for the antibody. But along with AIDS, doctors feared that Sean may have had hepatitis. Susan would have to be tested for that, as would their baby.

Bearing the news into the house, Sean broke down in tears. He had never meant to hurt her, never meant to hurt his baby.

The first time it happened with another man he'd been married for just a year. They'd barely broken in the wedding gifts, and there was Bobby, his best friend from grade school. It had been so long that Sean had almost forgotten the times when they were kids and some strange things just *happened* between them. Now they both were married men — with beautiful wives, executive jobs, and houses in the suburbs. "Of course, I'm happy," they told each other. Then they held each other tight and made love.

At first Sean tried to pretend that these occasional encounters couldn't really mean he was gay. He hated the thought of the gay scene; it seemed so lonely, so *temporary*. What he and Susan had was real. There were anniversaries to celebrate, families to spend Christmas with, Sunday afternoons when they'd go for a walk or take a drive to the museum. So what if the sex wasn't all he thought it was supposed to be? It was an effort to get turned on, but once he *was,* it all felt the same. And Susan never complained. Surely she must have felt empty, he thought, surely she must have thought marriage meant more than sex once a month with a man who hardly held her. But they never did talk about it, except once when he found her crying because she thought there was another woman. He told her there wasn't.

By the fourth year of their marriage, he had started frequenting gay bars in Center City. Then it was gay bath houses. He hated how he felt afterward, but he kept going back. In the fifth year of their marriage, Susan became pregnant. Sean swore to himself that it would never happen again.

Less than a year later, Sean discovered the lumps in his neck. He told himself it was just a cold. Susan had had a cold, so had the baby, and Sean had suffered with swollen glands so many times before. But three months later, the lumps hadn't disappeared — in fact, they had grown bigger.

By 1984, when he found the first spot of Kaposi's sarcoma, a harbinger of AIDS — just a funny purple mark on his leg one morning, barely the size of a dime — his marriage was already over, and he was living by himself in an apartment he'd rented in town. He had known it would all unravel, but never like this. He reached into the medicine cabinet, pulled out a Band-Aid, and covered the spot on his leg. It looked just like a bruise.

Lynne Gold's relationship with AIDS was also deepening by this point. Five months after Steven died, Lynne learned that she was no longer just a carrier of AIDS. From the start, she knew there was a bump on her neck — a hard bump, in the back, right in the middle, and almost the size of a quarter. But the word ARC just never came up. It was important, her doctor had been telling her, that she continue to have hope. And she did hope — she hoped that there'd be a cure in time for her to one day have a baby. In time so that nothing terrible would happen, so she'd never have to tell her parents. It wasn't simply that she thought they'd disown her. She just knew that every time they looked at her, they'd be looking at a daughter with AIDS. And that's one thing she swore she'd never do to them.

It was last October when she started to fear that things had gotten worse. 72
She was sitting in the examining room of her doctor's office, waiting for her checkup and reading *Time* magazine. There was an article about ARC, how more and more of those who had it were going on to develop AIDS. And that the symptoms were things you'd get with routine illnesses — swollen glands, night sweats, and fevers. She felt the lump on her neck. And remembered how many mornings she'd wake up and feel the drenched sheets. It was the first time she'd really read about ARC.

She put the magazine down and noticed her patient folder on the desk. A nurse had left it in the room; it was sitting right under Lynne's eyes. For a minute she felt like she was snooping. Files, she knew from her own job, were confidential property. She actually felt guilty, but she opened it. And read: "*HTLV-3*"-dash-"*ARC*."

When the doctor walked in, she closed it quickly, as though it wasn't hers to look at. Instead of letting on, she said, "I was just reading this article about ARC. . . ."

"Yes," he said. "You have ARC."

Lynne never told him she'd seen her file and never did question why he 76 hadn't explained it earlier. In fact, she wished she still hadn't known. As she left that day, all that went through her mind was, "Just don't tell me anything worse."

It's been more than three years since Sean Taylor was diagnosed, making him a long-term survivor of AIDS. In that time, he's gotten a divorce, obtained permission to see his son once a week, and taken an indefinite leave of absence from his job as a marketing executive. He has also found three more purple lesions. Last fall, on a trip to Florida, he walked into a gay bar and noticed a man who was cruising him from the other side of the room. They spent the next three days together, without ever making love. Sean's new friend, Tony, was afraid to ask why. Finally, Sean broke down and told him.

Today they share an apartment near Rittenhouse Square. They celebrate the monthly anniversaries since the night they met, argue over who will do the cooking, and once a month they walk through the park together, on the way to Sean's chemotherapy treatments. That's the hardest part for Tony — not the condoms, not the fear of AIDS, but the fear that he might lose Sean. Tony has chosen not to be tested, because if he's been exposed there's nothing he can do. He also knows that if he has been exposed to AIDS it was probably long before he met Sean.

It's been more than a year since Georgianna Cox learned she'd been exposed. In that time her kids have returned to eat dinner at her house. She remains an asymptomatic carrier and tries not to read the articles she sees in the papers. Her husband, Joe, still watches the AIDS reports on *Nightline*,

but she chooses not to. At night when she goes to sleep, he still tells her that he loves her.

And it's been a year and a half since Lynne Gold got her letter. In that time, she's buried a boyfriend, gotten a big raise at work, and bought a new fur coat.

She keeps the crumpled letter from the Red Cross in a drawer of her bedside table. Every now and then she'll reread it, as though the words might have changed. In the morning, she wakes up to the news on the radio and listens to the death toll. Then she lies back, particularly on those mornings when the sheets are soaked, and wonders.

At work she remains mute when someone makes a crack about AIDS. It amazes her how many people she works with still think you can get it from a toilet seat or a drinking cup. Just the other day, her supervisor asked Lynne if she wanted to try out a shade of lipstick. It wasn't her color, Lynne said. "What's the matter," the woman cracked, "you think I'm gonna give you *AIDS*?"

Life goes on. She keeps her standing haircut appointment at Duskin's, makes her car payments on time. Meets her parents for dinner at the country club. Of course, they've never guessed and she continues to vow she'll never tell them. And every now and then, she feels exactly the kinds of things she always felt when she meets a man who's interested in her.

It happened just a month ago, on the tennis courts. For a moment, he reminded her of Steven — handsome and muscular. When they began to date, she knew where it would lead. But she figured she'd ease into it by insisting that they use condoms.

"What do you think, I'm gonna give you *AIDS*?" he cracked, and laughed at her. But finally he gave in.

Despite the fact that the condoms remind her of her disease, it feels good to be made love to, Lynne says. She just doesn't know if she'll ever find the words to tell him.

Points to Consider

1. By choosing three very different people to write about, what does De-Paulo hope to illustrate about the nature of AIDS? Of what significance is the fact that two of the three AIDS victims are heterosexual?

2. At one point Lynne Gold asks, "I know who *I've* slept with, . . . but how do I know who *they've* slept with?" What does her question imply about our ability to protect ourselves from the disease? What kind of role do you think trust will play in our relationships as AIDS spreads?

3. Georgianna Cox reports that her adult children refused to eat in her

house after learning she had AIDS. Do you think they acted incorrectly? How is their reaction indicative of the level of knowledge about AIDS?

4. DePaulo writes that since contracting AIDS, Sean Taylor has begun a new relationship. He told his new companion, Tony, of his condition almost immediately, and Tony participates in Sean's treatments. But Lynne Gold has not informed her new lover about her condition. How would you evaluate the differences in the behavior of the two AIDS victims?

RANDY SHILTS

Talking AIDS to Death   [ESQUIRE / March 1989]

I'm talking to my friend Kit Herman when I notice a barely perceptible spot on the left side of his face. Slowly, it grows up his cheekbone, down to his chin, and forward to his mouth. He talks on cheerfully, as if nothing is wrong, and I'm amazed that I'm able to smile and chat on, too, as if nothing were there. His eyes become sunken; his hair turns gray; his ear is turning purple now, swelling into a carcinomatous cauliflower, and still we talk on. He's dying in front of me. He'll be dead soon, if nothing is done.

Dead soon, if nothing is done.

"Excuse me, Mr. Shilts, I asked if you are absolutely sure, if you can categorically state that you definitely can*not* get AIDS from a mosquito."

I forget the early-morning nightmare and shift into my canned response.   4
All my responses are canned now. I'm an AIDS talk-show jukebox. Press the

RANDY SHILTS (b. 1951) is considered the most expert journalist on the AIDS epidemic in the nation. His articles have appeared in newspapers and magazines all over the country, including the San Francisco Chronicle, *the* Washington Post, *the* Chicago Tribune, *the* Village Voice, *and* Christopher Street. *Shilts is the author of the internationally acclaimed* And the Band Played On: Politics, People, and the AIDS Epidemic *(1987).*

button, any button on the AIDS question list, and I have my canned answer ready. Is this Chicago or Detroit?

"Of course you can get AIDS from a mosquito," I begin.

Here, I pause for dramatic effect. In that brief moment, I can almost hear the caller murmur, "I *knew* it."

"If you have unprotected anal intercourse with an infected mosquito, you'll get AIDS," I continue. "Anything short of that and you won't."

The talk-show host likes the answer. All the talk-show hosts like my answers because they're short, punchy, and to the point. Not like those boring doctors with long recitations of scientific studies so overwritten with maybes and qualifiers that they frighten more than they reassure an AIDS-hysteric public. I give good interview, talk-show producers agree. It's amazing, they say, how I always stay so cool and never lose my temper.

"Mr. Shilts, has there ever been a case of anyone getting AIDS from a gay waiter?"

"In San Francisco, I don't think they allow heterosexuals to be waiters. This fact proves absolutely that if you could get AIDS from a gay waiter, all northern California would be dead by now."

I gave that same answer once on a Bay Area talk show, and my caller, by the sound of her a little old lady, quickly rejoined: "What if that gay waiter took my salad back into the kitchen and ejaculated into my salad dressing? Couldn't I get AIDS then?"

I didn't have a pat answer for that one, and I still wonder at what this elderly caller thought went on in the kitchens of San Francisco restaurants. Fortunately, this morning's phone-in—in Chicago, it turned out—is not as imaginative.

"You know, your question reminds me of a joke we had in California a couple of years back," I told the caller. "How many heterosexual waiters in San Francisco does it take to screw in a light bulb? The answer is both of them."

The host laughs, the caller is silent. Next comes the obligatory question about whether AIDS can be spread through coughing.

I had written a book to change the world, and here I was on talk shows throughout America, answering questions about mosquitoes and gay waiters.

This wasn't exactly what I had envisioned when I began writing *And the Band Played On*. I had hoped to effect some fundamental changes. I really believed I could alter the performance of the institutions that had allowed AIDS to sweep through America unchecked.

AIDS had spread, my book attested, because politicians, particularly those in charge of federal-level response, had viewed the disease as a political issue, not an issue of public health—they deprived researchers of anything near the resources that were needed to fight it. AIDS had spread because government health officials consistently lied to the American people about the need for more funds, being more concerned with satisfying their political bosses and protecting their own jobs than with telling the truth and protecting the public health. And AIDS had spread because indolent news organizations shunned their responsibility to provide tough, adversarial reportage, instead basing stories largely on the Official Truth of government press releases. The response to AIDS was never even remotely commensurate with the scope of the problem.

I figured the federal government, finally exposed, would stumble over itself to accelerate the pace of AIDS research and put AIDS-prevention programs on an emergency footing. Once publicly embarrassed by the revelations of its years of shameful neglect, the media would launch serious investigative reporting on the epidemic. Health officials would step forward and finally lay bare the truth about how official disregard had cost this country hundreds of thousands of lives. And it would never happen again.

I was stunned by the "success" of my book. I quickly acquired all the trappings of bestsellerdom: *60 Minutes* coverage of my "startling" revelations, a Book of the Month Club contract, a miniseries deal with NBC, translation into six languages, book tours on three continents, featured roles in movie-star-studded AIDS fund-raisers, regular appearances on network news shows, and hefty fees on the college lecture circuit. A central figure in my book became one of *People* magazine's "25 Most Intriguing People of 1987," even though he had been dead for nearly four years, and the *Los Angeles Herald Examiner* pronounced me one of the "in" authors of 1988. The mayor of San Francisco even proclaimed my birthday last year "Randy Shilts Day."

And one warm summer day as I was sunning at a gay resort in the   20
redwoods north of San Francisco, a well-toned, perfectly tanned young man slid into a chaise next to me and offered the ultimate testimony to my fifteen minutes of fame. His dark eyelashes rising and falling shyly, he whispered, "When I saw you on *Good Morning America* a couple weeks ago, I wondered what it would be like to go to bed with you."

"You're the world's first AIDS celebrity," enthused a friend at the World Health Organization, after hearing one of WHO's most eminent AIDS authorities say he would grant me an interview on one condition—that I autograph his copy of my book. "It must be great," he said.

It's not so great.

The bitter irony is, my role as an AIDS celebrity just gives me a more elevated promontory from which to watch the world make the same mistakes in the handling of the AIDS epidemic that I had hoped my work would help to change. When I return from network tapings and celebrity glad-handing, I come back to my home in San Francisco's gay community and see friends dying. The lesions spread from their cheeks to cover their faces, their hair falls out, they die slowly, horribly, and sometimes, suddenly, before anybody has a chance to know they're sick. They die in my arms and in my dreams, and nothing at all has changed.

Never before have I succeeded so well; never before have I failed so miserably.— 24

I gave my first speech on the college lecture circuit at the University of California [at] Los Angeles in January 1988. I told the audience that there were fifty thousand diagnosed AIDS cases in the United States as of that week and that within a few months there would be more people suffering from this deadly disease in the United States than there were Americans killed during the Vietnam War. There were audible gasps. During the question-and-answer session, several students explained that they had heard that the number of AIDS cases in America was leveling off.

In the next speech, at the University of Tennessee, I decided to correct such misapprehension by adding the federal government's projections—the 270,000 expected to be dead or dying from AIDS in 1991, when the disease would kill more people than any single form of cancer, more than car accidents. When I spoke at St. Cloud State University in Minnesota three months later, I noted that the number of American AIDS cases had that week surpassed the Vietnam benchmark. The reaction was more a troubled murmur than a gasp.

By the time I spoke at New York City's New School for Social Research in June and there were sixty-five thousand AIDS cases nationally, the numbers were changing so fast that the constant editing made my notes difficult to read. By then as many as one thousand Americans a week were learning that they, too, had AIDS, or on the average, about one every fourteen minutes. There were new government projections to report, too: by 1993, some 450,000 Americans would be diagnosed with AIDS. In that year, one American will be diagnosed with the disease every thirty-six seconds. Again, I heard the gasps.

For my talk at a hospital administrators' conference in Washington in August, I started using little yellow stick-ons to update the numbers on my outline. That made it easier to read; there were now seventy-two thousand AIDS cases. Probably this month, or next, I'll tell another college audience that the nation's AIDS case load has topped one hundred thousand and there will be gasps again. 28

The gasps always amaze me. Why are they surprised? In epidemics, people get sick and die. That's what epidemics do to people and that's why epidemics are bad.

When Kit Herman was diagnosed with AIDS on May 13, 1986, his doctor leaned over his hospital bed, took his hand, and assured him, "Don't worry, you're in time for AZT." The drug worked so well that all Kit's friends let themselves think he might make it. And we were bolstered by the National Institutes of Health's assurance that AZT was only the first generation of AIDS drugs, and that the hundreds of millions of federal dollars going into AIDS treatment research meant there would soon be a second and third generation of treatments to sustain life beyond AZT's effectiveness. Surely nothing was more important, considering the federal government's own estimates that between 1 and 1.5 million Americans were infected with the Human Immunodeficiency Virus (HIV), and virtually all would die within the next decade if nothing was done. The new drugs, the NIH assured everyone, were "in the pipeline," and government scientists were working as fast as they possibly could.

Despite my nagging, not one of dozens of public-affairs-show producers chose to look seriously into the development of those long-sought second and third generations of AIDS drugs. In fact, clinical trials of AIDS drugs were hopelessly stalled in the morass of bureaucracy at the NIH, but this story tip never seemed to cut it with producers. Clinical trials were not sexy. Clinical trials were boring.

I made my third *Nightline* appearance in January 1988 because new estimates had been released revealing that one in sixty-one babies born in New York City carried antibodies to the AIDS virus. And the link between those babies and the disease was intravenous drug use by one or both parents. Suddenly, junkies had become the group most likely to catch and spread AIDS through the heterosexual community. Free needles to junkies—now there was a sizzling television topic. I told the show's producers I'd talk about that, but that I was much more interested in the issue of AIDS treatments—which seemed most relevant to the night's program, since Ted Koppel's other guest was Dr. Anthony Fauci, associate NIH director for AIDS, and the Reagan administration's most visible AIDS official.

After fifteen minutes of talk on the ins and outs and pros and cons of free needles for intravenous drug users, I raised the subject of the pressing need for AIDS treatments. Koppel asked Fauci what was happening. The doctor launched into a discussion of treatments "in the pipeline" and how government scientists were working as fast as they possibly could.

I'd heard the same words from NIH officials for three years: drugs were in the pipeline. Maybe it was true, but when were they going to come out of their goddamn pipeline? Before I could formulate a polite retort to Fauci's stall, however, the segment was over, Ted was thanking us, and the red light on the camera had blipped off. Everyone seemed satisfied that the government was doing everything it possibly could to develop AIDS treatments.

Three months later, I was reading a week-old *New York Times* in Kit's room in the AIDS ward at San Francisco General Hospital. It was April, nearly two years after my friend's AIDS diagnosis. AZT had given him two years of nearly perfect health, but now its effect was wearing off, and Kit had suffered his first major AIDS-related infection since his original bout with pneumonia—cryptococcal meningitis. The meningitis could be treated, we all knew, but the discovery of this insidious brain infection meant more diseases were likely to follow. And the long-promised second and third generations of AIDS drugs were still nowhere on the horizon.

While perusing the worn copy of the *Times*, I saw a story about Dr. Fauci's testimony at a congressional hearing. After making Fauci swear an oath to tell the truth, a subcommittee headed by Representative Ted Weiss of New York City asked why it was taking so long to get new AIDS treatments into testing at a time when Congress was putting hundreds of millions of dollars into NIH budgets for just such purposes. At first Fauci talked about unavoidable delays. He claimed government scientists were working as fast as they could. Pressed harder, he finally admitted that the problem stemmed "almost exclusively" from the lack of staffing in his agency. Congress had allocated funds, it was true, but the Reagan administration had gotten around spending the money by stingily refusing to let Fauci hire anybody. Fauci had requested 127 positions to speed the development of AIDS treatments; the administration had granted him 11. And for a year, he had not told anyone. For a year, this spokesman for the public health answered reporters that AIDS drugs were in the pipeline and that government scientists had all the money they needed. It seemed that only when faced with the penalty of perjury would one of the administration's top AIDS officials tell the truth. That was the real story, I thought, but for some reason nobody else had picked up on it.

At the international AIDS conference in Stockholm two months later, the other reporters in "the AIDS pack" congratulated me on my success and asked what I was working on now. I admitted that I was too busy promoting the British and German release of my book to do much writing myself, and next month I had the Australian tour. But if I *were* reporting, I added with a vaguely conspiratorial tone, *I'd* look at the *scandal* in the NIH. Nobody had picked up that *New York Times* story from a few months ago about staffing shortages on AIDS clinical trials. The lives of 1.5 million HIV-infected Americans hung in the balance, and the only way you could get a straight answer out of an administration AIDS official was to put him under oath and make him face the charge of perjury. Where I went to journalism school, *that* was a news story.

One reporter responded to my tip with the question: "But who's going to play *you* in the miniseries?"

A few minutes later, when Dr. Fauci came into the press room, the world's leading AIDS journalists got back to the serious business of transcribing his remarks. Nobody asked him if he was actually telling the truth, or whether they should put him under oath to ensure a candid response to questions about when we'd get AIDS treatments. Most of the subsequent news accounts of Dr. Fauci's comments faithfully reported that many AIDS treatments were in the pipeline. Government scientists, he said once more, were doing all they possibly could.

The producer assured my publisher that Morton Downey, Jr., would be 40 "serious" about AIDS. "He's not going to play games on this issue," the producer said, adding solemnly: "His brother has AIDS. He understands the need for compassion." The abundance of Mr. Downey's compassion was implicit in the night's call-in poll question: "Should all people with AIDS be quarantined?"

Downey's first question to me was, "You *are* a homosexual, aren't you?"

He wasn't ready for my canned answer: "Why do you ask? Do you want a date or something?"

The show shifted into an earnest discussion of quarantine. In his television studio, Clearasil-addled high school students from suburban New Jersey held up MORTON DOWNEY FAN CLUB signs and cheered aggressively when the truculent, chain-smoking host appeared to favor a kind of homespun AIDS Auschwitz. The youths shouted down any audience member who stepped forward to defend the rights of AIDS sufferers, their howls growing particularly vitriolic if the speakers were gay. These kids were the ilk from which Hitler drew his Nazi youth. In the first commercial break, the other guest, an AIDS activist, and I told Downey we would walk off the show if he didn't tone down his gay-baiting rhetoric. Smiling amiably, Downey took a long drag on his cigarette and assured us, "Don't worry, I have a fallback position."

That comment provided one of the most lucid moments in my year as 44 an AIDS celebrity. Downey's "fallback position," it was clear, was the opposite of what he was promoting on the air. Of course, he didn't *really* believe that people with AIDS, people like his brother, should all be locked up. This was merely a deliciously provocative posture to exploit the working-class resentments of people who needed someone to hate. AIDS sufferers and gays would do for this week. Next week, if viewership dropped and Downey needed a new whipping boy, maybe he'd move on to Arabs, maybe Jews. It didn't seem to matter much to him, since he didn't believe what he was saying anyway. For Morton Downey, Jr., talking about AIDS was not an act of conscience; it was a ratings ploy. He knew it, he let his guests know it, his producers certainly knew it, and his television station knew it. The only people left out of the joke were his audience.

The organizers of the Desert AIDS Project had enlisted actor Kirk Douglas and CBS morning anchor Kathleen Sullivan to be honorary cochairs of the Palm Springs fund-raiser. The main events would include a celebrity tennis match pitting Douglas against Mayor Sonny Bono, and a fifteen-hundred-dollar-a-head dinner at which I would receive a Lucite plaque for my contributions to the fight against AIDS. The next morning I would fly to L.A. to speak at still another event, this one with Shirley MacLaine, Valerie Harper, and Susan Dey of *L.A. Law*.

The desert night was exquisite. There were 130 dinner guests, the personification of elegance and confidence, who gathered on a magnificent patio of chocolate-brown Arizona flagstone at the home of one of Palm Springs's most celebrated interior designers. A lot of people had come simply to see what was regarded as one of the most sumptuous dwellings in this sumptuous town.

When I was called to accept my reward, I began with the same lineup of jokes I use on talk shows and on the college lecture circuit. They work every time.

I told the crowd about how you get AIDS from a mosquito. 48

Kirk Douglas laughed; everybody laughed.

Next, I did the how-many-gay-waiters joke.

Kirk Douglas laughed; everybody laughed.

Then I mentioned the woman who asked whether she could get AIDS 52 from a waiter ejaculating in her salad dressing.

That one always has my college audiences rolling in the aisles, so I paused for the expected hilarity.

But in the utter stillness of the desert night air, all that could be heard was the sound of Kirk Douglas's steel jaw dropping to the magnificent patio of chocolate-brown Arizona flagstone. The rest was silence.

"You've got to remember that most of these people came because they're my clients," the host confided later. "You said that, and all I could think was how I'd have to go back to stitching slipcovers when this was done."

It turned out that there was more to my lead-balloon remark than 56 a misjudged audience. Local AIDS organizers told me that a year earlier, a rumor that one of Palm Springs's most popular restaurants was owned by a homosexual, and that most of its waiters were gay, had terrified the elite community. Patronage at the eatery quickly plummeted, and it had nearly gone out of business. Fears that I dismissed as laughable were the genuine concerns of my audience, I realized. My San Francisco joke was a Palm Springs fable.

As I watched the busboys clear the tables later that night, I made a mental note not to tell that joke before dinner again. Never had I seen so many uneaten salads, so much wasted iceberg lettuce.

A friend had just tested antibody positive, and I was doing my best to cheer him up as we ambled down the sidewalk toward a Castro Street restaurant a few blocks from where I live in San Francisco. It seems most of my conversations now have to do with who has tested positive or lucked out and turned up negative, or who is too afraid to be tested. We had parked our car near Coming Home, the local hospice for AIDS patients and others suffering from terminal illnesses, and as we stepped around a nondescript, powder-blue van that blocked our path, two men in white uniforms emerged from the hospice's side door. They carried a stretcher, and on the stretcher was a corpse, neatly wrapped in a royal-blue blanket and secured with navy-blue straps. My friend and I stopped walking. The men quickly guided the stretcher into the back of the van, climbed in the front doors, and drove away. We continued our walk but didn't say anything.

I wondered if the corpse was someone I had known. I'd find out Thursday when the weekly gay paper came out. Every week there are at least two pages filled with obituaries of the previous week's departed. Each week, when I turn to those pages, I hold my breath, wondering whose picture I'll see. It's the only way to keep track, what with so many people dying.

Sometimes I wonder if an aberrant mother or two going to mass at the Most Holy Redeemer Church across the street from Coming Home Hospice has ever warned a child, "That's where you'll end up if you don't obey God's law." Or whether some youngster, feeling that first awareness of a different sexuality, has looked at the doorway of this modern charnel house with an awesome, gnawing dread of annihilation.

"Is the limousine here? Where are the dancers?"

The room fell silent. Blake Rothaus had sounded coherent until that moment, but he was near death now and his brain was going. We were gathered around his bed in a small frame house on a dusty street in Oklahoma City. The twenty-four-year-old was frail and connected to life through a web of clear plastic tubing. He stared up at us and seemed to recognize from our looks that he had lapsed into dementia. A friend broke the uncomfortable silence.

"Of course, we all brought our dancing shoes," he said. "Nice fashionable pumps at that. I wouldn't go out without them."

Everyone laughed and Blake Rothaus was lucid again.

Blake had gone to high school in a San Francisco suburb. When he was a sophomore, he told us, he and his best friend sometimes skipped school, sneaking to the city to spend their afternoons in the gay neighborhood around Castro Street.

It's a common sight, suburban teenagers playing hooky on Castro Street. I could easily imagine him standing on a corner not far from my house. But back in 1982, when he was eighteen, I was already writing about a mysterious, unnamed disease that had claimed 330 victims in the United States.

Blake moved back to Oklahoma City with his family after he graduated from high school. When he fell ill with AIDS, he didn't mope. Instead, he started pestering Oklahoma health officials with demands to educate people about this disease and to provide services for the sick. The state health department didn't recoil. At the age of twenty-two, Blake Rothaus had become the one-man nucleus for Oklahoma's first AIDS-patient services. He was the hero of the Sooner State's AIDS movement and something of a local legend.

Though the state had reported only 250 AIDS cases, Oklahoma City had a well-coordinated network of religious leaders, social workers, health-care providers, gay-rights advocates, state legislators, and businessmen, all committed to providing a sane and humane response to this frightening new disease.

"I think it's the old Dust Bowl mentality," suggested one AIDS organizer. "When the hard times come, people pull together."

My past year's travels to twenty-nine states and talks with literally thousands of people have convinced me of one thing about this country and AIDS: most Americans want to do the right thing about this epidemic. Some might worry about mosquitoes and a few may be suspicious of their salad dressing. But beyond these fears is a reservoir of compassion and concern that goes vastly underreported by a media that needs conflict and heartlessness to fashion a good news hook.

In Kalamazoo, Michigan, when I visited my stepmother, I was buttonholed by a dozen middle-aged women who wondered anxiously whether we were any closer to a vaccine or a long-term treatment. One mentioned a hemophiliac nephew. Another had a gay brother in Chicago. A third went to a gay hairdresser who, she quickly added, was one of the finest people you'd ever meet. When I returned to my conservative hometown of Aurora, Illinois, nestled among endless fields of corn and soy, the local health department told me they receive more calls than they know what to do with from women's groups, parishes, and community organizations that want to do something to help. In New Orleans, the archconservative, pronuke, antigay bishop had taken up the founding of an AIDS hospice as a personal mission because, he said, when people are sick, you've got to help them out.

Scientists, reporters, and politicians privately tell me that of course *they* want to do more about AIDS, but they have to think about the Morton Downeys of the world, who argue that too much research or too much news space or too much official sympathy is being meted out to a bunch of miscreants. They do as much as they can, they insist; more would rile the resentments of the masses. So the institutions fumble along, convinced they must pander to the lowest common denominator, while the women and men of America's heartland pull me aside to fret about a dying cousin or co-worker and to plead, "When will there be a cure? When will this be over?"

"I think I'll make it through this time," Kit said to me, "but I don't have it in me to go through it again."

We were in room 3 in San Francisco General Hospital's ward 5A, the AIDS ward. The poplar trees outside Kit's window were losing their leaves, and the first winter's chill was settling over the city. I was preparing to leave for my fourth and, I hoped, final media tour, this time for release of the book in paperback and on audiocassette; Kit was preparing to die.

The seizures had started a week earlier, indicating he was suffering either from toxoplasmosis, caused by a gluttonous protozoa that sets up housekeeping in the brain; or perhaps it was a relapse of cryptococcal meningitis; or, another specialist guessed, it could be one of those other nasty brain infections that nobody had seen much of until the past year. Now that AIDS patients were living longer, they fell victim to even more exotic infections than in the early days. But the seizures were only part of it. Kit had slowly been losing the sight in his left eye to a herpes infection. And the Kaposi's sarcoma lesions that had scarred his face were beginning to coat the inside of his lungs. When Kit mentioned he'd like to live until Christmas, the doctors said he might want to consider having an early celebration this year, because he wasn't going to be alive in December.

"I can't take another infection," Kit said.

"What does that mean?"

"Morphine," Kit answered, adding mischievously, "lots of it."

We talked briefly about the mechanics of suicide. We both knew people who'd made a mess of it, and people who had done it right. It was hardly the first time the subject had come up in conversation for either of us. Gay men facing AIDS now exchange formulas for suicide as casually as housewives swap recipes for chocolate-chip cookies.

Kit was released from the hospital a few days later. He had decided to take his life on a Tuesday morning. I had to give my first round of interviews in Los Angeles that day, so I stopped on the way to the airport to say goodbye on Monday. All day Tuesday, while I gave my perfectly formed sound bites in a round of network radio appearances, I wondered: is this the moment he's slipping out of consciousness and into that perfect darkness? When I called that night, it turned out he'd delayed his suicide until Thursday to talk to a few more relatives. I had to give a speech in Portland that day, so on the way to the airport I stopped again. He showed me the amber-brown bottle with the bubble-gum-pink morphine syrup, and we said another good-bye.

The next morning, Kit drank his morphine and fell into a deep sleep. That afternoon, he awoke and drowsily asked what time it was. When told it was five hours later, he murmured, "That's amazing. I should have been dead hours ago."

And then he went back to sleep.

That night, Kit woke up again.

"You know what they say about near-death experiences?" he asked. "Going toward the light?"

Shaking his head, he sighed, "No light. Nothing."

His suicide attempt a failure, Kit decided the timing of his death would now be up to God. I kept up on the bizarre sequence of events by phone and called as soon as I got back to San Francisco. I was going to tell Kit that his theme song should be "Never Can Say Good-by," but then the person on the other end of the phone told me that Kit had lapsed into a coma.

The next morning, he died.

Kit's death was like everything about AIDS—anticlimactic. By the time he actually did die, I was almost beyond feeling.

The next day, I flew to Boston for the start of the paperback tour, my heart torn between rage and sorrow. All week, as I was chauffeured to my appearances on *Good Morning America, Larry King Live,* and various CNN shows, I kept thinking, it's all going to break. I'm going to be on a TV show with some officious government health spokesman lying to protect his job, and I'm going to start shouting, "You lying son of a bitch. Don't you know there are people, real people, people I love out there dying?" Or I'll be on a call-in show and another mother will phone about her thirty-seven-year-old son who just died and it will hit me all at once, and I'll start weeping.

But day after day as the tour went on, no matter how many official lies I heard and how many grieving mothers I talked to, the crackup never occurred. All my answers came out rationally in tight little sound bites about institutional barriers to AIDS treatments and projections about 1993 case loads.

By the last day of the tour, when a limousine picked me up at my Beverly Hills hotel for my last round of satellite TV interviews, I knew I had to stop. In a few weeks I'd return to being national correspondent for the *Chronicle,* and it was time to get off the AIDS celebrity circuit, end the interviews and decline the invitations to the star-studded fund-raisers, and get back to work as a newspaper reporter. That afternoon, there was just one last radio interview to a call-in show in the San Fernando Valley, and then it would be over.

The first caller asked why his tax money should go toward funding an AIDS cure when people got the disease through their own misdeeds.   92

I used my standard jukebox answer about how most cancer cases are linked to people's behavior but that nobody ever suggested we stop trying to find a cure for cancer.

A second caller phoned to ask why her tax money should go to funding an AIDS cure when these people clearly deserved what they got.

I calmly put a new spin on the same answer, saying in America you usually don't sentence people to die for having a different lifestyle from yours.

Then a third caller phoned in to say that he didn't care if all those queers   96
and junkies died, as did a fourth and fifth and sixth caller. By then I was shouting, "You stupid bigot. You just want to kill off everybody you don't like. You goddamn Nazi."

The talk-show host sat in stunned silence. She'd heard I was so *reasonable.* My anger baited the audience further, and the seventh and eighth callers began talking about "you guys," as if only a faggot like myself could give a shit about whether AIDS patients all dropped dead tomorrow.

In their voices, I heard the reporters asking polite questions of NIH officials. Of course, they had to be polite to the government doctors; dying queers weren't anything to lose your temper over. I heard the dissembling NIH researchers go home to their wives at night, complain about the lack of personnel, and shrug; this was just how it was going to have to be for a while. They'd excuse their inaction by telling themselves that if they went public and lost their jobs, worse people would replace them. It was best to go along. But how would they feel if *their* friends, *their* daughters were dying of this disease? Would they be silent—or would they shout? Maybe they'll forgive me for suspecting they believed that ultimately a bunch of fags weren't worth losing a job over. And when I got home, I was going to have to watch my friends get shoved into powder-blue vans, and it wasn't going to change.

The history of the AIDS epidemic, of yesterday and of today, was echoing in the voices of those callers. And I was screaming at them, and the show host just sat there stunned, and I realized I had rendered myself utterly and completely inarticulate.

I stopped, took a deep breath, and returned to compound-complex   100
sentences about the American tradition of compassion and the overriding need to overcome institutional barriers to AIDS treatments.

When I got home to San Francisco that night, I looked over some notes I had taken from a conversation I'd had with Kit during his last stay in the hospital. I was carping about how frustrated I was at the prospect of returning to my reporting job. If an internationally acclaimed best seller hadn't done shit to change the world, what good would mere newspaper stories do?

"The limits of information," Kit said. "There's been a lot written on it."
"Oh," I said.

Kit closed his eyes briefly and faded into sleep while plastic tubes fed   104
him a cornucopia of antibiotics. After five minutes, he stirred, looked up, and added, as if we had never stopped talking, "But you don't really have a choice. You've got to keep on doing it. What else are you going to do?"

Points to Consider

1. What does Randy Shilts think is the major cause of the spread of AIDS in America? Why did the government not increase federal grants to AIDS research once it was clear that the disease had become an epidemic?

2. What did Dr. Anthony Fauci of the National Institutes for Health reveal under oath before a congressional committee? How did this information differ from that which he supplied on *Nightline* a few months earlier? According to Shilts, did any publications other than the *New York Times* pick up the story about Fauci's testimony?

3. What important lesson did Shilts learn when he agreed to appear on the controversial *Morton Downey, Jr., Show*? What was Downey's attitude toward the AIDS crisis? Does Downey's attitude reveal anything about the coverage of the crisis elsewhere in the American media?

4. Why does Shilts include the anecdote about the AIDS fund-raiser he

attended in Palm Springs? Why was he surprised at the audience's re-action to his final joke? What did their reaction tell Shilts about hetero-sexuals' perceptions about AIDS?

SUSAN SONTAG

The Way We Live Now [THE NEW YORKER / November 24, 1986]

At first he was just losing weight, he felt only a little ill, Max said to Ellen, and he didn't call for an appointment with his doctor, according to Greg, because he was managing to keep on working at more or less the same rhythm, but he did stop smoking, Tanya pointed out, which suggests he was frightened, but also that he wanted, even more than he knew, to be healthy, or healthier, or maybe just to gain back a few pounds, said Orson, for he told her, Tanya went on, that he expected to be climbing the walls (isn't that what people say?) and found, to his surprise, that he didn't miss cigarettes at all and reveled in the sensation of his lungs' being ache-free for the first time in years. But did he have a good doctor, Stephen wanted to know, since it would have been crazy not to go for a checkup after the pressure was off and he was back from the conference in Helsinki, even if by then he was feeling better. And he said, to Frank, that he would go, even though he was indeed frightened, as he admitted to Jan, but who wouldn't be frightened now, though, odd as that might seem, he hadn't been worrying until recently, he avowed to Quentin, it was only in the last six months that he had the metallic taste of panic in his mouth, because becoming seriously ill was something that happened to other people, a normal delusion, he observed to Paolo, if one was thirty-eight and had never had a serious illness; he wasn't, as Jan confirmed, a hypochondriac. Of course, it was hard not to

---

SUSAN SONTAG (b. 1933) is the author of many distinguished books of intellectual and cultural commentary, including Against Interpretation *(1966),* Styles of Radical Will *(1969),* On Photography *(1977), and* Illness as Metaphor *(1978). She has also published two novels and a collection of short stories. Her most recent work is* AIDS and Its Metaphors *(1988). "The Way We Live Now" was selected for* Best American Short Stories 1987.

worry, everyone was worried, but it wouldn't do to panic, because, as Max pointed out to Quentin, there wasn't anything one could do except wait and hope, wait and start being careful, be careful, and hope. And even if one did prove to be ill, one shouldn't give up, they had new treatments that promised an arrest of the disease's inexorable course, research was progressing. It seemed that everyone was in touch with everyone else several times a week, checking in, I've never spent so many hours at a time on the phone, Stephen said to Kate, and when I'm exhausted after the two or three calls made to me, giving me the latest, instead of switching off the phone to give myself a respite I tap out the number of another friend or acquaintance, to pass on the news. I'm not sure I can afford to think so much about it, Ellen said, and I suspect my own motives, there's something morbid I'm getting used to, getting excited by, this must be like what people felt in London during the Blitz. As far as I know, I'm not at risk, but you never know, said Aileen. This thing is totally unprecedented, said Frank. But don't you think he ought to see a doctor, Stephen insisted. Listen, said Orson, you can't force people to take care of themselves, and what makes you think the worst, he could be just run down, people still do get ordinary illnesses, awful ones, why are you assuming it has to be *that*. But all I want to be sure, said Stephen, is that he understands the options, because most people don't, that's why they won't see a doctor or have the test, they think there's nothing one can do. But is there anything one can do, he said to Tanya (according to Greg), I mean what do I gain if I go to the doctor; if I'm really ill, he's reported to have said, I'll find out soon enough.

And when he was in the hospital, his spirits seemed to lighten, according to Donny. He seemed more cheerful than he had been in the last months, Ursula said, and the bad news seemed to come almost as a relief, according to Ira, as a truly unexpected blow, according to Quentin, but you'd hardly expect him to have said the same thing to all his friends, because his relation to Ira was so different from his relation to Quentin (this according to Quentin, who was proud of their friendship), and perhaps he thought Quentin wouldn't be undone by seeing him weep, but Ira insisted that couldn't be the reason he behaved so differently with each, and that maybe he was feeling less shocked, mobilizing his strength to fight for his life, at the moment he saw Ira but overcome by feelings of hopelessness when Quentin arrived with flowers, because anyway the flowers threw him into a bad mood, as Quentin told Kate, since the hospital room was choked with flowers, you couldn't have crammed another flower into that room, but surely you're exaggerating, Kate said, smiling, everybody likes flowers. Well, who wouldn't exaggerate at a time like this, Quentin said sharply. Don't you think *this* is an exaggeration. Of course I do, said Kate gently, I was only teasing, I mean I didn't mean to tease. I know that, Quentin said, with tears in his eyes, and Kate hugged him and said well, when I go this evening I guess I won't bring flowers, what does he want, and Quentin said, according to Max, what he likes best is chocolate. Is there anything else, asked Kate, I mean like chocolate but not chocolate. Licorice, said Quentin, blowing his nose. And besides that. Aren't *you* exaggerating now, Quentin said, smiling. Right, said Kate, so if I want to bring him a whole raft of stuff, besides chocolate and licorice, what else. Jelly beans, Quentin said.

He didn't want to be alone, according to Paolo, and lots of people came in the first week, and the Jamaican nurse said there were other patients on the floor who would be glad to have the surplus flowers, and people weren't afraid to visit, it wasn't like the old days, as Kate pointed out to Aileen, they're not even segregated in the hospital anymore, as Hilda observed, there's nothing on the door of his room warning visitors of the possibility of contagion, as there was a few years ago; in fact, he's in a double room and, as he told Orson, the old guy on the far side of the curtain (who's clearly on the way out, said Stephen) doesn't even have the disease so, as Kate went on, you really should go and see him, he'd be happy to see you, he likes having people visit, you aren't not going because you're afraid, are you. Of course not, Aileen said, but I don't know what to say, I think I'll feel awkward, which he's bound to notice, and that will make him feel worse, so I won't be doing him any good, will I. But he won't notice anything, Kate said, patting Aileen's hand, it's not like that, it's not the way you imagine, he's not judging people or wondering about their motives, he's just happy to see his friends. But I never was really a friend of his, Aileen said, you're a friend, he's always liked you, you told me he talks about Nora with you, I know he likes me, he's even attracted to me, but he respects you. But, according to Wesley, the reason Aileen was so stingy with her visits was that she could never have him to herself, there were always others there already and by the time they left still others had arrived, she'd been in love with him for years, and I can understand, said Donny, that Aileen should feel bitter that if there could have been a woman friend he did more than occasionally bed, a woman he really loved, and my God, Victor said, who had known him in those years, he was crazy about Nora, what a heart-rending couple they were, two surly angels, then it couldn't have been she.

And when some of the friends, the ones who came every day, waylaid the doctor in the corridor, Stephen was the one who asked the most informed questions, who'd been keeping up not just with the stories that appeared several times a week in the *Times* (which Greg confessed to have stopped reading, unable to stand it anymore) but with articles in the medical journals published here and in England and France, and who knew socially one of the principal doctors in Paris who was doing some much-publicized research on the disease, but his doctor said little more than that the pneumonia was not life-threatening, the fever was subsiding, of course he was still weak but he was responding well to the antibiotics, that he'd have to complete his stay in the hospital, which entailed a minimum of twenty-one days on the IV, before she could start him on the new drug, for she was optimistic about the possibility of getting him into the protocol; and when Victor said that if he had so much trouble eating (he'd say to everyone when they coaxed him to eat some of the hospital meals, that food didn't taste right, that he had a funny metallic taste in his mouth) it couldn't be good that friends were bringing him all that chocolate, the doctor just smiled and said that in these cases the patient's morale was also an important factor, and if chocolate made him feel better she saw no harm in it, which worried Stephen, as Stephen said later to Donny, because they wanted to believe in the promises and taboos of today's high-tech medicine but here this reassuringly curt and silver-haired specialist in the disease, someone quoted frequently in the papers, was talking like some oldfangled country GP who tells the family that tea with honey or chicken soup may do as much for the patient as penicillin, which might mean, as Max said, that they were just going through the motions of treating him, that they were not sure about what to do, or rather, as Xavier interjected, that they didn't know what the hell they were doing, that the truth, the real truth, as Hilda said, upping the ante, was that they didn't, the doctors, really have any hope.

Oh, no, said Lewis, I can't stand it, wait a minute, I can't believe it, are you sure, I mean are they sure, have they done all the tests, it's getting so when the phone rings I'm scared to answer because I think it will be someone telling me someone else is ill; but did Lewis really not know until yesterday, Robert said testily, I find that hard to believe, everybody is talking about it, it seems impossible that someone wouldn't have called Lewis; and perhaps Lewis did know, was for some reason pretending not to know already, because, Jan recalled, didn't Lewis say something months ago to Greg, and not only to Greg, about his not looking well, losing weight, and being worried about him and wishing he'd see a doctor, so it couldn't come as a total surprise. Well, everybody is worried about everybody now, said Betsy, that seems to be the way we live, the way we live now. And, after all, they were once very close, doesn't Lewis still have the keys to his apartment, you know the way you let someone keep the keys after you've broken up, only a little because you hope the person might just saunter in, drunk or high, late some evening, but mainly because it's wise to have a few sets of keys strewn around town, if you live alone, at the top of a former commercial building that, pretentious as it is, will never acquire a doorman or even a resident super-intendent, someone whom you can call on for the keys late one night if you find you've lost yours or have locked yourself out. Who else has keys, Tanya inquired, I was thinking somebody might drop by tomorrow before coming to the hospital and bring some treasures, because the other day, Ira said, he was complaining about how dreary the hospital room was, and how it was like being locked up in a motel room, which got everybody started telling funny stories about motel rooms they'd known, and at Ursula's story, about the Luxury Budget Inn in Schenectady, there was an uproar of laughter around his bed, while he watched them in silence, eyes bright with fever, all the while, as Victor recalled, gobbling that damned chocolate. But, according to Jan, whom Lewis's keys enabled to tour the swank of his bachelor lair with an eye to bringing over some art consolation to brighten up the hospital room, the Byzantine icon wasn't on the wall over his bed, and that was a puzzle until Orson remembered that he'd recounted without seeming upset (this disputed by Greg) that the boy he'd recently gotten rid of had stolen it, along with four of the *maki-e* lacquer boxes, as if these were objects as easy to sell on the street as a TV or a stereo. But he's always been very generous, Kate said quietly, and though he loves beautiful things isn't really attached to them, to things, as Orson said, which is unusual in a collector, as Frank commented, and when Kate shuddered and tears sprang to her eyes and Orson inquired anxiously if he, Orson, had said something wrong, she pointed out that they'd begun talking about him in a retrospective mode, summing up what he was like, what made them fond of him, as if he were finished, completed, already a part of the past.

Perhaps he was getting tired of having so many visitors, said Robert, who was, as Ellen couldn't help mentioning, someone who had come only twice and was probably looking for a reason not to be in regular attendance, but there could be no doubt, according to Ursula, that his spirits had dipped, not that there was any discouraging news from the doctors, and he seemed now to prefer being alone a few hours of the day; and he told Donny that he'd begun keeping a diary for the first time in his life, because he wanted to record the course of his mental reactions to this astonishing turn of events, to do something parallel to what the doctors were doing, who came every morning and conferred at his bedside about his body, and that perhaps it wasn't so important what he wrote in it, which amounted, as he said wryly to Quentin, to little more than the usual banalities about terror and amazement that this was happening to him, to him also, plus the usual remorseful assessments of his past life, his pardonable superficialities, capped by resolves to live better, more deeply, more in touch with his work and his friends, and not to care so passionately about what people thought of him, interspersed with admonitions to himself that in this situation his will to live counted more than anything else and that if he really wanted to live, and trusted life, and liked himself well enough (down, ol' debbil Thanatos!), he *would* live, he would be an exception; but perhaps all this, as Quentin ruminated, talking on the phone to Kate, wasn't the point, the point was that by the very keeping of the diary he was accumulating something to reread one day, slyly staking out his claim to a future time, in which the diary would be an object, a relic, in which he might not actually reread it, because he would want to have put this ordeal behind him, but the diary would be there in the drawer of his stupendous Majorelle desk, and he could already, he did actually say to Quentin one late sunny afternoon, propped up in the hospital bed, with the stain of chocolate framing one corner of a heartbreaking smile, see himself in the penthouse, the October sun streaming through those clear windows instead of this streaked one, and the diary, the pathetic diary, safe inside the drawer.

It doesn't matter about the treatment's side effects, Stephen said (when talking to Max), I don't know why you're so worried about that, every strong treatment has some dangerous side effects, it's inevitable, you mean otherwise the treatment wouldn't be effective, Hilda interjected, and anyway, Stephen went on doggedly, just because there *are* side effects it doesn't mean he has to get them, or all of them, each one, or even some of them. That's just a list of all the possible things that could go wrong, because the doctors have to cover themselves, so they make up a worst-case scenario, but isn't what's happening to him, and to so many other people, Tanya interrupted, a worst-case scenario, a catastrophe no one could have imagined, it's too cruel, and isn't everything a side effect, quipped Ira, even *we* are all side effects, but we're not bad side effects, Frank said, he likes having his friends around, and we're helping each other, too; because his illness sticks us all in the same glue, mused Xavier, and, whatever the jealousies and grievances from the past that have made us wary and cranky with each other, when something like this happens (the sky is falling, the sky is falling!) you understand what's really important. I agree, Chicken Little, he is reported to have said. But don't you think, Quentin observed to Max, that being as close to him as we are, making time to drop by the hospital every day, is a way of our trying to define ourselves more firmly and irrevocably as the well, those who aren't ill, who aren't going to fall ill, as if what's happened to him couldn't happen to us, when in fact the chances are that before long one of us will end up where he is, which is probably what he felt when he was one of the cohort visiting Zack in the spring (you never knew Zack, did you?), and, according to Clarice, Zack's widow, he didn't come very often, he said he hated hospitals, and didn't feel he was doing Zack any good, that Zack would see on his face how uncomfortable he was. Oh, he was one of those, Aileen said. A coward. Like me.

And after he was sent home from the hospital, and Quentin had volunteered to move in and was cooking meals and taking telephone messages and keeping the mother in Mississippi informed, well, mainly keeping her from flying to New York and heaping her grief on her son and confusing the household routine with her oppressive ministrations, he was able to work an hour or two in his study, on days he didn't insist on going out, for a meal or a movie, which tired him. He seemed optimistic, Kate thought, his appetite

8

was good, and what he said, Orson reported, was that he agreed when Stephen advised him that the main thing was to keep in shape, he was a fighter, right, he wouldn't be who he was if he weren't, and was he ready for the big fight, Stephen asked rhetorically (as Max told it to Donny), and he said you bet, and Stephen added it could be a lot worse, you could have gotten the disease two years ago, but now so many scientists are working on it, the American team and the French team, everyone bucking for that Nobel Prize a few years down the road, that all you have to do is stay healthy for another year or two and then there will be good treatment, real treatment. Yes, he said, Stephen said, my timing is good. And Betsy, who had been climbing on and rolling off macrobiotic diets for a decade, came up with a Japanese specialist she wanted him to see but thank God, Donny reported, he'd had the sense to refuse, but he did agree to see Victor's visualization therapist, although what could one possibly visualize, said Hilda, when the point of visualizing disease was to see it as an entity with contours, borders, here rather than there, something limited, something you were the host of, in the sense that you could disinvite the disease, while this was so total; or would be, Max said. But the main thing, said Greg, was to see that he didn't go the macrobiotic route, which might be harmless for plump Betsy but could only be devastating for him, lean as he'd always been, with all the cigarettes and other appetite-suppressing chemicals he'd been welcoming into his body for years; and now was hardly the time, as Stephen pointed out, to be worried about cleaning up his act, and eliminating the chemical additives and other pollutants that we're all blithely or not so blithely feasting on, blithely since we're healthy, healthy as we can be; so far, Ira said. Meat and potatoes is what I'd be happy to see him eating, Ursula said wistfully. And spaghetti and clam sauce, Greg added. And thick cholesterol-rich omelets with smoked mozzarella, suggested Yvonne, who had flown from London for the weekend to see him. Chocolate cake, said Frank. Maybe not chocolate cake, Ursula said, he's already eating so much chocolate.

And when, not right away but still only three weeks later, he was accepted into the protocol for the new drug, which took considerable behind-the-scenes lobbying with the doctors, he talked less about being ill, according to Donny, which seemed like a good sign, Kate felt, a sign that he was not feeling like a victim, feeling not that he *had* a disease but, rather, was living *with* a disease (that was the right cliché, wasn't it?), a more hospitable arrangement, said Jan, a kind of cohabitation which implied that it was something temporary, that it could be terminated, but terminated how, said Hilda, and when you say hospitable, Jan, I hear hospital. And it was encouraging, Stephen insisted, that from the start, at least from the time he was finally persuaded to make the telephone call to his doctor, he was willing to say the name of the disease, pronounce it often and easily, as if it were just another word, like boy or gallery or cigarette or money or deal, as in no big deal, Paolo interjected, because, as Stephen continued, to utter the name is a sign of health, a sign that one has accepted being who one is, mortal, vulnerable, not exempt, not an exception after all, it's a sign that one is willing, truly willing, to fight for one's life. And we must say the name, too, and often, Tanya added, we mustn't lag behind him in honesty, or let him feel that, the effort of honesty having been made, it's something done with and he can go on to other things. One is so much better prepared to help him, Wesley replied. In a way he's fortunate, said Yvonne, who had taken care of a problem at the New York store and was flying back to London this evening, sure, fortunate, said Wesley, no one is shunning him, Yvonne went on, no one's afraid to hug him or kiss him lightly on the mouth, in London we are, as usual, a few years behind you, people I know, people who would seem to be not even remotely at risk, are just terrified, but I'm impressed by how cool and rational you all are; you find us cool, asked Quentin. But I have to say, he's reported to have said, I'm terrified, I find it very hard to read (and you know how he loves to read, said Greg; yes, reading is his television, said Paolo) or to think, but I don't feel hysterical. I feel quite hysterical, Lewis said to Yvonne. But you're able to *do* something for him, that's wonderful, how I wish I could stay longer, Yvonne answered, it's rather beautiful, I can't help thinking, this utopia of friendship you've assembled around him (this pathetic utopia, said Kate), so that the disease, Yvonne concluded, is not, anymore, out there. Yes, don't you think we're more at home here, with him, with the disease, said Tanya, because the imagined disease is so much worse than the reality of him, whom we all love, each in our fashion, having it. I know for me his getting it has quite demystified the disease, said Jan, I don't feel afraid, spooked, as I did before he became ill, when it was only news about remote acquaintances, whom I never saw again after they became ill. But you know you're not going to come down with the disease, Quentin said, to which Ellen replied, on her behalf, that's not the point, and possibly untrue, my gynecologist says that everyone is at risk, everyone who has a sexual life, because sexuality is a chain that links each of us to many others, unknown others, and now the great chain of being has become a chain of death as well. It's not the same for you, Quentin insisted, it's not the same for you as it is for me or Lewis or Frank or Paolo or Max, I'm more and more frightened, and I have every reason to be. I don't think about whether I'm at risk or not, said Hilda, I know that I was afraid to know someone with the disease, afraid of what I'd see, what I'd feel, and after the first day I came to the hospital I felt so relieved. I'll never feel that way, that fear, again; he doesn't seem different from me. He's not, Quentin said.

According to Lewis, he talked more often about those who visited more often, which is natural, said Betsy, I think he's even keeping a tally. And among those who came or checked in by phone every day, the inner circle as it were, those who were getting more points, there was still a further competition, which was what was getting on Betsy's nerves, she confessed to Jan; there's always that vulgar jockeying for position around the bedside of the gravely ill, and though we all feel suffused with virtue at our loyalty to him (speak for yourself, said Jan), to the extent that we're carving time out of every day, or almost every day, though some of us are dropping out, as Xavier pointed out, aren't we getting at least as much out of this as he is. Are we, said Jan. We're rivals for a sign from him of special pleasure over a visit, each stretching for the brass ring of his favor, wanting to feel the most wanted, the true nearest and dearest, which is inevitable with someone who doesn't have a spouse and children or an official in-house lover, hierarchies that no one would dare contest, Betsy went on, so we are the family he's founded, without meaning to, without official titles and ranks (we, we, snarled Quentin); and is it so clear, though some of us, Lewis and Quentin and Tanya and Paolo, among others, are ex-lovers and all of us more or less than friends, which one of us he prefers, Victor said (now it's us, raged Quentin), because sometimes I think he looks forward more to seeing Aileen, who has visited only three times, twice at the hospital and once since he's been home, than he does you or me; but, according to Tanya, after being very disappointed that Aileen hadn't come, now he was angry, while, according to Xavier, he was not really hurt but touchingly passive, accepting Aileen's absence as something he somehow deserved. But he's happy to have people around, said Lewis; he says when he doesn't have company he gets very sleepy, he sleeps (according to Quentin), and then perks up when someone arrives, it's important that he not feel ever alone. But, said Victor, there's one person he hasn't heard from, whom he'd probably like to hear from more than most of us; but she didn't just vanish, even right after she broke away from him, and he knows exactly where she lives now, said Kate, he told me he put in a call to her last Christmas Eve, and she said it's nice to hear from you and Merry Christmas, and he was shattered, according to Orson, and furious and disdainful, according to Ellen (what do you expect of her, said Wesley, she was burned out), but Kate wondered if maybe he hadn't phoned Nora in the middle of a sleepless night, what's the time difference, and Quentin said no, I don't think so, I think he wouldn't want her to know.

And when he was feeling even better and had regained the pounds he'd shed right away in the hospital, though the refrigerator started to fill up with organic wheat germ and grapefruit and skimmed milk (he's worried about his cholesterol count, Stephen lamented), and told Quentin he could manage by himself now, and did, he started asking everyone who visited how he looked, and everyone said he looked great, so much better than a few weeks ago, which didn't jibe with what anyone had told him at that time; but then it was getting harder and harder to know how he looked, to answer such a question honestly when among themselves they wanted to be honest, both for honesty's sake and (as Donny thought) to prepare for the worst, because he'd been looking like *this* for so long, at least it seemed so long, that it was as if he'd always been like this, how did he look before, it was only a few months, and those words, pale and wan looking and fragile, hadn't they always applied? And one Thursday Ellen, meeting Lewis at the door of the building, said, as they rode up together in the elevator, how is he *really*? But you see how he is, Lewis said tartly, he's fine, he's perfectly healthy, and Ellen understood that of course Lewis didn't think he was perfectly healthy but that he wasn't worse, and that was true, but wasn't it, well, almost heartless to talk like that. Seems inoffensive to me, Quentin said, but I know what you mean, I remember once talking to Frank, somebody, after all, who has volunteered to do five hours a week of office work at the Crisis Center (I know, said Ellen), and Frank was going on about this guy, diagnosed almost a year ago, and so much further along, who'd been complaining to Frank on the phone about the indifference of some doctor, and had gotten quite abusive about the doctor, and Frank was saying there was no reason to be so upset, the implication being that *he,* Frank, wouldn't behave so irrationally, and I said, barely able to control my scorn, but Frank, Frank, he has every reason to be upset, he's dying, and Frank said, said according to Quentin, oh, I don't like to think about it that way.

And it was while he was still home, recuperating, getting his weekly treatment, still not able to do much work, he complained, but, according to Quentin, up and about most of the time and turning up at the office several days a week, that bad news came about two remote acquaintances, one in Houston and one in Paris, news that was intercepted by Quentin on the ground that it could only depress him, but Stephen contended that it was wrong to lie to him, it was so important for him to live in the truth; that had been one of his first victories, that he was candid, that he was even willing to crack jokes about the disease, but Ellen said it wasn't good to give him this end-of-the-world feeling, too many people were getting ill, it was becoming such a common destiny that maybe some of the will to fight for his life would be drained out of him if it seemed to be as natural as, well, death. Oh, Hilda said, who didn't know personally either the one in Houston or the one in Paris, but knew *of* the one in Paris, a pianist who specialized in twentieth-century Czech and Polish music, I have his records, he's such a valuable person, and, when Kate glared at her, continued defensively, I know every life is equally sacred, but that *is* a thought, another thought, I mean, all these valuable people who aren't going to have their normal four score as it is now, these people aren't going to be replaced, and it's such a loss to the culture. But this isn't going to go on forever, Wesley said, it can't, they're bound to come up with something (they, they, muttered Stephen), but did you ever think, Greg said, that if some people don't die, I mean even if they can keep them alive (they, they, muttered Kate), they continue to be carriers, and that means, if you have a conscience, that you can never make love, make love fully, as you'd been wont — wantonly, Ira said — to do. But it's better than dying, said Frank. And in all his talk about the future, when he allowed himself to be hopeful, according to Quentin, he never mentioned the prospect that even if he didn't die, if he were so fortunate as to be among the first generation of the disease's survivors, never mentioned, Kate confirmed, that whatever happened it was over, the way he had lived until now, but, according to Ira, he did think about it, the end of bravado, the end of folly, the end of trusting life, the end of taking life for granted, and of treating life as something that, samurai-like, he thought himself ready to throw away lightly, impudently; and Kate recalled, sighing, a brief exchange she'd insisted on having as long as two years ago, huddling on a banquette covered with steel-gray industrial carpet on an upper level of The Prophet and toking up for their next foray onto the dance floor: she'd said hesitantly, for it felt foolish asking a prince of debauchery to, well, take it easy, and she wasn't keen on playing big sister, a role, as Hilda confirmed, he inspired in many women, are you being careful, honey, you know what I mean. And he replied, Kate went on, no, I'm not, listen, I can't, I just can't, sex is too important to me, always has been (he started talking like that, according to Victor, after Nora left him), and if I get it, well, I get it. But he wouldn't talk like that now, would he, said Greg; he must feel awfully foolish now, said Betsy, like someone who went on smoking, saying I can't give up cigarettes, but when the bad X-ray is taken even the most besotted nicotine addict can stop on a dime. But sex isn't like cigarettes, is it, said Frank, and, besides, what good does it do to remember that he was reckless, said Lewis angrily, the appalling thing is that you just have to be unlucky once, and wouldn't he feel even worse if he'd stopped three years ago and had come down with it anyway, since one of the most terrifying features of the disease is that you don't know when you contracted it, it could have been ten years ago, because surely this disease has existed for years and years, long before it was recognized; that is, named. Who knows how long (I think a lot about that, said Max) and who knows (I know what you're going to say, Stephen interrupted) how many are going to get it.

I'm feeling fine, he's reported to have said whenever someone asked him how he was, which was almost always the first question anyone asked. Or: I'm feeling better, how are you? But he said other things, too. I'm playing leapfrog with myself, he is reported to have said, according to Victor. And: There must be a way to get something positive out of this situation, he's reported to have said to Kate. How American of him, said Paolo. Well, said Betsy, you know the old American adage: when you've got a lemon, make lemonade. The one thing I'm sure I couldn't take, Jan said he said to her, is becoming disfigured, but Stephen hastened to point out the disease doesn't

take that form very often anymore, its profile is mutating, and, in conversation with Ellen, wheeled up words like blood-brain barrier; I never thought
there was a barrier *there,* said Jan. But he mustn't know about Max, Ellen
said, that would really depress him, please don't tell him, he'll have to know,
Quentin said grimly, and he'll be furious not to have been told. But there's
time for that, when they take Max off the respirator, said Ellen; but isn't it
incredible, Frank said, Max was fine, not feeling ill at all, and then to wake
up with a fever of a hundred and five, unable to breathe, but that's the way
it often starts, with absolutely no warning, Stephen said, the disease has so
many forms. And when, after another week had gone by, he asked Quentin
where Max was, he didn't question Quentin's account of a spree in the
Bahamas, but then the number of people who visited regularly was thinning
out, partly because the old feuds that had been put aside through the first
hospitalization and the return home had resurfaced, and the flickering enmity
between Lewis and Frank exploded, even though Kate did her best to mediate
between them, and also because he himself had done something to loosen
the bonds of love that united the friends around him, by seeming to take
them all for granted, as if it were perfectly normal for so many people to
carve out so much time and attention for him, visit him every few days, talk
about him incessantly on the phone with each other; but, according to Paolo,
it wasn't that he was less grateful, it was just something he was getting used
to, the visits. It had become, with time, a more ordinary kind of situation, a
kind of ongoing party, first at the hospital and now since he was home,
barely on his feet again, it being clear, said Robert, that I'm on the B list;
but Kate said, that's absurd, there's no list; and Victor said, but there is,
only it's not he, it's Quentin who's drawing it up. He wants to see us, we're
helping him, we have to do it the way he wants, he fell down yesterday on
the way to the bathroom, he mustn't be told about Max (but he already
knew, according to Donny), it's getting worse.

When I was home, he is reported to have said, I was afraid to sleep, as
I was dropping off each night it felt like just that, as if I were falling down
a black hole, to sleep felt like giving in to death, I slept every night with the
light on; but here, in the hospital, I'm less afraid. And to Quentin he said,
one morning, the fear rips through me, it tears me open; and, to Ira, it presses
me together, squeezes me toward myself. Fear gives everything its hue, its
high. I feel so, I don't know how to say it, exalted, he said to Quentin.
Calamity is an amazing high, too. Sometimes I feel *so* well, so powerful, it's
as if I could jump out of my skin. Am I going crazy, or what? Is it all this
attention and coddling I'm getting from everybody, like a child's dream of
being loved? Is it the drugs? I know it sounds crazy but sometimes I think
this is a *fantastic* experience, he said shyly; but there was also the bad taste
in the mouth, the pressure in the head and at the back of the neck, the red,
bleeding gums, the painful, if pink-lobed, breathing, and his ivory pallor,

color of white chocolate. Among those who wept when told over the phone that he was back in the hospital were Kate and Stephen (who'd been called by Quentin), and Ellen, Victor, Aileen, and Lewis (who were called by Kate), and Xavier and Ursula (who were called by Stephen). Among those who didn't weep were Hilda, who said that she'd just learned that her seventy-five-year-old aunt was dying of the disease, which she'd contracted from a transfusion given during her successful double bypass of five years ago, and Frank and Donny and Betsy, but this didn't mean, according to Tanya, that they weren't moved and appalled, and Quentin thought they might not be coming soon to the hospital but would send presents; the room, he was in a private room this time, was filling up with flowers, and plants, and books, and tapes. The high tide of barely suppressed acrimony of the last weeks at home subsided into the routines of hospital visiting, though more than a few resented Quentin's having charge of the visiting book (but it was Quentin who had the idea, Lewis pointed out); now, to insure a steady stream of visitors, preferably no more than two at a time (this, the rule in all hospitals, wasn't enforced here, at least on this floor; whether out of kindness or inefficiency, no one could decide), Quentin had to be called first, to get one's time slot, there was no more casual dropping by. And his mother could no longer be prevented from taking a plane and installing herself in a hotel near the hospital; but he seemed to mind her daily presence less than expected, Quentin said; said Ellen it's we who mind, do you suppose she'll stay long. It was easier to be generous with each other visiting him here in the hospital, as Donny pointed out, than at home, where one minded never being alone with him; coming here, in our twos and twos, there's no doubt about what our role is, how we should be, collective, funny, distracting, undemanding, light, it's important to be light, for in all this dread there is gaiety, too, as the poet said, said Kate. (His eyes, his glittering eyes, said Lewis.) His eyes looked dull, extinguished, Wesley said to Xavier, but Betsy said his face, not just his eyes, looked soulful, warm; whatever is there, said Kate, I've never been so aware of his eyes; and Stephen said, I'm afraid of what my eyes show, the way I watch him, with too much intensity, or a phony kind of casualness, said Victor. And, unlike at home, he was clean-shaven each morning, at whatever hour they visited him; his curly hair was always combed; but he complained that the nurses had changed since he was here the last time, and that he didn't like the change, he wanted everyone to be the same. The room was furnished now with some of his personal effects (odd word for one's things, said Ellen), and Tanya brought drawings and a letter from her nine-year-old dyslexic son, who was writing now, since she'd purchased a computer; and Donny brought champagne and some helium balloons, which were anchored to the foot of his bed; tell me about something that's going on, he said, waking up from a nap to find Donny and Kate at the side of his bed, beaming at him; tell me a story, he said wistfully, said Donny, who couldn't think of anything to say; *you're* the story, Kate said. And Xavier brought an eighteenth-century Guatemalan wooden statue of

Saint Sebastian with upcast eyes and open mouth, and when Tanya said what's that, a tribute to eros past, Xavier said where I come from Sebastian is venerated as a protector against pestilence. Pestilence symbolized by arrows? Symbolized by arrows. All people remember is the body of a beautiful youth bound to a tree, pierced by arrows (of which he always seems oblivious, Tanya interjected), people forget that the story continues, Xavier continued, that when the Christian women came to bury the martyr they found him still alive and nursed him back to health. And he said, according to Stephen, I didn't know Saint Sebastian didn't die. It's undeniable, isn't it, said Kate on the phone to Stephen, the fascination of the dying. It makes me ashamed. We're learning how to die, said Hilda, I'm not ready to learn, said Aileen; and Lewis, who was coming straight from the other hospital, the hospital where Max was still being kept in ICU, met Tanya getting out of the elevator on the tenth floor, and as they walked together down the shiny corridor past the open doors, averting their eyes from the other patients sunk in their beds, with tubes in their noses, irradiated by the bluish light from the television sets, the thing I can't bear to think about, Tanya said to Lewis, is someone dying with the TV on.

He has that strange, unnerving detachment now, said Ellen, that's what upsets me, even though it makes it easier to be with him. Sometimes he was querulous. I can't stand them coming in here taking my blood every morning, what are they doing with all that blood, he is reported to have said; but where was his anger, Jan wondered. Mostly he was lovely to be with, always saying how are *you,* how are you feeling. He's so sweet now, said Aileen. He's so nice, said Tanya. (Nice, nice, groaned Paolo.) At first he was very ill, but he was rallying, according to Stephen's best information, there was no fear of his not recovering this time, and the doctor spoke of his being discharged from the hospital in another ten days if all went well, and the mother was persuaded to fly back to Mississippi, and Quentin was readying the penthouse for his return. And he was still writing his diary, not showing it to anyone, though Tanya, first to arrive one late-winter morning, and finding him dozing, peeked, and was horrified, according to Greg, not by anything she read but by a progressive change in his handwriting: in the recent pages, it was becoming spidery, less legible, and some lines of script wandered and tilted about the page. I was thinking, Ursula said to Quentin, that the difference between a story and a painting or photograph is that in a story you can write, He's still alive. But in a painting or a photo you can't show "still." You can just show him being alive. He's still alive, Stephen said.

Points to Consider

1. This story of an AIDS victim is told entirely through various reports of his friends' conversations. Who seems to be telling the story? By pre-

senting her narrative in this manner, what is Sontag able to reveal about the AIDS epidemic that otherwise might go unnoticed?

2. Throughout "The Way We Live Now" neither the name of the sick man nor the name of the disease is mentioned. How do these omissions affect your reading of the story?

3. Do you feel that the characters are acting unselfishly or that certain characters are exploiting the illness of their friend? Which of the characters seem to have the most concern for the AIDS victim? Does Sontag seem to prefer some characters to others? How can you tell?

4. At one point in the story, the friends of the AIDS victim withhold from him the news that another friend has been infected with AIDS. Do you think their behavior is justified?

Discussing the Unit

Suggested Topic for Discussion

In the last several years, many antidiscrimination cases involving AIDS victims have appeared in our courtrooms. Many dealt with the rights of people with AIDS in the work place; others have been concerned with the right of children with AIDS to attend school. Discuss whether the desire to preserve the rights of people infected with the AIDS virus conflicts with public health and safety standards.

Preparing for Class Discussion

1. Most people have encountered a wide range of attitudes about AIDS — from the print and broadcast media, from church groups, from health education groups, from conversation with friends, and so on. Make a list of all the different attitudes about AIDS that you have encountered (include sources if you can remember them and include the selections you have just read in this book). Try putting the various attitudes into a scale of perceived social hazard, from "highly dangerous" to "nothing for most people to worry about." How does your list break down? Consider how your own attitude about AIDS has been affected by this range of responses.

2. Many politicians and commentators have suggested ways to slow the spread of AIDS, including the quarantining or tattooing of AIDS victims. What do you think of such measures? Do you think they reveal anything about those who propose them other than their concern for public safety? What proposal to contain the spread of the disease would you support?

From Discussion to Writing

Randy Shilts maintains that the fight against AIDS is being hindered by government inaction and public ignorance. Do you agree with Shilts that victims of the disease are *still* stigmatized by our society? Does Shilts ignore the possibility that there may now be more understanding for AIDS victims than at first? How have your own attitudes about AIDS changed as you continue to learn about the disease? Write an essay in which you describe the evolution of your own views regarding AIDS. Be sure to record your initial impressions of the disease as well as significant moments in your education about AIDS.

22

The Drug Crisis:
Is Legalization a Solution?

The debate over legalization of drugs has resurfaced in the wake of the United States's apparent failure to significantly curtail drug sales and consumption within its borders. An increasing number of politicians and public figures, conservatives and liberals alike, support legalization. In "Drugs: Could Legalization Work?" Eric Scigliano argues that this extreme measure might be an effective tactic in battling drug abuse and the crime engendered by the underground narcotics trade.

Many opponents of legalization believe that such a measure would amount to surrender, and consequently consign a generation of young people to an uncertain future under the influence of drugs. In "Against the Legalization of Drugs," James Q. Wilson questions the social benefits of lifting the ban on drugs. He argues that while the drug problem may never be eliminated, it may be contained by strict enforcement of drug laws. As an example, he recalls his own experience battling the "heroin epidemic" of the 1970s.

As you read these pieces, consider your own position on legalization. Is your position supported by evidence provided by either author? Or do they compel you to rethink your position on the issue?

ERIC SCIGLIANO

funds are being waste

Drugs: Could Legalization Work?

[SEATTLE WEEKLY / October 26, 1988]

What a trip. You'd think America couldn't get any higher on drug wars than it did in 1986, the year of Len Bias, "Just Say No," urinalysis, and the drug bill that was supposed to end all drug bills. No such luck. Consider a few dispatches from the Great Drug War of 1988, which mingles a congressional election with a presidential sweepstakes:

Item. Now not only reports of past pot-smoking but reports of past encouragement of pot legalization are grist for the campaign-smear mill. Senatorial candidate Slade Gorton unleashes a ferocious TV ad accusing opponent Mike Lowry of supporting "legalizing marijuana in 1979"—solely because, according to a student reporter for the UW *Daily,* Lowry told some folks at a community-college meeting that "he would support their quest to legalize marijuana" and argued that alcohol should not be banned, because "prohibition of anything doesn't work." Lowry demands an apology, telling the *Seattle Times,* "I have never been for legalization."

Item. On the presidential primary trail, Bob Dole calls for the death penalty for drug smugglers. George Bush, like Gorton milking the drug terror for all it's worth, makes the only raise he can. He urges "swift execution" of smugglers. When asked how that might jibe with the constitutional guarantee of due process of law, Bush replies, "I don't know the answer to that. I'm not a lawyer."

Item. Intravenous-drug abusers now comprise a quarter of all HIV virus carriers. With safe sex taking hold in the gay world, needle sharing is the leading means of AIDS transmission. The obvious way to protect IV-drug abusers, their partners, their children, and everyone else from the epidemic is to provide them with clean needles for drugs they'll shoot anyway. The public conscience rises not in support of humane common sense but in

---

ERIC SCIGLIANO (b. 1953) is senior editor at Seattle Weekly, *where he has worked for over eight years. Scigliano has published in the* Washington Post, Newsweek, *the* Nation, *and* Mother Jones, *as well as other magazines and newspapers. He has also worked in drug and alcohol treatment centers in Boston and Santa Fe.*

outrage at such an "endorsement" of drug use. In the absence of any publicly sponsored needle exchange, a civic-minded ex–drug counselor sets up his own sidewalk needle swap in Tacoma. He's lucky he isn't in one of the states that make possession of hypodermics without prescription a crime.

Item. Stampeded by another election year, the U.S. House of Representatives passes, 375–30, yet another tough-talking Omnibus Drug Bill. It includes a death penalty for those who murder in the course of a drug enterprise, responding to wide outrage over the killing of policemen and drug-enforcement agents by ruthless drug gangsters. Funny thing is, according to FBI statistics, from 1977 through 1986 precisely eight law enforcement officers at the federal, state, and local levels were killed in drug cases. When they kill, drug traffickers and dealers tend overwhelmingly to kill each other. Congress thus declares that killing a drug trafficker is one of the most heinous crimes that can be committed. Call it the Drug Trafficker Protection Act. Given the hazards they already face at each other's hands, it's not likely to deter many traffickers from their fantastically profitable enterprise, but it will deter other countries that don't sanction the death penalty from extraditing traffickers to the United States.

Welcome, in short, to the age of overkill, rhetorical and otherwise. The House drug bill, for instance, orders up to ten thousand dollars in civil fines for possession of even small quantities of prohibited drugs—a blank check for prosecutors, who would be freed from the burden of proving their cases beyond a reasonable doubt in criminal trials.

The Senate, only a third of whose members stand for election at a time, subsequently provided its usual secondary treatment on the House's work. It and a House/Senate compromise ameliorated many of the other more extreme measures in the original House bill. Defendants can now appeal these civil fines for drug possession to a full criminal trial by jury. And judges now have discretion in assigning the House's extra penalty for drug offenders: withholding public housing, student loans, and licenses, which would save people from ruining their lives on drugs by leaving them nothing else to turn to. To save the addict, it was necessary to destroy him.

Mike Lowry was the only member of this state's delegation with the guts to oppose the House bill—opening himself up to Gorton's attacks. Dan Evans quipped wishfully that Congress should be barred from passing drug bills in election years, and turned in one of three votes against the Senate version. Nevertheless, the Senate and compromise versions did excise the most conspicuously unconstitutional elements of the House bill: restrictions on habeas corpus; an exemption to the exclusionary rule that would allow the admission of evidence obtained illegally but in "good faith" in drug cases; and widespread mandatory drug testing. The Senate did, however, insert a pilot program for testing driver's license applicants' pee.

The Senate bill did take one big step toward sweet reason, by proposing to balance expenditures for drug-law enforcement, interdiction, and eradication with outlays for treatment and education. In the last fiscal year enforcement and other measures against drug supply ate up 72 percent of the federal drug war chest, a percentage that would probably be much higher if hidden expenditures by the military, customs, and other agencies could be factored in (not to mention $5 billion a year in state and local drug-law enforcement). The Senate bill would reduce enforcement's share to 50 percent in the first year (the level sought by Republicans) and 40 in the second (the Democratic target), leaving 60 percent for treatment and education to stem demand.

Nice as this sounded, however, it proved to be fiscal voodoo. In order to boost prevention and fund the enforcement increases mandated at the same time, $1.6 billion would have to be added to the current $3.5 billion drug budget. But Congress was pushing against its Gramm-Rudman budget ceiling, and only $500 million in new drug funding was finally assigned. When the going gets tight, the story has consistently been the same: as U.S. Attorney Gene Anderson says, "It's just a lot easier for government to get tough on law enforcement than to support treatment and education. I don't know why that is."

Ray Milstead, Arizona's Director of Public Safety and a twenty-eight-year cop and former narcotics officer, puts it even more bluntly: "Instead of pumping more money into law enforcement, let's spend it on education. We've got to have a truce, because our prisons are full." Our lawmakers haven't listened; from 1981 to 1987 they cut treatment and rehabilitation funding 40 percent (in real dollars), while more than doubling funds for interdiction.

Still, the would-be drug-busters stamp about, trying to muster their   12
posses to ride out, hang the fiends high, and purge the land of demon dope. On the one hand, despair is spreading at the failure of tried-and-untrue antidrug strategies; on the other hand is new hope for strategies that were widely scorned as defeatist and even destructive just a few months ago. No less a heresy than drug legalization is finally getting its hearing in the courts of policy and public opinion. What follows is an attempt to look at this radical prescription soberly. It makes a lot more sense than you would ever think, here in the middle of an election-year frenzy of false panaceas.

Conventional ideological lines get muddied at once over this concept. Legalization is for the most part not finding voice on the left. In his presidential-nomination campaign, Jesse Jackson gave eloquent voice to the frustration and fear of inner cities besieged by crack and crime. As a nominee he might have stolen the drug issue from Bush and turned it around. But Dukakis has failed to do so, beyond needling Bush for past links to General Noriega. He and other liberals, terrified of looking like wimps on drugs and crime, hardly dare question drug orthodoxy—look what happened to Mike Lowry.

So the calls for legalization or decriminalization have come first from the right: William F. Buckley, free-market economist Milton Friedman, the Thatcherite British newsmagazine *The Economist,* and the American Libertarian Party. They argue for it from two basic principles. First, the libertarian one: drug use, as long as it is does not entail actual crimes against others' persons or property, is a private choice into which government has no right to intrude. Second, an economic one: drug prohibition wildly distorts the drug market, creating vastly inflated prices for the substances, huge, untaxed cash transfers from the drug-consuming to the drug-producing nations, and a vast criminal economy. The way to clean up this mess is to get government out, let the market find its natural price, and then, *shhh,* tax the heck out of drugs. Or, if you're not ready to unleash drugs on the open market, follow the state-monopoly model of the lottery and liquor stores. It's hardly a novel notion; government has always depended upon the profits of vice.

At the same time, academe is starting to take up the cause of legalization. This position was for most of the past fifteen years the lonely province of American University law and justice professor Arnold Trebach. In *The Heroin Solution, The Great Drug War,* and many other books and articles, Trebach has argued persuasively for looser controls on, and legal medical use of, heroin, marijuana, and other banned substances, and tighter controls on legal tobacco and alcohol. He has been joined by a growing, vocal academic minority, in particular Princeton public affairs professor Ethan Nadelmann, whose articles this year in *Foreign Affairs* and the neoconservative *Public Interest* have stirred a firestorm of debate.

The academics might have continued arguing with each other till the tropic poppy fields froze over, but for the startling legitimacy granted the legalization case by a few brave politicians. Two members of the House Select Committee on Narcotics Abuse and Control, James Scheuer of New York and Pete Stark of California, have broken ranks to urge consideration of all drug-policy options, including even what Scheuer calls "the L and the D words," legalization and decriminalization. Stark even urges outright decriminalization of all drug possession. In New York, State Senator Joseph Galiber of the Bronx, who represents one of the most drug-afflicted constituencies in the nation, has introduced sweeping legalization legislation.

But the legalization option has been legitimized and publicized most of all by Baltimore Mayor Kurt Schmoke, a spokesman uniquely equipped for this message. Though educated at Yale, Oxford, and Harvard Law, Schmoke is no pointy-headed elitist conservative eager to opiate the masses to make them stop menacing the upper classes. He is black, a Baltimore native, and fought his way to heresy in the trenches of that city's drug wars. After a stint on President Carter's Domestic Policy staff, Schmoke prosecuted federal

16

drug cases as an assistant U.S. attorney. In 1982 he was elected state's attorney (chief prosecutor) for Baltimore. Astounded at the volume of drug cases, he created a full-time narcotics unit and claimed one of the highest incarceration rates for such cases in the nation. "I am not soft on either drug use or drug dealers," Schmoke insists. "I am a soldier in the war on drugs." As a soldier, he watched that war being lost, and began to ask how it should be fought.

Last spring Schmoke brought that question before the National Conference of Mayors, calling for a national debate on legalization and decriminalization. Mayors Marion Barry of Washington, D.C., and Donald Fraser of Minneapolis joined the call. The House Select Committee on Narcotics consented to convene hearings on legalization at the end of September. Its chairman, Charles Rangel of Harlem, a more conventional drug warrior, publicly hoped that "when the questions are answered, the very dangerous idea of legalization of drugs will be put to rest once and for all." But Schmoke, after massive study of the issue over the summer, progressed from asking questions to advocacy: "The case for decriminalization is overwhelming. . . . Our current policy is destined to fail."

That policy, as Schmoke puts it, "can be stated with almost child-like simplicity. Our policy is zero use of all illicit drugs all the time. . . . It's a policy that is both unambiguous and unimaginative. It is also unattainable." It has also been profoundly ambivalent as to means, veering cyclically between attempts to cut off the supply of, and the demand for, drugs.

The United States first stumbled into drug prohibition through a process 20 as haphazard and hysterical as today's policy-making. It first tried to restrict supply, with a 1909 ban on the importation of smoking opium. (Several states had already taken such action, prompted by disapproval of interracial fraternization and supposed debauchery in Chinese opium dens rather than by fear of addiction.) As usual with attempts at prohibition—notably with alcohol—lots of backfires set in. The net effect of the opium ban was to make many opium smokers start injecting much-stronger morphine and heroin (the "hero drug" originally developed as a cure for morphine addiction). Even after morphine and heroin were likewise restricted, they remained attractive and lucrative for smugglers because they are more compact and concealable. . . . The pattern continues today, where interdiction encourages traffickers to switch from bulky, smelly marijuana to cocaine and heroin.

The first comprehensive U.S. drug law, the Harrison Act of 1914, seemed worded to control supply in a fashion very like that proposed by today's advocates of medical heroin and cocaine dispensation. Importers, manufacturers, physicians, and pharmacists were still to be able to supply opiates and cocaine, under tight regulation. In that Temperance era, however, public opinion and prosecutorial discretion soon interpreted regulation as an outright ban. Doctors and pharmacists, weary of public stigma and police harassment, stopped dispensing heroin and other controlled substances to addicts. In 1922, the maximum penalty for drug violations was doubled from five to ten years and continued to climb until the 1950s, when some states instituted death penalties and mandatory life sentences for repeat offenses.

Britain's Dr. Harry Campbell visited the States in 1922 and reported a situation eerily like today's:

> In the United States of America a drug addict is regarded as a malefactor even though the habit has been acquired through the medicinal use of the drug, as in the case, e.g., of American soldiers who were gassed and otherwise maimed in the Great War. . . . In consequence of this stringent law, a vast clandestine commerce in narcotics has grown up in that country. The small bulk of these drugs renders the evasion of the law comparatively easy, and the country is overrun by an army of peddlers who extort exorbitant prices from their helpless victims. It appears that not only has the Harrison Law failed to diminish the number of drug takers—some contend, indeed, that it has increased their number—but, far from bettering the lot of the opiate addict, it has actually worsened it; for without curtailing the supply of the drug it has sent the price up tenfold, and this has the effect of impoverishing the poorer class of addicts and reducing them to a condition of such abject misery as to render them incapable of gaining an honest livelihood.

After observing the U.S. experience, Britain decided to continue the medical prescription of heroin, for addiction and other needs. In 1914, after decades of open dispensation in patient medicines and epidemic use, the United States had a little over 200,000 heroin, morphine, and opium addicts. Today, after 74 years of prohibition, it has almost 500,000 heroin addicts. The estimated numbers of regular marijuana smokers (about 18 million), cocaine users (5.5 million), and cocaine addicts (600,000) have climbed much more dramatically.

Until the 1960s, enforcement tended to target drug users and small-time vendors (who tend to be users) rather than traffickers, in part because the former were more numerous and vulnerable. This attack on the demand side broke down in the face of the 1960s counterculture; there was neither prison space nor public will for locking up millions of young middle-class potheads. And thus what seemed an unarguable battle cry arose: bust the big traffickers, send out the military to seal the borders, cut off the supplies! 24

That first great War on Drugs was born at the peak of the Vietnam War. By 1973, Nixon saw the light at the end of the tunnel and declared, "We have turned the corner on drug addiction in the United States." There's little novel about the current war, except its costs and the range of forces, including the military, FBI, and CIA, that the Reagan administration has been willing to deploy. Echoing Nixon, Reagan last year declared the drug war one of the great successes of his tenure.

The drug war bears striking parallels to the Vietnam War. It is a war we are neither willing nor able to wage as total war, to a final dreary victory: an all-out law-enforcement attack on 30 million consumers of illicit drugs, the moral equivalent of bombing Vietnam back to the Stone Age. Aside from the cost and the reaction, where would we put the culprits? The federal prison system is already bursting with 44,000 inmates, a third of them drug-law violators. Fifteen years hence, it is expected to hold 100,000 to 150,000, according to Princeton's Nadelmann—half of them in for drug raps. That doesn't count the 80,000 state and county inmates jailed for drugs, or the many thousands more jailed for "drug-related" violence, stealing to buy drugs, and so on. And despite avowals of going for the big fish, more than three quarters of the 750,000 or so drug arrests each year are for simple possession, usually of marijuana, rather than for dealing, trafficking, or manufacture.

Like the generals in Vietnam, we measure our drug-war "victories" not in strategic gains (we haven't any) but in body counts: pleas bargained, trafficking rings broken, and tons of contraband seized, along with sundry planes, yachts, and Porsches. At this statistical game, our police, prosecutors, and customs guards grow ever more efficient. Their booty is staggering—40 tons of cocaine interdicted at the borders in 1987. (Before you cheer too loudly, imagine all the rapists and car thieves our watchdogs could catch, if we'd free them from drug work.) All the while, other, younger dealers, other, more ingenious smugglers, and other, larger sources of supply keep reappearing to replace those cut off. By a General Accounting Office estimate, 178 tons of cocaine, 12 tons of heroin, and 600,000 tons of marijuana got to market in 1987. As U.S. Attorney Anderson admits, "Body counts don't really matter. In the end, we're just fighting a holding action. We're taking a lot of prisoners, but we're not winning the war."

Each strategy for cutting off supply falls down against what Nadelmann   28 calls "the push-down/pop-up factor": whatever drug crop you push down will pop up somewhere else. Crop substitution—paying and persuading peasants to grow green beans and coffee instead of coca and opium—may have some merit as backdoor development aid, but we can't bribe all the world's farmers. More coercive forms of eradication tend to be counterproductive in obvious and unexpected ways. Spraying paraquat on Mexican pot fields merely worked to poison some *campesinos* and domestic consumers. Sending the helicopter gunships out to destroy Bolivian coca labs bolsters militaristic tendencies, stirs anti-*yanqui* resentment, and gives corrupt generals a second chance to cash in, on drug-war aid as on drug-traffic profits.

Peru's Sendero Luminoso guerrillas, for instance, have a recruiting field day with peasants horrified to see the troops burning the coca they've grown and used for centuries and which is now their best cash crop. It's no easy task to explain why some North Americans so want to destroy what millions of other North Americans will pay so much money for.

Even when eradication and substitution succeed in one country, they merely stimulate agriculture in others. Turkey, the main source of heroin in the 1970s, undertook an unusually thorough and severe poppy eradication. Burma, Thailand, Mexico, and other countries quickly filled the opium gap. Left to their own devices, Turkish farmers returned to growing poppies, too. Paraquat-tainted Mexican marijuana was soon replaced by much more potent and trustworthy sinsemilla[1] from Oregon glens and Ballard[2] basements.

Interdiction is an equally wishful strategy. In 1986 the U.S. House of Representatives passed an amendment to the drug megabill ordering the president to have the military "seal the borders" within 45 days. The Senate dropped this vain demand after Sam Nunn sneered that it was "the equivalent of passing a law saying the president shall, by Thanksgiving, find a cure for the common cold." The choice of entries and smuggling techniques is virtually limitless. "We've used AWACS aircraft, P-3 Orion aircraft, and a tethered observation balloon to watch for smugglers," says Arizona's disillusioned top cop, Milstead. "But only 10 to 20 percent of drugs come into Arizona by air. The smugglers land a little short of the border and shotgun the stuff in backpacks, automobiles, train cars, tile trucks, produce trucks. Interdiction simply doesn't work." At best it acts upon smugglers as wolves act upon elk, culling the weak and inept and inspiring the remainder to better defenses.

Even if interdiction were to succeed perfectly and keep all cocaine or opiates out of the United States, it wouldn't eliminate the abuse that goes with them. Consumers would switch to manufactured substitutes. Various "designer drugs"—synthetic opiate analogs—may be more potent than heroin and, with a sufficient market to support large production, much cheaper. Methedrine and other amphetamines—which, though not so addictive, can be as ravaging of mind and body as cocaine—have for decades alternated with cocaine as the stimulants of choice, according to shifts in price and supply. Here in the Northwest, underground amphetamine labs are becoming so widespread their toxic pollution is cause for concern.

Only in their most intoxicated moments have the drug-busters claimed that interdiction and other enforcement could eliminate drugs. They just hope to reduce supplies and force prices high enough to discourage demand. As for reducing supply, interdiction has manifestly failed. Only marijuana falls into shortages these days. For hard drugs, the economic incentive is just too great. By Reuter's calculations, the hill of coca leaf needed to extract a kilogram of cocaine costs just $1,000—still much bigger money than an Andean farmer can make off potatoes. By the time it gets to the Bahamas or Mexico, that kilo is worth about $15,000; it finally reaches the retail market at $250,000.

[1] A form of marijuana containing a high level of THC.
[2] A part of Seattle.

Moreover, the price is falling. The current $50 to $70 for a gram of cocaine is a bargain compared to $120 for a much more adulterated gram a decade ago. Heroin has likewise gotten much stronger, causing the rash of black-tar overdoses a few years ago.

So the word from the frontlines of this longest-running war of the century is grim and getting grimmer. The dealers and traffickers are outpacing the greatest mobilization against contraband in history. All our efforts only succeed in sustaining an enormous black market. We spend over $10 billion a year on drug enforcement (at all levels) so that traffickers can make $140 billion. Even defense contractors don't get such a sweet deal from the government.

We all pay the costs of this futile war in lots of other ways, too. Drug abusers affect the rest of us most directly by stealing our VCRs, tape decks, and wallets, in order to buy drugs that the law deliberately makes expensive. The law-abiding majority in the inner cities must live amid brazen, ubiquitous drug dealing. What aggrieves them most is the constant threat of violence and the sense of violation and intimidation that the drug biz brings: trigger-happy Crips and Bloods[3] swaggering down the street, indiscriminate drive-by shootings, rockhouses armed like bunkers. These plagues result from competition for the illicit market.

On it goes: the violence visited on the citizens of Colombia, the suborning of entire governments in Bolivia, bizarre foreign-policy entanglements like Bush's tango with Noriega, and the worst U.S. police corruption (over one hundred prosecuted cases a year) since alcohol prohibition. Anticipating just that danger, J. Edgar Hoover kept the FBI out of drug investigations for half a century. No sooner did the Reagan administration drag the Bureau into the drug war than its first known case of bribe-taking surfaced.

Add all of this up and you are about to make the first, irrefutable argument for legalization: it's not surrender to the drug traffickers, it's the only way to beat them. To strangle the fish, dry up their sea of money.

That may be logical, but it's a long way from how legalization looks on paper to the practical consequences of adopting such a policy. What would be the costs to the health, wealth, and morale of the rest of society? Opponents of legalization raise an ominous list of forecasts and arguments:

Legalization would be morally wrong. Obviously, something sticks in the craw about legitimizing any use of demon drugs like cocaine and heroin. But in nearly all religious and ethical traditions, except Islam and some Christian strains, there's nothing inherently immoral about mood-altering substances. In many, certain types of chemical intoxication, carefully and purposefully entered into, are seen as necessary and instructive holy states, bringing worshippers closer to their gods through contemplation or jubila-

36

40

---

[3] Rival gangs.

tion. We sanction the use of hundreds of mood alterers, from coffee and aspirin to alcohol and Valium. Judgments about the use of each must be based upon their effects upon individual physical and mental health. One person's soothing glass of wine or joint, or occasional eye-opener of LSD or toot of coke, is another man's poison.

Legalization would send the wrong message to potential victims of drugs, especially the young. It certainly could; great effort would be required to make clear that we don't endorse what we admit the law cannot effectively prohibit. (Abortion is a case in point.) We already have to make that point clearer, because we've been sending the wrong message for decades in our free use of alcohol and tobacco—which are more dangerous than most of the controlled substances. Alcohol is involved in two-fifths of motor-vehicle fatalities and in half of violent crimes, and causes some 100,000 deaths a year and contributes to 100,000 more. Nicotine is at least as addictive as heroin; smoking kills about 320,000 Americans a year. By contrast, the 1985 death toll from *all* illicit drugs together was 3,562, with 643 involving cocaine.

When we reinstated legal alcohol, we knew that it was a dangerous drug, but realized that the dangers of legal use were outweighed by the penalties of prohibition: crime and violence, corruption, poisoning from bathtub gin, the immoderation that goes with surreptitious indulgence. But we failed to attach a suitable program of education and warnings as to alcohol's dangers. We are now catching up and sending the right messages about alcohol and tobacco—with impressive results in moderation with the former and abstinence from the latter.

We can make a better start with any other pleasure drug we allow into the legal market, through a conscientious system of consumer information and warning labels. ("The Surgeon General has determined that frequent smoking of marijuana may lower your sperm count, fuzz up your chromosomes, and make you laugh helplessly at stupid jokes.") We could ban *all* advertising of recreational drugs, including alcohol and tobacco. (The cigarette barons cynically plaster billboards and youth-oriented magazines with seductive images of young vitality to lure novice smokers. And do you think MTV-style Michelob spots are directed at mature beer drinkers?) We could also institute severe laws against the sale to kids of all recreational drugs, including tobacco. In these ways, legalization can be coupled with serious efforts to cut down usage, paradoxical as that may seem on the surface.

In addition, by eliminating the illicit market, legalization would silence   44
a terribly destructive and seductive message that's now getting through to inner-city kids: that drugs spell wealth and power, the most (and sometimes the only) visible means of upward mobility. Indeed, harsh penalties induce dealers to employ children, who are subject only to milder juvenile codes or no prosecution at all, as couriers.

Other countries have tried legalization and abandoned it; why can't we learn from their mistakes? Time to clear away some myths. The two oft-cited examples of failed legalization, Britain's and the Netherlands's are neither full legalization nor clear failures. Britain's system of prescribing heroin for addicts, many of them hooked on it as a surgical painkiller and many of them respectable citizens, worked pretty well for half a century. In the 1950s and 1960s the system, which allowed any general practitioner to prescribe the stuff, started leaking. Patients got excessive prescriptions and sold their surplus in a black market abetted by the rise of the general drug culture and, as elsewhere, imported heroin. But the notorious British heroin "epidemic" was nothing next to the entirely bootleg U.S. epidemic at the same time; in 1967 the Home Office counted 1,290 "nontherapeutic" addicts. The government cracked down, restricting heroin prescription first to specially licensed doctors, then to addiction clinics that provided counseling and close scrutiny. The Brits didn't "ban" prescription heroin. They phased it out in favor of the American model, methadone—a synthetic opiate that staves off heroin withdrawal. Taken orally, methadone lasts longer than injected heroin and doesn't give the same high. (The Brits, unlike the Americans, also provide methadone for injection.) Some addicts and physicians believe it is more enervating and harder to kick than heroin.

Holland likewise hasn't formally legalized any of the no-no drugs. Its official penalty for personal marijuana possession, thirty days, is stiffer than Seattle's decriminalized fine. But the Dutch like to keep their vices out in the open where they can be monitored. They make a tolerance policy of not enforcing the pot laws or cracking down on other personal drug possession; marijuana and hashish are sold in cafés.

Contrary to a dire report in *Time,* L. J. S. Wever of the Dutch Welfare, Health, and Cultural Affairs Ministry reports considerable success from this policy. It has succeeded in "separating" the marijuana and heroin markets "in order to prevent soft drug users from becoming hard drug users." Drug use has leveled off, and users on average are older. Tolerance helps draw heroin addicts into drug-free treatment centers. That and widespread needle exchange make for a much lower percentage of junkies among AIDS cases (4 percent) than in the rest of Europe (17 percent). The Dutch report just half as many drug-related deaths on average as in the rest of Europe. Some authorities propose lifting restrictions on all drugs as they have on marijuana.

Wouldn't legalization encourage many more people to take drugs? Certainly more people, who now eschew drug experimentation out of respect for or fear of the law or because of lack of convenient access, would try more drugs. More might continue to use some drugs. Whether more would *abuse* drugs is problematic. To steer around the pitfalls of legalization and decriminalization, we will have to learn to distinguish between controlled, responsible use and compulsive, self-destructive abuse of all drugs, just as we distinguish between use and abuse of alcohol.

We may decide that some drugs—say, PCP "angel dust" and crack cocaine—are simply not amenable to safe use. We may also be forced to make some startling admissions. Heroin, for example, is a relatively benign substance, causing no organic damage to compare with that from heavy alcohol or tobacco use. Its main ill effects are constipation, brief drowsy euphoria, and of course addiction—plus the contagion, abscesses, and collapsed veins that result from improper injection and overdoses from unmeasured dosage and potency. Remove the stigma, poverty, and general desperation that result from heroin's illegality, and some addicts are able to function well—such as the British novelist Anthony Burgess, a registered addict for decades, and a millionaire investment whiz who claims he can forecast the market better while high on smack.

Then, too, legalization would undercut some of the attraction of drugs, especially for the young: the allure of prohibition, rebellion, and putting one over on the authorities, the glamour of an exclusive underground subculture.

A related objection to legalization is the charge that marijuana is a "gateway" to harder stuff. That case is overstated, and alcohol and tobacco are more universal "gateways" that precede use of harder drugs. The vast majority of marijuana smokers do not proceed to abuse other drugs, or even to abuse marijuana. But pot does provide an initiation into the criminal subculture; kids buying it learn how to make an illegal connection and where to score other drugs.

Chuck Pillon, the former Seattle Police sergeant driven from the force because of his iconoclastic zeal in attacking drug dealing, sees the real, and more dangerous, "gateway" syndrome on the supply side. "Kids start out at twelve or thirteen as marijuana couriers and then move on to the hard-drug business. The cash flow from marijuana funds them for other things." While vehemently believing other drug legalization is "sheer madness," Pillon believes it's time to decriminalize weed. "We can no longer afford to wrestle with trying to drive marijuana out of our system. When people can grow the plant at home, engage in private barter and giving—what's the problem?" Alaska reports no noticeable increase in marijuana use or related problems since it decriminalized the stuff.

Any drugs that we cannot "drive out of our system" we must learn to live with. The "compelling argument" for legalization, in the words of University of Washington sociologist and drug-abuse scholar Roger Roffman, is, "Legalize the drugs and society will find its own normative system to live with them, the way it's learned to live with alcohol." (Roffman himself is not ready to endorse full-scale legalization, only decriminalization of personal possession.) Trouble is, how long does it take for society to strike a norm with unfamiliar substances that can be dangerous and addictive?

On the scary side, most Eskimo and Indian groups have not struck such a balance with alcohol after a century or so of exposure, and are ravaged by its ill physical and social effects. But cultural dislocation and particular genetic factors, resulting from long isolation from alcohol, may have made many Native Americans especially vulnerable to it. Various Asian and Mediterranean cultures have had thousands of years to establish their patterns of moderate alcohol use. But the United States has come around to largely moderate use in a much shorter time. Two and even one hundred years ago, drinking was much more nearly synonymous with drunkenness than it is today. The quantities of whiskey swilled down in the Colonies and the Wild West leave one wondering how anyone could see straight enough to tame the frontier.

The 1960s counterculture left more than its share of drug victims, but it also provided a hopeful example of rapid accommodation to moderate use. Around 1966, the psycho wards and drop-in centers were filled with LSD freak-outs. Five years later, these cases had nearly disappeared and crisis clinics were fishing about for something else to justify their grants. Pundits declared that hallucinogens had been driven out of style and off the market. In fact, they were, and remain, very much with us, but absorbed into less visible, more informed usage. Millions of people just got tired of heavy acid dropping and pot smoking and went on to grad school and other things, with maybe a little weekend indulgence on the side.

Education, antidrug advertising, and other voluntary inducements seem   56
to work better to deter destructive drug use than prohibition (though prohibition may be more effective against widespread moderate use). The great, though unfinished, American success story in reforming destructive drug habits is cigarette smoking. Through persuasion rather than coercion, the percentage of Americans who smoke has dropped from 41 to 26.

One of the marvels of the illicit drug boom is that people who might worry about preservatives and cholesterol in their food have been willing to play chemical roulette with outlaw concoctions. Many bad "LSD" and "mescaline" trips were really taken on speed and PCP. Legalization, regulation, and labeling would end such misrepresentations, as well as accidental overdoses.

Licit drug use conduces to restraint and measured dosage, while illicit use lends an urgency that impels toward excess. Americans have consciously shifted to lower doses of tobacco and alcohol: low-tar cigarettes, and beer and wine in place of spirits. Conversely, they have moved to sinsemilla marijuana, with ten times as much active THC as the old Acapulco Gold, and much faster-acting and more dangerous freebase rock cocaine. Asians and South Americans for centuries got along just fine on, respectively, mild opium and coca. But attempts to restrict those vegetable substances, and the growth of export markets for their concentrated derivatives, have nurtured epidemics of heroin addiction in Nepal and Pakistan and of cocaine and highly poisonous coca-residue paste in Ecuador and Colombia.

Legalization is elitist and racist. By this argument, advanced most fervently by *Newsweek*, proponents of legalization would consign the underclass to a perpetual hell of addiction in order to be free of the threat of crime.

But the inner cities are already awash in expensive crack and other drugs, and all the violence and waste that go with high prices. Inexpensive crack is not the solution in itself. But by freeing our attention and resources from futile enforcement, we can begin to attack the immense and complex problems of education, unemployment, family structure, and internalized racism that nurture a growing and entrenched underclass. As Dr. Richard Blum observes in Horace Judson's *Heroin Addiction in Britain*, drugs "are the chemical tracer that diagnoses the problems of society. An avenue of discovery for the doctor and sociologist."

Legalization would be terribly difficult to implement consistently, given   60
the wide differences in state laws and customs. All the better. Let the federal government pull back from drug regulation and encourage the states to set their own rules, as they do with alcohol, and find their own "normative patterns." The various experiments will tell us much more about what (and perhaps what varied) approaches work.

Reasonable as all these counterarguments for legalization may seem, they still butt up against a void of unknowable possible consequences. Drug-buster Pillon puts the dilemma piquantly: "If we're going to legalize cocaine, put *your* kid first in line when the state starts to sell it." Immediate, blanket legalization of all illicit drugs is a terrifying prospect. We might well adjust eventually to ready, cheap access to every sort of high, but too many of us would be kids set loose in a candy store; the initial casualties could be high.

Decriminalization of personal possession has more visceral appeal; why penalize the victims of drugs by making them the victims of the law? Zero tolerance and "user accountability" are so manifestly unfair and disproportionate that they will only encourage public receptivity to decriminalization. So long as some interdiction were maintained to keep prices up, decriminalization would probably not boost drug abuse, though it would encourage more experimentation. But neither it nor any other half-measures short of legalization will achieve the longed-for ends of getting the gangsters, guns, and corruption out of the drug market and restoring neighborhood and geopolitical security.

Legalization is thus the end we should work toward, though we're not ready to embrace it yet. How can we start preparing for the burdens of responsibility that it would impose?

First and most important, we must undertake unstinting development   64
of drug treatment, rehabilitation, and education. The Senate's fifty-fifty split is not enough; let's start by switching all eradication and all but a minimum of interdiction funds to these more constructive measures. As it stands now, only one in ten addicts who seek public treatment receives it. According to John Edgell, legislative assistant to Congressman Pete Stark, "Massachusetts is the only state that offers treatment upon request, and Massachusetts has the lowest crime rate in the nation." (Not true, though it has less crime than

most industrial states.) Sure, various treatment and education approaches have proven to be very pricey and overhyped hooey. But we're also learning which ones work, and how well they can work. Some of the best cost just a tenth to fifth as much as imprisonment.

On those lines, we should make methadone maintenance available upon request, rather than requiring proof of a year's heroin addiction (and indoctrination in the criminal culture) first. We should undertake closely monitored trials in actual *heroin* maintenance, serving addicts in various regions and economic classes, and compare the results. And we should provide clean needles for every intravenous drug user; banning paraphernalia is a hang-up that no one should have to die for.

Heroin is three times as potent as morphine, with fewer side effects; it may be the best painkiller for severe cancer pain. Britain has long used it and whatever else works against pain (including the famous hospice "cocktails" of heroin and cocaine); Canada has recently reinstated heroin as a painkiller. Marijuana can provide unparalleled relief for glaucoma and the nausea of cancer chemotherapy. And yet both remain federal Schedule 1 drugs, forbidden as having no medically redeeming value whatsoever. Both should be available by prescription to patients in need. And research into medical applications of these and other proscribed drugs should no longer be blocked or snarled in red tape.

Take a hint from Alaska, Chuck Pillon, and common sense, and decriminalize small-scale possession, growing, and exchange of marijuana. We should test legal production and sale—perhaps through state liquor stores— and track their effect on local use (among adults and children), illicit prices, auto accident rates, and other indicators. Legal, restricted sale could hardly let more of the stuff get to kids than the underground market provides; as it is, they can score grass or crack more easily than beer. It's absurd to squander overburdened police, court, and jail resources on a nonaddicting drug we've largely learned to live with, even if we won't admit it.

Get tough where tough makes sense: on cigarette and other drug advertising, on driving under the influence of marijuana and other intoxicants, on sales of tobacco and other drugs to juveniles. We must have these weapons in place, along with our treatment and social-service infrastructures, before undertaking large-scale legalization. And we must undertake a basic change of viewpoint: to see drug abuse as a medical and social problem, with medical and social solutions, rather than as a target for "an all-out war, like World War II," which is what Ben Gilman, a Republican on the House Narcotics Select Committee, calls for.

To get anywhere at this, we must get the drug issue out of the sweaty hands of congressmen who stand for election every two years. Only a more impartial and independent authority will dare voice incendiary truths. Schmoke calls for "a high-level commission to study the potential impact of decriminalization" and design policies based on the specific dangers of each

68

drug—rather than a blanket declaration of war. Even some hardliners like Congressman Gilman call for a top-flight commission to develop some kind of better drug policy. The new act's provision of a "drug czar" to command the Great War could also help, if the right czar were chosen. Here's a second to the *New Republic*'s nomination of Surgeon General C. Everett Koop, who has led us to a rational attack upon the dangers of tobacco, alcohol, and AIDS. Under a general like him, we may finally start fighting drug abuse instead of waging war on drug users.

Points to Consider

1. According to Eric Scigliano, why does more government funding go to the enforcement of drug laws than to education and treatment programs? Why do most politicians call for increasingly tough measures against drug dealers and users when it seems as though such measures have little effect on the narcotics trade?

2. According to Scigliano, why are liberal politicians backing away from legalization? Who are the strongest proponents of legalization? What reasons do proponents offer as support for legalization?

3. How could legalization be coupled with efforts to curtail drug use? According to Scigliano, why would legalization not necessarily imply endorsement of drug use? How might legalization actually reduce drug use, especially among the young?

4. Consider the following statement by Scigliano: "Licit drug use conduces to restraint and measured dosage, while illicit use lends an urgency that impels toward excess." Based on evidence supplied by the author and others, do you agree with this statement? Can both halves of the statement be verified through the use of statistics?

JAMES Q. WILSON

Against the Legalization of Drugs

[COMMENTARY / February 1990]

In 1972, the president appointed me chairman of the National Advisory Council for Drug Abuse Prevention. Created by Congress, the Council was charged with providing guidance on how best to coordinate the national war on drugs. (Yes, we called it a war then, too.) In those days, the drug we were chiefly concerned with was heroin. When I took office, heroin use had been increasing dramatically. Everybody was worried that this increase would continue. Such phrases as "heroin epidemic" were commonplace.

That same year, the eminent economist Milton Friedman published an essay in *Newsweek* in which he called for legalizing heroin. His argument was on two grounds: as a matter of ethics, the government has no right to tell people not to use heroin (or to drink or to commit suicide); as a matter of economics, the prohibition of drug use imposes costs on society that far exceed the benefits. Others, such as the psychoanalyst Thomas Szasz, made the same argument.

We did not take Friedman's advice. (Government commissions rarely do.) I do not recall that we even discussed legalizing heroin, though we did discuss (but did not take action on) legalizing a drug, cocaine, that many people then argued was benign. Our marching orders were to figure out how to win the war on heroin, not to run up the white flag of surrender.

That was 1972. Today, we have the same number of heroin addicts that   4
we had then—half a million, give or take a few thousand. Having that many heroin addicts is no trivial matter; these people deserve our attention. But not having had an increase in that number for over fifteen years is also something that deserves our attention. What happened to the "heroin epidemic" that many people once thought would overwhelm us?

James Q. Wilson (b. 1931) is Collins Professor of Management and Public Policy at the University of California, Los Angeles. He is the author of Thinking About Crime *(1975) and coauthor (with Richard Herrnstein) of* Crime and Human Nature *(1985). His most recent book is* Bureaucracy *(1989). Wilson has served on several presidential task forces and national advisory committees on crime, law enforcement, and drug abuse prevention.*

The facts are clear: a more or less stable pool of heroin addicts has been getting older, with relatively few new recruits. In 1976 the average age of heroin users who appeared in hospital emergency rooms was about twenty-seven; ten years later it was thirty-two. More than two-thirds of all heroin users appearing in emergency rooms are now over the age of thirty. Back in the early 1970s, when heroin got onto the national political agenda, the typical heroin addict was much younger, often a teenager. Household surveys show the same thing—the rate of opiate use (which includes heroin) has been flat for the better part of two decades. More fine-grained studies of inner-city neighborhoods confirm this. John Boyle and Ann Brunswick found that the percentage of young blacks in Harlem who used heroin fell from 8 percent in 1970–71 to about 3 percent in 1975–76.

Why did heroin lose its appeal for young people? When the young blacks in Harlem were asked why they stopped, more than half mentioned "trouble with the law" or "high cost" (and high cost is, of course, directly the result of law enforcement). Two-thirds said that heroin hurt their health; nearly all said they had had a bad experience with it. We need not rely, however, simply on what they said. In New York City in 1973–75, the street price of heroin rose dramatically and its purity sharply declined, probably as a result of the heroin shortage caused by the success of the Turkish government in reducing the supply of opium base and of the French government in closing down heroin-processing laboratories located in and around Marseilles. These were short-lived gains for, just as Friedman predicted, alternative sources of supply—mostly in Mexico—quickly emerged. But the three-year heroin shortage interrupted the easy recruitment of new users.

Health and related problems were no doubt part of the reason for the reduced flow of recruits. Over the preceding years, Harlem youth had watched as more and more heroin users died of overdoses, were poisoned by adulterated doses, or acquired hepatitis from dirty needles. The word got around: heroin can kill you. By 1974 new hepatitis cases and drug-overdose deaths had dropped to a fraction of what they had been in 1970.

Alas, treatment did not seem to explain much of the cessation in drug use. Treatment programs can and do help heroin addicts, but treatment did not explain the drop in the number of *new* users (who by definition had never been in treatment) nor even much of the reduction in the number of experienced users.

No one knows how much of the decline to attribute to personal observation as opposed to high prices or reduced supply. But other evidence suggests strongly that price and supply played a large role. In 1972 the National Advisory Council was especially worried by the prospect that U.S. servicemen returning to this country from Vietnam would bring their heroin habits with them. Fortunately, a brilliant study by Lee Robins of Washington University in St. Louis put that fear to rest. She measured drug use of Vietnam veterans shortly after they had returned home. Though many had used heroin regularly while in Southeast Asia, most gave up the habit when back in the United States. The reason: here, heroin was less available and sanctions on its use were more pronounced. Of course, if a veteran had been willing to pay enough—which might have meant traveling to another city and would certainly have meant making an illegal contact with a disreputable dealer in a threatening neighborhood in order to acquire a (possibly) dangerous dose— he could have sustained his drug habit. Most veterans were unwilling to pay this price, and so their drug use declined or disappeared.

Reliving the Past

Suppose we had taken Friedman's advice in 1972. What would have happened? We cannot be entirely certain, but at a minimum we would have placed the young heroin addicts (and, above all, the prospective addicts) in a very different position from the one in which they actually found themselves. Heroin would have been legal. Its price would have been reduced by 95 percent (minus whatever we chose to recover in taxes). Now that it could be sold by the same people who make aspirin, its quality would have been assured—no poisons, no adulterants. Sterile hypodermic needles would have been readily available at the neighborhood drugstore, probably at the same counter where the heroin was sold. No need to travel to big cities or unfamiliar neighborhoods—heroin could have been purchased anywhere, perhaps by mail order.

There would no longer have been any financial or medical reason to avoid heroin use. Anybody could have afforded it. We might have tried to prevent children from buying it, but as we have learned from our efforts to prevent minors from buying alcohol and tobacco, young people have a way of penetrating markets theoretically reserved for adults. Returning Vietnam veterans would have discovered that Omaha and Raleigh had been converted into the pharmaceutical equivalent of Saigon.

Under these circumstances, can we doubt for a moment that heroin use 12 would have grown exponentially? Or that a vastly larger supply of new users would have been recruited? Professor Friedman is a Noble Prize–winning economist whose understanding of market forces is profound. What did he think would happen to consumption under his legalized regime? Here are his words: "Legalizing drugs might increase the number of addicts, but it is not clear that it would. Forbidden fruit is attractive, particularly to the young."

Really? I suppose that we should expect no increase in Porsche sales if we cut the price by 95 percent, no increase in whiskey sales if we cut the price by a comparable amount—because young people only want fast cars and strong liquor when they are "forbidden." Perhaps Friedman's uncharacteristic lapse from the obvious implications of price theory can be explained by a misunderstanding of how drug users are recruited. In his 1972 essay he said that "drug addicts are deliberately made by pushers, who give likely prospects their first few doses free." If drugs were legal it would not pay anybody to produce addicts, because everybody would buy from the cheapest source. But as every drug expert knows, pushers do not produce addicts. Friends or acquaintances do. In fact, pushers are usually reluctant to deal with nonusers because a nonuser could be an undercover cop. Drug use spreads in the same way any fad or fashion spreads: somebody who is already a user urges his friends to try, or simply shows already-eager friends how to do it.

But we need not rely on speculation, however plausible, that lowered prices and more abundant supplies would have increased heroin usage. Great Britain once followed such a policy and with almost exactly those results. Until the mid-1960s, British physicians were allowed to prescribe heroin to certain classes of addicts. (Possessing these drugs without a doctor's prescription remained a criminal offense.) For many years this policy worked well enough because the addict patients were typically middle-class people who had become dependent on opiate painkillers while undergoing hospital treatment. There was no drug culture. The British system worked for many years, not because it prevented drug abuse, but because there was no problem of drug abuse that would test the system.

All that changed in the 1960s. A few unscrupulous doctors began passing out heroin in wholesale amounts. One doctor prescribed almost 600,000 heroin tablets—that is, over thirteen pounds—in just one year. A youthful drug culture emerged with a demand for drugs far different from that of the older addicts. As a result, the British government required doctors to refer users to government-run clinics to receive their heroin.

But the shift to clinics did not curtail the growth in heroin use. Throughout the 1960s the number of addicts increased—the late John Kaplan of Stanford estimated by fivefold—in part as a result of the diversion of heroin from clinic patients to new users on the streets. An addict would bargain with the clinic doctor over how big a dose he would receive. The patient wanted as much as he could get, the doctor wanted to give as little as was needed. The patient had an advantage in this conflict because the doctor could not be certain how much was really needed. Many patients would use some of their "maintenance" dose and sell the remaining part to friends, thereby recruiting new addicts. As the clinics learned of this, they began to shift their treatment away from heroin and toward methadone, an addictive drug that, when taken orally, does not produce a "high" but will block the withdrawal pains associated with heroin abstinence.

Whether what happened in England in the 1960s was a miniepidemic or an epidemic depends on whether one looks at numbers or at rates of change. Compared to the United States, the numbers were small. In 1960 there were sixty-eight heroin addicts known to the British government; by 1968 there were two thousand in treatment and many more who refused treatment. (They would refuse in part because they did not want to get methadone at a clinic if they could get heroin on the street.) Richard Hartnoll estimates that the actual number of addicts in England is five times the number officially registered. At a minimum, the number of British addicts increased by thirtyfold in ten years; the actual increase may have been much larger.

In the early 1980s the numbers began to rise again, and this time nobody doubted that a real epidemic was at hand. The increase was estimated to be 40 percent a year. By 1982 there were thought to be twenty thousand heroin users in London alone. Geoffrey Pearson reports that many cities—Glasgow, Liverpool, Manchester, and Sheffield among them—were now experiencing a drug problem that once had been largely confined to London. The problem, again, was supply. The country was being flooded with cheap, high-quality heroin, first from Iran and then from Southeast Asia.

The United States began the 1960s with a much larger number of heroin addicts and probably a bigger at-risk population than was the case in Great Britain. Even though it would be foolhardy to suppose that the British system, if installed here, would have worked the same way or with the same results, it would be equally foolhardy to suppose that a combination of heroin available from leaky clinics and from street dealers who faced only minimal law-enforcement risks would not have produced a much greater increase in heroin use than we actually experienced. My guess is that if we had allowed either doctors or clinics to prescribe heroin, we would have had far worse results than were produced in Britain, if for no other reason than the vastly larger number of addicts with which we began. We would have had to find some way to police thousands (not scores) of physicians and hundreds (not dozens) of clinics. If the British civil service found it difficult to keep heroin in the hands of addicts and out of the hands of recruits when it was dealing with a few hundred people, how well would the American civil service have accomplished the same tasks when dealing with tens of thousands of people?

Back to the Future

Now cocaine, especially in its potent form, crack, is the focus of atten-   20
tion. Now as in 1972 the government is trying to reduce its use. Now as then some people are advocating legalization. Is there any more reason to yield to those arguments today than there was almost two decades ago?[1]

I think not. If we had yielded in 1972 we almost certainly would have had today a permanent population of several million, not several hundred thousand, heroin addicts. If we yield now we will have a far more serious problem with cocaine.

[1] I do not here take up the question of marijuana. For a variety of reasons—its widespread use and its lesser tendency to addict—it presents a different problem from cocaine or heroin. For a penetrating analysis, see Mark Kleiman, *Marijuana: Costs of Abuse, Costs of Control* (Greenwood Press, 217 pp., $37.95). [Au.]

Crack is worse than heroin by almost any measure. Heroin produces a pleasant drowsiness and, if hygienically administered, has only the physical side effects of constipation and sexual impotence. Regular heroin use incapacitates many users, especially poor ones, for any productive work or social responsibility. They will sit nodding on a street corner, helpless but at least harmless. By contrast, regular cocaine use leaves the user neither helpless nor harmless. When smoked (as with crack) or injected, cocaine produces instant, intense, and short-lived euphoria. The experience generates a powerful desire to repeat it. If the drug is readily available, repeat use will occur. Those people who progress to "bingeing" on cocaine become devoted to the drug and its effects to the exclusion of almost all other considerations—job, family, children, sleep, food, even sex. Dr. Frank Gawin at Yale and Dr. Everett Ellinwood at Duke report that a substantial percentage of all high-dose, binge users become uninhibited, impulsive, hypersexual, compulsive, irritable, and hyperactive. Their moods vacillate dramatically, leading at times to violence and homicide.

Women are much more likely to use crack than heroin, and if they are pregnant, the effects on their babies are tragic. Douglas Besharov, who has been following the effects of drugs on infants for twenty years, writes that nothing he learned about heroin prepared him for the devastation of cocaine. Cocaine harms the fetus and can lead to physical deformities or neurological damage. Some crack babies have for all practical purposes suffered a disabling stroke while still in the womb. The long-term consequences of this brain damage are lowered cognitive ability and the onset of mood disorders. Besharov estimates that about thirty thousand to fifty thousand such babies are born every year, about seven thousand in New York City alone. There may be ways to treat such infants, but from everything we now know the treatment will be long, difficult, and expensive. Worse, the mothers who are most likely to produce crack babies are precisely the ones who, because of poverty or temperament, are least able and willing to obtain such treatment. In fact, anecdotal evidence suggests that crack mothers are likely to abuse their infants.

The notion that abusing drugs such as cocaine is a "victimless crime" is 24 not only absurd but dangerous. Even ignoring the fetal drug syndrome, crack-dependent people are, like heroin addicts, individuals who regularly victimize their children by neglect, their spouses by improvidence, their employers by lethargy, and their co-workers by carelessness. Society is not and could never be a collection of autonomous individuals. We all have a stake in ensuring that each of us displays a minimal level of dignity, responsibility, and empathy. We cannot, of course, coerce people into goodness, but we can and should insist that some standards must be met if society itself—on which the very existence of the human personality depends—is to persist. Drawing the line that defines those standards is difficult and contentious, but if crack and heroin use do not fall below it, what does?

The advocates of legalization will respond by suggesting that my picture is overdrawn. Ethan Nadelmann of Princeton argues that the risk of legalization is less than most people suppose. Over twenty million Americans between the ages of eighteen and twenty-five have tried cocaine (according to a government survey), but only a quarter million use it daily. From this Nadelmann concludes that at most 3 percent of all young people who try cocaine develop a problem with it. The implication is clear: make the drug legal and we only have to worry about 3 percent of our youth.

The implication rests on a logical fallacy and a factual error. The fallacy is this: the percentage of occasional cocaine users who become binge users *when the drug is illegal* (and thus expensive and hard to find) tells us nothing about the percentage who will become dependent when the drug is legal (and thus cheap and abundant). Drs. Gawin and Ellinwood report, in common with several other researchers, that controlled or occasional use of cocaine changes to compulsive and frequent use "when access to the drug increases" or when the user switches from snorting to smoking. More cocaine more potently administered alters, perhaps sharply, the proportion of "controlled" users who become heavy users.

The factual error is this: the federal survey Nadelmann quotes was done in 1985, *before* crack had become common. Thus the probability of becoming dependent on cocaine was derived from the responses of users who snorted the drug. The speed and potency of cocaine's action increases dramatically when it is smoked. We do not yet know how greatly the advent of crack increases the risk of dependency, but all the clinical evidence suggests that the increase is likely to be large.

It is possible that some people will not become heavy users even when the drug is readily available in its most potent form. So far there are no scientific grounds for predicting who will and who will not become dependent. Neither socioeconomic background nor personality traits differentiate between casual and intensive users. Thus, the only way to settle the question of who is correct about the effect of easy availability on drug use, Nadelmann or Gawin and Ellinwood, is to try it and see. But that social experiment is so risky as to be no experiment at all, for if cocaine is legalized and if the rate of its abusive use increases dramatically, there is no way to put the genie back in the bottle, and it is not a kindly genie. 28

Have We Lost?

Many people who agree that there are risks in legalizing cocaine or heroin still favor it because, they think, we have lost the war on drugs. "Nothing we have done has worked" and the current federal policy is just "more of the same." Whatever the costs of greater drug use, surely they would be less than the costs of our present, failed efforts.

That is exactly what I was told in 1972—and heroin is not quite as bad a drug as cocaine. We did not surrender and we did not lose. We did not win, either. What the nation accomplished then was what most efforts to save people from themselves accomplish: the problem was contained and the number of victims minimized, all at a considerable cost in law enforcement and increased crime. Was the cost worth it? I think so, but others may disagree. What are the lives of would-be addicts worth? I recall some people saying to me then, "Let them kill themselves." I was appalled. Happily, such views did not prevail.

Have we lost today? Not at all. High-rate cocaine use is not commonplace. The National Institute of Drug Abuse (NIDA) reports that less than 5 percent of high-school seniors used cocaine within the last thirty days. Of course this survey misses young people who have dropped out of school and miscounts those who lie on the questionnaire, but even if we inflate the NIDA estimate by some plausible percentage, it is still not much above 5 percent. Medical examiners reported in 1987 that about fifteen hundred died from cocaine use; hospital emergency rooms reported about thirty thousand admissions related to cocaine abuse.

These are not small numbers, but neither are they evidence of a nationwide plague that threatens to engulf us all. Moreover, cities vary greatly in the proportion of people who are involved with cocaine. To get city-level data we need to turn to drug tests carried out on arrested persons, who obviously are more likely to be drug users than the average citizen. The National Institute of Justice, through its Drug Use Forecasting (DUF) project, collects urinalysis data on arrestees in twenty-two cities. As we have already seen, opiate (chiefly heroin) use has been flat or declining in most of these cities over the last decade. Cocaine use has gone up sharply, but with great variation among cities. New York, Philadelphia, and Washington, D.C., all report that two-thirds or more of their arrestees tested positive for cocaine, but in Portland, San Antonio, and Indianapolis the percentage was one-third or less.

In some neighborhoods, of course, matters have reached crisis proportions. Gangs control the streets, shootings terrorize residents, and drug dealing occurs in plain view. The police seem barely able to contain matters. But in these neighborhoods—unlike at Palo Alto cocktail parties—the people are not calling for legalization, they are calling for help. And often not much help has come. Many cities are willing to do almost anything about the drug problem except spend more money on it. The federal government cannot change that; only local voters and politicians can. It is not clear that they will.

It took about ten years to contain heroin. We have had experience with crack for only about three or four years. Each year we spend perhaps eleven billion dollars on law enforcement (and some of that goes to deal with marijuana) and perhaps two billion dollars on treatment. Large sums, but not sums that should lead anyone to say, "We just can't afford this any more."

The illegality of drugs increases crime, partly because some users turn to crime to pay for their habits, partly because some users are stimulated by certain drugs (such as crack or PCP) to act more violently or ruthlessly than they otherwise would, and partly because criminal organizations seeking to control drug supplies use force to manage their markets. These also are serious costs, but no one knows how much they would be reduced if drugs were legalized. Addicts would no longer steal to pay black-market prices for drugs, a real gain. But some, perhaps a great deal, of that gain would be offset by the great increase in the number of addicts. These people, nodding on heroin or living in the delusion-ridden high of cocaine, would hardly be ideal employees. Many would steal simply to support themselves, since snatch-and-grab, opportunistic crime can be managed even by people unable to hold a regular job or plan an elaborate crime. Those British addicts who get their supplies from government clinics are not models of law-abiding decency. Most are in crime, and though their per-capita rate of criminality may be lower thanks to the cheapness of their drugs, the total volume of crime they produce may be quite large. Of course, society could decide to support all unemployable addicts on welfare, but that would mean that gains from lowered rates of crime would have to be offset by large increases in welfare budgets.

Proponents of legalization claim that the costs of having more addicts 36 around would be largely if not entirely offset by having more money available with which to treat and care for them. The money would come from taxes levied on the sale of heroin and cocaine.

To obtain this fiscal dividend, however, legalization's supporters must first solve an economic dilemma. If they want to raise a lot of money to pay for welfare and treatment, the tax rate on the drugs will have to be quite high. Even if they themselves do not want a high rate, the politicians' love of "sin taxes" would probably guarantee that it would be high anyway. But the higher the tax, the higher the price of the drug, and the higher the price the greater the likelihood that addicts will turn to crime to find the money for it and that criminal organizations will be formed to sell tax-free drugs at below-market rates. If we managed to keep taxes (and thus prices) low, we would get that much less money to pay for welfare and treatment and more people could afford to become addicts. There may be an optimal tax rate for drugs that maximizes revenue while minimizing crime, bootlegging, and the recruitment of new addicts, but our experience with alcohol does not suggest that we know how to find it.

The Benefits of Illegality

The advocates of legalization find nothing to be said in favor of the current system except, possibly, that it keeps the number of addicts smaller than it would otherwise be. In fact, the benefits are more substantial than that.

First, treatment. All the talk about providing "treatment on demand" implies that there is a demand for treatment. That is not quite right. There are some drug-dependent people who genuinely want treatment and will remain in it if offered; they should receive it. But there are far more who want only short-term help after a bad crash; once stabilized and bathed, they are back on the street again, hustling. And even many of the addicts who enroll in a program honestly wanting help drop out after a short while when they discover that help takes time and commitment. Drug-dependent people have very short time horizons and a weak capacity for commitment. These two groups—those looking for a quick fix and those unable to stick with a long-term fix—are not easily helped. Even if we increase the number of treatment slots—as we should—we would have to do something to make treatment more effective.

One thing that can often make it more effective is compulsion. Douglas 40 Anglin of UCLA, in common with many other researchers, has found that the longer one stays in a treatment program, the better the chances of a reduction in drug dependency. But he, again like most other researchers, has found that dropout rates are high. He has also found, however, that patients who enter treatment under legal compulsion stay in the program longer than those not subject to such pressure. His research on the California civil commitment program, for example, found that heroin users involved with its required drug-testing program had over the long term a lower rate of heroin use than similar addicts who were free of such constraints. If for many addicts compulsion is a useful component of treatment, it is not clear how compulsion could be achieved in a society in which purchasing, possessing, and using the drug were legal. It could be managed, I suppose, but I would not want to have to answer the challenge from the American Civil Liberties Union that it is wrong to compel a person to undergo treatment for consuming a legal commodity.

Next, education. We are now investing substantially in drug-education programs in the schools. Though we do not yet know for certain what will work, there are some promising leads. But I wonder how credible such programs would be if they were aimed at dissuading children from doing something perfectly legal. We could, of course, treat drug education like smoking education: inhaling crack and inhaling tobacco are both legal, but you should not do it because it is bad for you. That tobacco is bad for you is easily shown; the Surgeon General has seen to that. But what do we say about crack? It is pleasurable, but devoting yourself to so much pleasure is not a good idea (though perfectly legal)? Unlike tobacco, cocaine will not give you cancer or emphysema, but it will lead you to neglect your duties to family, job, and neighborhood? Everybody is doing cocaine, but you should not?

Again, it might be possible under a legalized regime to have effective drug-prevention programs, but their effectiveness would depend heavily, I think, on first having decided that cocaine use, like tobacco use, is purely a matter of practical consequences; no fundamental moral significance attaches to either. But if we believe—as I do—that dependency on certain mind-altering drugs *is* a moral issue and that their illegality rests in part on their immorality, then legalizing them undercuts, if it does not eliminate altogether, the moral message.

That message is at the root of the distinction we now make between nicotine and cocaine. Both are highly addictive; both have harmful physical effects. But we treat the two drugs differently, not simply because nicotine is so widely used as to be beyond the reach of effective prohibition, but because its use does not destroy the user's essential humanity. Tobacco shortens one's life, cocaine debases it. Nicotine alters one's habits, cocaine alters one's soul. The heavy use of crack, unlike the heavy use of tobacco, corrodes those natural sentiments of sympathy and duty that constitute our human nature and make possible our social life. To say, as does Nadelmann, that distinguishing morally between tobacco and cocaine is "little more than a transient prejudice" is close to saying that morality itself is but a prejudice.

The Alcohol Problem

Now we have arrived where many arguments about legalizing drugs 44 begin: is there any reason to treat heroin and cocaine differently from the way we treat alcohol?

There is no easy answer to that question because, as with so many human problems, one cannot decide simply on the basis either of moral principles or of individual consequences; one has to temper any policy by a common-sense judgment of what is possible. Alcohol, like heroin, cocaine, PCP, and marijuana, is a drug—that is, a mood-altering substance—and consumed to excess it certainly has harmful consequences: auto accidents, barroom fights, bedroom shootings. It is also, for some people, addictive. We cannot confidently compare the addictive powers of these drugs, but the best evidence suggests that crack and heroin are much more addictive than alcohol.

Many people, Nadelmann included, argue that since the health and financial costs of alcohol abuse are so much higher than those of cocaine or heroin abuse, it is hypocritical folly to devote our efforts to preventing cocaine or drug use. But as Mark Kleiman of Harvard has pointed out, this comparison is quite misleading. What Nadelmann is doing is showing that a *legalized* drug (alcohol) produces greater social harm than *illegal* ones (cocaine and heroin). But of course. Suppose that in the 1920s we had made heroin and cocaine legal and alcohol illegal. Can anyone doubt that Nadelmann would now be writing that it is folly to continue our ban on alcohol because cocaine and heroin are so much more harmful?

And let there be no doubt about it—widespread heroin and cocaine use are associated with all manner of ills. Thomas Bewley found that the mortality rate of British heroin addicts in 1968 was twenty-eight times as high as the death rate of the same age group of nonaddicts, even though in England at the time an addict could obtain free or low-cost heroin and clean needles from British clinics. Perform the following mental experiment: suppose we legalized heroin and cocaine in this country. In what proportion of auto fatalities would the state police report that the driver was nodding off on heroin or recklessly driving on a coke high? In what proportion of spouse-assault and child-abuse cases would the local police report that crack was involved? In what proportion of industrial accidents would safety investi-gators report that the forklift or drill-press operator was in a drug-induced stupor or frenzy? We do not know exactly what the proportion would be, but anyone who asserts that it would not be much higher than it is now would have to believe that these drugs have little appeal except when they are illegal. And that is nonsense.

An advocate of legalization might concede that social harm—perhaps 48 harm equivalent to that already produced by alcohol—would follow from making cocaine and heroin generally available. But at least, he might add, we would have the problem "out in the open" where it could be treated as a matter of "public health." That is well and good, *if* we knew how to treat—that is, cure—heroin and cocaine abuse. But we do not know how to do it for all the people who would need such help. We are having only limited success in coping with chronic alcoholics. Addictive behavior is immensely difficult to change, and the best methods for changing it—living in drug-free therapeutic communities, becoming faithful members of Alcoholics Anony-mous or Narcotics Anonymous—require great personal commitment, a qual-ity that is, alas, in short supply among the very persons—young people, disadvantaged people—who are often most at risk for addiction.

Suppose that today we had, not fifteen million alcohol abusers, but half a million. Suppose that we already knew what we have learned from our long experience with the widespread use of alcohol. Would we make whiskey legal? I do not know, but I suspect there would be a lively debate. The surgeon general would remind us of the risks alcohol poses to pregnant women. The National Highway Traffic Safety Administration would point to the likelihood of more highway fatalities caused by drunk drivers. The Food and Drug Administration might find that there is a nontrivial increase in cancer associated with alcohol consumption. At the same time the police would report great difficulty in keeping illegal whiskey out of our cities, officers being corrupted by bootleggers, and alcohol addicts often resorting to crime to feed their habit. Libertarians, for their part, would argue that every citizen has a right to drink anything he wishes and that drinking is, in any event, a "victimless crime."

However the debate might turn out, the central fact would be that the problem was still, at that point, a small one. The government cannot legislate away the addictive tendencies in all of us, nor can it remove completely even

the most dangerous addictive substances. But it can cope with harms when the harms are still manageable.

Science and Addiction

One advantage of containing a problem while it is still containable is that it buys time for science to learn more about it and perhaps to discover a cure. Almost unnoticed in the current debate over legalizing drugs is that basic science has made rapid strides in identifying the underlying neurological processes involved in some forms of addiction. Stimulants such as cocaine and amphetamines alter the way certain brain cells communicate with one another. That alteration is complex and not entirely understood, but in simplified form it involves modifying the way in which a neurotransmitter called dopamine sends signals from one cell to another.

When dopamine crosses the synapse between two cells, it is in effect   52
carrying a message from the first cell to activate the second one. In certain parts of the brain that message is experienced as pleasure. After the message is delivered, the dopamine returns to the first cell. Cocaine apparently blocks this return, or "reuptake," so that the excited cell and others nearby continue to send pleasure messages. When the exaggerated high produced by cocaine-influenced dopamine finally ends, the brain cells may (in ways that are still a matter of dispute) suffer from an extreme lack of dopamine, thereby making the individual unable to experience any pleasure at all. This would explain why cocaine users often feel so depressed after enjoying the drug. Stimulants may also affect the way in which other neurotransmitters, such as serotonin and noradrenaline, operate.

Whatever the exact mechanism may be, once it is identified it becomes possible to use drugs to block either the effect of cocaine or its tendency to produce dependency. There have already been experiments using desipramine, imipramine, bromocriptine, carbamazepine, and other chemicals. There are some promising results.

Tragically, we spend very little on such research, and the agencies funding it have not in the past occupied very influential or visible posts in the federal bureaucracy. If there is one aspect of the "war on drugs" metaphor that I dislike, it is its tendency to focus attention almost exclusively on the troops in the trenches, whether engaged in enforcement or treatment, and away from the research-and-development efforts back on the home front where the war may ultimately be decided.

I believe that the prospects of scientists in controlling addiction will be strongly influenced by the size and character of the problem they face. If the problem is a few hundred thousand chronic, high-dose users of an illegal product, the chances of making a difference at a reasonable cost will be much greater than if the problem is a few million chronic users of legal substances. Once a drug is legal, not only will its use increase but many of those who then use it will prefer the drug to the treatment: they will want

the pleasure, whatever the cost to themselves or their families, and they will resist—probably successfully—any effort to wean them away from experiencing the high that comes from inhaling a legal substance.

If I Am Wrong . . .

No one can know what our society would be like if we changed the law 56 to make access to cocaine, heroin, and PCP easier. I believe, for reasons given, that the result would be a sharp increase in use, a more widespread degradation of the human personality, and a greater rate of accidents and violence.

I may be wrong. If I am, then we will needlessly have incurred heavy costs in law enforcement and some forms of criminality. But if I am right, and the legalizers prevail anyway, then we will have consigned millions of people, hundreds of thousands of infants, and hundreds of neighborhoods to a life of oblivion and disease. To the lives and families destroyed by alcohol we will have added countless more destroyed by cocaine, heroin, PCP, and whatever else a basement scientist can invent.

Human character is formed by society; indeed, human character is inconceivable without society, and good character is less likely in a bad society. Will we, in the name of an abstract doctrine of radical individualism, and with the false comfort of suspect predictions, decide to take the chance that somehow individual decency can survive amid a more general level of degradation?

I think not. The American people are too wise for that, whatever the academic essayists and cocktail-party pundits may say. But if Americans today are less wise than I suppose, then Americans at some future time will look back on us now and wonder, what kind of people were they that they could have done such a thing?

Points to Consider

1. To what factors does Wilson attribute the decline of heroin use by young blacks in Harlem? Does Wilson believe that treatment programs caused this decrease?

2. According to Wilson, what is wrong with Friedman's argument that the number of "new users" would not increase if legalization occurred? Who is usually responsible for the creation of addicts?

3. At one point in his essay Wilson writes that "we all have a stake in ensuring that each of us displays a minimal level of dignity, responsibility, and empathy." What are the assumptions underlying this statement? What are the possible social consequences of such a belief?

4. What does Wilson believe is the connection between legality and public

morality? Do you attach moral significance to drug use? How would legalization undermine the moral message against drugs?

Discussing the Unit

Suggested Topic for Discussion

While most of us are used to hearing statistics on drug addiction, the number of lives drugs take each year, and the increase in drug-related crimes, we seldom hear about the more subtle effects of drugs on society. What are the psychological and social effects of drugs on the life of a habitual user? What effect does the drug problem have on nonusers? How would these effects change with legalization?

Preparing for Class Discussion

1. The authors of both essays offer statistical evidence as support for their arguments. Make a list of the instances in each essay when statistics are used. Do you think that either author relies too heavily on statistics? Do you think that either author uses statistics misleadingly?

2. In his essay, James Q. Wilson seems to offer indirect replies to many of the individual arguments made by Eric Scigliano. Construct a chart in which you list the major points made by Scigliano and Wilson's objections to those points. Where Wilson does not seem to offer an objection or parallel argument, supply one of your own, even if you favor legalization. Besides their basic disagreement over legalization, how do the authors' approaches to the issue differ?

From Discussion to Writing

What do you think about the legalization of drugs? Should all drugs that are currently illegal continue to be illegal? Should some be legalized? Write an essay in which you construct an argument defending your position on legalization. Be sure to take into account opposing views and to consider the advantages to society that would result if your position gained national approval.

23

Animal Rights:
The Next Big Cause?

Few topics elicit as much emotion and as wide a range of responses as the growing animal rights movement, which today numbers about ten million people. Yet neither side in the debate seems to be listening to the other. In their fervor to advance their own positions, participants in the debate often fail to acknowledge the weaknesses in their arguments.

In "Animal Rights," Melvin Maddocks enters a plea for tolerance and reasoned discussion. According to Jean Bethke Elshtain in "Why Worry About the Animals?" humans don't deserve peace of mind over the fates of animals in our society. Elshtain examines recent efforts by the animal rights movement to curtail the abuses administered to nonhuman creatures in the name of progress. This movement holds as its major premise that, as Elshtain puts it, "animals have rights, and violating them constitutes oppression." The unit closes with a philosophical exploration of the ideas that have led animal rights activists to this conclusion. In "Are Animals People Too?" Robert Wright offers a searching analysis of a position that just a few years ago would have been considered extremist by most people. Is America poised at the brink of another great social revolution? According to Wright, the animal rights people are making progress and continue to win followers. It may not be long before the rest of America begins to think more carefully about the other creatures living among us.

MELVIN MADDOCKS

Animal Rights [WORLD MONITOR / October 1989]

Animal rights could just be "the next big cause," a *Fortune* magazine editor has speculated in one of those end-of-the-decade predictions beloved by journalists.

Well, the numbers are certainly there. In the United States alone some seven thousand animal protection groups exist, totaling some ten million members. Indeed, one may get the impression that no subject (including nuclear war) captures the impassioned attention of so many people, at least in those parts of the world rich enough to afford a certain luxury in their scruples, as in other matters.

It would take an Aesop—who knew his humans as well as his animals—to do justice to the cacophony of voices now declaring confidently what animals think and feel and want and are entitled to. Or do not think, do not feel, do not want, and are not entitled to. For The Enemy—principally furriers, the meat industry, and the scientists in animal experiment laboratories—also can and do participate in this most variegated debate, along with every kind of animal-rights activist from vegetarians carrying polite petitions to especially radical antivivisectionists carrying bombs.

As the naturalist Roger Caras has put it: "Everybody is so angry at everybody else nobody is really listening." In an apt metaphor he compares the shouting matches to "feeding time in the monkey house"—nor is he excluding the quarrels within the ranks of animal-rights activists.

Such muggings in the guise of reasoned discussion! Even moderate activists are routinely dismissed by their critics as "cranks" or "kooks," and nastily confused with the militant minority that vandalizes biomedical laboratories and spits on fur coats and, on occasion, assaults the people inhabiting both. For their part, animal-rights activists are likely to call scientists performing animal experiments "butchers" and to accuse even pet owners of being "supremacist" in patronizing their cats and dogs.

4

Melvin Maddocks (b. 1924) is a contributing columnist for World Monitor *and a contributing writer for* Time. *He has also published articles in* Sports Illustrated, *the* Atlantic Monthly, Smithsonian, *and other publications. He says that "Animal Rights" set a record for protest mail at the* World Monitor.

As for meat-consumers: "Those who still eat flesh when they could do otherwise have no claim to be serious moralists," according to one vegetarian absolutist.

No wonder a lover of animals (and a lover of humans) may not be sure he wants the "cause" of animal rights to grow even bigger. Until these polemicists become less dogmatic, less confrontational, who will learn what there is to learn from the ironies inherent in both sides of the issue?

Let the lesson in ambiguity begin with the activists:

The glue in the binding of animal-rights books contains animal byprod-   8
ucts. So does the ink and the paper used to create demonstration signs reading "Stop torturing animals." When activists picket against fur coats, they march in leather shoes, tanned from animal skins. If they break into an animal lab, the very film they use to document animal abuse depends upon photographic gelatin, composed from ground animal bones. And if, in their outrage, they are tempted to blow up the lab, what will the dynamite list in its recipe of destruction? Glycerin or glycerol—commonly using animal oils and fats in its natural form.

Where are the clean hands?

Meanwhile, the chief ideologues of the opposition—the scientists—are driven to their own absurdities in their competing pretenses to purity. If only they are allowed to continue with their animal experiments, what "magic bullets" they promise to discover to cure cancer and AIDS—while inventing the perfectly tear-free shampoo on the side. Enough! Must they and their apologists leave the impression that every time a laboratory rat dies, a child's life is saved?

This whole cold war is badly in need of its own détente—its recess from the din of ideology. All the talk about "rights"!—the "right" to research vs. the "rights" of animals, not to mention the "rights" of consumers. The word is invoked as a debater's reflex. "Rights" are claimed so automatically that they threaten to become morally meaningless, simply the "I want!" on the tip of everybody's tongue, on the top of everybody's placard thrust toward the camera for the evening news.

Should "rights" be given a cooling-down period in public rhetoric?   12
Temporarily the word might be reserved for children who are starving, women who are treated like chattels, and the 200 million human beings now estimated to be in slavery, including those sold in the Sudan for £10—like animals.

In fact, animal protection would benefit from being approached as a pragmatic business rather than a "cause." The hunting of animals on wildlife refuges, the slaughter of African elephants for ivory, the application by cosmetics manufacturers of eye-irritancy tests to guinea pigs or rabbits— these are specific abuses that deserve to be rectified specifically. (Toward that end, a handful of cosmetics companies—including Avon, Revlon, and Faberge—have recently ceased testing their products on animals.) To turn them into "rights," to turn the "rights" into a "cause" is more theater than substance, and not always persuasive theater at that. For all the melodrama, there can be a curious coldness at the heart of a "cause." As the rote arguments grow captious, obsessed with perceived villains, they leave little sense of the delights—the gifts—of either animal life or human life, or the rewarding interplay between the two.

Not infrequently a low-level materialism hangs over the controversy. Do the adversaries realize how close they come to agreement in their rather dreary shared assumption about the practically identical nature of humans and animals? For what real difference does it make whether you're talking about human-like animals as a "rights" activist or about animal-like humans as an experimenting biologist?

It is noticeable that Albert Schweitzer's once-famous phrase "reverence for life," with its religious implication, gets cited rarely nowadays. As many (though not all) "rights" activists see it, religion supports a hierarchy of human dominance in nature—a "speciesism"—that they take to be as offensive as racism. Many (though not all) biologists find religion guilty of wincing at their brute Darwinian facts.

There is idealism in the scientist's dedication to saving human life.   16

There is equal idealism in the "rights" activist's dedication to saving animal life, on the premise that the survival of the truly fittest lies in abetting the survival of all life.

Still, where else but in awe, in piety—in poetry—is nature finally viewed whole? Transcending any and all "causes," Gerard Manley Hopkins wrote as if he were witnessing the first day of creation:

> Glory be to God for dappled things—
> For skies as couple-colour as a brindled cow;
> For rose-moles all in stipple upon trout that swim

If the entire poem, "Pied Beauty," were stuck above the desks of scientists in animal labs, and written on the placards of "rights" activists picketing outside, and posted by the entrance to fur salons, hunting clubs, and abattoirs, everybody would be gloriously reminded at least of what they are fighting over.

Points to Consider

1. According to Maddocks, what is the greatest problem facing the participants in the animal rights debate? Does Maddocks believe that reasoned discussion is possible in the case of animal rights? How does he characterize most of the rhetoric surrounding the debate?

2. What irony does Maddocks find inherent in the activists' position? What

irony does he find inherent in the scientists' position? Does he feel that such contradictions can be reconciled?

3. According to the author, how do most people on both sides of the issue use the word "rights"? What has the word come to mean in the animal protection debate?

4. Why does Maddocks believe that the adversaries in the debate hold practically the same basic assumptions? What place does religious principle have in the debate? Why does Maddocks include a passage from the work of the poet Gerald Manley Hopkins?

<hr>

JEAN BETHKE ELSHTAIN

Why Worry About the Animals?

[THE PROGRESSIVE / March 1990]

These things are happening or have happened recently:

- The wings of seventy-four mallard ducks are snapped to see whether crippled birds can survive in the wild. (They can't.)
- Infant monkeys are deafened to study their social behavior, or turned into amphetamine addicts to see what happens to their stress level.
- Monkeys are separated from their mothers, kept in isolation, addicted to drugs, and induced to commit "aggressive" acts.

<hr>

JEAN BETHKE ELSHTAIN (b. 1941) is Centennial Professor of Political Science at Vanderbilt University. She holds a Ph.D. from Brandeis University and has contributed many scholarly essays to books and such periodicals as Quest, *the* Nation, *the* Progressive, *and* Dissent. *Elshtain is the author of* Public Man, Private Woman: Women in Social and Political Thought *(1981),* Meditations on Modern Political Thought *(1986), and* Women and War *(1987). Most recently, she coedited (with Sheila Tobias)* Women, Militarism, and the Arms Race *(1990).*

- Pigs are blowtorched and observed to see how they respond to third-degree burns. No painkillers are used.
- Monkeys are immersed in water and vibrated to cause brain damage.
- For thirteen years, baboons have their brains bashed at the University of Pennsylvania as research assistants laugh at signs of the animals' distress.
- Monkeys are dipped in boiling water; other animals are shot in the face with high-powered rifles.

The list of cruelties committed in the name of "science" or "research" could be expanded endlessly. "Fully 80 percent of the experiments involving rhesus monkeys are either unnecessary, represent useless duplication of previous work, or could utilize nonanimal alternatives," says John E. McArdle, a biologist and specialist in primates at Illinois Wesleyan University.

Growing awareness of animal abuse is helping to build an increasingly militant animal-welfare movement in this country and abroad—a movement that is beginning to have an impact on public policy. Secretary of Health and Human Services Frederick Goodwin complained recently that complying with new federal regulations on the use—or abuse—of animals will drain off some 17 percent of the research funds appropriated to the National Institutes of Health. (It is cheaper to purchase, use, and destroy animals than to retool for alternative procedures.) One of the institutes, the National Institute of Mental Health, spends about thirty million dollars a year on research that involves pain and suffering for animals.

The new animal-welfare activists are drawing attention in part because   4
of the tactics they espouse. Many preach and practice civil disobedience, violating laws against, say, breaking and entering. Some have been known to resort to violence against property and—on a few occasions—against humans.

Some individuals and groups have always fretted about human responsibility toward nonhuman creatures. In the ancient world, the historian Plutarch and the philosopher Porphyry were among those who insisted that human excellence embodied a refusal to inflict unnecessary suffering on all other creatures, human and nonhuman.

But with the emergence of the Western rationalist tradition, animals lost the philosophic struggle. Two of that tradition's great exponents, René Descartes and Immanuel Kant, dismissed out of hand the moral worth of animals. Descartes's view, which has brought comfort to every human who decides to confine, poison, cripple, infect, or dismember animals in the interest of human knowledge, was the more extreme: he held that animals are simply machines, devoid of consciousness or feeling. Kant, more sophisticated in his ethical reasoning, knew that animals could suffer but denied that they were self-conscious. Therefore, he argued, they could aptly serve as means to human ends.

To make sure that human sensibilities would not be troubled by the groans, cries, and yelps of suffering animals—which might lead some to suspect that animals not only bleed but feel pain—researchers have for a century subjected dogs and other animals to an operation called a centriculocordectomy, which destroys their vocal cords.

Still, there have long been groups that placed the suffering of animals   8
within the bounds of human concern. In the nineteenth and early twentieth centuries, such reform movements as women's suffrage and abolitionism made common cause with societies for the prevention of cruelty to animals. On one occasion in 1907, British suffragettes, trade-unionists, and their animal-welfare allies battled London University medical students in a riot triggered by the vivisection of a dog.

Traditionally, such concern has been charitable and, frequently, highly sentimental. Those who perpetrated the worst abuses against animals were denounced for their "beastly" behavior—the farmer who beat or starved his horse; the householder who chained and kicked his dog; the aristocratic hunter who, with his guests, slew birds by the thousands in a single day on his private game preserve.

For the most part, however, animals have been viewed, even by those with "humane" concerns, as means to human ends. The charitable impulse, therefore, had a rather condescending, patronizing air: alas, the poor creatures deserve our pity.

The new animal-welfare movement incorporates those historic concerns but steers them in new directions. Philosophically, animal-rights activists seek to close the gap between "human" and "beast," challenging the entire Western rationalist tradition which holds that the ability to reason abstractly is *the* defining human attribute. (In that tradition, women were often located on a scale somewhere between "man" and "beast," being deemed human but not quite rational.)

Politically, the new abolitionists, as many animal-welfare activists call   12
themselves, eschew sentimentalism in favor of a tough-minded, insistent claim that animals, too, have rights, and that violating those rights constitutes oppression. It follows that animals must be liberated—and since they cannot liberate themselves in the face of overwhelming human hegemony, they require the help of liberators much as slaves did in the last century.

Thus, the rise of vocal movements for animal well-being has strong historic antecedents. What is remarkable about the current proliferation of efforts is their scope and diversity. Some proclaim animal "rights." Others speak of animal "welfare" or "protection." Still others find the term "equality" most apt, arguing that we should have "equal concern" for the needs of all sentient creatures.

When so many issues clamor for our attention, when so many problems demand our best attempts at fair-minded solution, why animals, why now? There is no simple explanation for the explosion of concern, but it is clearly linked to themes of peace and justice. Perhaps it can be summed up this way: those who are troubled by the question of who is or is not within the circle of moral concern; those who are made queasy by our use and abuse of living beings for our own ends; those whose dreams of a better world are animated by some notion of a peaceable kingdom, *should* consider our relationship with the creatures that inhabit our planet with us—the creatures that have helped sustain us and that may share a similar fate with us unless we find ways to deflect if not altogether end the destruction of our earthly habitat.

Dozens of organizations have sprung up, operating alongside—and sometimes in conflict with—such older mainline outfits as the Humane Society, the Anti-Vivisection League, and the World Wildlife Fund. Among the new groups are People for the Ethical Treatment of Animals (PETA), Trans-Species Unlimited, In Defense of Animals, the Gorilla Foundation, Primarily Primates, Humane Farming Association, Farm Animal Reform, Alliance for Animals, Citizens to End Animal Suffering and Exploitation (CEASE), Whale Adoption Project, Digit Fund—the list goes on and on.

Some organizations focus on the plight of animals on factory farms, 16 especially the condition of anemic, imprisoned veal calves kept in darkness and unable to turn around until they are killed at fourteen weeks. Others are primarily concerned with conditions in the wild, where the habitat of the panda, among others, is being destroyed or where great and wonderful creatures like the black rhinoceros and the African elephant or magnificent cats like the snow leopard or the Siberian tiger are marching toward extinction, victims of greedy buyers of illegal tusks or pelts.

Another group of activists clusters around the use of animals in such profitable pursuits as greyhound racing, where dogs by the hundreds are destroyed once they cease "earning their keep," or in tourist attractions where such wonderfully intelligent social beings as the orca and the dolphin are turned into circus freaks for profit. In the wild, orcas can live for up to one hundred years; in captivity, the average, sadly misnamed "killer whale" lasts about five.

Those wonderful chimpanzees that have been taught to speak to us through sign-language also arouse concern. If the funding ends or a researcher loses interest, they are sometimes killed, sometimes turned over to the less-than-tender mercies of laboratory researchers to be addicted to cocaine, infected with a virus, or subjected to some other terrible fate. Eugene Linden describes, in his study *Silent Partners,* chimps desperately trying to convey their pain and fear and sadness to uncomprehending experimenters.

Use of animals in war research is an industry in itself, though one usually shielded from public view. Monkeys are the most likely subjects of experiments designed to measure the effects of neutron-bomb radiation and the toxicity of chemical-warfare agents. Beginning in 1957, monkeys were placed at varying distances from ground zero during atomic testing; those that didn't die immediately were encaged so that the "progress" of their various cancers might be noted.

Radiation experiments on primates continue. Monkeys' eyes are irradiated, and the animals are subjected to shocks of up to twelve hundred volts. Junior researchers are assigned the "death watch," and what they see are primates so distressed that they claw at themselves and even bite hunks from their own arms or legs in a futile attempt to stem the pain. At a government proving ground in Aberdeen, Maryland, monkeys are exposed to chemical-warfare agents. 20

Dolphins, animals of exquisite intelligence, have been trained by the military in such scenarios as injecting carbon dioxide cartridges into Vietnamese divers and planting and removing mines. The Navy announced in April 1989 that it would continue its thirty-million-dollar clandestine program, expanded in the Reagan years, to put dolphins to military use. The aim, the *New York Times* reported, is to use dolphins captured in the Gulf of Mexico to guard the Trident Nuclear Submarine Base at Bangor, Washington.

Several years ago, when I was writing a book on women and war, I came across references to the use of dogs in Vietnam. When I called the Pentagon and was put through to the chief of military history, Southeast Asia Branch, he told me that no books existed on the subject, but he did send me an excerpt from the *Vietnam War Almanac* that stated the U.S. military "made extensive use of dogs for a variety of duties in Vietnam, including scouting, mine detecting, tracking, sentry duty, flushing out tunnels, and drug detecting." Evidently, many of these dogs were killed rather than returned home, since it was feared their military training ill-suited them for civilian life.

Much better known, because of an increasingly successful animal-rights campaign, is the use of animals to test such household products as furniture polish and such cosmetics as shampoo and lipstick.

For years, industry has determined the toxicity of floor wax and detergents by injecting various substances into the stomachs of beagles, rabbits, and calves, producing vomiting, convulsions, respiratory illness, and paralysis. The so-called LD (lethal dose) 50 test ends only when half the animals in a test group have died. No anesthesia or pain killers are administered. 24

Dr. Andrew Rowan, assistant dean of the Tufts University School of Medicine, has offered persuasive evidence that such testing methods are crude and inaccurate measures of a product's safety. For one thing, a number of potentially significant variables, including the stress of laboratory living, are not taken into account, thus tainting any comparison of the effect of a given substance on human consumers.

The LD50 is notoriously unreproducible; the method for rating irritation is extremely subjective; and interspecies variations make test results highly suspect when applied to the human organism.

Most notorious of the "tests" deployed by the multibillion-dollar cosmetics industry is the Draize, which has been used since the 1940s to measure the potential irritative effects of products. Rabbits—used because their eyes do not produce tears and, therefore, cannot cleanse themselves—are placed into stocks and their eyes are filled with foreign substances. When a rabbit's eyes ulcerate—again, no pain killers are used—the cosmetics testers (who are usually not trained laboratory researchers) report a result. To call this procedure "scientific" is to demean authentic science.

Curiously, neither the LD50 test nor the Draize is required by law. They 28 continue in use because manufacturers want to avoid alarming consumers by placing warning labels on products. More accurate methods available include computer simulations to measure toxicity, cell-culture systems, and organ-culture tests that use chicken-egg membranes.

The disdainful response by corporate America to animal-protection concerns seems, at least in this area, to be undergoing a slow shift toward new laboratory techniques that abandon wasteful, crude, and cruel animal testing. Several large cosmetics manufacturers, including Revlon, have only recently announced that they will phase out animal testing, confirming the claim of animal-welfare groups that the tests are unnecessary.

Among the nastier issues in the forefront of the "animal wars" is the controversy over hunting and trapping.

It's estimated that about seventeen million fur-bearing animals (plus "trash" animals—including pets—the trapper doesn't want) are mangled each year in steel-jaw leg-hold traps that tear an animal's flesh and break its bones. Many die of shock or starvation before the trapper returns. Some animals chew off part of a limb in order to escape. More than sixty countries now ban the leg-hold trap, requiring the use of less painful and damaging devices.

Protests against the manufacture, sale, and wearing of fur coats have 32 been aggressively—and successfully—mounted in Western Europe. In Holland, fur sales have dropped 80 percent in the last few years. Radical groups in Sweden have broken into fur farms to release minks and foxes. An effort to shame women who wear fur has had enormous impact in Great Britain.

Similar campaigns have been mounted in the United States, but the fur industry is waging a well-financed counterattack in this country. Curiously, the industry's efforts have been tacitly supported by some rights-absolutists within feminism who see wearing a fur coat as a woman's right. It's difficult to think of a greater reductio ad absurdum of the notion of "freedom of choice," but it seems to appeal to certain adherents of upwardly mobile, choice-obsessed political orthodoxy.

Hunting may be the final frontier for animal-welfare groups. Because hunting is tied to the right to bear arms, any criticism of hunting is construed as an attack on constitutional freedoms by hunting and gun organizations, including the powerful and effective National Rifle Association. A bumper sticker I saw on a pickup truck in Northampton, Massachusetts, may tell the tale: MY WIFE, YES. MY DOG, MAYBE. BUT MY GUN, NEVER.

For some animal protectionists, the case against hunting is open and shut. They argue that the vast majority of the estimated 170 million animals shot to death in any given year are killed for blood sport, not for food, and that the offspring of these slaughtered creatures are left to die of exposure or starvation. Defenders of blood sports see them as a skill and a tradition, a lingering relic of America's great frontier past. Others—from nineteenth century feminists to the Norman Mailer of *Why Are We in Vietnam?*—link the national mania for hunting with a deeper thirst for violence.

I am not convinced there is an inherent connection between animal 36 killing and a more general lust for violence, but some disquieting evidence is beginning to accumulate. Battered and abused women in rural areas often testify, for example, that their spouses also abused animals, especially cows, by stabbing them with pitchforks, twisting their ears, kicking them, or, in one reported incident, using a board with a nail in it to beat a cow to death.

But even people who recoil from hunting and other abuses of animals often find it difficult to condemn such experiments as those cited at the beginning of this article, which are, after all, conducted to serve "science" and, perhaps, to alleviate human pain and suffering. Sorting out this issue is no easy task if one is neither an absolute prohibitionist nor a relentless defender of the scientific establishment. When gross abuses come to light, they are often reported in ways that allow and encourage us to distance ourselves from emotional and ethical involvement. Thus the case of the baboons whose brains were bashed in at the University of Pennsylvania prompted the *New York Times* to editorialize, on July 31, 1985, that the animals "seemed" to be suffering. They *were* suffering, and thousands of animals suffer every day.

Reasonable people should be able to agree on this: that alternatives to research that involves animal suffering must be vigorously sought; that there is no excuse for such conditions as dogs lying with open incisions, their entrails exposed, or monkeys with untreated, protruding broken bones, exposed muscle tissue, and infected wounds, living in grossly unsanitary conditions amidst feces and rotting food; that quick euthanasia should be administered to a suffering animal after the conclusion of a pain-inducing procedure; that pre- and postsurgical care must be provided for animals; that research should not be needlessly duplicated, thereby wasting animal lives, desensitizing generations of researchers, and flushing tax dollars down the drain.

What stands in the way of change? Old habits, bad science, unreflective cruelty, profit, and, in some cases, a genuine fear that animal-welfare groups want to stop all research dead in its tracks. "Scientists fear shackles on research," intones one report. But why are scientists so reluctant to promote such research alternatives as modeling, in-vitro techniques, and the use of lower organisms? Because they fear that the public may gain wider knowledge of what goes on behind the laboratory door. Surely those using animals should be able to explain themselves and to justify their expenditure of the lives, bodies, and minds of other creatures.

There is, to be sure, no justification for the harassment and terror tactics   40
used by some animal-welfare groups. But the scientist who is offended when an animal-welfare proponent asks, "How would you feel if someone treated your child the way you treat laboratory animals?" should ponder one of the great ironies in the continuing debate: research on animals is justified on grounds that they are "so like us."

I *do* appreciate the ethical dilemma here. As a former victim of polio, I have thought long and hard for years about animal research and human welfare. This is where I come down, at least for now:

First, most human suffering in this world cannot be ameliorated in any way by animal experimentation. Laboratory infliction of suffering on animals will not keep people healthy in Asia, Africa, and Latin America. As philosopher Peter Singer has argued, we already know how to cure what ails people in desperate poverty; they need "adequate nutrition, sanitation, and health care. It has been estimated that 250,000 children die each week around the world, and that one-quarter of these deaths are by dehydration due to diarrhea. A simple treatment, already known and needing no animal experimentation, could prevent the deaths of these children."

Second, it is not clear that a cure for terrible and thus far incurable diseases such as AIDS is best promoted with animal experimentation. Some American experts on AIDS admit that French scientists are making more rapid progress toward a vaccine because they are working directly with human volunteers, a course of action Larry Kramer, a gay activist, has urged upon American scientists. Americans have been trying since 1984 to infect chimpanzees with AIDS, but after the expenditure of millions of dollars, AIDS has not been induced in any nonhuman animal. Why continue down this obviously flawed route?

Third, we could surely agree that a new lipstick color, or an even more   44
dazzling floor wax, should never be promoted for profit over the wounded bodies of animals. The vast majority of creatures tortured and killed each year suffer for *nonmedical* reasons. Once this abuse is eliminated, the really hard cases having to do with human medical advance and welfare can be debated, item by item.

Finally, what is at stake is the exhaustion of the eighteenth century model of humanity's relationship to nature, which had, in the words of philosopher

Mary Midgley, "built into it a bold, contemptuous rejection of the nonhuman world."

Confronted as we are with genetic engineering and a new eugenics, with the transformation of farms where animals ranged freely into giant factories where animals are processed and produced like objects, with callous behavior on a scale never before imagined under the rubric of "science," we can and must do better than to dismiss those who care as irrational and emotional animal-lovers who are thinking with their hearts (not surprisingly, their ranks are heavily filled with women), and who are out to put a stop to the forward march of rationalism and science.

We humans do not deserve peace of mind on this issue. Our sleep should be troubled and our days riddled with ethical difficulties as we come to realize the terrible toll one definition of "progress" has taken on our fellow creatures.

We must consider our meat-eating habits as well. Meat-eating is one of 48 the most volatile, because most personal, of all animal-welfare questions. Meat-eaters do not consider themselves immoral, though hard-core vegetarians find meat-eating repugnant—the consumption of corpses. Such feminist theorists as Carol Adams insist that there is a connection between the butchering of animals and the historic maltreatment of women. Certainly, there is a politics of meat that belongs on the agenda along with other animal-welfare issues.

I, for one, do not believe humans and animals have identical rights. But I do believe that creatures who can reason in their own ways, who can suffer, who are mortal beings like ourselves, have a value and dignity we must take into account. Animals are not simply a means to our ends.

When I was sixteen years old, I journeyed on a yellow school bus from LaPorte, Colorado, to Fairbanks, Iowa, on a 4-H Club "exchange trip." On the itinerary was a visit to a meat-packing plant in Des Moines. As vivid as the day I witnessed it is the scene I replay of men in blood-drenched coats "bleeding" pigs strung up by their heels on a slowly moving conveyer belt. The pigs—bright and sensitive creatures, as any person who has ever met one knows—were screaming in terror before the sharp, thin blade entered their jugular veins. They continued to struggle and squeal until they writhed and fell silent.

The men in the slaughter room wore boots. The floor was awash in blood. I was horrified. But I told myself this was something I should remember. For a few months I refused to eat pork. But then I fell back into old habits—this was Colorado farm country in the late 1950s, after all.

But at one point, a few years ago, that scene and those cries of terror 52 returned. This time I decided I would not forget, even though I knew my peace of mind would forever be disturbed.

Points to Consider

1. Jean Bethke Elshtain draws our attention to the sometimes violent tactics of the animal rights activists. Is there any evidence in her essay that she supports such activities? Do you believe that such actions can be justified?

2. At one point in her essay, Elshtain states that "philosophically, animal-rights activists seek to close the gap between 'human' and 'beast.'" What is the traditional distinction between the two? What assumptions underlie this distinction? On what grounds can activists argue against this distinction?

3. While the author admits that she is "not convinced there is an inherent connection between animal killing and a more general lust for violence," she does offer possible evidence of such a connection. What is the nature of this evidence? Do you find it conclusive?

4. What arguments does Elshtain offer in favor of ending most animal research? Why does she invoke the problem of world poverty as the source of most human suffering? Does she believe that human suffering can be alleviated through animal experimentation?

ROBERT WRIGHT

Are Animals People Too? [THE NEW REPUBLIC / March 12, 1990]

I recently interviewed several animal rights activists in hopes that they would say some amusing, crazy-sounding things that might liven up this article. More often than not I was disappointed. They would come close to making unreservedly extremist pronouncements but then step back from the

---

ROBERT WRIGHT (b. 1957) is senior editor of the New Republic. A 1979 graduate of Princeton University, Wright has worked as a newspaper reporter, an editor at the Wilson Quarterly, and an editor at the Sciences. His writing has also appeared in the Atlantic Monthly. He is the author of Three Scientists and Their Gods (1988).

brink, leaving me with a quote that was merely provocative. For example, Ingrid Newkirk, cofounder of People for the Ethical Treatment of Animals (PETA), seemed on the verge of conceding that Frank Perdue is no better than Adolf Hitler—a proposition that technically follows her premise that animals possess the moral status of humans (and from references in animal rights literature to the ongoing "animal holocaust"). But she wouldn't go all the way. "He's the animals' Hitler, I'll give you that," she said. "If you were a chicken . . . you wouldn't think he was Mother Teresa." The other cofounder of PETA, Alex Pacheco, was not much more helpful. "You and I are equal to the lobsters when it comes to being boiled alive," he said, raising my hopes. But, he added, "I don't mean I couldn't decide which one to throw in, myself or the lobster."

The biggest disappointment was a woman who went by the pseudonym "Helen." She was a member of the Animal Liberation Front, a shadowy group that goes around breaking into scientific laboratories, documenting the conditions therein, and sometimes burning down the labs (minus the animals, which are typically "liberated"—taken somewhere else—in the process). Given all the intrigue involved in interviewing "Helen"—I had to "put out the word" that I wanted to talk with an ALF member, and when she called she always used a street-side phone booth and never left a number—I expected a rich encounter. This hope grew when I found out that she had participated in a recent lab-burning at the University of Arizona. But as professed arsonists go, Helen seemed like a very nice and fairly reasonable person. She was a combination of earnest moral anguish ("For the most part, people just aren't aware of how much suffering and death goes into what they eat and wear. . . . Most people just literally don't know") and crisp professionalism ("Whether I have any animosity toward [laboratory researchers] is irrelevant. . . . I just do everything I can to move them into a different job category"). And though her reverence for life may strike you as creepy—she picks up spiders off the floor and moves them outdoors, rather than squash them—it is not unbounded. She assured me that if termites were destroying her home, she would call an exterminator.

One reason for this general failure to gather satisfactorily extremist quotes is that animal rights activists have become more media-savvy, developing a surer sense for when they are being baited. But another reason is my own failure to find their ideas extremist. Slowly I seem to be getting drawn into the logic of animal rights. I still eat meat, wear a leather belt, and support the use of animals in important scientific research. But not without a certain amount of cognitive dissonance.

The animal rights movement, which has mushroomed during the past decade, most conspicuously in the growth of PETA (membership around three hundred thousand), is distinguished from the animal welfare movement, as represented by, for example, the Humane Society of the United States. Animal *welfare* activists don't necessarily claim that animals are the moral equivalent of humans, just that animals' feelings deserve some consideration; we shouldn't needlessly hurt them—with pointless experimentation, say, or by making fur coats. And just about every thinking person, if pressed, will agree that animal welfare is a legitimate idea. Hardly anyone believes in kicking dogs.

But the truth is that animal welfare is just the top of a slippery slope that leads to animal rights. Once you buy the premise that animals can experience pain and pleasure, and that their welfare therefore deserves *some* consideration, you're on the road to comparing yourself with a lobster. There may be some exit ramps along the way—plausible places to separate welfare from rights—but I can't find any. And if you don't manage to find one, you wind up not only with a rather more sanguine view of animal rights but also with a more cynical view of the concept of human rights and its historical evolution.

None of this is to say that a few minutes of philosophical reflection will lead you to start wearing dumpling-shaped fake-leather shoes, sporting a "Meat is Murder" button, or referring to your pet dog as your "companion animal." The stereotype about the people who do these things—that they're ill at ease in human society, even downright antagonistic toward other humans—is generally wrong, but the stereotype that they're, well, *different* from most people is not. These are dyed-in-the-wool activists, and if they weren't throwing themselves into this cause, they would probably be throwing themselves into some other cause. (Pacheco, for example, had originally planned to become a priest.) Moreover, very few of them were converted to the movement solely or mainly via philosophy. Many will say they were critically influenced by the book *Animal Liberation* (1975), written by the Australian ethicist Peter Singer, but reading Singer was for most of them merely a ratifying experience, a seal of philosophical approval for their intuitive revulsion at animal suffering. Pacheco received a copy of the book the same week he got grossed out while touring a Canadian slaughterhouse. He later gave a copy to Newkirk, who was then chief of Animal Disease Control for the District of Columbia. Around that time she spent a day trying to rescue some starving, neglected horses that were locked in their stalls and mired in mud. That's when it hit her: "It didn't make sense. I had spent the whole day trying to get some starving horses out of a stall and here I was going home to eat some other animal." This gut perception is a recurring theme, as crystallized by Helen: "I just realized that if I wouldn't eat my dog, why should I eat a cow?"

Good question. And implicit in it is the core of the case for animal rights: the modest claim—not disputed by anyone who has ever owned a dog or cat, so far as I know—that animals are sentient beings, capable of pleasure and pain. People who would confine natural rights to humans commonly talk about the things we have that animals don't—complex language, sophisticated reasoning, a highly evolved culture. But none of these is important, for moral purposes, in the way that sheer sentience is.

One way to appreciate this is through a simple thought experiment. Suppose there's a planet populated by organisms that look and act exactly like humans. They walk, talk, flirt, go to law school, blush in response to embarrassing comments, and discuss their impending deaths in glum tones. Now suppose it turns out they're automatons, made out of silicon chips— or even made out of flesh and blood. The important thing is that all their behavior—their blushing, their discussion of death—is entirely a product of the physical circuitry inside their heads and isn't accompanied by any subjective experience; they can't feel pain, pleasure, or anything else. In other words (to use the terminology of Thomas Nagel), it isn't like anything to be them. 8

Is there anything particularly immoral about slapping one of them in the face? Most everyone would say: obviously not, since it doesn't hurt. How about killing one of them? Again, no; their death doesn't preclude their future experience of happiness, as with real live humans, or cause any pain for friends and relatives. There is no apparent reason to bestow any moral status whatsoever on these creatures, much less the exalted status that the human species now enjoys. They have powerful brains, complex language, and high culture, but none of this makes them significant.

Now rearrange the variables: subtract all these attributes and add sentience. In other words, take all the robots off the planet and populate it with nonhuman animals: chimps, armadillos, dogs, etc. Is there anything immoral about gratuitously hurting or killing one of these? Do they have individual rights? Most people would answer yes to the first question, and some would answer yes to the second. But the main point is that few people would quickly and easily say "no" to either, because these are harder questions than the robot question. Sentience lies at the core of our moral thinking, and language, intelligence, etc., lie nearer the periphery. Sentience seems definitely a necessary and arguably a sufficient condition for the possession of high moral status (experiments 1 and 2, respectively), whereas the other attributes are arguably necessary but definitely not sufficient (experiments 2 and 1, respectively).

The best way to get a better fix on exactly which traits are prerequisites for moral status is simply to try to explain why they *should* be. Take sentience first. We all agree from personal experience that pain is a bad thing, that no one should have the right to inflict it on us, and consistency (part of any moral system) dictates that we agree not to inflict it on anyone else. Makes sense. But now try to say something comparably compelling about why great reasoning ability or complex language are crucial to moral status. Also, try to do the same with self-consciousness—our awareness of our own existence. (This is another uniquely human attribute commonly invoked in these discussions, but we couldn't isolate it in experiment 1 above because an organism can't have it without having sentience.)

If you accept this challenge, you'll almost certainly go down one of two   12
paths, neither of which will get you very far. First, you may try to establish that self-consciousness, complex language, etc., are the hallmarks of "spirit," the possession of which places us in some special category. This is a perfectly fine thing to believe, but it's hard to *argue* for. It depends much more on religious conviction than on any plausible line of reasoning.

The second path people take in asserting the moral significance of uniquely human attributes is even less successful, because it leads to a booby trap. This is the argument that self-consciousness and reason and language give humans a dimension of suffering that mere animals lack: because we can anticipate pain and death; and because we know that death will represent the end of our consciousness forever; and because we recognize that threats to one citizen may represent a threat to us all—because of all this, the protection of human rights is essential to everyone's peace of mind; the torture or murder of anyone in town, as conveyed to the public via language and then reflected upon at length, makes everyone tremendously fearful. So a robust conception of individual rights is essential for the welfare of a human society in a way that it isn't for, say, the welfare of a chicken society.

Sounds nice, but it amounts to philosophical surrender. To rely completely on this argument is to concede that language, reason, and self-consciousness are morally important *only* to the extent that they magnify suffering or happiness. Pain and pleasure, in other words, are the currency of moral assessment. The several uniquely human attributes may revaluate the currency, but the currency possesses some value with or without them. And many, if not all, nonhuman animals seems to possess the currency in some quantity. So unless you can come up with a nonarbitrary reason for saying that their particular quantities are worthless while our particular quantities are precious, you have to start thinking about animals in a whole new light. This explains why Peter Singer, in *Animal Liberation,* readily admits that the human brain is unique in its ability to thus compound suffering.

Once the jaws of this philosophical trap have closed on the opponents of animal rights, no amount of struggling can free them. Let them insist that language, reason, and self-consciousness *immensely* raise the moral stakes for humans. Let them add, even, that our sheer neurological complexity makes us experience raw pain more profoundly than, say, dogs or even mice do. Grant them, in other words, that in the grand utilitarian calculus, one day of solid suffering by a single human equals one day's suffering by ten thousand laboratory rats. Grant them all of this, and they still lose, because the point is that animals have now been *admitted* to the utilitarian calculus. If it is immoral, as we all believe it is, to walk up to a stranger and inflict 1/10,000 of one day's suffering (nine seconds' worth), then it is equally immoral to walk up and inflict one day's suffering on a single laboratory rat.

Actually, granting animals utilitarian value doesn't technically mean you have to extend individual rights to them. As far as sheer philosophical consistency goes, you can equally well take rights away from humans. You can say: sure, it makes sense to kill one hundred baboons to save the life of one human, but it also makes sense to kill a human to save the life of one hundred baboons. Whatever you say, though, you have to go one way or the other, letting such equations work either in both directions or in neither. Unless you can create a moral ratchet called "human rights"—and I don't see any way to do it—you have to choose between a planet on which every sentient creature has rights and a planet on which none does.

And of course if no creature on earth has rights, then it can make sense to kill a human not just for the sake of one hundred baboons, but for the sake of two humans—or just in the name of the greater good. In other words, the logic used by animal rights activists turns out to play into the hands of the Adolf Hitlers of the world no less than the Albert Schweitzers. In *Darkness at Noon*, when Ivanov describes Stalin's rule as belonging to the school of "vivisection morality," Arthur Koestler is onto something more than good allegory.

Before figuring out whether to follow this logic toward vegetarianism or totalitarianism, let's remove it from the realm of abstraction. Spending an evening watching videotapes supplied by PETA—such as *The Animals Film*, narrated by Julie Christie—is a fairly disturbing experience. This is partly because the people who made it gave it a subtle shrillness that reflects what is most annoying about the animal rights movement. There are man-on-the-street interviews conducted by an obnoxious, self-righteous interrogator demanding to know how people can own dogs and eat Big Macs; there is the assumption that viewers will find the late McDonald's founder Ray Kroc—a seemingly likable guy shown innocently discussing how he settled on the name "McDonald's"—abhorrent; there is a simple-minded anticapitalist undercurrent (as if factory farmers in socialist countries spent their time giving foot massages to hogs); and there is grating atonal music meant to make the sight of blood more disturbing than it naturally is.

And that's plenty disturbing, thank you. Take, for example, the chickens hung by their feet from a conveyer belt that escorts them through an automatic throat slicing machine—this is the culmination of a life spent on the poultry equivalent of a New York subway platform at rush hour. Or consider the deep basketfuls of male chicks, struggling not to smother before they're ground into animal feed. There's also, naturally, the veal: a calf raised in a crate so small that it can't even turn around, much less walk—the better to keep the flesh tender. There are wild furry animals cut almost in half by steel-jawed traps but still conscious. There are rabbits getting noxious chemicals sprayed in their eyes by cosmetics companies.

And these are the animals that *don't* remind you of human beings. [20] Watching these portions of *The Animals Film* is a day at the zoo compared with watching nonhuman primates suffer. If you don't already have a strong sense of identity with chimpanzees, gorillas, and the like—if you doubt that they're capable of crude reasoning, anticipating pain, feeling and expressing deep affection for one another—I suggest you patronize your local zoo (or prison, as animal rights activists would have it) and then get hold of a copy of the ethologist Frans de Waal's two amazing books, *Peace-making Among Primates* and *Chimpanzee Politics*. The commonly cited fact that chimps share about 98 percent of our genes is misleading, to be sure; a handful of genes affecting the brain's development can make a world of difference. Still, if you can watch a toddler chimp or gorilla for long without wanting to file for adoption, you should seek professional help.

In videotapes that Helen helped steal in 1984 from the University of Pennsylvania's Head Injury Clinical Research Center, anesthetized baboons are strapped down and their heads placed in boxlike vices that are violently snapped sixty degrees sideways by a hydraulic machine. Some of the baboons have what appear to be seizures, some go limp, and none looks very happy. Some of the lab workers—as callous as you'd have to become to do their job, perhaps—stand around and make jokes about it all. It's hard to say how much scientific good came of this, because the scientist in question refuses to talk about it. But watching the tapes, you have to hope that the data were markedly more valuable than what's already available from the study of injured humans. In any event, the experiments were halted after PETA publicized the tapes (though ostensibly for sloppy lab technique, such as occasionally inadequate anesthesia, not because of the violent nature of the experiments).

There are certainly many kinds of animal research that seem justified by any reasonable utilitarian calculus. A case in point is the lab Helen helped set afire at the University of Arizona. Among the researchers whose work was destroyed in the attack is a man named Charles Sterling, who is studying a parasite that causes diarrhea in both animals and humans and kills many children in the Third World every year. There is no way fruitfully to study this parasite in, say, a cell culture, so he uses mice, infecting them with the parasite and thereby inducing a nonlethal spell of diarrhea. (The idea repeated mindlessly by so many animal rights activists—that there's almost always an equally effective nonanimal approach to experimentation—is wrong.)

Sterling is one of a handful of workers in this area, and he figures, in over-the-phone, off-the-cuff calculations, that all together they cause around ten thousand to twenty thousand mice-weeks of diarrheal discomfort every year. The apparently realistic goal is to find a cure for a disease that kills more than a hundred thousand children a year. Sounds like a good deal to me. Again, though, the hitch is that to endorse this in a philosophically impeccable way, you have to let go of the concept of human rights, at least as classically conceived.

Then again, human rights isn't what it's classically conceived as being. 24
It isn't some divine law imparted to us from above, or some Platonic truth apprehended through the gift of reason. The idea of individual rights is simply a nonaggression pact among everyone who subscribes to it. It's a deal struck for mutual convenience.

And, actually, it's in some sense a very old deal. A few million years ago, back when human ancestors were not much smarter than chimps, they presumably abided by an implicit and crude concept of individual rights, just as chimps do. Which is to say: life within a troop of, say, fifty or sixty individuals was in practical terms sacred. (Sure, chimps occasionally murder fellow troop members, just as humans do, but this is highly aberrant behavior. Rituals that keep bluster and small-scale aggression from escalating to fatality are well developed. And when they fail, and death occurs, an entire chimp colony may be solemn and subdued for hours or longer as if in mourning.) At the same time, these prehuman primates were presumably much like chimps in being fairly disdainful of the lives of fellow species-members who didn't belong to the troop. At some point in human history, as troops of fifty became tribes of thousands, the circle of morally protected life grew commensurately. But the circle didn't at first extend to other tribes. Indeed, wide acceptance of the idea that people of all nations have equal moral rights is quite recent.

How did it all happen? In one of Singer's later and less famous books, *The Expanding Circle* (Farrar, Straus & Giroux, 1981), whose title refers to exactly this process, he writes as if the circle's expansion has been driven almost Platonically, by the "inherently expansionist nature of reasoning." Once people became civilized and started thinking about the logic behind the reciprocal extension of rights to one another, he says, they were on an intellectual "escalator," and there was no turning back. The idea of uniformly applied ethical strictures "emerges because of the social nature of human beings and the requirements of group living, but in the thought of reasoning beings, it takes on a logic of its own which leads to its extension beyond the bounds of the group."

This, alas, is perhaps too rosy a view. The concept of human rights has grown more inclusive largely through raw politics. Had tribes not found it in their interest to band together—sometimes to massacre other tribes—they wouldn't have had to invent the concept of intertribal rights. Necessity was similarly the mother of moral invention in modern societies. Had the suffragists not deftly wielded political clout, men mightn't have seen the logic of giving women the vote. Had the abolition of slavery not acquired political moment in a war that slaughtered millions, slavery might have long persisted.

Certainly in advances of this sort an important role can be played by intellectual persuasion, by sympathy, by empathy. These can fuse with political power and reinforce it. South Africa today exemplifies the mix. President F. W. de Klerk may or may not truly buy the moral logic behind his (relatively) progressive initiatives, but he definitely has felt the accompanying political pressure, ranging from international sanctions to domestic protest and unrest. On the other hand, behind those sanctions has been, among other things, some genuine empathy and some pure moral logic. 28

The bad news for animals is twofold. First, in all of these cases—women's rights, the abolition of slavery, ending apartheid—a good part of the political momentum comes from the oppressed themselves. Progress in South Africa never would have begun if blacks there hadn't perceived their own dignity and fought for it. Second, in all of these cases, empathy for the oppressed by influential outsiders came because the outsiders could identify with the oppressed—because, after all, they're people, too. With animal rights, in contrast, (1) the oppressed can never by themselves exert leverage; and (2) the outsiders who work on their behalf, belonging as they do to a different species, must be exquisitely, imaginatively compassionate in order to be drawn to the cause. To judge by history, this is not a recipe for success. It may forever remain the case that, when it comes time to sit down and do the moral bargaining, nonhuman animals, unlike all past downtrodden organisms, don't have much to bring to the table.

Notwithstanding these handicaps, the animal rights movement has made progress. American fur sales are by some accounts down (perhaps more out of fear of social disapproval than out of newfound sympathy). Some cosmetics companies have stopped abusing rabbit's eyes, finding that there are gentler ways to test products. And the university panels that administer federal laboratory regulations—designed to ensure that animal experimentation is worthwhile and not needlessly cruel—are undoubtedly, in the present climate, being at least as scrupulous as they've ever been (however scrupulous that is).

Even I—never quick to bring my deeds into sync with my words—am making minor gains. I hereby vow never again to eat veal. And it's conceivable that the dovetailing of moral concerns and health fears will get me to give up all red meat, among the most (formerly) sentient kind of flesh on the market. Also: no leather couches or leather jackets in my future. Shoes, yes, couches, no; the least we can do is distinguish between the functionally valuable and the frivolous. (Which also means, of course: people who wear fur coats to advertise their social status—which is to say all people who wear fur coats—should indeed, as the Humane Society's ads have it, be ashamed of themselves.) Finally, for what it's worth, I plan to keep intact my lifelong record of never eating pâté de foie gras, the preternaturally enlarged liver of a goose force-fed through a large tube.

But so long as I so much as eat tuna fish and support the use of primates   32
in AIDS research, how can I still endorse the idea of human rights? How can I consider Stalin guilty of a moral crime and not just a utilitarian arithmetic error? One answer would be to admit that my allegiance to human rights isn't philosophical in the pure sense, but pragmatic; I've implicitly signed a nonaggression pact with all other humans, and Stalin violated the pact, which is immoral in this practical sense of the term. But I'd rather answer that, yes, I think moral law should be more than a deal cut among the powerful, but, no, I haven't been any more successful than the next guy in expunging all moral contradictions from my life. I'll try to do what I can.

If there is a half-decent excuse for this particular contradiction, I suppose it is that human civilization is moving in the right direction. Given where our moral thinking was two hundred, five hundred, five thousand years ago, we're not doing badly. The expanding circle will never get as big as Singer would like, perhaps, but if it grows even slowly and fitfully, we'll be justified in taking a certain chauvinistic pride in our species.

Points to Consider

1. Why was Robert Wright disappointed by his encounters with animal rights activists? To what does he attribute his failure to gather the kinds of quotes he desired?

2. What is the distinction between "animal welfare" and "animal rights"? Why does Wright believe that this is an important distinction?

3. Wright believes that "sentience lies at the core of our moral thinking." Do you agree with him, however, that language and intelligence lie at the periphery of such thinking? Do you feel that linguistic expression and the ability to reason are crucial to moral status?

4. What does Wright think is the fundamental difference between the animal rights movement and human rights movements like women's rights, civil rights, and the ending of apartheid? Why does this difference make it difficult for animal rights activists to succeed in their efforts?

Discussing the Unit

The animal rights debate has raised a number of difficult questions that go to the very heart of our thinking about the concept of rights. What does it mean to say that someone has "rights"? Can a person demand rights for another person? Is a person justified in demanding rights for animals? How can we be sure that by extending rights to animals we would be acting in their best interest? If animals have rights, do they also have responsibilities? Should *their* actions be judged morally?

Participating in Class Discussion

1. Every day we are faced with consumer decisions that might increase or decrease animal suffering. Make a list of the choices you make each day that affect animal life. (These could range from eating a hamburger to using a hair-care product that has been tested on animals to riding in a car with an all-leather interior.) Which animal products or products that are linked to animal testing would you be willing to forgo? For those products you would continue to use, how would you defend your choice?

2. One of the more difficult aspects of the animal rights debate is deciding what constitutes animal abuse. While most people would say that inflicting unnecessary pain upon animals constitutes abuse, would the necessary suffering of animals also be considered abuse? For example, scientists may argue that the suffering of animals is sometimes necessary to test vaccines such as the polio vaccine that has saved thousands of human lives. Make a list of ten acts that you think constitute animal abuse. Determine which of these abuses can be avoided and how ending such abuses would affect our lives.

From Discussion to Writing

How would you characterize your own views on animal rights? Where do you draw the line between responsibility and compassion toward animals, and emotionalism and absurdity? Write an essay in which you consider what the reasonable bounds of a person's reverence for life might be. Consider also what contradictions even the most animal rights–conscious of us might be forced to live with if we are concerned with maintaining our moral responsibilities toward other human beings.

24

The Farm Crisis:
Are Rural Values Obsolete?

In the last several decades we have witnessed the decline of America's farmlands and the place of the farm in the national consciousness. In 1985 only 3 percent of all Americans still lived and worked on farms. While many farmers have been forced to leave the land because of drought, dropping land values, and large debts, some farm families have managed to survive. In "Pulling Things Back to Earth," Michael Martone considers the life of one such family. He observes and participates in its daily routine and draws his own conclusions about farm life in America. His personal account supplies much-needed insight into the lives behind the statistics about the farm crisis.

By carefully recording his experience of rural life, Martone may have been enacting the very approach Wendell Berry feels we must adopt when thinking about the country. In "An Argument for Diversity," essayist Berry maintains that a true understanding, and hence better use, of the land depends upon an individual's careful attention to the unique qualities of the place in which he or she lives. While not especially hopeful, Berry at least offers some possible solutions to the problems of today's rural communities.

While reading these essays, consider your own views about rural life and how those views were originally shaped. Do you think the American farm can endure as the symbol of a simpler — and therefore better — time?

Can the farm still stand as the embodiment of the ideals of hard work and communal feeling?

MICHAEL MARTONE

Pulling Things Back to Earth

[THE NORTH AMERICAN REVIEW / June 1985]

"There's one," Tom said. We were in the pickup truck driving through Hepburn, Iowa. On the outskirts of town was a little house. In the backyard, a satellite dish.

"That one's got a motor drive," Tom said. The truck was slowing down. There was a stack of wood propped against the south wall of the house. The plastic on the windows was ripped and flapping in the wind. The yard was mud. The dish was turned away from the house to the south. It didn't rock or sway in the wind, though the stalk it was attached to seemed puny. The dish was the color of used soap.

"They can aim the thing from inside the house." He smiled a little. "I'd say it's pulling in the Playboy channel right now." He could tell, he told me. There were really only two satellites up there. Low in the southern sky and a little lower. I asked him about scrambling the signal. He said that the cable companies keep threatening to do it.

We'd been out in the country around Villisca in Montgomery County in southwest Iowa. Tom was showing me the neighborhood. We'd been through Nodaway and Guss and Hawleyville, and now we were on the way

MICHAEL MARTONE (b. 1955) has taught at Iowa State University and the University of Northern Iowa, and he currently teaches at Harvard. His fiction and essays have appeared in such periodicals as Antaeus, Indiana Review, *the* Iowa Review, *and the* North American Review. *Martone is the author of two collections of short stories,* Alive and Dead in Indiana *(1984) and* Safety Patrol *(1988). He has also edited a collection of essays on the Midwest,* A Place Sense *(1988). His newest collection is* Fort Wayne Is Seventh on Hitler's List *(1990).*

back to his farm. It was the first thaw of the year, and the roads were sweaty and slick. And it did seem, as we wandered around, that the satellite dish was replacing the old metal, many-bladed, windmill water pump. Again it struck me how steady these dish antennae are, cocked ears, in the landscape that pitches and rolls even in the slightest breeze. The old windmills were constantly turning, creaking, the red fish tail bearing the blades into the wind. I suppose school children in the cities would still make the windmill the centerpiece of a farm portrait. Windmill, barn, silo. That's a farm. But in the country, farms are more likely to be made up of grain bins and sheds, and long low confinement buildings that look something like mobile homes. And now these dishes: big plastic platters, pie pans, some made out of a metal netting with overlapping panels like a vegetable steamer, a black mesh strainer. Kitchen utensils grown big, gone feral.

I imagine that the windmills that look so natural on the farm today looked pretty silly when they were put up late last century, the newest item from the Sears and Roebuck catalogue. The way we change our thinking about industrial artifacts is curious. Iowa celebrates a covered bridge festival every summer near Winterset. Wooden covered bridges, there is no doubt, have entered a realm of celebration, a time to marvel at the beauty and craft of these old things, to urge their preservation. I've noticed a change of wind in the feelings directed toward the iron and steel truss bridges that replaced the covered bridge. As concrete replaces the rusting hulks, the I-beams, the rivets, the tie bars, the scroll work in upper reaches of the iron, the rust itself, take on new meanings. Nostalgia. Awe. Delight. There will be a metal bridge festival soon.

They stood out — the old windmill towers and the new dishes, the superstructure of ships at sea, the identifying silhouette. Sometimes the dish was rigged right into the ruins of the old well. The yard lights were coming on. We headed back to Tom's house to change for dinner.

When you drive in the country you have to use the odometer. The odometer becomes something more than a rough measure of engine life considered in the used car lot. The roads on the map to Tom's house and farm were marked off in quarter miles, half miles. And landmarks. The white house, the bridge, the railroad track. The directions were like the old guide-books before signs. Before, signs were the only thing that stayed the same.

I had rented a white car and I was taking much pleasure plowing along those roads, picturing the spray of mud along the sides. The roads were straight. I watched the numbers slip around. A seven and I'd look up from the dash. There would be a turn, another straight road going up and down over the next hill.

This part of Iowa has hills. That's a big surprise to people, hills in Iowa. Every summer the *Des Moines Register* sponsors a bike ride across the state which attracts many out-of-state participants. The newspaper files reports daily as the bikes head east. There is only one story to report, and the newspaper reports it over and over: the out-of-state riders are amazed at how hilly Iowa is. Below Interstate 80 are the foothills, then further south, the Alps of Iowa.

Because there are hills, more farms have more animals, the land in pasture grass and alfalfa instead of row crops. I saw plenty of cattle and hogs and sheep on both sides of the road. And the fields were fenced yet, which might indicate a pretty good chance of animals still on the place and sheltering since the sky was close and wet snow would come and go.

Of course, I found the house. Tom probably had been giving those directions for years. I remember a class in junior high school called language arts that consisted, it seemed, of giving directions to get to places in the city I myself had never been.

I pulled into the driveway between the house where Tom had been born 12 and the one where he grew up and now lived. I scrambled out of the car without my jacket. Really, I wanted to see the pattern of mud the front wheel drive had created. It was cold in the wind. Tom came out of the feed mill and over the scale, up to where I was parked. I started in about how great his directions were, how great what I'd seen of the farm so far, how great it was for him to have me visit.

He was wearing blue striped coveralls and a winter COOP hat with the flaps down. Resting on the bill was a white cloth mask he used when he worked in the confinement buildings. He looked younger because he'd shaved off his mustache. "It freezes outside in the winter and melts when I go in the buildings."

Tom had just started farming on his own, a partner with his father. He had graduated a couple of months earlier, in December, from Iowa State. Tom's brief time at home, his short time being a farmer, had nearly coincided with this year's farm crisis. There had been inklings of problems — bank closings, foreclosures, protests at farm auctions — before and through the election in November. But as he graduated, these regional news stories began to attract the attention of the nation. I visited him the weekend before the farm rally in Ames.

The events this winter and spring had that classic narrative structure as it was shaped and presented by the storytellers of newspapers, radio, and television. I think it began with other stories, the "farm" movies that prefigured the rising action: white crosses in the town squares, the formation of a farm coalition, the Farm Bureau's convention in Hawaii. The climax of the Big Rally. The swift reversal: the veto. The falling action: the tattoo of President Reagan's remarks this week, a joke or wince, that he should have kept the grain and exported the farmers, that he shouldn't have said anything since it didn't get a laugh. There is a closure there. It signals enough already. There are other stories to tell. And I think we've grown used to things being told this way, the world itself adhering to the unities of some ancient aesthetics or modern attention spans.

The farm rally, the debate in Congress, the lobbying; the veto hadn't 16 happened yet. Tom was farrowing twelve sows — twelve sows were due to farrow this weekend. I wanted to see that. And I wanted to see how the drama was affecting him. Maybe try and detect if he realized or even noticed he had been cast in this larger story, a character in somebody else's play.

I met his father, Don. He was dressed like his son. He took off the glove to shake my hand. Tom said, "This is Don." Don looked me up and down. I had worn what I consider my work clothes. I was ready to go. Don said, "Well, you better get him something to wear."

They wanted to feed the cattle before the ground got any softer that day or in case it rained or snowed and melted, which would make everything worse. The tractor would tear up the pasture as we'd go through it feeding from the hay wagon. Tom told me that his dad would be happy this summer because they'd be building terraces. "You get to build some terraces, don't you, Don?" As we headed to the pasture to feed the cattle, Tom began the task of sorting out the land for me. His neighbors', his uncle's, his folks', his own. Their own land, terraces and pastures and animals. The terraces give the look of play to the landscape, the childish glee of the sandbox. Serious business though, long-term and short-term costs. It was remarkably clear to Tom and his dad. Build terraces. Don't break open the ground.

I had to climb a ladder. I realized the only time I climb ladders is when I visit farms. Always I am amazed to find out that my body is as heavy as it is when I have to haul it up. I expect there will be something to support my back, something to lean against, because this isn't the inclined stepladder on the farm, my center of gravity tricked along the steep incline, but a straight shot up. Halfway up the side of a bin I always remember I don't climb ladders, don't really know how to. This ladder was wired to the outside of a pole shed where they kept the hay. I believe it was a ladder salvaged from a windmill, a mere wisp of a ladder.

I was in boots I'd never worn before. I had deerskin gloves that didn't 20 move. Tom, of course, scrambled up ahead of me. The wind was blowing. The birds Tom had startled from the loft above blew away, their wings of no use.

Now we all put ourselves in these positions. I was here, a volunteer, jaunty, a good student, wishing to perform, to please. But I was already, at the foot of the ladder, in way over my head. I'm only a generation away from all of this, as are many of you out there. I know lots of things, but not too many of them have to do with physical laws. It is like learning to crawl but without the instincts or genetic triggers a baby's got. Climbing a ladder. And I understood that to climb a ladder is why I visit farms in the first place. It's the old nagging doubt of the office worker. It's *doing* things. I'm not a participatory journalist. I don't want to farm and tell. *The Paper Farmer.*[1]

[1] An allusion to journalist George Plimpton's book about his experiences with the Detroit Lions, *Paper Lion.*

My curiosity brought me to the base of this flimsy ladder wobbling up the side of a swaying shed. When I moved to Iowa six years ago I would have drawn a farm with a silo, a barn, and a spinning windmill in the sun. I'm just getting to know my way around, getting to feel at home. As I made ready to climb that ladder on the farm near Villisca, Iowa, there were in other parts of the country many people talking about what was happening on The Farm. I reminded myself, as a kind pep talk, that those people didn't know the first thing about what was going on. As I swung onto the ladder I also understood that important things would be decided anyway without that knowledge.

We went to the new place to feed some more cattle. The farms I visit are made up of new places and home places. If you ask a man who farms four hundred acres what size is the right size for a family farm, he'll say four hundred acres. Ask a man who farms twelve hundred acres and he is likely to say the same. Couldn't make it below twelve hundred. The problems of this spring have a lot to do with scale — farming too much or not enough, growing or shrinking or disappearing. Don told me that this new place might have been a mistake. What he says is all understated. I'll never know the details. They bought when the land was much more expensive than it is now, now that it is falling rapidly. Don adds quickly that he isn't worried, that one good thing about Tom being a part owner is that they won't have to pay him.

Before they got the land, the hills had been cropped out in corn and soybeans. They put it into pasture. Terraces soon. We walked square bales from a barn to a stand of trees and there kicked the hay loose, another operation that I handled clumsily. The steers snuck up on us as we went back and forth, the ground sucking at our feet. Don talked a little about family history, more because he thought I wanted to hear it, I think, thought I expected it of a farmer. I remember his family history being a series of accidents, guesses, and compromises, like all histories. And I remember thinking that he was trying to disguise the haphazard past that brought us here, make it sound like there was a plan. Someone had sat down and thought all of this out. I kept kicking at the bales, pulling the twine. The cattle were patient with me. In the barn, Don pointed out the joints in the beams. Pegs instead of nails. It is his barn and he is proud of it, but nobody any of us knew built it.

Don and Cherryl live in a new house they designed. I liked it. It has one 24 big room — kitchen, dining room, living room. A fireplace and woodstove are across the room from a big window that looks out back over the hills and terraces. You can see three valleys on a clear day, Cherryl tells me. I could see, off in the middle distance, the pole shed, the one with the ladder.

I stayed the night here in a daughter's bedroom. She's away in college. Tom has his own house now.

The front yard is fenced, and if times were better, Cherryl says, they'd run sheep there. On the wall next to the big window hangs the same scene done on a loom in wool, dyed the way it must look in fall. The house was designed so there was a room for Cherryl's looms and yarns.

During lunch Cherryl asked Tom if I knew what I was getting into. Tom let me answer, ate, listened to the basketball game. Don told us what we had done, looked outside, and was happy we'd beat the snow. I looked up. It was snowing. "Guessed right." Tom joked about how Don kept his knife dull. They figured out where everyone was going to be in the afternoon, including me. They asked me, and I told them what brought me here. We adjourned.

In the basement there was another room with an outside entrance where we changed again back into work clothes. When we came in earlier we took turns using the bootjack. My shoes had come off in the boots. Tom teased his dad again about a knife he had loaned me to cut twine on the bales, how dull it was. I gave Don back his knife. It was still in the coverall pocket. But we weren't going to work exactly. And when we came in before lunch we hadn't really left work the way we left our clothes in the special changing room. It feels funny, not being used to it, not going to work, not going home. I'm a tourist here.

Driving from the new house to Tom's house and the hog houses, we   28
almost clipped a mailbox planted close to a road on a curve. I sat between Tom and Don, who was driving. They talked about the history of the mailbox. How many times it's been knocked over, the motives the neighbor might have for putting it back up in the same place after each time. How they always forget it is there.

We all waved at a car going by in the other direction. Don — two fingers off the wheel. Tom — flick of the hand from the dash. Me — more of a nod of the head, trying to pass. It is in the timing actually. Make a move too soon and the other folks can't see your subtleness. Too late, and they've gone talking about you. The people in the other car waved back.

At Tom's house we stopped on the road. Tom got out to get the mail. It's a clump of four mailboxes all with the family name. An important moment. Towns are towns because of post offices. Mail can be a daily confirmation that you are where you're supposed to be. Tom stood sorting the envelopes. Suddenly, a horn went off in the buildings. It sounded like a submarine about to submerge, general quarters. Tom sprang into the cab. Don gunned into the drive, shouting instructions to Tom. "I'll let you off at the barn!" My God, I thought, something's happened in one of the hog houses — a fire, they can't breathe, pigs are being born. We bounced over the yard. Tom had the door open, leapt and ran to the barn. "Dive! Dive!" the buzzer said.

It was the phone. Cherryl had called to say that Iowa had lost again.

Tom got me a mask from the little shed that houses the scale. They keep the masks there for when buyers come on the farm. The mask I got was like the ones Tom and his father had perched on the bills of their COOP caps. Mine was whiter. It felt like felt. It had subtle indentations pressed into it, a ribbing, that made it cup my nose and mouth. There was a metal strip at the top. I crimped it around my nose. I fiddled the mask into place. Every time I went into the hog houses for the rest of the visit, I had to get a new mask out of the shed. They were in a box, nestled inside one another. I never learned the trick of storing one out of the way, like a visor, on my cap, whipping it down and in place when it was needed. My masks looked like used tissue after a few minutes, crumpled, stove in. The metal clip whitened where I tried to bend it back in shape, snapped in two. I'd wrestle the thing off my head, wedge the rubber band from my ears, stuff it in my pocket.

After all that, the mask didn't do any good. I had brought some allergy pills, antihistamines. I knew what I was getting into.

The houses are closed up tight in the winter. I was surprised by the flies. You forgot flies over the winter, get to know them again slowly in the spring. They don't go away in the confinement hog house where it is always like it is — warm, close, moist. The manure from the animals goes through slats in the floor, into holding tanks right below us. In late winter the pits were nearly full, four foot deep. It wasn't that it smelled bad. It just smelled. Sensitive sense. I wasn't used to using it. But the mask has nothing to do with smell. It's beyond smell. I was breathing, breathing in the pit gases, and my lungs were closing up shop.

Tom was showing me a table full of medicines, drugs. He had told me before how the use of the stuff concerned him, especially subtherapeutically, not for curing a disease in the animal but to stimulate its growth. We were in a house that had thirty crates, a sow and a litter of a dozen more or less in each. I was trying to breathe and listen and see. A sow would stand up in her cage. Her pigs crashed around the pen getting out of the way. The tubular cage keeps the sow from rolling on the pigs when she lies down. It leaves room for the pigs to maneuver. I could hear water running, the snuffling at the automatic fountains, the squealing, the jostling. The pigs nearest me were curious, sniffing. It seemed Tom might be talking to himself, thinking out loud about the drugs. These were his animals, his building, his drugs. But he had bought into this system. He'd have done things differently, tried to think things through. But he could get no distance, elbow room. There were the pressures, forces that were beyond his control — bankers and markets and this system. These systems were new, still evolving. They had no track record. These things — the buildings, the economy, the method of production — had lives of their own. And in the building this other life, the pigs, still after all the study, finally, unknown and unknowable. They were looking up at us. Tom stabbed at a big syringe. The mask made it even more difficult for me to breathe. I felt that panic — suffocation, drowning, choking. It was the air. Tom was in it every day. "You get used to it," he said. "But you do hear about what they're calling farmer's lung. Just like the miners get." My own drugs weren't doing a thing.

In the farrowing house Tom was rearranging the crates, preparing the ones where the sow was about to give birth. He slid mesh flooring in over the slats so the newborn pigs wouldn't slip through. He gathered heat lamps, hung them on either side of the laboring sow.

36

The sows were due anytime. Tom had written to me saying, "Come on out." Attached to the letter was a list of dates and numbers of sows. The letter was done on his computer, a dot matrix printer. Tom had majored in computers and math at Iowa State. Farm operations and agriculture classes hadn't interested him. He liked telling me about a farm operation class he took where the instructor insisted a certain mower-conditioner be pulled by a sixty-five-horsepower tractor.

"I had cut thousands of acres with that very implement back home," he said, "and we never used more than thirty-five horsepower. I told the guy that. He didn't believe me. I went back home one weekend and looked it up in the manual. It suggested twenty-five."

In the arguments during those weeks of the farm crisis, the position that farming was a business like any other business came up often. It seems that the decision to return to farming or to leave it and work somewhere else does not come easily to farm kids. It is not like the usual vocational choice, this job or that one. It might be true that farming is like other businesses. But it *is* true that there are few businesses anymore that involve children the way farming still does. A land of opportunity implies a model of the world that is out there off your folks' land. Farm kids are different from city and suburban kids because they have this decision to make: stay or go. To the rest, to go is a given.

Tom came back to the farm. That means he will work with and be near his mother and father every day for a very long time. It is a state of affairs that is, by definition, insulated and it is, by its rarity, a state further removed from the rest of America.

40

Tom's a quiet man. He does things. He may not talk about what motivated him because he believes I could not begin to understand the reasons that brought him home to Villisca, or because he doesn't believe in words themselves, their processing, that matrix of dots.

One sow had been laboring too long, Tom thought. He slid on a clear plastic glove that covered his whole arm. He squirted on a disinfectant and reached up inside the sow. He said, "Everything seems all right. I don't get it." The sow was grunting and panting. Tom pulled his arm back out. He clutched a pig. It was alive. We watched for a bit, seeing if any more would follow. The newborn stumbled around on the mesh flooring. Tom put him under the heat lamp. We went on about other chores. Every time we came back into the farrowing house, Tom checked the sow. He didn't want to induce contractions, the drugs again, but decided finally to go ahead. Tom has told me about the vet who wanted to abort bred gilts so that they would cycle at the same time, give birth all at once, take the guesswork out of it.

I was able to breathe easier in the farrowing house. I don't know why. Tom went back to the nursery. I watched the sow and the one pig.

I wandered around the yard. It was snowing again, big heavy globs of 44 snow. It wasn't sticking. My mask hung around my neck. It had somehow gotten turned inside out. I met Don coming out of the feed mill. He had been grinding feed. "The smartest thing my dad did," he said about the mill. He showed me the boars in their pens. He called a huge spotted one a wimp, said he was much happier with the Durocs. The sow I'd been watching was one of the group that had been artificially inseminated. He showed me an old hog house that he thought might start up again after a little work. I saw the honey wagon, the manure tank. Don wished the ground would freeze so he could pump the pits and spread it on the fields. He would have to do something with it. He didn't want to think about pumping it over the hill.

I asked him if he was coming up to the rally in Ames. He said he didn't think he had the time. He went on. His feelings about the whole thing were mixed. He thought some might have deserved it, borrowed too much. But there was bad luck, the breaks. He told about a neighbor who might be helping his neighbors *too* much, dropping things on his own place to go help. Tom and he had tried to translate what they did on the farm into the terms of a regular job, so many hours a week. They were working enough. Who wasn't? You compete with your neighbors as well as the folks in Canada.

I thought then of the telling phrase from the Vietnam War, of destroying the village to save it. What were those farmers going to fight for up in Ames? It seemed that what was being said about farms wasn't meshing. Was the farm the innovative frontier of agricultural science and enterprise? Or was it the repository of traditional beliefs and values? It also seemed that no one could approach farming without nostalgia both for the past and the future. It was this tug of war between longings. But what seemed to be longed for most was that the problems should be settled, fixed, taken care of, finished. No more manure in the pits or flies or problems in the farrowing pens, no more arguing in the commodity pits or congresses. Wanting it to be over and done with — that was the one clear message of the farm rally. By calling it a crisis, by treating these problems as if they were like a bad Midwestern snow storm, we were able to ignore the fundamental issues as well as the daily realities that finally have no answers or solutions, like life or death. Some things simply must be done, not finished.

Outside the nursery door was a dead pig. Its mother had crushed it. It was smashed on one side, waffled flat by the slats on the floor. It should have been big enough, smart enough, fast enough to get out of the way. There is a steady loss of pigs. It is hard to tell if the crates and pens constructed with this type of thing in mind might also contribute to it. In the alleys and gutters of both houses were dead pigs. Some were born dead. Some were runts that couldn't compete with the rest of the litter. There were not that many. But it didn't take many to notice.

Cherryl has told me how much Tom hates to kill the ones that have been 48 crushed but aren't dead yet. Don has been taking care of that for a long time. Tom does it, but he can't get used to it.

I think about the Midwest sometimes as being the great graveyard for the country. People leave the Midwest to go live somewhere else. But bodies are always being shipped back to be buried here. I wonder if the rest of the country doesn't think of the Midwest as they would think of their local cemetery. Both are even landscaped the same — not too hilly, few sturdy trees, plastic flowers. People who don't live here are kind of proud that they can't be bothered with sorting out the I states — Iowa, Illinois, Indiana. They lose track of the family plots in the same way. Out of sight, out of mind. Only two seasons here. Winter and summer. Even to call the Midwest the heart of the country is not to get it right. It is more the gut. It is the gut of the nation. So why should we expect anyone to come visit? They fly over. They pass through (even better). The Midwest busies itself with changing the living into the dead, the dead into the living.

It's just messy here. Confinement houses, slaughter houses. Our houses. If the whole country were zoned by one big planning board, we all know what would be allowed to go on here. It goes on here anyway. Dirt. Dirt is us.

I was outside the nursery door trying to catch my breath. It was raining now. I was balancing on a board that bridged a pool of muddy water. They had to regrade this part of the yard. The crushed pig was by the door.

Inside Tom was putting a litter of pigs into an old wood milk crate 52 suspended from a scale. I had tried to gather up the pigs as they scampered around the pen, but I got winded instantly. I went back into the house. Tom was working smoothly, quickly. He was taking the gilts out of the milk crate, putting them back with their mother. I was trying to help Tom as he castrated the boars. I held their hind legs up, the pig head rested against my belly. Tom felt between their legs, pushed up, made two quick cuts with a scalpel. He squeezed out the testicles and cut the connecting cords. He swabbed on some disinfectant. I took the barrow back to the litter. Tom reached for the next pig.

I could do one litter at a time before I had to get outside in the cold air. Outside the nursery door was the dead pig. Water ran in sheets off the metal roof of the building. The board floated on the pool of mud until I stepped on it. The mill was grinding and mixing feed. I could hear the clanking of the lids on the feed bunks down in the finishing barns. Now it was snowing.

Tom lives in the house he grew up in. The house where he was born is across the driveway. When he moved back home, he moved into that house. But it was too cold, too old, too big. He moved over to the newer house.

We changed out of our work clothes in the basement. The basement was filled with work clothes, boots, gloves, hats. Tom had told me he never had to buy a coat since all the companies give coats to him.

It is a big old farm house, the type of house a city kid might draw when 56 drawing a farm house. But there is nothing in it except a couch and TV in the living room, a bed in the bedroom, a computer in the dining room. He has two cats. They were waiting for us at the head of the stairs.

He showed me his records, entered the litter weights he'd just recorded. Don hadn't kept detailed records. School paid off here. We were waiting to go up to his parents' house for dinner. We talked about basketball a little. Bobby Knight[2] had just thrown a chair at a referee. Tom told me he wanted to get one of those satellite dishes so he could watch basketball. At college he played pickup games with the team, ran around with the players. Cherryl describes her son with the help of basketball.

"Tom," she said, "is always one on one."

We played a game on the computer that had to do with outer space. Tom said it was the only game he had. The program recorded all of his scores from all the games he'd played. He purposely lost so we could watch the starship explode.

I looked at the catalogue from the semen company. 60

Tom waved his tax form at me. "Won't have to pay anything this year."

We sat on the couch. The cats roamed over us.

Later, I drove us to the new house in my muddy rented car. After dinner, after his parents had talked with me, Tom's father drove him home. Together they checked the sows, walked the yard.

Tom got the day off Sunday. He gets only every other Sunday off. He'll 64 sometimes save up the days and take the whole weekend off. He wants to go to the Big Eight basketball finals in Kansas City. Tom had said that he didn't want to work for the big computer companies, didn't want to work for anybody. Of course, he is working for himself, and he does boss himself

---

[2] Indiana University basketball coach.

around. Still, in complex ways, he is an employee of the large companies that sell him equipment, chemicals, seeds, and the sperm that he depends upon, that give him bright jackets and caps, his uniform. He is aware of this. There is irony on the farm. It mixes with those sincere, rarely stated beliefs in hard work, family, and independence. But finally it isn't true independence at all. The debate that is going on in agriculture, beyond the immediate problems of debt restructuring, seems to be about what ways farmers will lose their independence. Will they become parts of corporate structures or of the ones that emanate from nature? Does happiness derive from subordination to instead of domination over the world? Which family are they to be part of? Which kind of work?

Since Tom had the day off, Cherryl and I were in the farrowing house doing teeth and tails and inoculations. Don had come home the night before saying that the sow Tom was worried about had had her litter. The twelve pigs were nosing into the teats, constantly arranging their order, swarming. A sow in another crate was standing up, scraping the floor. She was lactating, the colostrum in pools beneath her. She would be next.

Cherryl was dressed in brown coveralls, the boots and hat. She didn't like to use the masks. She was standing in the alley between the crates trying to read the labels on the bottles. We were going to give the six-hour-old pigs injections to prevent scouring, a virulent form of diarrhea. There might have been an iron shot too. We took the bottles and the needles and syringes over to the crate. I put a board across the top of the pen and we set up store. Cherryl reached in, grabbed a pig, and cradled it behind the front legs. She gave a shot into the right shoulder, put down the syringe, picked up the other one, and shot the left shoulder. She put down the syringe and picked up a livestock marker, a big crayon, and striped the pig's back. The stripe was bright pink, flamingo pink. The pink turned a kind of tangerine color under the heat lamp when she set him down. Him. That had to be done too today. Cherryl had to notch the ear to identify the pig as male or female. The day before when we were castrating, Tom could read the ears on the pigs as we pulled them out. We found one notched wrong. "Cherryl must've done this group," he said. He asked me to remind him to tease her. He forgot. I forgot to remind him. As Cherryl readied for another pig I told her about the day before. She laughed.

I had just been watching her work, juggle all those operations. She asked me if I wanted to inject while she grabbed and marked.

I thought the pig was more nervous about being held than being shot. It settled down, stopped squirming in my hand after a moment. It thrummed, a little engine. No, that's not fair. It was not like a machine. But there was this tension and power. The belly was tight, harmonies under the skin. The cord was turning brown and trailed down along my arm.

When we were talking about sheep, and later, when he urged me to come back out for the calving, Tom had said that all baby animals are cute.

Even this pig was cute. I gave him his shots. I was too gentle with the needle at first. I felt like I was trying to open a new jar of olives while I was in new clothes. Such fine tuning of strength. I tried to keep my eye steady on the correct dosage mark as the plunger went down. One big mark for one. Two half marks for the other. We finished the litter that way. It had gotten easier. The pigs were back in business, the pink stripes punching in and out. By that time I was having trouble breathing again. With my last breath I was making excuses to Cherryl, apologizing.

I waited outside the building. Snow now. Cherryl brought out a pig so I could see how the teeth and tails were clipped, the ear notched. These pigs will be in pens, and crowded in with other pigs. They'll nip at each other, bite tails and ears. Cutting out the teeth, docking the tails is one response. The other, of course, is to change the whole system. Yesterday, as we worked, Tom talked about animal rights and people who do not farm who are concerned with the rights of animals. It was another delicate balance. He explained to me, perhaps a bit defensively, why he was doing this or that. No anesthesia for castrating.

Wouldn't do it at all if boars brought a price. It's another drug. Lose fewer pigs to weather, more to accidents. Fewer people have to raise the food.

I wondered if he thought about these moral ambiguities, these practical considerations while he worked, as he most often does, alone without the benefit of my naiveté. I imagine he does since the consequences of his actions are oftentimes right at hand. That is not to say that what he does or feels he has to do to animals is right or wrong, just that he is conscious. He considers. As I tried to breathe outside the farrowing house, I also understood that the way we all eat contributes to the way Tom works and the way Tom lives. Tom is as humane with his animals as he can be. Can we be more humane with Tom? Saying he has a will, a choice is not enough, I think, at least not enough until we look to our own choices, our own will.

Cherryl pried open the pig's mouth and showed me the needle teeth. She worked the cutters in and snipped off the ends. She held the pig between her legs. It seems there is a point with any animal where it will stop struggling, trying to get free. It is a kind of freeze. Just a moment. Then more wiggling, twisting. In that moment, between breaths, Cherryl snipped the teeth, the tails. "Most times," she said, "there's little blood." The ears are encoded with a series of v'ed nips. Sex, litter, number in the litter. She'll work around the big ears. Clock positions. The edge of the cut flushed red, a pencil line. There had been so little color that weekend.

Cherryl went back in the house to finish the pigs. I stood out in the yard, cold and tired and sick. I would leave for home after lunch. I was alone and unable, really, to make sense yet of the weekend. Up in an oak tree, an old tree house, wet and rotting. I couldn't see any ladder or rope, no way up.

Tom came out of his house in his work clothes. He had his hands in his

72

pockets. I didn't think he was going to work — it was his day off — but he might have thought he was going to watch other people work. Sometimes that is the best entertainment.

That's when we went for a ride through the country. We saw things that did not look too good, dirt pooled in the ditches, equipment out in the open rusting, a new Butler building abandoned in the field. In the middle of another field was a used car lot that Tom had never seen before. Everything looked worse because of the weather, the time of the year. The main streets of the towns were in ruins, not old enough yet to be transformed into places to come see, not ghost towns because there were people here. We could tell by the new dish in the side yard. There were people here watching TV.

In the yard outside the coliseum at Ames the day of the rally, semitrailers circled a stand of satellite dishes. All the networks were there sending these pictures out into space. It might have been a basketball game, a graduation. Looking at the bright trucks, the gleaming dishes, I guess I felt connected to something. I thought of the dish Tom wanted, wanting to pull the whole world back down to earth.

Why should his life be more pure than my own, why should he conform to my notion of the farm generated by butter and bread commercials I've seen on TV, or to my image of what is rural or even poor? Our ghost towns are on the air, our ghosts. Pictures without context. I think you should visit some of the hidden places of the country, farms and factories. Schools and offices. Get authorization to be admitted, become the author of what you witness.

Tom writes to me. They are out in the field collecting new calves. He tells me of the largest calf. His mother, for some unknown reason, has rejected him. They have to put her in a squeeze pen so she'll sit still and nurse. He writes to say that calving will go on for several more weeks, that he has twelve new litters of pigs. He writes to say he is a tired young farmer. He writes to say I should come out.

76

Points to Consider

1. Why does Martone note the presence of satellite dishes in farm country? What does the replacement of some of the more traditional features of farm life by modern developments indicate?

2. Why does Martone compare the Midwest to a graveyard? Is his comparison appropriate? Does his essay alter your attitudes about the Midwest? Explain.

3. Why does Martone include a graphic description of the castration of baby pigs (paragraph 52)? Has this description any symbolic value?

4. Consider Martone's suggestion: "I think you should visit some of the hidden places of the country, farms and factories. Schools and offices."

Why does he feel these are "hidden places"? Why does he feel it is important to record these aspects of American life?

WENDELL BERRY

An Argument for Diversity

[THE HUDSON REVIEW / Winter 1990]

> Elegant solutions will be predicated upon the uniqueness of place.
> —*John Todd*

I live in and have known all my life the northern corner of Henry County, Kentucky. The country here is narrowly creased and folded; it is a varied landscape whose main features are these:

1. A rolling upland of which some of the soil is excellent and some, because of abuse, is less so. This upland is well suited to mixed farming which was, in fact, traditional to it, but which is less diversified now than it was twenty-five years ago. Some row-cropping is possible here, but even the best-lying ridges are vulnerable to erosion and probably not more than 10 percent should be broken in any year. It is a kind of land that needs grass and grazing animals, and it is excellent for this use.

2. Wooded bluffs where the upland breaks over into the valleys of the creeks and the Kentucky River. Along with virtually all of this region, most of these bluffs have been cleared and cropped at one time or another. They should never have been cropped, and because of their extreme vulnerability to erosion they should be logged only with the greatest skill and care. Most of these bluffs are now forested, though not many old growth stands remain.

WENDELL BERRY (b. 1934) farms his own land in Kentucky, using traditional methods rather than modern machinery. He is a faculty member at the University of Kentucky, as well as a well-known poet, novelist, short story writer, essayist, and translator. Berry is the author of several books, including Remembering *(1988),* Sabbaths *(1987), and* Home Economics *(1987).*

3. Slopes of gentler declivity below the bluffs. Some of these slopes are grassed, and, with close care, are maintainable as pasture. Until World War II they were periodically cropped, in a version of slash-and-burn agriculture, which resulted in serious damage by erosion. Now much of this land is covered with trees thirty or forty years old.

4. Finally, there are the creek and river bottoms, some of which are subject to flooding at varying frequencies. Much of this land is suitable for intensive row-cropping, which, under the regime of industrial agriculture, has sometimes been too intensive.

Within these four general divisions, this country is extremely diverse. To familiarity and experience, the landscape divides into many small facets or aspects differentiated by the kind or quality of soil, and by slope, exposure, drainage, rockiness, etc. In the two centuries during which European races have occupied this part of the country, the best of the land has sometimes been well used, under the influence of good times and good intentions. But virtually none of it has escaped ill use under the influence of bad times or ignorance, need or greed. Some of it—the steeper, more marginal areas— has never been well used. Of virtually all of this land it may be said that the national economy has prescribed ways of use but not ways of care. It is now impossible to imagine any immediate way that most of this land might receive excellent care. The economy, as it now is, prescribes plunder of the land owners and abuse of the land.

The connection of the American economy to this place—in comparison, say, to the connection of the American economy to just about any university—has been unregarding and ungenerous. Indeed, the connection has been almost entirely exploitive. It has never been more exploitive than it is now. Increasingly, from the beginning, most of the money made on the products of this place has been made in other places. Increasingly the ablest young people of this place have gone away to receive a college education, which has given them a "professional status" too often understood as a license to predatorize such places as this one that they came from. The destruction of the human community, the local economy, and the natural health of such a place as this is now looked upon, not as a "tradeoff," a possibly regrettable "price of progress," but as a good, virtually a national goal.

Recently I heard, on an early morning radio program, a university economist explaining the benefits of off-farm work for farm women: that farm women are increasingly employed off the farm, she said, has made them "full partners" in the farm's economy. Never mind that this is a symptom of economic desperation and great unhappiness on the farm. And never mind the value, which was more than economic, of these women's previous contribution *on* the farm to the farm family's life and economy— which was, many of them would have said, a full partnership. *Now* they are "earning 45 percent of total family income," *now* they are playing "a major role." The 45 percent and the "major role" are allowed to defray all other costs. That the farm family now furnishes labor and (by its increased consumption) income to the economy that is destroying it is seen simply as an improvement. Thus the abstract and extremely tentative value of money is thoughtlessly allowed to replace the particular and fundamental values of the lives of household and community. Obviously, we need to stop thinking about the economic functions of individuals for a while, and try to learn to think of the economic functions of communities and households. We need to try to understand the long-term economies of places—places, that is, that are considered as dwelling places for humans and their fellow creatures, not as exploitable resources.

What happens when farm people take up "off-farm work"? The immediate result is that they must be replaced by chemicals and machines and other purchases from an economy adverse and antipathetic to farming, which means that the remaining farmers are put under yet greater pressure to abuse their land. If under the pressure of an adverse economy, the soil erodes, soil and water and air are poisoned, the woodlands are wastefully logged, and everything not producing an immediate economic return is neglected, that is apparently understood by most of the society as merely the normal cost of production.

One thing that this means is that the land and its human communities are not being thought about in places of study and leadership, and this failure to think is causing damage. But if one lives in a country place, and if one loves it, one must think about it. Under present circumstances, it is not easy to imagine what might be a proper human economy for the country I have just described. And yet, if one loves it, one must make the attempt; if one loves it, in fact, the attempt is irresistible.

Two facts are immediately apparent. One is that the present local economy, based exclusively on the export of raw materials, like the economies of most rural places, is ruinous. Another is that the influence of a complex, aggressive national economy upon a simple, passive local economy will also be ruinous. In a varied and versatile countryside, fragile in its composition and extremely susceptible to abuse, requiring close human care and elaborate human skills, able to produce a great variety of products from its soils, what is needed, obviously, is a highly diversified local economy.

We should be producing the fullest variety of foods to be consumed 12 locally, in the countryside itself and in nearby towns and cities: meats, grains, table vegetables, fruits and nuts, dairy products, poultry and eggs. We should be harvesting a sustainable yield of fish from our ponds and streams. Our woodlands, managed for continuous yields, selectively and carefully logged, should be yielding a variety of timber for a variety of purposes: firewood, fence posts, lumber for building, fine woods for furniture makers.

And we should be adding value locally to these local products. What is needed is not the large factory so dear to the hearts of government "developers" and local "boosters." To set our whole population to making computers or automobiles would be as gross an error as to use the whole countryside for growing corn or Christmas trees or pulpwood; it would discount everything we have to offer as a community and a place; it would despise our talents and capacities as individuals.

We need, instead, a system of decentralized, small-scale industries to transform the products of our fields and woodlands and streams: small creameries, cheese factories, canneries, grain mills, saw mills, furniture factories, and the like. By "small" I mean simply a size that would not be destructive of the appearance, the health, and the quiet of the countryside. If a factory began to "grow" or to be noisy at night or on Sunday, that would mean that another such factory was needed somewhere else. If waste should occur at any point, that would indicate the need for an enterprise of some other sort. If poison or pollution resulted from any enterprise, that would be understood as an indication that something was absolutely wrong, and a correction would be made. Small scale, of course, makes such changes and corrections more thinkable and more possible than does large scale.

I realize that, by now, my argument has crossed a boundary line of which everyone in our "realistic" society is keenly aware. I will be perceived to have crossed over into "utopianism" or fantasy. Unless I take measures to prevent it, I am going to hear somebody say, "All that would be very nice, if it were possible. Can't you be realistic?"

Well, let me take measures to prevent it. I am not, I admit, optimistic about the success of this kind of thought. Otherwise, my intention, above all, is to be realistic; I wish to be practical. The question here is simply that of convention. Do I want to be realistic according to the conventions of the industrial economy and the military state, or according to what I know of reality? To me, an economy that sees the life of a community or a place as expendable, and reckons its value only as money, is not acceptable because it is *not* realistic. I am thinking as I believe we must think if we wish to discuss the *best* uses of people, places, and things, and if we wish to give affection some standing in our thoughts.

If we wish to make the *best* use of people, places, and things, then we are going to have to deal with a law that reads about like this: as the quality of use increases, the scale of use (that is, the size of operations) will decline, the tools will become simpler, and the methods and the skills will become more complex. That is a difficult law for us to believe, because we have assumed otherwise for a long time, and yet our experience overwhelmingly suggests that it *is* a law, and that the penalties for disobeying it are severe.

I am making a plea for diversity not only because diversity exists and is pleasant, but because it is necessary and we need more of it. For an example, let me return to the countryside I described at the beginning. From birth, I have been familiar with this place, and have heard it talked about and thought about. For the last twenty-four years I have been increasingly involved in the use and improvement of a little part of it. As a result of some failures and some successes, I have learned some things about it. I am certain, however, that I do not know the best way to use this land. I do not believe that anyone else does. I no longer expect to live to see it come to its best use. But I am beginning to see what is needed, and everywhere the need is for diversity. This is the need of every American rural landscape that I am acquainted with. We need a greater range of species and varieties of plants and animals, of human skills and methods, so that the use may be fitted ever more sensitively and elegantly to the place. Our places, in short, are asking us questions, some of them urgent questions, and we do not have the answers.

The answers, if they are to come, and if they are to work, must be developed in the presence of the user and the land; they must be developed to some degree *by* the user *on* the land. The present practice of handing down from on high policies and technologies developed without consideration of the nature and the needs of the land and the people has not worked, and it cannot work. Good agriculture and forestry cannot be "invented" by self-styled smart people in offices and laboratories and then sold at the highest possible profit to the supposedly dumb country people. That is not the way good land use comes about. And it does not matter how the methodologies so developed and handed down are labeled; whether "industrial" or "conventional" or "organic" or "sustainable," the professional or professorial condescension that is blind to the primacy of the union between the individual people and individual places is ruinous. The challenge to the would-be scientists of an ecologically sane agriculture, as David Ehrenfeld has written, is "to provide unique and particular answers to questions about a farmer's unique and particular land." The proper goal, he adds, is *not* merely to "substitute the cult of the benevolent ecologist for the cult of the benevolent sales representative."

The question of what a beloved country is to be used for quickly becomes 20
inseparable from the questions of who is to use it or who is to prescribe its uses, and what will be the ways of using it. If we speak simply of the use of "a country," then only the first question is asked, and it is asked only by its would-be users. It is not until we speak of "a beloved country"—a particular country, particularly loved—that the question about ways of use will arise. It arises because, loving our country, we see where we are, and we see that present ways of use are not adequate. They are not adequate because such local cultures and economies as we had have been stunted or destroyed. As a nation, we have attempted to substitute the *concepts* of "land use," "agribusiness," "development," and the like, for the *culture* of stewardship and husbandry. And this change is not a result merely of economic pressure and adverse social values; it comes also from the state of affairs in our educational system, especially in our universities.

It is readily evident, once affection is allowed into the discussion of "land use," that the life of the mind, as presently constituted in the universities, is of no help. The sciences are of no help, indeed are destructive, because they work, by principle, outside the demands, checks, and corrections of affection. The problem with this "scientific objectivity" becomes immediately clear when science undertakes to "apply" itself to land use. The problem simply is that land users are using people, places, and things that cannot be well used without affection. To be well used, creatures must be used sympathetically, just as they must be known sympathetically to be well known. The economist to whom it is of no concern whether or not a family loves its farm will almost inevitably aid and abet the destruction of family farming. The "animal scientist" to whom it is of no concern whether or not animals suffer will almost inevitably aid and abet the destruction of the decent old ideal of animal husbandry and, as a consequence, increase the suffering of animals. I hope that my country may be delivered from the remote, cold abstractions of university science.

But "the humanities," as presently constituted in the universities, are of no help either, and indeed, with respect to the use of a beloved country, they too have been destructive. (The closer I have come to using the term "humanities" the less satisfactory it has seemed to me; by it, I mean everything that is not a "science," another unsatisfactory term.) The humanities have been destructive not because they have been misapplied, but because they have been so frequently understood by their academic stewards as not applicable. The scientific ideals of objectivity and specialization have now crept into the humanities and made themselves at home. This has happened, I think, because the humanities have come to be infected with a suspicion of their uselessness or worthlessness in the face of the provability or workability or profitability of the applied sciences. The conviction is now widespread, for instance, that "a work of art" has no purpose but to be itself: "A poem should not mean / But be." Or if it is allowed that a poem has a meaning, then it is a meaning peculiar to its author, its time, or its convention. A poem, in short, is a relic as soon as composed; it can be taught, but it cannot teach. The issue of its truth and pertinence is not raised because literary study is conducted with about the same anxiety for "control" as is scientific study. The context of a poem is its text, or the context of its history and criticism as a text. I have not, of course, read all the books or sat in all the classrooms, but my impression is that not much importance is attached to the question of the truth of poems. My impression is that "Comus," for example, is not often taught as an argument with a history and a sequel, with the gravest importance for us in our dilemma now. My impression is that the great works are less and less taught as Ananda Coomaraswamy said they should be: with the recognition "that nothing will have been accomplished unless men's lives are affected and their values changed by what we have to show." My impression is that in the humanities as in the sciences the world is increasingly disallowed as a context. I hope that my country may be delivered from the objectivity of the humanities.

Without a beloved country as context, the arts and the sciences become oriented to the careers of their practitioners, and the intellectual life to intellectual (and bureaucratic) procedures. And so in the universities we see forming an intellectual elite more and more exclusively accomplished in intellectual procedures: promotion, technological innovation, publication, and grant-getting. The context of a beloved country, moreover, implies an academic standard that is not inflatable or deflatable. The standard—the physical, intellectual, political, ecological, economic, and spiritual health of the country—cannot be too high; it is as high, simply, as we have the love, the vision, and the courage to make it.

I would like my country to be seen and known with an attentiveness   24
that is schooled and skilled. I would like it to be loved with a minutely particular affection and loyalty. I would like the work in it to be practical and loving and respectful and forbearing. In order for these things to happen the sciences and the humanities are going to have to come together again in the presence of the practical problems of individual places, and of local knowledge and local love in individual people—people able to see, know, think, feel, and act coherently and well without the modern instinct of deference to the "outside expert."

What should the sciences have to say to a citizen in search of the criteria by which to determine the best use of a beloved place or countryside, or of the technical or moral means by which to limit the use of it to its best use? What should the humanities have to say to a scientist—or, for that matter, a citizen—in search of the cultural instructions that might effectively govern the use of a beloved place? These questions or such questions could reunite the sciences and the humanities. That a scientist and an artist can speak and work together in response to such questions I know from my own experience. All that is necessary is a mutuality of concern and a mutual willingness to speak common English. When friends speak across these divisions or out of their "departments," in mutual concern for a beloved country, then it is clear that these diverse disciplines are not "competing interests," as the university structure and academic folklore suggest, but interests with legitimate claims on all minds. It is only when the country becomes an abstraction, a prize of conquest, that these interests compete—though, of course, when that has happened *all* interests compete.

But in order to assure that a beloved country might be lovingly used, the sciences and the humanities will have to do more than mend their divorce at "the university level"; they will also have to mend their divorce from the common culture, by which I do not mean the "popular culture," but rather the low and local wisdom that is now either relegated to the compartments of anthropology or folklore or "oral history," or not attended to at all.

Some time ago, after I had given a lecture at a college in Ohio, a gentleman came up and introduced himself to me as a fellow Kentuckian.

"Where in Kentucky are you from?" I asked.   28

"Oh, a little place you probably never heard of—North Middletown."

"I *have* heard of North Middletown," I said. "It was the home of my father's great friend and colleague, John W. Jones."

"Well, John W. Jones was my uncle."

I told him then of my father's and my own respect for Mr. Jones.

"I want to tell you a story about Uncle John," he said. And he told me this:

When his Uncle John was president of the bank in North Middletown, his policy was to give a loan to any graduate of the North Middletown high school who wanted to go to college and needed the money. This practice caused great consternation to the bank examiners who came and found those unsecured loans on the books, and found no justification for them except for Mr. Jones's conviction that it was right to make them.

As it turned out, it was right in more than principle, for in the many years that Mr. Jones was president of the bank, making those "unsound loans," *all* of the loans were repaid; he never lost a dime on a one of them.

I do not mean to raise here the question of the invariable goodness of a   36
college education, which I doubt. My point in telling this story is that Mr. Jones was acting from a kind of knowledge, inestimably valuable and probably indispensable, that comes out of common culture, and that cannot be taught as a part of the formal curriculum of a school. The students whose education he enabled were not taught it at the colleges they attended. What he knew—and this involved his knowledge of himself, his tradition, his community and everybody in it—was that trust, in the circumstances then present, could beget trustworthiness. This is the kind of knowledge, obviously, that is fundamental to the possibility of community life and to certain good possibilities in the characters of people. Though I don't believe that it can be taught and learned in a university, I think that it should be known about and respected in a university, and I don't know where, in the sciences and the humanities as presently constituted, students would be led to suspect, much less to honor, its possible existence. It is certainly no part of banking or of economics as now taught and practiced. It is a part of community life, which most scientists ignore in their professional pursuits, and which most people in the humanities seem to regard as belonging to a past now useless or lost or dispensed with.

Let me give another, more fundamental example. My brother, who is a lawyer, recently had as a client an elderly man named Bennie Yeary who had farmed for many years a farm of about three hundred acres of hilly and partly forested land. His farm and the road to his house had been damaged by a power company.

Seeking to determine the value of the land, my brother asked him if he had ever logged his woodlands.

Mr. Yeary answered: "Yes, sir, since 1944 . . . I have never robbed [the land]. I have always just cut a little out where I thought it needed it. I have got as much timber right now, I am satisfied . . . as I had when I started mill runs here in '44."

That we should not rob the land is a principle to be found readily enough   40
in the literary culture. That it came into literature out of the common culture

is suggested by the fact that it is commonly phrased in this way by people who have not inherited the literary culture. That we should not rob the land, anyhow, is a principle that can be learned from books. But the ways of living on the land so as not to rob it probably cannot be learned from books, and this is made clear by a further exchange between my brother and Mr. Yeary.

They came to the question of what was involved in the damage to the road, and the old farmer said that the power company had destroyed thirteen or fourteen water breaks. A water break is a low mound of rock and earth built across a hilly road to divert the water out of it. It is a means of preventing erosion both of the roadbed and of the land alongside it, one of the ways of living on the land without robbing it.

"How long . . . had it been since you had those water breaks constructed in there?"

"I had been working on them . . . off and on, for about twelve years, putting them water breaks in. I hauled rocks out of my fields . . . and I would dig out, bury these rocks down, and take the sledgehammer and beat rock in here and make this water break."

The way to make a farm road that will not rob the land cannot be 44 learned from books, then, because the long use of such a road is a part of the proper way of making it, and because the use and improvement of the road are intimately involved with the use and improvement of the place. It is of the utmost importance that the rocks to make the water breaks were hauled from the fields. Mr. Yeary's solution did not, like the typical industrial solution, involve the making of a problem, or a series of problems, elsewhere. It involved the making of a solution elsewhere: the same work that improved the road improved the fields. Such work requires not only correct principles, skill, and industry, but a knowledge of local particulars, and many years; it involves slow, small adjustments in response to questions asked by a particular place. And this is true in general of the patterns and structures of a proper human use of a beloved country, as examination of the traditional landscapes of the Old World will readily show: they were made by use as much as by skill.

This implication of use in the making of essential artifacts and the maintenance of the landscape—which are to so large an extent the making and the maintenance of culture—brings us to the inescapable final step in an argument for diversity: the realization that without a diversity of people we cannot maintain a diversity of anything else. By a diversity of people I do not mean a diversity of specialists, but a diversity of people elegantly suited to live in their places and to bring them to their best use, whether the use is that of uselessness, as in a place left wild, or that of the highest sustainable productivity. The most abundant diversity of creatures and ways cannot be maintained in preserves, zoos, museums, and the like, but only in the occupations and the pleasures of an appropriately diversified human economy.

The proper ways of using a beloved country are humanities, I think, and are as complex, difficult, interesting, and worthy as any of the rest. But they defy the present intellectual and academic categories. They are *both* science and art, knowing and doing. Indispensable as these ways are to the success of human life, they have no place and no standing in the present structures of our intellectual life. The purpose, indeed, of the present structures of our intellectual life has been to educate them out of existence. I think I know where in any university my brother's client, Mr. Yeary, would be laughed at or ignored or tape-recorded or classified. I don't know where he would be appropriately honored. The scientific disciplines certainly do not honor him, and the "humane" ones almost as certainly do not. We would have to go some distance back in the literary tradition—back to Thomas Hardy, at least, and before Hardy to Wordsworth—to find the due respect paid to such a person. He *has* been educated almost out of existence, and yet an understanding of his importance and worth would renew the life of the mind in this country, in the university and out.

Points to Consider

1. Why does Wendell Berry object to the university economist's assessment of off-farm work for farm women? What does the fact that more women are taking off-farm jobs signify to Berry?

2. In Berry's analysis, what is the relation of the farm to the American economy? Why does Berry believe people need to think more about "the economic functions of communities and households"? What does he mean by "diversity" and why is it necessary for the health of rural economies?

3. To "make the best use of people, places, and things," what "law" does Berry think must be obeyed? Why does Berry feel this will be a difficult "law" for most of us to accept?

4. According to Berry, what role do the sciences and the humanities currently play in the life of the farm? How must these disciplines change if they are going to exert a positive influence? What is Berry's reason for including the story about the banker, Mr. Jones?

Discussing the Unit

Suggested Topic for Discussion

What were your ideas and attitudes about farm life and its values before reading the essays in this unit? How did the essays affect those ideas and attitudes? Do you think that the values associated with the family farm are obsolete or are they worth preserving?

Preparing for Class Discussion

1. While Michael Martone's essay is based on the experiences of an outsider to rural life, Wendell Berry's essay is the result of knowledge derived from many years of living on a farm. How does each perspective help the author successfully convey his message?

2. Make a list of popular ideas about farm life in America. Using what you have learned from the essays by Martone and Berry, examine which ideas are no longer appropriate in describing the family farm. What kinds of values are beginning to take their place?

From Discussion to Writing

Having considered the way traditional values and images often affect the public's response to rural life, you might now examine how such values and images affect other ways of life. Choose a way of life with which you are familiar and write an essay in which you examine your assumptions about life in that community. (If you are most familiar with rural life, you might try to examine features of that life not covered in either essay in this unit.) In your essay, consider the prevailing images associated with the way of life you've chosen to write about. Does your view agree with or reject those popular images? Be sure to defend your position against opposing views.

25

America's Cultural Diversity: Is It a Good Thing?

America's population is growing more culturally diverse. What impact will this diversity have on our society? How will it affect our schools, our jobs, our relations with one another? In "Multiculturalism: E Pluribus Plures," Diane Ravitch examines what she regards as the positive and negative sides of ethnic pluralism. Though she applauds the educational accomplishments of those who have opened up American culture to women and minorities, she sees these achievements as jeopardized by those who now advocate separatist or ethnocentric modes of "culturally relevant" education.

Diversity is also becoming a pressing issue for American business. In "From Affirmative Action to Affirming Diversity," R. Roosevelt Thomas, Jr., argues that our homogeneous society is a thing of the past and American business needs to explore ways to handle a rapidly changing work force. In Thomas's view, business must scrap some of its cherished metaphors (such as the company as "family") and develop new ones to ensure that workers will have the freedom to achieve their potential and equality of opportunity. Just how difficult it may be to achieve those goals is the subject of "Free and Equal," Lalita Gandbhir's short story about the difficulties of finding a job in America.

DIANE RAVITCH

Multiculturalism:
E Pluribus Plures [THE AMERICAN SCHOLAR / Summer 1990]

Questions of race, ethnicity, and religion have been a perennial source of conflict in American education. The schools have often attracted the zealous attention of those who wish to influence the future, as well as those who wish to change the way we view the past. In our history, the schools have been not only an institution in which to teach young people skills and knowledge, but an arena where interest groups fight to preserve their values, or to revise the judgments of history, or to bring about fundamental social change. In the nineteenth century, Protestants and Catholics battled over which version of the Bible should be used in school, or whether the Bible should be used at all. In recent decades, bitter racial disputes—provoked by policies of racial segregation and discrimination—have generated turmoil in the streets and in the schools. The secularization of the schools during the past century has prompted attacks on the curricula and textbooks and library books by fundamentalist Christians, who object to whatever challenges their faith-based views of history, literature, and science.

Given the diversity of American society, it has been impossible to insulate the schools from pressures that result from differences and tensions among groups. When people differ about basic values, sooner or later those disagreements turn up in battles about how schools are organized or what the schools should teach. Sometimes these battles remove a terrible injustice, like racial segregation. Sometimes, however, interest groups politicize the curriculum and attempt to impose their views on teachers, school officials, and textbook publishers. Across the country, even now, interest groups are pressuring local school boards to remove myths and fables and other imaginative literature from children's readers and to inject the teaching of creationism in biology. When groups cross the line into extremism, advancing

---

DIANE RAVITCH (b. 1938) is an adjunct professor of history and education at Teachers College, Columbia University. She has written and edited several books, most recently What Do Our Seventeen-Year-Olds Know? *(1987) and* The American Reader *(1990).*

their own agenda without regard to reason or to others, they threaten public education itself, making it difficult to teach any issues honestly and making the entire curriculum vulnerable to political campaigns.

For many years, the public schools attempted to neutralize controversies over race, religion, and ethnicity by ignoring them. Educators believed, or hoped, that the schools could remain outside politics; this was, of course, a vain hope since the schools were pursuing policies based on race, religion, and ethnicity. Nonetheless, such divisive questions were usually excluded from the curriculum. The textbooks minimized problems among groups and taught a sanitized version of history. Race, religion, and ethnicity were presented as minor elements in the American saga; slavery was treated as an episode, immigration as a sidebar, and women were largely absent. The textbooks concentrated on presidents, wars, national politics, and issues of state. An occasional "great black" or "great woman" received mention, but the main narrative paid little attention to minority groups and women.

With the ethnic revival of the 1960s, this approach to the teaching of history came under fire, because the history of national leaders—virtually all of whom were white, Anglo-Saxon, and male—ignored the place in American history of those who were none of the above. The traditional history of elites had been complemented by an assimilationist view of American society, which presumed that everyone in the American melting pot would eventually lose or abandon those ethnic characteristics that distinguished them from mainstream Americans. The ethnic revival demonstrated that many groups did not want to be assimilated or melted. Ethnic studies programs popped up on campuses to teach not only that "black is beautiful," but also that every other variety of ethnicity is "beautiful" as well; everyone who had "roots" began to look for them so that they too could recover that ancestral part of themselves that had not been homogenized. 4

As ethnicity became an accepted subject for study in the late 1960s, textbooks were assailed for their failure to portray blacks accurately; within a few years, the textbooks in wide use were carefully screened to eliminate bias against minority groups and women. At the same time, new scholarship about the history of women, blacks, and various ethnic minorities found its way into the textbooks. At first, the multicultural content was awkwardly incorporated as little boxes on the side of the main narrative. Then some of the new social historians (like Stephan Thernstrom, Mary Beth Norton, Gary Nash, Winthrop Jordan, and Leon Litwack) themselves wrote textbooks, and the main narrative itself began to reflect a broadened historical understanding of race, ethnicity, and class in the American past. Consequently, today's history textbooks routinely incorporate the experiences of women, blacks, American Indians, and various immigrant groups.

Although most high school textbooks are deeply unsatisfactory (they still largely neglect religion, they are too long, too encyclopedic, too superficial, and lacking in narrative flow), they are far more sensitive to pluralism than their predecessors. For example, the latest edition of Todd and Curti's *Triumph of the American Nation,* the most popular high school history text, has significantly increased its coverage of blacks in America, including profiles of Phillis Wheatley, the poet; James Armistead, a revolutionary war spy for Lafayette; Benjamin Banneker, a self-taught scientist and mathematician; Hiram Revels, the first black to serve in the Congress; and Ida B. Wells-Barnett, a tireless crusader against lynching and racism. Even better as a textbook treatment is Jordan and Litwack's *The United States,* which skillfully synthesizes the historical experiences of blacks, Indians, immigrants, women, and other groups into the mainstream of American social and political history. The latest generation of textbooks bluntly acknowledges the racism of the past, describing the struggle for equality by racial minorities while identifying individuals who achieved success as political leaders, doctors, lawyers, scholars, entrepreneurs, teachers, and scientists.

As a result of the political and social changes of recent decades, cultural pluralism is now generally recognized as an organizing principle of this society. In contrast to the idea of the melting pot, which promised to erase ethnic and group differences, children now learn that variety is the spice of life. They learn that America has provided a haven for many different groups and has allowed them to maintain their cultural heritage or to assimilate, or—as is often the case—to do both; the choice is theirs, not the state's. They learn that cultural pluralism is one of the norms of a free society; that differences among groups are a national resource rather than a problem to be solved. Indeed, the unique feature of the United States is that its common culture has been formed by the interaction of its subsidiary cultures. It is a culture that has been influenced over time by immigrants, American Indians, Africans (slave and free), and by their descendants. American music, art, literature, language, food, clothing, sports, holidays, and customs all show the effects of the commingling of diverse cultures in one nation. Paradoxical though it may seem, the United States has a common culture that is multicultural.

Our schools and our institutions of higher learning have in recent years 8 begun to embrace what Catherine R. Stimpson of Rutgers University has called "cultural democracy," a recognition that we must listen to a "diversity of voices" in order to understand our culture, past and present. This understanding of the pluralistic nature of American culture has taken a long time to forge. It is based on sound scholarship and has led to major revisions in what children are taught and what they read in school. The new history is—indeed, must be—a warts-and-all history; it demands an unflinching examination of racism and discrimination in our history. Making these changes is difficult, raises tempers, and ignites controversies, but gives a more interesting and accurate account of American history. Accomplishing these changes is valuable, because there is also a useful lesson for the rest of the world in America's relatively successful experience as a pluralistic society.

Throughout human history, the clash of different cultures, races, ethnic groups, and religions has often been the cause of bitter hatred, civil conflict, and international war. The ethnic tensions that now are tearing apart Lebanon, Sri Lanka, Kashmir, and various republics of the Soviet Union remind us of the costs of unfettered group rivalry. Thus, it is a matter of more than domestic importance that we closely examine and try to understand that part of our national history in which different groups competed, fought, suffered, but ultimately learned to live together in relative peace and even achieved a sense of common nationhood.

Alas, these painstaking efforts to expand the understanding of American culture into a richer and more varied tapestry have taken a new turn, and not for the better. Almost any idea, carried to its extreme, can be made pernicious, and this is what is happening now to multiculturalism. Today, pluralistic multiculturalism must contend with a new, particularistic multiculturalism. The pluralists seek a richer common culture; the particularists insist that no common culture is possible or desirable. The new particularism is entering the curriculum in a number of school systems across the country. Advocates of particularism propose an ethnocentric curriculum to raise the self-esteem and academic achievement of children from racial and ethnic minority backgrounds. Without any evidence, they claim that children from minority backgrounds will do well in school *only* if they are immersed in a positive, prideful version of their ancestral culture. If children are of, for example, Fredonian ancestry, they must hear that Fredonians were important in mathematics, science, history, and literature. If they learn about great Fredonians and if their studies use Fredonian examples and Fredonian concepts, they will do well in school. If they do not, they will have low self-esteem and will do badly.

At first glance, this appears akin to the celebratory activities associated with Black History Month or Women's History Month, when schoolchildren learn about the achievements of blacks and women. But the point of those celebrations is to demonstrate that neither race nor gender is an obstacle to high achievement. They teach all children that everyone, regardless of their race, religion, gender, ethnicity, or family origin, can achieve self-fulfillment, honor, and dignity in society if they aim high and work hard.

By contrast, the particularistic version of multiculturalism is unabashedly filiopietistic[1] and deterministic. It teaches children that their identity is determined by their "cultural genes." That something in their blood or their race memory or their cultural DNA defines who they are and what they may achieve. That the culture in which they live is not their own culture, even though they were born here. That American culture is "Eurocentric," and therefore hostile to anyone whose ancestors are not European. Perhaps the most invidious implication of particularism is that racial and ethnic

[1] In anthropology, pertaining to an excessive reverence of ancestors.

minorities are not and should not try to be part of American culture; it implies that American culture belongs only to those who are white and European; it implies that those who are neither white nor European are alienated from American culture by virtue of their race or ethnicity; it implies that the only culture they do belong to or can ever belong to is the culture of their ancestors, even if their families have lived in this country for generations.

The war on so-called Eurocentrism is intended to foster self-esteem   12
among those who are not of European descent. But how, in fact, is self-esteem developed? How is the sense of one's own possibilities, one's potential choices, developed? Certainly, the school curriculum plays a relatively small role as compared to the influence of family, community, mass media, and society. But to the extent that curriculum influences what children think of themselves, it should encourage children of all racial and ethnic groups to believe that they are part of this society and that they should develop their talents and minds to the fullest. It is enormously inspiring, for example, to learn about men and women from diverse backgrounds who overcame poverty, discrimination, physical handicaps, and other obstacles to achieve success in a variety of fields. Behind every such biography of accomplishment is a story of heroism, perseverance, and self-discipline. Learning these stories will encourage a healthy spirit of pluralism, of mutual respect, and of self-respect among children of different backgrounds. The children of American society today will live their lives in a racially and culturally diverse nation, and their education should prepare them to do so.

The pluralist approach to multiculturalism promotes a broader interpretation of the common American culture and seeks due recognition for the ways that the nation's many racial, ethnic, and cultural groups have transformed the national culture. The pluralists say, in effect, "American culture belongs to us, all of us; the United States is us, and we remake it in every generation." But particularists have no interest in extending or revising American culture; indeed, they deny that a common culture exists. Particularists reject any accommodation among groups, any interactions that blur the distinct lines between them. The brand of history that they espouse is one in which everyone is either a descendant of victims or oppressors. By doing so, ancient hatreds are fanned and recreated in each new generation. Particularism has its intellectual roots in the ideology of ethnic separatism and in the black nationalist movement. In the particularist analysis, the nation has five cultures: African American, Asian American, European American, Latino/Hispanic, and Native American. The huge cultural, historical, religious, and linguistic differences within these categories are ignored, as is the considerable intermarriage among these groups, as are the linkages (like gender, class, sexual orientation, and religion) that cut across these five groups. No serious scholar would claim that all Europeans and white Americans are part of the same culture, or that all Asians are part of the same culture, or that all people of Latin-American descent are of the same culture, or that all people of African descent are of the same culture. Any categorization this broad is essentially meaningless and useless.

Several districts—including Detroit, Atlanta, and Washington, D.C.—are developing an Afrocentric curriculum. *Afrocentricity* has been described in a book of the same name by Molefi Kete Asante of Temple University. The Afrocentric curriculum puts Africa at the center of the student's universe. African Americans must "move away from an [sic] Eurocentric framework" because "it is difficult to create freely when you use someone else's motifs, styles, images, and perspectives." Because they are not Africans, "white teachers cannot inspire in our children the visions necessary for them to overcome limitations." Asante recommends that African Americans choose an African name (as he did), reject European dress, embrace African religion (not Islam or Christianity) and love "their own" culture. He scorns the idea of universality as a form of Eurocentric arrogance. The Eurocentrist, he says, thinks of Beethoven or Bach as classical, but the Afrocentrist thinks of Ellington or Coltrane as classical; the Eurocentrist lauds Shakespeare or Twain, while the Afrocentrist prefers Baraka, Shange, or Abiola. Asante is critical of black artists like Arthur Mitchell and Alvin Ailey who ignore Afrocentricity. Likewise, he speaks contemptuously of a group of black university students who spurned the Afrocentrism of the local Black Student Union and formed an organization called Inter-race: "Such madness is the direct consequence of self-hatred, obligatory attitudes, false assumptions about society, and stupidity."

The conflict between pluralism and particularism turns on the issue of universalism. Professor Asante warns his readers against the lure of universalism: "Do not be captured by a sense of universality given to you by the Eurocentric viewpoint; such a viewpoint is contradictory to your own ultimate reality." He insists that there is no alternative to Eurocentrism, Afrocentrism, and other ethnocentrisms. In contrast, the pluralist says, with the Roman playwright Terence, "I am a man: nothing human is alien to me." A contemporary Terence would say "I am a person" or might be a woman, but the point remains the same: you don't have to be black to love Zora Neale Hurston's fiction or Langston Hughes's poetry or Duke Ellington's music. In a pluralist curriculum, we expect children to learn a broad and humane culture, to learn about the ideas and art and animating spirit of many cultures. We expect that children, whatever their color, will be inspired by the courage of people like Helen Keller, Václav Havel, Harriet Tubman, and Feng Lizhe. We expect that their response to literature will be determined by the ideas and images it evokes, not by the skin color of the writer. But particularists insist that children can learn only from the experiences of people from the same race.

Particularism is a bad idea whose time has come. It is also a fashion spreading like wildfire through the education system, actively promoted by 16 organizations and individuals with a political and professional interest in strengthening ethnic power bases in the university, in the education profession, and in society itself. One can scarcely pick up an educational journal without learning about a school district that is converting to an ethnocentric curriculum in an attempt to give "self-esteem" to children from racial minorities. A state-funded project in a Sacramento high school is teaching young black males to think like Africans and to develop the "African Mind Model Technique," in order to free themselves of the racism of American culture. A popular black rap singer, KRS-One, complained in an op-ed article in the *New York Times* that the schools should be teaching blacks about their cultural heritage, instead of trying to make everyone Americans. "It's like trying to teach a dog to be a cat," he wrote. KRS-One railed about having to learn about Thomas Jefferson and the Civil War, which had nothing to do (he said) with black history.

Pluralism can easily be transformed into particularism, as may be seen in the potential uses in the classroom of the Mayan contribution to mathematics. The Mayan example was popularized in a movie called *Stand and Deliver,* about a charismatic Bolivian-born mathematics teacher in Los Angeles who inspired his students (who are Hispanic) to learn calculus. He told them that their ancestors invented the concept of zero; but that wasn't all he did. He used imagination to put across mathematical concepts. He required them to do homework and to go to school on Saturdays and during the Christmas holidays, so that they might pass the Advanced Placement mathematics examination for college entry. The teacher's reference to the Mayans' mathematical genius was a valid instructional device: it was an attention-getter and would have interested even students who were not Hispanic. But the Mayan example would have had little effect without the teacher's insistence that the class study hard for a difficult examination.

Ethnic educators have seized upon the Mayan contribution to mathematics as the key to simultaneously boosting the ethnic pride of Hispanic children and attacking Eurocentrism. One proposal claims that Mexican-American children will be attracted to science and mathematics if they study Mayan mathematics, the Mayan calendar, and Mayan astronomy. Children in primary grades are to be taught that the Mayans were first to discover the zero and that Europeans learned it long afterwards from the Arabs, who had learned it in India. This will help them see that Europeans were latecomers in the discovery of great ideas. Botany is to be learned by study of the agricultural techniques of the Aztecs, a subject of somewhat limited relevance to children in urban areas. Furthermore, "ethnobotanical" classifications of plants are to be substituted for the Eurocentric Linnaean system. At first glance, it may seem curious that Hispanic children are deemed to have no cultural affinity with Spain; but to acknowledge the cultural tie would confuse the ideological assault on Eurocentrism.

This proposal suggests some questions: is there any evidence that the teaching of "culturally relevant" science and mathematics will draw Mexican-American children to the study of these subjects? Will Mexican-American children lose interest or self-esteem if they discover that their ancestors were Aztecs or Spaniards, rather than Mayans? Are children who learn in this way prepared to study the science and mathematics that are taught in American colleges and universities and that are needed for advanced study in these fields? Are they even prepared to study the science and mathematics taught in *Mexican* universities? If the class is half Mexican-American and half something else, will only the Mexican-American children study in a Mayan and Aztec mode or will all the children? But shouldn't all children study what is culturally relevant for them? How will we train teachers who have command of so many different systems of mathematics and science?

The efficacy of particularist proposals seems to be less important to their   20
sponsors than their value as ideological weapons with which to criticize existing disciplines for their alleged Eurocentric bias. In a recent article titled "The Ethnocentric Basis of Social Science Knowledge Production" in the *Review of Research in Education*, John Stanfield of Yale University argues that neither social science nor science are objective studies, that both instead are "Euro-American" knowledge systems which reproduce "hegemonic racial domination." The claim that science and reason are somehow superior to magic and witchcraft, he writes, is the product of Euro-American ethnocentrism. According to Stanfield, current fears about the misuse of science (for instance, "the nuclear arms race, global pollution") and "the power-plays of Third World nations (the Arab oil boycott and the American-Iranian hostage crisis) have made Western people more aware of nonscientific cognitive styles. These last events are beginning to demonstrate politically that which has begun to be understood in intellectual circles: namely, that modes of social knowledge such as theology, science, and magic are different, not inferior or superior. They represent different ways of perceiving, defining, and organizing knowledge of life experiences." One wonders: if Professor Stanfield broke his leg, would he go to a theologian, a doctor, or a magician?

Every field of study, it seems, has been tainted by Eurocentrism, which was defined by a professor at Manchester University, George Ghevarughese Joseph, in *Race and Class* in 1987, as "intellectual racism." Professor Joseph argues that the history of science and technology—and in particular, of mathematics—in non-European societies was distorted by racist Europeans who wanted to establish the dominance of European forms of knowledge. The racists, he writes, traditionally traced mathematics to the Greeks, then claimed that it reached its full development in Europe. These are simply Eurocentric myths to sustain an "imperialist/racist ideology," says Professor Joseph, since mathematics was found in Egypt, Babylonia, Mesopotamia, and India long before the Greeks were supposed to have developed it. Professor Joseph points out too that Arab scientists should be credited with major discoveries traditionally attributed to William Harvey, Isaac Newton,

Charles Darwin, and Sir Francis Bacon. But he is not concerned only to argue historical issues; his purpose is to bring all of these different mathematical traditions into the school classroom so that children might study, for example, "traditional African designs, Indian *rangoli* patterns and Islamic art" and "the language and counting systems found across the world."

This interesting proposal to teach ethnomathematics comes at a time when American mathematics educators are trying to overhaul present practices, because of the poor performance of American children on national and international assessments. Mathematics educators are attempting to change the teaching of their subject so that children can see its uses in everyday life. There would seem to be an incipient conflict between those who want to introduce real-life applications of mathematics and those who want to teach the mathematical systems used by ancient cultures. I suspect that most mathematics teachers would enjoy doing a bit of both, if there were time or student interest. But any widespread movement to replace modern mathematics with ancient ethnic mathematics runs the risk of disaster in a field that is struggling to update existing curricula. If, as seems likely, ancient mathematics is taught mainly to minority children, the gap between them and middle-class white children is apt to grow. It is worth noting that children in Korea, who score highest in mathematics on international assessments, do not study ancient Korean mathematics.

Particularism is akin to cultural Lysenkoism,[2] for it takes as its premise the spurious notion that cultural traits are inherited. It implies a dubious, dangerous form of cultural predestination. Children are taught that if their ancestors could do it, so could they. But what happens if a child is from a cultural group that made no significant contribution to science or mathematics? Does this mean that children from that background must find a culturally appropriate field in which to strive? How does a teacher find the right cultural buttons for children of mixed heritage? And how in the world will teachers use this technique when the children in their classes are drawn from many different cultures, as is usually the case? By the time that every culture gets its due, there may be no time left to teach the subject itself. This explosion of filiopietism (which, we should remember, comes from adults, not from students) is reminiscent of the period some years ago when the Russians claimed that they had invented everything first; as we now know, this nationalistic braggadocio did little for their self-esteem and nothing for their economic development. We might reflect, too, on how little social prestige has been accorded in this country to immigrants from Greece and Italy, even though the achievements of their ancestors were at the heart of the classical curriculum.

Filiopietism and ethnic boosterism lead to all sorts of odd practices. In   24

---

[2] T. F. Lysenko (1898–1976) was a Soviet biologist and geneticist who maintained that acquired characteristics could be inherited.

New York State, for example, the curriculum guide for eleventh grade American history lists three "foundations" for the United States Constitution, as follows:

A. Foundations.
    1. 17th and 18th century Enlightenment thought
    2. Haudenosaunee political system
        a. Influence upon colonial leadership and European intellectuals (Locke, Montesquieu, Voltaire, Rousseau)
        b. Impact on Albany Plan of Union, Articles of Confederation, and U.S. Constitution
    3. Colonial experience

Those who are unfamiliar with the Haudenosaunee political system might wonder what it is, particularly since educational authorities in New York State rank it as equal in importance to the European Enlightenment and suggest that it strongly influenced not only colonial leaders but the leading intellectuals of Europe. The Haudenosaunee political system was the Iroquois confederation of five (later six) Indian tribes in upper New York State, which conducted war and civil affairs through a council of chiefs, each with one vote. In 1754, Benjamin Franklin proposed a colonial union at a conference in Albany; his plan, said to be inspired by the Iroquois Confederation, was rejected by the other colonies. Today, Indian activists believe that the Iroquois Confederation was the model for the American Constitution, and the New York State Department of Education has decided that they are right. That no other state sees fit to give the American Indians equal billing with the European Enlightenment may be owing to the fact that the Indians in New York State (numbering less than forty thousand) have been more politically effective than elsewhere or that other states have not yet learned about this method of reducing "Eurocentrism" in their American history classes.

Particularism can easily be carried to extremes. Students of Fredonian descent must hear that their ancestors were seminal in the development of all human civilization and that without the Fredonian contribution, we would all be living in caves or trees, bereft of art, technology, and culture. To explain why Fredonians today are in modest circumstances, given their historic eminence, children are taught that somewhere, long ago, another culture stole the Fredonians' achievements, palmed them off as their own, and then oppressed the Fredonians.

I first encountered this argument almost twenty years ago, when I was a graduate student. I shared a small office with a young professor, and I listened as she patiently explained to a student why she had given him a D on a term paper. In his paper, he argued that the Arabs had stolen mathematics from the Nubians in the desert long ago (I forget in which century this theft allegedly occurred). She tried to explain to him about the necessity of historical evidence. He was unconvinced, since he believed that he had uncovered a great truth that was beyond proof. The part I couldn't understand was how anyone could lose knowledge by sharing it. After all, cultures are constantly influencing one another, exchanging ideas and art and technology, and the exchange usually is enriching, not depleting.

Today, there are a number of books and articles advancing controversial theories about the origins of civilization. An important work, *The African Origin of Civilization: Myth or Reality*, by Senegalese scholar Cheikh Anta Diop, argues that ancient Egypt was a black civilization, that all races are descended from the black race, and that the achievements of "western" civilization originated in Egypt. The views of Diop and other Africanists have been condensed into an everyman's paperback titled *What They Never Told You in History Class* by Indus Khamit Kush. This latter book claims that Moses, Jesus, Buddha, Mohammed, and Vishnu were Africans; that the first Indians, Chinese, Hebrews, Greeks, Romans, Britains, and Americans were Africans; and that the first mathematicians, scientists, astronomers, and physicians were Africans. A debate currently raging among some classicists is whether the Greeks "stole" the philosophy, art, and religion of the ancient Egyptians and whether the ancient Egyptians were black Africans. George G. M. James's *Stolen Legacy* insists that the Greeks "stole the Legacy of the African Continent and called it their own." James argues that the civilization of Greece, the vaunted foundation of European culture, owed everything it knew and did to its African predecessors. Thus, the roots of western civilization lie not in Greece and Rome, but in Egypt and, ultimately, in black Africa.

Similar speculation was fueled by the publication in 1987 of Martin Bernal's *Black Athena: The Afroasiatic Roots of Classical Civilization*, Volume 1, *The Fabrication of Ancient Greece, 1785–1985*, although the controversy predates Bernal's book. In a fascinating foray into the politics of knowledge, Bernal attributes the preference of Western European scholars for Greece over Egypt as the fount of knowledge to nearly two centuries of racism and "Europocentrism," but he is uncertain about the color of the ancient Egyptians. However, a review of Bernal's book last year in the *Village Voice* began, "What color were the ancient Egyptians? Blacker than Mubarak,[3] baby." The same article claimed that white racist archeologists chiseled the noses off ancient Egyptian statues so that future generations would not see the typically African facial characteristics. The debate reached the pages of the *Biblical Archeology Review* last year in an article titled "Were the Ancient Egyptians Black or White?" The author, classicist Frank J. Yurco, argues that some Egyptian rulers were black, others were not, and

28

[3] Mohammed Hosni Mubarak, the president of Egypt since 1981.

that "the ancient Egyptians did not think in these terms." The issue, wrote Yurco, "is a chimera, cultural baggage from our own society that can only be imposed artificially on ancient Egyptian society."

Most educationists are not even aware of the debate about whether the ancient Egyptians were black or white, but they are very sensitive to charges that the schools' curricula are Eurocentric, and they are eager to rid the schools of the taint of Eurocentrism. It is hardly surprising that America's schools would recognize strong cultural ties with Europe since our nation's political, religious, educational, and economic institutions were created chiefly by people of European descent, our government was shaped by European ideas, and nearly 80 percent of the people who live here are of European descent. The particularists treat all of this history as a racist bias toward Europe, rather than as the matter-of-fact consequences of European immigration. Even so, American education is not centered on Europe. American education, if it is centered on anything, is centered on itself. It is "Americentric." Most American students today have never studied any world history; they know very little about Europe, and even less about the rest of the world. Their minds are rooted solidly in the here and now. When the Berlin Wall was opened in the fall of 1989, journalists discovered that most American teenagers had no idea what it was, nor why its opening was such a big deal. Nonetheless, Eurocentrism provides a better target than Americentrism.

In school districts where most children are black and Hispanic, there has been a growing tendency to embrace particularism rather than pluralism. Many of the children in these districts perform poorly in academic classes and leave school without graduating. They would fare better in school if they had well-educated and well-paid teachers, small classes, good materials, encouragement at home and school, summer academic programs, protection from the drugs and crime that ravage their neighborhoods, and higher expectations of satisfying careers upon graduation. These are expensive and time-consuming remedies that must also engage the larger society beyond the school. The lure of particularism is that it offers a less complicated anodyne, one in which the children's academic deficiencies may be addressed—or set aside—by inflating their racial pride. The danger of this remedy is that it will detract attention from the real needs of schools and the real interests of children, while simultaneously arousing distorted race pride in children of all races, increasing racial antagonism, and producing fresh recruits for white and black racist groups.

The particularist critique gained a major forum in New York in 1989, 32 with the release of a report called "A Curriculum of Inclusion," produced by a task force created by the State Commissioner of Education, Thomas Sobol. In 1987, soon after his appointment, Sobol appointed a Task Force on Minorities to review the state's curriculum for instances of bias. He did this not because there had been complaints about bias in the curriculum, but because—as a newly appointed state commissioner whose previous job had been to superintend the public schools of a wealthy suburb, Scarsdale—he wanted to demonstrate his sensitivity to minority concerns. The Sobol task force was composed of representatives of African American, Hispanic, Asian American, and American Indian groups.

The task force engaged four consultants, one from each of the afore-mentioned racial or ethnic minorities, to review nearly one hundred teachers' guides prepared by the state. These guides define the state's curriculum, usually as a list of facts and concepts to be taught, along with model activities. The primary focus of the consultants, not surprisingly, was the history and social studies curriculum. As it happened, the history curriculum had been extensively revised in 1987 to make it multicultural, in both American and world history. In the 1987 revision the time given to Western Europe was reduced to one-quarter of one year, as part of a two-year global studies sequence in which equal time was allotted to seven major world regions, including Africa and Latin America.

As a result of the 1987 revisions in American and world history, New York State had one of the most advanced multicultural history–social studies curricula in the country. Dozens of social studies teachers and consultants had participated, and the final draft was reviewed by such historians as Eric Foner of Columbia University, the late Hazel Hertzberg of Teachers College, Columbia University, and Christopher Lasch of the University of Rochester. The curriculum was overloaded with facts, almost to the point of numbing students with details and trivia, but it was not insensitive to ethnicity in American history or unduly devoted to European history.

But the Sobol task force decided that this curriculum was biased and Eurocentric. The first sentence of the task force report summarizes its major thesis: "African Americans, Asian Americans, Puerto Ricans/Latinos, and Native Americans have all been the victims of an intellectual and educational oppression that has characterized the culture and institutions of the United States and the European American world for centuries."

The task force report was remarkable in that it vigorously denounced bias without identifying a single instance of bias in the curricular guides under review. Instead, the consultants employed harsh, sometimes inflammatory, rhetoric to treat every difference of opinion or interpretation as an example of racial bias. The African American consultant, for example, excoriates the curriculum for its "White Anglo-Saxon (WASP) value system and norms," its "deep-seated pathologies of racial hatred" and its "white nationalism"; he decries as bias the fact that children study Egypt as part of the Middle East instead of as part of Africa. Perhaps Egypt should be studied as part of the African unit (geographically, it is located on the African continent); but placing it in one region rather than the other is not what most people think of as racism or bias. The "Latino" consultant criticizes the use of the term "Spanish-American War" instead of "Spanish-Cuban-

36

American War." The Native American consultant complains that tribal languages are classified as "foreign languages."

The report is consistently Europhobic. It repeatedly expresses negative judgments on "European Americans" and on everything Western and European. All people with a white skin are referred to as "Anglo-Saxons" and "WASPs." Europe, says the report, is uniquely responsible for producing aggressive individuals who "were ready to 'discover, invade and conquer' foreign land because of greed, racism and national egoism." All white people are held collectively guilty for the historical crimes of slavery and racism. There is no mention of the "Anglo-Saxons" who opposed slavery and racism. Nor does the report acknowledge that some whites have been victims of discrimination and oppression. The African American consultant writes of the Constitution, "There is something vulgar and revolting in glorifying a process that heaped undeserved rewards on a segment of the population while oppressing the majority."

The New York task force proposal is not merely about the reconstruction of what is taught. It goes a step further to suggest that the history curriculum may be used to ensure that "children from Native American, Puerto Rican/ Latino, Asian American, and African American cultures will have higher self-esteem and self-respect, while children from European cultures will have a less arrogant perspective of being part of the group that has 'done it all.' "

In February 1990, Commissioner Sobol asked the New York Board of Regents to endorse a sweeping revision of the history curriculum to make it more multicultural. His recommendations were couched in measured tones, not in the angry rhetoric of his task force. The board supported his request unanimously. It remains to be seen whether New York pursues the particularist path marked out by the Commissioner's advisory group or finds its way to the concept of pluralism within a democratic tradition.

The rising tide of particularism encourages the politicization of all curricula in the schools. If education bureaucrats bend to the political and ideological winds, as is their wont, we can anticipate a generation of struggle over the content of the curriculum in mathematics, science, literature, and history. Demands for "culturally relevant" studies, for ethnostudies of all kinds, will open the classroom to unending battles over whose version is taught, who gets credit for what, and which ethno-interpretation is appropriate. Only recently have districts begun to resist the demands of fundamentalist groups to censor textbooks and library books (and some have not yet begun to do so). 40

The spread of particularism throws into question the very idea of American public education. Public schools exist to teach children the general skills and knowledge that they need to succeed in American society, and the specific skills and knowledge that they need in order to function as American citizens. They receive public support because they have a public function. Historically, the public schools were known as "common schools" because they were schools for all, even if the children of all the people did not attend them. Over the years, the courts have found that it was unconstitutional to teach religion in the common schools, or to separate children on the basis of their race in the common schools. In their curriculum, their hiring practices, and their general philosophy, the public schools must not discriminate against or give preference to any racial or ethnic group. Yet they are permitted to accommodate cultural diversity by, for example, serving food that is culturally appropriate or providing library collections that emphasize the interests of the local community. However, they should not be expected to teach children to view the world through an ethnocentric perspective that rejects or ignores the common culture. For generations, those groups that wanted to inculcate their religion or their ethnic heritage have instituted private schools—after school, on weekends, or on a full-time basis. There, children learn with others of the same group—Greeks, Poles, Germans, Japanese, Chinese, Jews, Lutherans, Catholics, and so on—and are taught by people from the same group. Valuable as this exclusive experience has been for those who choose it, this has not been the role of public education. One of the primary purposes of public education has been to create a national community, a definition of citizenship and culture that is both expansive and *inclusive*.

The curriculum in public schools must be based on whatever knowledge and practices have been determined to be best by professionals—experienced teachers and scholars—who are competent to make these judgments. Professional societies must be prepared to defend the integrity of their disciplines. When called upon, they should establish review committees to examine disputes over curriculum and to render judgment, in order to help school officials fend off improper political pressure. Where genuine controversies exist, they should be taught and debated in the classroom. Was Egypt a black civilization? Why not raise the question, read the arguments of the different sides in the debate, show slides of Egyptian pharaohs and queens, read books about life in ancient Egypt, invite guest scholars from the local university, and visit museums with Egyptian collections? If scholars disagree, students should know it. One great advantage of this approach is that students will see that history is a lively study, that textbooks are fallible, that historians disagree, that the writing of history is influenced by the historian's politics and ideology, that history is written by people who make choices among alternative facts and interpretations, and that history changes as new facts are uncovered and new interpretations win adherents. They will also learn that cultures and civilizations constantly interact, exchange ideas, and influence one another, and that the idea of racial or ethnic purity is a myth. Another advantage is that students might once again study ancient history, which has all but disappeared from the curricula of American schools. (California recently introduced a required sixth grade course in ancient civilizations, but ancient history is otherwise *terra incognita*[4] in American education.)

The multicultural controversy may do wonders for the study of history, which has been neglected for years in American schools. At this time, only half of our high school graduates ever study any world history. Any serious attempt to broaden students' knowledge of Africa, Europe, Asia, and Latin America will require at least two, and possibly three years of world history (a requirement thus far only in California). American history, too, will need more time than the one-year high-school survey course. Those of us who have insisted for years on the importance of history in the curriculum may not be ready to assent to its redemptive power, but hope that our new allies will ultimately join a constructive dialogue that strengthens the place of history in the schools.

As cultural controversies arise, educators must adhere to the principle of "E Pluribus Unum." That is, they must maintain a balance between the demands of the one—the nation of which we are common citizens—and the many—the varied histories of the American people. It is not necessary to denigrate either the one or the many. Pluralism is a positive value, but it is also important that we preserve a sense of an American community—a society and a culture to which we all belong. If there is no overall community with an agreed-upon vision of liberty and justice, if all we have is a collection of racial and ethnic cultures, lacking any common bonds, then we have no means to mobilize public opinion on behalf of people who are not members of our particular group. We have, for example, no reason to support public education. If there is no larger community, then each group will want to teach its own children in its own way, and public education ceases to exist.

History should not be confused with filiopietism. History gives no grounds for race pride. No race has a monopoly on virtue. If anything, a study of history should inspire humility, rather than pride. People of every racial group have committed terrible crimes, often against others of the same group. Whether one looks at the history of Europe or Africa or Latin America or Asia, every continent offers examples of inhumanity. Slavery has existed in civilizations around the world for centuries. Examples of genocide can be found around the world, throughout history, from ancient times right through to our own day. Governments and cultures, sometimes by edict, sometimes simply following tradition, have practiced not only slavery, but human sacrifice, infanticide, cliterodectomy,[5] and mass murder. If we teach children this, they might recognize how absurd both racial hatred and racial chauvinism are.

What must be preserved in the study of history is the spirit of inquiry, the readiness to open new questions and to pursue new understandings. History, at its best, is a search for truth. The best way to portray this search

[4] Latin; unknown or unexplored region.
[5] Excision of the clitoris; female circumcision.

is through debate and controversy, rather than through imposition of fixed beliefs and immutable facts. Perhaps the most dangerous aspect of school history is its tendency to become Official History, a sanctified version of the Truth taught by the state to captive audiences and embedded in beautiful mass-market textbooks as holy writ. When Official History is written by committees responding to political pressures, rather than by scholars synthesizing the best available research, then the errors of the past are replaced by the politically fashionable errors of the present. It may be difficult to teach children that history is both important and uncertain, and that even the best historians never have all the pieces of the jigsaw puzzle, but it is necessary to do so. If state education departments permit the revision of their history courses and textbooks to become an exercise in power politics, then the entire process of state-level curriculum-making becomes suspect, as does public education itself.

The question of self-esteem is extraordinarily complex, and it goes well beyond the content of the curriculum. Most of what we call self-esteem is formed in the home and in a variety of life experiences, not only in school. Nonetheless, it has been important for blacks—and for other racial groups—to learn about the history of slavery and of the civil rights movement; it has been important for blacks to know that their ancestors actively resisted enslavement and actively pursued equality; and it has been important for blacks and others to learn about black men and women who fought courageously against racism and who provide models of courage, persistence, and intellect. These are instances where the content of the curriculum reflects sound scholarship, and at the same time probably lessens racial prejudice and provides inspiration for those who are descendants of slaves. But knowing about the travails and triumphs of one's forebears does not necessarily translate into either self-esteem or personal accomplishment. For most children, self-esteem—the self-confidence that grows out of having reached a goal—comes not from hearing about the monuments of their ancestors but as a consequence of what they are able to do and accomplish through their own efforts.

As I reflected on these issues, I recalled reading an interview a few years 48 ago with a talented black runner. She said that her model is Mikhail Baryshnikov. She admires him because he is a magnificent athlete. He is not black; he is not female; he is not American-born; he is not even a runner. But he inspires her because of the way he trained and used his body. When I read this, I thought how narrow-minded it is to believe that people can be inspired *only* by those who are exactly like them in race and ethnicity.

Points to Consider

1. Ravitch argues that the United States has "a common culture that is multicultural." Do you agree with her on this point? What evidence does she offer to support her claim that there is a common culture?

2. What are the origins of the "particularistic multiculturalism"? Why does Ravitch believe that this position is "spreading like wildfire through the education system"? What do you think is the basis for its appeal?

3. Why does Ravitch bring up the question of whether ancient Egyptians were black or white? Of what importance is it to the issue being discussed? How does she think this question should be handled? Do you think particularists would agree with her?

4. Why does Ravitch bring up the topic of "self-esteem"? Why does she believe it is important to those who promote ethnocentrism? What place do you think it occupies in the argument? Do you agree or disagree with the way she interprets the black runner's comment on role models in her final paragraph?

R. ROOSEVELT THOMAS, JR.

From Affirmative Action to Affirming Diversity

[HARVARD BUSINESS REVIEW / March–April 1990]

Sooner or later, affirmative action will die a natural death. Its achievements have been stupendous, but if we look at the premises that underlie it, we find assumptions and priorities that look increasingly shopworn. Thirty years ago, affirmative action was invented on the basis of these five appropriate premises:

1. Adult, white males make up something called the U.S. business mainstream.

R. ROOSEVELT THOMAS, JR., (b. 1944) is executive director and founder of the American Institute for Managing Diversity. Thomas, who earned his doctor of business administration degree in organizational behavior from Harvard University, has served as dean of the Atlanta University Graduate School of Business, assistant professor at the Harvard Business School, and instructor at Morehouse College. He is currently at work on a book about managing diversity.

2. The U.S. economic edifice is a solid, unchanging institution with more than enough space for everyone.

3. Women, blacks, immigrants, and other minorities should be allowed in as a matter of public policy and common decency.

4. Widespread racial, ethnic, and sexual prejudice keeps them out.

5. Legal and social coercion are necessary to bring about the change.

Today all five of these premises need revising. Over the past six years, I have tried to help some fifteen companies learn how to achieve and manage diversity, and I have seen that the realities facing us are no longer the realities affirmative action was designed to fix.

To begin with, more than half the U.S. work force now consists of minorities, immigrants, and women, so white, native-born males, though undoubtedly still dominant, are themselves a statistical minority. In addition, white males will make up only 15 percent of the increase in the work force over the next ten years. The so-called mainstream is now almost as diverse as the society at large.

Second, while the edifice is still big enough for all, it no longer seems   4
stable, massive, and invulnerable. In fact, American corporations are scrambling, doing their best to become more adaptable, to compete more successfully for markets and labor, foreign and domestic, and to attract all the talent they can find.

Third, women and minorities no longer need a boarding pass, they need an upgrade. The problem is not getting them in at the entry level; the problem is making better use of their potential at every level, especially in middle-management and leadership positions. This is no longer simply a question of common decency, it is a question of business survival.

Fourth, although prejudice is hardly dead, it has suffered some wounds that may eventually prove fatal. In the meantime, American businesses are now filled with progressive people—many of them minorities and women themselves—whose prejudices, where they still exist, are much too deeply suppressed to interfere with recruitment. The reason many companies are still wary of minorities and women has much more to do with education and perceived qualifications than with color or gender. Companies are worried about productivity and well aware than minorities and women represent a disproportionate share of the undertrained and undereducated.

Fifth, coercion is rarely needed at the recruitment stage. There are very few places in the United States today where you could dip a recruitment net and come up with nothing but white males. Getting hired is not the problem—women and blacks who are seen as having the necessary skills and energy can get *into* the work force relatively easily. It's later on that many of them plateau and lose their drive and quit or get fired. It's later on that their managers' inability to manage diversity hobbles them and the companies they work for.

In creating these changes, affirmative action had an essential role to play   8
and played it very well. In many companies and communities it still plays
that role. But affirmative action is an artificial, transitional intervention
intended to give managers a chance to correct an imbalance, an injustice, a
mistake. Once the numbers mistake has been corrected, I don't think affirmative action alone can cope with the remaining long-term task of creating
a work setting geared to the upward mobility of *all* kinds of people, including
white males. It is difficult for affirmative action to influence upward mobility
even in the short run, primarily because it is perceived to conflict with the
meritocracy we favor. For this reason, affirmative action is a red flag to every
individual who feels unfairly passed over and a stigma for those who appear
to be its beneficiaries.

Moreover, I doubt very much that individuals who reach top positions
through affirmative action are effective models for younger members of their
race or sex. What, after all, do they model? A black vice president who got
her job through affirmative action is not necessarily a model of how to rise
through the corporate meritocracy. She may be a model of how affirmative
action can work for the people who find or put themselves in the right place
at the right time.

If affirmative action in upward mobility meant that no person's competence and character would ever be overlooked or undervalued on account
of race, sex, ethnicity, origins, or physical disability, then affirmative action
would be the very thing we need to let every corporate talent find its niche.
But what affirmative action means in practice is an unnatural focus on one
group, and what it means too often to too many employees is that someone
is playing fast and loose with standards in order to favor that group. Unless
we are to compromise our standards, a thing no competitive company can
even contemplate, upward mobility for minorities and women should always
be a question of pure competence and character unmuddled by accidents of
birth.

And that is precisely why we have to learn to manage diversity—to move
beyond affirmative action, not to repudiate it. Some of what I have to say
may strike some readers—mostly those with an ax to grind—as directed at
the majority white males who hold most of the decision-making posts in our
economy. But I am speaking to all managers, not just white males, and I
certainly don't mean to suggest that white males somehow stand outside
diversity. White males are as odd and as normal as anyone else.

The Affirmative Action Cycle

If you are managing diverse employees, you should ask yourself this   12
question: am I fully tapping the potential capacities of everyone in my
department? If the answer is no, you should ask yourself this follow-up: is
this failure hampering my ability to meet performance standards? The answer
to this question will undoubtedly be yes.

Think of corporate management for a moment as an engine burning pure gasoline. What's now going into the tank is no longer just gas, it has an increasing percentage of, let's say, methanol. In the beginning, the engine will still work pretty well, but by and by it will start to sputter, and eventually it will stall. Unless we rebuild the engine, it will no longer burn the fuel we're feeding it. As the work force grows more and more diverse at the intake level, the talent pool we have to draw on for supervision and management will also grow increasingly diverse. So the question is: can we burn this fuel? Can we get maximum corporate power from the diverse work force we're now drawing into the system?

Affirmative action gets blamed for failing to do things it never could do. Affirmative action gets the new fuel into the tank, the new people through the front door. Something else will have to get them into the driver's seat. That something else consists of enabling people, in this case minorities and women, to perform to their potential. This is what we now call managing diversity. Not appreciating or leveraging diversity, not even necessarily understanding it. Just managing diversity in such a way as to get from a heterogeneous work force the same productivity, commitment, quality, and profit that we got from the old homogeneous work force.

The correct question today is not "How are we doing on race relations?" or "Are we promoting enough minority people and women?" but rather "Given the diverse work force I've got, am I getting the productivity, does it work as smoothly, is morale as high, as if every person in the company was the same sex and race and nationality?" Most answers will be, "Well, no, of course not!" But why shouldn't the answer be, "You bet!"?

When we ask how we're doing on race relations, we inadvertently put our finger on what's wrong with the question and with the attitude that underlies affirmative action. So long as racial and gender equality is something we grant to minorities and women, there will be no racial and gender equality. What we must do is create an environment where no one is advantaged or disadvantaged, an environment where "we" is everyone. What the traditional approach to diversity did was to create a cycle of crisis, action, relaxation, and disappointment that companies repeated over and over again without ever achieving more than the barest particle of what they were after.

Affirmative action pictures the work force as a pipeline and reasons as follows: "If we can fill the pipeline with *qualified* minorities and women, we can solve our upward mobility problem. Once recruited, they will perform in accordance with our promotional criteria and move naturally up our regular developmental ladder. In the past, where minorities and women have failed to progress, they were simply unable to meet our performance standards. Recruiting qualified people will enable us to avoid special programs and reverse discrimination."

This pipeline perspective generates a self-perpetuating, self-defeating, recruitment-oriented cycle with six stages:

1. *Problem Recognition.* The first time through the cycle, the problem takes this form—We need more minorities and women in the pipeline. In later iterations, the problem is more likely to be defined as a need to retain and promote minorities and women.

2. *Intervention.* Management puts the company into what we may call an Affirmative Action Recruitment Mode. During the first cycle, the goal is to recruit minorities and women. Later, when the cycle is repeated a second or third time and the challenge has shifted to retention, development, and promotion, the goal is to recruit *qualified* minorities and women. Sometimes, managers indifferent or blind to possible accusations of reverse discrimination will institute special training, tracking, incentive, mentoring, or sponsoring programs for minorities and women.

3. *Great Expectations.* Large numbers of minorities and women have been recruited, and a select group has been promoted or recruited at a higher level to serve as highly visible role models for the newly recruited masses. The stage seems set for the natural progression of minorities and women up through the pipeline. Management leans back to enjoy the fruits of its labor.

4. *Frustration.* The anticipated natural progression fails to occur. Minorities and women see themselves plateauing prematurely. Management is upset (and embarrassed) by the failure of its affirmative action initiative and begins to resent the impatience of the new recruits and their unwillingness to give the company credit for trying to do the right thing. Depending on how high in the hierarchy they have plateaued, alienated minorities and women either leave the company or stagnate.

5. *Dormancy.* All remaining participants conspire tacitly to present a silent front to the outside world. Executives say nothing because they have no solutions. As for those women and minorities who stayed on, calling attention to affirmative action's failures might raise doubts about their qualifications. Do they deserve their jobs, or did they just happen to be in the right place at the time of an affirmative action push? So no one complains, and if the company has a good public relations department, it may even wind up with a reputation as a good place for women and minorities to work.

If questioned publicly, management will say things like "Frankly, affirmative action is not currently an issue," or "Our numbers are okay," or "With respect to minority representation at the upper levels, management is aware of this remaining challenge."

In private and off the record, however, people say things like "Premature plateauing is a problem, and we don't know what to do," and "Our top people don't seem to be interested in finding a solution," and "There's plenty of racism and sexism around this place—whatever you may hear."

6. *Crisis.* Dormancy can continue indefinitely, but it is usually broken by a crisis of competitive pressure, governmental intervention, external pressure from a special interest group, or internal unrest. One company found

that its pursuit of a Total Quality program was hampered by the alienation of minorities and women. Senior management at another corporation saw the growing importance of minorities in their customer base and decided they needed minority participation in their managerial ranks. In another case, growing expressions of discontent forced a break in the conspiracy of silence even after the company had received national recognition as a good place for minorities and women to work.

Whatever its cause, the crisis fosters a return to the Problem Recognition phase, and the cycle begins again. This time, management seeks to explain the shortcomings of the previous affirmative action push and usually concludes that the problem is recruitment. This assessment by a top executive is typical:

> The managers I know are decent people. While they give priority to performance, I do not believe any of them deliberately block minorities or women who are qualified for promotion. On the contrary, I suspect they bend over backward to promote women and minorities who give some indication of being qualified.
>
> However, they believe we simply do not have the necessary talent within those groups, but because of the constant complaints they have heard about their deficiencies in affirmative action, they feel they face a no-win situation. If they do not promote, they are obstructionists. But if they promote people who are unqualified, they hurt performance and deny promotion to other employees unfairly. They can't win. The answer, in my mind, must be an ambitious new recruitment effort to bring in quality people.

And so the cycle repeats. Once again blacks, Hispanics, women, and immigrants are dropped into a previously homogeneous, all-white, all-Anglo, all-male, all native-born environment, and the burden of cultural change is placed on the newcomers. There will be new expectations and a new round of frustration, dormancy, crisis, and recruitment.   28

Ten Guidelines for Learning to Manage Diversity

The traditional American image of diversity has been assimilation: the melting pot, where ethnic and racial differences were standardized into a kind of American purée. Of course, the melting pot is only a metaphor. In real life, many ethnic and most racial groups retain their individuality and express it energetically. What we have is perhaps some kind of American mulligan stew; it is certainly no purée.

At the workplace, however, the melting pot has been more than a metaphor. Corporate success has demanded a good deal of conformity, and employees have voluntarily abandoned most of their ethnic distinctions at the company door.

Now those days are over. Today the melting pot is the wrong metaphor even in business, for three good reasons. First, if it ever was possible to melt down Scotsmen and Dutchmen and Frenchmen into an indistinguishable broth, you can't do the same with blacks, Asians, and women. Their differences don't melt so easily. Second, most people are no longer willing to be melted down, not even for eight hours a day—and it's a seller's market for skills. Third, the trust of today's nonhierarchical, flexible, collaborative management requires a ten- or twentyfold increase in our tolerance for individuality.

So companies are faced with the problem of surviving in a fiercely   32
competitive world with a work force that consists and will continue to consist of *unassimilated diversity*. And the engine will take a great deal of tinkering to burn that fuel.

What managers fear from diversity is a lowering of standards, a sense that "anything goes." Of course, standards must not suffer. In fact, competence counts more than ever. The goal is to manage diversity in such a way as to get from a diverse work force the same productivity we once got from a homogeneous work force, and to do it without artificial programs, standards—or barriers.

Managing diversity does not mean controlling or containing diversity, it means enabling every member of your work force to perform to his or her potential. It means getting from employees, first, everything we have a right to expect, and, second—if we do it well—everything they have to give. If the old homogeneous work force performed dependably at 80 percent of its capacity, then the first result means getting 80 percent from the new heterogeneous work force too. But the second result, the icing on the cake, the unexpected upside that diversity can perhaps give as a bonus, means 85 to 90 percent from everyone in the organization.

For the moment, however, let's concentrate on the basics of how to get satisfactory performance from the new diverse work force. There are few adequate models. So far, no large company I know of has succeeded in managing diversity to its own satisfaction. But any number have begun to try.

On the basis of their experience, here are my ten guidelines: 36
1. *Clarify Your Motivation.* A lot of executives are not sure why they should want to learn to manage diversity. Legal compliance seems like a good reason. So does community relations. Many executives believe they have a social and moral responsibility to employ minorities and women. Others want to placate an internal group or pacify an outside organization. None of these are bad reasons, but none of them are business reasons, and given the nature and scope of today's competitive challenges, I believe only business reasons will supply the necessary long-term motivation. In any case, it is the business reasons I want to focus on here.

In business terms, a diverse work force is not something your company ought to have; it's something your company does have, or soon will have. Learning to manage that diversity will make you more competitive.

2. *Clarify Your Vision.* When managers think about a diverse work force, what do they picture? Not publicly, but in the privacy of their minds?

One popular image is of minorities and women clustering on a relatively low plateau, with a few of them trickling up as they become assimilated into the prevailing culture. Of course, they enjoy good salaries and benefits, and most of them accept their status, appreciate the fact that they are doing better than they could do somewhere else, and are proud of the achievements of their race or sex. This is reactionary thinking, but it's a lot more common than you might suppose. 40

Another image is what we might call "heightened sensitivity." Members of the majority culture are sensitive to the demands of minorities and women for upward mobility and recognize the advantages of fully utilizing them. Minorities and women work at all levels of the corporation, but they are the recipients of generosity and know it. A few years of this second-class status drives most of them away and compromises the effectiveness of those that remain. Turnover is high.

Then there is the coexistence-compromise image. In the interests of corporate viability, white males agree to recognize minorities and women as equals. They bargain and negotiate their differences. But the win-lose aspect of the relationship preserves tensions, and the compromises reached are not always to the company's competitive advantage.

"Diversity and equal opportunity" is a big step up. It presupposes that the white male culture has given way to one that respects difference and individuality. The problem is that minorities and women will accept it readily as their operating image, but many white males, consciously or unconsciously, are likely to cling to a vision that leaves them in the driver's seat. A vision gap of this kind can be a difficulty.

In my view, the vision to hold in your own imagination and to try to communicate to all your managers and employees is an image of fully tapping the human resource potential of every member of the work force. This vision sidesteps the question of equality, ignores the tensions of coexistence, plays down the uncomfortable realities of difference, and focuses instead on individual enablement. It doesn't say "Let *us* give *them* a chance." It assumes a diverse work force that includes us and them. It says, "Let's create an environment where everyone will do their best work." 44

Several years ago, an industrial plant in Atlanta with a highly diverse work force was threatened with closing unless productivity improved. To save their jobs, everyone put their shoulders to the wheel and achieved the results they needed to stay open. The senior operating manager was amazed.

For years he had seen minorities and women plateauing disproportionately at the lower levels of the organization, and he explained that fact away with two rationalizations. "They haven't been here that long," he told himself. And "This is the price we pay for being in compliance with the law."

When the threat of closure energized this whole group of people into a level of performance he had not imagined possible, he got one fleeting glimpse of people working up to their capacity. Once the crisis was over, everyone went back to the earlier status quo—white males driving and everyone else sitting back, looking on—but now there was a difference. Now, as he put it himself, he had been to the mountaintop. He knew that what he was getting from minorities and women was nowhere near what they were capable of giving. And he wanted it, crisis or no crisis, all the time.

3. *Expand Your Focus.* Managers usually see affirmative action and equal employment opportunity as centering on minorities and women, with very little to offer white males. The diversity I'm talking about includes not only race, gender, creed, and ethnicity but also age, background, education, function, and personality differences. The objective is not to assimilate minorities and women into a dominant white male culture but to create a dominant heterogeneous culture.

The culture that dominates the United States socially and politically is heterogeneous, and it works by giving its citizens the liberty to achieve their potential. Channeling that potential, once achieved, is an individual right but still a national concern. Something similar applies in the workplace, where the keys to success are individual ability and a corporate destination. Managing disparate talents to achieve common goals is what companies learned to do when they set their sights on, say, Total Quality. The secrets of managing diversity are much the same.

4. *Audit Your Corporate Culture.* If the goal is not to assimilate diversity into the dominant culture but rather to build a culture that can digest unassimilated diversity, then you had better start by figuring out what your present culture looks like. Since what we're talking about here is the body of unspoken and unexamined assumptions, values, and mythologies that make your world go round, this kind of cultural audit is impossible to conduct without outside help. It's a research activity, done mostly with in-depth interviews and a lot of listening at the water cooler.

The operative corporate assumptions you have to identify and deal with are often inherited from the company's founder. "If we treat everyone as a member of the family, we will be successful" is not uncommon. Nor is its corollary "Father Knows Best."

Another widespread assumption, probably absorbed from American culture in general, is that "cream will rise to the top." In most companies, what passes for cream rising to the top is actually cream being pulled or pushed to the top by an informal system of mentoring and sponsorship.

Corporate culture is a kind of tree. Its roots are assumptions about the company and about the world. Its branches, leaves, and seeds are behavior. You can't change the leaves without changing the roots, and you can't grow peaches on an oak. Or rather, with the proper grafting, you *can* grow peaches on an oak, but they come out an awful lot like acorns—small and hard and not much fun to eat. So if you want to grow peaches, you have to make sure the tree's roots are peach-friendly.

5. *Modify Your Assumptions.* The real problem with this corporate culture tree is that every time you go to make changes in the roots, you run into terrible opposition. Every culture, including corporate culture, has root guards that turn out in force every time you threaten a basic assumption.

Take the family assumption as an example. Viewing the corporation as a family suggests not only that father knows best; it also suggests that sons will inherit the business, that daughters should stick to doing the company dishes, and that if Uncle Deadwood doesn't perform, we'll put him in the chimney corner and feed him for another thirty years regardless. Each assumption has its constituency and its defenders. If we say to Uncle Deadwood, "Yes, you did good work for ten years, but years eleven and twelve look pretty bleak; we think it's time we helped you find another chimney," shock waves will travel through the company as every family-oriented employee draws a sword to defend the sacred concept of guaranteed jobs.

But you have to try. A corporation that wants to create an environment with no advantages or disadvantages for any group cannot allow the family assumption to remain in place. It must be labeled dishonest mythology.

Sometimes the dishonesties are more blatant. When I asked a white male middle manager how promotions were handled in his company, he said, "You need leadership capability, bottom-line results, the ability to work with people, and compassion." Then he paused and smiled. "That's what they say. But down the halls there's a guy we call Captain Kickass. He's ruthless, mean-spirited, and he steps on people. That's the behavior they really value. Forget what they say."

In addition to the obvious issue of hypocrisy, this example also raises a question of equal opportunity. When I asked this young middle manager if he thought minorities and women could meet the Captain Kickass standard, he said he thought they probably could. But the opposite argument can certainly be made. Whether we're talking about blacks in an environment that is predominantly white, whites in one predominantly black, or women in one predominantly male, the majority culture will not readily condone such tactics from a member of a minority. So the corporation with the unspoken kickass performance standard has at least one criterion that will hamper the upward mobility of minorities and women.

Another destructive assumption is the melting pot I referred to earlier. The organization I'm arguing for respects differences rather than seeking to smooth them out. It is multicultural rather than culture-blind, which has an important consequence: when we no longer force people to "belong" to a common ethnicity or culture, then the organization's leaders must work all the harder to define belonging in terms of a set of values and a sense of

56

purpose that transcend the interests, desires, and preferences of any one group.

6. *Modify Your Systems.* The first purpose of examining and modifying 60 assumptions is to modify systems. Promotion, mentoring, and sponsorship comprise one such system, and the unexamined cream-to-the-top assumption I mentioned earlier can tend to keep minorities and women from climbing the corporate ladder. After all, in many companies it is difficult to secure a promotion above a certain level without a personal advocate or sponsor. In the context of managing diversity, the question is not whether this system is maximally efficient but whether it works for all employees. Executives who only sponsor people like themselves are not making much of a contribution to the cause of getting the best from every employee.

Performance appraisal is another system where unexamined practices and patterns can have pernicious effects. For example, there are companies where official performance appraisals differ substantially from what is said informally, with the result that employees get their most accurate performance feedback through the grapevine. So if the grapevine is closed to minorities and women, they are left at a severe disadvantage. As one white manager observed, "If the blacks around here knew how they were really perceived, there would be a revolt." Maybe so. More important to your business, however, is the fact that without an accurate appraisal of performance, minority and women employees will find it difficult to correct or defend their alleged shortcomings.

7. *Modify Your Models.* The second purpose of modifying assumptions is to modify models of managerial and employee behavior. My own personal hobgoblin is one I call the Doer Model, often an outgrowth of the family assumption and of unchallenged paternalism. I have found the Doer Model alive and thriving in a dozen companies. It works like this:

Since father knows best, managers seek subordinates who will follow their lead and do as they do. If they can't find people exactly like themselves, they try to find people who aspire to be exactly like themselves. The goal is predictability and immediate responsiveness because the doer manager is not there to manage people but to do the business. In accounting departments, for example, doer managers do accounting, and subordinates are simply extensions of their hands and minds, sensitive to every signal and suggestion of managerial intent.

Doer managers take pride in this identity of purpose. "I wouldn't ask 64 my people to do anything I wouldn't do myself," they say. "I roll up my sleeves and get in the trenches." Doer managers love to be in the trenches. It keeps them out of the line of fire.

But managers aren't supposed to be in the trenches, and accounting managers aren't supposed to do accounting. What they are supposed to do is create systems and a climate that allow accountants to do accounting, a climate that enables people to do what they've been charged to do. The right goal is doer subordinates, supported and empowered by managers who manage.

8. *Help Your People Pioneer.* Learning to manage diversity is a change process, and the managers involved are change agents. There is no single tried and tested "solution" to diversity and no fixed right way to manage it. Assuming the existence of a single or even a dominant barrier undervalues the importance of all the other barriers that face any company, including, potentially, prejudice, personality, community dynamics, culture, and the ups and downs of business itself.

While top executives articulate the new company policy and their commitment to it, middle managers—most or all of them still white males, remember—are placed in the tough position of having to cope with a forest of problems and simultaneously develop the minorities and women who represent their own competition for an increasingly limited number of promotions. What's more, every time they stumble they will themselves be labeled the major barriers to progress. These managers need help, they need a certain amount of sympathy, and, most of all, perhaps, they need to be told that they are pioneers and judged accordingly.

In one case, an ambitious young black woman was assigned to a white   68
male manager, at his request, on the basis of her excellent company record. They looked forward to working together, and for the first three months, everything went well. But then their relationship began to deteriorate, and the harder they worked at patching it up, the worse it got. Both of them, along with their superiors, were surprised by the conflict and seemed puzzled as to its causes. Eventually the black woman requested and obtained reassignment. But even though they escaped each other, both suffered a sense of failure severe enough to threaten their careers.

What could have been done to assist them? Well, empathy would not have hurt. But perspective would have been better yet. In their particular company and situation, these two people had placed themselves at the cutting edge of race and gender relations. They needed to know that mistakes at the cutting edge are different—and potentially more valuable—than mistakes elsewhere. Maybe they needed some kind of pioneer training. But at the very least they needed to be told that they were pioneers, that conflicts and failures came with the territory, and that they would be judged accordingly.

9. *Apply the Special Consideration Test.* I said earlier that affirmative action was an artificial, transitional, but necessary stage on the road to a truly diverse work force. Because of its artificial nature, affirmative action requires constant attention and drive to make it work. The point of learning once and for all how to manage diversity is that all that energy can be focused somewhere else.

There is a simple test to help you spot the diversity programs that are going to eat up enormous quantities of time and effort. Surprisingly, perhaps, it is the same test you might use to identify the programs and policies that created your problem in the first place. The test consists of one question: does this program, policy, or principle give special consideration to one group? Will it contribute to everyone's success, or will it only produce an advantage for blacks or whites or women or men? Is it designed for *them* as opposed to *us*? Whenever the answer is yes, you're not yet on the road to managing diversity.

This does not rule out the possibility of addressing issues that relate to a single group. It only underlines the importance of determining that the issue you're addressing does not relate to other groups as well. For example, management in one company noticed that blacks were not moving up in the organization. Before instituting a special program to bring them along, managers conducted interviews to see if they could find the reason for the impasse. What blacks themselves reported was a problem with the quality of supervision. Further interviews showed that other employees too—including white males—were concerned about the quality of supervision and felt that little was being done to foster professional development. Correcting the situation eliminated a problem that affected everyone. In this case, a solution that focused only on blacks would have been out of place. 72

Had the problem consisted of prejudice, on the other hand, or some other barrier to blacks or minorities alone, a solution based on affirmative action would have been perfectly appropriate.

10. *Continue Affirmative Action.* Let me come full circle. The ability to manage diversity is the ability to manage your company without unnatural advantage or disadvantage for any member of your diverse work force. The fact remains that you must first have a work force that is diverse at every level, and if you don't, you're going to need affirmative action to get from here to there.

The reason you then want to move beyond affirmative action to managing diversity is because affirmative action fails to deal with the root causes of prejudice and inequality and does little to develop the full potential of every man and woman in the company. In a country seeking competitive advantage in a global economy, the goal of managing diversity is to develop our capacity to accept, incorporate, and empower the diverse human talents of the most diverse nation on earth. It's our reality. We need to make it our strength.

Points to Consider

1. Why does Thomas believe that affirmative action programs are obsolete? How does he suggest we replace them?

2. Why does Thomas think that business needs new models and metaphors? What is wrong with the old ones? What assumptions are they based on?

3. What kind of cycle does affirmative action lead to? What causes this cycle? How does Thomas propose to break the cycle?

4. What audience is Thomas addressing in this article? How does his awareness of this audience's needs and interests shape his terminology and reasoning?

LALITA GANDBHIR

Free and Equal [THE MASSACHUSETTS REVIEW / Winter 1989]

Ramesh carefully studied his reflection in the mirror hung in the hallway. His hair, shirt, tie, suit, nothing escaped his scrutiny. His tie seemed a little crooked, so he undid it and fixed it with slow deliberate movements. Then he reexamined the tie. A conservative shade of maroon, not too wide, not too narrow, just right for the occasion, for the image he wanted to project.

All of a sudden he was aware of two eyes staring at him. He turned to Jay, his little son. Jay sat on the steps leading to the second floor, his eyes focused on his father.

"Why are you staring at me?" Ramesh inquired.

"Going to work now?" Jay intimated the reason for the surprised stare.   4

Ramesh understood the reason behind Jay's confusion. He used to go to work dressed like this in the mornings. Jay had not seen him dressed in a suit in the evening.

For a moment Ramesh was proud of his son. "What a keen observer Jay is!" Ramesh thought to himself. "For six months I have not worked, yet he noticed a change in my old routine."

However, the implications behind the question bothered Ramesh.

"I am going to a job fair," he answered irritably and again attempted to   8
focus his attention on his tie.

"Can I come?" Jay promptly hurled a question in Ramesh's direction. To him a fair was a fun event. He had been to fairs with his mother before and did not wish to miss this one.

Lalita Gandbhir (b. 1938) has lived and worked in the greater Boston area since she came to the United States in 1963. She has published stories in several journals and magazines, including Toronto South Asian Review, Massachusetts Review, *and* Spotlight. *She has also published two short story collections in India. Gandbhir works as a physician.*

"Jay, this is not the kind of fair you are thinking of. This is a job fair."

"Do they sell jobs at job fairs?"

"Yes." Jay's question struck a sensitive spot. "No, they don't sell jobs.   12
They are buyers. They shop for skills. It's me who is selling my skills. Unfortunately, it's a buyer's market."

The question had stimulated Ramesh's chain of thought. "Is my skill for sale?" Ramesh wondered. "If that is true, then why did I dress so carefully? Why did I rehearse answers to imaginary questions from interviewers?"

"No, this job hunting is no longer a simple straightforward business transaction like it used to be when engineers were in demand. I am desperate. I am selling my soul. The job market is no longer a two-way street. I have no negotiating power. I just have to accept what I can get."

Ramesh pulled on his socks mechanically and longingly thought of the good old days like a sick old man thinking of his healthful youth.

Just ten years ago he had hopped from job to job at will. Money,   16
interesting work, more responsibility, benefits, a whim for any reason that appealed to him, and he had switched jobs. Responding to advertisements was his hobby. Head hunters called him offering better and better situations. He went to job fairs casually dressed and never gave a second thought to his attire.

He had job offers, not one or two, but six or seven. The industry needed him then. It was so nice to be coveted!

Ramesh wiped his polished, spotless shoes with a soft cloth.

How carefree he used to be! He dressed like this every morning in five minutes and, yes, Jay remembers.

He never polished his shoes then. His hand moving the cloth on his   20
shoes stood still for a minute. Yes, Rani, his wife, did it for him. Nowadays she seemed to do less and less for him. Why? he asked himself.

Rani had found a part-time job on her own when companies in the area had started to lay off engineers. She had not bothered to discuss the matter with him, just informed him of her decision. In a year she had been promoted once and was recently offered another promotion if she accepted a full-time slot. "How did she manage to receive promotions so soon?" Ramesh wondered.

Rani still ran the home and cared for their young children. Ramesh had seen her busy at all kinds of tasks from early morning until late at night.

Over the last three months she did less and less for Ramesh. She no longer did his laundry or ironing. She had stopped polishing his shoes and did not wait up for him when he returned late from job fairs.

"She is often tired," Ramesh tried to understand, but he felt that she   24
had let him down, wronged him just when his spirit was sinking and he needed her most.

"She should have made an effort for the sake of appearance. It was her duty toward a jobless, incomeless husband."

He pushed all thoughts out of his mind.

He tied his polished shoes, dragged his heavy winter coat out of the closet, and picked up his keys.

"Tell your Ma that I have left," he ordered Jay, and closed the door without saying good-bye to Rani. 28

In the car, thoughts flooded his mind again.

Perhaps he made a mistake in coming to study abroad for his Masters in engineering. No! That was not the error. He should not have stayed on after he received his Masters. He should have returned home as he originally planned.

He intended to return, but unfortunately he attended a job fair after graduation just for fun and ended up accepting a job offer. A high salary in dollars converted into a small fortune in rupees, proved impossible to resist. He always converted dollars into rupees then, before buying or selling. He offered himself an excuse of short-term American experience and stayed on. The company that hired him sponsored him for a green card.

He still wanted to return home, but he postponed it, went for a visit instead and picked Rani from several prospective brides, married her and returned to the United States. 32

The trip left bitter memories, especially for Rani. He could not talk his mother out of accepting a dowry.

"Mother, Rani will earn the entire sum of a dowry in a month in the United States. A dowry is a hardship for her middle-class family. Let us not insist on it. Just accept what her family offers."

But Mother, with Father's tacit support, insisted. "You are my only son. I have waited for this occasion all my life. I want a proper wedding, the kind of wedding our friends and relatives will remember forever."

Ramesh gave in to her wishes and had a wedding with pomp and special traditional honors for his family. His mother was only partially gratified because she felt that their family did not get what was due them with her foreign returned son! The dowry, however, succeeded in upsetting Rani, who looked miserable throughout the ceremony. 36

"We will refund all the money once you come to the United States," Ramesh promised her. "It's a minor sum when dollars are converted to rupees."

Instead of talking in his conciliatory tone, Rani demanded, too harshly for a bride, "If it is a minor sum, why did you let your family insist on a dowry? You know my parents' savings are wiped out."

Later he found out that Rani wanted to back out of the match because of the dowry, but her family would not let her.

Over a few years they refunded the money, but Rani's wounds never healed and during fights she referred to the dowry spitefully. 40

Her caustic remarks did not bother Ramesh before, but now with her income supporting the family, they were beginning to hurt. "Write your mother that your wife works and makes up for part of the dowry her father failed to provide!" she had remarked once.

"Don't women ever forgive?" he had wondered.

"I am being extra sensitive." He brushed off the pain that Rani's words caused.

The job fair was at a big hotel. He followed the directions and turned into a full parking lot. As he pulled into the tight space close to the exit, he glanced at the hotel lobby. Through the glass exterior wall, underneath a brightly lit chandelier, he could see a huge crowd milling in the lobby. 44

Panic struck him. He was late. So many people had made it there ahead of him. All applicants with his experience and background might be turned away.

Another car approached and pulled into the last parking space in the lot. The engine noise died and a man roughly his height and build stepped out, just as Ramesh shut his car door. Out on the walkway Ramesh heard a greeting.

"Hello, how are you?"

Ramesh looked up. 48

In the fluorescent lights his eyes met friendly blue eyes. He noticed a slightly wrinkled forehead and receding hairline, like his own.

"Hello," Ramesh responded.

The stranger smiled. "Sometimes I wonder why I come to these fairs. In the last six months I must have been to at least ten."

"Really? So have I!" He must have been laid off at the same time, Ramesh thought. 52

"We must have attended the same ones. I don't remember seeing you," the newcomer said.

"Too many engineers looking for a job—you know," Ramesh offered as explanation.

The pair had approached the revolving lobby doors. Ramesh had a strong urge to turn back and return home.

"Come on, we must try." The newcomer apparently had sensed the urge. 56 "My name is Bruce. Would you like to meet me at the door in an hour? We will have a drink before we go home. It will—kind of lift my spirits."

"All right," Ramesh agreed without thinking and added, "I am Ramesh."

Bruce waited for Ramesh to step into the revolving door.

Ramesh mechanically pushed into the lobby. His heart sagged even further. "With persons like Bruce looking for a job, who will hire a foreigner like me?" he wondered. He looked around. Bruce had vanished into the crowd.

Ramesh looked at a row of booths set up by the side wall. He approached 60 one looking for engineers with his qualifications. A few Americans had already lined up to talk to the woman screening the applicants.

She looked at him and repeated the same questions she had asked applicants before him. "Your name, sir?"

He had to spell it. She made a mistake in noting it down. He had to correct her.

"Please fill out this application." He sensed a slight irritation in her voice.

"Thank you," he said. His accent seemed to have intensified. He took the application and retreated to a long table. 64

He visited six or seven booths of companies who might need—directly, indirectly, or remotely—someone of his experience and education; challenge, benefit package, location, salary, nothing mattered to him any more. He had to find a job.

An hour and a half later, as he approached the revolving door, he noticed Bruce waiting for him.

During the discussion over drinks, he discovered that Bruce had the same qualifications as himself. However, Bruce had spent several years wandering around the world, so he had only four years of experience. Ramesh had guessed right. Bruce had been laid off the same time as himself.

"It's been very hard," Bruce said. "What little savings we had are wiped out and my wife is fed up with me. She thinks I don't try hard. This role reversal is not good for a man's ego." 68

"Yes," Ramesh agreed.

"I may have to move but my wife doesn't want to. Her family is here."

"I understand."

"I figure you don't have that problem." 72

"No. You must have guessed I'm from India."

After a couple of drinks they walked out into an empty lobby and empty parking lot.

Two days later Bruce called. "Want to go to a job fair? It's in Woodland, two hundred miles from here. I hate to drive out alone." Ramesh agreed.

"Who will hire me when Americans are available?" he complained to Rani afterward. 76

"You must not think like that. You are as good as any of them," Rani snapped. "Remember what Alexander said."

Ramesh remembered. Alexander was a crazy history student with whom he had shared an apartment. Rani always referred to Alexander's message.

Ramesh had responded to an advertisement on his university's bulletin board and Alexander had answered the phone.

"You have to be crazy to share an apartment with me. My last roommate left because he could not live with me." 80

"What did you do? I mean, why did he leave?" Ramesh asked.

"I like to talk. You see, I wake up people and tell them about my ideas at night. They call me crazy Alexander . . ."

"I will get back to you." Ramesh put the receiver down and talked to the student who had moved out.

"You see, Alexander's a nut. He sleeps during the day and studies at night. He's a history buff. He studies revolutions. He wakes up people just to talk to them, about theories, others and his own! He will offer to discount the rent if you put up with him."

Short of funds, Ramesh moved in with Alexander.

Much of Alexander's oratory bounced off Ramesh's half-asleep brain, but off and on a few sentences made an impression and stuck in his memory.

"You must first view yourself as free and equal," Alexander had said.

"Equal to whom?"

"To those around you who consider you less than equal . . ."

"Me? Less than equal?"

"No! Not you, stupid. The oppressed person. Oppression could be social, religious, foreign, traditional."

"Who oppressed me?"

"No! No! Not you! An imaginary oppressed person who must first see himself as the equal of his oppressors. The idea of equality will ultimately sow seeds of freedom and revolution in his mind. That idea is the first step. You see . . . stop snoring . . . That's the first step toward liberation."

Soon Ramesh walked like a zombie.

In another month, he too moved out.

After his marriage he told Rani some of his conversations with Alexander.

"Makes sense," she said, looking very earnest.

"Really! You mean you understand?" Rani's reaction amazed Ramesh.

"Yes, I do. I am an oppressed person, socially and traditionally. That's why my parents had to come up with a dowry."

A month went by and Ramesh was called for an interview.

Bruce telephoned the same night. He and some other engineers he knew had also been called. Had Ramesh received a call, too?

Ramesh swallowed hard. "No, I didn't." He felt guilty and ashamed. He had lied to Bruce, who was so open, friendly, and supportive, despite his own difficulties.

Ramesh's ego had already suffered a major trauma. He was convinced that he would not get a job if Americans were available and he did not wish to admit to Bruce later on, "I had an interview, but they didn't hire me." It was easier to lie now.

The interview over, Ramesh decided to put the job out of his mind. His confidence at a low ebb, he dared not hope.

Three weeks went by and he received a phone call from the company that interviewed him. He had the job.

"They must have hired several engineers," Ramesh thought, elated.

Bruce called again. "I didn't get the job. The other guys I know have also received negative replies."

The news stunned Ramesh. He could not believe that he had the job and the others did not. As he pondered this, he realized he owed an embarrassing explanation to Bruce. How was he going to tell him that he had the job? 108

As Bruce jabbered about something, Ramesh collected his courage.

"I have an offer from them," he stated in a flat tone and strained his ear for a response.

After a few unbearable seconds of silence, Bruce exclaimed, "Congratulations! At least one of us made it. Now we can all hope. I know you have better qualifications."

Ramesh knew that the voice was sincere, without a touch of the envy he had anticipated. 112

They agreed to meet Saturday for a drink, a small celebration, Bruce suggested.

"Rani, I got the job. The others didn't." Ramesh hung up the receiver and bounded up to Rani.

"I told you you are as good as any of them," Rani responded nonchalantly and continued to fold laundry.

Maybe . . . possibly . . . they needed a minority candidate," Ramesh muttered. 116

Rani stopped folding. "Ramesh," she said as her eyes scanned Ramesh's face, "You may have the job and the knowledge and the qualifications, but you are not free and equal."

"What do you mean?" Ramesh asked.

Points to Consider

1. How does the job market affect Ramesh's self-image? How is this conveyed by the opening paragraph of the story?

2. Why is Rani's dowry an issue in their marriage? How has this problem followed them to America? What does it suggest about their marriage?

3. Why is Alexander an important character in the story? Why is he "crazy"? Do you think the writer of the story regards him as crazy?

4. Why does the story end with Ramesh's question? What does his question indicate about him? How would you answer his question?

Discussing the Unit

Suggested Topic for Discussion

In all of the selections in this unit, success plays a key role. Ravitch believes that students will be inspired by people from diverse backgrounds who overcame obstacles to achieve success. Thomas wants both management and labor to reach high levels of individual success. And Gandbhir's short story is about an immigrant's desire to be a successful American. Consider the idea of success. Can everyone be successful? Or does the success of some people depend upon the failure of others? Some cultures don't value material success as others do. In what ways does the individual drive to be successful conflict with social and communal values? How important is success to self-esteem?

Preparing for Discussion

1. Both Ravitch and Thomas believe that the concept of America as a great "melting pot" is obsolete. Why do they believe this? Do you think this is correct? What image do you think best describes today's America? Jot down a few metaphors (Thomas suggests "mulligan stew") that you believe could replace the "melting pot" image.

2. Previous generations of immigrants believed in the process of assimilation. Many desired to become citizens and to "blend in" with mainstream America. To these generations "self-esteem" was closely connected to one's social adaptation and material success. To what extent do you think this is still true? Do you think most of today's immigrants or ethnic groups really want to be part of the mainstream, or has the nature of self-esteem changed? Consider the selections in this unit in terms of this question.

From Discussion to Writing

Having considered a few of the images that might replace the old "melting pot" image of America, write an essay in which you propose the image that you personally think works best today. Describe why you think this is the best image for contemporary America and defend your image against other ways of picturing the nation. Be sure to discuss how your image portrays the way you think Americans should now view our cultural diversity.

26

Business and the Public Interest: Can They Work in Harmony?

In 1980, Ronald Reagan campaigned for the presidency on the promise "to get government off the backs of business." He kept his promise. By Reagan's second term of office American business had fewer regulations—and greater prosperity—than it had at any time since Calvin Coolidge's presidency in the 1920s. But as the 1980s wore on, a number of scandals and instances of corruption—from insider trading to toxic waste problems—altered public perceptions of corporate responsibility. In "Murder, Inc.," Robert Sherrill takes a hard look at recent corporate crime and cover-up. Sherrill introduces us to a number of business executives who, he feels, because of deliberate negligence and dangerous products, are as guilty of murder as any of the killers on death row. Though he thinks it would be legally futile, he proposes that in the interests of applying capital punishment fairly, our "corporate murderers" should also be given the death sentence.

But if business has the power to destroy human lives, might it also have the power to save them? In "Revolution in the Marketplace," Marjorie Kelly explores this question and reports that there is a new respect for human resources and the environment emerging in the business world. According to Kelly, some people have come to believe that business might be the last best hope of humanity. Will American business really grow kinder and gentler in the 1990s? In "Buying In," Eve Pell examines the recent trend of corporate funding for environmental groups. The businesses themselves profess to have adopted a more enlightened attitude toward the public sector, but Pell exposes the darker side of these "philanthropic" activities. All three pieces in this unit point up some of the major difficulties that those hoping for more publicly accountable corporations must face.

ROBERT SHERRILL

Murder, Inc. [GRAND STREET / Spring 1986]

There are something over fifteen hundred men and women on the death rows of America. Given the social context in which they operated, one might reasonably assume that they were sentenced to be executed not because they are murderers but because they were inefficient. Using guns and knives and the usual footpad paraphernalia, they dispatched only a few more than their own number. Had they used asbestos, mislabeled pharmaceutical drugs and devices, defective autos, and illegally used and illegally disposed chemicals, they could have killed, crippled, and tortured many thousands of people. And they could have done it without very much fuss.

Corporate criminals, as we all know, live charmed lives. Not until 1978 had a corporation ever been indicted for murder (Ford Motor Company, which was acquitted), and not until 1985 had corporate executives ever been brought to trial for murder because of the lethal mischief done by their company.

The executives who made history last year were the president, plant manager, and plant foreman of Film Recovery Systems Corporation, a ratty little silver-rendering operation in Elm Grove Village outside Chicago. The silver was recovered by cooking used X-ray films in vats of boiling cyanide. Film Recovery hired mostly illegal immigrants, who were afraid to protest

---

ROBERT SHERRILL (b. 1924), a contributing editor to the Nation, has written nine books and hundreds of magazine articles, forty of which have been published in the New York Times Magazine. Sherrill has been a visiting professor at several colleges and is the author of The Oil Follies: 1970–1980 (1983).

working conditions so foul that they made employees vomit and faint. The illegals were preferred also because they couldn't read much English and would not be spooked by the written warnings on the drums of cyanide. To make doubly sure that fright wouldn't drive workers away, management had the skull-and-cross-bones signs scraped off the drums. Although the antidote for cyanide poisoning is cheap and easy to obtain, Film Recovery Systems didn't keep any on hand.

So it came to pass that Stefan Golab, a sixty-one-year-old illegal immi-   4
grant from Poland, took too hefty a lungful of cyanide fumes and died. Charged with murder on the grounds that they had created such unsafe working conditions as to bring about "a strong probability of death and great bodily harm," the three officials were convicted and sentenced to twenty-five years in prison.

Will executives at other villainous corporations be similarly charged and convicted? Don't bet on it. In this instance the law was applied so properly, so rightly, so common-sensically that one would be foolish to expect such usage to appear again soon. It was a sort of Halley's Comet of Justice.

The idea of treating corporate murderers as just plain murderers strikes many people as excessive. Some lawyers who cautiously approved the conviction in principle said they were afraid it would confuse people generally because a bald murder charge is usually associated with a bullet in the gut or an ice pick in the neck, and nice people would have a hard time adapting the charge to the way things are sometimes accomplished in the front office. Speaking for this timid viewpoint, Alan Dershowitz, Harvard's celebrated criminal law specialist, said he thought the Film Recovery case showed we need a new category of crime. "We should have one that specifically reflects our condemnation of this sort of behavior," he said, "without necessarily assimilating it into the most heinous forms of murder" — as if the St. Valentine's Day massacre were any more heinous than Bhopal.[1]

During the trial, the Illinois prosecutor accused the defendants of "callousness, disregard of human lives, and exposing people to dangerous products all for the sake of profits." No wonder the verdict has been so modestly praised. If that's enough to rate a murder charge, our whole commercial system is at risk. If it were to become the rule, we could look forward to a lineup of accused corporate executives extending out the courthouse and around the block several times. Since there is no statute of limitations on murder, prosecutors would be obliged to charge those executives at Firestone who, a few years back, allegedly killed and injured no telling how many people by flooding the market with ten million tires they knew to be defective; and the executives at Ford who sent the Pinto into circulation knowing its gas tank was so poorly designed that a rear-end collision could turn the car

[1] Indian city, site of the Union Carbide industrial accident that produced one of the worst chemical disasters in history on December 3, 1984.

into a fire trap (several dozen men, women, and children were burned alive). From the pharmaceutical fraternity would come such as Dr. William Shedden, former vice-president and chief medical officer for Eli Lilly Research Laboratories, who recently pleaded guilty to fifteen criminal counts relating to the marketing of Oraflex, an arthritis drug that the Food and Drug Administration says has been "possibly" linked to forty-nine deaths in the United States and several hundred abroad, not to mention the hundreds who have suffered nonfatal liver and kidney failure. Seems as how the folks at Lilly, when they sought approval from the FDA, forgot to mention that the drug was already known to have killed at least twenty-eight people in Europe. (Shedden was fined $15,000; Lilly, which earned $3.1 billion in 1984, was fined $25,000.) And let's be sure to save an early murder indictment for those three sly dogs at SmithKline Beckman Corporation who whizzed their product, Selacryn, through the FDA without mentioning that it had caused severe liver damage in some patients in France. False labels were used to peddle it in this country, where it has been linked to thirty-six deaths and five hundred cases of liver and kidney damage.

Now comes a ripple of books that, were there any justice, would put a dozen or so hangdog executives in the dock. Three of the books make particularly persuasive cases. Paul Brodeur's *Outrageous Misconduct: The Asbestos Industry on Trial* (Pantheon) is an account of how the largest manufacturer of asbestos products, Manville Corporation (previously known as Johns-Manville Corporation), and other asbestos companies committed over the years what one plaintiff's attorney called "the greatest mass murder in history," which is possibly true if one means industrial mass murder, not political. People who regularly inhale asbestos fibers are likely to die, or at least be crippled, from the lung disease called asbestosis or the even worse (at least it sounds worse) mesothelioma. It sometimes takes twenty or thirty years for asbestosis to appear, so a measure of the slaughter from it is somewhat vague. But the best experts in the field, which means Dr. Irving J. Selikoff and his staff at the Mount Sinai Hospital in New York City, estimate that aside from the many thousands who have died from asbestos diseases in the past, there will be between eight and ten thousand deaths from asbestos-related cancer each year for the next twenty years. These deaths are not accidental. Manville et al. knew exactly what they were doing. Brodeur's book is mainly an account of how the asbestos companies, though they claimed to be ignorant of the deadly quality of their product until a study by Dr. Selikoff was released in 1964, had for forty years known about, and had suppressed or disregarded, hundreds of studies that clearly showed what asbestos was doing to the people who inhaled it. Did the companies even care what was happening? Typically, at a Manville asbestos mine in Canada, company doctors found that of seven hundred and eight workers, only four — who had worked there less than four years — had

8

normal lungs. Those who were dying of asbestosis were not told of their ailment.

The other two books, Susan Perry and Jim Dawson's *Nightmare: Women and the Dalkon Shield* (Macmillan) and Morton Mintz's *At Any Cost: Corporate Greed, Women, and the Dalkon Shield* (Pantheon), remind me of what Dr. Jules Amthor said to my favorite detective: "I'm in a very sensitive profession, Mr. Marlowe. I'm a quack." The murderous quackery of the Dalkon Shield, an intrauterine device, was committed by A. H. Robins, a company that should have stuck to making Chap Stick and Sergeant's Flea & Tick Collars, and left birth-control gadgets to those who knew how to make them properly. These two books should convince anyone, I think, that compared to the fellows at A. H. Robins, the Film Recovery executives were pikers when it came to showing disregard for human lives for the sake of profits. Profits were plentiful, that's for sure. A. H. Robins sold more than 4.5 million Dalkon Shields worldwide (2.8 million in the United States) for $4.35 each; not bad for a device that cost only twenty-five cents to produce. The death count among women who wore the shield still isn't complete; the last I heard it was twenty. But wearers of the shield also have reported stillbirths, babies with major congenital defects, punctured uteri, forced hysterectomies, sterilization from infection, and various tortures and illnesses by the thousands — some generous portion, we may presume, of the 9,230 lawsuits that A. H. Robins has settled out of court. And as both books make clear, the company launched the Dalkon Shield fully aware of the shield's dangers, sold it with false advertising, kept on selling it for several years after the company knew what its customers were going through, and pulled a complicated cover-up of guilt.

Dershowitz is right in one respect: corporate murderers are not like your typical killer on death row. Corporate murderers do not set out to kill. There's no profit in that. They are simply willing to accept a certain amount of death and physical torment among their workers and customers as a sometimes necessary byproduct of the free enterprise system. Mintz has uncovered a dandy quote from history to illustrate this attitude. When it was suggested to Alfred P. Sloan, Jr., president of General Motors circa 1930, that he should have safety glass installed in Chevrolets, he refused with the explanation, "Accidents or no accidents, my concern in this matter is a matter of profit and loss."

The Sloan spirit is everywhere. Brodeur quotes from a deposition of Charles H. Roemer, once a prominent New Jersey attorney who handled legal matters for the Union Asbestos and Rubber Company. Roemer reveals that around 1942, when Union Asbestos discovered a lot of its workers coming down with asbestos disease, he and some of Union Asbestos's top officials went to Johns-Manville and asked Vandiver Brown, Manville's attorney, and Lewis Brown, president of Manville, if their physical examination program had turned up similar results. According to Roemer, Vandiver Brown said, in effect, Sure, our X-rays show many of our workers have that disease, but we don't tell them they are sick because if we did, they would stop working and sue us. Roemer recalled asking, "Mr. Brown, do you mean to tell me you would let them work until they dropped dead?" and Brown answering, "Yes, we save a lot of money that way."

Saving money, along with making money, was obviously the paramount objective of A. H. Robins, too. This was evident from the beginning, when Robins officials learned — *six months before marketing the device nationally* — that the Dalkon Shield's multifilament tail had a wicking tendency and could carry potentially deadly bacteria into the uterus. Did the company hold up marketing the shield until it could be further tested and made safe? No, no. That would have meant a delay, for one thing, in recovering the $750,000 they had paid the shield's inventors. Though Robins knew it was putting its customers in great jeopardy, it hustled the shield onto the market with promotional claims that it was "safe" and "superior" to all other intrauterine devices; and never, during the four years the shield was on the market, did A. H. Robins conduct wicking studies of the string. The shield's promotional literature, by the way, was a classic example of phony drugstore hype. A. H. Robins claimed the shield kept the pregnancy rate at 1.1 percent; the company was well aware that the shield allowed at least a 5 percent pregnancy rate, one of the most slipshod in the birth-control business. A. H. Robins also advertised that the device could be easily inserted in "even the most sensitive woman," although in fact many doctors, before inserting the shield, had to give patients an anesthetic, and many women were in pain for months.

Not long after the shield went on the market, Wayne Crowder, one of the few heroes in this sorry tale, a quality-control engineer at Chap Stick, which manufactured many of the shields for its parent firm, rejected ten thousand of them because he was convinced the strings could wick bacteria. His boss overruled him with the remark, "Your conscience doesn't pay your salary." Crowder also suggested a method for stopping the wicking, but his technique was rejected because it would have cost an extra five cents per device. Crowder kept on complaining (he would ultimately be fired as an irritant) and he finally stirred Daniel French, president of Chap Stick, to convey Crowder's criticisms to the home office. French was told to mind his own business and not worry about the safety of the shield, which prompted him to go into the corporate softshoe routine he knew would please. He wrote A. H. Robins: "It is not the intention of Chap Stick Company to attempt any unauthorized improvements in the Dalkon Shield. My only interest in the Dalkon Shield is to produce it at the lowest possible price and, therefore, increase Robins' gross profit level."

Of course, when thousands of women begin dying, screaming, cursing, and suing, it gets a little difficult to pretend that all is well with one's product, but for more than a decade A. H. Robins did its best, never recalling the gadget, never sending a warning to doctors about possible deadly side effects, and continuing to the last — continuing right up to the present even after losing hundreds of millions of dollars in lawsuits — to argue that the shield is just hunkydory. The A. H. Robins school spirit was beautifully capsulated by one of its officials who told the *National Observer,* "But after all, we are in business to sell the thing, to make a profit. I don't mean we're trying to go out and sell products that are going to be dangerous, fatal, or what have you. But you don't put all the bad things in big headlines."

Where is the corporate executive who will not savor the easy insouciance of "or what have you"?

One of the more fascinating characteristics of corporate murderers is   16
the way these fellows cover up their dirty work. They are really quite bold and successful in their deviousness. When one considers how many top officials there are at places like Manville and Robins, and when one assumes (obviously naïvely) among the lot of them surely there must be at least one or two with a functioning conscience, the completeness of their cover-ups is indeed impressive. Which isn't to say that their techniques are very sophisticated. They simply lie, or hide or burn the incriminating material. When the litigation flood began to break over Manville Corporation in the late 1960s, the asbestos gang began thwarting their victims' attorneys by claiming certain Manville executives couldn't give depositions because they were dead (when they were very much alive), by refusing to produce documents ordered by the court, and by denying that certain documents existed when in fact they did. A. H. Robins was just as expert at that sort of thing. According to Mintz, "Thousands of documents sought by lawyers for victims of the Dalkon Shield sank from sight in suspicious circumstances. A few were hidden for a decade in a home basement in Tulsa, Oklahoma. Other records were destroyed, some admittedly in a city dump in Columbus, Indiana, and some allegedly in an A. H. Robins furnace. And despite court orders, the company did not produce truckloads of documents for judicial rulings on whether the women's lawyers could see the papers."

A. H. Robins's most notorious effort at a cover-up ultimately failed, thanks to one Roger Tuttle, a classic example of what can happen when the worm turns.

Tuttle was an attorney for A. H. Robins in the early 1970s. He says that immediately after the company lost its first Dalkon Shield lawsuit, his superiors ordered him (they deny it) to search through the company's files and burn every document that he thought might be used against A. H. Robins in future lawsuits — documents that, in Tuttle's words, indicated "knowledge and complicity, if any, of top officials in what at that stage of the game appeared to be a grim situation." Unfortunately for the company, Tuttle did not fully obey orders. He took possession of some of the juiciest documents and kept them. Just why he rebelled isn't clear. Perhaps it was because Tuttle, a plain little guy who admits he isn't the smartest attorney in the world, was tired of having his employers push him around, which they often did. He says he did it because he was ashamed that "I personally lacked the courage" to challenge the order and "I wanted some sop for my own conscience as an attorney." Whatever his motivation, Tuttle sat on the purloined files for nearly ten years. He moved on to other jobs, finally winding up, a born-again Christian, on the Oral Roberts University law faculty. Watching the Dalkon Shield trials from afar, troubled by the plaintiffs' inability to cope with A. H. Robins's cover-up, Tuttle finally decided to step forward and provide the material their attorneys needed for the big breakthrough.

A lucky windfall like that is the only way victims can overcome the tremendous imbalance in legal firepower. In the way they muster defense, corporate murderers bear no resemblance to the broken-down, half-nuts, penniless drifters on death row, dozens of whom have no attorney at all. Corporate killers are like the Mafia in the way they come to court with a phalanx of attorneys. They are fronted by the best, or at least the best known. Griffin Bell, President Carter's Attorney General, has been one of A. H. Robins's attorneys.

There are two other significant differences between corporate killers and 20 the habitués of death rows. In the first place, the latter generally did not murder as part of doing business, except for the relatively few who killed coincidental to a holdup. They did not murder to protect their rackets or territory, as the Mafia does, and they did not murder to exploit a patent or to increase production and sales, as corporate murderers do. One judge accused A. H. Robins officials of taking "the bottom line as your guiding beacon and the low road as your route." Killing for the bottom line has probably not sent a single murderer to death row anywhere. In the second place, most of the men and women on death row were lonely murderers. No part of society supported what they did. But just as the Mafia can commit murder with impunity only because it has the cooperation of police and prosecutors, so too corporate murderers benefit from the collusion of re-spectable professions, particularly doctors (who, for a price, keep quiet), and insurance companies (who, to help Manville, did not reveal what their actuarial tables told about the risks to asbestos workers; and, for Robins, worked actively backstage to conceal the Dalkon Shield's menace to public health), and government agencies who are supposed to protect public health but look the other way.

It was an old, and in its way valid, excuse that Film Recovery's officials gave the court: "We were just operating like other plants, and none of the government health and safety inspectors who dropped around — neither the Elm Grove Village Public Health Department nor the Environmental Pro-tection Agency — told us we shouldn't be letting our workers stick their heads in vats of boiling cyanide." They were probably telling the truth. That's the way health and safety regulators have usually operated.

Brodeur tells us that a veritable parade of government inspectors marched through the Pittsburgh Corning asbestos plant in Tyler, Texas, over a period of six and a half years without warning the workers that the asbestos dust levels were more than twenty times the maximum recommended for health safety. One Department of Labor official later admitted he had not worn a respirator when inspecting the plant because he did not want to excite the workers into asking questions about their health. Though the Public Health Service several times measured the fallout of asbestos dust, never did it warn the workers that the stuff was eating up their lungs. Finally things got so bad at Tyler that federal inspectors, forced to bring charges against the owners for appalling infractions of health standards, recommended that they be fined $210. Today the men and women who worked in that plant (since closed) are dying of lung cancer at a rate five times greater than the national average.

The most impressive bureaucratic collusion A. H. Robins received was, not surprisingly, from the Food and Drug Administration. When trial attorneys brought evidence that the Dalkon Shield's rotting tail strings were endangering thousands of women and asked FDA officials to remove the device from the market, the agency did nothing. When the National Women's Health Network petitioned the FDA for a recall — paid for by Robins — that would remove the shield from all women then wearing it, the FDA did nothing. For a full decade it pretended to be helpless.

There is one more significant difference between the people on death row and the corporate murderers: the former sometimes say they are sorry; the latter never do. Midway through 1985, Texas executed Charles Milton, thirty-four, because when he stuck up a liquor store the owner and his wife wrestled Milton for the gun, it went off, and the woman died. Shortly before the state killed him with poison, Milton said, "I am sorry Mrs. Denton was killed in the struggle over the gun." There. He said it. It wasn't much, but he said it. And that's more than the folks at Manville have ever said about the thousands of people they killed with asbestos. When it comes to feeling no remorse, A. H. Robins doesn't take a back seat to anybody. In a famous courtroom confrontation between Federal Judge Miles W. Lord and three A. H. Robins officials, including company president E. Claiborne Robins, Jr., Judge Lord asked them to read silently to themselves a long reprimand of their actions. The most scathing passage, quoted both by Mintz and by Perry and Dawson, was this:

> Today as you sit here attempting once more to extricate yourselves from the legal consequences of your acts, none of you has faced up to the fact that more than nine thousand women [the figure two years ago (in 1984)] have made claims that they gave up part of their womanhood so that your company

might prosper. It is alleged that others gave their lives so you might so prosper. And there stand behind them legions more who have been injured but who had not sought relief in the courts of this land. . . .

If one poor young man were by some act of his — without authority or consent — to inflict such damage upon one woman, he would be jailed for a good portion of the rest of his life. And yet your company, without warning to women, invaded their bodies by the millions and caused them injuries by the thousands. And when the time came for these women to make their claims against your company, you attacked their characters. You inquired into their sexual practices and into the identity of their sex partners. You exposed these women — and ruined families and reputations and careers — in order to intimidate those who would raise their voices against you. You introduced issues that had no relationship whatsoever to the fact that you planted in the bodies of these women instruments of death, of mutilation, of disease.

Judge Lord admitted that he did not have the power to make them recall the shield but he begged them to do it on their own: "You've got lives out there, people, women, wives, moms, and some who will never be moms. . . . You are the corporate conscience. Please, in the name of humanity, lift your eyes above the bottom line."

It was a pretty stirring piece of writing (later, when Judge Lord got so pissed off he read it aloud, they say half the courtroom was in tears), and the judge asked them if it had had any impact on them.

Looking sulky, they just stared at him and said nothing.

A few weeks later, at A. H. Robins's annual meeting, E. Claiborne 28 Robins, Jr., dismissed Lord's speech as a "poisonous attack." The company did not recall the shield for another eight months.

Giving deposition in 1984, Ernest L. Bender, Jr., senior vice-president for corporate planning and development, was asked if he had ever heard an officer or employee say he or she was "sorry or remorseful about any infection that's been suffered by any Dalkon Shield wearer." He answered, "I've never heard anyone make such remarks because I've never heard anyone that said the Dalkon Shield was the cause."

What punishment is fitting for these fellows?

If they are murderers, why not the death sentence? Polls show that 84 percent of Americans favor the death penalty, but half think the penalty is unfairly applied. Let's restore their faith by applying justice equally and poetically. In Georgia recently it took the state two 2,080 volts spaced over nineteen minutes to kill a black man who murdered during a burglary. How fitting it would be to use the same sort of defective electric chair to execute, for example, auto manufacturers and tire manufacturers who knowingly kill people with defective merchandise. In Texas recently it took the state executioners forty minutes to administer the lethal poison to a drifter who had killed a woman. Could anything be more appropriate than to tie down drug and device manufacturers who have killed many women and let slow-witted executioners poke around their bodies for an hour or so, looking for just the right blood vessel to transport the poison? At a recent Mississippi execution, the prisoner's protracted gasping for breath became such an ugly spectacle that prison authorities, in a strange burst of decorum, ordered witnesses out of the death chamber. That sort of execution for Manville executives who specialized in spreading long-term asphyxiation over thousands of lives would certainly be appropriate.

But these things will never happen. For all our popular declarations of democracy, most Americans are such forelock-tugging toadies that they would be horrified to see, say, Henry Ford II occupying the same electric chair that cooked black, penniless Alpha Otis Stephens.

Nor will we incarcerate many corporate murderers. Though some of us with a mean streak may enjoy fantasizing the reception that our fat-assed corporate killers would get from some of their cellmates in America's more interesting prisons — I like to think of the pious chaps from A. H. Robins spending time in Tennessee's notorious Brushy Mountain Prison — that is not going to happen very often either, the precedent of Film Recovery to the contrary notwithstanding. The Film Recovery trio had the misfortune of working for a crappy little corporation that has since gone defunct. Judges will not be so stern with killers from giant corporations.

So long as we have an army of crassly aggressive plaintiff attorneys to rely on, however, there is always the hope that we can smite the corporations and the men who run them with a punishment they probably fear worse than death or loss of freedom: to wit, massive loss of profits. Pamela C. Van Duyn, whose use of the Dalkon Shield at the age of twenty-six destroyed one Fallopian tube and critically damaged the other (her childbearing chances are virtually nil), says: "As far as I'm concerned, the last dime that is in Claiborne Robins's pocket ought to be paid over to all the people that have suffered." Author Brodeur dreams of an even broader financial punishment for the industry he hates:

> When I was a young man, out of college in 1953, I went into the Army Counterintelligence Corps and went to Germany, where I saw one of the death camps, Dachau. And I saw what the occupational army had done to Dachau. They had razed it, left the chimneys standing, and the barbed wire as a monument — quite the same way the Romans left Carthage. What I would do with some of these companies that are nothing more or less than killing grounds would be to sell their assets totally, reimburse the victims, and leave the walls as a reminder — just the way Dachau was — that a law-abiding and decent society will not tolerate this kind of conduct.

He added, "I know perfectly well that this is not going to happen in the private enterprise system."

How right he is. The laws, the court system, federal and state legislatures, most of the press, the unions — most of the establishment is opposed to applying the final financial solution to killer corporations.

As it became evident that juries were inclined to agree with Mrs. Van Duyn's proposal to wring plenty of money from A. H. Robins, the corporation in 1985 sought protection under Chapter 11 of the Federal Bankruptcy Code. It was a sleazy legal trick they had picked up from Manville Corporation, which had declared bankruptcy in August 1982. Although both corporations had lost hundreds of millions in court fights, neither was actually in financial trouble. Indeed, at the time it copped out under Chapter 11, Manville was the nation's 181st largest corporation and had assets of more than $2 billion. Bankruptcy was a transparent ploy — or, as plaintiff attorneys put it, a fraudulent abuse and perversion of the bankruptcy laws — but with the connivance of the federal courts it is a ploy that has worked. Not a penny has been paid to the victims of either corporation since they declared bankruptcy, and the 16,500 pending lawsuits against Manville and the five thousand lawsuits pending against A. H. Robins (those figures are climbing every day) have been frozen.

Meanwhile, companies are not even mildly chastised. Quite the contrary. Most major newspapers have said nothing about Manville's malevolent cover-up but have clucked sympathetically over its courtroom defeats. The *New York Times* editorially seemed to deplore the financial problems of the asbestos industry almost as much as it deplored the industry's massacre of workers: "Asbestos is a tragedy, most of all for the victims and their families but also for the companies, which are being made to pay the price for decisions made long ago." Senator Gary Hart, whose home state, Colorado, is corporate headquarters for Manville, pitched in with legislation that would lift financial penalty from the asbestos companies and dump it on the taxpayers. And in Richmond, Virginia, corporate headquarters for the makers of the Dalkon Shield, civic leaders threw a banquet for E. Claiborne Robins, Sr. The president of the University of Virginia assured Robins that "Your example will cast its shadow into eternity, as the sands of time carry the indelible footprint of your good works. We applaud you for always exhibiting a steadfast and devoted concern for your fellow man. Truly, the Lord has chosen you as one of His most essential instruments."

After similar encomiums from other community leaders, the top man behind the marketing of the Dalkon Shield was given the Great American Tradition Award.

Points to Consider

1. Why does Sherrill think that many people don't like the "idea of treating corporate murderers as just plain murderers"? What term would most people use instead of "corporate murderers"? How does Sherrill try to change people's attitude toward corporate crime?

2. Why does Sherrill believe that corporate murderers are in some ways *worse* than "your typical killer on death row"? What examples does he give to convince readers of this?

3. Why does Sherrill propose the death penalty for corporate murderers? Would most people agree that they deserve it? What is Sherrill's tone when he proposes the death sentence? Do you think he generally favors the death penalty? Explain.

4. Why does Sherrill believe that the best way to punish corporations may be through "massive loss of profits"? Why does he believe that such punishment is highly unlikely?

MARJORIE KELLY

Revolution in the Marketplace

[THE UTNE READER / January–February 1989]

The names come like a litany: Bhopal, the Dalkon Shield, Ivan Boesky, Three Mile Island. It is a litany of the tragedy of business in our time, the tragedy of ruined lives and a tainted earth. And not only in our time, but throughout modern history. The trail of industrialization has been a trail of bloody footprints: stripping native Americans of their homeland, raping the earth, polluting the rivers and the skies and the soil. The history of business is a tale of child labor, robber barons, snake oil salesmen, and sweat shops. In the future, our history will tell of plant closings, nuclear accidents, toxic waste, and ozone depletion.

Business is destroying the earth: if that seems to you an inescapable conclusion, it is with good reason. But there are some today who suggest a surprising sequel to this tale of destruction. There are some who say business might be the last best hope of humanity.

If business has the power to destroy the earth, might it also have the

---

MARJORIE KELLY (b. 1953) is editor and publisher of Business Ethics *magazine, which she founded in 1987. Kelly has worked as a journalist for fifteen years. She writes a regular column for* Business Ethics *called "Musings."*

power to heal it? If business has the ability to ruin human lives, might it also have the ability to save them?

The answer may be yes. From many sectors—inside and outside the 4 corporation, among academics, activists, and New Age thinkers—there are signs that a new life-affirming paradigm is emerging for business. Just as physics is shifting paradigms of the physical world from matter to energy, and as medicine is shifting paradigms of health care from treatment to prevention, so too is a shift under way in business. It is a shift from the inhuman to the human or, in consultant Michael Ducey's phrase, "from jungle to community."

The new paradigm has to do with respect for the human resources in business, and the acknowledgment that workers aren't obedient automatons but team players. It concerns employees demanding jobs with substance and meaning, and with corporations beginning to offer flextime, day care, and worker ownership. The new paradigm has corporations taking a role in helping the schools, reducing pollution, or fighting illiteracy. And it means tougher community standards, with public outcry against animal testing, nuclear power, and business in South Africa. The new paradigm has to do, in short, with making a better world—and using business as a tool.

No, the millennium has not arrived. But there are signs that the way we think about business—and the way business thinks about itself—are beginning to change.

A good example is the idea of "stakeholders," an increasingly popular concept in corporate circles. The premise is that it's not only stockholders who count, but all who have a stake in a company: employees, customers, suppliers, government, the community, anyone affected by corporate actions. NCR is one corporation that has been carrying this banner high, taking out a series of full-page ads in the *Wall Street Journal* and *Business Week*, proclaiming its commitment to various stakeholder groups. And in June, NCR sponsored the First International Symposium on Stakeholders, inviting corporate leaders to examine questions like this one, taken verbatim from the program: "Can Marxist claims about the 'internal contradictions of capitalism' be countered with a stakeholder approach to management?" Also: "Is stakeholder goodwill a fundamental component of success?"

It's respectable these days to be a good corporate citizen. When *Fortune* 8 magazine ranks America's Most Admired Corporations each year, it uses a list of "Eight Key Attributes of Reputation." Right up there alongside "Financial Soundness" is "Community and Environmental Responsibility."

Even conservative *Forbes* shows a few signs of change. In its May 1988 cover story on "The 800 Most Powerful People in Corporate America," it used a headline that could have come straight from a New Age workshop: "Not power but empower." *Forbes* told readers, "The most efficient way to wield power is to democratize it." Describing its talks with powerful corporate leaders, the magazine reported: "These executives reached reflexively for words like 'participatory management,' 'collegiality,' and 'consensus-building' to describe what they do."

A more humane vocabulary seems to be entering the management lexicon. According to *Business Week*'s April article on "Management for the 1990s," leadership today calls for "a new ingredient, caring." The magazine quoted one corporate chairman as saying, "The more you want people to have creative ideas and solve difficult problems, the less you can afford to manage them with terror."

In management practices, a key sign of change is the move toward decentralization, and giving workers a greater voice. In union-management relations, for example, an adversarial stance is giving way to a spirit of cooperation, in some sectors. Since 1980, the United Steelworkers and a handful of steelmakers have been experimenting with labor-management participation teams (LMPT), where ten to fifteen workers meet each week to explore how to do their jobs better—and how to improve life in the mills. One LMPT reduced the chances for burns from a caustic solution by devising a better delivery system: driving the truck directly to the bath, eliminating a messy transfer step. "I think both sides feel that LMPTs can improve the industry," said one union official. Recently, eight companies and the United Steelworkers began an unusual joint effort to set up LMPTs throughout the industry.

At Pitney Bowes, communication lines are kept open with the Council 12
of Personnel Relations, which brings together an equal number of managers and employees twice each month, to discuss issues ranging from salaries to new products. Kollmorgen Corporation believes so strongly in decentralization that it keeps even key decisions—such as capital expansion, the research and development budget, and the hiring of senior management—at the division level. And divisions are kept deliberately small, so employees can feel part of a group where their contribution matters.

From inhuman to human. From jungle to community. A new corporate ethic may be gradually emerging—and it has to do with external as well as internal constituencies. Indeed, the very idea of a corporate "constituency" is being broadened to include the local community, the nation, even the Earth itself.

"The terms of the contract between business and society are changing," Henry Ford II observed. "Now we are being asked to serve a wider range of human values and to accept an obligation to members of the public with whom we have no commercial transactions."

Du Pont seems to have been acting in that spirit, responding to its global constituency, when it decided last spring to phase out the production of chlorofluorocarbons (CFCs), which destroy ozone. Similarly responsive moves were made by McDonald's, when it decided to eliminate styrofoam cartons made with CFCs, and by Toys "R" Us, when it decided to stop selling realistic toy guns. If operating from a jungle mentality—as many corporations still do—these companies might have dug in and refused to change, leaving society's problems to society. But operating from a community mindset, they realized that society's problems *are* their problems.

Increasingly, the terms of the new contract between business and society are being written into law. Much has been made of Reagan's move to deregulate industry, but in addition new legislation is quietly being enacted that places greater demands on companies, and holds them to higher standards of accountability. In the wake of Bhopal and Chernobyl, the new Community Right to Know Act requires companies to inform the public about hazardous materials in use. When the law took effect last summer, Pennsylvania residents had the surprising experience of seeing a full-page ad from Rohm & Haas, saying that it releases one million pounds of chemicals into the environment each year. Texas residents heard Texaco tell about its annual release of seventy-six thousand pounds of benzene, which is known to cause leukemia. The ultimate intent of the law is for public pressure to force companies to reduce their use of toxic materials. 16

In other legislation, a law passed last summer sharply restricts employers' use of polygraph tests, and another requires advance notice of plant closings. Communities in California and New York have banned certain kinds of plastic packaging, and a dozen states are considering similar restrictions— moving chemical companies to work faster on developing biodegradable plastics. Pending legislation would raise the minimum wage, and require businesses above a certain size to offer health insurance to workers.

The public welfare is increasingly becoming a private concern. We're accustomed to thinking that nonprofit institutions do good, while profit-making companies are greedy and uncaring. But as futurist Hazel Henderson says, we're beginning to tear down the wall between the two. Nonprofits are developing profit-making businesses to help themselves survive, while corporations are taking a greater hand in community welfare.

One example is the growing role of business in education. General Electric, the nation's largest defense contractor and the target of a national consumers boycott, spends fifty thousand dollars a year working with top students at a public school in New York's Spanish Harlem, helping its GE Scholars get into prestigious universities. The well-known Boston Compact—a pledge by Boston businesses to hire one thousand graduates a year from inner-city schools—has added a new Compact Ventures program, providing remedial education and mentors for high school students in an effort to stem dropout rates.

Another area where public and private interests blend is in pollution cleanup. The public problem of hazardous waste has been solved in an ingenious way by the private company Marine Shale Processors, which turns toxic materials like paint solvent and chemicals into street paving. In a 20 different approach, Detox Industries of Sugarland, Texas, has developed a method that breaks down polychlorinated biphenyls, or PCBs, biologically— using microorganisms. Even more elegantly, the Environmental Concern company restores native wetlands on the Atlantic Coast, building new marshes, reconstructing lost habitat, and planting vegetation.

Outside of industry, there are further signs of change. Activists have brought nuclear power to a virtual standstill and successfully fought for animal rights. Revlon, Bausch & Lomb, and Clorox are among the companies now supporting research into alternatives to the Draize test, which calls for toxic substances to be tested on the eyes of rabbits. Colgate has reduced animal use 80 percent in six years, while Avon and Procter & Gamble have eliminated animal tests entirely.

In the religious community, the Interfaith Center on Corporate Responsibility acts as a central clearinghouse for shareholder activism by churches— and in recent years, that activism has reached all-time highs, with record numbers of resolutions on topics like South African divestment, poison-pill takeover defenses, and the environment. Churches have also been active in the Royal Dutch/Shell boycott, with the United Church of Christ, United Methodist, and the Episcopal Church, among others, endorsing a boycott against Shell's presence in South Africa.

In the financial community, the field of socially responsible investing has grown geometrically, from forty billion dollars in investments in 1985 to ten times that amount today. It's been called the fastest growing new niche in the investing world—supporting some two dozen funds, a number of specialty newsletters, and a trade association called the Social Investment Forum.

Academia has shown a burgeoning interest in business ethics, with a 24 growing number of universities offering required courses in the topic, several conferences being offered each year, and three dozen campus centers of ethics enjoying rising popularity.

In the alternative community, socially responsible companies find a national market for their goods and services through Co-op America, which lets thousands of consumers put their dollars where their hearts are. This year Co-op America director Paul Freundlich is working to create a new entity called Fair Trade, to bring wider U.S. distribution to products from the Third World.

The growing trend toward employee ownership is nourished by the Industrial Cooperative Association of Massachusetts, which offers both financial and technical assistance to worker-owned firms. When a brass company in Connecticut was threatened with closure, for example, ICA helped structure an Employee Stock Ownership Plan that put control of the company in the hands of its 227 employees. And in the first eight months after the company agreed to sell to the workers, the mill made more money than in the previous three years.

In the New Age community, there are groups like the Business Initiative—part of the Open Center in New York—which critically examines topics like "manipulation and trust in the field of sales," or "personal growth within large corporations." In Santa Monica, the company InSynergy runs "summit teams"—ongoing support groups where executives can explore their own spiritual growth, and work on being more effective and sensitive leaders. Last summer Boulder's Buddhist-inspired Naropa Institute sponsored a conference called Good Work, exploring "the relationship of spiritual journey and business."

All this activity on so many fronts adds up to an emerging new paradigm—a new picture of what's expected of business, and what's possible. It's a picture of workplaces that are healthy for employees, of corporate citizens who are powerful yet responsive, of companies that are tools for social change, and of a corporate community that is a humane presence on the earth. 28

Beyond this new picture, there seems to be a groundswell of change, driven by a variety of powerful forces. In this age of environmental limits, we simply cannot afford widespread corporate carelessness anymore. And with the coming of age of the baby boom generation, sixties values are being transformed into responsible professional values of the eighties. Faced with coming shortages of skilled labor, corporations need all available hands—and they need them functioning at their best. To reverse America's trade imbalance, companies need creativity at every level, including the shop floor. And that makes union-management cooperation a necessity. With the rise of service industries, employees are coming to function more as autonomous professionals, requiring a wholly new style of management: less autocratic, more democratic, more collegial.

Society *needs* a more humane business environment—and it's beginning to develop. But that's not to say everything is sliding effortlessly into place; far from it. Even companies that appear to espouse new values may be operating from the same old jungle mentality.

Some companies do good with their right hand only to do harm with the left. Tobacco companies, for instance, are dragged into court for product liability lawsuits, while they're lauded as the darling philanthropists of the art world. Other companies specialize in window dressing—as in IBM's "departure" from South Africa, which, through transfer of assets to an independent company, left sales intact.

There are grand schemes that sound good but will never go anywhere—like a plan for Universal Stock Ownership, which would solve poverty by handing corporate equity around like food stamps. There are corporations that institute employee stock ownership plans merely as fancy tax dodges. Others set up generous severance benefits for workers—tin parachutes to match executive golden parachutes—which turn out to be nothing but take- 32 over defenses. We may have a new picture of what we want from business, yet we certainly don't have the full reality. Yet if we allow ourselves a flight of optimism, the possibilities are tantalizing.

If it's illiteracy we want to tackle, business can help. Dayton Hudson has spent millions on a literacy program, encouraging employees to serve as tutors, and is working to recruit thousands of volunteers at other companies. The New York ad agency of Benton & Bowles put together a public service campaign about literacy—and McGraw-Hill's chairman funded a clearinghouse to handle calls the ads generated.

If homelessness is the issue, business can help. Meredith Corporation's *Better Homes & Gardens* has set up a foundation to help homeless families, with a goal of raising ten million dollars from its eight million readers. Meredith also hopes to convince advertisers in areas like home furnishings and building materials to donate both supplies and money.

If poverty is the problem, business can help. The South Shore Bank in Chicago is channeling funds into development of its decaying inner-city neighborhood, and has succeeded in sparking a real estate renaissance—with benefits going not to outsiders, but to the largely minority community. IBM has a network of sixty job training centers for disadvantaged youth, and has graduated more than fourteen thousand students—with a job placement record of better than 80 percent.

There's no denying that we live in a troubled world, and that the corporate community has had a hand in creating those troubles. With its soiled past and its powerful self-interest, business may never be a wholly reliable force for the public good. But in a search for the most powerful tool for social change in the world, the most effective lever available might just turn out to be business. It may be an unavoidable truth: business is our last best hope.

36

Points to Consider

1. What examples does Marjorie Kelly cite as indications of the new attitude emerging in corporate America? How does the concept of "stakeholder" differ from the concept of "stockholder"?

2. Why are corporations more willing, in the words of Henry Ford II, "to accept an obligation to members of the public with whom [they] have no commercial transactions"? What is the hoped-for effect of new legislation holding businesses to higher standards of accountability?

3. According to Kelly, what kinds of problems can businesses most effectively help solve? What measures taken by businesses to benefit the public strike you as self-interested rather than community-minded?

4. Does Kelly believe that business can be considered a reliable force for the public good? Does she think our knowledge of past business practices

should influence our attitudes toward the more enlightened practices of today's corporations?

Buying In   [MOTHER JONES / April–May 1990]

If the 1980s taught us anything, it is that almost everything is for sale. Even the environmental movement now risks slipping under the influence of some of the most powerful corporations in the United States.

As the public increasingly supports environmental activism, corporate executives are gaining access to environmental organizations. Governing boards of some major environmental groups now include the chair of the New York Stock Exchange as well as executives of such corporations as Exxon, Stroh Brewery, Philip Morris, and the giant paper and pulp maker, Union Camp Corporation. Moreover, as the competition for foundation grants intensifies, corporations are giving more and more money to conservation groups. Consider that:

- The World Wildlife Fund/Conservation Foundation, one of the top ten environmental groups in the country, now lists as major donors Chevron and Exxon, which each donated more than $50,000 in 1988, as well as Philip Morris, Mobil, and Morgan Guaranty Trust.

- The National Audubon Society, which in 1986 received only $150,000   4 in corporate contributions, expects to receive nearly $1 million in such funds in 1989.

- The National Wildlife Federation recently added three new members to its Corporate Council. It costs each company $10,000 to join. Among

---

EVE PELL (b. 1937) is a staff reporter at the Center for Investigative Reporting. She has written news and feature articles for the Nation, New West, In These Times, *and many other publications. She is the editor of* Maximum Security, *a book of letters by convicts describing conditions in California's toughest prisons. She is also coauthor of* To Serve the Devil, *a two-volume history of ethnic groups in the United States.*

632   **Business and the Public Interest: Can They Work in Harmony?**

the fourteen members are Arco, DuPont, and Ciba-Geigy. The Council promotes cooperation between industry leaders and environmentalists.

- The Sierra Club, after considerable agonizing, turned down $700,000 from McDonald's, which wanted to sponsor an environmental education project. McDonald's sought another environmental organization to fund. The National Audubon Society turned down a similar offer shortly afterward.

Businesses say they are just being good citizens, and the environmental groups claim they can remain independent while taking corporate money. But critics charge that the reality is far more sinister. "These corporations claim to be environmentalists, but they are buying off the groups who are opposing them," says David Rapaport of Greenpeace. "And the corporations are buying legitimacy as well. Dow funds environmental groups and schools in Michigan, and the chemical companies do the same in the Louisiana chemical corridor."

The relationship between Waste Management, Inc. (WMI), and the   8 Environmental Grantmakers Association (EGA) is a prime example of the growing connection between big business and the environmental movement. Perhaps the most sophisticated of the corporate infiltrators, WMI is a world-wide conglomerate with an annual gross income of more the $3 billion and nearly nine hundred subsidiaries. Although WMI is the nation's largest and most advanced handler of wastes, it is also known for its leaky landfills, its conviction for price-fixing, and its violations of environmental regulations that resulted in more than $30 million in fines being assessed from 1982 to 1987. For those reasons it has become a prime target for many grassroots activists around the country.

Strange as it may seem, Waste Management has been admitted to the Environmental Grantmakers Association, an association of foundation executives who have studied, worked with, and financially supported most of the varied organizations that make up the U.S. environmental movement today. The diversity of the funders mirrors the diversity of the environmental movement itself, which spans a wide spectrum of environmental policies and goals—from simple preservation of rain forests to lawsuits against polluters. By deciding which organizations get money, the grant-makers help set the agenda of the environmental movement and influence the programs and strategies that activists carry out.

A latecomer to philanthropy, WMI, in the past three years, has donated more than $900,000 to organizations such as the National Wildlife Federation, the National Audubon Society, and the Trust for Public Land. Because of these contributions to environmental causes, WMI's public affairs director, Dr. William Y. Brown, was invited to attend the EGA's 1988 meeting in Princeton; his presence there made several funders very uncomfortable.

Admission to the EGA gives the controversial WMI unusual access to the inner sanctum of the environmental movement. Since the funders hold frank, detailed discussions about the activists they are considering for support, EGA members learn the movement's plans and tactics. As a major target of some of those activist groups, WMI is now in the position that the fox might envy: guarding, and even financing, the henhouse.

Dr. Brown says that his company likes to fund legislative advocacy, 12 especially laws to strengthen regulations governing hazardous waste. If, for instance, laws prohibit dumping waste at sea, that means more business for WMI. "Stricter legislation is environmentally good and it also helps our business," he says. Conceding that his company "is not perfect," he says that because of the nature of its operations, it can't have "a squeaky clean record as if we made yogurt." And Brown readily admits, "The EGA has been useful for me to share information about environmental groups."

That's just what some environmentalists fear. "We don't want to be worried about giving information to the enemy," says a funder who wishes to remain anonymous. The debate over WMI has polarized the EGA into groups roughly paralleling divisions in the environmental movement, where groups that favor compromising with polluters square off against those that favor confrontation. Some funders feel that to keep lines of communication open to all, WMI must be included. Others, who believe that the EGA should hew to higher standards, refuse to attend any meeting where Dr. Brown shows up. "I have met with the parents who come from the bedsides of kids in hospitals as a result of pollution," says another foundation officer. "It's a matter of conscience for me that if he is admitted, I will leave."

Greenpeace, which accepts neither corporate nor foundation money, took the unprecedented step of picketing the Environmental Grantmakers' November 1989 meeting in San Francisco. There, Greenpeace activists marched around with placards telling EGA members about the local groups across the United States that are currently battling to keep WMI landfills out of their communities. Among the signs: "People for Clean Air and Water Is Fighting WMI in Kettleman, CA"; "Dumpstoppers Are Fighting WMI, Inc., in Ft. Wayne, IN"; "Alabamans for a Clean Environment Is Fighting WMI, Inc., in Emelle, AL"; "Citizens United to Recover the Environment Is Fighting WMI, Inc., in Chicago, IL."

To many, the question of whether to exclude WMI from the EGA dramatizes the issues facing the environmental movement in the United States today: where is its soul? And can money buy that soul?

Grassroots groups, such as the Citizen's Clearinghouse for Hazardous 16 Wastes, Inc., are already suspicious of the three-way revolving door connecting many large environmental organizations (like the National Wildlife Federation and the National Audubon Society), government regulatory agencies, and big business. For example, William Ruckelshaus, the Environmental Protection Agency's first director, now chairs Browning-Ferris Industries, second in size only to WMI in the waste disposal field. Ruckelshaus also sits on the governing board of the World Wildlife Fund/Conservation Foundation. The current EPA head, William Reilly, joined the Bush administration from the World Wildlife Fund/Conservation Foundation, which he headed. This revolving door allows established Beltway insiders to move so easily from one sector to another that it is not always clear just whose interests they are serving.

For those who say that the dangers of accepting corporate money are exaggerated, critics point to the way WMI appeared to benefit from its relationship with the National Wildlife Federation. In 1987, WMI began giving money to the NWF. That same year, WMI chief executive officer Dean Buntrock was appointed a director of the NWF, a development that caused considerable controversy. NWF director Jay D. Hair, a figure in the upper reaches of the environmental elite, defended Buntrock and, in letters to critics of the appointment, called WMI's environmental record "responsible."

Buntrock then parlayed his connection with Hair into a cozy breakfast meeting with EPA chief William Reilly. Afterward, Reilly softened an EPA position on waste disposal regulations, to the benefit of WMI.

The events leading up to that meeting illustrate the workings of the insider network. Last March, NWF director Hair, a friend of Reilly's, suggested that Reilly meet with him and Buntrock. The invitation was written on a newspaper clipping describing a South Carolina state regulation that spelled trouble for WMI's business practices—and which the EPA had the power to affect. In the note, Hair suggested that Reilly discuss the "national implications" of the South Carolina regulation and "get to know Dean." After the breakfast, Reilly said he was reversing the EPA policy WMI disliked, telling a reporter that Buntrock had lobbied him to make the change. However, Reilly later denied to in-house investigators that any lobbying had taken place.

Publicly, NWF director Hair opposed the EPA policy change, but the   20
WMI breakfast controversy shows the difficulty of determining whose side environmentalists are on once the corporate nose enters the environmental tent.

While corporations wishing to improve their images are able to saturate the air waves with public-relations campaigns, corporate influence over environmental organizations through quiet funding is less easily detected. Chevron's "People Do" campaign—which gives the impression that Chevron is in the business of raising eagles rather than selling oil—may be offensive, but at least viewers recognize it as a paid message.

Why have businesses suddenly begun funding some of their most effective adversaries—groups that have cost them billions of dollars in government regulations, court actions, fines, and other headaches? The companies are buying credibility and access to insider networks because they cannot win a free and open war of ideas, and because nothing covers up depredations like large checks.

Not everyone agrees with this analysis. EGA president Joe Kilpatrick asserts, "Even if corporations have adopted what they call an 'enlightened strategy' to make grants to environmental groups in order to 'inject reason' into their tactics, the grantees have their eyes open."

Nevertheless, it seems naive to believe that environmental groups will act any differently than politicians or judges or journalists when confronted with gobs of cold cash.

Do people *really* respond to large amounts of money? People do.

24

Points to Consider

1. What does Eve Pell report is the main incentive for corporate funding of environmental groups? Why does she think that corporate sponsors negatively influence the groups to which they provide aid?

2. According to Pell, why has Waste Management, Inc. (WMI), become a target of many environmental groups? Why did WMI seek membership in the Environmental Grantmakers Association (EGA)? What is the primary function of EGA?

3. Why could information about environmental groups provided by the EGA to its members harm the very groups the EGA is trying to help? Why do many environmental groups deem it necessary to maintain an adversarial relationship with corporate America?

4. What means other than donations to conservation groups do businesses have to improve their public images? Why might corporate funding be a more effective means for businesses seeking better public relations?

Discussing the Unit

Suggested Topic for Discussion

Robert Sherrill strongly believes that the only concern of business is the "bottom line"—profits. Even Marjorie Kelly, who seems more sympathetic to corporations than Sherrill, admits that business's "powerful self-interest" may get in the way of doing any real public good. Given this economic reality, do you think that corporations would become more responsible of their own volition? Or are public pressure and regulation the only means to make corporations more accountable? What are the national dangers of regulation? What are the dangers of allowing corporations to maintain their freedom? Which alternative—regulation or freedom—do you think is ultimately best for the nation?

Participating in Class Discussion

1. As Eve Pell points out, many corporations turn to unorthodox advertising strategies to improve their public image. In particular she cites a recent Chevron commercial that might have given "the impression that Chevron is in the business of raising eagles rather than selling oil." What other recent corporate advertising campaigns can you think of that use similar tactics? Do you think that such campaigns are intended to deceive the general public? Why do you think that advertisers resort to this strategy?

2. A recent Gallup poll reported that 75 percent of Americans considered themselves to be environmentalists, yet the dismantling of environmental regulations that began under Ronald Reagan has gone so far that many activists believe that they must start all over again. How do you explain this phenomenon? Would you say that businesses are responsible for the undoing of much of our environmental safety legislation? Think about what kinds of corporations are most affected by such regulation. Make a list of corporations that profess to be environmentally aware but continue to endanger the environment, and consequently human life.

From Discussion to Writing

Despite recent efforts by American businesses to improve their images, surveys continue to show increasing public dissatisfaction with corporate behavior. Though the polls indicate a certain level of public approval for corporate involvement in technology, research, and the creation of new products for the consumer, they also indicate many areas of public disapproval besides environmental issues, including executive ethics, pricing, foreign competition, and the corporate share of taxation. Select one aspect of recent business practice that you think represents either the best or the worst side of American corporations and write an essay in which you discuss your position and defend your attitude against opposite views.

27

The Changing World Picture: What Does It Mean for America?

The revolutionary changes in Eastern Europe and the Soviet Union over the past few years have forced Americans to ask themselves some tough questions about their own commitment to our democratic heritage. In "Coming to America," the essayist Roger Rosenblatt confronts many of these questions directly as he examines the increasing problems in our society: do they mean that we have abandoned our ideals of freedom and equality? Felix Rohatyn in "Becoming What They Think We Are" also interprets the events in Europe in light of America's problems and prospects. He agrees with Rosenblatt that the ideals of the European revolution are based on "the American model," and he, too, is uncertain whether we still represent those ideals. He worries that the American system may not be what other nations think it is. When they look at America, he wonders, are they merely "seeing the light of a distant star which, some time ago, may have ceased to shine so brightly"?

Rohatyn sees an America that has been practically gutted by the economic policies of the 1980s. He proposes a concrete plan that he believes would enable us to enter the next century with our democratic ideals intact and our economy on an equal footing with Europe and Japan. Especially Japan, Bill Powell and Bradley Martin would argue. In "What Japan Thinks of Us" they provide an unflattering picture of a whiny, immature America that for the first time since World War II must wake up to the fact that "what the Japanese think of us matters enormously."

ROGER ROSENBLATT

Coming to America [LIFE / February 1990]

Yes, we know that they were not doing it for our benefit: the Czechs not swarming in Prague's Wenceslas Square for our amazement; the Hungarians not filling Budapest's Parliament Square with candlelight so that we would be impressed. Not for our pleasure did the Poles vote Solidarity in and the Communists out. Not for our satisfaction did Soviet republics wield their national flags like clubs against the state. When the Berlin Wall was dismantled slab by slab, it was not to engender our approval, nor did the ecstatic East Germans dance all night to make us clap. The Romanians did not bloody their streets to shock our senses. The Chinese university students did not take their heroic stand in Beijing's Tiananmen Square to win our hearts.

But watching all the astonishing eruptions month after month in the past year, seeing the words "freedom" and "democracy" hoisted on placards by crowds the size of parks, what American could help but feel that the once huddled masses of the world were in some way coming to us? If they were not racing to embrace America's version of democracy wholesale, at least they were reaching for the ideas at America's core. At the general strike in Prague in late November, Zdenek Janicek, a Czech brewery worker, climbed up on a platform, looked out at his audience, and recited the following: "We hold these truths to be self-evident, that all men are created equal. . . ."

ROGER ROSENBLATT (b. 1940) is an editor-at-large for Life *magazine, where he writes a monthly column as well as feature stories. He holds a Ph.D. in English and American Literature from Harvard University, where he taught creative writing and journalism from 1968 to 1973, prior to his career in journalism. Rosenblatt has written three books:* Black Fiction *(1974),* Children of War *(1983), and* Witness: The World Since Hiroshima *(1985).*

From an idea came a word, from a word a footstep, from a footstep a body in motion, then several bodies, moving together toward an open place where they were joined by other bodies, a few hundred, a few thousand, then hundreds of thousands, rubbing up against one another until there was a kind of fusion into one vast body speaking with one vast voice that seemed to roll between an ancient cry of human fury and sorrow and a fierce declaration of dignity and purpose. A titanic no, a no the height of an Alp, suddenly stood up in the countries freeing themselves, or seeking to free themselves, from their oppressors. Not in our lifetime did we ever expect that such a thing could happen, so implacable did the forces seem that locked whole civilizations in cages for decades. Yet on the meeting grounds of the antique cities the most basic human protest was born so quickly and completely, it was as if the deadening powers had never existed.

Inside the grand spectacle of events, then, there was something grander 4 still. The unceasing blasts of the throngs in the squares, the overheated speeches of the reformers, the panicky abdication of the tyrants, the busy reconstruction of the governments—all that stemmed from a moral idea: that people are of equal value; that they have equal rights to their thoughts and to the conduct of their lives. Communism promised them equality but delivered sameness without freedom—equality under the thumb. But tie equality to democracy and you really have something. The idea existed long before this generation of revolutionaries. It sat brooding in the minds of their parents and their grandparents like the genie waiting patiently for Aladdin. The strength of the genie, said the poet Richard Wilbur, comes from the fact that it lives in the bottle. If the democratic impulses of these countries had not been corked for many years, they never would have exploded in such a shot.

For us in the grandstand it was like having someone play our music for us, and play it very well, perhaps better than we. "We hold . . . that all men are created equal." Americans have heard those words somewhere before. Hearing them shouted by people in the process of self-realization has been elating, overwhelming.

It should be chastening too.

America finds itself, or ought to find itself, in a strangely embarrassing position these days. Here are the oppressed peoples of the world intoxicated by our slogans about human equality. And here we are, two hundred-plus years from the earliest expression of equality as a national ideal, with the distance between the hope and the fact unconscionably wide. Certainly there is greater equal opportunity in America. But equal opportunity can be elusive, even taunting: tell someone without legs that he has equal opportunity in a foot race. If the poor, the sick, and [the] uneducated truly had the capacity to take advantage of American opportunities today, we would be offering the world not just the best words of democracy but also the best form.

In the February 17, 1941, issue of *Life*, Henry Luce published his brilliant   8
and irritating essay on "The American Century," the immediate objective of
which was to urge his countrymen into war against the Axis. Lustily as ever,
Luce told America to seize the day. Our national mission was to be the leader
and protector of world trade, to send abroad industrialists, entertainers, and
teachers, to reach out to the hungry and destitute, to promote freedom and
"a feeling for the equality of opportunity." That most of all. America, said
Luce, must show the world the value of its soul.

Today, whatever one thinks of some of Luce's other ideas, his vision of
the American Century has pretty much been achieved. The way to that
achievement has been sloppy and often wrong-headed. It has consisted of
grand ventures such as America's entry into the Second World War, the
Marshall Plan, the Truman Doctrine; of costly and frustrating ventures such
as Korea; of self-punishing ventures such as Vietnam. Most recently the way
led to Panama. In the name of the American Century former enemies have
been hauled to their feet again, refugees rescued, refugees denied, dictators
supported, dictators deposed, continents fed and clothed, cultures upended,
products hawked and sold, skills disseminated, languages changed, whole
economies redirected and redistributed. America's economic prominence has
shrunk drastically in recent years (good-bye world trade), but no organized
power in the past half century has so affected the policies, attitudes, and
destinies of other places.

What America has not achieved for the world in that period is what it
has not achieved for itself. More alarmingly, in the last decade the idea of
equality seems to have been abandoned as a national goal. This tendency is
due largely, though hardly exclusively, to reductions in federal poverty programs made by the Reagan administration, accompanied by an emerging, if
silent, public attitude that the disadvantaged lie beyond the reach of help.

But if America has any place and mission in the world right now, if the
American Century is to be given a modest extension, the idea of equality
ought to be retrieved. Every serious internal problem tearing at the country
derives from a fundamental inequality of circumstance and station. Return
to first principles, and we may lessen the problems.

Survey the threats and the messes before us: 12

Crime. A record 627,561 men and women were in federal and state
prisons at the end of 1988, an increase of 7.3 percent over 1987. Since 1980,
eighteen states have more than doubled their prison populations. Alaska,
California, New Hampshire, and New Jersey have seen threefold increases.
As many as three-quarters of the men arrested for serious offenses in twelve
major cities tested positive for illicit drugs.

Education. About 17 percent of all American high school students drop
out before graduating. Of the students who do graduate, one of four has the
equivalent of an eighth grade education. Of the 3.8 million eighteen-year-
old Americans in 1988, fully 532,000 (14 percent) had dropped out of school,

and another 700,000 could not read their high school diplomas. Illiteracy among minority students is as high as 40 percent—and by the year 2000, minorities will make up the majority of the school populations in ten states. As a result of undereducation, hundreds of thousands, perhaps millions of people find themselves without a place in today's job market: 84 percent of the twenty-three thousand people who took an exam for entry-level jobs at New York Telephone in 1988 failed.

Health. The United States ranks nearly last among industrialized nations in infant mortality—eighteenth in the world, behind Hong Kong and Singapore, and twenty-eighth in black infant mortality, behind Cuba. In 1986 nearly one fifth of all children younger than eighteen, and one third of all poor children, had no health insurance, public or private. Thirty-seven million Americans are without health insurance coverage. The number of AIDS cases is growing, the latest count by the Centers for Disease Control being 115,158 cases. Fifty-nine percent of the patients have died. Blacks and Hispanics are disproportionately represented. Blacks make up 27 percent of AIDS cases, Hispanics 15 percent. Of the total population, 12 percent is black, 6 percent Hispanic.

The Economy. The deficit stands at more than $150 billion, roughly double what it was in 1980. The national debt is close to $2.9 trillion, three times what it was in 1980. Almost all the national debt has gone to finance current consumption rather than infrastructure or investment in people or in productive capacity. Paying interest on all our loans cost $169.3 billion the past fiscal year. 16

The Elderly. People eighty-five and older are the fastest growing age group in the U.S. elderly population. Over the next twenty years, before the baby boom generation begins to enter the ranks of the elderly, the number of people age sixty-five or older is projected to increase 1.3 percent a year, while the population age eighty-five and older is projected to increase at more than three times that rate, 4.3 percent. In thirty years the number of nursing home residents will grow to 2.8 million from 1.3 million today. Nursing home care now costs $40.6 billion, and out-of-pocket expenses not covered by government or private insurance make up $20 billion of that amount. The Brookings Institution projects that out-of-pocket expenses will more than double to $50.3 billion in the next thirty years.

Poverty. The Center on Budget and Policy Priorities reports that in 1987 nearly one in every seven Americans lived below the poverty line. Child poverty, in particular, is on the increase. One in five children under eighteen is poor; one in four children under the age of three is poor; two in five Hispanic children are poor; nearly one out of two black children is poor. The number of "working poor" has grown from 6.5 million in 1979 to 8.5 million in 1987. For the heads of families younger than thirty, earnings fell 40 percent from 1973 to 1986. In 1988, 33.5 percent of families headed by women were poor, compared with 10.4 percent of all families.

Housing. Between 600,000 and 1.2 million Americans are homeless, a great many of them simply because they cannot find affordable shelter. Nearly two-thirds of the nation's renters who are poor spend at least half their income for living quarters. There exists an "affordable housing gap" for families earning less than ten thousand dollars a year, with 3.7 million fewer low-cost units available than are needed. The housing squeeze on low- and moderate-income families is projected to leave seven million people without affordable housing by 1993, meaning that families will have to double or triple up in homes or be out on the streets.

Those are some of the numbers, but no American really needs statistics   20
to verify the situation. In the blue-lit hallways of tenement houses in Denver, Boston, and St. Louis drug addicts lazily pass needles from one to the other, while their kids, furtive and sullen, sit on stoops supporting their heads in their hands. At a neonatal ICU in Atlanta, one-and-a-half-pound babies twitch in their incubators, tubes arcing from every part of their bodies. The homeless in New York make little villages on the steps of churches at night. They look like carpets rolled in carpets. Stupefied street gangs roam in packs, hungry to do harm. In the countryside, old couples sell farms for trailers; they live alone. Girls of thirteen use cocaine as an abortifacient or shop for maternity wear. At the dark end of the day they walk home with their fifteen-year-old boyfriends past the dilapidated schoolhouse where a discouraged teacher stares blankly at a student staring back.

To be sure, the whole picture is not so grim. In the area of crime, if the prisons are overcrowded, at least that suggests that more serious offenders are serving time. In education, we have the world's highest percentage (57) of young people going to college, even if that number is undercut by the quality of their high school educations. The number of high school dropouts is very high at 25 to 30 percent, but no higher than it was fifteen years ago. If the growth of the elderly population places a strain on Social Security and health care, people are also generally healthier and living longer. Inflation has fallen from 14 percent to 4 percent since 1980. Real take-home pay is more than twelve thousand dollars per capita, up from ten thousand dollars in 1980. The economy has gone from a decline in 1980 to the longest peacetime expansion in history.

Yet what one notices in even a superficial scanning of national troubles is that almost all the good news is short term, and the worst news long term. Everyone acknowledges that the most severe problem areas are interconnected: education is related to drugs, drugs to health, drugs to crime. Housing is related to poverty, poverty to teenage pregnancy, teenage pregnancy to infant mortality and to education, and so forth. But the central fact that ties all these areas together is the division between those with plenty and those with nothing or nearly nothing. If the country is going to get at these problems, some basic inequities will have to be attended to.

Exactly how America should look to achieve greater equality in these areas—the means and methods by which the problems are confronted—has sensibly to be a matter of trial and balance. Federal help is indispensable. The antigovernment line trumpeted during the Reagan years and continued, though in muted tones, in the Bush administration is based on the flimsiest evidence, and reports of the failures of federal programs have been exaggerated. The era of federal poverty programs (not welfare programs) lasted until the first Reagan budget, during which time the percentage of poor Americans decreased substantially. Time has proved that some intelligent combination of federal and local assistance, given sufficient chance to work, does the most sustained good. The tendency of the times is toward small-scale solutions to large social problems; the country would need to experiment with combinations of different forms. Private business has already contributed a great deal, to education especially.

Why we should strive for greater equality—the intellectual and moral 24 reasons for solving our internal problems—brings us back to the country's place and mission in the world. There are at least three strong reasons for Americans to push for greater equality. One has to do with our history, one with our role as international exemplar, one with simply doing right.

America's obsession with equality has been constant throughout its history. Equality was the nation's first idea, occurring even before there was a nation. The American Revolution was propelled by the unequal treatment dealt the colonies, and all the egalitarian sentiments that eventually became the prescriptions for the independent country arose from our experience with the British. De Tocqueville, the first observer to detect that the idea of equality was more important to Americans even than freedom, saw the progress of American equality as "something fated. The main features of this progress are the following," he said. "It is universal and permanent, it is daily passing beyond human control, and every event and every man helps it along."

As the country moved along, the force of the idea proved anything but irresistible, and human control regularly held it back. The administrations of Jefferson and Jackson were high on rhetoric about equality but low on results. The Civil War enforced the principle of equal protection under the laws, but the language of protection in the Fourteenth and Fifteenth Amendments was manipulable for mischief. The national commitment to equality persisted through the Depression, the New Deal, and WWII, with continued advancements and backslides. The civil rights movement and the women's movement of the 1960s and 1970s rode the egalitarian dream. They, too, have gained and slipped.

For two hundred years, nonetheless, equality as a goal and ideal never left the American mind. A straight emotional line runs from Jefferson through Martin Luther King, Jr. There are several reasons why that line was broken in the last ten years. For one thing, equality has grown a lot more difficult and subtle to achieve. No one who participates in battles for civil rights thinks them easy, but until recently all such battles have had the advantage of visible, concrete goals—a school desegregation law, a voting rights act. It is when the laws have all been passed, when formal opportunity is ready and in place, that equality becomes elusive. If the results are disappointing, one is tempted to feel that all that can be done has been done: how is the disadvantaged individual ever to walk on his own if he has to be pulled to his feet again and again? If there is a close second to the proposition of equality in American thought, it is that of individual achievement in a free market system. Those who cannot achieve without considerable help seem to contradict, undermine, even insult the American Dream.

Then, too, Americans are undoubtedly more than a little weary of 28
fighting the good fight. We have cause to be weary. Historically, the achievement of equality always entails a revolutionary upheaval; even when a small and temporary portion of equality is won, the toll on the country is enormous. The issue of equality has been at the center of not only the Revolutionary War but also the ages of Jackson, the Civil War and Reconstruction, the Populist-Progressive era, and all the civil protests of recent decades. No matter how giddily it is advertised, equality is always a radical idea involving radical consequences by threatening an unequal status quo.

There may even be a business tendency behind the abandonment of egalitarian thought in the 1980s. The 1980s was the decade of the specialized markets, after all, the wisdom arising and taking hold that the only way to ensure the success of a commercial venture was to isolate well-researched fractions of the country and sell to them according to specific needs. Thus blooms the era of customer-focused magazines. To insist on seeing the country as an amalgam of isolable markets is logically to refute the idea that America exists as a general social intelligence with commonly shaped desires. In a country so divided, the notion of equality is quaint.

Whatever the causes of our recent break with the idea of equality, the break should be recognized for what it is. By stepping away from that idea, we also step out of our history—a bad move for a successful civilization. Why would we toss away the one element of our past that, more than any other, has held the union together?

The second reason for recovering our goal of equality gets us back to Henry Luce's zeal to improve other nations, an ambition America has grown increasingly leery of over the years. It was one thing for the country to propose itself as savior to the world in the postwar 1940s and 1950s, when the world clearly needed saving. With the pain of Vietnam still throbbing, however, Americans may feel that they have nothing certain left to tell the world, and that the transformation of other nations is none of our business.

In fact, our moral center is still our best export. The ideal of equality is 32
exactly what the country should be demonstrating right now, especially as

so much of the world is turning like a heliotrope toward democracy. The most shameful and perplexing manifestation of inequality is racism—still and always racism. The Civil War, America's flash point of original sin, resolved the most outrageous aspect of the issue, but the virulence spread in different ways. The civil rights laws of the 1960s resolved other aspects of the issue, and still the poison spread. Today racism is not only suffered by blacks, it is practiced by blacks—against Jews, against Hispanics, who practice it back. Various ethnic groups in America—Irish, Italians, Slavs—retain and refurbish old tribal hatreds. Asians are reviled for being successful. WASPs have not permitted their diminished prominence to dilute their contempt for the lower orders. From one perspective every item on the national problem list is connected to race—health, education, crime, housing, drugs. What more morally useful message could America send an increasingly democratizing world than to attack its most demoralizing and destructive inequality?

One may counter with the question: why should the other countries of the world be at all concerned with the problem of racial equality? No other power, the Soviet Union excepted, needs to handle so heterogeneous a population. True. But in Europe, for example, where each individual country has a comparatively homogeneous makeup, the ancient antipathies of the countries toward one another create a continent of frictions. In Europe, East and West, no matter how heady the democratic spirits at any given moment, old-fashioned bellicose nationalism is always murmuring in the cellar. If the national boundaries of prewar Europe are reestablished, atavistic forces could let fly again.

Observe the treatment accorded the Turks by the Germans, the way Muslims are regarded in France, Hungarians in Romania, Pakistanis in England. Note the resurgence of anti-Semitism in Russia. Consider the stature of Koreans in Japan, Sikhs in India, Baha'is in Iran, Tibetans in China. Examine the internecine hatreds in the Mideast, in Northern Ireland. Then judge if the world could not use a model of racial and religious equality.

To sell the idea of equality, of course, America must first manufacture the product, and the third, and best, reason for working toward equality is simply that it is right—not easily realized or even intellectually provable, but right. One must never underestimate the appeal of pure moral motives to Americans. What more experienced countries may see as naive and callow impulses have always been the stuff of life to us.

The idea of acting on moral motives would certainly not be strange to 36 the Czechs, Poles, Hungarians, and others going through their upheavals now. Having tapped their moral power, these peoples are only beginning to test its full extent. Skeptics might wonder: if Communism had been an economic success, if there were chickens in every pot and soap to wash the pots, would there still be democratic rebellions? One has to believe that the rebellions would have occurred even if the economy of the system had worked—because the basic humanity of the people, their moral self-respect, could not forcibly be denied forever. They could not live a lie forever. Neither should we.

The moral center of a society is stronger than any political structure created for that society. That applies as much to democracies as to dictatorships. Democracy without humanity is merely people governing themselves, to any end. With its peculiar emphasis on equality, American democracy has implied something more than self-government. It has implied that people, left to govern themselves, will behave more decently than not toward one another. If the people who are casting off Communism did not see democracy as potentially offering something closer to their souls, there would be no point in embracing it. All they would be doing is exchanging an unworkable form of modern industrial society for one that makes a profit. That they wholeheartedly seek democracy obliges democracy to be good and do right.

Look at the crowds packed in Wenceslas Square or Parliament Square or Tiananmen Square and imagine that they are all the Americans in need. We would not be cheering then. Nor would they be protesting, because the disadvantaged are too weak, too ill, too dazed or ignorant to protest. They are our countrymen, still. Let them drown and disappear, and we let the foundation of the country disintegrate. Can democracy exist without equality? Probably. But equality gives it a reason for existing, connects the structure of government to the people's self-regard.

It is time to look ourselves and the world in the eye again. The price of a permanently divided society is awfully steep. And it is plainly wrong not to correct an immoral situation when it bellows in your face. The aim of the country ought not be to create a melting pot; that was always a false and self-deceiving goal. The aim is to create a country that we may live with uncomfortably, one that will probably have to suffer perpetual distinctions of race and class but that still works zealously to narrow those distinctions and to make them irrelevant to opportunity. America has always managed to live with a personality split between competitiveness and altruism. The country may require a split personality in the pursuit of equality as well, one that accepts certain frictions as inevitable, while striving to ameliorate the consequences of those frictions.

Equality may be America's last frontier, just as it was its first, a more   40
difficult frontier to reach than the outer planets and a rougher terrain than the Rocky Mountains. But the achievement or near achievement of equality would raise the entire level, the entire nature of democracy, presenting an invention at least as remarkable as those with which we once dazzled the Old World. The Old World, rocking with revival, might appreciate a little dazzle these days, though that cannot be the sole reason for America's fulfilling its most cherished and self-defining goal. Equality ought to be

sought because it is the right thing to do. So would we join those other nations of the world coming to see the light.

Points to Consider

1. What does Rosenblatt mean by his title? Who or what is coming to America?

2. Why have the changes in Eastern Europe placed America in an "embarrassing position"? What, according to Rosenblatt, should we be embarrassed about?

3. How do you interpret the problems Rosenblatt outlines in his essay? To what extent are these essentially American problems? In what sense are we as a nation responsible for these problems?

4. Why does Rosenblatt perceive racism as being at the root of America's problems? Do you agree with him on this point, or do you see other problems that are more fundamental?

FELIX ROHATYN

Becoming What They Think We Are

[THE NEW YORK REVIEW OF BOOKS / April 12, 1990]

The ideals of the revolutions in Poland, Hungary, Czechoslovakia, and even Bulgaria owe much to the American model, with its combination of political freedom and an economic system that seems to guarantee an ever-rising standard of living. It is important to recognize that it is a version of American political democracy, and not Japanese discipline or German efficiency, that the new leaders of these countries say they are striving for. Whether and how they will succeed is impossible to predict; their struggle

---

FELIX ROHATYN (b. 1928) is coeditor of Vision for the 1990s: U.S. Strategy and the Global Economy *(1989). He is a senior partner of the New York investment banking house Lazard Freres & Company. He serves on the board of directors of a number of U.S. and foreign corporations.*

will be long and may not always be peaceful. It is worth examining, however, whether the American system is all that they think it is, or whether they are seeing the light of a distant star which, some time ago, may have ceased to shine so brightly.

Clearly, military power is no longer the ultimate test of influence in the world. As the Soviet Union struggles simply to survive, the main competition for the United States is no longer communist ideology or military expansion, but European and Japanese financial and economic power. The so-called American century lasted barely twenty-five years. We are still, in many ways, the richest and most powerful country in the world. However, since the mid-1970s, the competitive position of many of our industries has steadily eroded, our position as the world's largest creditor has turned into the world's largest debtor, and our dependence on foreign capital has become worrisome to many. It is ironic that, as one country after another seeks freedom from foreign domination, our own economic independence is more and more constrained as a result of our needs for borrowing.

Americans are smug in claiming that "we beat communism." To some extent, the strength and steadfastness of the western alliance account for the recent changes; but if the command economies have failed, our own experiment with the free market and a deregulated economy is far from a success. Communism destroyed itself because it is philosophically and psychologically untenable and economically unworkable in the modern world. In many ways, communism was defeated by people who believed in the ideal possibilities of both democracy and the "social market" rather than by the American reality; the real question for the United States is whether it can become what these countries think it is.

First, as these Central European countries are striving to do, we should 4 have a real multiparty political system. At the least, we should have two functioning political parties. This is no longer the case today. I have been a Democrat ever since I came to the United States in 1942, at the age of fourteen, from Occupied France. There was never any question in my mind whether to support FDR, Truman, Stevenson, Kennedy, or Johnson. They stood for what I believed in: internationalism, the defense of freedom, equality of opportunity, fairness in the distribution of wealth. The Republican party, it seemed to me, was a party of the status quo, of isolationism, and of the simple, unadulterated pursuit of wealth.

Today the political choice, if there is any, is quite different. The Republican party is internationalistic and expansionist, both militarily and economically; it is conservative, not to say reactionary, on social issues such as abortion, school prayer, and gun control; it is dedicated to the pursuit of wealth through lower taxes and the absence of regulation, without any seeming concern for the appropriate role of government. But what does the Democratic party stand for, in opposition to this program? It is exceedingly hard to tell because the Democrats are not an opposition party; they share power, they do not seek it. Seeking power requires putting forward alternatives to the voters and competing for their allegiance; sharing power is an entirely different matter. The Democratic leaders in the Congress are excellent men, but they are part of the existing political power structure, and have formed something close to a coalition government with a Republican administration. Congressman Dan Rostenkowski's proposal to cut the federal budget deficit and to eliminate the Gramm-Rudman law is a courageous exception to this situation. However, in the main, we no longer have a true multiparty system, certainly not at the national level.

The legacy of Ronald Reagan, which has entirely paralyzed the Democratic party, is twofold:

1. The conviction, throughout America, that the country is overtaxed, with a 28 percent top income tax rate; and
2. The conviction that government is the enemy, especially when it intervenes in the economy to control the social consequences of excess or to protect the poor.

The result of these convictions is that two important notions have been wholly eliminated from American political discourse. The dread of taxes means that no rational discussion of resource allocation or of fairness can take place; and the dread of being associated with "liberalism" means that no rational discussion of an active policy of government intervention in economic life can take place either.

The Republican administrations of the 1980s, together with the Democratic Congresses, are jointly responsible for the present situation. Excessive tax cuts together with steep increases in defense spending created huge deficits, which were financed with $2 trillion of debt. The low domestic savings pool resulted in a growing foreign debt, high real interest rates, and the sale of more and more domestic assets abroad. A haphazard policy of deregulation under the Reagan administration brought about the fiasco of the S and Ls as well as the tendency of the securities industry to act like a gambling casino, the demise of half of the U.S. airlines, and the increasing destruction of the environment.

In order to create a facade of fiscal respectability, the administration and the Congress enacted the Gramm-Rudman-Hollings Act, which pretends to limit the yearly budget deficit to $100 billion. The act is really an accounting fantasy, at once cynical and grotesque, since, to avoid the automatic effects of the act, the government, among other bookkeeping devices, claims contributions to Social Security as assets and fails to show its bailout of the S and Ls as liabilities. It is as if a private company used its employee pension funds to offset operating losses, while not reporting the huge debts one of its branches had incurred. The directors, management, and auditors of such a company would be indicted and convicted. But each year the U.S. government solemnly performs this charade, which gives the administration and the Congress the excuse to borrow another $150 to $200 billion, and to pretend that they are reducing the deficit. The Gramm-Rudman-Hollings Act provides a convenient excuse to do nothing about our real problems, other than to suggest that state and local governments deal with them. The most recent example of this policy is the suggestion by Secretary of Transportation Skinner that the states pay a larger proportion of the federal highway program through increases in local fuel taxes. The United States did not become a great power through such evasions.

The events occurring in the world today can give the United States a unique opportunity to deal with its internal needs and, by doing so, to maintain the strong international position that is rapidly slipping away from us. These needs include large new domestic investment, both in the private and the public sectors; a significant reduction in the cost of capital to American businesses; and a willingness on the part of the federal government to deal with many urgent social and economic problems, in partnership with local governments as well as with business.

A few weeks ago, I watched former French Prime Minister Jacques Chirac on television talking about the world of the 1990s. He spoke of the dominant role of a Europe of 500 million people, East and West, educated, skilled, increasingly well-to-do, and cohesive. He spoke of the Pacific rim, of Japan, Korea, Taiwan, Singapore, with their economic power, discipline, and high growth. I waited to hear what he would say of the United States and where we fit into his vision of the future. It never came; neither we nor the Soviet Union were mentioned as having any international influence or presence. I do not believe that this is a correct analysis, but more and more, in Europe and in Japan, the United States is seen as a marginal country. Sooner or later, perception will become reality.

With or without the addition of Eastern Europe, the Western European countries will together be an increasingly formidable competitor. With a unified market, a common currency, financial institutions more powerful than ours, more investment in public facilities, higher and higher educational standards, and strong social welfare institutions acting as a safety net, Europe will be a powerhouse in the twenty-first century. So will Japan and the Pacific rim nations, as their often interconnected financial institutions and manufacturing enterprises continue to grow swiftly. And, unless we begin to change, we will gradually slip permanently into the position of a large, less than first-rate economic power, still strong militarily, but less and less competitive, burdened by huge levels of debt, the sagging leader of a continent whose southern nations are also burdened by debt and declining living standards. This does not have to happen but it will, unless there is a growing consciousness that a national effort must be made. The leaders of the Democratic party, the Congress, and state governments should be trying to conceive of programs to remedy such failures. This will mean that they will have to defy the conventional political wisdom.

The United States today has gigantic problems. These include a decaying infrastructure, whether in roads, bridges, or transport, as well as inadequate public education, increasing use of drugs, greater numbers of deaths from AIDS, and a lack of adequate housing—and these are only a few. Dealing with these problems is now hampered by the claims of the federal deficit and the need for the budget to remain within the artificial arithmetic limits of the Gramm-Rudman law. Even though the social, physical, and economic problems that we face are daunting, our fiscal problems, centering as they do on insufficient public revenue and excessive federal deficits, need not be. To deal with our fiscal problems would require relatively little real sacrifice. I was a member of the National Economic Commission created by the Congress to make recommendations to solve such problems, and a decisive bipartisan majority of the Commission was ready to propose a program of budget cuts and new taxes that would have increased revenues and steadily reduced the deficit. The administration was not interested in such a program; the Congressional leadership was not willing to endorse it without presidential support, and so the Commission was disbanded. But such a program, consisting of budget cuts, particularly in military spending, but also in entitlement programs, and a relatively small increase in taxes, should not be difficult for American citizens to absorb. Dan Rostenkowski's recent proposal would certainly be one way to do it. Certainly the sacrifices involved would be derisory compared to those that are being accepted in Western and Eastern Europe today.

What could have been done by the National Economic Commission in 1989, with relatively little pain, can be done even more readily in 1990 in view of the new world situation. Therein lies our greatest opportunity. The so-called peace dividend, however, is not something that will magically appear. The peace dividend will become reality only when it is decided upon and planned for over a period of years, as a matter of national policy, and enacted into laws. Furthermore, the peace dividend will not by itself provide for the needs of new public investment in America; nor will cutting the deficit, by itself, do the job; they should, however, form an important part of an ambitious three-part strategy: to invest an additional $1 trillion (in today's dollars) in America by the year 2000; to cut the costs of capital—particularly interest rates—significantly; and to reduce the tax burden of state and local government.

Such objectives are not as far-fetched as they sound. Military spending, if sustained at current levels in constant dollars, would amount to $3 trillion between 1990 and the year 2000. Reducing this expenditure by $500 billion, or slightly over 15 percent, does not appear to be excessively ambitious. In addition to savings in defense spending, another $500 billion over ten years can easily be raised by a combination of gasoline taxes (50 cents per gallon alone would accomplish it); a small increase in the maximum income tax rate, to 33 percent at the most; and a moderate slowing of the growth of some entitlement programs, for example health care costs, which are growing at three times the rate of inflation and must be brought under control. Our increasing dependence on foreign oil alone would justify a small gasoline tax as a conservation measure; it would still leave American fuel costs at less than half of Europe's and Japan's. Appropriate safeguards would be provided to the poor.

Of such a trillion-dollar program, one-half could be allocated to reducing the borrowing of the federal government, and one half could be returned to state and local governments for repairing infrastructure and for other urgent needs. Reduced federal borrowings would result in lower interest rates. The costs of a tax increase would be offset to a large extent by the reduction in interest costs to the individual and corporate borrower, and by the increased value of assets ranging from securities portfolios to real estate, which would come about as a result of lower interest rates.

Is it excessively bold to suggest investing an additional $1 trillion in our economy over the next decade? Not if you look at European countries investing $100 billion in high-speed railway transportation alone. Not if you look at the savings rate of the Japanese economy—at least double our own—and at the fact that the cost of capital to Japanese companies is about half of our own capital costs in real terms. Or if you look at the state of our infrastructure, with an estimated need for $2 trillion to restore to an acceptable condition interstate roads, city facilities such as bridges and waterworks, and airports; or if you take account of the fiscal condition of state and local governments, which have in many cases reached the fiscal limits of their capacities to deal with many of the problems I have mentioned. One trillion dollars is probably a minimum.

To talk seriously about such goals involves two subjects that are currently taboo in American political discourse. The first is active government. When a significant reduction in military spending takes place, the consequences of that reduction must be carefully worked out if it is to produce the hoped-for savings and, at the same time, avoid serious industrial and social dislocations. This requires some kinds of coordination and planning among the federal government, local communities, and the existing defense industries. Defense companies should be encouraged, through tax benefits or direct contracting, to convert to nonmilitary activities such as rapid rail and mass transit systems, large-scale waste disposal systems, or large supersonic commercial airplanes, to mention only three of many possibilities. The antitrust laws should be reviewed to permit mergers among large defense contractors facing significant cutbacks. Reductions in jobs should be planned far ahead of time and cushioned by retraining and relocation programs. If any of this smacks of another dreaded phrase, that is, "industrial policy," it is time for the United States to outgrow such slogans and observe how other industrial transitions have successfully been carried out in such different capitalist countries as Japan, France, and Austria.

The second political taboo is a rise in taxes. The resistance to tax increases is all the more understandable when the money seems to be wasted in fraud, corruption, and political waste. However, taxes are also the price we pay for a civilized society, for clean and safe streets, a decent system of education, a workable health care system, and a genuine protection of poor and incapacitated citizens from degradation. No other advanced Western industrialized democracy functions today with a top income tax rate as low as 28 percent or with gasoline prices less than double our own. And yet Japan and West Germany are more productive than we are in many industries, and save more than we do, while producing at least as much security for their citizens. We must break out of the trap we have created by purely reflexive reactions to tax policy.

Recently, Senator Moynihan attempted to do so by suggesting a cut in the Social Security payroll tax. Moynihan was trying to point out a long-concealed reality: since 1981, the United States has cut income taxes and increased military spending by a combined total of about $3 trillion. We have financed this program with (1) increases in Social Security payroll taxes, (2) domestic and foreign borrowing of $2 trillion, and (3) increases in state and local taxes to make up for federal cutbacks. This has been an economically self-destructive means of financing, and a socially regressive one as well—its burdens have not been allotted according to people's ability to pay. Moynihan and the Democratic leaders were, however, inhibited from stating the logical conclusion from the reality Moynihan pointed to: if payroll taxes are to be cut, income taxes or other taxes must be increased. No leading politician today seems able to say this.

Proposals for tax increases, if they are to be accepted, should be presented as part of a long-term domestic public investment program that will simultaneously lower the cost of capital to American business and reduce the fiscal pressure on local governments. The high cost of capital in America is caused, in large part, by the huge borrowing requirements of the government and by the general propensity of American private business to make use of debt during a period of low national savings. This country's overall debt structure is a financial San Andreas fault which puts the entire economy at risk. The tendency to borrow was compounded in the 1980s by financial deregulation, high levels of speculation, and the extensive use of junk bonds and other forms of credit in takeovers and corporate restructurings. Financial deregulation of the thrift industry, together with lax oversight and widely tolerated corruption, produced the scandal of the S and Ls. The use by unscrupulous bankers of federally guaranteed deposits to rescue a savings and loan industry that should have been liquidated a decade ago will ultimately cost the taxpayers between $300 and $500 billion; ten years ago, the costs could have been limited to perhaps $10 billion. The colossal amounts of money wasted by the savings and loan industry in investments in worthless real estate, in junk bonds, in speculation and corruption of all kinds, could have been invested in new, productive investments. Instead, half a trillion dollars were diverted from productive investment to the most blatant kind of fraud. The enormous capital drain caused by the S and Ls is one reason for our high cost of capital.

Another reason for the high cost of capital is the more general trend of the 1980s to substitute debt for equity. The invention of junk bonds, the relaxation of credit regulation, and the rush for high immediate returns by financial institutions led to the huge wave of debt-financed takeovers, leveraged buyouts, and corporate restructurings of the last decade. During the last five years alone, some $500 billion of equity disappeared—as companies were acquired or bought back their own shares—and was replaced by debt. The leading instrument for promoting this debt was the junk bond, which, because of its lack of covenants or any real restrictions on the borrower, for the first time gave almost any raider, no matter how small, the ability to acquire almost any company, no matter how big. All that was needed to create an ocean of debt was large-scale institutional demand for junk bonds, a demand that was stimulated by very high interest rates (quite often beyond any realistic prospect of profitability by the business that would be responsible for the payments) and the promise of something like a functioning market. The S and Ls, banks, pension funds, and insurance companies rushed to acquire over $200 billion of this junk paper, and together with the commercial banks largely created the financial boom of the 1980s.

A slowing economy, an increasing number of large bankruptcies, the collapse of the junk-bond market, and the demise of Drexel Burnham brought the world back to harsh reality. First, there is no real junk-bond market, only a collection of financial institutions holding questionable paper; second, far from being the new way to finance American growth, the excessive use of junk bonds, particularly for LBOs and takeovers, is now destroying both borrowers and lenders, at great cost to the U.S. economy. It was a destructive experiment which also had, as one of its principal effects, that of raising the cost of capital to American business. But it was not the free market alone that belatedly started the demise of junk bonds. It was regulation by the Federal Reserve and other federal agencies that tightened the use of bank credit; and it was federal legislation that took the S and Ls out of junk bonds. These actions were long overdue.

Additional regulation and legislation is probably required to reduce the   24
cost of capital by making equity financing more attractive than acquiring
debt. Making dividends tax deductible should be studied as an alternative
to reductions in the capital gains tax, which offer no real overall economic
benefits. Such changes in tax policy should obviously be related to their
effects on the budget. In addition, to restore full confidence in our financial
institutions, regulation of the financial markets should be tightened by increasing the capital requirements of the securities firms and adopting the
initial recommendations of the Brady Commission, for example, raising
margin requirements on options and futures trading as well as making the
Federal Reserve the overall regulator of the adequacy of capital in the
securities industry.

Ultimately, to reduce significantly the cost of capital will require a
significant decrease in real interest rates. This can only occur if U.S. government borrowing requirements are reduced—an outcome that will be made
all the more difficult to achieve by the huge international demands for capital
for the development of Eastern Europe. As a result of our own capital
constraints we will, in my view, unfortunately have to leave the financing of
development in Eastern Europe largely to West Germany, the European
Community and Japan, and to private investors.

We must concentrate on putting our own house in order. If the United
States were to make available $1 trillion in new resources over the next
decade through a combination of new taxes and cuts in expenditures, roughly
one-half, or $500 billion, should be dedicated to bringing down the deficit
and to reducing the borrowing requirements of the government. This should
allow the Federal Reserve System to bring interest rates down significantly.
Such a decrease in the real cost of capital would have a dramatic effect on
U.S. economic growth; our objective should be a prime rate of interest of 5
percent within two years. In addition, such a reduction would reduce significantly the costs of (1) the government in bailing out the S and Ls, (2) U.S.
banks in carrying shaky Third World and real estate loans on their books,
and (3) companies that must, if they are to continue, struggle with high
interest payments.

The current arguments about including or excluding Social Security
pension funds from the federal budget are missing the central issue. Social
Security is, and always will be, a pay-as-you-go system; the level of payroll
taxes and benefits will be set by future Congresses, and there is no way of
insuring exactly what they will be. We should not become fascinated by the
accounting dodges of the Gramm-Rudman law. The one public financial
obligation of decisive importance is the net borrowing requirement of the
government. For the five years from fiscal year 1986 through fiscal year 1990
the national debt held by the public grew by about $900 billion despite the
existence of the Gramm-Rudman restrictions. It will probably continue to
increase at between $150 and $200 billion per year as a result of continued

deficits together with greater financial requirements for the S and L bailout. The growth of the national debt must be contained. The likely result of doing so could be a rise in the securities markets, which would in turn lower the cost of capital further and help to stabilize the dollar. Both our balance of trade and our ability to invest abroad would be strengthened.

Of the one trillion dollars in new resources that is needed, the balance of about $500 billion should, as I have noted, be returned to the states. One half of this $500 billion should, in my view, be devoted entirely to rebuilding decaying infrastructure; the other half should directly augment the budgets of state and local governments. If some $250 billion of the $500 billion were devoted to rebuilding infrastructure over the decade, it would still only represent a fraction of our total needs. New York City alone estimates that between $40 and $50 billion will be required for the next decade. However, annual increases in investment in the infrastructure by the states would be of significant help to the general economy. The federal funds returned to the states for investment in infrastructure should be deposited in state trust funds adapted to such purposes.

The reasons for allotting $250 billion for direct assistance to local governments should be clear. Enormous pressure has been put on state and local governments to deal with social problems that are national in scope: education, medical care, crime, drugs, housing, the environment, etc. With a slowing national economy and continuing federal cutbacks, local governments have had to raise taxes and cut services time and time again. The new federalism of the Reagan years has mainly consisted of transferring responsibilities to local governments and having them financed locally. This is being continued by the Bush administration and has been extremely destructive. A national investment program would assist local governments by making it possible for them to finance vital social services and/or reduce their own taxes—including local sales taxes, property taxes, and income taxes—by an amount equal to the federal contribution that they receive. Such a program—a different kind of revenue sharing—would stimulate local economies and allow them to devote more resources to deal with national problems, while causing a rollback in some of the more regressive local taxes. It is not enough for the president and the nation's governors to set ambitious goals for public education by the year 2000. The states have to be given the means to carry out those goals.

If we continue on our present course of borrowing and spending and selling our national assets; of neglecting our environment, our cities, and our children; of giving up one industry after another to foreign competition, we will surely see a decline in America's position in the world, whether or not we have a financial crisis. We will see a steady erosion in our standard of living and an increasing polarization of our society.

None of this is necessary; dealing with our budget problems should not be difficult if we stop acting like a poor country that cannot afford taxes that are proportionally equivalent to those of other advanced industrial countries. But for a change to occur, more imaginative political leadership will have to come forward. The Democratic party should produce that leadership by proposing to invest in the United States, by defining how the government can act in partnership with other forces in society, and finally by showing how both a balanced program of reduced military and entitlement costs and moderate federal tax increases are needed to save both public and private institutions from deterioration. It is time for the Democrats to raise their sights and to make real for Americans the ideals that other countries still ascribe to us.

Points to Consider

1. Note the references to talk, discussion, and discourse in Rohatyn's essay. Why are these important to his political attitude and program? How, for example, are taxes related to discussion, and why is the relationship politically significant?

2. Rohatyn concentrates on economic solutions to our national problems. To what extent do you see these problems as economic ones? Why does Rohatyn focus on economic solutions?

3. Do you think Rohatyn's plan could work? Do you think it could be seriously entertained by the government? By the voters? Why or why not?

4. How does Rohatyn's identification of himself as a lifelong Democrat shape the direction of his article? What does he think of the Democratic party? What changes would he like to see in its political philosophy?

BILL POWELL AND BRADLEY MARTIN

What Japan Thinks of Us   [NEWSWEEK / April 2, 1990]

In Japan Kent Derricott is what's known as a *gaijin talento*. A blond, blue-eyed American who speaks perfect Japanese, he works the Tokyo talk shows, often defending his homeland. It's a tough job, but someone's got to do it.

"Aren't American workers lazy?" asks a Japanese host. Absolutely not, Derricott responds. "They just lead a more balanced life than you do. They don't work all the time." Well then, the bemused host replies, what if we asked some Americans whether they would continue working if they suddenly got rich. "How many do you think would say 'No?' "

"Very few," says Derricott confidently. "Americans *like* to work."

The camera cuts to a Wall Street health club. A group of yuppies are   4
lined up, the same question put to them. Nearly all vote for quitting. One says he'd go off and live on a boat. Back in the studio, the audience is laughing uproariously, and a battered Kent protests, "But that doesn't mean *anything*, that doesn't mean anything!"

For nearly four decades after World War II, most Americans didn't much care *what* the Japanese thought about them. Geographic isolation, economic might, and a bristling nuclear arsenal allowed America the luxury of indifference. The State Department politely called Japan a "partner" in the vital task of securing the West's interests in Northeast Asia. Former prime minister Yasuhiro Nakasone was more candid: in 1983, he said that "the whole

---

BILL POWELL *is* Newsweek's *Asia economics editor, based in the magazine's Tokyo bureau since January 1989. He had been a senior writer in* Newsweek's *business sections since 1987, writing on trends and developments in the world of economics and commerce. Powell's recent assignments include covering insider trading scandals, the crash on Wall Street, and trade with Asian nations.*

BRADLEY MARTIN *is the Tokyo bureau chief for* Newsweek *magazine. He has lived and worked in Japan since 1977. Before joining* Newsweek, *Martin worked for the Asian* Wall Street Journal, *the* Baltimore Sun, *and the* Charlotte Observer. *He received an A.B. in history from Princeton University in 1964. He also attended Emory Law School and, at the University of Hawaii, studied Thai language and received Peace Corps training.*

Japanese archipelago . . . should be like an unsinkable aircraft carrier" off the coast of Vladivostok. As long as the Japanese didn't object, the United States was content to use the islands as a military staging ground, and let the Japanese tend to their business. Which, it turned out, was business.

Today the following truth should be self-evident: what the Japanese think of us matters enormously. No other foreign country comes close to exerting so much influence on our daily lives. They've known that for a long time now in the industrial Midwest, where Japanese competition eviscerated the auto, steel, and machine-tool industries. They're learning as well in Silicon Valley, on Route 128 outside Boston, and in the Pentagon, where many fear that if the United States doesn't wake up, Japan will overtake the industries that will spur economic growth in the twenty-first century: semiconductors, supercomputers, industrial robots, biotechnology.

As Japan's trade surpluses with the United States have mounted, so, too, have the dollars the Japanese pour back into this country. Tokyo has become America's de facto banker. The interest rate you pay for a car or a mortgage now depends greatly on the attitudes and actions of investors and policymakers in Japan. That's why the Treasury Department worries more when Nippon Life Insurance Co. fails to show up for a government bond auction than it does about the Travelers or Prudential. Japanese financial institutions have allowed America to run mammoth budget deficits and yet avoid economic disaster.

Like it or not, the Japanese are in a position to tell the United States 8 what they think. The message, delivered with increasingly un-Japanese candor, is simple: grow up, America. The Japanese believe Americans are overwrought crybabies, grousing about trade problems primarily of their own making—product of a flaccid fiscal policy, an inability to make goods anyone would want to buy. And, many Japanese say, Americans display utter indifference to those facts. Most corrosive now are trade issues; Japan is tired of the whining about the difficulty of penetrating its market. Asks Ako Wakai, a thirty-two-year-old magazine writer, "Why do they even push? We might as well just buy good solid German products."

Some in Japan now talk about America with an avuncular sadness, as if they were composing an obituary for a relative they were once fond of: "Affluence made many Americans content with their lives, and lazy," says Yoshiko Taniguchi, a forty-year-old Tokyo housewife who made her first trip to the United States twenty-three years ago. "In the end, they lost the work ethic their grandparents had cherished. This has begun to show in their products."

Others, though still a minority, are harsher still. With a trade war looming between the United States and Japan, the themes of American decline and chronic conflict between the two countries are common. *Nichibei Senso wa Owatteinai (The War Between Japan and America Is Not Over)* by Jun Eto, a professor of comparative literature at the Tokyo Institute of Technology, and *Amerika no Botsuraku (America's Decline)* by Seiki Sha are representative titles. Sha's book hits all the popular notes: America's crumbling educational system, crime-ridden cities, fiscal irresponsibility, and corporate shortsightedness make it a spent force in the world marketplace. Like the Romans, some Japanese intellectuals believe, America can bear neither its ills nor the cures for them.

At the same time, many Japanese are mystified and hurt by polls in the United States showing that Americans now view Tokyo's economic power as a greater threat to the United States than the Soviet military. A *Newsweek/Gallup* Poll taken in Japan in late January suggests the dimensions of the resentment. For example, 64 percent of those questioned said that negative American attitudes toward Japan were simple scapegoating—a result of "new anger at America's slipping economic performance." Fully one third said they had less respect for Americans now than they did five years ago. That was clear in an editorial cartoon last year in the news magazine *AERA*. It pictured an overweight American sitting in front of his television set, beer and popcorn by his side. In frame one, he watched serenely as Soviet troops goose-step by on the screen. In frame two, tanks, fighter jets, and huge missiles rolled by, and the American didn't bat an eye. The last frame showed a short, squinting Japanese tourist with a camera slung around his neck on the TV screen—and the American cowered behind his chair in fear. For large numbers of his countrymen, says Kazuo Nukazawa, an economist at the Keidanren, Japan's big business federation, "the United States at this moment is over the hill and blaming the discomfort on an easy target, its most formidable competitor."

Publicly, Japanese leaders tend to dismiss the significance of those polls. 12 But attitudes among the country's elites in both government and business are gradually hardening. Japan's intransigence during a recent round of trade talks prompted George Bush to summon Prime Minister Toshiki Kaifu for a quickie summit in Palm Springs. In Tokyo, there was much grumbling about Kaifu looking like Bush's "toady," as one Japanese journalist said privately. It was not a hopeful sign. "The Japanese establishment is still pro-American," says Kan Ito, a Washington-based Japanese journalist and political consultant, "but it is pro-Americanism tempered with sadness, disappointment and pessimism about the future."

The creeping pessimism is apparently far-reaching. Throughout most of the postwar period Japanese feelings toward the United States were over-whelmingly favorable; they admired America for its military and technological prowess, respected the relatively benign nature of the Occupation, and were grateful for U.S. aid in rebuilding the country. But when the *Newsweek* Poll asked, "How likely do you think it is that Japan could again become an enemy of the United States?" a dismaying 45 percent of the respondents answered "Somewhat likely," and 9 percent "Very likely." Still, many continued to believe that the two countries' destinies are linked: 57 percent said that America's problems are "bad news for Japan."

But the poll figures may appear more ominous than they really are. For one thing, to the Japanese ear the connotation of the word "enemy," when translated, is not harshly militaristic, but more akin to "antagonist." In the midst of the current trade problems—which get saturation coverage in Japan's press—the response is less surprising. Conceivably, those disputes could fade if, as many economists expect, Japan's trade surplus continues to fall. Moreover, the vast majority of the Japanese polled said they still had "somewhat" or "a lot" of respect for America.

But America's stature in Japan is undeniably eroding. The most notorious expression of that change was last year's bootleg publication of *The Japan That Can Say No*—the book written by right-wing politician Shintaro Ishihara and Sony chairman Akio Morita. It was in fact the first inkling many Americans got that the Japanese were getting a bit irritated. The book captured U.S. attention with two points: Ishihara's assertion that Japan could alter the balance of power by selling microchips to the Soviets instead of to the Americans, and his attribution of increasing tension between the United States and Japan to American racism.

It also struck a chord in Japan, where the book has sold more than one million copies. "It shows that the people are taking problems in the U.S. relationship a lot more seriously than the government thinks," Ishihara says. Six first- and second-year Tokyo University students, sitting in a coffee shop five minutes from the campus, pondered the book's success. For nearly a minute, no one said anything. Finally, Tetsuo Kojima blurted out: "Because *that's* the way most Japanese think!" By which he meant what? he was asked. That Ishihara is going to be prime minister of Japan and cozy up to the Soviets because they're not racist? No, Kojima said, "the point is, he spoke out, he stood up to America. Japan is just getting tired of being pushed around."

This is beyond dispute. Americans should not misunderstand the significance of Ishihara, even if he does seem like a Japanese Jesse Helms. It is not what he said specifically, but rather that he said it at all. In Japanese terms, as Jun Eto puts it, Ishihara dropped the *tatemae* (pretense, or false front) and gave them *honne* (what he really thinks). He speaks, Eto says, for Japan's "inarticulate population," and for many of them it is the first time anyone has.

The roots of the problem go back to the Occupation and beyond. Few Japanese go as far as Yuji Aida, professor emeritus of Western cultural history at Kyoto University, who recently wrote that the Occupation was a time of "sweeping self-betrayal whereby postwar Japan forfeited its identity and pride." Most Japanese accept that occupation was bound to follow defeat. But Japan's new confidence is disrupting the equilibrium enforced by the Occupation, much to both sides' surprise. The Japanese, outwardly humble and accustomed to accommodation, are openly expressing pride—and sometimes running down the United States in the process. "Our sense of accomplishment—of excellence, if you will, on an international scale—has come

16

only in the last five years," says Toshio Yamaguchi, a former minister of Labor and now a member of Parliament. "If the question is whether Japan's system is archaic or whether America's system is an industrial castoff, I think we can say that Japan's system is at the leading edge."

For the last six months, at the government's prodding, many giant Japanese companies have tried to do their bit to ease current trade tensions with the United States. All have announced voluntary programs to increase significantly their purchases of foreign-made parts over the next few years. What's unusual now is that the effort plainly irks some of them—and they're willing to say so. The deals have more to do with politics than economics, Japanese executives say. The programs are nothing less than a kind of commercial charity: Japanese firms giving money to U.S. companies for a cause, in this case to forestall U.S. protectionism. "Our shareholders wouldn't like to think of us as a philanthropic institution," a high-ranking electronics-industry executive said recently, "but that's exactly right."

The Japanese have had doubts for years about the way the United States does business—and the 1980s didn't reassure them. Unlike the Japanese, Americans "deserted their factories to play the stock market," says Tsuneo Iida, a Nagoya University economist. Today, Japanese may be exaggerating U.S. weakness. Yotaro Kobayashi, president of Fuji-Xerox Corp. in Tokyo, contends the common image of the U.S. businessman as "totally interested in the bottom line, ruthless with people, and overly interested in the short-term interests of shareholders" has been "greatly overemphasized in Japan." 20

In fact, many average Japanese citizens would be surprised to learn that as a percent of U.S. gross national product, manufacturing is only a shade less now than it was in 1980. Some would be shocked to learn that America's share of total world exports remains significantly higher than Japan's. Finally, for all the talk in Japan about American decline, overall U.S. productivity is about half again as high as Japan's.

But facts right now seem to be less important than atmospherics in U.S.-Japanese relations—and the atmospherics are deteriorating steadily. The whole thrust of U.S. policy toward Japan since the war has been to contain trade disputes so they didn't upset the alliance. But burying trade issues is going to be difficult now that the Soviets no longer appear to be such a threat. There is danger in that for U.S.-Japan cooperation on foreign policy. If the debate on trade becomes the central dialogue between the two countries, that means almost inevitably the loudest voices belong to the harshest critics. Says Kan Ito: "Constant Japan-bashing in the United States has created a dangerous reaction in Japan—resentful, nationalistic, America-bashing."

The danger is compounded by how excruciatingly sensitive the Japanese are to what *we* think of *them*. The reason for the sensitivity is simple. The United States has been far more important to Japan than Japan has been to the United States; and since the war, the United States has been the country against which Japan relentlessly measured itself. Journalist Yoichi Funabashi says some Japanese feel especially hurt when Americans criticize. They tend "to personalize their feelings toward Americans who criticize them . . . the tendency is to think that whoever is not for us is against us."

In the current environment, that means the United States is going to   24
hear a lot more pointed criticism from Japan. Ishihara himself told *Newsweek* that the greatest threat to American auto workers is not Japanese competition, but American managers and politicians. "Look what Lee Iacocca did when the yen went up and Japanese cars were losing competitive power—why in the world did he raise the prices of *his* cars?" he said. "In Japan, a manager like him would have been fired."

And listen, for example, to Hajime Karatsu, a former top executive at Matsushita Electric Corp. who now teaches at Tokai University. Addressing current U.S. trade concerns in the English-language *Japan Times,* Karatsu let it all hang out. On alleged exclusionary purchasing practices by Japan's closely knit business groups (known as *keiretsu*), he says: "As for Japan's corporate groupings, the Americans who criticize them only betray their ignorance of the situation here." On the competence of American negotiators in general: "It is annoying when these Americans come to the negotiating table armed with knowledge gained only from newspaper clippings."

In the current environment, strident voices are already starting to drown out all others. Though you wouldn't know it from listening to Karatsu, many Japanese economists actually favor the structural reforms the United States advocates because they *would* benefit Japanese consumers. In fact, the U.S. side is only making arguments that several Japanese analysts—Mckinsey & Co.'s Kenichi Ohmae, for one—have made for years. "U.S. officials are butting into Japan's domestic affairs by demanding an end to high land prices here," says Junichi Kada, an economist in Tokyo, "but they're right, and social justice requires radical reform."

At least Karatsu limits his invective to trade issues. Others make invidious comparisons of the two countries overall. The Japanese are justifiably proud that there is virtually no crime in their cities and no drugs. (The group of young Tokyo University students responded with blank stares of disbelief when a reporter asked them if "you or any of your friends had ever tried marijuana or cocaine.") Japanese couples divorce at only a quarter the U.S. rate. Rates for unemployment and school dropouts are similarly low.

But the comparison game can compound misconceptions that already   28
exist in Japan. Many Japanese, for example, have doubts about multiracial societies. In the *Newsweek* Poll, when respondents were asked to rank each of seven factors as either a "very serious, serious, or not serious" problem for the U.S. economy, 31 percent put "too many different racial and ethnic groups" in the "very serious" category. That was tied for second place with "lazy workers," but both trailed "drugs and alcohol addiction," which a remarkable 82 percent cited as a very serious problem. By contrast, only 23 percent put "inadequate education" in that category.

As Foreign Ministry spokesman Taizo Watanabe points out, those Japanese citing "too many minorities" do so mainly out of ignorance, not mean-spirited racism. "Most Japanese haven't been to the United States and they don't know how things are," says Watanabe. Indeed, they just figure that the racial mix of the United States stands in stark contrast to the homogeneity of Japan—so it must be a big problem. Still, this attitude invites scrutiny of Japan's own level of racial and ethnic tolerance—scrutiny it can ill afford. There's widespread discrimination, for example, against Koreans living in Japan. "We're not the country to lecture others about racism," says Tadashi Yamamoto, president of the Japan Center for International Exchange.

However unwittingly, press coverage further skews Japan's perception of what racial and ethnic diversity means in the United States. Taking its cues from the U.S. press, Japanese coverage of America tends to be heavy on inner-city drug stories these days—stories that inevitably portray blacks in a negative light and major urban areas as crime- and drug-ridden hellholes. "On my way home late one night, three men mugged me and left me lying in the street," wrote Kanji Shibata, a former correspondent in New York for the *Mainichi Shimbun*. "That doesn't happen in Tokyo. Fear of personal safety aside, the mixture of races and ethnic groups in the United States means you have to be very careful not to offend people."

Former ambassador to Japan Mike Mansfield used to call the alliance between the two countries "the most important bilateral relationship in the world, bar none." Today, for all the negative imagery and invective on both sides, the United States remains fortunate in one respect: though it may be squandering a lot of good will in Japan, it has a lot to squander. "There is in the Japanese mind a built-in resistance to drastic changes in the images of America," scholar Hiroshi Kitamura once wrote. In survey after survey, the United States comes up as Japan's favorite foreign country. Three million Japanese visited the United States last year. A concrete illustration that Japan's affection still runs deep came after last year's San Francisco earthquake. Japanese neighborhoods, civic clubs, and businesses donated millions of dollars.

For young Japanese in particular, the United States has powerful allure. 32
The influence of the country's pop culture remains enormously positive. Tom Cruise is a bigger sex symbol in Tokyo than he is in Los Angeles. Satin warm-up jackets that say "San Francisco 49ers," "Oakland A's" or "L.A. Lakers"—the Japanese love winners—are worn all over Tokyo. To many Japanese some aspects of the United States resemble nothing less than a giant theme park—Americaland—full of open spaces, uncrowded beaches, inexpensive golf courses, things so many Japanese crave but don't have at home. Every Saturday night a popular television show called *USA Express* tells what's hot and hip in the United States. It even portrays New York favorably, capturing its excitement, not merely its danger.

The majority of Japanese, in the end, may have more faith in the United States than a lot of Americans do. However irritated they are by our carping and growing sloth, they are, after all, investing in the United States at record levels. If only we were doing the same. Only 16 percent of those *Newsweek* polled said they thought the United States was in "irreversible decline." The average Japanese seem to know, more than most Americans seem to, how disastrous a rupture between the two countries would be. Nearly three-fifths of those polled said America's problems "are bad news for Japan." And notwithstanding the popularity of *The Japan That Can Say No,* Tokyo's establishment fears nothing more today than the political and economic isolation that a split with the United States could conceivably bring.

Japan is challenging the United States for power and influence in the world, to be sure. But in adjusting to that, urges Kuniko Inoguchi, a political scientist in her late thirties at Sophia University, the United States mustn't lose sight of the fact "that deep down we are really pro-American. You should realize the value of it." In the end there is not much choice, if both sides are to avoid a crippling break. Amid the rising acrimony lies a simple reality: if a split comes, both sides lose.

Points to Consider

1. What are some of the stereotypes that Japanese have of Americans? Where do you think they derived these stereotypes? How accurate do you think they are?

2. To what do the Japanese attribute America's problems? Why do they view our ethnic diversity as a major part of our national problem? Do you agree or disagree with their assessment?

3. According to the authors, what do the Japanese seem to respect most about American culture? Do you think the things they respect are more important than those they don't?

4. Besides trade, what other sources of antagonism add to Japanese-American friction? Of all the potential sources of conflict, which do you consider most critical?

Discussing the Unit

Both Rosenblatt and Rohatyn talk about the twentieth century as the American Century. Why do you think this century has been called that? Do you think that as we head toward a new century the United States will play a much smaller role in the world? What do you think America should do if it is to retain its world leadership?

Preparing for Class Discussion

1. Consider all of the problems that Rosenblatt and Rohatyn introduce. Which do you think are the most serious? Based on the readings in this chapter, make your own list of America's five biggest problems. Bring this list to class to compare it with other lists.

2. Consider the interconnection of the problems you listed. In what ways are the problems separate and in what ways are they interdependent? Will solving one problem aggravate another? Consider, too, to what extent these problems can be solved through economic, social, or cultural means.

From Discussion to Writing

One of the prevailing images of America is that it is a young nation, a "new world." In keeping with the image, immigrants used to call their homelands the "old country." But do you think America is still a young nation? Is it possible that some of the Japanese critics are correct and that we are "over the hill"? Write an essay in which you discuss how you think we will enter a new century and a new millennium: will we still be the "new world" or will we have become the "old country"?

The Periodicals:
Information for Subscription

The American Scholar: quarterly. $5.50/issue, $19/yr. Journal published by the Phi Beta Kappa honorary society. Contains scholarly criticism, fiction, poetry, book reviews. Subscription address: The Phi Beta Kappa Society, 1811 Q Street NW, Washington, DC 20077-3632.

The American Voice: quarterly. $4/issue, $12/yr. Journal of fiction, nonfiction, and poetry with a special focus on women's experience. Subscription address: The Kentucky Foundation for Women, Inc., 332 West Broadway, Louisville, KY 40202.

The Boston Globe Magazine: Sunday supplement to *The Boston Globe*, a Boston daily newspaper. Prices vary according to location in the United States. For subscription information, call (617) 929-2222.

Change: bimonthly $3.50/issue, $23/yr. Subtitled "The Magazine of Higher Learning," covers current issues in academia across the country. Controversial articles on teaching, liberal arts education, culture, books. Subscription address: *Change*, 4000 Albemarle St. NW, Washington, DC 20016; or call 1-800-365-9753.

The Chronicle of Higher Education: weekly. $2/issue, $57.50/yr. Weekly academic news. Includes extensive education want ads, news about professors, business, students, coming events, calls for papers. Subscription address: Box 1955, Marion, OH 43305.

Commentary: monthly. $3.75/issue, $39/yr. Analyses of current events in politics, social sciences, and culture. Special focus on Jewish affairs. Subscription address: American Jewish Committee, 165 East 56th Street, New York, NY 10022; or call (212) 751-4000.

Cosmopolitan: monthly. $2.50/issue, $24.97/yr. Audience is young women; focuses on fashion, makeup, careers, entertainment, and the arts. Subscription address: Box 10074, Des Moines, IA 50340.

Esquire: monthly. $2.50/issue, $17.94/yr. Male audience; subjects include business, sports, fashion, the arts, interviews, and fiction. Subscription address: 1255 Portland Place, Boulder, CO 80323; or call 1-800-888-5400.

Essence: Monthly. $1.75/issue, $12/yr. Audience is young black women; information concerning health and beauty, parenting, the arts. Subscription address: *Essence*, Box 51300, Boulder, CO 80321-1300.

Frontiers: $8/issue, $16/1 volume (3 issues). A journal of women's studies, addressing issues of gender, race, class, feminism, politics. Book reviews, poetry, fiction, art, photography, and criticism. Subscription address: *Frontiers*, Women's Studies, Box 246, University of Colorado at Boulder, Boulder, CO 80309.

Gentlemen's Quarterly (GQ): monthly. $3/issue, $20/yr. Men's fashion magazine, with articles on arts and entertainment, the professional male, office politics, etc. Subscription address: Box 53816, Boulder, CO 80322; or call 1-800-289-9330.

Good Housekeeping: monthly. $1.95/issue, $16.97/yr. Articles of interest to homemakers, half of whom work outside of the home. Food, fashion, decorating, fiction, health. Subscription address: Box 7189, Red Oak, IA 51591-0186; or call 1-800-888-7788.

Grand Street: quarterly. $6/issue, $24/yr. Stories, poems, articles, translations, and photographs by both well-known and lesser-known writers. Subscription address: 50 Riverside Drive, New York, NY 10024.

Harper's Magazine: monthly. $2/issue, $18/yr. Articles by prominent writers on contemporary issues, including politics, the arts, entertainment, and business. Subscription address: *Harper's Magazine*, Box 1937, Marion, OH 43305.

Harvard Business Review: 6 issues/yr. $12/issue, $65/yr. A hefty business review covering marketing, technology, foreign investments, national and international economies. Subscription address: *Harvard Business Review*, Subscription Service Department, Soldiers Field Road, Boston, MA 02163-9901; or call 1-800-274-3214.

Hudson Review: quarterly. $6/issue, $20/yr. Journal containing literary essays, fiction, poetry, reviews. Subscription address: 684 Park Avenue, New York, NY 10021.

The Humanist: 6 issues/yr. $3.75/issue, $19.75/yr. Self-described as "a nontheistic, secular, naturalistic approach to philosophy, science, and broad areas of personal and social concern. It focuses on humanistic ideas, developments, and revolutions." Subscription address: 7 Harwood Drive, Box 146, Amherst, NY 14226-0146; (716) 839-5080.

Life: monthly, except semimonthly in October. $2.95/issue, $32.50/13 issues. Photojournalism, with articles covering current events. Subscription address: *Life*, P.O. Box 30605, Tampa, FL 33630-0605; or call 1-800-621-6000.

Los Angeles: monthly. $2.50/issue, $19/yr. Cultural events, interviews, travel, and entertainment. Focuses on the Los Angeles metropolitan and suburban area. Subscription address: Box 10742, Des Moines, IA 50340; or call 1-800-876-5222.

The Los Angeles Times: daily and Sunday. Cost varies according to location. Daily newspaper covering Los Angeles area, national and international news. Call 1-800-LA-TIMES for subscription information.

Mademoiselle: monthly. $2.50/issue, $15/yr. Audience is college educated, single working women. Articles on fitness, relationships, fashion, entertainment. Subscription address: Box 54348, Boulder, CO 80322; or call 1-800-274-4750.

The Massachusetts Review: quarterly. $4/copy, $12/yr. Fiction, poetry, criticism, cultural theory, politics, and the arts. Subscription address: *The Massachusetts Review*, Memorial Hall, University of Massachusetts, Amherst, MA 01003.

Mother Jones: ten times per year. $2.95/issue, $24/yr. Investigative reporting, national news, arts, health, and environment. Subscription address: *Mother Jones*, Box 58249, Boulder, CO 80322; or call 1-800-288-7683.

Ms.: bimonthly. $4.50/issue, $40/yr. Articles on women's issues, personalities, health, politics. Subscription address: P.O. Box 57132, Boulder, CO 80322-7132; or call 1-800-365-5232.

National Review: biweekly. $1.95/issue, $39/yr. Conservative takes on national and international developments. Subscription address: *National Review*, P.O. Box 96639, Washington, DC 20077-7471; or call 1-800-222-6806.

New England Monthly: monthly. $2.50/issue, $12/yr. in New England, $15/yr. elsewhere in the United States. Topics pertinent to the New England economy, social life, travel, and entertainment. Subscription address: P.O. Box 446, Haydenville, MA 01039; or call 1-800-288-8388.

The New Republic: weekly. $2.95/issue, $59.97/yr. Political reporting and analysis; literature and arts reviews. Subscription address: Box 56515, Boulder, CO 80322; or call 1-800-274-6686.

Newsweek: weekly. $2/issue, $41.08/yr. News and commentary on the week's events in national and international affairs. Subscription address: The Newsweek Building, Livingston, NJ 07039.

New York: 50 issues/yr. $1.95/issue, $37/yr. Lifestyles and personalities in the New York metropolitan area. Subscription address: Box 54661, Boulder, CO 80322-4661; or call 1-800-678-0900.

The New Yorker: weekly. $1.75/issue, $32/yr. Current events, cartoons, criticism, biographical profiles, short fiction, and poetry. Subscription address: *The New Yorker*, Box 56447, Boulder, CO 80322; or call 1-800-825-2510.

The New York Review of Books: 22 issues/yr. $2.25/issue, $37.50/yr. Literary journal with articles by American and European writers. Book reviews and topical international issues. Subscription address: Box 2094, Knoxville, IA 50197-2094; or call 1-800-227-7585.

The New York Times: daily, with large Sunday edition that contains the *New York Times Magazine* and the *New York Times Book Review*, as well as other supplements. Rates vary according to location and frequency of delivery. The *Times* is considered the definitive source for current events, daily national and international news, business and arts reporting. Subscription information: call 1-800-631-2500.

The North American Review: quarterly. $3/issue, $11/yr. Features on contemporary issues, fiction and poetry, book reviews, foreign correspondence. Subscription address: University of Northern Iowa, Cedar Falls, IA 50614.

Outweek: weekly. $2.95/issue, $101.40/yr. Weekly newsmagazine focusing on gay and lesbian issues, arts and entertainment, politics, reviews. Subscription address: 159 West 25th Street, 7th Floor, New York, NY 10001; or call 1-800-OUT-WEEK.

People: weekly. $1.95/issue, $75.06/yr. "Personality journalism." Articles on people in news, television, and film. Subscription address: Box 30603, Tampa, FL 33630-0603; or call 1-800-541-9000.

Philadelphia: monthly. $2.50/issue, $15/yr. Features, travel and entertainment, food, with a special focus on the Philadelphia metropolitan and suburban area. Subscription address: 1500 Walnut Street, Philadelphia, PA 19102; or call 1-800-777-1003.

Playboy: monthly. $4/issue, $26/yr. Entertainment magazine for men. Fiction, reviews, interviews, "picture stories" of women. Subscription address: Box 2002, Harlan, IA 51593-2217.

Profession: yearly. Journal published by the Modern Language Association of America, and self-described as "a journal of opinion about and for the modern language profession." Includes essays on aspects of the study and teaching of modern language and literature. Subscription address: Modern Language Association, 10 Astor Place, New York, NY 10003-6981.

The Progressive: monthly. $2.50/issue, $27.50/yr. Investigative reporting, analysis, and commentary on major political, social, and economic issues. Subscription address: *The Progressive*, Box 54615, Boulder, CO 80321-4615; or call 1-800-525-0643.

Psychology Today: 10 issues/yr. $1.95/issue, $15.99/yr. Psychological information for the popular reader. Covers personal and organizational issues from the behavioral viewpoint. Subscription address: Box 55046, Boulder, CO 80322-5046; or call 1-800-525-0643.

The Sciences: bimonthly. $3.50/issue, $14.50/yr. (6 issues). Essays, commentary, reviews concerning the social and natural sciences. Subscription address: *The Sciences*, 2 East 63rd Street, New York, NY 10021; or call (212) 838-0230.

Seattle Weekly: weekly. $.75/issue, $29.95/yr. in Washington state; $39.95/yr. outside of Washington. News and arts coverage, as well as timely and controversial topics. Subscription address: 1931 Second Avenue, Seattle, WA 98101; or call (206) 441-6262.

The South Atlantic Quarterly: quarterly. $6/issue, $14/yr. Journal for the humanities. Includes critical essays, fiction, interviews, poetry. Subscription address: Duke University Press, Box 6697, College Station, Durham, NC 27708.

Spin: monthly. $2.50/issue, $18/yr. Features on the latest news in rock, metal, rap, alternative, and club music. Interviews with music personalities and celebrities. Articles on current issues. Subscription address: Box 235, Palm Coast, FL 32142-0235; or call 1-800-829-9080.

Sports Illustrated: weekly. $2.75/issue, $69.66/54 issues. Weekly update of sports news and information. Articles concerning sports issues, personalities, politics. Subscription address: P.O. Box 30602, Tampa, FL 33630-0602; or call 1-800-528-5000.

Tikkun: bimonthly. $5/issue, $30/6 issues. Self-described as "a bimonthly Jewish critique of politics, culture, and society." Subscription address: Box 6406, Syracuse, NY 13217; or call 1-800-825-0061.

TV Guide: weekly. $.79/issue, $37.44/yr. Television, cable, and pay-TV reporting. Subscription address: Box 440, Radnor, PA 19088.

U.S. News and World Report: weekly. $1.95/issue, $34.50/yr. National and world news for an educated audience. Subscription address: Box 2629, Boulder, CO 80322; or call 1-800-333-8130.

The Utne Reader: bimonthly. $4/issue, $24/yr. News, opinion, and humor about current events and culture, with articles excerpted from alternative magazines and journals nationwide. Subscription address: Box 1974, Marion, OH 43305.

The Village Voice: weekly. $1/issue, $39.95/yr. New York–area (New York, New Jersey, Connecticut) rate, $44.20/yr. national rate. Liberal commentary and analysis of political and social issues. Features on New York City fashion, night life, the arts. Articles on controversial public figures. Subscription address: Village Voice Subscription, Box 1905, Marion, OH 43306; or call 1-800-526-4859.

World Monitor: monthly. $3.50/issue, $29.94/yr. The *Christian Science Monitor* monthly, with articles on national and international politics and contemporary social and religious issues. Subscription address: Box 10544, Des Moines, IA 50340-0544; or call 1-800-888-6261.

The Yale Review: quarterly. $6/issue, $16/yr. Journal of fiction, nonfiction, poetry. Subscription address: Yale University Press, 92A Yale Station, New Haven, CT 06520.

Acknowledgments (continued from p. ii)

Cheryl A. Davis, "A Day on Wheels," *The Progressive*, November 1987, reprinted by permission from *The Progressive*, 409 East Main Street, Madison, Wisconsin 53703. Copyright © 1987, The Progressive, Inc.

Lisa DePaulo, "Love and AIDS," *Philadelphia*, May 1987, reprinted by permission of the author and *Philadelphia* Magazine.

Bob Dylan, from "Don't Think Twice, It's All Right." Copyright © 1963 Warner Bros., Inc. All rights reserved. Used by permission.

Bob Dylan, from "Queen Jane Approximately." Copyright © 1965 Warner Bros., Inc. All rights reserved. Used by permission.

Bob Dylan, from "You're Gonna Make Me Lonesome When You Go." Copyright © 1974, 1975 by Ram's Horn Music. All rights reserved. International copyright secured. Reprinted by permission.

Barbara Ehrenreich, "The Wretched of the Hearth," *The New Republic*, April 2, 1990, reprinted by permission of the author.

Riane Eisler, "Our Lost Heritage: New Facts on How God Became a Man," reprinted by permission of Riane Eisler. Originally published in the *Humanist*, May/June 1985. Copyright © 1985 by Riane Eisler.

Trey Ellis, "Disillusioned in the Promised Land." Copyright © 1989 by Trey Ellis. Reprinted by permission of Donadio and Ashworth. Originally appeared in *Playboy* Magazine.

Jean Bethke Elshtain, "Why Worry About the Animals?" Reprinted by permission of *The Progressive*, 409 East Main Street, Madison, WI 53703.

Stephen Fried, "*thirtysomething*: A Fun House Mirror on American Men." Copyright © 1989 by Stephen Fried. Reprinted by permission of the author.

Lalita Gandbhir, "Free and Equal," reprinted from *The Massachusetts Review*, © 1989 The Massachusetts Review, Inc.

Henry Louis Gates, Jr., "2 Live Crew, Decoded," copyright © 1990 by The New York Times Company. Reprinted by permission.

David Gelman, "A Much Riskier Passage," from *Newsweek*, Special Edition Summer–Fall 1990. Copyright © 1990, Newsweek, Inc. All rights reserved. Reprinted by permission.

Richard Goldstein, "The Art of Outing," reprinted by permission of the author and *The Village Voice*.

Vivian Gornick, "Twice an Outsider: On Being Jewish and a Woman." Reprinted by permission of the author and of *Tikkun*, a bimonthly Jewish critique of politics, culture, and society based in Oakland, California.

Pete Hamill, "Black and White at Brown," copyright © Pete Hamill. Reprinted by permission of the author. First appeared in *Esquire*.

Louis Harris, "Mirror, Mirror on the Wall: Worry over Personal Appearance," from *Inside America* by Louis Harris. Copyright © 1987, 1988 by Louis Harris. Reprinted by permission of Random House, Inc.

Nat Hentoff, "Free Speech on the Campus," first published in *The Progressive*. Reprinted by permission of the author.

Richard Hill, "Could We Please Have Some Quiet, Please?" First published in *The American Voice*, 1989. Reprinted by permission of the author.

Gerri Hirshey, "The Comedy of Hate." Copyright © 1989 by Gerri Hirshey. Reprinted by permission of the author and Sterling Lord Literistic.

June Jordan, "Waiting for a Taxi." Copyright © 1989 by June Jordan. Reprinted by permission of the author.

Joanmarie Kalter and Jane Marion, "The Big Stories TV News Is Missing—and Why," reprinted with permission from *TV Guide®* Magazine. Copyright © 1989 by News America Publications Inc., Radnor, Pennsylvania.

Diane Ravitch, "Multiculturalism: E Pluribus Plures," reprinted from *The American Scholar*, Volume 59, Number 3, Summer 1990. Copyright © 1990 by the author. By permission of the publishers.

Ishmael Reed, "Antihero," copyright © 1990 by Ishmael Reed. First published in *Spin* Magazine. Reprinted by permission. Mr. Reed's eight novels, two collections of essays, and collection of poetry are published by Atheneum Publishers, New York.

Felix Rohatyn, "Becoming What They Think We Are," reprinted with permission from *The New York Review of Books*. Copyright © 1990 Nyrev, Inc.

Roger Rosenblatt, "Coming to America," *Life* Magazine, copyright © 1990 the Time Inc. Magazine Company.

Roy Rowan, "Homeless Bound," copyright © 1990 the Time Inc. Magazine Company.

Ann Rule, "Rape on Campus." Copyright © 1989 by Ann Rule. Reprinted by permission of the author.

Roberto Santiago, "Black *and* Latino," copyright © Roberto Santiago. Reprinted by permission of the author.

Eric Scigliano, "Drugs: Could Legalization Work?" First published October 26, 1988. Reprinted by permission of *Seattle Weekly*.

Robert Sherrill, "Murder, Inc.," *Grand Street*, Spring 1986, reprinted by permission of the author.

Randy Shilts, "Talking AIDS to Death," copyright © Randy Shilts.

Susan Sontag, "The Way We Live Now." Copyright © 1986 by Susan Sontag. Originally appeared in *The New Yorker*. Reprinted by permission of Farrar, Straus & Giroux, Inc.

Brent Staples, "Just Walk on By: A Black Man Ponders His Power to Alter Public Space," *Ms.*, September 1986, reprinted by permission of the author.

Shelby Steele, "The Recoloring of Campus Life." Copyright © 1989 by *Harper's Magazine*. All rights reserved. Reprinted from the February issue by special permission.

Steely Dan, from "Hey Nineteen" and "Third World Man." Used by permission of Freejunket Music and Zeon Music. All rights reserved.

Laurence Steinberg, "Bound to Bicker," *Psychology Today*, September 1987, reprinted with permission from *Psychology Today* Magazine. Copyright © 1987 (PT Partners, L. P.).

Ellen Sweet, "Date Rape: The Story of an Epidemic and Those Who Deny It," *Ms.*, October 1985, reprinted by permission of the author.

Rick Telander, "Senseless," reprinted courtesy of *Sports Illustrated* from the May 14, 1990, issue. Copyright © 1990, the Time Inc. Magazine Company. All rights reserved.

R. Roosevelt Thomas, "From Affirmative Action to Affirming Diversity." Reprinted by permission of *Harvard Business Review*. "From Affirmative Action to Affirming Diversity," by R. Roosevelt Thomas, March/April 1990. Copyright © 1990 by the President and Fellows of Harvard College; all rights reserved.

Rusty Unger, "Oh, Goddess!" Copyright © 1990 News America Publishing, Inc. All rights reserved. Reprinted with the permission of *New York* Magazine.

James Q. Wilson, "Against the Legalization of Drugs," reprinted from *Commentary*, February 1990, by permission of the author; all rights reserved.

Robert Wright, "Are Animals People Too?" Reprinted by permission of *The New Republic*, copyright © 1990, The New Republic, Inc.

Neil Young, from "I Believe in You." Copyright © 1970 Cotillion Music, Inc., & Broken Fiddle Music, Inc. All rights on behalf of Cotillion Music, Inc., administered by Warner-Tamerlane Publishing Corp. All rights reserved. Used by permission.

Index of Authors and Titles